Business Law and the Legal Environment

Texas State University

7th Edition

Jeffrey F. Beatty | Susan S. Samuelson | Patricia Sánchez Abril

CENGAGE
Learning·

Australia • Brazil • Japan • Korea • Mexico • Singapore • Spain • United Kingdom • United States

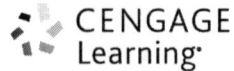
CENGAGE
Learning·

**Business Law and the Legal Environment:
Texas State University, 7th Edition**

Business Law and the Legal Environment, Seventh Edition
Jeffrey F. Beatty | Susan S. Samuelson | Patricia Sánchez Abril

For product information and technology assistance, contact us at
Cengage Learning Customer & Sales Support, 1-800-354-9706
For permission to use material from this text or product,
submit all requests online at **cengage.com/permissions**
Further permissions questions can be emailed to
permissionrequest@cengage.com

This book contains select works from existing Cengage Learning resources and
was produced by Cengage Learning Custom Solutions for collegiate use. As such,
those adopting and/or contributing to this work are responsible for editorial
content accuracy, continuity and completeness.

Compilation © 2015 Cengage Learning

ISBN: 978-1-305-75470-6

WCN: 01-100-101

Cengage Learning
20 Channel Center Street
Boston, MA 02210
USA

Cengage Learning is a leading provider of customized learning solutions with
office locations around the globe, including Singapore, the United Kingdom,
Australia, Mexico, Brazil, and Japan. Locate your local office at:
www.international.cengage.com/region.

Cengage Learning products are represented in Canada by Nelson Education, Ltd.

For your lifelong learning solutions, visit **www.cengage.com/custom.**

Visit our corporate website at **www.cengage.com.**

Brief Contents

Looking for more examples for class? Find all the latest developments on our blog at **bizlawupdate.com.** To be notified when we post updates, just "like" our Facebook page at Beatty Business Law or follow us on Twitter @bizlawupdate.

NOTE FROM THE AUTHORS

New to This Edition

Cyberlaw and Privacy

We all face profound issues about how to maintain privacy in a digital world. Yes, we want to use the Internet but we also want to protect our personal data. The cyberlaw chapter now includes a thorough discussion of privacy both on and offline. It is essential information for anyone who has ever connected to the Internet or worried that private data could become public. This chapter has been moved to the Torts unit.

A New Chapter: Employment Discrimination

Prior editions included one chapter on employment law and another on labor law. But because discrimination issues have become an increasingly important part of the employment landscape, this topic has been expanded to a full chapter. Other employment law issues are included in a joint chapter with labor law.

International Law

In a global world, students clamor for more international law and many schools require coverage of international issues in every course. The international law chapter has been completely rewritten to provide students with an understanding of the basic structure and impact of international law. It includes a discussion of: (1) how international law is created, (2) major treaties and other sources of international law, (3) the world's different legal systems, (4) the application of U.S. law overseas, and (5) the enforceability of foreign laws and treaties in the United States.

A Focus on Students

We have increased coverage of topics that are of particular interest to students, such as social media and technology. Also, the bankruptcy chapter includes a new section on student loans. The Crime chapter explores the application of constitutional standards of privacy to new technology such as DNA tests, digital cameras, social media, cellphones, and computers. The consumer law chapter looks at the legal issues raised when students spend money through direct debit, ATM cards, and prepaid debit cards.

Enhanced Digital Content—*MindTap*™

Our goal—and yours—is for the students to learn the material. With that goal in mind, we have created a *MindTap*™ product for this book. *MindTap*™ is a fully online, highly personalized learning experience that is easy to use and benefits both instructors and students. The MindTap for our book contains a prebuilt Learning Path consisting of four different activities: Worksheets that test basic knowledge of the chapter; Brief Hypotheti-cals that require students to apply what they have learned; Video Activities that reinforce course concepts; and Case Problem Blueprints that require critical thinking skills. **As an assurance to you, we (the authors) have reviewed every question in the** *MindTap* **product to ensure that it meets the high standards of our book.**

When students are assigned (and required) to complete the *MindTap* Worksheet ques-tions prior to class, they will be **prepared** for class discussions and you will know the topics with which they struggle. Recent research indicates that students who are pretested in this way learn the material more fully and perform better on final exams.

MindTap guides students through their course with ease and engagement. Instructors can personalize the prebuilt Learning Path by customizing Cengage Learning resources and adding their own content via apps that integrate into the *MindTap* framework seamlessly with Learning Management Systems.

We recognize that the online experience is as important to the students—and you—as the book itself. Each and every item in the Learning Path is assignable and gradable. This gives instructors the knowledge of class standings and concepts that may be difficult. Additionally, students gain knowledge about where they stand—both individually and compared to the highest performers in class.

To view a demo video and learn more about *MindTap*, please visit **www.cengage.com/ mindtap/**.

The Beatty/Samuelson Difference

It has been 21 years since we began work on the first edition of this textbook. At the time, publishers warned us that our undertaking was risky because there were already so many business law texts. Despite these warnings, we were convinced that there was a market for a business law book that was different from all the others. Our goal was to capture the passion and excitement, the sheer enjoyment, of the law. Business law is notoriously complex, and as authors, we are obsessed with accuracy. Yet this intriguing subject also abounds with human conflict and hard-earned wisdom, forces that we wanted to use to make this book sparkle.

Once we have the students' attention, our goal is to provide the information they will need as businesspeople and as informed citizens. Of course, we present the *theory* of how laws work, but we also explain when *reality* is different. To take some examples, tradition-ally business law textbooks have simply taught students that shareholders elect the directors of public companies. Even Executive MBA students rarely understand the reality of corporate elections. But our book explains the truth of corporate power. The practical contracts chapter focuses not on the theory of contract law but on the real-life issues involved in making an agreement: Do I need a lawyer? Should the contract be in writing? What happens if the contract has an unclear provision or an important typo? What does all that boilerplate mean anyway?

Nobel laureate Paul Samuelson famously said, "Let those who will write the nation's laws, if I can write its textbooks." As authors, we never forget the privilege—and responsibility—of educating a generation of business law students. Our goal is to write a business law text like no other—a book that is authoritative, realistic, and yet a pleasure to read.

Strong Narrative.   The law is full of great stories, and we use them. Your students and ours should come to class curious and excited. Look at Chapter 3, on dispute resolution. No tedious list of next steps in litigation, this chapter teaches the subject by tracking a double-indemnity lawsuit. An executive is dead. Did he drown accidentally, obligating the insur-ance company to pay? Or did the businessman commit suicide, voiding the policy? The student follows the action from the discovery of the body, through each step of the lawsuit, to the final appeal.

Every chapter begins with a story, either fictional or real, to illustrate the issues in the chapter. Over the years, we have learned how much more successfully we can teach when our students are intrigued. They only learn when they want to learn.

Context.   Many of our students were not yet born when Bill Clinton was elected president. They come to college with varying levels of preparation; many arrive from other countries. We have found that to teach business law most effectively we must provide its context. In the chapter on employment discrimination, we provide an historical perspective to help students understand how the laws developed. In the chapter on securities laws, we discuss the impact of the Depression on the major statutes. Only with this background do students grasp the importance and impact of our laws.

Student Reaction.   Students have responded enthusiastically to our approach. One professor asked a student to compare our book with the one that the class was then using. This was the student's reaction: "I really enjoy reading the [Beatty/Samuelson] textbook, and I have decided that I will give you this memo ASAP, but I am keeping the book until Wednesday so that I may continue reading. Thanks! :-)"

This text has been used in courses for undergraduates, MBAs, and Executive MBAs, with students ranging in age from 18 to 55. This book works, as some unsolicited comments indicate:

From Amazon:

- "Glad I purchased this. It really helps put the law into perspective and allows me as a leader to make intelligent decisions. Thanks."

- "I enjoyed learning business law and was happy my college wanted this book. THUMBS UP!"

From Undergraduates:

- "This is the best textbook I have had in college, on any subject."

- "The textbook is awesome. A lot of the time I read more than what is assigned—I just don't want to stop."

- "I had no idea business law could be so interesting."

From MBA students:

- "Actually enjoyed reading the textbook, which is a rarity for me."

- "The law textbook was excellent through and through."

From a Fortune 500 vice president, enrolled in an Executive MBA program:

- "I really liked the chapters. They were crisp, organized, and current. The information was easy to understand and enjoyable."

From business law professors:

- "The clarity of presentation is superlative. I have never seen the complexity of contract law made this readable."

- "Until I read your book I never really understood UCC 2-207."

- "With your book, we have great class discussions."

From a state supreme court justice:

- "This book is a valuable blend of rich scholarship and easy readability. Students and professors should rejoice with this publication."

Current. This seventh edition contains more than 50 new cases. Almost all were reported within the last two or three years, and many within the last 12 months. We never include a new court opinion merely because it is recent. Yet the law evolves continually, and our willingness to toss out old cases and add important new ones ensures that this book—and its readers—remain on the frontier of legal developments.

Authoritative. We insist, as you do, on a law book that is indisputably accurate. A professor must teach with assurance, confident that every paragraph is the result of exhaustive research and meticulous presentation. Dozens of tough-minded people spent thousands of hours reviewing this book, and we are delighted with the stamp of approval we have received from trial and appellate judges, working attorneys, scholars, and teachers.

We reject the cloudy definitions and fuzzy explanations that can invade judicial opinions and legal scholarship. To highlight the most important rules, we use bold print, and then follow with vivacious examples written in clear, forceful English. We cheerfully venture into contentious areas, relying on very recent decisions. Can a creditor pierce the veil of an LLC? Are stop and frisk policies constitutional? Is discrimination based on attractiveness legal? Are employees protected against bullying in the workplace? Where there is doubt about the current (or future) status of a doctrine, we say so. In areas of particularly heated debate, we footnote our work: We want you to have absolute trust in this book.

Humor. Throughout the text we use humor—judiciously—to lighten and enlighten. Not surprisingly, students have applauded—but is it appropriate? How dare we employ levity in this venerable discipline? We offer humor because we take law seriously. We revere the law for its ancient traditions, its dazzling intricacy, and its relentless though imperfect attempt to give order and decency to our world. Because we are confident of our respect for the law, we are not afraid to employ some levity. Leaden prose masquerading as legal scholarship does no honor to the field.

Humor also helps retention. Research shows that the funnier or more bizarre the example, the longer students will remember it. Students are more likely to remember a contract problem described in an original setting, and from that setting recall the underlying principle. By contrast, one widget is hard to distinguish from another.

Features

We chose the features for our book with great care. Each feature responds to an essential pedagogical goal. Here are some of those goals and the matching feature.

Exam Strategy

GOAL: To help students learn more effectively and to prepare for exams. In developing this feature, we asked ourselves: What do students want? The short answer is—a good grade in the course. How many times a semester does a student ask you, "What can I do to study for the exam?" We are happy to help them study and earn a good grade because that means that they will also be learning.

About six times per chapter, we stop the action and give students a two-minute quiz. In the body of the text, again in the end-of-chapter review, and also in the *Instructor's Manual*, we present a typical exam question. Here lies the innovation: We guide the student in analyzing the issue. We teach the reader—over and over—how to approach a question: to start with the overarching principle, examine the fine point raised in the question, apply the analysis that courts use, and deduce the right answer. This skill is second nature to lawyers but not to students. Without practice, too many students panic, jumping at a convenient answer, and leaving aside the tools they have spent the course acquiring. Let's change that. Students love the Exam Strategy feature.

You Be the Judge

GOAL: Get them thinking independently. When reading case opinions, students tend to accept the court's "answer." Judges, of course, try to write decisions that appear indisputable, when in reality they may be controversial—or wrong. From time to time we want students to think through the problem and reach their own answer. Virtually every chapter contains a You Be the Judge feature, providing the facts of the case and conflicting appellate arguments. The court's decision, however, appears only in the *Instructor's Manual*. Because students do not know the result, discussions are more complex and lively.

Ethics

GOAL: Make ethics real. We ask ethical questions about cases, legal issues, and commercial practices. Is it fair for one party to void a contract by arguing, months after the fact, that there was no consideration? What is a manager's ethical obligation when asked to provide a reference for a former employee? What is wrong with bribery? We believe that asking the questions, and encouraging discussion, reminds students that ethics is an essential element of justice, and of a satisfying life.

Cases

GOAL: Let the judges speak. Each case begins with a summary of the facts and a statement of the issue. Next comes a tightly edited version of the decision, in the court's own language, so that students "hear" the law developing in the diverse voices of our many judges. In the principal cases in each chapter, we provide the state or federal citation, unless it is not available, in which case we use the LEXIS and Westlaw citations. We also give students a brief description of the court.

End-of-Chapter Exam Review and Questions

GOAL: Encourage students to practice! At the end of the chapters we provide a list of review points and several additional Exam Strategy exercises in the Question/Strategy/Result format. We also challenge the students with 15 or more problems—Multiple-Choice Questions, Essay Questions, and Discussion Questions. The questions include the following:

- *You Be the Judge Writing Problem*. The students are given appellate arguments on both sides of the question and must prepare a written opinion.

- *Ethics*. This question highlights the ethical issues of a dispute and calls upon the student to formulate a specific, reasoned response.

- *CPA Questions*. For topics covered by the CPA exam, administered by the American Institute of Certified Public Accountants, the Exam Review includes questions from previous CPA exams.

Answers to all the odd-numbered questions are available in Appendix C of the book.

Author Transition

Jeffrey Beatty fought an unremitting ten-year battle against a particularly aggressive form of leukemia, which, despite his great courage and determination, he ultimately lost. Jeffrey, a gentleman to the core, was an immensely kind, funny, and thoughtful human being, someone who sang and danced, and who earned the respect and affection of colleagues and students alike. In writing these books he wanted students to see and understand the impact of law in their everyday lives as well as its role in supporting human dignity, and what's more, he wanted students to laugh.

Jeffrey was a hard act to follow. We feel immensely grateful to have found a worthy successor in Patricia Sánchez Abril. A tenured member of the faculty at the University of Miami School of Business Administration, Patricia is a devoted teacher who has won awards for her teaching in both the undergraduate and graduate programs. She has also published widely in scholarly journals and has won awards for her scholarship. In 2011, the Academy of Legal Studies in Business honored her with its Distinguished Junior Faculty Award.

TEACHING MATERIALS

For more information about any of these ancillaries, contact your Cengage Learning/South-Western Legal Studies Sales Representative, or visit the Beatty & Samuelson Business Law (Standard Edition) website at **www.cengagebrain.com.**

MindTap.   *MindTap*™ is a fully online, highly personalized learning experience combining readings, multimedia, activities, and assessments into a singular Learning Path. Instructors can personalize the Learning Path by customizing Cengage Learning resources and adding their own content via apps that integrate into the *MindTap* framework seamlessly with Learning Management Systems. To view a demo video and learn more about *MindTap*, please visit **www.cengage.com/mindtap.**

Instructor's Manual.   The *Instructor's Manual*, available on the Instructor's Support Site at **www.cengagebrain.com**, includes special features to enhance class discussion and student progress:

- Exam Strategy Problems. If your students would like more of these problems, there is an additional section of Exam Strategy problems in the *Instructor's Manual*.

- Dialogues. These are a series of questions and answers on pivotal cases and topics.

- The questions provide enough material to teach a full session. In a pinch, you could walk into class with nothing but the manual and use the Dialogues to conduct an exciting class.

- Action learning ideas: interviews, quick research projects, drafting exercises, classroom activities, commercial analyses, and other suggested assignments that get students out of their chairs and into the diverse settings of business law.

- A chapter theme and a quote of the day.

- Current Focus. This feature offers updates of text material.

- Additional cases and examples.

- Answers to You Be the Judge cases from the text and to the Exam Review questions found at the end of each chapter.

Cengage Learning Testing Powered by Cognero

Cognero is a flexible online system that allows you to author, edit, and manage test bank content from multiple Cengage Learning solutions; create multiple test versions in an instant; and deliver tests from your LMS, your classroom, or wherever you want.

PowerPoint Lecture Review Slides

PowerPoint slides are available for use by instructors for enhancing their lectures and to aid students in note taking. Download these slides at **www.cengagebrain.com.**

Business Law Digital Video Library

This dynamic online video library features over 60 video clips that spark class discussion and clarify core legal principles. Access to the Business Law Digital Video Library is available as an optional package with each new student text at no additional charge. Students with used books can purchase access to the video clips online. For more information about the Business Law Digital Video Library, visit **www.cengagebrain.com.**

Interaction with the Authors

This is our standard: Every professor who adopts this book must have a superior experience. We are available to help in any way we can. Adopters of this text often call us or email us to ask questions, obtain a syllabus, offer suggestions, share pedagogical concerns, or inquire about ancillaries. (And if you would like to share your course syllabus, please send it to us so that we can post it on our blog, bizlawupdate.com.) One of the pleasures of working on this project has been this link to so many colleagues around the country. We value those connections, are eager to respond, and would be happy to hear from you.

Jeffrey F. Beatty

Susan S. Samuelson
Phone: (617) 353-2033
Email: ssamuels@bu.edu

Patricia Sánchez Abril
Phone: (305) 284-6999
Email: pabril@miami.edu

ACKNOWLEDGMENTS

We are grateful to the following reviewers who gave such helpful comments on the first seven editions:

Joseph Adamo
Cazenovia College

Joy M. Alessi
New York City College of
Technology

J. Mark Anderson
Athens State University

John H. Bailey, III
Vanderbilt University

Robert Bird
University of Connecticut

Weldon Blake
Bethune Cookman College

Karl Boedecker
University of San Francisco

Jeff W. Bruns
Bacone College

Martin Carrigan
The University of Findlay

Machiavelli Chao
University of California, Irvine

Amy Chataginer
Mississippi Gulf Coast
Community College

Eric Chen
Saint Joseph College

Brad Childs
Belmont University

Wade M. Chumney
Georgia Institute of
Technology

George Oscar Darkenwald
South Puget Sound
Community College

Irene K. Rudnick
University of South Carolina,
Aiken

Linda Samuels
The University of Akron

Kurt M. Saunders
California State University, Northridge

Minna Schiller
Bellevue Community College

Sean D. K. Scott
St. Petersburg College

Lara Short
Middle Tennessee State University

Yolanda I. Smith
Northern Virginia Community College

Charles Soos
Rutgers School of Business

Alexis Stokes
Texas State University

Susan Marie Taylor
Andrews University

Ben Thompson
Georgia Southern University

Jan Tucker
Western Governors University

Bob Young
University of Nebraska at Kearney

David B. Washington
Augsburg College

Scott White
University of Wisconsin–Platteville

Melanie Williams
California State University, Northridge

Asher Wilson
Central Washington University–Des
Moines

Dexter Woods
Ohio Northern University

ABOUT THE AUTHORS

Jeffrey F. Beatty was an associate professor of Business Law at the Boston University School of Management. After receiving his B.A. from Sarah Lawrence and his J.D. from Boston University, he practiced with the Greater Boston Legal Services representing indigent clients. At Boston University, he won the Metcalf Cup and Prize, the university's highest teaching award. Professor Beatty also wrote plays and television scripts that were performed in Boston, London, and Amsterdam.

Susan S. Samuelson is a professor of Business Law at Boston University's School of Management. After earning her A.B. at Harvard University and her J.D. at Harvard Law School, Professor Samuelson practiced with the firm of Choate, Hall and Stewart. She has written many articles on legal issues for scholarly and popular journals, including the *American Business Law Journal, Ohio State Law Journal, Boston University Law Review, Harvard Journal on Legislation, National Law Journal, Sloan Management Review, Inc. Magazine, Better Homes and Gardens,* and *Boston Magazine.* At Boston University she won the Broderick Prize for excellence in teaching. For more than a decade, Professor Samuelson was the faculty director of the Boston University Executive MBA program.

Patricia Sánchez Abril is an associate professor of Business Law at the University of Miami School of Business Administration. Professor Abril's research has appeared in the *American Business Law Journal, Harvard Journal of Law & Technology, Florida Law Review, Houston Law Review, Wake Forest Law Review, Northwestern Journal of Technology and Intellectual Property,* and *Columbia Business Law Journal,* among other journals. In 2011, the *American Business Law Journal* honored her with its Distinguished Junior Faculty Award, in recognition of exceptional early career achievement. In 2014, one of her articles on privacy won the Outstanding Proceedings competition at the annual conference of the Academy of Legal Studies in Business. Professor Abril has won awards for her teaching in both the undergraduate and graduate programs at the University of Miami.

For Jeffrey, best of colleagues and dearest of friends.

S.S.S.

The Legal Environment

CHAPTER 1

INTRODUCTION TO LAW

© Creative Travel Projects/Shutterstock.com

The Pagans were a motorcycle gang with a reputation for violence. Two of its rougher members, Rhino and Backdraft, entered a tavern called the Pub Zone, shoving their way past the bouncer. The pair wore gang insignia, in violation of the bar's rules. For a while, all was quiet, as the two sipped drinks at the bar. Then they followed an innocent patron toward the men's room, and things happened fast.

"Wait a moment," you may be thinking. "Are we reading a chapter on business law or one about biker crimes in a roadside tavern?" Both.

Law is powerful, essential, and fascinating. We hope this book will persuade you of all three ideas. Law can also be surprising. Later in the chapter, we will return to the Pub Zone (with armed guards) and follow Rhino and Backdraft to the back of the pub. Yes, the pair engaged in street crime, which is hardly a focus of this text. However, their criminal acts will enable us to explore one of the law's basic principles—negligence. Should a pub owner pay money damages to the victim of gang violence? The owner herself did nothing aggressive. Should she have prevented the harm? Does her failure to stop the assault make her liable?

We place great demands on our courts, asking them to make our large, complex, and sometimes violent society into a safer, fairer, more orderly place. The Pub Zone case is a good example of how judges reason their way through the convoluted issues involved. What began as a gang incident ends up as a matter of commercial liability. We will traipse after Rhino and Backdraft because they have a lesson to teach anyone who enters the world of business.

> **Should a pub owner pay money damages to the victim of gang violence?**

1-1 THE ROLE OF LAW IN SOCIETY

1-1a Power

The strong reach of the law touches nearly everything we do, especially at work. Consider a mid-level manager at Sublime Corp., which manufactures and distributes video games.

During the course of a day's work, she might negotiate a deal with a game developer (contract law). Before signing any deals, she might research whether similar games already exist, which might diminish her ability to market the proposed new game (intellectual property law). One of her subordinates might complain about being harassed by a coworker (employment law). Another worker may complain about being required to work long hours (administrative law). And she may consider investing her own money in her company's stock, but she may wonder whether she will get into trouble if she invests based on inside information (securities law).

It is not only as a corporate manager that you will confront the law. As a voter, investor, juror, entrepreneur, and community member, you will influence and be affected by the law. Whenever you take a stance about a legal issue, whether in the corporate office, in the voting booth, or as part of local community groups, you help to create the fabric of our nation. Your views are vital. This book will offer you knowledge and ideas from which to form and continually reassess your legal opinions and values.

1-1b Importance

Law is also essential. *Every* society of which we have any historical record has had some system of laws. For example, consider the Visigoths, a nomadic European people who overran much of present-day France and Spain during the fifth and sixth centuries A.D. Their code admirably required judges to be "quick of perception, clear in judgment, and lenient in the infliction of penalties." It detailed dozens of crimes.

Our legal system is largely based upon the English model, but many societies contributed ideas. The Iroquois Native Americans, for example, played a role in the creation of our own government. Five major nations made up the Iroquois group: the Mohawk, Cayuga, Oneida, Onondaga, and Seneca. Each nation governed its own domestic issues. But each nation also elected "sachems" to a League of the Iroquois. The league had authority over any matters that were common to all, such as relations with outsiders. Thus, by the fifteenth century, the Iroquois had solved the problem of *federalism:* how to have two levels of government, each with specified powers. Their system impressed Benjamin Franklin and others and influenced the drafting of our Constitution, with its powers divided between state and federal governments.[1]

1-1c Fascination

In 1835, the young French aristocrat Alexis de Tocqueville traveled through the United States, observing the newly democratic people and the qualities that made them unique. One of the things that struck de Tocqueville most forcefully was the American tendency to file suit: "Scarcely any political question arises in the United States that is not resolved, sooner or later, into a judicial question."[2] De Tocqueville got it right: For better or worse, we do expect courts to resolve many problems.

Not only do Americans litigate—they watch each other do it. Every television season offers at least one new courtroom drama to a national audience breathless for more

---

[1]Jack Weatherford, *Indian Givers* (New York: Fawcett Columbine, 1988), pp. 133–150.
[2]Alexis de Tocqueville, *Democracy in America* (1835), Vol. 1, Ch. 16.

cross-examination. Almost all of the states permit live television coverage of real trials. The most heavily viewed event in the history of the medium was the O. J. Simpson murder trial, in which a famous football star was accused of killing his wife. In most nations, coverage of judicial proceedings is not allowed.[3]

The law is a big part of our lives, and it is wise to know something about it. Within a few weeks, you will probably find yourself following legal events in the news with keener interest and deeper understanding. In this chapter, we develop the background for our study. We look at where law comes from: its history and its present-day institutions. In the section on jurisprudence, we examine different theories about what "law" really means. And finally we see how courts—and students—analyze a case.

1-2 ORIGINS OF OUR LAW

It would be nice if we could look up "the law" in one book, memorize it, and then apply it. But the law is not that simple, and *cannot* be that simple, because it reflects the complexity of contemporary life. In truth, there is no such thing as "the law." Principles and rules of law actually come from *many different* sources. This is so, in part, because we inherited a complex structure of laws from England.

Additionally, ours is a nation born in revolution, and created, in large part, to protect the rights of its people from the government. The Founding Fathers created a national government but insisted that the individual states maintain control in many areas. As a result, each state has its own government with exclusive power over many important areas of our lives. To top it off, the Founders guaranteed many rights to the people alone, ordering national *and* state governments to keep clear. This has worked, but it has caused a multilayered system, with 50 state governments and one federal government all creating and enforcing law.

1-2a English Roots

England in the tenth century was a rustic agricultural community with a tiny population and very little law or order. Vikings invaded repeatedly, terrorizing the Anglo-Saxon peoples. Criminals were hard to catch in the heavily forested, sparsely settled nation. The king used a primitive legal system to maintain a tenuous control over his people.

England was divided into shires, and daily administration was carried out by a "shire reeve," later called a sheriff. The shire reeve collected taxes and did what he could to keep peace, apprehending criminals and acting as mediator between feuding families. Two or three times a year, a shire court met; lower courts met more frequently. Today, this method of resolving disputes lives on as mediation, which we will discuss in Chapter 3.

Because there were so few officers to keep the peace, Anglo-Saxon society created an interesting method of ensuring public order. Every freeman belonged to a group of 10 freemen known as a "tithing," headed by a "tithingman." If anyone injured a person outside his tithing or interfered with the king's property, all 10 men of the tithing could be forced to pay. Today, we still use this idea of collective responsibility in business partnerships. All partners are personally responsible for the debts of the partnership. They could potentially lose their homes and all assets because of the irresponsible conduct of one partner. That liability has helped create new forms of business organization, including limited liability companies.

When cases did come before an Anglo-Saxon court, the parties would often be represented by a clergyman, by a nobleman, or by themselves. There were few professional lawyers. Each

---

[3]Regardless of whether we allow cameras, it is an undeniable benefit of the electronic age that we can obtain information quickly. From time to time, we will mention websites of interest. Some of these are for nonprofit groups, while others are commercial sites. We do not endorse or advocate on behalf of any group or company; we simply wish to alert you to what is available.

party produced "oath helpers," usually 12, who would swear that one version of events was correct. The Anglo-Saxon oath helpers were forerunners of our modern jury of 12 persons.

In 1066, the Normans conquered England. William the Conqueror made a claim never before made in England: that he owned all of the land. The king then granted sections of his lands to his favorite noblemen, as his tenants in chief, creating the system of feudalism. These tenants in chief then granted parts of their land to *tenants in demesne*, who actually occupied a particular estate. Each tenant in demesne owed fidelity to his lord (hence, "landlord"). So what? Just this: Land became the most valuable commodity in all of England, and our law still reflects that. One thousand years later, American law still regards land as special. The Statute of Frauds, which we study in the section on contracts, demands that contracts for the sale or lease of property be in writing. And landlord-tenant law, vital to students and many others, still reflects its ancient roots. Some of a landlord's rights are based on the 1,000-year-old tradition that land is uniquely valuable.

In 1250, Henry de Bracton (d. 1268) wrote a legal treatise that still influences us. *De Legibus et Consuetudinibus Angliae (On the Laws and Customs of England)*, written in Latin, summarized many of the legal rulings in cases since the Norman Conquest. De Bracton was teaching judges to rule based on previous cases. He was helping to establish the idea of **precedent**. **The doctrine of precedent, which developed gradually over centuries, requires that judges decide current cases based on previous rulings.** This vital principle is the heart of American common law. Precedent ensures predictability. Suppose a 17-year-old student promises to lease an apartment from a landlord, but then changes her mind. The landlord sues to enforce the lease. The student claims that she cannot be held to the agreement because she is a minor. The judge will look for precedent, that is, older cases dealing with the same issue, and he will find many holding that a contract generally may not be enforced against a minor. That precedent is binding on this case, and the student wins. **The accumulation of precedent, based on case after case, makes up the common law.**

Today's society is dramatically different from that of medieval English society. But interestingly, legal disputes from hundreds of years ago are often quite recognizable today. Some things have changed but others never do.

Here is an actual case from more than six centuries ago, in the court's own language. The plaintiff claims that he asked the defendant to heal his eye with "herbs and other medicines." He says the defendant did it so badly that he blinded the plaintiff in that eye.

Medieval tenants in demesne harrowing, plowing and seeding a field.

North Wind/North Wind Picture Archives

Precedent

The tendency to decide current cases based on previous rulings.

Common law

Judge-made law

The Oculist's Case (1329)

LI MS. Hale 137 (1), fo. 150, Nottingham[4]

Attorney Launde [for defendant]: Sir, you plainly see how [the plaintiff claims] that he had submitted himself to [the defendant's] medicines and his care; and after that he can assign no trespass in his person, inasmuch as he submitted himself to his care: But this action, if he has any, sounds naturally in breach of covenant. We demand [that the case be dismissed].

---

[4]J. Baker and S. Milsom, *Sources of English Legal History* (London: Butterworth & Co., 1986).

Excerpts from Judge Denum's Decision: I saw a Newcastle man arraigned before my fellow justice and me for the death of a man. I asked the reason for the indictment, and it was said that he had slain a man under his care, who died within four days afterwards. And because I saw that he was a [doctor] and that he had not done the thing feloniously but [accidentally]

I ordered him to be discharged. And suppose a blacksmith, who is a man of skill, injures your horse with a nail, whereby you lose your horse: You shall never have recovery against him. No more shall you here.

Afterwards the plaintiff did not wish to pursue his case any more.

This case from 1329 is an ancient medical malpractice action. Attorney Launde does not deny that his client blinded the plaintiff. He claims that the plaintiff has brought the wrong kind of lawsuit. Launde argues that the plaintiff should have brought a case of "covenant"; that is, a lawsuit about a contract.

Judge Denum decides the case on a different principle. He gives judgment to the defendant because the plaintiff voluntarily sought medical care. He implies that the defendant would lose only if he had attacked the plaintiff. As we will see when we study negligence law, this case might have a different outcome today. Note also the informality of the judge's ruling. He rather casually mentions that he came across a related case once before and that he would stand by that outcome. The idea of precedent is just beginning to take hold.

1-2b Law in the United States

The colonists brought with them a basic knowledge of English law, some of which they were content to adopt as their own. Other parts, such as religious restrictions, were abhorrent to them. Many had made the dangerous trip to America precisely to escape persecution, and they were not interested in recreating their difficulties in a new land. Finally, some laws were simply irrelevant or unworkable in a world that was socially and geographically so different. American law ever since has been a blend of the ancient principles of English common law and a zeal and determination for change.

During the nineteenth century, the United States changed from a weak, rural nation into one of vast size and potential power. Cities grew, factories appeared, and sweeping movements of social migration changed the population. Changing conditions raised new legal questions. Did workers have a right to form industrial unions? To what extent should a manufacturer be liable if its product injured someone? Could a state government invalidate an employment contract that required 16-hour workdays? Should one company be permitted to dominate an entire industry?

In the twentieth century, the rate of social and technological change increased, creating new legal puzzles. Were some products, such as automobiles, so inherently dangerous that the seller should be responsible for injuries even if no mistakes were made in manufacturing? Who should clean up toxic waste if the company that had caused the pollution no longer existed? If a consumer signed a contract with a billion-dollar corporation, should the agreement be enforced even if the consumer never understood it? New and startling questions arise with great regularity. Before we can begin to examine the answers, we need to understand the sources of contemporary law.

1-3 SOURCES OF CONTEMPORARY LAW

Throughout the text, we will examine countless legal ideas. But binding rules come from many different places. This section describes the significant categories of laws in the United States.

1-3a **United States Constitution**

America's greatest legal achievement was the writing of the United States Constitution in 1787. It is the supreme law of the land.[5] Any law that conflicts with it is void. This federal Constitution does three basic things. First, it establishes the national government of the United States, with its three branches. Second, it creates a system of checks and balances among the branches. And third, the Constitution guarantees many basic rights to the American people.

Branches of Government

The Founding Fathers sought a division of government power. They did not want all power centralized in a king or in anyone else. And so, the Constitution divides legal authority into three pieces: legislative, executive, and judicial power.

Legislative power gives the ability to create new laws. In Article I, the Constitution gives this power to the Congress, which is comprised of two chambers—a Senate and a House of Representatives. Voters in all 50 states elect representatives who go to Washington, D.C., to serve in the Congress and debate new legal ideas.

The House of Representatives has 435 voting members. A state's voting power is based on its population. Large states (Texas, California, and Florida) send dozens of representatives to the House. Some small states (Wyoming, North Dakota, and Delaware) send only one. The Senate has 100 voting members—two from each state.

Executive power is the authority to enforce laws. Article II of the Constitution establishes the president as commander in chief of the armed forces and the head of the executive branch of the federal government.

Judicial power gives the right to interpret laws and determine their validity. Article III places the Supreme Court at the head of the judicial branch of the federal government. Interpretive power is often underrated, but it is often every bit as important as the ability to create laws in the first place. For instance, the Supreme Court ruled that privacy provisions of the Constitution protect a woman's right to abortion, although neither the word "privacy" nor "abortion" appears in the text of the Constitution.[6]

At times, courts void laws altogether. For example, in 1995, the Supreme Court ruled that the Gun-Free School Zones Act of 1990 was unconstitutional because Congress did not have the authority to pass such a law.[7]

Checks and Balances

The authors of the Constitution were not content merely to divide government power three ways. They also wanted to give each part of the government some power over the other two branches. Many people complain about "gridlock" in Washington, but the government is slow and sluggish by design. The Founding Fathers wanted to create a system that, without broad agreement, would tend towards inaction.

The president can veto Congressional legislation. Congress can impeach the president. The Supreme Court can void laws passed by Congress. The president appoints judges to the federal courts, including the Supreme Court, but these nominees do not serve unless approved by the Senate. Congress (with help from the 50 states) can override the Supreme

---

[5]The Constitution took effect in 1788, when 9 of 13 colonies ratified it. Two more colonies ratified it that year, and the last of the 13 did so in 1789, after the government was already in operation. The complete text of the Constitution appears in Appendix A.

[6]Roe v. Wade, 410 U.S. 113 (1973).

[7]United States v. Alfonso Lopez, Jr., 514 U.S. 549 (1995).

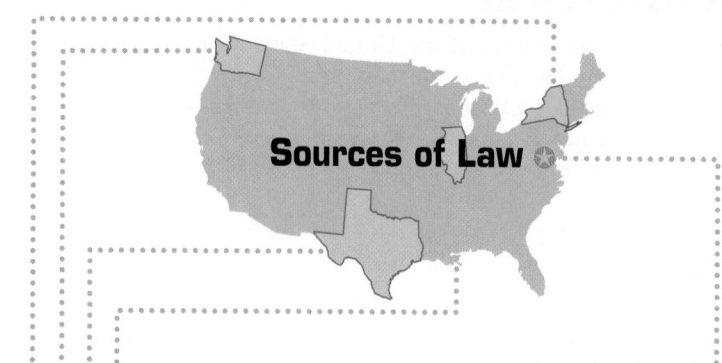

Sources of Law

50 State Governments

State Constitution
establishes the state government
guarantees the rights of state residents

Legislative Branch	Executive Branch	Judicial Branch

State Legislature
passes statutes on state law
creates state agencies

Governor
proposes statutes
signs or vetoes statutes
oversees state agencies

State Courts
create state common law
interpret statutes
review constitutionality of statutes and other acts

Administrative Agencies
oversee day-to-day application of law in dozens of commercial and other areas

One Federal Government

United States Constitution
establishes limited federal government
protects states' power
guarantees liberty of citizens

Legislative Branch	Executive Branch	Judicial Branch

Congress
passes statutes
ratifies treaties
creates administrative agencies

President
proposes statutes
signs or vetoes statutes
oversees administrative agencies

Federal Courts
interpret statutes
create (limited) federal common law
review the constitutionality of statutes and other legal acts

Administrative Agencies
oversee day-to-day application of law in dozens of commercial and other areas

Federal Form of Government. Principles and rules of law come from many sources. The government in Washington creates and enforces law throughout the nation. But 50 state governments exercise great power in local affairs. And citizens enjoy constitutional protection from both state and federal government. The Founding Fathers wanted this balance of power and rights, but the overlapping authority creates legal complexity.

Court by amending the Constitution. The president and the Congress influence the Supreme Court by controlling who is placed on the court in the first place.

Many of these checks and balances will be examined in more detail later in this book, starting in Chapter 4.

Fundamental Rights

The Constitution also grants many of our most basic liberties. For the most part, they are found in the amendments to the Constitution. The First Amendment guarantees the rights of free speech, free press, and the free exercise of religion. The Fourth, Fifth, and Sixth Amendments protect the rights of any person accused of a crime. Other amendments ensure that the government treats all people equally and that it pays for any property it takes from a citizen.

By creating a limited government of three branches, and guaranteeing basic liberties to all citizens, the Constitution became one of the most important documents ever written.

1-3b Statutes

The second important source of law is statutory law. The Constitution gave to the United States Congress the power to pass laws on various subjects. These laws are called **statutes**, and they can cover absolutely any topic, so long as they do not violate the Constitution.

> **Statute**
> A law created by a legislature

Almost all statutes are created by the same method. An idea for a new law—on taxes, body. health care, texting while driving, or any other topic, big or small—is first proposed in the Congress. This idea is called a *bill*. The House and Senate then independently vote on the bill. To pass Congress, the bill must win a simple majority vote in each of these chambers.

If Congress passes a bill, it goes to the White House for the president's approval. If the president signs it, a new statute is created. It is no longer a mere idea; it is the law of the land. If the president refuses to approve, or *vetoes* a bill, it does not become a statute unless Congress overrides the veto. To do that, both the House and the Senate must approve the bill by a two-thirds majority. If this happens, it becomes a statute without the president's signature.

1-3c Common Law

Binding legal ideas often come from the courts. Judges generally follow *precedent*. When courts decide a case, they tend to apply the legal rules that other courts have used in similar cases.

The principle that precedent is binding on later cases is called *stare decisis*, which means "let the decision stand." *Stare decisis* makes the law predictable and this, in turn, enables businesses and private citizens to plan intelligently.

It is important to note that precedent is binding only on *lower* courts. For example, if the Supreme Court decided a case in one way in 1965, it is under no obligation to follow precedent if the same issue arises in 2015.

Sometimes, this is quite beneficial. In 1896, the Supreme Court decided (unbelievably) that segregation—separating people by race in schools, hotels, public transportation, and other public services—was legal under certain conditions.[8] In 1954, on the exact same issue, the court changed its mind.[9]

In other circumstances, it is more difficult to see the value in breaking with an established rule.

---

[8]Plessy v. Ferguson, 163 U.S. 537 (1896).
[9]Brown v. Board of Education of Topeka, 347 U.S. 483 (1954).

1-3d **Court Orders**

Judges have the authority to issue court orders that place binding obligations on specific people or companies. An injunction, for example, is a court order to stop doing something. A judge might order a stalker to stay more than 500 yards away from an ex-boyfriend or -girlfriend. An alcoholic might be ordered to stop drinking and enter rehab. Courts have the authority to imprison or fine those who violate their orders.

1-3e **Administrative Law**

In a society as large and diverse as ours, the executive and legislative branches of government cannot oversee all aspects of commerce. Congress passes statutes about air safety, but United States senators do not stand around air traffic towers, serving coffee to keep everyone awake. The executive branch establishes rules concerning how foreign nationals enter the United States, but presidents are reluctant to sit on the dock of the bay, watching the ships come in. Administrative agencies do this day-to-day work.

> **United States senators do not stand around air traffic towers, serving coffee to keep everyone awake.**

Most government agencies are created by Congress. Familiar examples are the Environmental Protection Agency (EPA), the Securities and Exchange Commission (SEC), and the Internal Revenue Service (IRS), whose feelings are hurt if it does not hear from you every April 15. Agencies have the power to create laws called *regulations*.

1-3f **Treaties**

The Constitution authorizes the president to make treaties with foreign nations. These must then be ratified by the United States Senate by a two-thirds vote. When they are ratified, they are as binding upon all citizens as any federal statute. In 1994, the Senate ratified the North American Free Trade Agreement (NAFTA) with Mexico and Canada. NAFTA was controversial then and remains so today—but it is the law of the land.

1-4 CLASSIFICATIONS

We have seen where law originated. Now we need to classify the various types of laws. First, we will distinguish between criminal and civil law. Then, we will take a look at the intersection between law and morality.

1-4a **Criminal and Civil Law**

Criminal law

Criminal law prohibits certain behavior for the benefit of society.

It is a crime to embezzle money from a bank, to steal a car, to sell cocaine. **Criminal law concerns behavior so threatening that society outlaws it altogether.** Most criminal laws are statutes, passed by Congress or a state legislature. The government itself prosecutes the wrongdoer, regardless of what the bank president or car owner wants. A district attorney, paid by the government, brings the case to court. The victim is not in charge of the case, although she may appear as a witness. The government will seek to punish the defendant with a prison sentence, a fine, or both. If there is a fine, the money goes to the state, not to the injured party.

Civil law

Civil law regulates the rights and duties between parties.

Civil law is different, and most of this book is about civil law. **The civil law regulates the rights and duties between parties.** Tracy agrees in writing to lease you a 30,000-square-foot store in her shopping mall. She now has a *legal duty* to make the space available. But then another tenant offers her more money, and she refuses to let you move in. Tracy has violated her duty, but she has not committed a crime. The government will not prosecute the case. It is up to you to file a civil lawsuit. Your case will be based on the common law of contract. You will also seek equitable relief, namely, an injunction ordering Tracy not to lease to anyone else. You should win the suit, and you will get your injunction and some monetary damages. But Tracy will not go to jail.

Some conduct involves both civil and criminal law. Suppose Tracy is so upset over losing the court case that she becomes drunk and causes a serious car accident. She has committed the crime of driving while intoxicated, and the state will prosecute. Tracy may be fined or imprisoned. She has also committed negligence, and the injured party will file a lawsuit against her, seeking money. We will again see civil and criminal law joined together in the *Pub Zone* case, later in the chapter.

1-4b Law and Morality

Law is different from morality, yet the two are obviously linked. There are many instances when the law duplicates what all of us would regard as a moral position. It is negligent to drive too fast in a school zone, and few would dispute the moral value of seeking to limit harm to students. And the same holds with contract law: If the owner of land agrees in writing to sell property to a buyer at a stated price, both the buyer and the seller must go through with the deal, and the legal outcome matches our moral expectations.

On the other hand, we have had laws that we now clearly regard as immoral. At the turn of the century, a factory owner could typically fire a worker for any reason at all—including, for example, his religious or political views. It is immoral to fire a worker because she is Jewish—and today the law prohibits it.

Finally, there are legal issues where the morality is less clear. You are walking down a country lane and notice a three-year-old child playing with matches near a barn filled with hay. Are you obligated to intervene? No, says the law, though many think that is preposterous. (See Chapter 4, on common law, for more about this topic.) A company buys property and then discovers, buried under the ground, toxic waste that will cost $300,000 to clean up. The original owner has gone bankrupt. Should the new owner be forced to pay for the cleanup? If the new owner fails to pay for the job, who will? (See Chapter 40, on environmental law, for more discussion on this issue.)

Chapter 2 will further examine the bond between law and morality, but our ethics discussion does not end there. Throughout the text, you will find ethics questions and features, like the one that follows, which ask you to grapple with the moral dimensions of legal questions.

Do we want to live in a world where no one ever pays attention in public places?

Ethics It was a cold winter's day. In one of New York City's dank, dark subway stations, dozens of people waited for the next train, most of them engrossed in their smartphones. All of a sudden, a man was shoved onto the subway tracks. He screamed for help and struggled to climb up onto the platform. Because no one helped him, he was crushed to death by an oncoming train.[10]

---

[10]Christine Rosen, "The Gadget and the Bad Samaritan," *The Wall Street Journal*, Oct. 26–27, 2013.

Some of the bystanders were so busy peering at their smartphones, they did not even hear the man's screams for help. Use of technology has changed our awareness of our surroundings and our sense of civility and duty to those around us. Did these onlookers have an obligation to be more aware of their environment? Do we want to live in a world where no one ever pays attention in public places?

The second group saw what was happening, but still did not help. Sociologists call this the "bystander effect." Studies have shown that people in a group are much less likely to help others than are individuals on their own. In a crowd, responsibility is diffused. Everyone assumes that someone else will act.

A third group pulled out their phones to capture images and videos of the last minutes of the man's life. One man sold his picture of the episode to the *New York Post*, which published it on the cover the next day. Other witnesses shared their videos on YouTube. Some of these witnesses might argue that their images informed many people about the incident and brought awareness of it. Did they behave ethically?

What are the moral obligations of each of these groups of witnesses? Who has acted most unethically (if anyone)? Remember that the decision to help (or not) is one that is made in a split second. What would you have done?

1-5 JURISPRUDENCE

jurisprudence
The philosophy of law

We have had a glimpse of legal history and a summary of the present-day sources of American law. But what *is* law? That question is the basis of a field known as **jurisprudence**. What is the real nature of law? Can there be such a thing as an "illegal" law?

1-5a **Legal Positivism**

Sovereign
The recognized political power, whom citizens obey.

This philosophy can be simply stated: Law is what the sovereign says it is. The sovereign is the recognized political power whom citizens obey, so in the United States, both state and federal governments are sovereign. A legal positivist holds that whatever the sovereign declares to be the law *is* the law, whether it is right or wrong.

The primary criticism of legal positivism is that it seems to leave no room for questions of morality. A law permitting a factory owner to fire a worker because she is Catholic is surely different from a law prohibiting arson. Do citizens in a democracy have a duty to consider such differences? Consider the following example.

Most states allow citizens to pass laws directly at the ballot box, a process called voter referendum. California voters often do this, and during the 1990s, they passed one of the state's most controversial laws. Proposition 187 was designed to curb illegal immigration into the state by eliminating social spending for undocumented aliens. Citizens debated the measure fiercely but passed it by a large margin. One section of the new law forbade public schools from educating illegal immigrants. The law obligated a principal to inquire into the immigration status of all children enrolled in the school and to report undocumented students to immigration authorities. Several San Diego school principals rejected the new rules, stating that they would neither inquire into immigration status nor report undocumented aliens. Their statements produced a heated response. Some San Diego residents castigated the school officials as lawbreakers, claiming that:

- A school officer who knowingly disobeyed a law was setting a terrible example for students, who would assume they were free to do the same;

- The principals were advocating permanent residence and a free education for anyone able to evade our immigration laws; and

- The officials were scorning grass-roots democracy by disregarding a law passed by popular referendum.

Others applauded the principals' position, asserting that:

- The referendum's rules would transform school officials from educators into border police, forcing them to cross-examine young children and their parents;

- The new law was foolish because it punished innocent children for violations committed by their parents; and

- Our nation has long respected civil disobedience based on humanitarian ideals, and these officials were providing moral leadership to the whole community.

Ultimately, no one had to decide whether to obey Proposition 187. A federal court ruled that only Congress had the power to regulate immigration and that California's attempt was unconstitutional and void. The debate over immigration reform—and ethics—did not end, however. It continues to be a thorny issue.

1-5b Natural Law

St. Thomas Aquinas (1225–1274) answered the legal positivists even before they had spoken. In his *Summa Theologica*, he argued that an unjust law is no law at all and need not be obeyed. It is not enough that a sovereign makes a command. The law must have a moral basis.

Where do we find the moral basis that would justify a law? Aquinas says that "good is that which all things seek after." Therefore, the fundamental rule of all laws is that "good is to be done and promoted, and evil is to be avoided." This sounds appealing, but also vague. Exactly which laws promote good and which do not? Is it better to have a huge corporation dominate a market or many smaller companies competing? Did the huge company get that way by being better than its competitors? If Wal-Mart moves into a rural area, establishes a mammoth store, and sells inexpensive products, is that "good"? Yes, if you are a consumer who cares only about prices. No, if you are the owner of a Main Street store driven into bankruptcy. Maybe, if you are a resident who values small-town life but wants lower prices.

1-5c Legal Realism

Legal realists take a very different tack. They claim it does not matter what is written as law. What counts is who enforces that law and by what process it is enforced. All of us are biased by issues such as income, education, family background, race, religion, and many other factors. These personal characteristics, they say, determine which contracts will be enforced and which ignored, why some criminals receive harsh sentences while others get off lightly, and so on.

Judge Jones hears a multimillion dollar lawsuit involving an airplane crash. Was the airline negligent? The law is the same everywhere, but legal realists say that Jones's background will determine the outcome. If she spent 20 years representing insurance companies, she will tend to favor the airline. If her law practice consisted of helping the "little guy," she will favor the plaintiff.

Other legal realists argue, more aggressively, that those in power use the machinery of the law to perpetuate their control. The outcome of a given case will be determined by the needs of those with money and political clout. A court puts "window dressing" on a decision, they say, so that society thinks there are principles behind the law. A problem with legal realism, however, is its denial that any lawmaker can overcome personal bias. Yet clearly some do act unselfishly.

SUMMARY OF JURISPRUDENCE

Legal Positivism	Law is what the sovereign says.
Natural Law	An unjust law is no law at all.
Legal Realism	Who enforces the law counts more than what is in writing.

No one school of jurisprudence is likely to seem perfect. We urge you to keep the different theories in mind as you read cases in the book. Ask yourself which school of thought is the best fit for you.

1-6 WORKING WITH THE BOOK'S FEATURES

In this section, we introduce a few of the book's features and discuss how you can use them effectively. We will start with *cases*.

1-6a Analyzing a Case

A law case is the decision a court has made in a civil lawsuit or criminal prosecution. Cases are the heart of the law and an important part of this book. Reading them effectively takes practice. This chapter's opening scenario is fictional, but the following real case involves a similar situation. Who can be held liable for the assault? Let's see.

KUEHN V. PUB ZONE

364 N. J. Super. 301
Superior Court of New Jersey, 2003

Facts: Maria Kerkoulas owned the Pub Zone bar. She knew that several motorcycle gangs frequented the tavern. From her own experience tending bar, and conversations with city police, she knew that some of the gangs, including the Pagans, were dangerous and prone to attack customers for no reason. Kerkoulas posted a sign prohibiting any motorcycle gangs from entering the bar while wearing "colors"; that is, insignia of their gangs. She believed that gangs without their colors were less prone to violence, and experience proved her right.

Rhino, Backdraft, and several other Pagans, all wearing colors, pushed their way past the tavern's bouncer and approached the bar. Although Kerkoulas saw their colors, she allowed them to stay for one drink. They later moved towards the back of the pub, and Kerkoulas believed they were departing. In fact, they followed a customer named Karl Kuehn to the men's room, where, without any provocation, they savagely beat him. Kuehn was knocked unconscious and suffered brain hemorrhaging, disc herniation, and numerous fractures of facial bones. He was forced to undergo various surgeries, including eye reconstruction.

Although the government prosecuted Rhino and Backdraft for their vicious assault, our case does not concern that prosecution. Kuehn sued the Pub Zone, and that is the case we will read. The jury awarded him $300,000 in damages. However, the trial court judge overruled the jury's verdict. He granted a judgment for the Pub Zone, meaning that the tavern owed nothing. The judge ruled that the pub's owner could not have foreseen the attack on Kuehn, and had no duty to protect him from an outlaw motorcycle gang. Kuehn appealed, and the appeals court's decision follows:

Issue: *Did the Pub Zone have a duty to protect Kuehn from the Pagans' attack?*

Excerpts from Judge Payne's Decision: Whether a duty exists depends upon an evaluation of a number of factors including the nature of the underlying risk of harm, that is, its foreseeability and severity, the opportunity and ability to exercise care to prevent the harm, the comparative interests of and the relationships between or among the parties, and, ultimately, based on considerations of public policy and fairness, the societal interest in the proposed solution.

Since the possessor [of a business] is not an insurer of the visitor's safety, he is ordinarily under no duty to exercise any care until he knows or has reason to know that the acts of the third person are occurring, or are about to occur. He may, however, know or have reason to know, from past experience, that there is a likelihood of conduct on the part of third persons in general which is likely to endanger the safety of the visitor, even though he has no reason to expect it on the part of any particular individual.

We find the totality of the circumstances presented in this case give rise to a duty on the part of the Pub Zone to have taken reasonable precautions against the danger posed by the Pagans as a group. In this case, there was no reason to suspect any particular Pagan of violent conduct. However, the gang was collectively known to Kerkoulas to engage in random violence. Thus, Kerkoulas had knowledge as the result of past experience and from other sources that there was a likelihood of conduct on the part of third persons in general that was likely to endanger the safety of a patron at some unspecified future time. A duty to take precautions against the endangering conduct thus arose.

We do not regard our recognition of a duty in this case to give rise to either strict or absolute liability on the part of the Pub Zone. To fulfill its duty in this context, the Pub Zone was merely required to employ "reasonable" safety precautions. It already had in place a prohibition against bikers who were wearing their colors, and that prohibition, together with the practice of calling the police when a breach occurred, had been effective in greatly diminishing the occurrence of biker incidents on the premises. The evidence establishes that the prohibition was not enforced on the night at issue, that three Pagans were permitted entry while wearing their colors, and the police were not called. Once entry was achieved, the Pub Zone remained under a duty to exercise reasonable precautions against an attack.

The jury's verdict must therefore be reinstated.

Analysis

Let's take it from the top. The case is called *Kuehn v. Pub Zone*. Karl Kuehn is the **plaintiff**, the person who is suing. The Pub Zone is being sued, and is called the **defendant**. In this example, the plaintiff's name happens to appear first, but that is not always true. When a defendant loses a trial and files an appeal, *some* courts reverse the names of the parties.

The next line gives the legal citation, which indicates where to find the case in a law library. We explain in the footnote how to locate a book if you plan to do research.[11]

The *Facts* section provides a background to the lawsuit, written by the authors of this text. The court's own explanation of the facts is often many pages long, and may involve complex matters irrelevant to the subject covered in this book, so we relate only what is necessary. This section will usually include some mention of what happened at the trial court. Lawsuits always begin in a trial court. The losing party often appeals to a court of appeals, and it is usually an appeals court decision that we are reading. The trial judge ruled in favor of Pub Zone, but later, in the decision we are reading, Kuehn wins.

Plaintiff
The party who is suing

Defendant
The party being sued

---

[11] If you want to do legal research, you need to know where to find particular legal decisions. A citation is the case's "address," which guides you to the official book in which it is published. Look, for example at *Kuehn v. Pub Zone*, which has this citation: 364 N. J. Super. 301, Superior Court of New Jersey, 2003. The string of numbers identifies the volume and page of the official court reporter for the state of New Jersey (N. J. Super) in which you can find the full text of this decision. New Jersey, like most states, reports its law cases in a series of numbered volumes. This case appears in volume 364 of the New Jersey Superior Court reporters. If you go to a law library and find that book, you can then turn to page 301 and—*voila!*—you have the case. Because some of the cases in this text are so new, the official books that will eventually contain them have not yet been published, so their citations will be incomplete. In this event, we will also give you an alternate "address" where you can find the full case. For example, one citation for *National Federation of Independent Business v. Sebelius*, which examined whether Obamacare was constitutional, is 567 U.S. ___ (2012). Notice that it is missing a page number because it will not be published in the U.S. Reports for a few years. However, since we can also find that case in another reporter at 132 S. Ct. 2566 (2012), we will also provide this citation. Most cases are now available online. Your professor or librarian can show you how to find them electronically.

The *Issue* section is very important. It tells you what the court had to decide—and also why you are reading the case. In giving its decision, a court may digress. If you keep in mind the issue and relate the court's discussion to it, you will not get lost.

Excerpts from Judge Payne's Decision begins the court's discussion. This is called the *holding*, meaning a statement of who wins and who loses. The holding also includes the court's *rationale*, which is the reasoning behind the decision.

The holding that we provide is an edited version of the court's own language. Some judges write clear, forceful prose; others do not. Either way, their words give you an authentic feel for how judges think and rule, so we bring it to you in the original. Occasionally we use brackets [] to substitute our language for that of the court, either to condense or to clarify. Notice the brackets in the second paragraph of the Pub Zone decision. Judge Payne explains the point at much greater length, so we have condensed some of his writing into the phrase "of a business."

We omit a great deal. A court's opinion may be 3 pages, or it may be 75. We do not use ellipses (…) to indicate these deletions, because there is more taken out than kept in, and we want the text to be clean. When a court quotes an earlier decision verbatim but clearly adopts those words as its own, we generally delete the quotation marks, as well as the citation to the earlier case. If you are curious about the full holding, you can always look it up.

Let us look at a few of Judge Payne's points. The holding begins with a discussion of *duty*. The court explains that whether one person (or bar) owes a duty to protect another depends upon several factors, including whether the harm could be foreseen, how serious the injury could be, and whether there was an opportunity to prevent it.

Judge Payne then points out that the owner of a business is not an insurer of a visitor's safety. Typically, the owner has a duty to a visitor *only* if he has a reason to know that some harm is likely to occur. How would a merchant know that? Based on the character of the business, suggests the judge, or the owner's experience with particular people.

The judge then applies this general rule to the facts of this case. He concludes that the Pub Zone did in fact have a duty to protect Kuehn from the Pagans' attack. Based on Kerkoulas's experience, and warnings received from the police, she knew that the gang was dangerous and should have foreseen that admitting them in their "colors" greatly increased the chance of an attack.

Next, the court points out that it is not requiring the Pub Zone to *guarantee* everyone's safety. The bar was merely obligated to do a *reasonable* job. The prohibition on colors was a good idea, and calling the police had also proven effective. The problem of course was that in this case, Kerkoulas ignored her own rule about gang insignia and failed to call the police.

Based on all the evidence, the jury's finding of liability was reasonable, and its verdict must be reinstated. In other words, Kuehn, who lost at the trial, wins on appeal. What the court has done is to *reverse* the lower court's decision, meaning to turn the loser into the winner. In other cases, we will see an appellate court *remand* the case, meaning to send it back down to the lower court for additional steps. Or the appellate judges could *affirm* the lower court's decision, meaning to leave it unchanged.

1-6b Exam Strategy

This feature gives you practice analyzing cases the way lawyers do—and the way *you* must on tests. Law exams are different from most others because you must determine the issue from the facts provided. Too frequently, students faced with a law exam forget that the questions relate to the issues in the text and those discussed in class. Understandably, students new to law may focus on the wrong information in the problem or rely on material learned elsewhere. Exam Strategies teach you to figure out exactly what issue is at stake, and then analyze it in a logical, consistent manner. Here is an example, relating to the element of "duty," which the court discussed in the Pub Zone case.

EXAM Strategy

Question: The Big Red Traveling (BRT) Carnival is in town. Tony arrives at 8:00 p. m., parks in the lot—and is robbed at gunpoint by a man who beats him and escapes with his money. There are several police officers on the carnival grounds, but no officer is in the parking lot at the time of the robbery. Tony sues, claiming that brighter lighting and more police in the lot would have prevented the robbery. There has never before been any violent crime—robbery, beating, or otherwise—at any BRT carnival. BRT claims it had no duty to protect Tony from this harm. Who is likely to win?

Strategy: Begin by isolating the legal issue. What are the parties disputing? They are debating whether BRT had a duty to protect Tony from an armed robbery, committed by a stranger. Now ask yourself: How do courts decide whether a business has a duty to prevent this kind of harm? The *Pub Zone* case provides our answer. A business owner is not an ensurer of the visitor's safety. The owner generally has no duty to protect a customer from the criminal act of a third party, unless the owner knows the harm is occurring or could foresee it is about to happen. (In the Pub Zone case, the business owner knew of the gang's violent history, and could have foreseen the assault.) Now apply that rule to the facts of this case.

Result: There has never been a violent attack of any kind at a BRT carnival. BRT cannot foresee this robbery, and has no duty to protect against it. The carnival wins.

1-6c **You Be the Judge**

Many cases involve difficult decisions for juries and judges. Often both parties have legitimate, opposing arguments. Most chapters in this book will have a feature called "You Be the Judge," in which we present the facts of a case but not the court's holding.

We offer you two opposing arguments based on the kinds of claims the lawyers made in court. We leave it up to you to debate and decide which position is stronger or to add your own arguments to those given.

The following case is another negligence lawsuit, with issues that overlap those of the *Pub Zone* case. This time the court confronts a fight that resulted in a death. The victim's distraught family sued the owner of a bar, claiming that one of his employees was partly responsible for the death. Once again, the defendant asked the court to dismiss the case, claiming that he owed no duty to protect the victim—the same argument made by the *Pub Zone*.

But there is a difference here—this time the defendant owned the bar across the street, not the one where the fight took place. Could he be held legally responsible for the death? You be the judge.

You be the Judge

SOLDANO V. O'DANIELS
141 Cal. App. 3d 443
Court of Appeal of California, 1983

Facts: In the days before cell phones, a fight broke out at Happy Jack's Saloon. A good Samaritan ran across the street to the Circle Inn. He asked the bartender at the Circle Inn to let him use the telephone to call the police, but he refused.

Back at Happy Jack's Saloon, the fight escalated, and a man shot and killed Soldano's father. Soldano sued the owner of the Circle Inn for negligence. He argued that the bartender violated a legal duty when he refused to hand over the inn's telephone and that, as the employer of the bartender, O'Daniels was partially liable for Soldano's father's death.

The lower court dismissed the case, citing the principle that generally a person does not have a legal responsibility to help another unless he created the dangerous situation in the first place. Soldano appealed.

You Be the Judge: *Did the bartender have a duty to allow the use of the Circle Inn's telephone?*

Argument for the Defendant: Your honors, my client did not act wrongfully. He did nothing to create the danger. The fight was not even on his property. We sympathize with the plaintiff, but it is the shooter, and perhaps the bar where the fight took place, that are responsible for his father's death. Our client was not involved. Liability can be stretched only so far.

The court would place a great burden on the citizens of California by going against precedent. The Circle Inn is Mr. O'Daniel's private property. If the court imposes potential liability on him in this case, would citizens be forced to open the doors of their homes whenever a stranger claims that there is an emergency? Criminals would delight in their newfound ability to gain access to businesses and residences by simply demanding to use a phone to "call the police."

The law has developed sensibly. People are left to decide for themselves whether to help in a dangerous situation. They are not legally required to place themselves in harm's way.

Argument for the Plaintiff: Your honors, the Circle Inn's bartender had both a moral and a legal duty to allow the use of his establishment's telephone. The Circle Inn may be privately owned, but it is a business and is open to the public. Anyone in the world is invited to stop by and order a drink or a meal. The Good Samaritan had every right to be there.

We do not argue that the bartender had an obligation to break up the fight or endanger himself in any way. We simply argue he had a responsibility to stand aside and allow a free call on his restaurant's telephone. Any "burden" on him or on the Circle Inn was incredibly slight. The potential benefits were enormous. The trial court made a mistake in concluding that a person *never* has a duty to help another. Such an interpretation makes for poor public policy.

There is no need to radically change the common law. Residences can be excluded from this ruling. People need not be required to allow telephone-seeking strangers into their homes. This court can simply determine that businesses have a legal duty to allow the placement of emergency calls during normal business hours.

Chapter Conclusion

We depend upon the law to give us a stable nation and economy, a fair society, a safe place to live and work. These worthy goals have occupied ancient kings and twenty-first-century lawmakers alike. But while law is a vital tool for crafting the society we want, there are no easy answers about how to create it. In a democracy, we all participate in the crafting. Legal rules control us, yet *we* create *them*. A working knowledge of the law can help build a successful career—and a solid democracy.

EXAM REVIEW

1. **THE FEDERAL SYSTEM** Our federal system of government means that law comes from a national government in Washington, D.C., and from 50 state governments.

2. **LEGAL HISTORY** The history of law foreshadows many current legal issues, including mediation, partnership liability, the jury system, the role of witnesses, the special value placed on land, and the idea of precedent.

3. **PRIMARY SOURCES OF LAW** The primary sources of contemporary law are:

   - United States Constitution and state constitutions;

   - Statutes, which are drafted by legislatures;

   - Common law, which is the body of cases decided by judges, as they follow earlier cases, known as precedent;

   - Court orders, which place obligations on specific people or companies;

   - Administrative law, the rules and decisions made by federal and state administrative agencies; and

   - Treaties, agreements between the United States and foreign nations.

EXAM Strategy

Question: The stock market crash of 1929 and the Great Depression that followed were caused, in part, because so many investors blindly put their money into stocks they knew nothing about. During the 1920s, it was often impossible for an investor to find out what a corporation was planning to do with its money, who was running the corporation, and many other vital things. Congress responded by passing the Securities Act of 1933, which required a corporation to divulge more information about itself before it could seek money for a new stock issue. What kind of law did Congress create?

Strategy: What is the question seeking? The question asks you which *type* of law Congress created when it passed the 1933 Securities Act. What are the primary kinds of law? Administrative law consists of rules passed by agencies. Congress is not a federal agency. Common law is the body of cases decided by judges. Congress is not a judge. Statutes are laws passed by legislatures. Congress is a legislature. (See the "Result" at the end of this section.)

4. **CRIMINAL AND CIVIL LAW** Criminal law concerns behavior so threatening to society that it is outlawed altogether. Civil law deals with duties and disputes between parties, not with outlawed behavior.

Question: Bill and Diane are hiking in the woods. Diane walks down a hill to fetch fresh water. Bill meets a stranger, who introduces herself as Katrina. Bill sells a kilo of cocaine to Katrina, who then flashes a badge and mentions how much she enjoys her job at the Drug Enforcement Agency. Diane, heading back to camp with the water, meets Freddy, a motorist whose car has overheated. Freddy is late for a meeting where he expects to make a $30 million profit; he's desperate for water for his car. He promises to pay Diane $500 tomorrow if she will give him the pail of water, which she does. The next day, Bill is in jail and Freddy refuses to pay for Diane's water. Explain the criminal law/civil law distinction and what it means to Bill and Diane. Who will do what to whom, with what results?

Strategy: You are asked to distinguish between criminal and civil law. What is the difference? The criminal law concerns behavior that threatens society and is therefore outlawed. The government prosecutes the defendant. Civil law deals with the rights and duties between parties. One party files a suit against the other. Apply those different standards to these facts. (See the "Result" at the end of this section.)

5. **JURISPRUDENCE**   Jurisprudence is concerned with the basic nature of law. Three theories of jurisprudence are

- Legal positivism: The law is what the sovereign says it is.

- Natural law: An unjust law is no law at all.

- Legal realism: Who enforces the law is more important than what the law says.

---

3. Result: The Securities Act of 1933 is a statute.

4. Result: The government will prosecute Bill for dealing in drugs. If convicted, he will go to prison. The government will take no interest in Diane's dispute. However, if she chooses, she may sue Freddy for $500, the amount he promised her for the water. In that civil lawsuit, a court will decide whether Freddy must pay what he promised; however, even if Freddy loses, he will not go to jail.

MULTIPLE-CHOICE QUESTIONS

1. The United States Constitution is among the finest legal accomplishments in the history of the world. Which of the following influenced Ben Franklin, Thomas Jefferson, and the rest of the Founding Fathers?

    (a) English common-law principles

    (b) The Iroquois's system of federalism

    (c) Both A and B

    (d) None of the above

2. Which of the following parts of the modern legal system are "borrowed" from medieval England?

(a) Jury trials

(b) Special rules for selling land

(c) Following precedent

(d) All of the above

3. Union organizers at a hospital wanted to distribute leaflets to potential union members, but hospital rules prohibited leafleting in areas of patient care, hallways, cafeterias, and any areas open to the public. The National Labor Relations Board, a government agency, ruled that these restrictions violated the law and ordered the hospital to permit the activities in the cafeteria and coffee shop. What kind of law was it creating?

(a) A statute

(b) Common law

(c) A constitutional amendment

(d) Administrative regulation

4. If the Congress creates a new statute with the president's support, it must pass the idea by a _____ majority vote in the House and the Senate. If the president vetoes a proposed statute and the Congress wishes to pass it without his support, the idea must pass by a _____ majority vote in the House and Senate.

(a) simple; simple

(b) simple; two-thirds

(c) simple; three-fourths

(d) two-thirds; three-fourths

5. What part of the Constitution addresses the most basic liberties?

(a) Article I

(b) Article II

(c) Article III

(d) Amendments

CASE QUESTIONS

1. Burglar Bob breaks into Vince Victim's house. Bob steals a flat-screen television and laptop and does a significant amount of damage to the property before he leaves. Fortunately, Vince has a state-of-the-art security system. It captures excellent images of Bob, who is soon caught by police.

Assume that two legal actions follow, one civil and one criminal. Who will be responsible for bringing the civil case? What will be the outcome if the jury believes that Bob burgled Vince's house? Who will be responsible for bringing the criminal case? What will be the outcome if the jury believes that Bob burgled Vince's house?

2. As *The Oculist's Case* indicates, the medical profession has faced a large number of lawsuits for centuries. In Texas, a law provides that, so long as a doctor was not reckless and did not intentionally harm a patient, recovery for "pain and suffering" is limited to $750,000. In many other states, no such limit exists. If a patient will suffer a lifetime of pain after a botched operation, for example, he might recover millions in compensation. Which rule seems more sensible to you - the "Texas" rule or the alternative?

3. **YOU BE THE JUDGE WRITING PROBLEM** Should trials be televised? Here are a few arguments on both sides of the issue. You be the judge. **Arguments against live television coverage:** We have tried this experiment and it has failed. Trials fall into two categories: those that create great public interest and those that do not. No one watches dull trials, so we do not need to broadcast them. The few that are interesting have all become circuses. Judges and lawyers have shown that they cannot resist the temptation to play to the camera. Trials are supposed to be about justice, not entertainment. If a citizen seriously wants to follow a case, she can do it by reading the daily newspaper. **Arguments for live television coverage:** It is true that some televised trials have been unseemly affairs, but that is the fault of the presiding judges, not the media. Indeed, one of the virtues of television coverage is that millions of people now understand that we have a lot of incompetent people running our courtrooms. The proper response is to train judges to run a tight trial by prohibiting grandstanding by lawyers. Access to accurate information is the foundation on which a democracy is built, and we must not eliminate a source of valuable data just because some judges are ill-trained or otherwise incompetent.

4. Leslie Bergh and his two brothers, Milton and Raymond, formed a partnership to help build a fancy saloon and dance hall in Evanston, Wyoming. Later, Leslie met with his friend and drinking buddy, John Mills, and tricked Mills into investing in the saloon. Leslie did not tell Mills that no one else was investing cash or that the entire enterprise was already bankrupt. Mills mortgaged his home, invested $150,000 in the saloon—and lost every penny of it. Mills sued all three partners for fraud. Milton and Raymond defended on the grounds that they did not commit the fraud; only Leslie did. The defendants lost. Was that fair? By holding them liable, what general idea did the court rely on? What Anglo-Saxon legal custom did the ruling resemble?

5. *Kuehn v. Pub Zone* and *Soldano v. O'Daniels* both involve attacks in a bar. Should they have the same result? If so, in which way—in favor of the injured plaintiffs or owner-defendants? If not, why should they have different outcomes? What are the key facts that lead you to believe as you do?

DISCUSSION QUESTIONS

1. In the 1980s, the Supreme Court ruled that it is legal for protesters to burn the American flag. This activity counts as free speech under the Constitution. If the Court hears a new flag-burning case in this decade, should it consider changing its ruling, or should it follow precedent? Is following past precedent something that seems sensible to you: always, usually, sometimes, rarely, or never?

2. When should a business be held legally responsible for customer safety? Consider the following statements, and consider the degree to which you agree or disagree:

- A business should keep customers safe from its own employees.

- A business should keep customers safe from other customers.

- A business should keep customers safe from themselves. (Example: an intoxicated customer who can no longer walk straight.)

- A business should keep people outside its own establishment safe if it is reasonable to do so.

3. In his most famous novel, *The Red and the Black*, the French author Stendhal (1783–1842) wrote: "There is no such thing as 'natural law': This expression is nothing but old nonsense. Prior to laws, what is natural is only the strength of the lion, or the need of the creature suffering from hunger or cold, in short, need." What do you think? Does legal positivism or legal realism seem more sensible to you?

4. Before becoming a Supreme Court justice, Sonia Sotomayor stated in a speech to students: "I would hope that a wise Latina woman with the richness of her experiences would more often than not reach a better conclusion than a white male who hasn't lived that life." During her Senate confirmation proceedings, this statement was heavily probed and criticized. One senator said that the focus of the hearings was to determine whether Judge Sotomayor would "decide cases based only on the law as made by the people and their elected representatives, not on personal feelings or politics." (Sotomayor convinced many of her critics, because the Senate confirmed her by a vote of 68–31.) Should judges ignore their life experiences and feelings when making judicial decisions?

5. Consider the following statements. To what extent do you agree or disagree with each?

- I believe that members of Congress usually try to do the right thing for America.

- I believe that presidents usually try to do the right thing for America.

- I believe that Supreme Court justices usually try to do the right thing for America.

ETHICS AND CORPORATE SOCIAL RESPONSIBILITY

© Creative Travel Projects/Shutterstock.com

Eating is one of life's most fundamental needs and greatest pleasures. Yet all around the world many people go to bed hungry. Food companies have played an important role in reducing hunger by producing vast quantities of food cheaply. So much food, so cheaply that, in America, one in three adults and one in five children are obese. Some critics argue that food companies bear responsibility for this overeating because they make their products *too* alluring. Many processed food products are calorie bombs of fat (which is linked to heart disease), sugar (which leads to diabetes), and salt (which causes high blood pressure). What obligation do food producers and restaurants have to their customers? After all, no one is forcing anyone to eat. Do any of the following examples cross the line into unethical behavior?

> **Food with high levels of fat, sugar and salt not only taste better, they are also more addictive.**

1. Increasing Addiction. Food with high levels of fat, sugar, and salt not only taste better, they are also more addictive.[1] Food producers hire neuroscientists who perform MRIs on consumers to gauge the precise level of fat, sugar, and salt that will create the most powerful cravings, the so-called "bliss point." To take one example, in some Prego tomato sauces, sugar is the second most important ingredient after tomatoes.

---

[1] Researchers report that rats find Oreo cookies as addictive as cocaine. And they like the creamy middle best, too. *Connecticut College News*, "Student-faculty research shows Oreos are just as addictive as drugs in lab rats."

Did you know you were getting two heaping teaspoons of sugar in a small serving of pasta sauce?[2]

2. Increasing Quantity. Food companies also work hard to create new categories of products that increase the number of times a day that people eat and the amount of calories in each session. For example, they have created a new category of food that is meant to be more than a snack but less than a meal, such as Hot Pockets. But some versions of this product have more than 700 calories, which would be a lot for lunch, never mind for just a snack. And candy companies carefully package their products to encourage consumers to nibble all day. For example, when Hershey's learned that the wrappers on a Reese's Peanut Butter Cup act as a deterrent to nonstop eating, the company created Reese's minis, which are unwrapped candies in a resealable bag. Feel free to chow down!

    Food executives argue that they are just providing what consumers want.

3. Increasing Calories. Uno Chicago Grill serves a macaroni and cheese dish that, by itself, provides more than two-thirds of the calories that a moderately active man should eat in one day, and almost three times the amount of saturated fat. But this dish is at least *food*. Dunkin, Donuts offers a Frozen Caramel Coffee Coolatta with more than one-third the calories that a male should have in a day and 50 percent more saturated fat. Of course, these items are even worse choices for women and children. Should restaurants serve items such as these? If they do, what disclosure should they make?

4. Targeting Children. Kraft Food developed Lunchables, packaged food designed for children to take to school. The first version contained bologna, cheese, crackers, and candy—all of which delivered unhealthy levels of fat, sugar, and salt. The company lured children by advertising on Saturday morning cartoons.

5. Targeting the Poor. Traditionally, Coca-Cola focused its marketing efforts on low-income areas in the United States. It then took this effort overseas, selling Coke in the slums of Brazil. One of its strategies is to provide small bottles that cost only 20 cents. Said Jeffrey Dunn, the former president and chief operating officer for Coca-Cola in North and South America, "These people need a lot of things, but they don't need a Coke.' I almost threw up."[3] When Dunn tried to develop more healthful strategies for Coke, he was fired.

---

[2]To find nutritional information on this or other products, search the Internet for the name of the product with the word "nutrition."
[3]Michael Moss, "The Extraordinary Science of Addictive Junk Food," *The New York Times*, Feb. 20, 2013.

2-1 INTRODUCTION

Ethics
How people should behave.

Ethics decision
Any choice about how a person should behave that is based on a sense of right and wrong.

This text, for the most part, covers legal ideas. The law dictates how a person *must* behave. This chapter examines **ethics**, or how people *should* behave. Any choice about how a person should behave that is based on a sense of right and wrong is an **ethics decision**. This chapter will explore ethics dilemmas that commonly arise in workplaces, and present tools for making decisions when the law does not require or prohibit any particular choice.

If a person is intent on lying, cheating, and stealing his way through a career, then he is unlikely to be dissuaded by anything in this or any other course. But for the large majority of people who want to do the right thing, it is useful to study new ways of recognizing and dealing with difficult problems.

Laws represent society's view of basic ethics rules. And most people agree that certain activities such as murder, assault, and fraud are wrong. **However, laws may permit behavior that some feel is wrong and it may criminalize acts that some feel are right.** For example, assisted suicide is legal in a few states. Some people believe it is wrong under all circumstances, while others think it is the right thing to do for someone suffering horribly from a terminal illness. Likewise, many people feel it is ethical to record videos of farm animals being mistreated, although some states now prohibit secret videotaping on farms.

In this chapter, the usual legal cases are replaced by Ethics Cases with discussion questions. In some of these cases, reasonable people may disagree about the right thing to do. In others, the right answer is obvious, but actually doing it is difficult. These cases give you the opportunity to practice applying your values to the types of ethics issues you will face in your life. It is also important during class discussions for you to hear different points of view. In your career, you will work with and manage a variety of people, so it is useful to have insight into different perspectives on ethics.

Life principles
The rules by which you live your life

We also hope that hearing these various points of view will help you develop your own **Life Principles**. These principles are the rules by which you live your life. As we will see, **research shows that people who think about the right rules for living are less likely to do wrong.** Developing your own Life Principles, based on your values, may be the most important outcome of reading this chapter and studying ethics.

How do you go about preparing a list of Life Principles? Think first of important categories. A list of Life Principles should include your rules on:

- Lying

- Stealing

- Cheating

- Applying the same or different standards at home and at work

- Your responsibility as a bystander when you see other people doing wrong, or being harmed

Specific is better than general. Many people say, for example, that they will maintain a healthy work/life balance, but such a vow is not as effective as promising to set aside certain specific times each week for family activities. Many religions honor the sabbath for this reason. Another common Life Principle is: "I will always put my family first." But what does that mean? That you are willing to engage in unethical behavior at work to make sure that you keep your job? Increase your income by cheating everyone you can? Or live your life so that you serve as a good example?

Some Life Principles focus not so much on right versus wrong but, rather, serve as a general guide for living a happier, more engaged life: I will keep promises, forgive those who harm me, say I'm sorry, appreciate my blessings every day, understand the other person's point of view, try to say "yes" when asked for a favor.

Remember that, no matter what you *say,* **every ethics decision you make illustrates your** *actual* **Life Principles.** For example, one MBA student told the story of how his boss had ordered him to cheat on his expense report. The company did not require any receipts for meals that cost less than $25. He and his fellow salespeople habitually ate at fast food restaurants where it was almost impossible to spend $25. Everyone else was reporting a lot of $24 meals while he was submitting bills for $12. His boss told him he was making everyone else look bad and he needed to increase the amounts he claimed. What is your Life Principle in this case? Understand that if you fudge the expense report, your Life Principle is effectively: I am willing to cheat if I am unlikely to get caught or if my boss authorizes it. An alternative would be: I will not cheat even if my boss tells me to—I'll look for another job instead.

It is important to think through your Life Principles now, so that you will be prepared when facing ethics dilemmas in the future.

In this chapter, we will present eight topics:

1. The Role of Business in Society

2. Why Be Ethical?

3. Theories of Ethics

4. Ethics Traps

5. Lying

6. Applying the Principles

7. When the Going Gets Tough: Responding to Unethical Behavior

8. Corporate Social Responsibility

2-2 THE ROLE OF BUSINESS IN SOCIETY

Nobel Prize-winning economist Milton Friedman is famous for arguing that a corporate manager's primary responsibility is to the owners of the organization, that is, to shareholders. Unless the owners explicitly provide otherwise, managers should make the company as profitable as possible while also complying with the law.[4]

Others have argued that corporations should instead consider all company stakeholders, not just the shareholders. Stakeholders include employees, customers, and the communities and countries in which a company operates. This choice can create an obligation to such broad categories as "society" or "the environment." For example, after the shooting in Newtown, Connecticut, in which 20 first-graders and 6 educators were murdered, General Electric Co. stopped lending funds to shops that sell guns. GE headquarters are near Newtown. Many of its employees lived in the area and some had children in the Sandy Hook Elementary School where the shooting took place. In this case, GE was putting its employees ahead of its investors.

Every executive will treat employees well if she believes that doing so leads to increased profits. All executives are in favor of giving money to charity if the donation improves the company's image and thereby increases profits enough to pay for itself. But such win-win cases are not ethics dilemmas. In a true dilemma, a company considers an action that would not increase shareholder returns in any certain or measureable way, but would benefit other stakeholders.

---

[4]He also mentions that managers should comply with "ethical custom," but never explains what that means. Milton Friedman, *The New York Times Magazine*, September 13, 1970.

As we will see in this chapter, managers face many choices in which the most profitable option is not the most ethical choice. For example, Michael Mudd, a former executive vice president of global corporate affairs for Kraft Foods, had this to say about his fellow executives:

> In so many other ways, these are good people. But, little by little, they strayed from the honorable business of feeding people appropriately to the deplorable mission of "increasing shareholder value" by enticing people to consume more and more high-margin, low-nutrition branded products.[5]

Of course, when profitability increases and, with it, a company's stock price, managers benefit because their compensation is often tied to corporate results, either explicitly or through ownership of stock and options. Thus, managers who say that they are just acting in the best interest of shareholders are also conveniently benefiting themselves. That connection creates an incentive to ignore stakeholders.

Conversely, doing the right thing will sometimes lead to a loss of profits or even one's job. For example, Hugh Aaron worked for a company that sold plastic materials.[6] One of the firm's major clients hired a new purchasing agent who refused to buy any product unless he was provided with expensive gifts, paid vacations, and prostitutes. When Aaron refused to comply with these requests, the man bought from someone else. And that was that—the two companies never did business again. Aaron did not regret his choice. He believed that his and his employees' self-respect were as important as profits. But if your *only* concern is maximizing your company's profitability in the short run, you will find yourself in a position of making unethical choices.

2-3 WHY BE ETHICAL?

An ethical decision may not be the most profitable, but it does generate a range of benefits for employees, companies, and society.

2-3a Society as a Whole Benefits from Ethical Behavior

John Akers, the former chairman of IBM, argued that without ethical behavior, a society could not be economically competitive. He put it this way:

> Ethics and competitiveness are inseparable. We compete as a society. No society anywhere will compete very long or successfully with people stabbing each other in the back; with people trying to steal from each other; with everything requiring notarized confirmation because you can't trust the other fellow; with every little squabble ending in litigation; and with government writing reams of regulatory legislation, tying business hand and foot to keep it honest. That is a recipe not only for headaches in running a company, but for a nation to become wasteful, inefficient, and noncompetitive. There is no escaping this fact: The greater the measure of mutual trust and confidence in the ethics of a society, the greater its economic strength.[7]

In short, ethical behavior builds trust, which is important in all of our relationships. It is the ingredient that allows us to live and work together happily.

---

[5]Michael Moss, "How to Force Ethics on the Food Industry," *The New York Times*, March 16, 2013.
[6]Virtually all of the examples in this chapter are true events involving real people. Only their first names are used unless the individual has consented or the events are a matter of public record.
[7]David Grier, "Confronting Ethical Dilemmas," unpublished manuscript of remarks at the Royal Bank of Canada, Sept. 19, 1989.

2-3b **People Feel Better When They Behave Ethically**

Every businessperson has many opportunities to be dishonest. But each of us must ask ourselves: What kind of person do we want to be? In what kind of world do we want to live? You might think about how you would like people who know you to describe you to others.

Managers want to feel good about themselves and the decisions they have made; they want to sleep well at night. Their decisions—to lay off employees, install safety devices in cars, burn a cleaner fuel—affect people's lives. And their unethical decisions are painful to remember.

To take an example, an executive, whom we will call "Hank," told a story that still haunts him. His boss had refused to pay his tuition for an MBA program, so Hank went over his head and asked Sam, an executive several levels higher. Sam interceded immediately and personally approved the tuition reimbursement. He then took Hank under his wing, checking with him regularly to find out how the program and his work were going. Naturally, Hank felt grateful and indebted. Then one day, some other higher ups told him that they were planning a coup against Sam. They were trying to get him fired in a complete blindside. They offered Hank a big promotion in return for his help. All went according to plan and Sam was fired. When Sam found out about Hank's betrayal, he called to tell the younger man exactly what he thought of his character. Hank said that he will carry that phone call and his guilt forever. And because he was so untrustworthy, he finds it hard to trust others.

2-3c **Unethical Behavior Can Be Very Costly**

Unethical behavior is a risky business strategy—it can harm not only the bad actors but entire industries and even countries. For example, when VIPshop recently offered its shares publicly in the United States, they plummeted in price. This was the first Chinese company to go public in the United States in nine months, since a series of accounting frauds in other Chinese companies had caused billions of dollars in losses. Although VIPshop had done nothing wrong, investors were skeptical of *all* Chinese companies.

Although unethical decisions may increase short-term profits, they can create a lot of long-term harm. Johnson & Johnson manufactured a new artificial hip that had more metal parts than the old version. In theory, the hip would last longer and thereby let the patient avoid difficult replacement surgery. But the theory turned out to be wrong. The two parts ground together, releasing microscopic bits of metal that not only failed quickly but also irreparably damaged the patient's bone and tissue. Even when Johnson & Johnson had data from an English surgeon revealing these problems, it denied and stonewalled while continuing to sell the product. J&J subsequently faced more than 10,000 lawsuits. The company not only paid more than $4 billion to settle these cases, it also found its reputation sullied.

What is the cost of a lost reputation? **Research indicates that consumers are willing to pay more for a product that they believe to be ethically produced.** And much less if they believe it was made using shoddy ethical practices.[8]

Unethical behavior can also cause other, subtler damage. In one survey, a majority of those questioned said that they had witnessed unethical behavior in their workplace and that this behavior had reduced productivity, job stability, and profits. **Unethical behavior in an organization creates a cynical, resentful, and unproductive workforce.**

Although there is no *guarantee* that ethical behavior pays in the short or long run, there is evidence that the ethical company is more *likely* to win financially. Ethical companies tend to have a better reputation, more creative employees, and higher returns than those that engage in wrongdoing.[9]

But if we decide that we want to behave ethically, how do we know what ethical behavior is?

---

[8]Remi Trudel and June Cotte, "Does It Pay to Be Good?" *Sloan Management Review*," January 8, 2009.
[9]For sources, see "Ethics: A Basic Framework," Harvard Business School case 9-307-059.

2-4 THEORIES OF ETHICS

When making ethical decisions, people sometimes focus on the reason for the decision—they want to do what is right. Thus, if they think it is wrong to lie, then they will tell the truth no matter what the consequence. Other times, people think about the outcome of their actions. They will do whatever it takes to achieve the right result, no matter what. This choice—between doing right and getting the right result—has been the subject of much philosophical debate.

2-4a Utilitarian Ethics

In 1863, Englishman John Stuart Mill wrote *Utilitarianism*. **To Mill, a correct decision is one that maximizes overall happiness and minimizes overall pain, thereby producing the greatest net benefit.** As he put it, his goal was to produce the greatest good for the greatest number of people. Risk management and cost-benefit analyses are examples of utilitarian business practices.

Suppose that an automobile manufacturer could add a device to its cars that would reduce air pollution. As a result, the incidence of strokes and lung cancer would decline dramatically, saving society hundreds of millions of dollars over the life of the cars. But by charging a higher price to cover the cost of the device, the company would sell fewer cars and shareholders would earn lower returns. A utilitarian would argue that, despite the decline in profits, the company should install the device.

Consider this example that a student told us:

> During college, I used drugs—some cocaine, but mostly prescription painkillers. Things got pretty bad. At one point, I would wait outside emergency rooms hoping to buy drugs from people who were leaving. But that was three years ago. I went into rehab and have been clean ever since. I don't even drink. I've applied for a job, but the application asks if I have ever used drugs illegally. I am afraid that if I tell the truth, I will never get a job. What should I say on the application?

A utilitarian would ask: What harm will be caused if she tells the truth? She will be less likely to get that job, or maybe any job—a large and immediate harm. What if she lies? She might argue that no harm would result because she is now clean, and her past drug addiction will not have an adverse impact on her new employer.

Critics of utilitarian thought argue that it is very difficult to *measure* utility accurately, at least in the way that one would measure distance or the passage of time. The car company does not really know how many lives will be saved or how much its profits might decline if the device is installed. It is also difficult to *predict* benefit and harm accurately. The recovered drug addict may relapse, or her employer may find out about her lie.

A focus on outcome can justify some really terrible behavior. Among other things, it can be used to legitimize torture. After the 9/11 terrorist attacks, Americans debated the acceptability of torture. Is it ethical to torture a terrorist with the hope of obtaining the details of an upcoming attack?

Or suppose that wealthy old Ebenezer has several chronic illnesses that cause him great suffering and prevent him from doing any of the activities that once gave meaning to his life. Also, he is such a nasty piece of work that everyone who knows him hates him. If he were to die, all of his heirs would benefit tremendously from the money they inherited from him, including a disabled grandchild who then could afford medical care that would improve his life dramatically. Would it be ethical to kill Ebenezer?

2-4b Deontological Ethics

Deontological

From the Greek word for *obligation*. The duty to do the right thing, regardless of the result

The word **deontological** comes from the Greek word for *obligation*. **Proponents of deontological ethics believe that utilitarians have it all wrong and that the *results* of a decision are not as important as the *reason* for making it.** To a deontological thinker, the ends do not justify the means. Rather, it is important to do the right thing, no matter the result.

The best-known proponent of the deontological model was the eighteenth-century German philosopher Immanuel Kant. He believed in what he called the **categorical imperative**. He argued that you should not do something unless you would be willing to have everyone else do it, too. Applying this idea, he concluded that one should always tell the truth because if *everyone* lied, the world would become an awful place. Thus, Kant would say that the drug user should tell the truth on job applications, even if that meant she could not find work. The truth should be told, no matter the outcome.

Kant also believed that human beings possess a unique dignity and that no decision that treats people as commodities could be considered just, even if the decision tended to maximize overall happiness, or profit, or any other quantifiable measure. Thus, Kant would argue against killing Ebenezer, no matter how unpleasant the man was.

The problem with Kant is that the ends *do* matter. Yes, it is wrong to kill, but a country might not survive unless it is willing to fight wars. Although many people disagree with some of Kant's specific ideas, most people acknowledge that a utilitarian approach is incomplete, and that winning in the end does not automatically make a decision right.

2-4c Rawlsian Justice

How did you manage to get into college or graduate school? Presumably owing to some combination of talent, hard work, and support from family and friends. Imagine that you had been born into different circumstances—say, in a country where the literacy rate is only 25 percent and almost all of the population lives in desperate poverty. Would you be reading this book now? Most likely not. People are born with wildly different talents into very different circumstances, all of which dramatically affect their outcomes. Even for people born poor in the United States, circumstances matter hugely. For example, poor children in San Francisco are almost three times more likely to be prosperous as adults than are children from Atlanta.[10]

John Rawls (1921–2002) was an American philosopher who referred to these circumstances into which we are born as **life prospects**. In his view, hard work certainly matters, but so does luck. Rawls argued that we should think about what rules for society we would propose if we faced a "**veil of ignorance**." In other words, suppose that there is going to be a lottery tomorrow that would determine all our attributes. We could be a winner, ending up a hugely talented, healthy person in a loving family, or we could be poor and chronically ill from a broken, abusive family in a violent neighborhood with deplorable schools and social services.

What type of society would we establish now, if we did not know whether we would be one of life's winners or losers? First, we would design some form of a democratic system that provided equal liberty to all and important rights such as freedom of speech and religion. Second, we would apply the **difference principle**. Under this principle we would *not* plan a system in which everyone received an equal income. Society is better off if people have an incentive to work hard, so we would reward the type of work that provides the most benefit to the community as a whole. We might decide, for example, to pay doctors more than baseball players.

Kant's categorical imperative
An act is only ethical if it would be acceptable for everyone to do the same thing.

Life prospects
The opportunities one has at birth, based on one's natural attributes and initial place in society.

Veil of ignorance
The rules for society that we would propose if we did not know how lucky we would be in life's lottery.

Difference principle
Rawls' suggestion that society should reward behavior that provides the most benefit to the community as a whole.

Healthy, talented children born into a loving family are lucky to have such good life prospects.

© Creativa/Shutterstock.com

---

[10]David Leonhardt, "In Climbing Income Ladder, Location Matters," *The New York Times*, July 22, 2013.

But maybe not *all* doctors; perhaps just the ones who research cancer cures or provide care for the poor, not cosmetic surgeons operating on the affluent. Rawls argues that everyone should have the opportunity to earn great wealth so long as the tax system provides enough revenue to provide decent health, education, and welfare for all. In thinking about ethical decisions, it is worth remembering that many of us have been winners in life's lottery and that the unlucky are deserving of our compassion.

2-4d Front Page Test

There you are, trying to decide what to do in a difficult situation. How would you feel if your actions went viral—on YouTube, the Huffington Post, all over Facebook, or on the front page of a national newspaper? Would that help you decide what to do? Would such exposure have caused Hank to tell Sam about the planned coup? Make the Johnson & Johnson executives manage their hip implant differently?

The Front Page test is not completely foolproof—there are times you might want to do something private for legitimate reasons. You might, for example, think that having an abortion is completely ethical, but still not want everyone to know. Or, if you live in a state that prohibits the videotaping of mistreated farm animals, you would not want everyone to know that you had done so, even if you thought it the right thing to do.

2-4e Moral Universalism and Relativism

Moral universalism

A belief that some acts are always right or always wrong

Moral relativism

A belief that a decision may be right even if it is not in keeping with our own ethical standards.

For many ethics dilemmas, reasonable people may well disagree about what is right. For example, we have seen that a Kantian approach may lead to a different decision than a utilitarian view. However, some people believe that particular acts are always right or always wrong, regardless of what others may think. This approach is called **moral universalism**. Alternatively, others believe that it is right to be tolerant of different viewpoints and customs. And, indeed, a decision may be acceptable even if it is not in keeping with one's own ethical standards. This approach is referred to as **moral relativism**. For example, Pope Benedict XVI wrote that homosexuality is "a strong tendency ordered toward an intrinsic moral evil," while his successor, Pope Francis, took a different approach, saying, "If someone is gay and he searches for the Lord and has good will, who am *I* to judge?"[11] Pope Benedict's view reflects a moral universalism—he believes that homosexuality is always wrong—while Pope Francis is taking a more relativistic approach—under certain circumstances, he will not judge.

There are at least two types of moral relativism: cultural and **individual.** To cultural relativists, what is right or wrong depends on the norms and practices in each society. For example, some societies permit men to have more than one wife, while others find that practice abhorrent. A cultural relativist would say that polygamy is an ethical choice in societies where such practice is long-standing and culturally significant. And, as outsiders to that society, who are we to judge? In short, culture defines what is right and wrong.

To individual relativists, people must develop their own ethical rules. And what is right for *me* might not be good for *you*. Thus, I might believe that monogamy is bad because it goes against human nature. Therefore, I might decide that it is right for me to have relationships with many partners while you believe that being faithful to one partner is the cornerstone of an ethical life. The danger of individual relativism is obvious: It can justify just about anything.

Like so much in ethics, none of these approaches will always be right or wrong. There are times when certain acts are just wrong, no matter what anyone says to the contrary. But, of course, truly ethical people may differ. It is, however, ethically lazy simply to default to moral relativism as an excuse for condoning any behavior.

---

[11]Rachel Donadio, "On Gay Priests, Pope Francis Asks, 'Who Am I to Judge?" *The New York Times*, July 30, 2013.

2-4f **Ethics Case: Lincoln at War**

In 1865, toward the end of the American Civil War, President Abraham Lincoln had to choose between two rival goals: an immediate end to a devastating, bloody war or a change to the Constitution that would make slavery illegal. If he ended the war immediately, the Southern states would return to the Union and then be eligible to vote on the anti-slavery amendment. They would have enough votes to defeat it. He ultimately decided to delay peace with the South, a decision that cost thousands of lives.

To obtain the votes he needed, Lincoln did whatever it took. He figured out how to win over each individual Congressman, appealing to one man's sense of idealism, another's greed. He made threats and promises, handed out jobs and cash. And, in the end, he succeeded in ending the barbarous practice of slavery.[12]

Questions

- What would Mill, Kant, and Rawls have said about Lincoln's actions?

- What would have been the result if Lincoln had applied the Front Page test?

- Did Lincoln do the right thing?

- Lincoln risked people's lives for his principles and made decisions that affected millions. Can you think of a similar scenario in a business context?

2-5 ETHICS TRAPS

Very few people wake up one morning and think, "Today I'll do something unethical." Then why do so many unethical things happen? Sometimes our brains trick us into believing wrong is right. It is important to understand the ethics traps that create great temptation to do what we know to be wrong or fail to do what we know to be right.

2-5a **Money**

Money is a powerful lure because most people believe that they would be happier if only they had more. But that is not necessarily true. Good health, companionship, and enjoyable leisure activities all contribute more to happiness than money does. And, regardless of income, 85 percent of Americans feel happy on a day-to-day basis anyway.

Money *can*, of course, provide some protection against the inevitable bumps in the road of life. Being hungry is no fun. If you lose your winter coat, you will be happier if you can replace it. It is easier to maintain friendships if you can afford to go out together occasionally. So money can contribute to happiness, but research indicates that this impact disappears when household income exceeds $75,000. Above that level, income seems to have no impact on day-to-day happiness. Indeed, there is some evidence that higher income levels actually *reduce* the ability to appreciate small pleasures. Interestingly, too, people who come into a windfall are happier if they spend it on others or save it, rather than blowing it in a spree.[13]

Money is also a way of keeping score. If my company pays me more, that must mean I am a better employee. So, although an increase in income above $75,000 does not affect

---

[12]The Steven Spielberg movie *Lincoln* illustrates this process.

[13]Elizabeth Dunn and Michael Norton, "Don't Indulge, Be Happy," *The New York Times*, July 8, 2012, and Daniel Kahneman and Angus Deaton, "High Income Improves Evaluation of Life but not Emotional Well-Being," in the Proceedings of the National Academy of Sciences of the United States of America, August 4, 2010.

day-to-day happiness, higher pay can make people feel more satisfied with their lives. They consider themselves more successful and feel that their life is going better.

In short, the relationship between money and happiness is complicated. Above a certain level, more money does not make for more day-to-day happiness. Higher pay can increase general satisfaction with life, but when people work so hard or so dishonestly that their health, friendships, and leisure activities suffer, it has the reverse effect.

2-5b Competition

Humans are social animals who cannot help but compare themselves with other people. Deep down, we all want to be better than the other fellow. In one telling experiment, young children elected to get *fewer* prizes for themselves, as long as they still got more than other participants. For example, a child chose to get one prize for herself and zero for the other

> **Humans are social animals who cannot help but compare themselves with other people.**

person, rather than two for herself and two for the other participant. For an adult example, consider Rajat Gupta, who retired as CEO of the consulting firm McKinsey, worth $100 million. As CEO, he had been top dog. But in retirement, he began spending time with far wealthier businesspeople, such as Bill Gates, who were *giving away* hundreds of millions of dollars. To keep up with the Gateses, Gupta began illegal insider trading. He was ultimately sentenced to two years in prison.

In a related phenomenon, researchers have found that the mere process of negotiating the price of a product reduces a person's sense of morality. Participants in an experiment were offered a payment of €10 but, in return, a young, healthy mouse would be euthanized. If they rejected the payment, the mouse would continue to live in a happy mouse environment to the end of its natural life, which was about two years. In a different version, two participants—a buyer and a seller—negotiated the payment for euthanizing the mouse. And in a third round, larger groups of buyers and sellers negotiated against each other. People in the multi-party negotiations were more likely to kill the mouse than were the pairs of two people, and those pairs were much more likely to choose death than individuals acting on their own. In short, being involved in a market reduced the players' sense of morality, at least when mice were involved.[14]

2-5c Rationalization

A recent study found that more creative people tend to be less ethical. The reason? They are better at rationalizing their bad behavior. Virtually any foul deed can be rationalized. Some common rationalizations:

- If I don't do it, someone else will.

- I deserve this because…

- They had it coming.

- I am not harming a *person*—it is just a big company.

- This is someone else's responsibility.

- Just this once.

---

[14]Armin Falk and Nora Szech, "Morals and Markets," *Science*, 340, 707 (2013).

For example, Duke professor Dan Ariely has found in his groundbreaking research that almost everyone is willing to cheat, at least on a small scale. We all want to get the greatest benefit, but we also want to think of ourselves as being honest. If we cheat—just a little— then we can tell ourselves it does not really count. Ariely did an experiment in which he paid people for solving math problems. Participants averaged four correct answers. But when people were allowed to grade the tests themselves without anyone checking up on them, all of a sudden they began averaging six correct answers.[15] You can imagine how they might have rationalized that behavior—"I was close on this one. I normally would have gotten that one right. Today was an off day for me." Surprisingly, when the participants were paid a lot for each correct answer ($10 as opposed to $0.50) they cheated *less*. Presumably, they would have felt worse about themselves if they stole a lot of money rather than a little.

To take a real example, mostly elderly volunteers ran the gift shop at the Kennedy Center for the Performing Arts in Washington, D.C.. The shop had revenues of $400,000 a year, but someone was stealing $150,000 of that. It turned out there was not one thief. Instead, dozens of volunteers were each stealing a little bit, which added up. These people felt good about themselves for being volunteers so they thought that stealing a little was fine.[16] When we do something wrong, we tend to be creative at explaining why it did not really count.

2-5d We Can't Be Objective About Ourselves

Do you do more than your fair share of work at home? On your team? In your study group? Of course you do! At least, that is what most people think. **In reality, people are not objective when comparing themselves to others.** Many studies looking at groups as various as married couples, athletes, MBA students, and organizational behavior professors have found a tendency for people to overestimate their own contribution to a group effort.[17] Even Nobel-prize winners fall prey to this trap. When Frederick Banting won the prize with John Macleod for discovering insulin, he boycotted the ceremony because he was outraged that Macleod had been given credit, too.[18]

Or, to take another example, participants in a study were put in the position of deciding whether they or someone else got an easy assignment. When asked in the abstract what would be a fair method for assigning tasks, everyone said that the computer should make the assignments randomly. But when another group of people was actually given the authority to decide, three-quarters ignored the computer option and just assigned themselves the easy jobs. And then they rated themselves high on a fairness scale.[19] In making a decision that affects you, it is important to remember that you are unlikely to be objective.

2-5e Conflicts of Interest

Suppose that your doctor is writing a prescription for you. Do you care that she does so with a pen given to her by a pharmaceutical company? You should. The evidence is that doctors are influenced by gifts and, indeed, small gifts are surprisingly influential

---

[15]Dan Ariely, "Why We Lie," *The Wall Street Journal*, May 26, 2012.

[16]David Brooks, "The Moral Diet," *The New York Times*, June 7, 2012.

[17]MBA students were asked what percentage of the work each had done in their study groups. The total credit claimed per group averaged 139%. Organizational behavior professors overestimated their own contribution by a similar amount. Mahzarin R. Banaji, Max H. Bazerman, and Dolly Chugh, "How (Un)Ethical Are You?", *Harvard Business Review*, December 2003.

[18]Eugene M. Caruso, Nicholas Epley, and Max H. Bazerman, "The Costs and Benefits of Undoing Egocentric Responsibility Assessments in Groups," *Journal of Personality and Social Psychology*, November 1, 2006.

[19]John Tierney, "Deep Down, We Can't Fool Even Ourselves," *The New York Times*, July 1, 2008.

Should Orlanda accept such a gift?

because the recipients do not make a conscious effort to overcome any bias these tokens may create. With larger gifts, the recipients are more aware and, therefore, take more effort in overcoming their biases. Doctors are not alone in their reaction. For everyone, the bias created by a conflict of interest tends to be unconscious and unintentionally self-serving. In short, if ethical decisions are your goal, it is better to avoid all conflicts of interest—both large and small. No one—including you—is good at overcoming the biases that these conflicts create.

2-5f **Conformity**

Famed investor Warren Buffett has been quoted as saying, "The five most dangerous words in business may be: 'Everybody else is doing it.'" Because humans are social animals, they are often willing to follow the leader, even to a place where they do not really want to go. If all the salespeople in a company cheat on their expense accounts, a new hire is much more likely to view this behavior as acceptable.

2-5g **Ethics Case: Diamonds in the Rough**

When Orlanda graduated from college, she got a job as a software engineer in Silicon Valley. After two years working in technical support, one of her customers offered her a job at his company. It turned out that her new firm was in shambles but, after months of killer hours, she managed to get the company on a better path. One of her biggest accomplishments was to help a major supplier solve its technical problems so that its product would work reliably. On her birthday, her contact at the supplier (who was a friend of her boss) gave her a diamond watch. Her company had no policy on accepting gifts, so she kept it. Afterward, she realized that she was spending even more time working on this supplier's issues. But, she said to herself, this was good for her company, too. Also, no one at her company had high ethical standards anyway.

Some months later, the same supplier offered to buy her a diamond necklace if she would make his company a preferred supplier. He said the necklace would look just like the one he had given her boss.

Questions

1. What ethics traps is Orlanda facing?

2. Is there anything wrong with accepting these gifts?

2-5h **Following Orders**

When someone in authority issues orders, even to do something clearly wrong, it is very tempting to comply. Fear of punishment, the belief in authority figures, and the ability to rationalize all play a role. In a true story (with the facts disguised), Amanda worked at a private school that was struggling to pay its bills. As a result, it kept the lights turned off in the hallways. On a particularly cloudy day, a visitor tripped and fell in one of these darkened passages. When the visitor sued, the principal told Amanda to lie on the witness stand and say that the lights had been on. The school's lawyer reinforced this advice. Amanda did as she was told. When asked why, she said, "I figured it must be the right thing to do if the lawyer said so. Also, if I hadn't lied, the principal would have fired me, and I might not have been able to get another job in teaching."

In your life, you are likely to face the dilemma of a boss who orders you to do something wrong. Executives have told us that they have been ordered to:

- Misrepresent data in a presentation to the board (so the boss could take on a project that was not as profitable as it should have been)

- Avoid hiring certain ethnic groups or pregnant women

- "Smooth" numbers, that is, report sales that had not, actually, taken place

- Support the boss's position, even if it was clearly wrong

Be aware, too, that setting goals for your subordinates carries risks, especially if the goals are too narrowly focused. A law firm partner once said, "If we tell associates they have to bill 2,000 hours a year, they will bill 2,000 hours. Whether they will *work* 2,000 hours is another matter." Research supports this view. Participants in an experiment were more likely to cheat if they had been assigned specific goals, whether or not they were actually being paid for meeting the targets.[20]

As you might expect, employees who work for firms with a culture of blind-obedience are twice as likely to report having seen unethical behavior as are workers at companies with a more collaborative environment.[21]

2-5i **Euphemisms and Reframing**

The term "friendly fire" has a cheerful ring to it, much better than "killing your own troops," which is what it really means. In a business setting, to "smooth earnings" sounds a lot better than to "cook the books" or "commit fraud." "Right-sizing" is more palatable than "firing a whole bunch of people." And "file sharing" sounds friendly and helpful, very different from "stealing intellectual property." In making ethical decisions, it is important to use accurate terminology. Anything else is just a variation on rationalization.

Aerospace engineer Roger Boisjoly (pronounced "Boh-zho-lay") tried to convince his superiors at Morton-Thiokol, Inc. to scrub the launch of the space shuttle *Challenger*. His superiors were engineers, too, so they were qualified to evaluate Boisjoly's concerns. But during the discussion, one of the bosses said, "We have to make a management decision." Once the issue was reframed as "management," not "engineering," their primary concern was to please their customer, NASA. The flight had already been postponed twice and, as managers, they felt they needed really clear data to justify another postponement. The Morton-Thiokol managers had to be convinced that it was *not* safe to fly. With that clear evidence lacking, these men approved the launch, which ended catastrophically when the space shuttle exploded 73 seconds after liftoff, killing all seven astronauts onboard. If they had asked an engineering question—"Is this spaceship definitely safe?"—they would have made a different decision. In answering a question, it is always a good idea to consider whether the frame is correct.

---

[20]Alina Tugend, "Experts' Advice to the Goal-Oriented: Don't Overdo It," *The New York Times*, October, 5, 2012.
[21]"The View from the Top and Bottom," *The Economist*, September 224, 2011.

2-5j **Lost in a Crowd**

After being struck by a car, a two-year-old child lies at the side of the road as people walk and ride by. No one stops to help, and the child dies. On a busy street, a man picks up a seven-year-old girl and carries her away while she screams, "You're not my dad—someone help me!" No one responds. The first incident was real; the second one was a test staged by a news station. It took hours and many repetitions before anyone tried to prevent the abduction.

When in a group, people are less likely to take responsibility, because they assume (hope?) that someone else will. They tend to check the reactions of others and, if everyone else seems calm, they assume that all is right. Bystanders are much more likely to react if they are alone and have to form an independent judgment.

Thus, in a business, if everyone is lying to customers, smoothing earnings, or sexually harassing the staff, it is tempting to go with the flow rather than protest the wrongdoing. In the example about food companies that began this chapter, one former executive says that producers shrug off responsibility for obesity in America by pointing to all the "other causes": a car culture; too much screen time; less outdoor play; fewer women at home to cook. And, Americans spend half of their food money outside the home anyway.

2-5k **Ethics Case: Man Down**

Wesley Autrey was standing on a train platform with his two young daughters and a man he did not know. Suddenly, this man had a seizure, causing him to fall on the tracks. Autrey could hear a train approaching so he knew he had only seconds to act. Leaping on to the track, he pulled the man between the rails and lay on top of him to protect him from the train. The train engineer tried to stop, but five cars passed over the two men. Both were unharmed.

Some years later in New York City, a homeless man pushed Ki-Suck Han onto subway tracks, in view of many people. No one reacted, except a photographer who took photos as Han was killed by a train.

Questions

- Why was Autrey more likely to act than the crowds watching Han?

- What are your ethical obligations to respond when someone needs help? Or you observe wrongdoing?

- Imagine that, at your work, you know that someone is:

  ○ Lying on an expense account

  ○ Wrongly booking sales that have not yet occurred

  ○ Sexually harassing staff members

What is your ethical obligation? What would you do, under what circumstances?

2-5l **Short-Term Perspective**

Many times, people make unethical decisions because they are thinking short-term. Your boss asks you to book sales in this quarter that actually will not happen until next. That "solution" would solve the immediate issue of low sales while potentially creating an enormous long-term problem that could lead to bankruptcy and prison-time. One manager told this story:

> A vice president from the customer service team told me that the company's largest customer was going to be conducting an on-site audit. In my area, the customer would be particularly interested in seeing the dedicated computing equipment that was part of their contract. As it turns out, we did not have any dedicated computing equipment. The VP was incredulous because the past director of my area had, on multiple occasions, told him that there was. As it turned out, the

former director had been lying. To survive the audit, the VP asked me to lie and also to put fake labels on some of the machines to show the customer. If I didn't agree, I knew the VP would be furious and we might lose this client.

In the short-run, lying is an appealing option in this case, as lying often is. But eventually the customer was likely to find out about the breach of contract, which could mean one client lost and one lawsuit acquired. The manager refused to lie and, in the end, was given the extra funds to comply with the contract.

2-5m Blind Spots

As Bob Dylan memorably sang, "How many times can a man turn his head and pretend that he just doesn't see?" The answer is: a whole lot. For example, Bernard Madoff will long be remembered for running one of the biggest frauds ever through his brokerage house. One of the mysteries yet unresolved is: Who else knew what was going on? His brother, Peter, was second in command at his brother's firm. He admitted that he had committed many crimes, including income tax evasion and filing false documents with regulators. But he has always insisted that he had no idea his brother was committing fraud.

And then there is the case of Barry Bonds, one of the greatest baseball players of all time. Although he quickly gained tremendous weight and muscle mass that was consistent with the illegal use of steroids, neither his team nor baseball executives took any action against him until the federal government began an investigation.[22]

Or a partner in a law firm who was consistently billing 2,000+ hours a year. Yet he seemed to have time to attend his children's school functions in the middle of the day and was rarely in the office early or late. Firm executives were shocked to discover that he had been overbilling clients.[23]

We all have a tendency to ignore even blatant evidence that we would rather not know. Just as tobacco manufacturers were very slow to learn that smoking caused cancer, officials at Pennsylvania State University overlooked compelling evidence that football coach Jerry Sandusky was molesting children.

2-5n Avoiding Ethics Traps

These ethics traps represent potential dangers for us all. But they are not, by any means, inevitable.

Three practices will help us avoid these pitfalls:

1. **Slow down.** We all make worse decisions when in a hurry. In one experiment, a group of students at Princeton Theological Seminary (that is, people in training to be ministers) were told to go to a location across campus to give a talk. On their walk over, they encountered a man lying in distress in a doorway. Only one-tenth of those participants who had been told they were late for their talk stopped to help the ill man, while almost two-thirds of those who thought they had plenty of time did stop.[24]

2. **Do not trust your first instinct.** You make many decisions without thinking. When sitting down for dinner, you do not ask yourself, "Which hand should I use to pick up the fork? How will I cut up my food?" You use System 1 thinking—an automatic, instinctual, sometimes emotional process. This approach is efficient but can also lead

---

[22]To see the drastic change in Bonds's physique, search the Internet for "steroids, Barry Bonds."

[23]For more on this topic, see Max Bazerman and Ann Tenbrunsel, *Blind Spots: Why We Fail To Do What's Right and What To Do About It,* Princeton University Press.

[24]John M. Darley and Daniel C. Batson, "From Jerusalem to Jericho: A Study of Situational and Dispositional Variables in Helping Behavior," *Journal of Personality and Social Psychology,* Vol. 27(1), July 1973, 100–108.

to more selfish and unethical decisions. When taking an exam, System 1 thinking would not get you far. For that, you need System 2 thoughts—those that are conscious and logical.

Being in a hurry, or in a crowd, being able to rationalize easily, using euphemisms, doing what every else does, receiving an order, being dazzled by money; these can all lead you to make a quick and wrong System 1 decision. Before making an important choice, bring in System 2 thinking.

3. **Remember your Life Principles.** In his research, Ariely found that participants were less likely to cheat if they were reminded of their school honor code or the Ten Commandments. This result was true even if the participants were atheists. Also, in the case of the seminary students, the topic of the talk mattered. Those who were speaking on the Parable of the Good Samaritan (in which a man offers aid to an injured person from a different clan) were twice as likely to provide help than those who were giving a talk on careers for seminarians. It is a good practice to remind yourself of your values. What about keeping a list of your Life Principles as wallpaper on your phone or computer?

2-6 LYING: A SPECIAL CASE

We are taught from an early age to tell the truth. Yet research shows that we tell between one and two lies a day.[25] Is honesty the best policy? The consequences of lying can be severe: Students are suspended, employees are fired, and witnesses are convicted of perjury. Sometimes the impact is subtler but still significant: a loss of trust or of opportunities.

When is lying acceptable? If poker players bluff their way through lousy hands, we consider them skilled because that is an accepted part of the game. What about white lies to make others feel better: I love your lasagna. You're not going bald. No, that sweater doesn't make you look fat. When Victoria McGrath suffered a terrible wound to her leg in the Boston Marathon bombing, Tyler Dodd comforted her at the scene by telling her that he had recovered from a shrapnel wound in Afghanistan. His story was not true—he had never been in combat or Afghanistan. McGrath was grateful to him for his lie because it gave her strength and hope. Was he right or wrong? What are your rules on lying?

Kant felt that any lie violated his principle of the categorical imperative. Because the world would be intolerable if everyone lied all the time, no one should lie ever. He gave the example of the murderer who knocks on your door and asks, "Where's Lukas?" You know Lukas is cowering just inside, but you might be tempted to lie and send the murderer off in the opposite direction. Kant preferred that you tell what is now called a **Kantian Evasion** or a **palter**. That is, you would make a truthful statement that is nonetheless misleading. So, you might say, truthfully, "I saw Lukas in the park just an hour ago." And off the murderer would go.

Kantian evasion or a palter

A truthful statement that is nonetheless misleading.

Is a Kantian Evasion really more ethical than a lie? For example, when a candidate for the presidency, Bill Clinton was asked if he had ever smoked marijuana. He answered that he "never broke the laws of my state or of the United States." Later, it was revealed that he had used marijuana while a student in England. So, although technically correct, his statement was misleading. Was that really better than lying about marijuana use?

One could argue that Clinton was at least honoring the importance of truth-telling. He went to some effort *not* to lie. However, some commentators argue that paltering is actually

---

[25]Bella M. DePaulo, Deborah A. Kashy, Susan E. Kirkendol, and Melissa M. Wyer, "Lying in Everyday Life," *Journal of Personality and Social Psychology*, 1996, Vol. 70, No. 5, 979–995.

worse than lying. Although the harm to the victim is the same, palterers are less likely to be caught and are, therefore, more likely to palter again.

What are your Life Principles on this issue? There may indeed be good reasons to lie but what are they? Would it be right to say that you would only lie to benefit other people? Hiding Lukas from the murderer? Deceiving children who believe in Santa Claus? It is useful to analyze this issue now rather than to rationalize later.

What about in business? Does the presence of *competition* make a difference? When do the ends justify the means?

2-6a Ethics Case: Truth (?) in Borrowing

Rob is in the business of buying dental practices. He finds solo practitioners, buys their assets, signs them to a long-term contract and then improves their management and billing processes so effectively that both he and the dentists are better off.

Rob has just found a great opportunity with a lot of potential profit. There is only *one* problem. The bank will not give him a loan to buy the practice without checking the dentist's financial record. Her credit rating is fine, but it turns out that she filed for bankruptcy 20 years ago. That event no longer appears on her credit record but, on the form it required her to sign, the bank asked about *all* bankruptcies. She is perfectly willing to lie. Rob refused to turn in the form with a lie. But when the bank learned about the bankruptcy, it denied his loan even though *her* bankruptcy in no way affects *his* ability to pay the loan. And the incident is ancient history—the dentist's current finances are strong. Subsequently four other banks also refused to make the loan.

Rob is feeling pretty frustrated. He figures the return on this deal would be 20 percent. Everyone would benefit—the dentist would earn more, her patients would have better technology, he could afford a house in a better school district, and the bank would make a profit. There is one more bank he could try.

Questions

1. Should Rob file loan documents with the bank, knowing the dentist has lied?

2. Who would be harmed by this lie?

3. What if Rob pays back the loan without incident? Was the lie still wrong? Do the ends justify the means?

4. What is your Life Principle about telling lies? When is making a misrepresentation acceptable? To protect someone's life or physical safety? To protect a job? To protect another person's feelings? To gain an advantage? When others are doing the same? When it makes sense from a cost-benefit perspective?

5. Do you have the same rule when lying to protect yourself, as opposed to benefiting others?

2-7 APPLYING THE PRINCIPLES

Having thought about ethics principles and traps, let's now practice applying them to situations that are similar to those you are likely to face in your life. Be aware that some of these ethical dilemmas illustrate the trade-off between shareholders and stakeholders. It is important to recognize explicitly the forces that push or pull you when making a decision. Unless you are aware of these factors, you cannot make a truly informed decision.

2-7a **Personal Ethics in the Workplace**

Should you behave in the workplace the way you do at home, or do you have a separate set of ethics for each part of your life? What if your employees behave badly outside of work—should that affect their employment? Consider the following case.

2-7b **Ethics Case: Weird Wierdsma**

Beatrix Szeremi immigrated to the United States from Hungary. But her American dream turned into a nightmare when she married Charles Wierdsma. He repeatedly beat her and threatened to suffocate and drown her. Ultimately, he pleaded guilty to one felony count and went to jail. Despite his son's guilt, Thomas Wierdsma pressured his daughter-in-law to drop the charges and delete photos of her injuries from her Facebook page. When she refused, he threatened her and her lawyer that he would report her to immigration officials. Father and son discussed how they could get her deported. Thomas also testified in a deposition that it was not wrong to lie to a federal agency. "It happens all the time," he said.[26] Thomas Wierdsma is the senior vice president at The GEO Group, Inc.

Research indicates that CEOs who break the law outside of the office are more likely to engage in workplace fraud. Although their legal infractions—driving under the influence, use of illegal drugs, domestic violence, even speeding tickets—were unrelated to their work, they seemed to indicate a disrespect for the rule of law and a lack of self-control.[27]

Questions

1. If you were the CEO of Thomas Wierdsma's company, would you fire him? Impose some other sanction?

2. Which is worse—threatening his daughter-in-law or stating that it is acceptable to lie to a federal agency?

3. Would you fire a warehouse worker who behaved this way? How high up in the hierarchy does an employee have to be for this behavior to be forgiven?

4. GEO runs prisons and immigration facilities for the government. Does that fact change any of your answers?

5. Wierdsma's woes were reported in major newspapers and his statement about lying to a federal agency is on YouTube (see footnote). Do these facts change any of your answers?

6. What would Kant and Mill say is the right thing to do in this case? What result under the Front Page Test?

7. What ethics traps might Wierdsma's boss face in this situation?

8. What is your Life Principle? What behavior are you willing to tolerate in the interest of profitability?

9. What would you say to someone who argues that the goal at work is to make as much money as possible, but at home it is to be a kind and honorable human being?

---

[26]Nancy Lofholm, "GEO Investigated in Son's Domestic Violence Case," *The Denver Post*, April 8, 2013. The YouTube video of his admission about lying to a federal agency is at http://www.youtube.com/watch?v=UTi9fbo202M.
[27]Robert Davidson, Aiyesha Dey, and Abbie Smith, "Executives' 'Off-the-Job' Behavior, Corporate Culture, and Financial Reporting Risk," Chicago Booth Paper No. 12-24.

2-7c The Organization's Responsibility to Society

Many products can potentially cause harm to customers or employees. Does it matter if they willingly accept exposure to these products? What constitutes informed agreement? What is the company's responsibility to those who are *unwittingly* harmed by its products?

2-7d Ethics Case: Breathing the Fumes

Every other year, the National Institutes of Health publish the Report on Carcinogens, which lists products that cause cancer. Among those in the most recent report was formaldehyde, found in furniture, cosmetics, building products, carpets, and fabric softeners. Unless we take heroic efforts to avoid this chemical, we are all exposed to it on a daily basis. Indeed, almost all homes have formaldehyde levels that exceed government safety rules. In an effort to shoot the messenger, the American Chemistry Council, which is an industry trade group, lobbied Congress to cut off funding for the Report on Carcinogens— not improve it, but defund it.

Questions

1. If you were one of the many companies using products that contain formaldehyde, what would you do? What would you be willing to pay to provide a safer product?

2. If you were an executive at Exxon, Dow, or DuPont, all members of the American Chemistry Council, how would you react to this effort to hide the facts on formaldehyde?

3. What would Mill and Kant recommend?

4. What ethics traps would you face in making a decision?

5. What Life Principle would you apply?

2-7e The Organization's Responsibility to Its Employees

Organizations cannot be successful without good workers. In many circumstances, the shareholder and stakeholder models agree that employees should be treated well. Disgruntled workers are likely to be unmotivated and unproductive. But sometimes doing what is best for employees may not lead to higher profits. In these cases, does an organization have a duty to take care of its workers? The shareholder model says no; the stakeholder model takes the opposite view.

Corporate leaders are often faced with difficult decisions when the issue of layoffs arises. Choices can be particularly difficult to navigate when outsourcing is an option. *Outsourcing* refers to cutting jobs at home and relocating operations to another country. That is the issue in the following scenario.

2-7f Ethics Case: The Storm After the Storm

Yanni is the CEO of Cloud Farm, a company that provides online data centers for Internet companies. Because these data centers are enormous, they are located in rural areas where they are often the main employer. A series of tornados has just destroyed a data center near Farmfield, Arkansas, a town with a population of roughly 5,000 people. Farmfield is a two-hour drive from the nearest city, Little Rock.

Here is the good news: The insurance payout will cover the full cost of rebuilding. Indeed, the payout will be so generous that Cloud Farm could build a bigger and better facility than the one destroyed. The bad news? Data centers are much more expensive to build and operate in the United States than in Africa, Asia, or Latin America. Yanni could take the money from the insurance company and build three data centers overseas. He has asked Adam and Zoe to present the pros and cons of relocating.

Adam says, "If we rebuild overseas, our employees will never find equivalent jobs. We pay $20 an hour, and the other jobs in town are mostly minimum wage. And remember how some of the guys worked right through Christmas to set up for that new client. They have been loyal to us—we owe them something in return. Going overseas is not just bad for Farmfield or Arkansas, it's bad for the country. We can't continue to ship jobs overseas."

Zoe responds, "That is the government's problem, not ours. We'll pay to retrain the workers, which, frankly, is a generous offer. Our investors get a return of 4 percent; the industry average is closer to 8 percent. If we act like a charity to support Farmfield, we could all lose our jobs. It is our obligation to do what's best for our shareholders—which, in this case, happens to be what's right for us, too."

Questions

1. Do you agree with Zoe's argument that it is the government's responsibility to create and protect American jobs, and that it is a CEO's job to increase shareholder wealth?

2. Imagine that you personally own shares in Cloud Farm. Would you be upset with a decision to rebuild the data center in the United States?

3. If you were in Yanni's position, would you rebuild the plant in Arkansas or relocate overseas?

4. If Cloud Farm decides to rebuild in Arkansas, should it pay the workers while the center is being rebuilt? If yes, should it pay all workers, or just the high-level ones who might leave if they were not paid?

5. What ethics traps does Yanni face in this situation?

6. What is your Life Principle on this issue? Would you be willing to risk your job to protect your employees?

2-7g An Organization's Responsibility to Its Customers

Customers are another group of essential stakeholders. A corporation must gain and retain loyal buyers if it is to stay in business for long. Treating customers well usually increases profits and helps shareholders.

But when, if ever, does an organization go too far? Is a leader acting appropriately when she puts customers first in a way that significantly diminishes the bottom line? The shareholder model says no. What do you say?

2-7h Ethics Case: Mickey Weighs In

As we have seen, many food companies manipulate products to maximize their appeal, without regard to the health of their customers. Disney is taking a different approach, announcing recently that only healthy foods can be advertised on its children's television channels, radio stations, and websites. Candy, fast food, and sugared cereals are banned from Mickey land.

Kicked to the curb are such childhood favorites as Lunchables and Capri Sun drinks. In addition, sodium must be reduced by one-quarter in food served at its theme parks. Nor does Disney permit its characters to associate with unhealthy foods. No more Mickey Pop-Tarts or Buzz Lightyear Happy Meals. Said Disney chairman, Robert Iger, "Companies in a position to help with solutions to childhood obesity should do just that."[28]

Disney will certainly lose advertising, but would not say how much. Food sales at its theme parks may decline if children find the options unappealing. Its licensing revenues are also affected by its decision to remove Disney characters from the likes of Pop-Tarts and Happy Meals.

On the other hand, this healthy initiative will enhance its reputation, at least with parents, who increasingly seek healthy food options for their children. Disney will profit from license fees it receives for the use of a Mickey Check logo on healthy food in grocery aisles and restaurants. This food initiative may also help forestall more onerous government regulation.

In contrast, the Nickelodeon television channel, home to SpongeBob SquarePants and Dora the Explorer, still allows ads for such nutritional failures as Trix and Cocoa Puffs cereals. It said that its goal is "to make the highest quality entertainment content in the world for kids … [while leaving] the science of nutrition to the experts." Food ads are the third highest source of advertising revenues for Nickelodeon. Also, it does not have as many other revenue streams as Disney does—no theme parks, for example.

Questions

1. What obligation do Disney and Nickelodeon have to their young customers? Do they owe anything other than entertainment?

2. How much advertising and licensing revenue would you be willing to give up to protect children from ads for unhealthy foods? Does your answer depend on how profitable the division is?

3. Does this information make you more likely to buy Disney products or allow your children to watch Disney TV? Less likely to watch Nickelodeon?

4. What would Mill or Kant have said? What result with the Front Page Test?

5. What ethics traps do Disney and Nickelodeon face?

6. What is your Life Principle? How much profitability (or income) would you be willing to give up to protect children you do not know?

2-7i Organization's Responsibility to Overseas Workers

What ethical duties does an American manager have overseas, to stakeholders in countries where the culture and economic circumstances are very different? Should American companies (and consumers) buy goods that are produced in sweatshop factories?

Industrialization has always been the first stepping-stone out of dire poverty—it was in England in centuries past, and it is now in the developing world. Eventually, higher productivity leads to higher wages. The results in

> Industrialization has always been the first stepping-stone out of dire poverty

---

[28]Brooks Barnes, "Promoting Nutrition, Disney to Restrict Junk-Food Ads," *The New York Times*, June 5, 2012.

China have been nothing short of remarkable. During the Industrial Revolution in England, per-capita output doubled in 58 years; in China, it took only 10 years.

During the past 50 years, Taiwan and South Korea welcomed sweatshops. During the same period, India resisted what it perceived to be foreign exploitation. Although all three countries started at the same economic level, Taiwan and South Korea today have much lower levels of infant mortality and much higher levels of education than India.[29]

In theory, then, sweatshops might not be all bad. But are there limits? Consider the following case.

2-7j Ethics Case: A Worm in the Apple

"Riots, Suicides and More," blares an Internet headline about a FoxConn factory where iPhones and other Apple products are assembled. Apple is not alone in facing supplier scandals. So have Nike, Coca-Cola, and Gap, among many others. Do companies have an obligation to the employees of their suppliers? If so, how can they, or anyone, be sure what is really going on in a factory on the other side of the world? Professor Richard Locke of MIT has studied supply chain issues.[30] His conclusions:

- The first step that many companies took to improve working conditions overseas was to establish a code of conduct and then conduct audits. Professor Locke found that these coercive practices do not work and that compliance is sporadic, at best. For example, despite Hewlett-Packard's best efforts, only a handful of its 276 overseas factories consistently met its standards.

- A more collaborative approach worked better—when the auditors sent by multinationals saw their role as less of a police officer and more as a partner, committed to problem solving and sharing of best practices.

- It can be hard to improve conditions without also changing a company's business model. One of the reasons that Apple uses Chinese manufacturers such as FoxConn is that its workers have fewer overtime restrictions. Just before the first iPhone was released, Steve Jobs decided that the screens had to be unscratchable glass instead of plastic. One Chinese company supplied a team of engineers that was housed in a dormitory and willing to work around the clock to design the right glass. When the glass arrived at FoxConn in the middle of the night, thousands of assemblers were put to work immediately.

What would you do if you were a manager in the following circumstances?

- In clothing factories, workers often remove the protective guards from their sewing machines, because the guards slow the flow of work. As a result, many workers suffer needle punctures. Factories resist the cost of buying new guards because the workers just take them off again. Is there a solution?

- In a factory in Central America, powerful chemicals were used to remove stains from clothing. The fumes from these chemicals were a health hazard but ventilation systems were too expensive. What could be done?

- Timberland, Nike, and Hewlett-Packard have recognized that selling large numbers of new products creates great variation in demand and therefore pressure on factory workers to work overtime. What can a company do to reduce this pressure?[31]

---

[29]The data in this and the preceding paragraph are from Nicholas D. Kristof and Sheryl Wu Dunn, "Two Cheers for Sweatshops," *New York Times Magazine*, Sept. 24, 2000, p. 70.

[30]"When the Jobs Inspector Calls," *The Economist*, March 31, 2012.

[31]These examples are from: Richard Locke, Matthew Amengual, and Akshay Mangla, "Virtue out of Necessity?: Compliance, Commitment and the Improvement of Labor Conditions in Global Supply Chains," available at Princeton.edu.

2-8 WHEN THE GOING GETS TOUGH: RESPONDING TO UNETHICAL BEHAVIOR

We have talked about the kinds of ethical issues that you are likely to face in your career. If you find yourself working for a company that tolerates an intolerable level of unethical behavior, you face three choices.

2-8a Loyalty

It is always important to pick one's battles. For example, a firm's accounting department must make many decisions about which reasonable people could disagree. Just because their judgment is different from yours does not mean that they are behaving unethically. Being a team player means allowing other people to make their own choices sometimes. However, the difference between being a team player and starting down the slippery slope can be very narrow. If you are carrying out a decision, or simply observing one, that makes you uncomfortable, then it is time to consult your Life Principles and review the section on ethics traps.

2-8b Exit

When faced with the unacceptable, one option is to walk out the door quietly. You resign "to spend more time with your family," "to explore other opportunities," or "to accept an offer that is too good to refuse." This approach may be the safest for you because you are not ruffling any feathers or making any enemies. It is a small world and you never know when someone you have offended will be in a position to do you harm. But a quiet exit leaves the bad guys in position to continue the unsavory behavior. For example, the CEO was sexually harassing Laura, but she left quietly for fear that if she reported him, he would harm her career. No one likes to hire a troublemaker. So the CEO proceeded to attack other women at the company until finally a senior man got wind of what was going on and confronted the chief. In short, the braver and better option may be to exit loudly—reporting the wrongdoing on the way out the door.

2-8c Voice

As we saw in our discussion of conformity, wrongdoing often occurs because everyone just goes along to get along. One valiant soul with the courage to say, "This is wrong," can be a powerful force for the good. But confrontation may not be the only, or even the best, use of your voice. Learning to persuade, cajole, or provide better options are all important leadership skills. For example, Keith felt that the CEO of his company was about to make a bad decision but he was unable to persuade the man to choose a different alternative. When Keith turned out to be correct, the CEO gave him no credit, saying, "You are equally responsible because your arguments weren't compelling enough." Keith thought the man had a point.

2-9 CORPORATE SOCIAL RESPONSIBILITY (CSR)

So far, we have largely been talking about a company's duty not to cause harm. But do companies have a **corporate social responsibility**—that is, an obligation to contribute positively to the world around them? Do businesses have an affirmative duty to do good?.

Corporate social responsibility
An organization's obligation to contribute positively to the world around it

You remember Milton Friedman's view that a manager's obligation is to make the company as profitable as possible while also complying with the law. Harvard Professor Michael Porter has written that CSR often benefits a company. For example, improving economic and social conditions overseas can create new customers with money to spend. Educational programs may provide a better workforce. However, in Porter's view, a company should not undertake a CSR project unless it is profitable for the company in its own right, regardless of any secondary benefits the company may receive from, say, an improved reputation.[32] Thus, for example, Yoplait has periodically run a "Save Lids to Save Lives" campaign. For every Yoplait lid mailed in, the company makes a donation to a breast cancer charity. During these campaigns, Yoplait gains market share. Should companies be willing to improve the world even if their efforts *reduce* profitability?

2-9a Ethics Case: The Beauty of a Well-Fed Child

Cosmetic companies often use gift-with-purchase offers to promote their products. For example, with any $45 Estee Lauder purchase at Bloomingdale's, you can choose a free seven-piece gift of creams and makeup valued at more than $165, plus a special-edition Lily Pulitzer cosmetic bag.

But Clarins has put a new spin on these offers with what it calls "gift with *purpose*." Buy two Clarins items at Macy's and you will receive six trial-size products *and* the company will pay the United Nations World Food Program enough for 10 school meals.

Because so many cosmetic companies do gift-with-purchase offers, it is difficult for any one business to stand out from the crowd. That is Clarins's goal with this offer. The company hopes that cosmetic buyers, many of whom are women with children, will find this opportunity to feed children particularly compelling. Says the Macy's vice president for national media relations and cause marketing, "With no energy or lift on the customers' part, they get this really feel-good element with the shopping experience."[33]

Questions

1. If you were an executive at Clarins or Macy's, what would you want to know before approving this promotion?

2. How important is it to improve the image of these two companies? Would this promotion do so?

3. Would you approve this promotion if it were not profitable on its own account? How much of a subsidy would you be willing to grant?

Chapter Conclusion

Many times in your life, you will be tempted to do something that you know in your heart of hearts is wrong. Referring to your own Life Principles, being aware of potential traps, will help you to make the right decisions. But it is also important that you be able to afford to do the right thing. Having a reserve fund to cover six months' living expenses makes it easier for you to leave a job that violates your personal ethics. Too many times, people make the wrong, and sometimes the illegal, decision for financial reasons.

---

[32]Michael E. Porter and Mark R. Kramer, "The Competitive Advantage of Corporate Philanthropy," *Harvard Business Review*, December 2002.

[33]Adam Andrew Newman, "A Cosmetic Freebie with a Cause," *The New York Times*, April 7, 2013.

Managers wonder what they can do to create an ethical environment in their companies. In the end, the surest way to infuse ethics throughout an organization is for top executives to behave ethically themselves. Few will bother to do the right thing unless they observe that their bosses value and support such behavior. Even employees who are ethical in their personal lives may find it difficult to uphold their standards at work if those around them behave differently. To ensure a more ethical world, managers must be an example for others, both within and outside their organizations.

EXAM REVIEW

1. **ETHICS** The law dictates how a person *must* behave. Ethics governs how people *should* behave.

2. **LIFE PRINCIPLES** Life Principles are the rules by which you live your life. If you develop these Life Principles now, you will be prepared when facing ethical dilemmas in the future.

3. **THE ROLE OF BUSINESS IN SOCIETY** An ongoing debate about whether managers should focus only on what is best for shareholders or whether they should consider the interests of other stakeholders as well.

4. **WHY BE ETHICAL?**

   - Society as a whole benefits from ethical behavior.

   - People feel better when they behave ethically.

   - Unethical behavior can be very costly.

5. **THEORIES OF ETHICS**

   - Utilitarian thinkers such as John Stuart Mill believe that the right decision maximizes overall happiness and minimizes overall pain.

   - Deontological thinkers such as Immanuel Kant believe that the ends do not justify the means. Rather, it is important to do the right thing, no matter the result.

   - With his categorical imperative, Kant argued that you should not do something unless you would be willing to have everyone else do it, too.

   - John Rawls asked us to consider what rules we would propose for society if we did not know how lucky we would be in life's lottery. He called this situation "the veil of ignorance."

   - Under the Front Page Test, you ask yourself what you would do if your actions were going to be reported publicly online or offline.

6. **ETHICS TRAPS**

   - Money

   - Competition

   - Rationalization

- We Can't Be Objective About Ourselves

- Conflicts of Interest

- Conformity

- Following Orders

- Euphemisms and Reframing

- Lost in a Crowd

- Short-Term Perspective

- Blind Spots

7. To avoid ethics traps:

   - Slow down.

   - Do not trust your first instinct.

   - Remember your Life Principles.

8. **KANTIAN EVASION**   A truthful statement that is nonetheless misleading.

9. **WHEN THE GOING GETS TOUGH**   When faced with unethical behavior in your organization, you have three choices:

   - Loyalty

   - Exit (either quiet or noisy)

   - Voice

10. **CORPORATE SOCIAL RESPONSIBILITY**   An organization's obligation to contribute positively to the world around it.

MULTIPLE-CHOICE QUESTIONS

1. Milton Friedman was a strong believer in the _____ model.
   He _____ argue that a corporate leader's sole obligation is to make money for the company's owners.
   (a) shareholder; did
   (b) shareholder; did not
   (c) stakeholder; did
   (d) stakeholder; did not

2. Which of the following wrote the book *Utilitarianism* and believed that ethical actions should "generate the greatest good for the greatest number"?
   (a) Milton Friedman
   (b) John Stuart Mill
   (c) Immanuel Kant
   (d) John Rawls

3. Which of the following believed that the dignity of human beings must be respected, and that the most ethical decisions are made out of a sense of obligation?

   (a) Milton Friedman

   (b) John Stuart Mill

   (c) Immanuel Kant

   (d) John Rawls

4. Kant believed that:

   (a) it is ethical to tell a lie if necessary to protect an innocent person from great harm.

   (b) it is ethical to tell a lie if the benefit of the lie outweighs the cost.

   (c) it is ethical to make a true, but misleading, statement.

   (d) it is wrong to tell an outright lie or to mislead.

5. The following statement is true:

   (a) Most people are completely honest most of the time.

   (b) Even people who do not believe in God are more likely to behave honestly after reading the Ten Commandments.

   (c) When confronted with the option of engaging in wrongdoing, most people accurately evaluate the ethics of these situations.

   (d) People make their best ethical decisions when in a hurry.

CASE QUESTIONS

1. The Senate recently released a report on wrongdoing at JPMorgan Chase & Co. It found that bank executives lied to investors and the public. Also, traders, with the knowledge of top management, changed risk limits to facilitate more trading and then violated even these higher limits. Executives revalued the bank's investment portfolio to reduce apparent losses. The bank's internal investigation failed to find this wrongdoing. Into what ethics traps did these JPMorgan employees fall? What options did the executives and traders have for dealing with this wrongdoing?

2. Located in Bath, Maine, Bath Iron Works builds high-tech warships for the Navy. Winning Navy contracts is crucial to the company's success—it means jobs for the community and profits for the shareholders. Navy officials held a meeting at Bath's offices with its executives and those of a competitor to review the specs for an upcoming bid. Both companies desperately wanted to win the contract. After the meeting, a Bath worker realized that one of the Navy officials had left a folder on a chair labeled: "Business Sensitive." It contained information about the competitors' bid that would be a huge advantage to Bath. William Haggett, the Bath CEO, was notified about the file just as he was walking out the door to give a luncheon speech. What should he do? What ethics traps did he face? What result if he considered Mill, Kant, or the Front Page test?

3. A group of medical schools conducted a study on very premature babies—those born between 24 and 27 weeks of gestation (instead of the normal 40 weeks). These children face a high risk of blindness and death. The goal of the study was to

determine which level of oxygen in a baby's incubator produced the best results. Before enrolling families in the study, the investigators did not tell them that being in the study could *increase* their child's risk of blindness or death. The study made some important discoveries about the best oxygen level. These results could benefit many children. What would Mill and Kant say about this decision *not* to tell the families?

4. I oversee the internal audit function at my company. Although we always use a Big Four accounting firm, we have no loyalty to any one particular firm. We hold periodic bid competitions to get the lowest price we can. At the moment, we are using Firm A. Recently, one of the partners at A offered me box seats to a Red Sox baseball game. I love the Red Sox, and even more important, I could have taken my father who, even though he has always been a big Sox fan, has never been to a game. However, I knew that we would soon be asking A to bid against the other Big Four firms for the right to do next year's audit. Needless to say, I was torn about what I should do.

   What traps does this person face? Would something as minor as Red Sox tickets affect his decision about which audit firm to use?

5. Each year, the sale of Girl Scout cookies is the major fund-raiser for local troops. But because the organization was criticized for promoting such unhealthy food, it introduced a new cookie, Mango Cremes with Nutrifusion. It promotes this cookie as a vitamin-laden, natural whole food. "A delicious way to get your vitamins." But these vitamins are a minuscule part of the cookie. The rest has more bad saturated fat than an Oreo. The Girl Scouts do much good for many girls. And to do this good, they need to raise money. What would Kant and Mill say about Mango Cremes? What about the Front Page test? What do you say?

6. In Japan, automobile GPS systems come equipped with an option for converting them into televisions so that drivers can watch their favorite shows, yes, while driving. "We can't help but respond to our customers' needs," says a company spokesperson.[34] Although his company does not recommend the practice of watching while driving, he explained that it is the driver's responsibility to make this decision. Is it right to sell a product that could cause great harm to innocent bystanders? Where does the company's responsibility end and the consumer's begin? What would Mill and Kant say?

DISCUSSION QUESTIONS

1. While waiting in line at a supermarket, you observe a woman trying to pay with food stamps. Under the law, food stamps cannot be used to pay for prepared items so the register would not accept the stamps in payment for a $6 container of chicken noodle soup from the deli counter. The woman explained that she was sick and did not have the energy to cook. She just wanted to go home and get in bed. In general, you agree that this law is reasonable—people on limited budgets should not be buying more expensive prepared food. But the woman is sick. Would it be ethical for you to buy her chicken soup if she agreed to buy $6 worth of your grocery items?

---

[34]Chester Dawson, "Drivers Use Navigation Systems to Tune In," *The Wall Street Journal*, April 23, 2013.

2. Because Raina processes payroll at her company, she knows how much everyone earns, including the top executives. This information could make for some good gossip, but she has kept it all completely confidential. She just found out, however, that it is against company policy for her to do payroll for C-level employees. And her boss knew it. Yesterday, the CEO went to her boss to confirm that he, the boss, was personally doing the processing for top management. Her boss lied to the CEO and said that he was. Then he begged Raina not to tell the truth if the CEO checked with her. Raina just got a message that the CEO wants to see her. What does she say if he asks about the payroll?

3. Darby has been working for 14 months at Holden Associates, a large management consulting firm. She is earning $85,000 a year, which *sounds* good but does not go very far in New York City. It turns out that her peers at competing firms are typically paid 20 percent more and receive larger annual bonuses. Darby works about 60 hours a week—more if she is traveling. A number of times, she has had to reschedule her vacation or cancel personal plans to meet client deadlines. She hopes to go to business school in a year and has already begun the application process.

   Holden has a policy that permits any employee who works as late as 8:00 p.m. to eat dinner at the company's expense. The employee can also take a taxi home. Darby is in the habit of staying until 8:00 p.m. every night, whether or not her workload requires it. Then she orders enough food for dinner, with leftovers for lunch the next day. She has managed to cut her grocery bill to virtually nothing. Sometimes she invites her boyfriend to join her for dinner. As a student, he is always hungry and broke. Darby often uses the Holden taxi to take them back to his apartment, although the cab fare is twice as high as to her own place.

   Sometimes Darby stays late to work on her business school applications. Naturally, she uses Holden equipment to print out and photocopy the finished applications. Darby has also been known to return online purchases through the Holden mailroom on the company dime. Many employees do that, and the mailroom workers do not seem to mind.

   Is Darby doing anything wrong? What ethics traps is she facing? What would your Life Principle be in this situation?

4. Steve supervises a team of account managers. One night at a company outing, Lawrence, a visiting account manager, made some wildly inappropriate sexual remarks to Maddie, who is on Steve's team. When she told Steve, he was uncertain what to do, so he asked his boss. She was concerned that if Steve took the matter further and Lawrence was fired or even disciplined, her whole area would suffer. Lawrence was one of the best account managers in the region, and everyone was overworked as it was. She told Steve to get Maddie to drop the matter. Just tell her that these things happen, and Lawrence did not mean anything by it.

   What should Steve do? What ethics traps does he face? What would be your Life Principle in this situation? What should Maddie do?

5. Many people enjoy rap music at least in part because of its edgy, troublemaking vibe. The problem is that some of this music could cause real trouble. Thus, Ice-T's song "Cop Killer" generated significant controversy when it was released. Among other things, its lyrics celebrated the idea of slitting a policeman's throat. Rick Ross rapped about drugging and raping a woman. Time Warner Inc. did not withdraw Ice-T's song but Reebok fired Ross over his lyrics. One difference: Time Warner was struggling with a $15 billion debt and a depressed stock price. Reebok at first refused to take

action but then singing group UltraViolet began circulating an online petition against the song and staged a protest at the main Reebok store in New York.

What obligation do companies have to their customers? What factors matter when making a decision about the content of entertainment.

6. You are negotiating a new labor contract with union officials. The contract covers a plant that has experienced operating losses over the past several years. You want to negotiate concessions from labor to reduce the losses. However, labor is refusing any compromises. You could tell them that, without concessions, the plant will be closed, although that is not true.

Is bluffing ethical? Under what circumstances? What would Kant and Mill say? What result under the Front Page test? What is your Life Principle?

7. When James Kilts became CEO of Gillette Co., the consumer products giant had been a mainstay of the Boston community for 100 years. But the organization was going through hard times: Its stock was trading at less than half its peak price, and some of its established brands of razors were suffering under intense competitive pressure. In four short years, Kilts turned Gillette around—strengthening its core brands, cutting jobs, and paying off debt. With the company's stock up 61 percent, Kilts had added $20 billion in shareholder value.

Then Kilts suddenly sold Gillette to Procter & Gamble (P&G) for $57 billion. So short was Kilts's stay in Boston that he never moved his family from their home in Rye, New York. The deal was sweet for Gillette shareholders—the company's stock price went up 13 percent in one day. And also for Kilts—his payoff was $153 million, including a $23.9 million reward from P&G for having made the deal and a "change in control" clause in his employment contract that was worth $12.6 million. In addition, P&G agreed to pay him $8 million a year to serve as vice chairman after the merger. When he retired, his pension would be $1.2 million per year. Moreover, two of his top lieutenants were offered payments totaling $57 million.

Was there any downside to this deal? Four percent of the Gillette workforce— 6,000 employees—were fired. If the payouts to the top three Gillette executives were divided among these 6,000, each unemployed worker would receive $35,000. The loss of this many employees (4,000 of whom lived in New England) had a ripple effect throughout the area's economy. Although Gillette shareholders certainly benefited in the short run from the sale, their profit would have been even greater without this $210 million payout to the executives. Moreover, about half the increase in Gillette revenues during the time that Kilts was running the show were attributable to currency fluctuations. A cheaper dollar increased revenue overseas. If the dollar had moved in the opposite direction, there might not have been any increase in revenue. Indeed, for the first two years after Kilts joined Gillette, the stock price declined. It was not until the dollar turned down that the stock price improved.

Do CEOs who receive incentives have too strong of a motivation to sell their companies? Should their incentives be based on factors that they do not control or even affect (such as the strength of the dollar)? Is it unseemly for them to be paid so much when many employees will lose their jobs?

8. Craig Newmark founded craigslist, the most popular website in the country for classified ads. Rather than maximizing its profits, craigslist instead focused on developing a community among its users. It was a place to find an apartment, a pet, a job, a couch, a date, a babysitter, and, it turned out, a prostitute. Most of the ads on

craigslist were free, but blatant ads for sex were not. Much of the company's revenue was from these illegal services. Many of the prostitutes available on craigslist were not independent entrepreneurs; they were women and girls bought and sold against their will. To fight sex trafficking, craigslist required credit cards and phone numbers, and it reported any suspicious ads. Law enforcement officials pressured craigslist to close the sex section of its website. But some people argued that blocking these ads was a violation of free speech and would just drive this business more underground where law enforcement officials were less likely to be able to find it. Others said that banning these ads made the business model of selling children for sex less profitable. Does it seem that trafficking women and children was in keeping with the founder's Life Principles? What were his options? Could he have had any real impact on this thriving industry? What traps did he face?

9.   You are a president of a small, highly rated, liberal college in California. Many of the dining hall workers are Latino. Some of these workers are trying to organize a union, which would dramatically increase the college's costs at a time of budget pressure. One of your vice presidents suggests hiring a law firm to review the college's employment records to make sure all employees have the proper documentation showing that they are in the United States legally. It seems likely that some of the rabble rousers will turn out to be illegal and could be deported, thereby solving your union problem. What would you do?

10.   Many socially responsible funds are now available to investors who want to make ethical choices. For example, the Appleseed Fund avoids tobacco products, alcoholic beverages, gambling, weapons systems, or pornography, while the TIAA-CREF Social Choice Equity Premier Fund invests in companies that are "strong stewards of the environment," devoted to serving local communities and committed to high labor standards. Are socially responsible funds attractive to you? Does it matter if they are less profitable than other alternatives? How much less profitable? Do you now, or will you in the future, use them in saving for your own retirement?

11.   David has just spoken with a member of his sales team who has not met her sales goals for some months. She has also missed 30 days of work in the past six months. It turns out that she is in the process of getting a divorce, and her teenage children are reacting very badly. Some of the missed days have been for court; others because the children have refused to go to school. If David's team does not meet its sales goals, no one will get a bonus and his job may be at risk. What should he do?

CHAPTER 3

INTERNATIONAL LAW

During periods of war and insecurity, international laws are hotly contested. The following is an excerpt of an unsigned letter published in the *London Times* during an uncertain time— the American Civil War. It puts great pressure on the authors of this book—and on any student of international law.

© Creative Travel Projects/Shutterstock.com

> The text-writer on international law assumes a noble task, but he at the same time accepts a grave responsibility. His speculations, if unsound, must too often be refuted by the sword. They deal out the lots of peace and of war; they affect the destinies of nations and determine the misery or the happiness of whole generations of mankind.
>
> Nevertheless, on most questions of international law, the student has to make for himself his own textbook; to extract from scattered documents the records of historical precedents; to deduce from judicial decisions the principles of established law.
>
> It is from these difficulties that ill-informed and shallow reasoners have question[ed] the existence of international law. Yet this idea is about as reasonable as if a man who had neither the instruments nor the knowledge requisite to take an observation, should dispute the possibility of a science of astronomy.[1]

They affect the misery or the happiness of whole generations of mankind.

---

[1] Excerpts from the Preamble to *Letters by Historicus on Some Questions of International Law*, v–viii (London: Macmillan & Co. 1863).

Many people throughout the ages have asked this basic question: What is international law? In Chapter 1, we learned that the law is a system of rules that predictably regulates our behavior. It secures our rights and balances government power. For any legal system to thrive, it must have clear rules, shared values, and a system of enforcement that its subjects acknowledge and respect.

International law is different. It has no single source of law or enforcement mechanism. It is a hodgepodge of different actors, legal systems, and cultures. For this reason, as the mysterious letter writer noted, some people have wondered whether international law exists at all. But it *does* exist, and is important to study, because our globalized world is more and more dependent on it each day. And luckily, you do not have to make your own textbook.

3-1 INTERNATIONAL LAW: PUBLIC VERSUS PRIVATE

International law covers a wide array of topics relevant to, well, everything and everyone in the world. **It consists of rules and principles that apply to the conduct of states,**[2] **international organizations, businesses, and individuals across borders.** It is important to distinguish between two branches of international law: public and private.

Public international law is the law governing relations among governments and international organizations. It includes the law of war (yes, we have to fight fair), the acquisition of territory, and the settlement of disputes among nations. Public international law also has rules governing the globe's shared resources and common elements: the sea, outer space, trade, and communications. Finally, it addresses people: Public international law sets out the basic rules of human rights and laws defining the treatment of refugees, prisoners of war, and international criminals.

Private international law applies to private parties (such as businesses and individuals) in international commercial and legal transactions. It deals with two fundamental issues: Which law applies to a private agreement? How will people from one country settle their private disputes with parties on foreign soil?

Private international law is highly influenced by treaties and other sources of public international law. Because this is a business law text, we will focus on private international law and those areas of public international law that affect business.

Public international law
Rules and norms governing relationships among states and international organizations

Private international law
International rules and standards applying to cross-border commerce

3-2 ACTORS IN INTERNATIONAL LAW

Unlike domestic law—in which the main actors are individuals, businesses, and the government—international law must balance the interests and roles of many different people, organizations, and states.

3-2a **The United Nations**

After World Wars I and II, people and governments around the world were intent on preventing future conflict. They sought the creation of a supranational organization that could ensure international peace and security, encourage economic and social cooperation, and protect human rights. So, in 1945, 50 nations signed the Charter of the United Nations, binding themselves to its terms and obligations. Today, 193 countries are members of the United Nations.

---

[2]Throughout the chapter, the authors use "state" to have the same meaning as "country" and "nation."

The UN Charter sets out the organization's governance:

- The **Secretariat**, headed by the Secretary General, administers the day-to-day operations of the UN.

- The **General Assembly** is the UN's lawmaking body. It is composed of all of its member nations, which propose and vote on resolutions.

- The **Security Council** is charged with maintaining international peace. It has 15 member nations. Ten are elected by the General Assembly; five are permanent members: China, France, Russia, the United Kingdom, and the United States. The five permanent members were the primary victors in World War II. They have the right to veto any Security Council resolution.

Much of the UN's work is done through its Specialized Agencies and related organizations, including influential agencies like the International Labor Organization (ILO), the World Health Organization (WHO), and the UN Educational, Scientific, and Cultural Organization (UNESCO).

The following agencies, which operate under the UN's umbrella, have great impact on world business:

- The **World Bank's** mandate is to end poverty by encouraging development. Among other activities, it loans money to the poorest countries on favorable terms.

- The **International Monetary Fund** (IMF) aims to foster worldwide economic growth and financial stability.

- The **World Intellectual Property Organization** (WIPO) was established to promote the protection of intellectual property: patents, copyrights, trademarks, and industrial design. The organization also has a system for domain name dispute resolution, to which private parties often resort when challenging the illicit international use of domain names.

International Court of Justice

The judicial branch of the United Nations

- The **UN Commission on International Trade Law** (UNCITRAL) aims to harmonize international business law by proposing model legislation on such topics as international payments and e-commerce. This agency was responsible for putting forth the UN Convention for the International Sale of Goods (CISG) and the Convention on the Recognition and Enforcement of Foreign Arbitral Awards (New York Convention), both significant business-related treaties discussed later in this chapter.

3-2b The International Court of Justice

In 1946, the UN opened the doors of the **International Court of Justice** (ICJ). Also known as the World Court, the ICJ settles international legal disputes and gives advisory opinions to the UN and its agencies. It is comprised of 15 elected judges from 15 countries representing the world's principal legal systems.

In its seven-decade history, the court has heard fewer than 200 cases. The ICJ has not been an important force in resolving international business disputes for several reasons:

Rob Keeris/AFP/Getty Images

The World Court sits in the Hague, Netherlands.

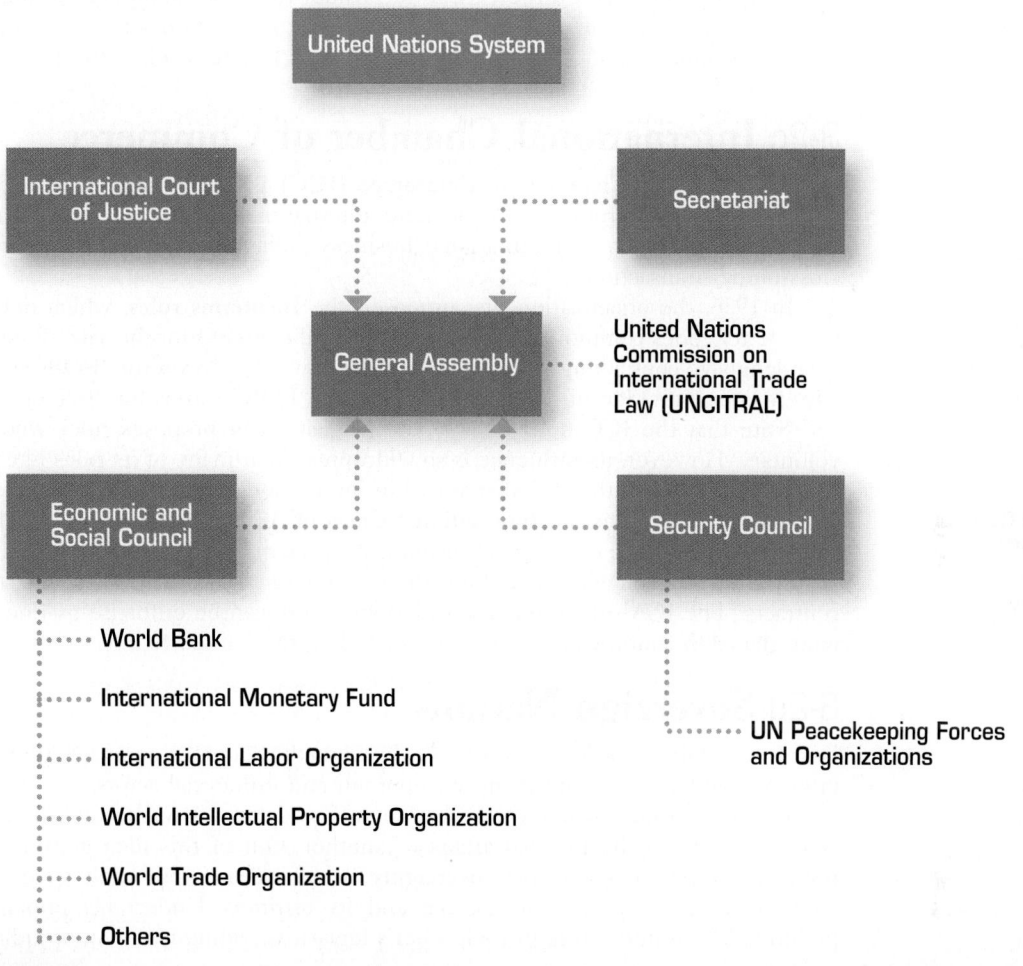

EXHIBIT 3.1 The Basic Structure of the UN

- **Only states can be a party to litigation before the ICJ.** To have their day in court, individuals and businesses must persuade their country to initiate a case on their behalf. Most states are reluctant to bring business associated with cases on behalf of their citizens because of the political and financial costs may result from suing another country.

- **The ICJ only has jurisdiction over states that have agreed to be bound by its decisions.** The United States had accepted the ICJ's authority—until it lost a case. When the ICJ determined that the U.S. violated international law by secretly supporting Nicaraguan rebels, the U.S. simply withdrew from ICJ jurisdiction.[3] Today the U.S. agrees to ICJ jurisdiction on a case-by-case basis.

- **The court has no enforcement power.** Mexico accused the United States of breaching its treaty obligations by failing to notify its consulate when the U.S. arrested Mexican citizens on U.S. soil. Fifty-four Mexican nationals on death row in the U.S. had been

---

[3]Case Concerning Military and Paramilitary Activities in and Against Nicaragua *(Nicaragua v. United States of America)*, 1986 I.C.J. 14 (June 27).

denied their right to consult with the local Mexican consulate. The ICJ agreed with Mexico and ordered the U.S. to reconsider the death sentences in these cases.[4] But the U.S. Supreme Court held that in this situation domestic law trumped treaty obligations—and that the United States was free to disobey the ICJ.[5]

3-2c International Chamber of Commerce

The International Chamber of Commerce (ICC) is the world's largest global business organization. Its purpose is to facilitate international business. To that end, the ICC advocates on matters of international business policy and develops uniform rules to aid cross-border transactions.

Incoterms

A series of three-letter codes used in international contracts for the sale of goods

In 1936, the organization first proposed the **Incoterms rules**, which define a series of three-letter codes commonly used in international contracts for the sale of goods. No matter what language contracting parties speak, it is known that Incoterm "FOB" means the buyer pays for transportation of the purchased goods. ("FOB" stands for "free on board.")

Note that the ICC does not make law. Instead, it proposes rules whose adoption is voluntary. However, its influence is so widespread that many of its rules like the Incoterms are now accepted as the global standard in international business.

International Court of Arbitration (ICA)

A forum for international dispute resolution, run by the ICC

The ICC also runs the **International Court of Arbitration (ICA)**, which hears over half of the world's private commercial disputes. Contracting parties seeking a politically neutral forum for arbitration agree to submit their claims to the ICA, usually when they sign their contracts. The ICA's decision, also called an award, can be enforced by domestic courts in more than 145 countries around world, including the United States.

3-2d Sovereign Nations

Last but certainly not least, we cannot discount the role that countries themselves play in international law. They are its most important and influential actors.

In ancient times, when kings were seen as gods, it was well-established that no "god" could interfere in the internal affairs of another. Out of this idea grew the fundamental principle of international law: **sovereignty**, which means that each government has the absolute authority to rule its people and its territory. Under this principle, states are prohibited from interfering in each other's legislative, administrative, or judicial activities.

Sovereign Immunity

Sovereign immunity holds that the courts of one nation lack the jurisdiction (power) to hear suits against foreign governments. Most nations respect this principle. In the United States, the **Foreign Sovereign Immunities Act** (FSIA) provides that American courts generally cannot hear suits against foreign governments. This is a difficult hurdle to overcome, but there are three possible exceptions.

Foreign Sovereign Immunities Act

A U.S. statute that provides that American courts generally cannot entertain suits against foreign governments.

Waiver.   A lawsuit is permitted against a foreign country that waives its immunity, that is, voluntarily gives up this protection. Suppose the Czech government wishes to buy fighter planes from an American manufacturer. If the manufacturer insists on a waiver in the sales contract, the Czech Republic might be willing to grant one to get the weapons it desires. If the planes land safely but the checks bounce, the manufacturer has the right to sue.

Commercial Activity.   A plaintiff in the United States can sue a foreign country engaged in commercial, but not political, activity. If a business can engage in the activity, it is considered to be commercial. If, however, the foreign government is doing something

---

[4]Avena and Other Mexican Nationals (Mexico v. United States of America), 2004 I.C.J. 12 (Mar. 31).
[5]Medellin v. Texas, 552 U.S. 491 (2008).

that only a government has the power to do (e.g., printing money, making laws), it is a state activity and the country is immune from litigation.

Suppose the government of Iceland hires an American consulting firm to help its fishermen replenish depleted fishing grounds. Because fishing is a for-profit activity, the contract is commercial, and if Iceland refuses to pay, the company may sue in American courts.

Violation of International Law. **A plaintiff in this country may sue a foreign government that has confiscated property in violation of international law**, provided that the property either ends up in the United States or is involved in commercial activity that affects someone in the United States. Suppose a foreign government, acting in violation of international law, confiscates a visiting American ship, and begins to use it for shipping goods for profit. Later, the ship carries some American produce. The taking was illegal, and it now affects American commerce. The original owner may sue.

EXAM Strategy

Question: Fabric World, a U.S. company, owns and operates a textile factory in the country of Parador. After a political revolution, the new government seizes the factory and refuses to pay for it. It also sells bonds to investors in the United States to raise money to fund government operations and then defaults on their payment. Both Fabric World and the bond investors sue Parador in New York, where it has some large bank accounts. Parador denies liability in both lawsuits, claiming "sovereign immunity." Will this argument succeed in either case?

Strategy: Examine the nature of the government's activities: Did it waive sovereign immunity? Are its activities commercial?

Result: Parador has never waived sovereign immunity. In the *Fabric World* case, the government enacted new laws that expropriated private property. This is an act of state—not something a business or private citizen could ever do—and so Parador retains immunity. In the case of the bonds, the investors win because the country is engaged in a commercial activity.

3-3 THE WORLD'S LEGAL SYSTEMS

In Chapter 1, we began to explore the origins of our Anglo-American legal tradition. But it is important for every international businessperson to recognize that the great majority—roughly 84 percent—of the world is governed by legal systems that take a very different approach from our own.

3-3a Common Law

As discussed in Chapter 1, we inherited our legal system from England. The United States shares this legacy with most former British colonies, including Australia, Canada, and India.
    The hallmarks of common law are:

- The use of an adversarial process of dispute resolution presided over by an impartial judge. After the Norman conquest of England, William the Conqueror introduced trial by combat to settle disputes: The winner of the battle was right.

This practice formed the basis of the common law's assumption that the role of lawyers is to battle on behalf of the client by making the most persuasive arguments.

- The doctrine of ***stare decisis***, which requires judges to base their decisions on prior cases.[6]

- The use of a jury to determine questions of fact.

Stare decisis

The principle that legal conclusions must be reached after an analysis of past judgments

3-3b Civil Law

More than 70 percent of the world's population is subject to civil law, including most European countries, Russia, Central and South America, China, large swaths of Asia, and parts of Africa.[7] Exhibit 3-2 shows the legal systems used throughout the world. You may be asking: How did Mexico end up with the same legal methodology as Germany?

| CIVIL LAW | COMMON LAW | ISLAMIC LAW | CUSTOMARY LAW | MIXED SYSTEM |

EXHIBIT 3.2   Legal Systems throughout the World

Source: http://www.juriglobe.ca/eng/; http://outsourceportfolio.com/mexicos-potential-nearshore-services-outsourcing-leader/; and http://chartsbin.com/view/aq2

---

[6]*Stare decisis* is Latin for "to let the decision stand."

[7]Note that "civil law," as referred to in this chapter, is a legal system based on codes (*i.e.,* civil law versus common law systems). In common law systems such as ours, the same term is also used to describe contract, tort, and other areas of private law (*i.e.,* civil law versus criminal law).

The civil code tradition grew out of Roman Emperor Justinian's *Corpus Juris Civilis* in the sixth century. To solidify his power, Justinian set out to organize and record Roman laws. A widespread empire demanded uniform laws—and their uniform application—so **the main principle of civil law is that the law is found primarily in the statute books, or codes.**

Centuries later, European legal scholars unearthed Justinian's code and spread its methodology to continental Europe—Germany, Italy, France, Spain, and Portugal. Under the Emperor Napoleon, the French adopted the code system, but infused it with its own ideals and values, resulting in the Napoleonic Code. Other countries similarly developed their own versions of the code before exporting them to most of the world through conquest (including Louisiana, where the Napoleonic Code is still the basis for that state's laws).

Statute-based systems also have a clear appeal to countries whose political systems demand strong central authority rather than a focus on individual rights. China and Russia both have code-based systems overlaid with socialist law.

The main characteristics of the civil code tradition are:

- The use of an inquisitorial process of dispute resolution, in which the judge acts as interrogator and investigator. Judges rely more on written submissions than on lawyers' oral arguments.

- Courts base their judgments on the code, and statutes, and on the writings of law professors.

- Civil code systems do not use juries.

3-3c **Islamic Law**

More than one-fifth of the world's population lives under legal systems influenced by the religion of Islam. Islamic law, also known as *shari'a*, is a legal system most commonly found in Africa, Asia, and the Middle East.[8] There is much variation in the interpretation and practice of both Islam and Islamic law.

***Shari'a* is based on the Muslim holy book, the Koran, and the teachings and actions of the Prophet Muhammed.** Early Islamic scholars gave definitive guidelines and interpretations on *shari'a* using a reasoning process known as *ijtihad*,[9] which incorporates religious and legal reasoning. While some Islamic groups prohibit any new interpretations of *shari'a*, other Muslims regularly use *ijtihad* to adapt *shari'a* to modern-day problems.

Although most of what Westerners hear about *shari'a* law involves harsh criminal punishments, Islamic law covers business relationships, personal and family matters, and daily life. Many of its doctrines are tailored to promote honesty and transparency in business relationships. **Some of its important principles are:**

- The payment and collection of interest is prohibited because it causes unfair enrichment.[10] Financial investments in companies or industries that do not align with Muslim values are also prohibited.

- The concept of **gharar**[11] prohibits any contract gain that is not clearly outlined at the time of contract, especially when it involves risk and deception.

Gharar

The Islamic prohibition on risk and deception

---

[8]*Shari'a* means "path" in Arabic.
[9]*Ijtihad* is Arabic for "independent reasoning" or "effort."
[10]McKesson Corp. v. Islamic Republic of Iran, 672 F.3d 1066 (2012).
[11]*Gharar* is Arabic for "deceptive uncertainty" and is the basis for other prohibitions in Islamic finance, such as risky deals whose outcome is unknown.

The following case may come as a surprise because most people do not realize that U.S. courts can apply foreign law to resolve disputes. The parties filed suit in a U.S. court, even though the dispute was governed by *shari'a* law.

SAUDI BASIC INDUSTRIES CORPORATION V. MOBIL YANBU PETROCHEMICAL COMPANY, INC. AND EXXON CHEMICAL ARABIA, INC.

A.2d 1
Delaware Supreme Court, 2005

Facts: Saudi Basic Industries Corporation (SABIC) was a Saudi Arabian corporation owned by the Saudi government. In the 1970s, it entered into joint ventures with Mobil and Exxon, under contracts governed by Saudi law. The agreements forbade the participants from charging a "mark-up" on any products purchased for the joint venture, but SABIC violated this provision for two decades.

ExxonMobil and SABIC sued each other in federal court in Delaware for breach of contract and tort.[12] Because the Delaware court was required to apply Saudi law, the judge brought in notable experts in *shari'a* law for instruction.

The jury found SABIC liable for Saudi tort of usurpation (*ghasb*) and awarded ExxonMobil $416 million. SABIC appealed to the Delaware Supreme Court for a new trial, arguing that that the trial court's application of Saudi law was flawed.

Issue: *Did the U.S. court err in its application of shari'a law?*

Excerpts from Justice Jacobs's Decision: In Saudi Arabia, Islamic law (*shari'a*), which is a fundamentally religious law based on both the Q'uran and the model behavior of the Prophet Muhammed, is the law of the land. Although early Islamic law scholars eventually coalesced into various guilds or schools, only four of those guilds have survived in modern times: the *Hanbali*, the *Hanafi*, the *Shafi'i* and the *Maliki*. In Saudi Arabia, the judges are instructed to rule exclusively in accordance with the teachings of the *Hanbali* guild.

The Saudi law system differs in critically important respects from the system of legal thought employed by the common law countries, including the United States. Perhaps most significant is that Islamic law does not embrace the common-law system of binding precedent and *stare decisis*. Indeed, in Saudi Arabia, judicial decisions are not in themselves a source of law, and with minor exceptions, court decisions in Saudi Arabia are not published or even open to public inspection. The trial judge was keenly mindful of this distinctive characteristic of Saudi law.

Instead of relying upon statutes or decisional precedent to discern the law applicable to a particular case, judges in Saudi Arabia must "first and last navigate within the boundaries" of the Hanbali school's authoritative works, which are the scholarly treatises. Using these writings as guides, Saudi judges identify a spectrum of possibilities on any given question, rather than a single 'correct' answer.

Thus, in this highly different legal environment, the predominate factor in determining the Saudi law on a given issue is the study and analysis, or *ijtihad*, that a judge brings to bear in each particular case. To state it in different terms, the critical inquiry is whether the proper analytical procedures are followed in reaching the results.

The judge made exceptional efforts to ensure that she was fully informed of the Hanbali teachings. Before trial, the parties presented [her] with seven reports from four Saudi law experts. [She also] retained an independent expert, who conduct[ed] additional research in Saudi Arabia. After reviewing a total of nine reports and over one thousand pages of testimony, the judge then held a day-long pretrial

[12]Exxon and Mobil entered into separate contracts with SABIC, but by the time of this lawsuit had merged to form one company named ExxonMobil.

hearing, to [hear] live testimony from [the experts]. Only after this extensive process did the trial court undertake to determine the disputed elements of *ghasb*.

It is remarkable that SABIC, having [purposefully] selected this forum instead of a Saudi Court, knowing the United States legal system is dramatically different than the Saudi legal system, comes forward after a verdict against it to claim that no American judge is qualified to interpret and apply Saudi law. This is particularly incredible in light of SABIC's vehement argument that this case should be tried by a U.S. judge.

For the foregoing reasons, the judgment of the Superior Court awarding damages to ExxonMobil is affirmed.

As we see from this case, the world—and the law—is increasingly internationalized. Greater interaction among societies has led to convergence among some legal traditions. In particular, common law and civil law systems have borrowed significant concepts from each other:

- Common law countries exhibit a trend toward codification. In the United States, many laws, notably in intellectual property, bankruptcy, banking, securities, and tax, are statute-based. The Uniform Commercial Code (UCC) now applies to contracts for the sale of goods in the U.S., an area of law previously governed only by common law.

- Civil law countries have begun to take precedents into account. One study found that German courts followed precedent in all but 12 out of 4,000 decisions.[13] Spain has enacted laws making the rulings of higher courts binding on lower courts.[14]

3-4 Sources of Law

This section outlines the three major sources of international law: treaties, custom, and general principles of law.

3-4a **Treaties**

Recall from Chapter 1 that the president makes treaties with foreign nations. According to the Vienna Convention on the Law of Treaties, a **treaty** is an international agreement governed by international law. Since treaties have their own treaty, they also have their own vocabulary:

- A **bilateral treaty** is between two countries—similar to a contract between states. The United States and the Bahamas have a bilateral **extradition** treaty, outlining the process that each country must follow when returning a fugitive to another country's legal system. A **multilateral treaty** involves three or more countries.

- A **convention** is a treaty on a specific issue that affects all the participants, like the UN Convention on Contracts for the International Sale of Goods or the Vienna Convention on the Law of Treaties.

Treaty

An agreement between two or more states that is governed by international law

---

[13]T. Lundmark, '*Stare decisis in der Rechtssprechung des Bundesverfassungsgerichts.*' Rechtstheorie (1999).
[14]Ley Orgánica 6/1985, de 1 de julio, del Poder Judicial §5.1.

- A **protocol** is an amendment to a treaty. In 1891, a group of countries signed the Madrid Agreement, a treaty creating a registration system for trademarks. Almost 100 years later, the Madrid Protocol updated and strengthened the original treaty to create a uniform process for registering trademarks worldwide.

- A treaty is said to be **adopted** when those who have drafted it agree that it is in final form.

- A treaty is **ratified** when a nation indicates its intent to be bound by it. **To take effect in the United States, treaties must be approved by at least two-thirds of the Senate.**

- A treaty **enters into force** when it becomes legally binding on its signatories. This date may be specified in the treaty or it may be the date on which the treaty receives a certain number of ratifications.

This section examines treaties that are critical to international business.

GATT

GATT is the General Agreement on Tariffs and Trade. Any discussion of international trade issues must begin with free trade, which has been a contentious issue since David Ricardo first advocated it in the early nineteenth century. He, and economists since him, have argued that citizens of the world will benefit overall if each country produces whatever goods it can make most efficiently and then trades them for goods that other countries make more efficiently. Thus, a developing country with unskilled labor should produce clothing and then trade it to the United States for commercial aircraft and semiconductors (two major categories of U.S. exports).

World Trade Organization (WTO)

An international organization whose mandate is to lower trade barriers

Most favored nation

WTO/GATT requires that favors offered to one country must be given to all member nations.

National treatment

The principle of nondiscrimination between foreigners and locals

Such a plan makes great economic sense, unless you happen to work in the clothing business in the United States. So countries are often tempted to impose tariffs and quotas on imports to protect local industries and workers. Thus, when David Ricardo was writing, England had recently passed the Corn Laws, which restricted the importation of wheat. These laws caused higher food prices in England, but helped maintain the value of farmland and the wages of farmworkers.

GATT is a massive international treaty that has been negotiated on and off since the 1940s as nations have sought to eliminate trade barriers and bolster commerce. To strengthen this treaty, GATT signatories created the **World Trade Organization (WTO)** in 1995. Its mandate is to stimulate international commerce and resolve trade disputes.

GATT and the WTO are founded on the following principles:

- **Free Trade.** The major focus of this treaty is to reduce trade barriers.

- **Most Favored Nation.** Although it sounds like a requirement to give someone special treatment, "**most favored nation**" means that countries must treat every other country equally. If Brazil grants Australia a special discount on customs duties for certain products, that treatment must be extended to all other WTO members.

- **National Treatment.** After imported products have entered the country, they must be treated the same as locally produced goods. In other words, countries may not discriminate against foreign goods by imposing additional sales taxes, requirements, or standards that do

Dinah Rogers/The Times-Picayune/Landov

The WTO found that shochu was like vodka and had to be taxed similarly.

not apply to domestic goods. Japan taxed imported vodka seven times higher than its own domestic version, *shochu*, even though both were distilled similarly. Because this tax violated national treatment provisions, the WTO required that Japan revise its laws.

The WTO tries to promote free trade by limiting countries' efforts to unfairly protect their domestic industries. **Among the techniques that countries use (and the WTO tries to limit) are:**

- **customs duties:** taxes imposed on goods when they enter a country

- **excise taxes:** taxes levied on a particular activity, such as the purchase of wine or cigarettes

- **non-tariff barriers:** such as quotas on the amount of a particular good that can be imported.

The WTO is empowered to settle trade disputes between its member states. It may order compliance and impose penalties in the form of trade sanctions. Suppose that the United States believes that Brazil is unfairly restricting trade. Via the WTO, the United States can request a consultation with Brazil's trade representative. In the majority of cases, these discussions lead to a satisfactory settlement. If the consultation does not resolve the problem, the United States asks the WTO's Dispute Settlement Body (DSB) to form a panel, which consists of three nations uninvolved in the dispute. After the panel hears testimony and arguments from both countries, it prepares a report. The DSB generally approves this report, unless either nation appeals. If there is an appeal, the WTO Appellate Body hears the dispute and generally makes the final decision, subject to approval by the entire WTO. No single nation has the power to block final decisions.

If a country refuses to comply with the WTO's ruling, affected nations may retaliate by imposing punitive tariffs or other measures. The United States and four Central American countries filed a complaint with the WTO alleging that the European Union (EU) had placed unfair restrictions on the importation of bananas. The WTO agreed, and then granted the United States and Ecuador the right to impose sanctions on EU imports into their countries.

GATT has had a considerable impact. In 1947, the worldwide average tariff on industrial goods was about 40 percent. Now it is about 4 percent. Over the past six decades, the world's economy has grown explosively. Leading supporters of WTO/GATT suggest that lower tariffs have vastly increased world trade. The United States is one of the biggest beneficiaries because, for decades, this country has imposed lower duties than most other nations. A typical American family's annual income has increased due to the more vigorous domestic economy, and at the same time, many goods are less expensive because they enter with low duties.

But opponents claim that the United States now competes against nations with unlimited pools of exploited labor. These countries dominate labor-intensive industries such as textiles, clothing, and manufacturing, and are steadily taking jobs from millions of American workers. Because domestic job losses come in low-end employment, those put out of work are precisely those least able to find a new job.

Ethics Child labor is a wrenching issue. The practice exists to some degree in all countries and is common throughout the developing world. The International Labor Organization estimates that more than 144 million children under the age of 14 work—many of them in hazardous and otherwise deplorable conditions, in households, fields, mines, and factories.[15]

---

[15]Yacouba Diallo, Alex Etienne, and Farhad Mehran, *Global child labour trends 2008–2012*, International Programme on the Elimination of Child Labour, International Labour Office (2013).

Child labor raises compelling moral questions, but the solution is not always obvious. Historically, poor children have worked. Indeed, for many people and for many centuries, the point of having children was to create a supply of free labor to help support the family. In England in 1860, almost 40 percent of 14-year-old boys worked, and that was not just a few hours at Burger Box, but more likely 60 hours a week. That percentage is higher than in Africa or India today. Children in desperately poor families work because, for them, the choice is not work or school, it is work, starvation, or prostitution.

Congress passed a statute prohibiting the importation of goods created by forced or indentured child labor. Is this law an example of humane legislation or cultural imperialism dressed as a nontariff barrier? Should the voters of this country or the WTO decide the issue?

Regional Trade Agreements

Regional trade agreements (RTAs)

Treaties that reduce trade restrictions and promote common policies among member nations.

Regional trade agreements (RTAs) reduce trade restrictions and promote common trade policies among member nations, who are located near each other. Today, RTAs cover more than half of international trade.

North American Free Trade Agreement (NAFTA)

A treaty that reduced trade barriers among Canada, the United States, and Mexico

NAFTA.   The **North American Free Trade Agreement (NAFTA)** is an RTA that has had a large impact on the United States. Signed by the United States, Canada, and Mexico in 1993, its principal goal was to eliminate almost all trade barriers among the three nations. This treaty has been controversial, for all the usual reasons.

Trade between the three nations has increased enormously. Mexico now exports more goods to the United States than do Germany, Britain, and Korea combined. Opponents of the treaty argue that NAFTA costs the United States jobs and lowers the living standards of American workers by forcing them to compete with low-paid labor. Swingline Staplers closed a factory in Queens, New York, after 75 years of operation and moved to Mexico. Instead of the $11.58 per hour that its American employees earned, Swingline can now pay Mexican workers 50 cents an hour to do the same job.

Proponents contend that although some jobs are lost, many others are gained, especially in fields with a promising future, such as high technology. They claim that as new jobs invigorate the Mexican economy, consumers there will be able to afford certain categories of American goods for the first time, providing an enormous new market. Also, NAFTA provides American consumers with more, and cheaper, products.

GATS and TRIPs

General Agreement on Trade in Services (GATS)

A treaty on transnational services

Agreement on Trade Related Aspects of Intellectual Property (TRIPs)

A treaty on intellectual property

The **General Agreement on Trade in Services, or GATS**, extends the WTO/GATT principles to transnational services; the **Agreement on Trade Related Aspects of Intellectual Property (TRIPs)** covers intellectual property (IP).[16] The WTO administers both treaties.

Before TRIPs, many countries had dissimilar and confusing IP rules covering copyright, trademark, and patents: One country might grant a patent for 20 years, while another offered only 10. TRIPs has succeeded in harmonizing the international practice.

The following case is about a tiny country with big dreams of becoming a gambling giant. Without access to the U.S. market, it was just a pipe dream. But would the United States obey the WTO's ruling? Don't bet on it.

---

[16]Annex 1C to the WTO Agreement.

UNITED STATES—MEASURES AFFECTING THE CROSS-BORDER SUPPLY OF GAMBLING AND BETTING SERVICES

WT/DS285/ARB
WTO Arbitral Body, 2007

Facts: Antigua is a small Caribbean nation. When it began hosting gambling websites, its economy thrived, boosted by U.S. gamblers. But when the United States started criminally prosecuting Internet gambling, Antigua's profits plummeted. The United States had the right to take this step, but it had to do so consistently—treating foreign and domestic sites the same. The problem was that it allowed Internet betting on horseracing within its borders.

Antigua challenged U.S. gambling laws in the WTO, arguing that they discriminated against foreign betting services. Both the United States and Antigua were members of GATS, under which each agree to free trade (including nondiscrimination and national treatment) in online services.

A WTO panel ruled that the United States' inconsistent gambling laws violated GATS and ordered that it bring them into compliance. Two years passed and the U.S. government did not act.

Frustrated, Antigua requested permission from the WTO to suspend its obligations to the United States under TRIPs. This suspension would mean that Antigua could freely use, reproduce, and distribute any U.S.-copyrighted, trademarked, or patented works—a real blow to the U.S. entertainment, pharmaceutical, and technology industries. The United States objected and submitted the matter to a panel of WTO experts.

Issue: *When one WTO Member refuses to comply with a WTO ruling, can the injured Member retaliate by suspending its duties under another treaty?*

Excerpts from the WTO Arbitrator's Decision: Antigua considers it unconscionable for the United States to have done nothing to come into compliance in the time that it should have, and now requests to be authorized to suspend [its] obligations under the TRIPS Agreement.

Antigua, a developing country, is by far the smallest WTO Member to have made a request for the suspension of concessions and realizes the difficulty of providing effective countermeasures against the world's dominant economy.

When a complaining party wishes to seek suspension in another agreement than that in which a violation was found, it must prove that (1) it is not effective for it to suspend the same agreement and (2) that the circumstances are serious enough to suspend obligations under another agreement.

Antigua considers that suspension of obligations in [GATS] would most likely impair the already limited options available to Antiguan citizens while having virtually no impact on the United States at all. The trade disparity [between the countries] is so great that United States service providers would suffer little harm at all, if any, while Antiguan consumers would be forced to scramble for replacement services at uncertain cost. The volume of its imports from the United States in services is nowhere near sufficient to absorb the level of suspension of concessions that it is entitled to.

In order to demonstrate the seriousness of the circumstances, Antigua first presents some basic figures comparing the population, size, GDP, exports and imports of the United States and Antigua, which illustrate a considerable disparity in all of these areas.

Antigua also highlights that it has extremely limited natural resources and very limited arable land, such that it cannot produce sufficient agricultural products to satisfy domestic needs, let alone for export. Antigua further notes that its economy has become highly dependent on tourism and associated services. Third, Antigua highlights the need to diversify its economy, and that in order to do this it has tried to develop trade in services, including trade in remote gambling.

In our view, the various considerations highlighted by Antigua are such as to exacerbate the difficulties in finding a way to suspend obligations in an effective manner under the GATS.

Accordingly, we find that Antigua may seek to suspend obligations under the TRIPS Agreement.

This issue has been in dispute for over a decade. The WTO has now authorized Antigua to violate up to $21 million worth of U.S. copyrights, trademarks, and patents in retaliation for U.S. noncompliance. As of this writing, Antigua is creating an online platform to openly sell American movies, music, and medications at a discounted price—and keep the profit. Critics argue that the WTO has set a dangerous precedent. Stay tuned.

EXAM Strategy

Question: To limit the number of cars on city streets, Shanghai, China, set up a system under which drivers could only acquire automobile license plates through a monthly auction. But Shanghai ran two different auctions: One for foreign-made cars, in which the government limited the number of license plates to 30 a month and set a high minimum bid and another for Chinese cars, in which 3,000 license plates a month were available, with no minimum bid. The United States complained that Shanghai's system had a direct effect on its imports. Is China in violation of WTO principles?

Strategy: As a signatory to the WTO, China committed to treating imported cars the same as its own domestic products. Does China have the right to impose these restrictions? Is traffic regulation a valid excuse?

Result: National treatment means that a WTO country cannot give special treatment or benefits to its own goods. Even though Shanghai may not have intended its rules to disrupt international trade, it did, because the license auctions had a direct effect on the price of imported cars. Shanghai's rules violated WTO principles.

CISG

The **United Nations Convention on Contracts for the International Sale of Goods (CISG)** aims to make sales law more uniform and predictable—and to make international contracting easier. To that end, the treaty relaxes some of the formal rules found in contract law throughout the world, making it simpler for parties to form contracts and live by them. The United States and most of its principal trading partners (except the United Kingdom) have adopted this important treaty, which governs over two-thirds of the world's trade.

The most important provisions are:

- **The CISG applies to contracts for the sale of commercial goods**, but not to consumer goods bought for personal use.

- **The CISG applies automatically when contracts are formed between two parties located in different signatory countries.** Note that the treaty's application does not depend on nationality, rather on location. Starbucks is a U.S. company with coffee shops in 62 countries. If the Starbucks store in Colombia contracts with a seller in Brazil, the CISG automatically applies because both Brazil and Colombia are members of the CISG. But if a Starbucks in England buys goods from a French seller, the CISG does not apply because, although France is a signatory, the United Kingdom is not.

- **Contracting parties can opt out.** If the parties want to be governed by other law, their contract must state very clearly that they exclude the CISG and elect, for example, French, Israeli, or any other country's law.

- **International sales contracts do not need to be in writing.** Unlike many nations' contract laws, the CISG does not require a writing to prove the existence of a contract. Parties can prove the terms of contracts by any means, including witnesses and their course of dealing.

- **Contracting parties must be flexible and fair.** The CISG requires parties to negotiate in good faith and modify the contract in case of unforeseen circumstances.

- **A buyer can avoid payment under a contract only after giving the seller notice and an opportunity to remedy.** As we will see in Unit 4 on sales, U.S. contract law excuses buyers from paying if the seller's performance is not absolutely perfect. The CISG is much less strict on sellers.

- **Countries may use their own national laws to (1) replace some CISG provisions or (2) fill in the blanks on issues that the CISG does not cover at all.** For example, the CISG does not provide rules for determining whether a contract is fraudulent: This substantive rule is left to the discretion of each country.

In the following case, each country had different contract rules and divergent interpretations of the CISG. The result? A huge mess, in any language. Which law applies?

FORESTAL GUARANI S.A. v. DAROS INTERNATIONAL, INC.

613 F.3d 395
United States Court of Appeals for the Third Circuit, 2010

Facts: Forestal Guarani S.A., in Argentina, entered into an oral agreement to sell wooden finger joints to Daros International, Inc. in New Jersey.[17] Forestal sent Daros the products but Daros declined to pay the full amount.

When Forestal sued Daros in the U.S. for breach of contract, Daros denied owing anything because, under New Jersey sales law, the contract would have had to be in writing to be enforceable. Further, it claimed, Argentina had not accepted the CISG's elimination of the writing requirement when it ratified the CISG. Since the contract was not in writing, it was also possible that Argentine law applied.

The district court dismissed Forestal's claim because the parties' agreement was not in writing. Forestal appealed.

Issue: *Which law applied to this contract—the CISG, Argentine law, or New Jersey law?*

Excerpts from Judge Fisher's Decision: The CISG applies to contracts of sale of goods between parties whose places of business are in different States when the States are Contracting States. Because both the United States, where Daros is based, and Argentina,

where Forestal is based, are signatories to the CISG and the alleged contract at issue involves the sale of goods, the CISG governs Forestal's claim.

The CISG dispenses with certain formalities associated with proving the existence of a contract. Specifically, a contract of sale need not be evidenced by writing and it may be proved by any means, including witnesses. [But the] elimination of formal writing requirements does not apply in all instances in which the CISG governs. A Contracting State whose legislation requires contracts of sale to be evidenced by writing may at any time make a declaration that [that rule] does not apply where any party has his place of business in that State. The United States has not made [such a] declaration. Argentina, however, has opted out of [this CISG rule].

There is no dispute here that Forestal's contract with Daros was verbal at best, so we could feasibly apply both New Jersey and Argentine law. In the end, we think it unwise to engage in a largely speculative exercise about the viability of Forestal's claim under either jurisdiction's law. Because these issues deserve a full airing, we conclude that remand is a better course of action.

---

[17]A finger joint is a method of attaching two pieces of wood. Rectangular cut-outs are made in the end of each piece. Then the pieces are joined together so that the cut-outs on one piece fit the projections on the other. It is as if you bent your fingers at the knuckle and then slid your hands together.

3-4b **Custom and General Principles of Law**

For hundreds of years, until treaties became common, custom was the main way international law was created. A custom is a widely accepted way of doing something. Over time, patterns of states' behavior, action, and inaction crystallized into the compulsory rules of **customary international law**.

Today, courts recognize a custom as binding international law if:

Customary international law

International rules that have become binding through a pattern of consistent, longstanding behavior.

- It is widespread and widely accepted,

- It is longstanding, and

- Nations follow it out of a sense of obligation to each other.

Customary international law governed behavior on the battlefield and the treatment of prisoners of war until the creation of the Geneva Conventions, which codified these customary practices.

Jus cogens

When rule of customary international law becomes a fundamental legal principle across all nations, it cannot be changed by custom or practice.

In addition, there is the concept of *jus cogens*, which means a fundamental principle that must be followed.[18] It is different from customary international law because it cannot be altered by custom or practice. Slavery, genocide, piracy, and torture are examples of *jus cogens*. Although these practices still exist in the modern world, no civilized state would say they are acceptable.

Ethics   Is torture always wrong? That issue has been deeply and bitterly debated in the United States ever since the terrorist attacks of 9/11. On one side of this debate are those who believe that torture should be used if necessary to obtain information that might help prevent other acts of terrorism. They believe that the harsh treatment of suspected terrorists has been successful in keeping America safe. On the other side are those who say that torture is less effective at eliciting useful information than other interrogation methods. The United States' use of brutality, these critics claim, undermines our legal and moral standing worldwide, and gives other countries a license to torture our citizens.

Under what circumstances, if any, should torture be permitted? What would Kant and Mill say?

3-5 INTERACTION OF FOREIGN AND DOMESTIC LAWS

You might be wondering how the laws and rulings of sovereign nations interact with one another. Do the laws of one nation have force in another? Can one country's court judgments be enforced in another? Predictably, these questions are not easy. Read on to decipher some of these sticky situations, with which international businesses and multinationals must contend on a daily basis.

---

[18]*Jus cogens* means "compelling law" in Latin.

3-5a **Application of U.S. Law Abroad**

When developing their own laws, countries sometimes look to other nations for models. The U.S. Constitution has served as a model for constitutions around the world. European nations have borrowed U.S. legal concepts, especially in the areas of contract and product liability laws. Australian antitrust law is based on American statutes. But it is one thing for a country to voluntarily adopt a U.S. law; it is quite another for the United States to impose its own laws in other countries.

Extraterritoriality is the power of one nation to impose its laws in other countries.[19] Many U.S. statutes regulate conduct outside the country. The Foreign Corrupt Practices Act, discussed in Chapter 7 on crime, prohibits bribery abroad. Price-fixing conducted abroad is a violation of the Sherman Act if it has an impact on the United States. **But, as a general rule, U.S. statutes do not apply abroad, unless they explicitly state that they do.**

In the following case, victims of *jus cogens* violations in Nigeria sought remedies in American law. No one disputed that what happened to them was horrific—and illegal. But could a U.S. statute grant them relief?

Extraterritoriality

The power of one country's laws to reach activities outside of its borders

---

KIOBEL V. ROYAL DUTCH PETROLEUM CO.

133 S. Ct. 1659
United States Supreme Court, 2013

Facts: Throughout the early 1990s, Royal Dutch Petroleum, a Dutch company, and Shell, a British company, were engaged in oil exploration and production in Nigeria. When local residents protested the oil companies' practices, the firms allegedly paid the Nigerian Government to suppress the protests by beating, raping, killing, and arresting locals.

A group of Nigerian victims of these attacks sued the oil companies in U.S. federal court for violations of customary international law under the Alien Tort Statute (ATS), a statute passed by the first Congress in 1789. The ATS allows U.S. district courts to hear certain lawsuits brought by non-U.S. citizens for violations of international law occurring in the United States or on the high seas, outside the sovereignty of any country. According to the plaintiffs, the oil companies violated customary international law and *jus cogens* by helping the Nigerian Government commit many crimes against humanity.

The appeals court dismissed the case. The Supreme Court granted *certiorari* on the question of

whether the ATS permitted U.S. courts to hear a suit for violations of customary international law that occurred outside the U.S.

Issue: *Does U.S. law extend to violations of customary international law occurring entirely outside the United States?*

Excerpt from Chief Justice Roberts's Decision:[20] The question here is whether a claim under the ATS may reach conduct occurring in the territory of a foreign sovereign. The oil companies contend the [it does] not. They rely primarily on the presumption of extraterritoriality [whose premise is] that United States law governs domestically but does not rule the world. This presumption serves to protect against unintended clashes between our laws and those of other nations which could result in international discord.

We typically apply the presumption of extraterritoriality to discern whether an Act of Congress regulating conduct applies abroad. The ATS allows federal courts to recognize certain causes of action based on sufficiently

---

[19]Extraterritoriality can also refer to exemption from local laws. For example, ambassadors are generally exempt from the law of the nation in which they serve.

[20]For ease of reading, "respondents" has been replaced with "oil companies" and "petitioners" with "Kiobel."

[
United States law governs domestically but does not rule the world.
]

definite norms of international law. But we think the principles of interpretation constrain courts considering causes of action that may be brought under the ATS.

Since many attempts by federal courts to craft remedies for the violation of new norms of international law would raise risks of adverse foreign policy consequences, they should be undertaken, if at all, with great caution. These concerns are all the more pressing when the question is whether a cause of action reaches conduct within the territory of another sovereign.

There is no indication that the ATS was passed to make the United States a uniquely hospitable forum for the enforcement of international norms. As Justice Story put it, "No nation has ever yet pretended to be the *custos morum*[21] of the whole world … ." It is implausible to suppose that the First Congress wanted their fledgling Republic—struggling to receive international recognition—to be the first. Indeed, the parties offer no evidence that any nation, meek or mighty, presumed to do such a thing.

Moreover, accepting Kiobel's view would imply that other nations could hale our citizens into their courts for alleged violations of the law of nations occurring in the United States, or anywhere else in the world. The presumption against extraterritoriality guards against our courts triggering such serious foreign policy consequences.

We therefore conclude that the presumption against extraterritoriality applies to claims under the ATS. Kiobel's case seeking relief for violations of the law of nations occurring outside the United States is barred. If Congress were to determine otherwise, a statute more specific than the ATS would be required.

The judgment of the Court of Appeals is affirmed.

Many American companies do business through international subsidiaries—foreign companies that they control. The subsidiary may be incorporated in a nation that denies workers the protection they would receive in the United States. What should happen when an employee of a foreign subsidiary argues that his rights under an American statute have been violated? You make the call.

---

[21]In Latin, *custos morum* means "guardian of manners or morals."

You be the Judge

Facts: Boston Scientific (BSC) was an American company that manufactured medical equipment. The company had its headquarters in Massachusetts but did business around the world through foreign subsidiaries. One of the company's subsidiaries was Boston Scientific Argentina (BSA), and it was there that Ruben Carnero began working. His employment contract stated he would work at BSA's headquarters in Buenos Aires and be paid in pesos. Argentine law was to govern the contract. Four years later, Carnero took an assignment to work as country manager for a different BSC subsidiary,

CARNERO V. BOSTON SCIENTIFIC CORPORATION
433 F.3d 1
United States Court of Appeals for the First Circuit, 2006

Boston Scientific do Brasil (BSB). Carnero frequently traveled to Massachusetts to meet with company executives, but he did most of his work in South America.

About a year later, BSB fired Carnero, and BSA soon did the same. Carnero claimed that the companies terminated him in retaliation for his reporting to BSC executives that the Argentine and Brazilian subsidiaries inflated sales figures and engaged in other accounting fraud. Carnero filed suit in Massachusetts, alleging that his firing violated an American statute, the Sarbanes-Oxley Act (SOX).

Congress passed that law to protect investors from fraud, but included a "whistleblower" provision designed to guard employees who informed superiors or investigating officials of fraud within the company. The law allows injured employees reinstatement and back pay.

BSC argued that SOX did not apply overseas and the District Court agreed, dismissing the case. Carnero appealed.

You Be the Judge: *Does SOX protect a whistleblower employed overseas by a subsidiary of an American company?*

Argument for Carnero: Congress passed SOX because the American people were appalled by the massive fraud in major corporations, and the resulting harm to employees, investors, the community, and the economy. The whistleblower protection is designed to encourage honest employees to come forward and report wrongdoing —an act that no employee wants to do, and one which has historically led to termination. Mr. Carnero knew his report would be poorly received, but believed he had an ethical obligation to protect his company. For that effort, he was fired, and now Boston Scientific attempts to avoid liability using the technicality of corporate hierarchy.

Yes, Mr. Carnero was employed by BSB and BSA. But both of those companies are owned and operated by Boston Scientific. It is the larger company, with headquarters in the United States, which called the shots.

That is why executives in Massachusetts frequently asked Mr. Carnero to report to them—and why he brought them his unhappy news.

Argument for Boston Scientific: The fact that Mr. Carnero was employed by companies incorporated in Argentina and Brazil is more than a technicality. He is asking an American court to go into two foreign countries—sovereign nations—and investigate accounting and employment practices of companies incorporated and operating there. Their laws, not ours, should apply to their companies.

If the United States can impose its whistleblowing law in foreign countries, may those nations impose their rules here? Suppose that a country forbids women to do certain work. May companies in those nations direct American subsidiaries to reject all female job applicants? Neither the citizens nor courts of this country would tolerate such interference.

Mr. Carnero's request is also impractical. How would an American court determine why he was fired? Must the trial judge here subpoena Brazilian witnesses and demand documentary evidence from that country?

Finally, SOX does not state that it applies overseas. Congress was well aware that American corporations operate subsidiaries abroad, but made no mention of those companies when it passed this statute.

EXAM Strategy

Question: U.S. citizens Alberto Vilar and Gary Tanaka managed $9 billion in investments through their companies, some of which were located in Panama. The two were arrested in the United States for a massive securities fraud: They had lied to their clients about investments—and used some of the money entrusted to them to repair their homes and buy horses. Vilar and Tanaka claimed that U.S. securities laws did not apply to sales that occurred outside the country. These laws were silent as to their application abroad. Do Vilar and Tanaka have a valid argument?

Strategy: Review the *Kiobel* court's discussion of the presumption of extraterritoriality.

Result: The court agreed with the defendants: When laws do not explicitly state that they cover conduct abroad, judges cannot interpret them to do so.[22] (Unfortunately for the defendants, they still went to jail on other charges.)

---

[22]United States v. Vilar, 729 F.3d 62 (2d Cir. 2013).

3-5b **Foreign Laws and Rulings in the United States**

One of the major legal debates of our time involves the blurring line between sovereignty and international law. While Americans are proud to say that our Constitution has influenced the laws of other countries, the debate becomes considerably more heated when it involves the influence of foreign or international law on the United States.

What is the proper role of foreign and international law within our own borders? Questions abound. Supreme Court Justice Ruth Bader Ginsburg has cited foreign court rulings and *jus cogens* to argue against the constitutionality of the death penalty. Should the decisions of foreign courts and international law inform our interpretation of our own Constitution?

Should the U.S. be bound by the rulings of international tribunals like the WTO and the ICJ? This chapter posed three examples of cases in which the United States refused to comply: the cases of gambling in Antigua (WTO), rebels in Nicaragua (ICJ), and imprisoned citizens of Mexico (ICJ). On one hand, sovereignty demands that others do not meddle in domestic affairs, especially laws. On the other, the United States was a founding member of both the WTO and the ICJ. If it ignores their rulings, what is the use of these international bodies?

Application of Foreign Law in U.S. Courts

Recall the *SABIC* case, in which a U.S. court applied the law of Saudi Arabia. Clearly, U.S. judges are not experts in the laws of every country, yet federal courts commonly apply the laws of other countries to resolve disputes. Judges may consult experts, request briefs from the parties, listen to testimony, and conduct their own extensive research on the foreign law. While this process may seem inefficient, some foreign litigants are willing to incur the expense for the benefits of the American judicial system, which is internationally regarded as fair and relatively free from political influence.

Recognition and Enforcement of Foreign Judgments

Imagine that you obtain a court judgment for a million dollars against a foreign seller who sent you defective goods. Great news, right? Well, you may not want to celebrate too soon: If the seller has no assets in the country where you won in court, your award may be worthless.

Foreign recognition

Means that a foreign judgment has legal validity in another country

To address this common situation, most major trading nations have rules for recognizing and enforcing foreign judgments within their borders. **Recognition** means that a decision by a court outside a country is legally valid inside. **Enforcement** means that a judgment rendered outside a country can be collected inside, just as an internal judgment can be.

Foreign enforcement

Means that the court system of a country will assist in enforcing or collecting on the verdict awarded by a foreign court

In the United States, most states have adopted the **Uniform Foreign Money Judgments Recognition Act. This act provides that U.S. courts will recognize foreign judgments if:**

- The award was based on a full and fair trial by an impartial tribunal with proper jurisdiction;

- The defendant was given notice and an opportunity to appear;

- The judgment was not fraudulent or against public policy; and

- The foreign court was the proper forum to hear the case.

The Ecuadorian Supreme Court awarded $9.5 billion to the Ecuadorian victims of a massive, decades-long environmental contamination of an area known as Lago Agrio by oil company Texaco (now Chevron). Because Chevron did not have sufficient assets in Ecuador for the victims to collect, the plaintiffs sought to enforce the judgment in the

United States. In a 500-page decision, a federal court in New York refused to recognize the award. The court found that the Ecuadorian judges were paid off, the decision was ghost written, and the investigation was replete with corruption and fraud.[23] The court concluded:

> Justice is not served by inflicting injustice. The ends do not justify the means. There is no "Robin Hood" defense to illegal and wrongful conduct. And the defendants' "this-is-the-way-it-is-done-in-Ecuador" excuses—actually a remarkable insult to the people of Ecuador—do not help them. The[se] wrongful actions would be offensive to the laws of any nation that aspires to the rule of law, including Ecuador.[24]

Arbitration

Parties who prefer to avoid courts altogether generally opt for arbitration. **Arbitration** is a binding process in which the parties submit their dispute to a neutral private body for resolution. It is especially advantageous when the disputing parties are from different countries because it is generally faster, more private, less expensive, and less political than litigating in foreign courts. International arbitral bodies, such as the ICC, issue arbitral awards, but enforcement depends upon the laws of the individual countries where the parties operate.

The Convention on the Recognition and Enforcement of Foreign Arbitral Awards (also known as the **New York Convention**) is an international treaty with 149 signatories that provides common rules for recognizing arbitration agreements. But each country has its own specific requirements. **In the United States, an arbitral award will generally be enforced if:**

- It is enforceable under the local law of the country where the award was granted;

- The arbitral tribunal had proper jurisdiction;

- The defendant was given notice of the arbitration and an opportunity to be heard; and

- Enforcement of the award is not fraudulent or contrary to public policy.

Arbitration
A binding process of resolving legal disputes by submitting them to a neutral third party

New York Convention
Widely accepted treaty on the court enforcement of arbitral awards

3-6 ESSENTIAL CLAUSES IN INTERNATIONAL CONTRACTS

International business brings great reward, but also carries significant risks. Distance, language, politics, culture, and different legal systems all pose potential hurdles to successful transactions.

However, some of these risks can be controlled by carefully thinking about contract terms beforehand. In this chapter, we witnessed what happened to Forestal, an Argentine company that made an oral agreement with a New Jersey buyer. First it was not paid—perhaps due to a miscommunication or cultural difference. Then, it was dragged into a common law court system in a foreign country more than 5,000 miles away, only to spend thousands of American dollars on pricey U.S. lawyers to figure out *which law* applied to their deal. Unfortunately, these outcomes are not uncommon in international business.

To ensure that you do not end up in a similar predicament, be sure to consider the following when you negotiate international deals:

- **Choice of Law: Which Law Governs?** As we have seen, there are a variety of legal systems and each country has a different way of applying whatever legal system it uses. Therefore, when making an agreement, it is *essential* to negotiate which country's law will control. Each side will prefer the law they are most familiar with.

---

[23]This legal saga was the subject of a 2009 documentary, Crude—which was made by the allegedly corrupt plaintiffs' legal team.

[24]Chevron Corp. v. Donzinger, __ F. Supp. 2d __, 2014 WL 815553 (S.D.N.Y. 2014).

How to compromise? Perhaps by using a neutral law. But before reaching any agreement, be sure to seek the advice of an attorney who specializes in the law of that country. It is a good idea to have a trusted legal advisor in any foreign country where you do business.

- **Choice of Forum: Where Will the Case Be Heard?** The parties must decide not only what law governs, but also where disagreements will be resolved. This can be a significant part of a contract, because legal and court systems are dramatically different in terms of speed, cost, transparency, and trustworthiness.

- **Choice of Language and Currency.** The parties must select a language for the contract and a currency for payment. Language counts because legal terms seldom translate literally. Currency is vital because the exchange rate may alter between the signing and payment.

Chapter Conclusion

International law is increasingly relevant to our globalized business world. While it was once the domain of nations, today it affects individuals, businesses, and groups all over the world. As the world gets smaller, these issues will become more and more pressing.

EXAM REVIEW

1. **PUBLIC INTERNATIONAL LAW** The law governing relations among governments and international organizations.

2. **PRIVATE INTERNATIONAL LAW** The law governing private parties in international commercial and legal transactions.

3. **INTERNATIONAL COURT OF JUSTICE (ICJ)** The World Court settles international legal disputes among states.

4. **THE INTERNATIONAL CHAMBER OF COMMERCE (ICC)** The world's largest global business organization.

5. **SOVEREIGN IMMUNITY** Sovereign immunity holds that the courts of one nation lack the jurisdiction (power) to hear suits against foreign governments, unless the foreign nation has waived immunity, is engaging in commercial activity, or has violated international law.

6. **COMMON LAW** The legal system based on precedent and adversarial process that was inherited by most British colonies, including the United States and Australia.

7. **CIVIL LAW** The most widespread legal system in the world, whose main principle is that law is found primarily in statutes rather than in judicial decisions.

8. **ISLAMIC LAW** Based on the Koran and the action and teachings of Mohammad.

Question: No matter where you are in the world, the relationship between landlords and tenants can be a tense one. How would judges in common law, civil law, and Islamic law jurisdictions approach a landlord/tenant controversy?

Strategy: Review the process that judges use to examine and apply the laws in each of these legal systems. (See the "Result" at the end of this section.)

9. **GATT, GATS, and TRIPs** The goal of the General Agreement on Tariffs and Trade (GATT) is to lower trade barriers worldwide. The General Agreement on Trade in Services (GATS) and the Trade Related Aspects of Intellectual Property (TRIPs) extend GATT principles to services and intellectual property, respectively.

10. **WTO** GATT created the WTO, which resolves disputes between signatories to the treaty.

Question: When fishermen trawled for shrimp, they often caught sea turtles as well. The U.S. Environmental Protection Agency (EPA) sought to protect the endangered sea turtles by requiring that fisherman use costly technology called a Turtle Excluder Device (TED). The United States prohibited the importation of shrimp caught without TEDs. Several developing nations claimed that American laws on shrimp fishing were unfair and illegal. Who won and why? The case demonstrated a conflict between two important values. What were the values? In your view, which is more important?

Strategy: Apply the GATT principles to determine the outcome. (See the "Result" at the end of this section.)

11. **REGIONAL TRADE AGREEMENTS** Trade agreements promoting common policies among member states.

12. **CISG** The goal of CISG is to make sales law more uniform and predictable—and to make international contracting easier. A sales agreement between an American company and a foreign company may be governed by American law, by the law of the foreign country, or by the CISG.

Question: Paula, a U.S. citizen, purchased a lamp for her home from Interieures, a lighting website based in Paris. The company's website stated that the governing law would be the law of France and only French courts could hear claims. When the company breached its contract, Paula sought to sue in the United States under the CISG. Does the CISG apply to Paula's claim?

Strategy: Review the scope and applicability of the CISG and the section on "Essential Clauses in International Contracts." (See the "Result" at the end of this section.)

13. **CUSTOMARY INTERNATIONAL LAW** Courts recognize custom as binding international law if it is (1) widespread and widely accepted, (2) longstanding, and (3) nations obey it out of a sense of obligation to each other.

14. *JUS COGENS* A fundamental principle of law that must be followed. It cannot be altered by custom or practice.

15. **EXTRATERRITORIALITY** The power of one nation to impose its laws in other countries.

16. **UNIFORM FOREIGN MONEY JUDGMENTS RECOGNITION ACT** A U.S. act requiring states to recognize foreign judgments under certain conditions.

17. **NEW YORK CONVENTION** An international treaty that provides rules for the recognition and enforcement of foreign arbitral awards.

---

8. Result: The common law judge would hear the arguments of lawyers, who formulate their argument based on prior courts' rulings. The civil law judge would consult the applicable code that deals with landlord and tenant disputes. The Islamic law judge would engage in a process of ijtihad, which incorporates legal knowledge with religious reasoning based on the Koran and teachings and actions of Mohammad.

10. Result: Small nations sued, claiming that American regulations made it difficult or impossible for them to fish, devastating their economic growth. The United States argued that vital environmental concerns mandated such rules. The WTO found in favor of the small nations, ruling that before the United States imposed its environmental standards on other countries, it must engage in multinational negotiations, seeking an acceptable compromise. Environmentalists argued that the decision was short-sighted, and contributed to the destruction of an endangered species. Supporters of the decision responded that long-term environmental concerns sound patronizing and hollow to people with empty stomachs.

12. Result: Paula is out of luck. First, the CISG only applies to commercial sales contracts, not personal ones. Even if it applied, Interieures has conspicuously opted out of it. As the section on choice of law clauses discusses, these clauses are widely acceptable internationally. The only way U.S. law would have applied is if the two parties had agreed to such a provision.

MULTIPLE-CHOICE QUESTIONS

1. For which of the following activities can a foreign sovereign be sued?
   (a) Operating a factory dangerously
   (b) Issuing a law that discriminates against a certain group
   (c) Suspending the civil rights of its people
   (d) None of the above

2. Outdoor Technologies (an Australian company) obtained a judgment for $500,000 against Silver Star (a Chinese company) in a court in Australia. Silver Star owned property in Iowa, so Outdoor filed suit in Iowa to collect the judgment. Which of the following statements is true?

(a) Outdoor cannot collect a judgment in the United States that was issued by an Australian court.

(b) Outdoor cannot collect in the United States because Silver is not an American company.

(c) Outdoor can collect in the United States if the Australian court was fair and proper.

(d) Outdoor can collect in the United States, because both the United States and Australia have common law systems.

3. The president negotiates a defense agreement with a foreign government. To take effect, the agreement must be ratified by which of the following?

(a) Two-thirds of the House of Representatives

(b) Two-thirds of the Senate

(c) The Supreme Court

(d) A and B

(e) A, B, and C

4. Lynn is an author living in Nevada. She contracted with a company in China, which promised to print her custom children's books. After receiving Lynn's payment, the company disappeared without performing. Lynn wants to sue for fraud, but the contract does not say anything about which country's law will be used to resolve disputes. Both China and the United States are signatories of the CISG. Will the CISG apply in this case?

(a) Yes, because both countries are signatories.

(b) Yes, because the parties did not opt out of the CISG.

(c) No, because the contract does not involve goods.

(d) No, because the CISG does not establish rules for fraud.

5. Austria, Indonesia, and Colombia are all members of the WTO. If Austria imposes a tariff on imports of coffee beans from Colombia, but not from Indonesia, is it in violation of WTO principles?

(a) Yes, the WTO prohibits tariffs.

(b) Yes, the WTO prohibits excise taxes.

(c) Yes, Austria is violating the WTO's most favored nation rules.

(d) No, the WTO's most favored nation rules permit Austria to do this.

CASE QUESTIONS

1. A Saudi Arabian government-run hospital hired American Scott Nelson to be an engineer. The parties signed the employment agreement in the United States. On the job, Nelson reported that the hospital had significant safety defects. For this, he was arrested, jailed, and tortured for 39 days. Upon his release to the United States, Nelson sued the Saudi government for personal injury. Can Nelson sue Saudi Arabia?

2. The Instituto de Auxilios y Viviendas is a government agency of the Dominican Republic. Dr. Marion Fernandez, the general administrator of the Instituto and Secretary of the Republic, sought a loan for the Instituto. She requested that Charles Meadows, an American citizen, secure the Instituto a bank loan of $12 million. If he obtained a loan on favorable terms, he would receive a fee of $240,000. Meadows did secure a loan, which the Instituto accepted. He then sought his fee, but the Instituto and the Dominican government refused to pay. He sued the government in United States federal court. The Dominican government claimed immunity. Comment.

3. Asante, located in California, purchased electronic parts from PMC, whose offices were in Canada. When Asante sued PMC for breach of contract, it alleged that California sales law should apply. PMC argued that the CISG automatically applied because both Canada and the United States have ratified the treaty. Who is right?

4. During the Spanish-American War in 1898, the United States blockaded Cuba. It seized two commercial fishing vessels sailing under a Spanish flag off the Cuban coast. The crew knew nothing about the war and had no arms on board. U.S. officials auctioned off the captured vessels, but their owners protested, claiming that since ancient times countries at war had respected each other's commercial ships. There was no law or treaty on this matter. Do the ship owners have a valid claim?

5. Many European nations fear the effects of genetically modified foods, so they choose to restrict their importation. The EU banned the entry of these foods and subjected them to strict labeling requirements. Does this policy contravene the principles of WTO/GATT?

DISCUSSION QUESTIONS

1. After reading this chapter, do you believe that international law exists? Has your concept of law and legal rules changed?

2. After the 9/11 terrorist attacks, the U.S. government imprisoned suspected terrorists in Guantanamo Bay, Cuba. Officials argued that these detainees did not enjoy constitutional rights because they were not on U.S. soil, even though they were held by Americans. Are the freedoms guaranteed by the U.S. Constitution reserved for U.S. citizens on U.S. soil or do they apply more broadly?

3. The United Kingdom has not signed the CISG. Until recently, major world traders like Japan and Brazil had refused to sign. Imagine that you are a legislator from one of these countries. What might your objections be to ratifying a treaty on sales law?

4. Generally speaking, should the United States pass laws that seek to control behavior outside its borders? Or, when in Rome, should our companies and subsidiaries be allowed to do as the Romans do?

5. What responsibility, if any, does the United States have to obey international law? Is it any different from other countries' responsibility to uphold international law? Why or why not?

CHAPTER 5

CONSTITUTIONAL LAW

TO MAJOR JOHN CARTWRIGHT.
MONTICELLO, June 5, 1824.

DEAR AND VENERABLE SIR,

I am much indebted for your kind letter…

Our Revolution presented us an album on which we were free to write what we pleased. We had no occasion to search into musty records, to hunt up royal parchments, or to investigate the laws and institutions of a semi-barbarous ancestry. We appealed to those of nature, and found them engraved on our hearts.

We had never been permitted to exercise self-government. When forced to assume it, we were novices in its science. Its principles and forms had entered little into our former education. We established, however, some, although not all, its important principles.

The constitutions of most of our States assert that all power is inherent in the people; that they may exercise it by themselves, or they may act by representatives, freely and equally chosen; that it is their right and duty to be at all times armed; that they are entitled to freedom of person, freedom of religion, freedom of property, and freedom of the press.

In the structure of our legislatures, we think experience has proved the benefit of subjecting questions to two separate bodies of deliberants. The wit of man cannot devise a more solid basis for a free, durable and well-administered republic.

[O]ur State and federal governments are coordinate departments of one simple and integral whole. To the State governments are reserved all legislation and administration, in affairs which concern their own citizens only, and to the federal government is given whatever concerns foreigners, or the citizens of other States.

You will perceive that we have not so far [made] our constitutions unchangeable. [W]e consider them not otherwise changeable than by the authority of the people.

Can one generation bind another, and all others, in succession forever? I think not. A generation may bind itself as long as its majority continues in life; when that has disappeared,

> **The wit of man cannot devise a more solid basis for a free, durable and well-administered republic.**

another majority is in place, holds all the rights and powers their predecessors once held, and may change their laws and institutions to suit themselves. Nothing is unchangeable but the inherent and unalienable rights of man.

Your age of eighty-four and mine of eighty-one years, insure us a speedy meeting. In the meantime, I pray you to accept assurances of my high veneration and esteem for your person and character.

Yours truly,

Thomas Jefferson

5-1 GOVERNMENT POWER

5-1a One in a Million

The Constitution of the United States is the greatest legal document ever written. No other written constitution has lasted so long, governed so many, or withstood such challenge. This amazing work was drafted in 1787, when two weeks were needed to make the horseback ride from Boston to Philadelphia, a pair of young cities in a weak and disorganized nation. Yet today, when that trip requires less than two hours by jet, the same Constitution successfully governs the most powerful country on Earth. This longevity is a tribute to the wisdom and idealism of the Founding Fathers. The Constitution is not perfect but, overall, it has worked astonishingly well and has become the model for many constitutions around the world.

The Constitution is short and relatively easy to read. Because the language is general, it is open to interpretation. Its brevity is potent. And so is its reach: The Constitution sits above everything else in our legal system. No law can conflict with it. As Thomas Jefferson recounts in the introduction to this chapter, the Founding Fathers, or **Framers**, wanted it to last for centuries, and they understood that would happen only if the document was not "unchangeable." Indeed, the Constitution has been amended 27 times. Also, the interpretation of its provisions has changed over the years. As a result, the Constitution has stayed relevant in the face of changing social mores, times, and technology. The Constitution's versatility is striking.

In this chapter, the first part provides an overview of the Constitution, discussing how it came to be and how it is organized. The second part describes the power given to the three branches of government. The third part explains the individual rights the Constitution guarantees to citizens.

5-2 OVERVIEW

Thirteen American colonies declared independence from Great Britain in 1776, and gained it in 1783. The new status was exhilarating. Ours was the first nation in modern history founded on the idea that the people could govern themselves, democratically. The idea was daring, brilliant, and fraught with difficulties. The states were governing themselves under the Articles of Confederation, but these articles gave the central government no real power. The government could not tax any state or its citizens and had no way to raise money. The national government also lacked the power to regulate commerce between the states or between foreign nations and any state. This was disastrous. States began to impose taxes on goods entering from other states. The young "nation" was a collection of poor relations, threatening to squabble themselves to death.

In 1787, the states sent a group of 55 delegates to Philadelphia. Rather than amend the old articles, the Framers set out to draft a new document and to create a government from scratch. In Jefferson's words, it was "an album on which we were free to write what we pleased." It was hard going. What structure should the government have? How much power? Representatives like Alexander Hamilton, a *federalist*, urged a strong central government. The new government must be able to tax and spend, regulate commerce, control the borders, and do all things that national governments routinely do. But Patrick Henry and other *antifederalists* feared a powerful central government. They had fought a bitter war precisely to get rid of autocratic rulers; they had seen the evil that a distant government could inflict. The antifederalists insisted that the states retain maximum authority, keeping political control closer to home.

The debate continues to this day, and periodically it plays a key role in elections. The "tea party" movement, for example, is a modern group of antifederalists.

Another critical question was how much power the *people* should have. Many of the delegates had little love for the common people and feared that extending this idea of democracy too far would lead to mob rule. Antifederalists again disagreed. The British had been thrown out, they insisted, to guarantee individual liberty and a chance to participate in the government. Power corrupted. It must be dispersed among the people to avoid its abuse.

How to settle these basic differences? By compromise, of course. **The Constitution is a series of compromises about power.** We will see many provisions granting power to one branch of the government while at the same time restraining the authority given.

5-2a Separation of Powers

The Framers did not want to place too much power in any single place. One method of limiting power was to create a national government divided into three branches, each independent and equal. Each branch would act as a check on the power of the other two. Article I of the Constitution created a Congress, which was to have legislative, or lawmaking, power. Article II created the office of president, defining the scope of executive, or enforcement, power. Article III established judicial, or interpretive, power by creating the Supreme Court and permitting additional federal courts.

Consider how the three separate powers balance one another: Congress was given the power to pass statutes, a major grant of power. But the president was permitted to veto, or block, proposed statutes, a nearly equal grant. Congress, in turn, had the right to override the veto, ensuring that the president would not become a dictator. The president was allowed to appoint federal judges and members of his cabinet, but only with a consenting vote from the Senate.

5-2b Individual Rights

The original Constitution was silent about the rights of citizens. This alarmed many who feared that the new federal government would have unlimited power over their lives. So in 1791, the first 10 amendments, known as the **Bill of Rights**, were added to the Constitution, guaranteeing many liberties directly to individual citizens.

In the next two sections, we look in more detail at the two sides of the great series of compromises: power granted and rights protected.

5-3 POWER GRANTED

5-3a Congressional Power

To recap two key ideas from Chapter 1:

1. Voters in all 50 states elect representatives who go to Washington, D.C., to serve in Congress.

2. The Congress is comprised of the House of Representatives and the Senate. The House has 435 voting members, and states with large populations send more representatives. The Senate has 100 members—two from each state.

Congress wields tremendous power. Its members create statutes that influence our jobs, money, health care, military, communications, and virtually everything else. But can Congress create *any* kind of law it wishes? No.

Article I, section 8 is a critically important part of the Constitution. It lists the 18 types of statutes that Congress is allowed to pass, such as imposing taxes, declaring war, and coining money. Thus, only the national government may create currency. The state of Texas cannot print $20 bills with George W. Bush's profile.

States like Texas *are* supposed to create all other kinds of laws for themselves because the Tenth Amendment says, "All powers not delegated to the United States by the Constitution … are reserved to the States."

The **Commerce Clause** is the specific item in Article I, section 8, most important to your future as a businessperson. It calls upon Congress "to regulate commerce… among the several States," and its impact is described in the next section.

Commerce Clause

The part of Article I, Section 8, that gives Congress the power to regulate commerce with foreign nations and among states

Interstate Commerce

With the Commerce Clause, the Framers sought to accomplish several things in response to the commercial chaos that existed under the Articles of Confederation. They wanted the federal government to speak with one voice when regulating commercial relations with foreign governments. The Framers also wanted to give Congress the power to bring coordination and fairness to trade among the states, and to stop the states from imposing the taxes and regulations that were wrecking the nation's domestic trade.

Virtually all of the numerous statutes that affect businesses are passed under the Commerce Clause. But what does it mean to regulate interstate commerce? Are all business transactions "interstate commerce," or are there exceptions? In the end, the courts must interpret what the Constitution means.

Substantial Effect Rule

An important test of the Commerce Clause came in the Depression years of the 1930s, in *Wickard v. Filburn*.[1] The price of wheat and other grains had fluctuated wildly, severely harming farmers and the national food market. Congress sought to stabilize prices by limiting the bushels per acre that a farmer could grow. Filburn grew more wheat than federal law allowed and was fined. In defense, he claimed that Congress had no right to regulate him because none of his wheat went into *interstate* commerce. He sold some locally and used the rest on his own farm as food for livestock and as seed. The Commerce Clause, Filburn claimed, gave Congress no authority to limit what he could do.

The Supreme Court disagreed and held that **Congress may regulate any activity that has a substantial economic effect on interstate commerce.** Filburn's wheat *affected* interstate commerce because the more he grew for use on his own farm, the less he would need to buy in the open market of interstate commerce. In the end, "interstate commerce" does not require that things travel from one state to another.

In *United States v. Lopez*,[2] however, the Supreme Court ruled that Congress *had* exceeded its power under the Commerce Clause. Congress had passed a criminal statute called the "Gun-Free School Zones Act," which forbade any individual from possessing a firearm in a school zone. The goal of the statute was obvious: to keep schools safe. Lopez was convicted of violating the act and appealed his conviction all the way to the high Court, claiming that Congress had no power to pass such a law. The government argued that the Commerce Clause gave it the power to pass the law, but the Supreme Court was unpersuaded:

> The possession of a gun in a local school zone is in no sense an economic activity that might, through repetition elsewhere, substantially affect any sort of interstate commerce. [Lopez] was a local student at a local school; there is no indication that he had recently moved in interstate

---

[1]317 U.S. 111 (1942).
[2]514 U.S. 549 (1995).

commerce, and there is no requirement that his possession of the firearm have any concrete tie to interstate commerce. To uphold the Government's contentions here, we would have to pile inference upon inference in a manner that would bid fair to convert congressional authority under the Commerce Clause to a general police power of the sort retained by the States. [The statute was unconstitutional and void.]

In the following case, the Supreme Court was faced with a decision that would profoundly affect the health care and pocketbook of every American: Does the Commerce Clause allow Congress to *compel* people to enter into commerce?

NATIONAL FEDERATION OF INDEPENDENT BUSINESS v. SEBELIUS

576 U.S. ___, 132 S. Ct. 2566
United States Supreme Court, 2012

Facts: In 2010, Congress enacted the Patient Protection and Affordable Care Act (the Act), which aimed to increase the number of Americans covered by health insurance and decrease the cost of health care. The Act required most Americans either to maintain health insurance coverage, or pay a "penalty" to the IRS. This provision was commonly referred to as the "individual mandate." The logic was that, if everyone—even healthy young people—had health insurance, health care costs would go down for all.

On the day president Obama signed the Act into law, 13 states challenged it, alleging that neither the Constitution's Commerce provision nor its Taxing Clause gave Congress the authority to enact the individual mandate. Both the federal district court and the appeals court agreed. The Supreme Court granted *certiorari*.

Issue: *Did Congress have the power to make every American purchase health insurance?*

Excerpts from Chief Justice Roberts's Decision: In our federal system, the National Government possesses only limited powers; the States and the people retain the remainder. In this case we must determine whether the Constitution grants Congress power to enact the individual mandate under the Commerce Clause or as an exercise of its power to tax.

The Constitution authorizes Congress to regulate interstate commerce and activities that substantially affect interstate commerce. [The Government argues] Congress may order individuals to buy health insurance because the failure to do so affects interstate commerce.

[But] the individual mandate does not regulate existing commercial activity. It instead compels individuals to become active in commerce by purchasing a product, on the ground that their failure to do so affects interstate commerce.

Every day individuals do not do an infinite number of things. Allowing Congress to justify federal regulation by pointing to the effect of inaction on commerce would bring countless decisions within the scope of federal regulation, and empower Congress to make those decisions.

[This] logic would justify a mandatory purchase to solve almost any problem. Many Americans do not eat a balanced diet. The failure of that group to have a healthy diet increases health care costs to a greater extent than the failure of the uninsured to purchase insurance. Under the Government's theory, Congress could address the diet problem by ordering everyone to buy vegetables.

The Commerce Clause is not a general license to regulate an individual from cradle to grave, simply because he will predictably engage in particular transactions. Any police power to regulate individuals as such, as opposed to their activities, remains vested in the States.

The individual mandate forces individuals into commerce precisely because they elected to refrain from commercial activity. Such a law cannot be sustained under a clause authorizing Congress to "regulate Commerce."

Congress also has the power to "lay and collect Taxes." Even if Congress lacks the power to direct individuals to buy insurance, the only effect of the individual mandate is to raise taxes on those who do not do so, and thus the law may be upheld as a tax.

Under the mandate, if an individual does not maintain health insurance, the only consequence is that he must pay the IRS. The mandate is not a legal command to buy insurance. Rather, it makes going without insurance just another thing the Government taxes, like buying gasoline or earning income. And if the mandate is in effect just a tax hike on certain taxpayers who do not have health insurance, it [is] within Congress's constitutional power to tax.

The [Act's penalty] looks like a tax in many respects, regardless of labels. It is paid into the Treasury by taxpayers when they file their tax returns. The IRS must assess and collect it in the same manner as taxes. This process yields the essential feature of any tax: It produces at least some revenue for the Government.

The Federal Government does not have the power to order people to buy health insurance. The Federal Government does have the power to impose a tax on those without health insurance. [The individual mandate] is therefore constitutional, because it can reasonably be read as a tax. Because the Constitution permits such a tax, it is not our role to forbid it, or to pass upon its wisdom or fairness.

The judgment of the Eleventh Circuit is *affirmed* in part and *reversed* in part.

State Legislative Power

The "dormant" or "negative" aspect of the Commerce Clause governs state efforts to regulate interstate commerce. **The dormant aspect holds that a state statute discriminating against interstate commerce is almost always unconstitutional.** Here is an example. Michigan and New York permitted in-state wineries to sell directly to consumers. They both denied this privilege to out-of-state producers, who were forced to sell to wholesalers, who offered the wine to retailers, who sold to consumers. This created an impossible barrier for many small vineyards, which did not produce enough wine to attract wholesalers. Even if they did, the multiple resales drove their prices prohibitively high.

Local residents and out-of-state wineries sued, claiming that the state regulations violated the dormant Commerce Clause. The Supreme Court ruled that these statutes obviously discriminated against out-of-state vineyards; the schemes were illegal unless Michigan and New York could demonstrate an important goal that could not be met any other way. The states' alleged motive was to prevent minors from purchasing wine over the Internet. However, Michigan and New York offered no evidence that such purchases were really a problem. The Court said that minors seldom drink wine and, when they do, they seek instant gratification, not a package in the mail. States that allowed direct shipment to consumers reported no increase in purchases by minors. This discrimination against interstate commerce, like most, was unconstitutional.[3]

Supremacy Clause

What happens when both the federal and state governments pass regulations that are permissible, but conflicting? For example, Congress passed the federal Occupational Safety and Health Act (OSHA) establishing many job safety standards, including those for training workers who handle hazardous waste. Congress had the power to do so under the Commerce Clause. Later, Illinois passed its own hazardous waste statutes, seeking to protect both the general public and workers. The state statute did not violate the Commerce Clause because it imposed no restriction on interstate commerce.

Each statute specified worker training and employer licensing. But the requirements differed. Which statute did Illinois corporations have to obey? Article VI of the Constitution contains the answer. **The Supremacy Clause** states that the Constitution, and federal statutes and treaties, shall be the supreme law of the land.

The Supremacy Clause

Makes the Constitution, and federal statutes and treaties, the supreme law of the land

- If there is a conflict between federal and state statutes, the federal law **preempts** the field, meaning it controls the issue. The state law is void.

---

[3]Granholm v. Heald, 544 U.S. 460 (2005).

- Even in cases where there is no conflict, if Congress demonstrates that it intends to exercise exclusive control over an issue, federal law preempts.

Thus state law controls only when there is no conflicting federal law *and* Congress has not intended to dominate the issue. In the Illinois case, the Supreme Court concluded that Congress intended to regulate the issue exclusively. Federal law therefore preempted the field, and local employers were obligated to obey only the federal regulations.

EXAM Strategy

Question: Dairy farming was more expensive in Massachusetts than in other states. To help its farmers, Massachusetts taxed all milk sales, regardless of where the milk was produced. The revenues went into a fund that was then distributed to in-state dairy farmers. Discuss.

Strategy: By giving a subsidy to local farmers, the state is treating them differently than out-of-state dairies. This raises Commerce Clause issues. The dormant aspect applies. What does it state? Apply that standard to theses facts.

Result: The dormant aspect holds that a state statute that discriminates against interstate commerce is almost always invalid. Massachusetts was subsidizing its farmers at the expense of those from other states. The tax violates the Commerce Clause and is void.

5-3b Executive Power

Article II of the Constitution defines executive power. The president's most basic job function is to enforce the nation's laws. Three of his key powers concern appointment, legislation, and foreign policy.

Appointment?

Administrative agencies play a powerful role in business regulation, and the president nominates the heads of most of them. These choices dramatically influence what issues the agencies choose to pursue and how aggressively they do it. For example, a president who seeks to expand the scope of regulations on air quality may appoint a forceful environmentalist to run the Environmental Protection Agency (EPA), whereas a president who dislikes federal regulations will choose a more passive agency head.[4]

Legislation

The president and his advisers propose bills to Congress. During the past 50 years, a vast number of newly proposed bills have come from the executive branch. Some argue that *too many* proposals come from the president and that Congress has become overly passive. When a president proposes controversial legislation on a major issue, such as Social Security

---

[4]For a discussion of administrative agency power, see Chapter 4, on administrative law.

reform, the bill can dominate the news—and Congress—for months or even years. The president, of course, also has the power to veto bills.[5]

Foreign Policy

The president conducts the nation's foreign affairs, coordinating international efforts, negotiating treaties, and so forth. The president is also the commander in chief of the armed forces, meaning that he heads the military. But Article II does not give him the right to declare war—only the Senate may do that. A continuing tension between the president and Congress has resulted from the president's use of troops overseas *without* a formal declaration of war.

5-3c Judicial Power

Article III of the Constitution creates the Supreme Court and permits Congress to establish lower courts within the federal court system.[6] Federal courts have two key functions: adjudication and judicial review.

Chief Justice John Marshall

North Wind Picture Archives/Alamy

Adjudicating Cases

The federal court system hears criminal and civil cases. Generally, prosecutions of federal crimes begin in United States District Court. That same court has limited jurisdiction to hear civil lawsuits, a subject discussed in Chapter 3, on dispute resolution.

Judicial Review

One of the greatest "constitutional" powers appears nowhere in the Constitution. In 1803, the Supreme Court decided *Marbury v. Madison*.[7] Congress had passed a relatively minor statute that gave certain powers to the Supreme Court, and Marbury wanted the Court to use those powers. The Court refused. In an opinion written by Chief Justice John Marshall, the Court held that the statute violated the Constitution because Article III of the Constitution did not grant the Court those powers. The details of the case were insignificant, but the ruling was profound: Because the statute violated the Constitution, said the Court, it was void. **Judicial review refers to the power of federal courts to declare a statute or governmental action unconstitutional and void.**

This formidable grab of power has produced two centuries of controversy. The Court was declaring that it alone had the right to evaluate acts of the other two branches of government—the legislative and the executive—and to decide which were valid and which void. The Constitution nowhere grants this power. Undaunted, Marshall declared that "[I]t is emphatically the province and duty of the

---

[5]For a discussion of the president's veto power and Congress's power to override a veto, see Chapter 4, on statutory law.

[6]For a discussion of the federal court system, see Chapter 3, on dispute resolution.

[7]5 U.S. 137(1803).

judicial department to say what the law is." In later cases, the Supreme Court expanded on the idea, holding that it could also nullify state statutes, rulings by state courts, and actions by federal and state officials. In this chapter, we have already encountered an example of judicial review in the *Lopez* case, where the justices declared that Congress lacked the power to pass local gun regulations.

Is judicial review good for the nation? Those who oppose it argue that federal court judges are all appointed, not elected, and that we should not permit judges to nullify a statute passed by elected officials because that diminishes the people's role in their government. Those who favor judicial review insist that there must be one cohesive interpretation of the Constitution and the judicial branch is the logical one to provide it. The following example of judicial review shows how immediate and emotional the issue can be. This is a criminal prosecution for a brutal crime. Cases like this force us to examine two questions about judicial review. What is the proper punishment for such a horrible crime? Just as important, *who should make that decision*—appointed judges, or elected legislators?

KENNEDY V. LOUISIANA

554 U.S. 407
United States Supreme Court, 2008

Facts: Patrick Kennedy raped his eight-year-old stepdaughter. Her injuries were the most severe that the forensic expert had ever seen. Kennedy was convicted of aggravated rape because the victim was under 12 years of age.

The jury voted to sentence Kennedy to death, which was permitted by the Louisiana statute. The state supreme court *affirmed* the death sentence, and Kennedy appealed to the United States Supreme Court. He argued that the Louisiana statute was unconstitutional. The Eighth Amendment prohibits cruel and unusual punishment, which includes penalties that are out of proportion to the crime. Kennedy claimed that capital punishment was out of proportion to rape and violated the Eighth Amendment.

Issues: *Did the Louisiana statute violate the Constitution by permitting the death penalty in a case of child rape? Is it proper for the Supreme Court to decide this issue?*

Excerpts from Justice Kennedy's Decision: The constitutional prohibition against excessive or cruel and unusual punishments mandates that the State's power to punish be exercised within the limits of civilized standards. Evolving standards of decency that mark the progress of a maturing society counsel us to be most hesitant before interpreting the Eighth Amendment to allow the extension of the death penalty, a hesitation that has special force where no life was taken in the commission of the crime.

Consistent with evolving standards of decency and the teachings of our precedents we conclude that, in determining whether the death penalty is excessive, there is a distinction between intentional first-degree murder on the one hand and nonhomicide crimes against individual persons, even including child rape, on the other. The latter crimes may be devastating in their harm, as here, but in terms of moral depravity and of the injury to the person and to the public, they cannot be compared to murder in their severity and irrevocability.

Louisiana reintroduced the death penalty for rape of a child in 1995. Five States have since followed Louisiana's lead: Georgia, Montana, Oklahoma, South Carolina, and Texas. By contrast, 44 states have not made child rape a capital offense. As for federal law, Congress in the Federal Death Penalty Act of 1994 expanded the number of federal crimes for which the death penalty is a permissible sentence, including certain nonhomicide offenses; but it did not do the same for child rape or abuse. [The court concludes that there is a national consensus against imposing the death penalty for rape, and strikes down the Louisiana statute.]

Justice Alito, dissenting: If anything can be inferred from state legislative developments, the message is very different from the one that the Court perceives. In just the past few years, five States have enacted targeted capital child-rape laws. Such a development would not be out of step with changes in our society's thinking. During that time, reported instances of child abuse have increased dramatically; and there are many indications of growing alarm about the sexual abuse of children.

Judicial Activism/Judicial Restraint.   The power of judicial review is potentially dictatorial. The Supreme Court nullifies statutes passed by Congress (*Marbury v. Madison*, *United States v. Lopez)* and executive actions. May it strike down any law it dislikes? In theory, no—the Court should nullify only laws that violate the Constitution. But in practice, yes—the Constitution means whatever the majority of the current justices says it means, because it is the Court that tells us which laws are violative.

> **Judicial activism**
>
> A court's willingness to decide issues on constitutional grounds
>
> **Judicial restraint**
>
> A court's attitude that it should leave lawmaking to legislators

Judicial activism refers to a court's willingness, or even eagerness, to become involved in major issues and to decide cases on constitutional grounds. Activists are sometimes willing to "stretch" laws beyond their most obvious meaning. **Judicial restraint** is the opposite, an attitude that courts should leave lawmaking to legislators and nullify a law only when it unquestionably violates the Constitution. Some justices believe that the Founding Fathers never intended the judicial branch to take a prominent role in sculpting the nation's laws and its social vision. In certain high-profile political cases, the Court has reminded us of its role. Notice the last sentence in the earlier *Sebelius* case: "Because the Constitution permits [the law], it is not our role to forbid it, or to pass upon its wisdom or fairness."

From the 1950s through the 1970s, the Supreme Court took an activist role, deciding many major social issues on constitutional grounds. The landmark 1954 decision in *Brown v. Board of Education* ordered an end to racial segregation in public schools, not only changing the nation's educational systems, but also forever altering its expectations about race.[8] The Court also struck down many state laws that denied minorities the right to vote. Beginning with *Miranda v. Arizona*, the Court began a sweeping reappraisal of the police power of the state and the rights of criminal suspects during searches, interrogations, trials, and appeals.[9] And in *Roe v. Wade*, the Supreme Court established certain rights to abortion, most of which remain after nearly 40 years of continuous litigation.[10]

Beginning in the late 1970s, and lasting to the present, the Court has pulled back from its social activism. Exhibit 5.1 illustrates the balance among Congress, the president, and the Court.

5-4 PROTECTED RIGHTS

The amendments to the Constitution protect the people of this nation from the power of state and federal government. The First Amendment guarantees rights of free speech, free press, and religion; the Fourth Amendment protects against illegal searches; the Fifth Amendment ensures due process; the Sixth Amendment demands fair treatment for defendants in criminal prosecutions; and the Fourteenth Amendment guarantees equal protection of the law. We consider the First, Fifth, and Fourteenth Amendments in this chapter and the Fourth, Fifth, and Sixth Amendments in Chapter 7, on crime.

The "people" who are protected include citizens and, for most purposes, corporations. Corporations are considered persons and receive most of the same protections. The great majority of these rights also extend to citizens of other countries who are in the United States.

Constitutional rights generally protect only against governmental acts. The Constitution generally does not protect us from the conduct of private parties, such as corporations or other citizens.

---

[8]347 U.S. 483 (1954).
[9]384 U.S. 436 (1966).
[10]410 U.S. 113 (1973).

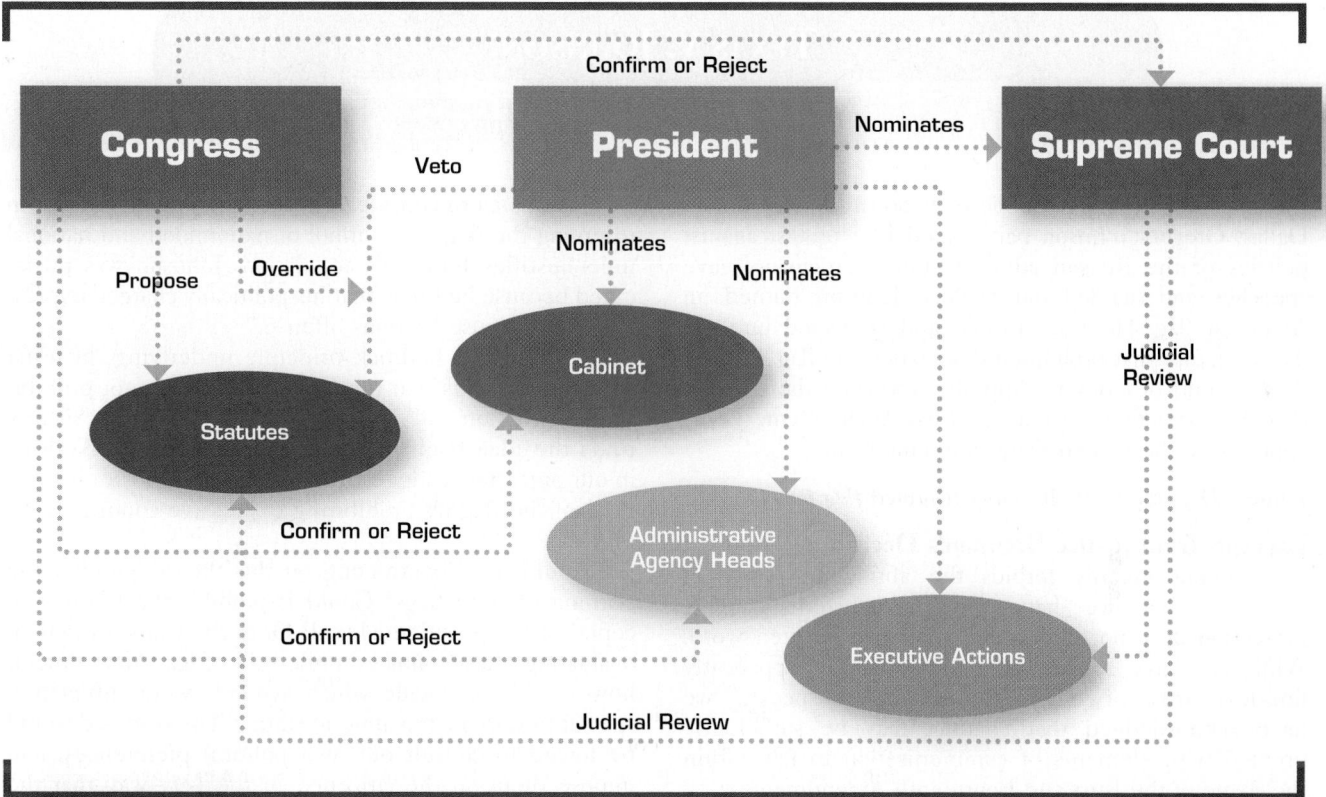

EXHIBIT 5.1 The Constitution established a federal government of checks and balances. Congress may propose statutes; the president may veto them; and Congress may override the veto. The president nominates cabinet officers, administrative heads, and Supreme Court justices, but the Senate must confirm his nominees. Finally, the Supreme Court (and lower federal courts) exercises judicial review over statutes and executive actions. Unlike the other checks and balances, judicial review is not provided for in the Constitution, but is a creation of the Court itself in *Marbury v. Madison*.

5-4a Incorporation

A series of Supreme Court cases has extended virtually all of the important constitutional protections to *all levels* of national, state, and local government. This process is called **incorporation** because rights explicitly guaranteed at one level are incorporated into rights that apply at other levels.

5-4b First Amendment: Free Speech

The First Amendment states that "Congress shall make no law … abridging the freedom of speech…" In general, we expect our government to let people speak and hear whatever they choose. The Founding Fathers believed democracy would work only if the members of the electorate were free to talk, argue, listen, and exchange viewpoints in any way they wanted. The people could only cast informed ballots if they were informed. "Speech" also includes symbolic conduct, as the following case flamingly illustrates.

TEXAS V. JOHNSON

491 U.S. 397
United States Supreme Court, 1989

Facts: Outside the Republican National Convention in Dallas, Gregory Johnson participated in a protest against policies of the Reagan administration. Participants gave speeches and handed out leaflets. Johnson burned an American flag. He was arrested and convicted under a Texas statute that prohibited desecrating the flag, but the Texas Court of Criminal Appeals *reversed* on the grounds that the conviction violated the First Amendment. Texas appealed to the United States Supreme Court.

Issue: *Does the First Amendment protect flag burning?*

Excerpts from Justice Brennan's Decision: The First Amendment literally forbids the abridgment only of "speech," but we have long recognized that its protection does not end at the spoken or written word. While we have rejected the view that an apparently limitless variety of conduct can be labeled "speech," we have acknowledged that conduct may be sufficiently imbued with elements of communication to fall within the scope of the First and Fourteenth Amendments.

In deciding whether particular conduct possesses sufficient communicative elements to bring the First Amendment into play, we have asked whether an intent to convey a particularized message was present, and [whether] the likelihood was great that the message would be understood by those who viewed it. Hence, we have recognized the expressive nature of students' wearing of black armbands to protest American military involvement in Vietnam; of a sit-in by blacks in a "whites only" area to protest segregation; of the wearing of American military uniforms in a dramatic presentation criticizing American involvement in Vietnam; and of picketing about a wide variety of causes.

[The Court concluded that burning the flag was in fact symbolic speech.]

It remains to consider whether the State's interest in reserving the flag as a symbol of nationhood and national unity justifies Johnson's conviction. Johnson was prosecuted because he knew that his politically charged expression would cause "serious offense."

If there is a bedrock principle underlying the First Amendment, it is that the Government may not prohibit the expression of an idea simply because society finds the idea itself offensive or disagreeable. Nothing in our precedents suggests that a State may foster its own view of the flag by prohibiting expressive conduct relating to it.

Could the Government, on this theory, prohibit the burning of state flags? Could it prohibit the burning of copies of the presidential seal? Or of the Constitution? In evaluating these choices under the First Amendment, how would we decide which symbols were sufficiently special to warrant this unique status? To do so, we would be forced to consult our own political preferences, and impose them on the citizenry, in the very way that the First Amendment forbids us to do.

The way to preserve the flag's special role is not to punish those who feel differently about these matters. It is to persuade them that they are wrong. We can imagine no more appropriate response to burning a flag than waving one's own, no better way to counter a flag-burner's message than by saluting the flag that burns, no surer means of preserving the dignity even of the flag that burned than by—as one witness here did—according its remains a respectful burial. We do not consecrate the flag by punishing its desecration, for in doing so we dilute the freedom that this cherished emblem represents.

The judgment of the Texas Court of Criminal Appeals is therefore *affirmed*.

Political Speech

Because the Framers were primarily concerned with enabling democracy to function, political speech has been given an especially high degree of protection. Such speech may not be barred even when it is offensive or outrageous. A speaker, for example, could accuse a U.S. senator of being insane and could use crude, violent language to describe him. The speech is still protected. **Political speech is protected unless it is intended and likely to create imminent lawless action.**[11] For example, suppose the speaker said, "The senator is

---

[11]Brandenburg v. Ohio, 395 U.S. 444 (1969).

inside that restaurant. Let's get some matches and burn the place down." Speech of this sort is not protected. The speaker could be arrested for attempted arson or attempted murder.

Time, Place, and Manner

Even when speech is protected, the government may regulate the *time, place,* and *manner* of such speech. A town may require a group to apply for a permit before using a public park for a political demonstration. The town may insist that the demonstration take place during daylight hours and that there be adequate police supervision and sanitation provided. However, the town may not prohibit such demonstrations outright.

Protected speech?

Many public universities have designated "free speech zones" located in high-traffic areas of campus that are not immediately adjacent to a large number of classrooms. The zones allow for debates to proceed and reach many students, but they minimize the chances that noisy demonstrations will interfere with lectures.

Morality and Obscenity

The regulation of morality and obscenity presents additional problems. Obscenity has never received constitutional protection. The Supreme Court has consistently held that obscenity does not play a valued role in our society and has refused to give protection to obscene works. That is well and good, but it merely forces the question: What is obscene?

In *Miller v. California*, the Court created a three-part test to determine if a creative work is obscene.[12] The basic guidelines for the fact finder are:

- Whether the average person, applying contemporary community standards, would find that the work, taken as a whole, appeals to the prurient interest;

- Whether the work depicts or describes, in a patently offensive way, sexual conduct specifically defined by the applicable state law; and

- Whether the work, taken as a whole, lacks serious literary, artistic, political, or scientific value.

If the trial court finds that the answer to all three of those questions is "yes," it may judge the material obscene; the state may then prohibit the work. If the state fails to prove any one of the three criteria, though, the work is not obscene. A United States District Court ruled that "As Nasty As They Wanna Be," recorded by 2 Live Crew, was obscene. The appeals court, however, *reversed*, finding that the state had failed to prove lack of artistic merit.[13]

Commercial Speech

This refers to speech that has a dominant theme to propose a commercial transaction. For example, most advertisements on television and in the newspapers are **commercial speech**. This sort of speech is protected by the First Amendment, but the government is permitted to regulate it more closely than other forms of speech. Commercial speech that is false or misleading may be outlawed altogether. **The government may regulate other commercial**

Commercial speech

Communication, such as advertisements, that has the dominant theme of proposing a business transaction

[12]413 U.S. 15 (1973).
[13]Luke Records, Inc. v. Navarro, 960 F. 2d 134, 1992 U.S. App. LEXIS 9592 (11th Cir. 1992).

speech, provided that the rules are reasonable and directed to a legitimate goal. Recall *R. J. Reynolds v. FCC*, discussed in Chapter 4, in which a court struck down the FDA's cigarette packaging rules because they were too broad and went beyond just educating consumers. The following case demonstrates the very different treatment given to this type of speech.

SALIB V. CITY OF MESA

133 P.3d 756
Arizona Court of Appeals, 2006

Facts: Edward Salib owned a Winchell's Donut House in Mesa, Arizona. To attract customers, he displayed large signs in his store window. The city ordered him to remove the signs, because they violated its Sign Code, which prohibited covering more than 30 percent of a store's windows with signs. Salib sued, claiming that the Sign Code violated his First Amendment free speech rights. The trial court gave summary judgment for Mesa, and the store owner appealed.

Issue: *Did Mesa's Sign Code violate the First Amendment?*

Excerpts from Judge Irvine's Decision: Under [a Supreme Court case called] *Central Hudson*, commercial speech that concerns unlawful activity or is misleading is not protected by the First Amendment. Commercial speech that falls into neither of these categories may be regulated if the government satisfies a three-prong test. First, the government must assert a substantial interest in support of the regulation. Mesa argues, and Salib concedes, that the governmental regulation of aesthetics constitutes a substantial interest, so the first prong of *Central Hudson* is not at issue.

Under the second prong of *Central Hudson*, the government must demonstrate that the challenged regulation advances its interest in a direct and material way. Salib argues that this prong has not been met because no studies were conducted to determine what aesthetic or safety problems existed and how the Sign Code could solve such problems.

Mesa responds that the Sign Code was enacted because of legitimate concerns among business owners that many businesses in the area had 100 percent coverage of their storefront windows and that this total coverage was unattractive and detracted from the aesthetics of the city. The First Amendment does not require a formal study before a regulation may be enacted. The record shows that the city council received considerable input on the subject of window coverage and aesthetics before enacting the Sign Code. Although its final adoption of the Sign Code may have rested on anecdote, history, consensus or simple common sense, rather than a formal study or survey addressed specifically to the window coverage provision, the constitution requires no greater proof.

Salib argues the restriction is not narrow enough and therefore violates the third prong of *Central Hudson*. It is clear from the First Amendment cases that "narrowly tailored" or "narrowly drawn" do not mean that the least restrictive means must be used. Rather, a "reasonable fit" between the intent and purpose of the regulation and the means chosen to accomplish those goals is required. The regulation does not have to be perfect, but its scope must be in proportion to the interest served.

Mesa argues that 30 percent is a reasonable compromise between 100 percent coverage and a total ban of signage. Further, Mesa argues, the Sign Code is narrow because it only addresses signs that are inside the pane, and the Code allows alternative methods of communication, including signs hanging outside of the window sill area. Additionally, Mesa conducted comparisons with other communities and found that the 30 percent restriction on window coverage was comparable to other cities' restrictions.

We are not in a position to determine what percentage of window coverage is optimal. Rather, we only decide if the 30 percent figure that was adopted by the Sign Code is a reasonable fit to further the goal of improving aesthetics. We conclude that it is. Reasonable minds can differ as to whether Mesa's interest would best be served by a 15 percent, 25 percent, 30 percent, or 40 percent limitation on window coverage, but under the facts of this case we cannot conclude that these differences of degree are of a constitutional dimension. The exact balance between the size of the signs and the aesthetic benefits attained is ultimately a subjective decision best left to the city council.

We conclude the Sign Code directly advances a substantial governmental interest and is narrowly tailored to directly advance the goal of improved aesthetics. We therefore affirm the trial court's granting of Mesa's Motion for Summary Judgment.

EXAM Strategy

Question: Maria owns a lot next to a freeway that passes through Tidyville. She has rented a billboard to Huge Mart, a nearby retailer, and a second billboard to Green, a political party. However, Tidyville prohibits off-premises signs (those not on the advertiser's property) that are visible from the freeway. Tidyville's rule is designed to make the city more attractive, to increase property values, and to eliminate distractions that may cause freeway accidents. Huge Mart and Green sue, claiming that Tidyville's law violates their First Amendment rights.

    A. Huge Mart is likely to win; Green is likely to lose.

    B. Green is likely to win; Huge Mart is likely to lose.

    C. Huge Mart and Green are both likely to win.

    D. Huge Mart and Green are both likely to lose.

Strategy: What is the difference between the two cases? Huge Mart wants the billboard for commercial speech; Green wants it for a political message. What are the legal standards for commercial and political free speech? Apply those standards.

Result: The government may regulate commercial speech, provided that the rules are reasonable and directed to a legitimate goal. Political speech is given much stronger protection, and can be prohibited only if it is intended and likely to create imminent lawless action. The regulation outlawing *advertising* will be upheld, but Tidyville will not be allowed to block political messages.

5-4c Fifth Amendment: Due Process and the Takings Clause

You are a senior at a major state university. You feel great about a difficult exam you took in Professor Watson's class. The Dean's Office sends for you, and you enter curiously, wondering if your exam was so good that the dean is awarding you a prize. Not quite. The exam proctor has accused you of cheating. Based on the accusation, Watson has flunked you. You protest that you are innocent and demand to know the accusation. The dean says that you will learn the details at a hearing, if you wish to have one. She reminds you that if you lose the hearing, you will be expelled from the university. Four years of work and your entire career is suddenly on the line.

> **Four years of work and your entire career is suddenly on the line.**

The hearing is run by Professor Holmes, who will make the final decision. Holmes is a junior faculty member in Watson's department. (Next year, Watson will decide Holmes's tenure application.) At the hearing, the proctor accuses you of copying from a student sitting in front of you. Both Watson and Holmes have already compared the two papers and concluded that they are strongly similar. Holmes tells you that you must convince him the charge is wrong. You examine the papers, acknowledge that there are similarities, but plead as best you can that you never copied. Holmes doesn't buy it. The university expels you, placing on your transcript a notation of cheating.

Have you received fair treatment? To answer that, we must look to the Fifth Amendment, which provides several vital protections. We will consider two related provisions, the Due Process Clause and the Takings Clause. Together, they state: "No person shall be ... deprived of life, liberty, or property without due process of law; nor shall private property be taken for public use, without just compensation." These clauses prevent the government from arbitrarily taking the most valuable possessions of a citizen or corporation. The government has the right to take a person's liberty or property. But there are three important limitations:

- **Procedural Due Process.** Before depriving anyone of liberty or property, the government must go through certain steps, or procedures, to ensure that the result is fair.

- **The Takings Clause**. When the government takes property for public use, such as to build a new highway, it has to pay a fair price.

- **Substantive Due Process.** Some rights are so fundamental that the government may not take them from us at all. The substance of any law or government action may be challenged on fundamental fairness grounds.

Procedural Due Process

The government deprives citizens or corporations of their property in a variety of ways. The Internal Revenue Service may fine a corporation for late payment of taxes. The Customs Service may seize goods at the border. As to liberty, the government may take it by confining someone in a mental institution or by taking a child out of the home because of parental neglect. The purpose of **procedural due process** is to ensure that before the government takes liberty or property, the affected person has a fair chance to oppose the action. There are two steps in analyzing a procedural due process case:

- Is the government attempting to take liberty or property?

- If so, how much process is due? (If the government is *not* attempting to take liberty or property, there is no due process issue.)

Is the Government Attempting to Take Liberty or Property?   Liberty interests are generally easy to spot: Confining someone in a mental institution and taking a child from her home are both deprivations of liberty. A property interest may be obvious. Suppose that, during a civil lawsuit, the court **attaches** a defendant's house, meaning it bars the defendant from selling the property at least until the case is decided. This way, if the plaintiff wins, the defendant will have assets to pay the judgment. The court has clearly deprived the defendant of an important interest in his house, and the defendant is entitled to due process. However, a property interest may be subtler than that. A woman holding a job with a government agency has a "property interest" in that job, because her employer has agreed not to fire her without cause, and she can rely on it for income. If the government does fire her, it is taking away that property interest, and she is entitled to due process. A student attending any public school has a property interest in her education. If a public university suspends a student as described earlier, it is taking her property, and she, too, should receive due process.

How Much Process Is Due?   Assuming that a liberty or property interest is affected, a court must decide how much process is due. Does the person get a formal trial, or an informal hearing, or merely a chance to reply in writing to the charges against her? If she gets a hearing, must it be held before the government deprives her of her property, or is it enough that she can be heard shortly thereafter? **What sort of hearing the government must offer depends upon how important the property or liberty interest is and on whether the government has a competing need for efficiency.** The more important the interest, the more formal the procedures must be.

Neutral Fact Finder.   Regardless of how formal the hearing, one requirement is constant: The fact finder must be neutral. Whether it is a superior court judge deciding a multimillion-dollar contract suit or an employment supervisor deciding the fate of a

Takings Clause
A clause in the Fifth Amendment that ensures that when any governmental unit takes private property for public use, it must compensate the owner

Procedural due process
The doctrine that ensures that before the government takes liberty or property, the affected person has a fair chance to oppose the action.

government employee, the fact finder must have no personal interest in the outcome. In *Ward v. Monroeville*, the plaintiff was a motorist who had been stopped for traffic offenses in a small town.[14] He protested his innocence and received a judicial hearing. But the "judge" at the hearing was the town mayor. Traffic fines were a significant part of the town's budget. The motorist argued that the town was depriving him of procedural due process because the mayor had a financial interest in the outcome of the case. The United States Supreme Court agreed and *reversed* his conviction.

Attachment of Property.   As described earlier, a plaintiff in a civil lawsuit often seeks to *attach* the defendant's property. This protects the plaintiff, but it may also harm the defendant if, for example, he is about to close a profitable real estate deal. Attachments used to be routine. In *Connecticut v. Doehr*, the Supreme Court required more caution.[15] Based on *Doehr*, when a plaintiff seeks to attach at the beginning of the trial, a court must look at the plaintiff's likelihood of winning. Generally, the court must grant the defendant a hearing *before* attaching the property. The defendant, represented by a lawyer, may offer evidence as to how attachment would harm him and why it should be denied.

Government Employment.   A government employee must receive due process before being fired. Generally, this means some kind of hearing, but not necessarily a formal court hearing. The employee is entitled to know the charges against him, to hear the employer's evidence, and to have an opportunity to tell his side of the story. He is not entitled to have a lawyer present. The hearing "officer" need only be a neutral employee. Further, in an emergency, where the employee is a danger to the public or the organization, the government may suspend with pay, before holding a hearing. It then must provide a hearing before the decision becomes final.

Academic Suspension.   There is still a property interest here, but it is the least important of those discussed. When a public school concludes that a student has failed to meet its normal academic standards, such as by failing too many courses, it may dismiss him without a hearing. Due process is served if the student receives notice of the reason and has some opportunity to respond, such as by writing a letter contradicting the school's claims.

In cases of disciplinary suspension or expulsion, courts generally require schools to provide a higher level of due process. In the hypothetical at the beginning of this section, the university has failed to provide adequate due process.[16] The school has accused the student of a serious infraction. The school must promptly provide details of the charge and cannot wait until the hearing to do so. The student should see the two papers and have a chance to rebut the charge. Moreover, Professor Holmes has demonstrated bias. He appears to have made up his mind in advance. He has placed the burden on the student to disprove the charges. And he probably feels obligated to support Watson's original conclusion, because Watson will be deciding his tenure case next year.

The Takings Clause

Florence Dolan ran a plumbing store in Tigard, Oregon. She and her husband wanted to enlarge it on land they already owned. But the city government said that they could expand only if they dedicated some of their own land for use as a public bicycle path and for other public use. Does the city have the right to make them do that? For an answer, we must look to a different part of the Fifth Amendment.

---

[14]409 U.S. 57 (1972).
[15]501 U.S. 1 (1991).
[16]See, e.g., University of Texas Medical School at Houston v. Than, (Tex. 1995).

The Takings Clause prohibits a state from taking private property for public use without just compensation. A town wishing to build a new football field may boot you out of your house. But the town must compensate you. The government takes your land through the power of **eminent domain**. Officials must notify you of their intentions and give you an opportunity to oppose the project and to challenge the amount the town offers to pay. But when the hearings are done, the town may write you a check and level your house, whether you like it or not.

More controversial issues arise when a local government does not physically take the property but passes regulations that restrict its use. Tigard is a city of 30,000 in Oregon. The city developed a comprehensive land use plan for its downtown area in order to preserve green space, to encourage transportation other than autos, and to reduce its flooding problems. Under the plan, when a property owner sought permission to build in the downtown section, the city could require some of her land to be used for public purposes. This has become a standard method of land use planning throughout the nation. States have used it to preserve coastline, urban green belts, and many environmental features.

When Florence Dolan applied for permission to expand, the city required that she dedicate a 15-foot strip of her property to the city as a bicycle pathway and that she preserve, as greenway, a portion of her land within a floodplain. She sued, and though she lost in the Oregon courts, she won in the United States Supreme Court. The Court held that Tigard City's method of routinely forcing all owners to dedicate land to public use violated the Takings Clause. The city was taking the land, even though title never changed hands.[17]

The Court did not outlaw all such requirements. What it required was that, **before a government may require an owner to dedicate land to a public use, it must show that this owner's proposed building requires this dedication of land.** In other words, it is not enough for Tigard to have a general plan, such as a bicycle pathway, and to make all owners participate in it. Tigard must show that it needs *Dolan's* land *specifically for a bike path and greenway.* This will be much harder for local governments to demonstrate than merely showing a citywide plan. A related issue arose in the following controversial case. A city used eminent domain to take property on behalf of *private developers.* Was this a valid public use?

The *Kelo* decision was controversial and, in response, some states passed statutes prohibiting eminent domain for private development.

Eminent domain

The power of the government to take private property for public use

KELO V. CITY OF NEW LONDON, CONNECTICUT

545 U.S. 469
United States Supreme Court, 2005

Facts: New London, Connecticut, was declining economically. The city's unemployment rate was double that of the state generally, and the population was at its lowest point in 75 years. In response, state and local officials targeted a section of the city, called Fort Trumbull, for revitalization. Located on the Thames River, Fort Trumbull comprised 115 privately owned properties and 32 additional acres of an abandoned naval facility. The development plan included one section for a waterfront conference hotel and stores; a second one for 80 private residences; and one for research facilities.

The state bought most of the properties from willing sellers. However, nine owners of 15 properties refused to

sell, and filed suit. The owners claimed that the city was trying to take land for *private* use, not public, in violation of the Takings Clause. The case reached the United States Supreme Court.

Issue: *Did the city's plan violate the Takings Clause?*

Excerpts from Justice Stevens's Decision: It has long been accepted that the sovereign may not take the property of A for the sole purpose of transferring it to another private party B, even though A is paid just compensation. On the other hand, it is equally clear that a State may transfer property from one private party to another if future "use by the public" is the purpose of the

---

[17]Dolan v. City of Tigard, 512 U.S. 374 (1994).

taking; the condemnation of land for a railroad with common-carrier duties is a familiar example.

This is not a case in which the City is planning to open the condemned land—at least not in its entirety—to use by the general public. Nor will the private lessees of the land in any sense be required to operate like common carriers, making their services available to all comers. But this Court long ago rejected any literal requirement that condemned property be put into use for the general public, [embracing] the broader and more natural interpretation of public use as "public purpose." Thus, in a case upholding a mining company's use of an aerial bucket line to transport ore over property it did not own, Justice Holmes' opinion for the Court stressed "the inadequacy of use by the general public as a universal test."

The City has carefully formulated an economic development plan that it believes will provide appreciable benefits to the community, including—but by no means limited to—new jobs and increased tax revenue. As with other exercises in urban planning and development, the City is endeavoring to coordinate a variety of commercial, residential, and recreational uses of land, with the hope that they will form a whole greater than the sum of its parts. Because that plan unquestionably serves a public purpose, the takings challenged here satisfy the public use requirement of the Fifth Amendment.

To avoid this result, petitioners urge us to adopt a new bright-line rule that economic development does not qualify as a public use. [However, promoting] economic development is a traditional and long-accepted function of government. There is, moreover, no principled way of distinguishing economic development from the other public purposes that we have recognized. In our cases upholding takings that facilitated agriculture and mining, for example, we emphasized the importance of those industries to the welfare of the States in question. Clearly, there is no basis for exempting economic development from our traditionally broad understanding of public purpose.

The judgment of the Supreme Court of Connecticut is *affirmed*.

Justice O'Connor, dissenting: The Court today significantly expands the meaning of public use. It holds that the sovereign may take private property currently put to ordinary private use, and give it over for new, ordinary private use, so long as the new use is predicted to generate some secondary benefit for the public—such as increased tax revenue, more jobs, maybe even aesthetic pleasure. But nearly any lawful use of real private property can be said to generate some incidental benefit to the public. Thus, if predicted (or even guaranteed) positive side effects are enough to render transfer from one private party to another constitutional, then the words "for public use" do not realistically exclude *any* takings, and thus do not exert any constraint on the eminent domain power.

Any property may now be taken for the benefit of another private party, but the fallout from this decision will not be random. The beneficiaries are likely to be those citizens with disproportionate influence and power in the political process, including large corporations and development firms. As for the victims, the government now has license to transfer property from those with fewer resources to those with more.

Substantive Due Process

This doctrine is part of the Due Process Clause, but it is entirely different from procedural due process and from government taking. During the first third of the twentieth century, the Supreme Court frequently nullified state and federal laws, asserting that they interfered with basic rights. For example, in a famous 1905 case, *Lochner v. New York*, the Supreme Court invalidated a New York statute that had limited the number of hours that bakers could work in a week.[18] New York had passed the law to protect employee health. But the Court declared that private parties had a basic constitutional right to contract. In this case, the statute interfered with the rights of the employer and the baker to make any bargain they wished. Over the next three decades, the Court struck down dozens of state and federal laws that were aimed at working conditions, union rights, and social welfare generally. This was called **substantive due process** because the Court was looking at the underlying rights being affected, such as the right to contract, not at any procedures.[19]

substantive due process
A form of due process that holds that certain rights are so fundamental that the government may not eliminate them

---

[18]198 U.S. 45 (1905).
[19]Be the first on your block to pronounce this word correctly. The accent goes on the first syllable: substantive.

Critics complained that the Court was interfering with the desires of the voting public by nullifying laws that the justices personally disliked (judicial activism). During the Great Depression, however, things changed. Beginning in 1934, the Court completely *reversed* itself and began to uphold the types of laws it had struck down earlier.

The Supreme Court made an important substantive due process ruling in the case of *BMW v. Gore*.[20] A BMW dealership sold Gore a car that had sustained water damage. Instead of telling him of the damage, they simply repainted the car and sold it as new.

In Chapter 6, we will examine two different types of cash awards that juries may make in tort cases. For now, let's call them "ordinary" and "punitive" damages. When plaintiffs win tort cases, juries may always award ordinary damages to offset real, measureable losses. In addition, juries are sometimes allowed to add to an award to further punish a defendant for bad behavior.

In the BMW case, the jury awarded Gore $4,000 in ordinary damages as the difference in value between a flawless new car and a water-damaged car. The jury then awarded a delighted Gore $4 *million* in punitive damages. In the end, the Supreme Court decided that the punitive award was so disproportionate to the harm actually caused that it violated substantive due process rights.

5-4d Fourteenth Amendment: Equal Protection Clause

Shannon Faulkner wanted to attend The Citadel, a state-supported military college in South Carolina. She was a fine student who met every admission requirement that The Citadel set except one: She was not a man. The Citadel argued that its long and distinguished history demanded that it remain all male. Faulkner responded that she was a citizen of the state and ought to receive the benefits that others got, including the right to a military education. Could the school exclude her on the basis of gender?

Equal Protection Clause
A clause in the Fourteenth Amendment that generally requires the government to treat people equally

The Fourteenth Amendment provides that "No State shall ... deny to any person within its jurisdiction the equal protection of the laws." This is the **Equal Protection Clause**, and it means that, generally speaking, **governments must treat people equally.** Unfair classifications among people or corporations will not be permitted. A notorious example of unfair classification would be race discrimination: Permitting only white children to attend a public school violates the Equal Protection Clause.

Yet clearly, governments do make classifications every day. People with high incomes pay a higher tax rate than those with low incomes; some corporations are permitted to deal in securities, while others are not. To determine which classifications are constitutionally permissible, we need to know what is being classified. There are three major groups of classifications. The outcome of a case can generally be predicted by knowing which group it is in.

- **Minimal Scrutiny: Economic and Social Relations.** Government actions that classify people or corporations on these bases are almost always upheld.

- **Intermediate Scrutiny: Gender.** Government classifications are sometimes upheld.

- **Strict Scrutiny: Race, Ethnicity, and Fundamental Rights.** Classifications based on any of these are almost never upheld.

Minimal Scrutiny: Economic and Social Regulation

Just as with the Due Process Clause, laws that regulate economic or social issues are presumed valid. They will be upheld if they are *rationally related to a legitimate goal*. This means a statute may classify corporations and/or people, and the classifications will be upheld if they make any sense at all. The New York City Transit Authority excluded all methadone users from any employment. The United States District Court concluded that this violated the Equal Protection Clause by unfairly excluding all those who were on

---

[20]517 U.S. 559 (1996).

methadone. The court noted that even those who tested free of any illegal drugs and were seeking non-safety-sensitive jobs, such as clerks, were turned away. That, said the district court, was irrational.

Not so, said the United States Supreme Court. The Court admitted that the policy might not be the wisest. It would probably make more sense to test individually for illegal drugs rather than automatically exclude methadone users. But, said the Court, it was not up to the justices to choose the best policy. They were only to decide if the policy was rational. Excluding methadone users related rationally to the safety of public transport and therefore did not violate the Equal Protection Clause.[21]

Intermediate Scrutiny: Gender

Classifications based on sex must meet a tougher test than those resulting from economic or social regulation. Such laws must *substantially relate to important government objectives.* Courts have increasingly nullified government sex classifications as societal concern with gender equality has grown.

At about the same time Shannon Faulkner began her campaign to enter The Citadel, another woman sought admission to the Virginia Military Institute (VMI), an all-male state school. The Supreme Court held that Virginia had violated the Equal Protection Clause by excluding women from VMI. The Court ruled that gender-based government discrimination requires an "exceedingly persuasive justification," and that Virginia had failed that standard of proof. The Citadel promptly opened its doors to women as well.[22]

Strict Scrutiny: Race, Ethnicity, and Fundamental Rights

Any government action that intentionally discriminates against racial or ethnic minorities, or interferes with a fundamental right, is presumed invalid. In such cases, courts will look at the statute or policy with *strict scrutiny;* that is, courts will examine it very closely to determine whether there is compelling justification for it. The law will be upheld only if it is *necessary to promote a compelling state interest.* Very few meet that test.

- **Racial and Ethnic Minorities.** Any government action that intentionally discriminates on the basis of race, or ethnicity, is presumed invalid. For example, in *Palmore v. Sidoti*, the state had refused to give child custody to a mother because her new spouse was racially different from the child.[23] The practice was declared unconstitutional. The state had made a racial classification, it was presumed invalid, and the government had no *compelling need* to make such a ruling.

- **Fundamental Rights**. A government action interfering with a fundamental right also receives strict scrutiny and will likely be declared void. For example, New York State gave an employment preference to any veteran who had been a state resident when he entered the military. Newcomers who were veterans were less likely to get jobs, and therefore this statute interfered with the right to travel, a fundamental right. The Supreme Court declared the law invalid.[24]

Fundamental rights

Rights so basic that any governmental interference with them is suspect and likely to be unconstitutional

---

[21]New York City Transit Authority v. Beazer, 440 U.S. 568 (1979).
[22]United States v. Virginia, 518 U.S. 515 (1996).
[23]466 U.S. 429 (1984).
[24]Attorney General of New York v. Soto-Lopez, 476 U.S. 898 (1986).

EXAM Strategy

Question: Megan is a freshman at her local public high school; her older sister Jenna attends a nearby private high school. Both girls are angry because their schools prohibit them from joining their respective wrestling teams, where only boys are allowed. The two girls sue based on the U.S. Constitution. Discuss the relevant law and predict the outcomes.

Strategy: One girl goes to private school and one to public school. Why does that matter? Now ask what provision of the Constitution is involved, and what legal standard it establishes.

Result: The Constitution offers protection from the *government*. A private high school is not part of the government, and Jenna has no constitutional case. Megan's suit is based on the Equal Protection Clause. This is gender discrimination, meaning that Megan's school must convince the court that keeping girls off the team *substantially relates to an important government objective*. The school will probably argue that wrestling with stronger boys will be dangerous for girls. However, courts are increasingly suspicious of any gender discrimination and are unlikely to find the school's argument persuasive.

Chapter Conclusion

The legal battle over power never stops. The obligation of a state to provide equal educational opportunity for both genders relates to whether Tigard, Oregon, may demand some of Ms. Dolan's store lot for public use. Both issues are governed by one amazing document. The same Constitution determines what tax preferences are permissible and even whether a state may require you to wear clothing. As social mores change in step with broad cultural developments, as the membership of the Supreme Court changes, the balance of power between federal government, state government, and citizens will continue to evolve. There are no easy answers to these constitutional questions because there has never been a democracy so large, so diverse, or so powerful.

EXAM REVIEW

1. **CONSTITUTION**   The Constitution is a series of compromises about power.

2. **ARTICLES I, II, AND III**   Article I of the Constitution creates the Congress and grants all legislative power to it. Article II establishes the office of president and defines executive powers. Article III creates the Supreme Court and permits lower federal courts; the article also outlines the powers of the federal judiciary.

3. **COMMERCE CLAUSE**   Under the Commerce Clause, Congress may regulate any activity that has a substantial effect on interstate commerce.

4. **INTERSTATE COMMERCE**   A state may not regulate commerce in any way that will interfere with interstate commerce.

Question: Maine exempted many charitable institutions from real estate taxes but denied this benefit to a charity that primarily benefited out-of-state residents. Camp Newfound was a Christian Science organization, and 95 percent of its summer campers came from other states. Camp Newfound sued Maine. Discuss.

Strategy: The state was treating organizations differently depending on what states their campers came from. This raised Commerce Clause issues. Did the positive aspect or dormant aspect of that clause apply? The dormant aspect applied. What does it state? Apply that standard to these facts. (See the "Result" at the end of this section.)

5. **SUPREMACY CLAUSE** Under the Supremacy Clause, if there is a conflict between federal and state statutes, the federal law preempts the field. Even without a conflict, federal law preempts if Congress intended to exercise exclusive control.

6. **PRESIDENTIAL POWERS** The president's key powers include making agency appointments, proposing legislation, conducting foreign policy, and acting as commander in chief of the armed forces.

7. **FEDERAL COURTS** The federal courts adjudicate cases and also exercise judicial review, which is the right to declare a statute or governmental action unconstitutional and void.

8. **FREEDOM OF SPEECH** Freedom of speech includes symbolic acts. Political speech by both people and organizations is protected unless it is intended and likely to create imminent lawless action.

9. **REGULATION OF SPEECH** The government may regulate the time, place, and manner of speech.

10. **COMMERCIAL SPEECH** Commercial speech that is false or misleading may be outlawed; otherwise, regulations on this speech must be reasonable and directed to a legitimate goal.

Question: A federal statute prohibits the broadcasting of lottery advertisements, except by stations that broadcast in states permitting lotteries. The purpose of the statute is to support efforts of states that outlaw lotteries. Truth Broadcasting operates a radio station in State A (a nonlottery state) but broadcasts primarily in State B (a lottery state). Truth wants to advertise State B's lottery but is barred by the statute. Does the federal statute violate Truth's constitutional rights?

Strategy: This case involves a particular kind of speech. What kind? What is the rule about that kind of speech? (See the "Result" at the end of this section.)

11. **PROCEDURAL DUE PROCESS**   Procedural due process is required whenever the government attempts to take liberty or property. The amount of process that is due depends upon the importance of the liberty or property threatened.

EXAM Strategy

> **Question:** Fox's Fine Furs claims that Ermine owes $68,000 for a mink coat on which she has stopped making payments. Fox files a complaint and also asks the court clerk to *garnish* Ermine's wages. A garnishment is a court order to an employer to withhold an employee's wages, or a portion of them, and pay the money into court so that there will be money for the plaintiff, if it wins. What constitutional issue does Fox's request for garnishment raise?
>
> **Strategy:** Ermine is in danger of losing part of her income, which is property. The Due Process Clause prohibits the government (the court) from taking life, liberty, or property without due process. What process is Ermine entitled to? (See the "Result" at the end of this section.)

12. **TAKINGS CLAUSE**   The Takings Clause prohibits a state from taking private property for public use without just compensation.

13. **SUBSTANTIVE DUE PROCESS**   A substantive due process analysis presumes that any economic or social regulation is valid, and presumes invalid any law that infringes upon a fundamental right.

14. **EQUAL PROTECTION CLAUSE**   The Equal Protection Clause generally requires the government to treat people equally. Courts apply strict scrutiny in any equal protection case involving race, ethnicity, or fundamental rights; intermediate scrutiny to any case involving gender; and minimal scrutiny to an economic or social regulation.

> **4. Result:** The dormant aspect holds that a state statute that discriminates against interstate commerce is almost always invalid. Maine was subsidizing charities that served in-state residents and penalizing those that attracted campers from elsewhere. The tax rule violated the Commerce Clause and was void.[25]
>
> **10. Result:** An advertisement is commercial speech. The government may regulate this speech so long as the rules are reasonable and directed to a legitimate goal. The goal of supporting nonlottery states is reasonable, and there is no violation of Truth's free speech rights.[26]
>
> **11. Result:** Ermine is entitled to notice of Fox's claim and to a hearing before the court garnishes her wages.[27]

---

[25]Camps Newfound/Owatonna, Inc. v. Town of Harrison, Maine, 520 U.S. 564 (1997).
[26]United States v. Edge Broadcasting, 509 U.S. 418 (1993).
[27]Sniadach v. Family Finance Corp., 395 U.S. 337 (1969).

MULTIPLE-CHOICE QUESTIONS

1. Greenville College, a public community college, has a policy of admitting only male students. If the policy is challenged under the Fourteenth Amendment, _____ scrutiny will be applied.

   (a) strict

   (b) intermediate

   (c) rational

   (d) none of the above

2. You begin work at Everhappy Corp. at the beginning of November. On your second day at work, you wear a political button on your overcoat, supporting your choice for governor in the upcoming election. Your boss glances at it and says, "Get that stupid thing out of this office or you're history, chump." Your boss _____ violated your First Amendment rights. After work, you put the button back on and start walking home. You pass a police officer who blocks your path and says, "Take off that stupid button or you're going to jail, chump." The officer _____ violated your First Amendment rights.

   (a) has; has

   (b) has; has not

   (c) has not; has

   (d) has not; has not

3. Which of the following statements accurately describes statutes that Congress and the president may create?

   (a) Statutes must be related to a power listed in Article I, section 8, of the Constitution.

   (b) Statutes must not infringe on the liberties in the Bill of Rights.

   (c) Both A and B

   (d) none of the above

4. Which of the following is true of the origin of judicial review?

   (a) It was created by Article II of the Constitution.

   (b) It was created by Article III of the Constitution.

   (c) It was created in the *Marbury v. Madison* case.

   (d) It was created by the Fifth Amendment.

   (e) It was created by the Fourteenth Amendment.

5. Consider *Kelo v. City of New London*, in which a city with a revitalization plan squared off against property owners who did not wish to sell their property. The key constitutional provision was the Takings Clause in the _____ Amendment. The Supreme Court decided the city _____ use eminent domain and take the property from the landowners.

   (a) Fifth; could

   (b) Fifth; could not

   (c) Fourteenth; could

   (d) Fourteenth; could not

CASE QUESTIONS

1. In 1996, California legalized the medical use of marijuana, even though it was still illegal under federal law. Californians Angel Raich and Diane Monson used homegrown medical marijuana. When federal agents destroyed their plants, Monson and Raich sued, claiming, among other things, that the Commerce Clause did not permit the federal government to regulate activities that took place in their backyards and homes. The federal government argued that because consuming locally grown marijuana for medical purposes affects the interstate market for marijuana, the federal government may regulate—and prohibit—such consumption. Whose argument should prevail?

2. In the landmark 1965 case of *Griswold v. Connecticut*, the Supreme Court examined a Connecticut statute that made it a crime for any person to use contraception. The majority declared the law an unconstitutional violation of the right of privacy. Justice Black dissented, saying, "I do not to any extent whatever base my view that this Connecticut law is constitutional on a belief that the law is wise or that its policy is a good one. [It] is every bit as offensive to me as it is to the majority. [There is no criticism by the majority of this law] to which I cannot subscribe—except their conclusion that the evil qualities they see in the law make it unconstitutional." What legal doctrines are involved here? Why did Justice Black distinguish between his personal views on the statute and the power of the Court to overturn it?

3. Carter was an employee of the Sheriff's office in Hampton, Virginia. When his boss, Sheriff Roberts, was up for reelection against Adams, Carter "liked" the Adams campaign's Facebook page. Upon winning reelection, Sheriff Roberts fired Carter, who then sued on free speech grounds. Is a Facebook "like" protected under the First Amendment?

4. David Lucas paid $975,000 for two residential lots on the Isle of Palms near Charleston, South Carolina. He intended to build houses on them. Two years later, the South Carolina legislature passed a statute that prohibited building seaward of a certain line, and Lucas's property fell in the prohibited zone. Lucas claimed that his land was now useless and that South Carolina owed him its value. Explain his claim. Should he win?

5. The federal Defense of Marriage Act (DOMA) defined marriage as a union between a man and a woman. As a result, same-sex couples were not eligible for the federal marriage benefits given to heterosexual couples. Edith Windsor and Thea Spyer had been together for 40 years, and married for two, when Spyer died. Because of DOMA, the federal government did not treat Windsor as a surviving spouse for purposes of estate taxes, so she was presented with a tax bill of $363,000. If she had been married to a man, she would not have owed any taxes. Windsor challenged the statute, claiming the government had violated her right to equal protection. Should she win?

DISCUSSION QUESTIONS

1. What is the proper role of a judge in interpreting the Constitution? Do you believe in judicial activism or judicial restraint?

2. **ETHICS** Lawmakers have traditionally struggled when asked to define obscenity. Justice Potter Stewart simply defined it as "I know it when I see it." This chapter

discusses the guidelines that determine if speech is obscene for purposes of the First Amendment. In Chapter 4, you read about the FCC's vague guidelines on obscenity in *Fox Television Stations v. FCC.* Should obscenity ever be protected under the First Amendment? Where you do draw the line?

3. Consider the "tea party" movement. Do you believe that the federal government should be able to create whatever laws it deems to be in the country's best interests, or do you believe that individual states, like Florida and California, should have more control over the laws within their own borders?

4. This chapter is filled with examples of statutes that have been struck down by the courts. A Texas law banning flag burning was rejected by the Supreme Court, as was a Louisiana death penalty statute. The Affordable Healthcare Act was voided by multiple lower court judges before the Supreme Court ultimately upheld the law.

   Do you like the fact that courts can void laws which they determine to be in violation of the Constitution? Or is it wrong for appointed judges to overrule "the will of the majority," as expressed by elected members of Congress and state legislatures?

5. Gender discrimination currently receives "intermediate" Fourteenth Amendment scrutiny. Is this right? Should gender receive "strict" scrutiny as does race? Why or why not?

CHAPTER 6

DISPUTE RESOLUTION

Tony Caruso had not returned for dinner, and his wife, Karen, was nervous. She put on some sandals and hurried across the dunes, a half mile to the ocean shore. She soon came upon Tony's dog, Blue, tied to an old picket fence. Tony's shoes and clothing were piled neatly nearby. Karen and friends searched frantically throughout the evening.

© Creative Travel Projects/Shutterstock.com

A little past midnight, Tony's body washed ashore, his lungs filled with water. A local doctor concluded he had accidentally drowned.

Karen and her friends were not the only ones who were distraught. Tony had been partners with Beth Smiles in an environmental consulting business, Enviro-Vision. They were good friends, and Beth was emotionally devastated. When she was able to focus on business issues, Beth filed an insurance claim with the Coastal Insurance Group. Beth hated to think about Tony's death in financial terms, but she was relieved that the struggling business would receive $2 million on the life insurance policy.

> **A little past midnight, Tony's body washed ashore, his lungs filled with water.**

Several months after filing the claim, Beth received this reply from Coastal: "Under the policy issued to Enviro-Vision, we are conditionally liable in the amount of $1 million in the event of Mr. Caruso's death. If his death is accidental, we are conditionally liable to pay double indemnity of $2 million. But pursuant to section H(5), death by suicide is not covered.

"After a thorough investigation, we have concluded that Anthony Caruso's death was an act of suicide, as defined in section B(11) of the policy. Your claim is denied in its entirety." Beth was furious. She was convinced Tony was incapable of suicide. And her company could not afford the $2 million loss. She decided to consult her lawyer, Chris Pruitt.

6-1 THREE FUNDAMENTAL AREAS OF LAW

This case is a fictionalized version of several real cases based on double indemnity insurance policies. In this chapter, we follow Beth's dispute with Coastal from initial interview through appeal, using it to examine three fundamental areas of law: the structure of our court systems, civil lawsuits, and alternative dispute resolution.

When Beth Smiles meets with her lawyer, Chris Pruitt brings a second attorney from his firm, Janet Booker, who is an experienced **litigator**; that is, a lawyer who handles court cases. If they file a lawsuit, Janet will be in charge, so Chris wants her there for the first meeting. Janet probes about Tony's home life, the status of the business, his personal finances, everything. Beth becomes upset that Janet doesn't seem sympathetic, but Chris explains that Janet is doing her job: She needs all the information, good and bad.

6-1a **Litigation versus Alternative Dispute Resolution**

Janet starts thinking about the two methods of dispute resolution: litigation and alternative dispute resolution. **Litigation** refers to lawsuits, the process of filing claims in court, and ultimately going to trial. **Alternative dispute resolution** is any other formal or informal process used to settle disputes without resorting to a trial. It is increasingly popular with corporations and individuals alike because it is generally cheaper and faster than litigation, and we will focus on this topic in the last part of this chapter.

Litigation
The process of filing claims in court and ultimately going to trial.

Alternative dispute resolution
Any other formal or informal process used to settle disputes without resorting to a trial

6-2 COURT SYSTEMS

The United States has more than 50 *systems* of courts. One nationwide system of *federal* courts serves the entire country. In addition, each individual state has its court system. The state and federal courts are in different buildings, have different judges, and hear different kinds of cases. Each has special powers and certain limitations.

6-2a **State Courts**

The typical state court system forms a pyramid, as Exhibit 6.1 shows. Some states have minor variations on the exhibit. For example, Texas has two top courts: a Supreme Court for civil cases and a Court of Criminal Appeals for criminal cases.

Trial Courts

Almost all cases start in trial courts, which are endlessly portrayed on television and in film. There is one judge, and there will often (but not always) be a jury. This is the only court to hear testimony from witnesses and receive evidence. **Trial courts** determine the facts of a particular dispute and apply to those facts the law given by earlier appellate court decisions.

In the Enviro-Vision dispute, the trial court will decide all important facts that are in dispute. How did Tony Caruso die? Did he drown? Assuming he drowned, was his death accidental or suicide? Once the jury has decided the facts, it will apply the law to those facts. If Tony Caruso died accidentally, contract law provides that Beth Smiles is entitled to double indemnity benefits. If the jury decides he killed himself, Beth gets nothing.

Facts are critical. That may sound obvious, but in a course devoted to legal principles, it is easy to lose track of the key role that factual determinations play in the resolution of any dispute. In the Enviro-Vision case, we will see that one bit of factual evidence goes undetected, with costly consequences.

Jurisdiction refers to a court's power to hear a case. In state or federal court, a plaintiff may start a lawsuit only in a court that has jurisdiction over that kind of case. Some courts have very limited jurisdiction, while others have the power to hear almost any case.

Trial courts
Determine the facts of a particular dispute and apply to those facts the law given by earlier appellate court decisions

Jurisdiction
A court's power to hear a case

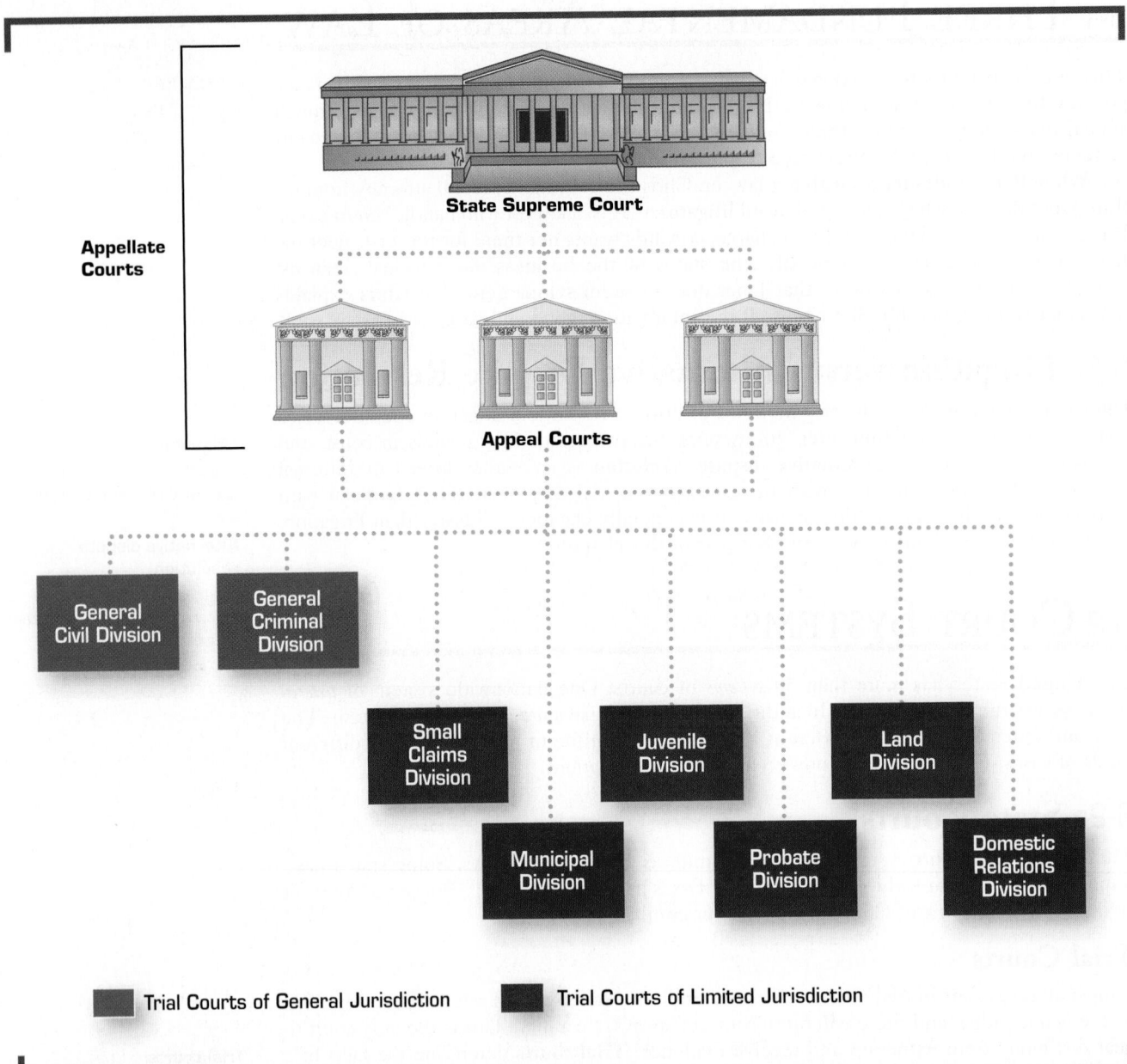

State Supreme Court

Appellate Courts

Appeal Courts

General Civil Division

General Criminal Division

Small Claims Division

Juvenile Division

Land Division

Municipal Division

Probate Division

Domestic Relations Division

Trial Courts of General Jurisdiction   Trial Courts of Limited Jurisdiction

EXHIBIT 6.1   A trial court determines facts, while an appeals court ensures that the lower court correctly applied the law to those facts.

Subject Matter Jurisdiction

Subject matter jurisdiction
A court's authority to hear a particular type of case

Subject matter jurisdiction means that a court has the authority to hear a particular type of case.

Trial Courts of Limited Jurisdiction.   These courts may hear only certain types of cases. Small claims court has jurisdiction only over civil lawsuits involving a maximum of, say, $5,000 (the amount varies from state to state). A juvenile court hears only cases involving minors. Probate court is devoted to settling the estates of deceased persons, though in some states it will hear certain other cases as well.

Trial Courts of General Jurisdiction.

Trial courts of general jurisdiction, however, can hear a very broad range of cases. The most important court, for our purposes, is the general civil division. This court may hear virtually any civil lawsuit. In one day it might hear a $450 million shareholders' derivative lawsuit, an employment issue involving freedom of religion, and a foreclosure on a mortgage. Most of the cases we study start in this court.[1] If Enviro-Vision's case against Coastal goes to trial in a state court, it will begin in the trial court of general jurisdiction.

Personal Jurisdiction

In addition to subject matter jurisdiction, courts must also have **personal jurisdiction** over the defendant. Personal jurisdiction is the legal authority to require the defendant to stand trial, pay judgments, and the like. When plaintiffs file lawsuits, defendants sometimes make *a special appearance* to challenge a court's personal jurisdiction. If the court agrees with the defendant's argument, the lawsuit will be dismissed.

> **Personal jurisdiction**
> A court's authority to bind the defendant to its decisions

Personal jurisdiction generally exists, if:

1. For individuals, the defendant is a resident of the state in which a lawsuit is filed. For companies, the defendant is doing business in that state.

2. The defendant takes a formal step to defend a lawsuit. Most papers filed with a court count as formal steps, but special appearances do not.

3. A **summons** is *served* on a defendant. A summons is the court's written notice that a lawsuit has been filed against the defendant. The summons must be delivered to the defendant when she is physically within the state in which the lawsuit is filed.

> **Summons**
> The court's written notice that a lawsuit has been filed against the defendant

Corporations are required to hire a registered agent in any state in which they do business. If a registered agent receives a summons, then the corporation is served.

4. A **long-arm statute** applies. If all else fails—the defendant does not reside in the state, does not defend the lawsuit, and has not been served with a summons while in the state—a court still can obtain jurisdiction under long-arm statutes. These statutes typically claim jurisdiction over someone who commits a tort, signs a contract, or conducts "regular business activities" in the state.

> **Long-arm statute**
> A statute that gives a court jurisdiction over someone who commits a tort, signs a contract, or conducts "regular business activities" in the state

As a general rule, courts tend to apply long-arm statutes aggressively, hauling defendants into their courtrooms. However, the due process guarantees in the United States Constitution require fundamental fairness in the application of long-arm statutes. Therefore, courts can claim personal jurisdiction only if a defendant has had *minimum contacts* with a state. In other words, it is unfair to require a defendant to stand trial in another state if he has had no meaningful interaction with that state.

In the following Landmark Case, the Supreme Court established the "minimum contacts" rule.

---

[1]Note that the actual name of the court of general jurisdiction will vary from state to state. In many states, it is called *superior court* because it has power superior to the courts of limited jurisdiction. In New York, it is called *supreme court* (anything to confuse the layperson); in some states, it is called *court of common pleas*; in Oregon and other states, it is a *circuit court*. Within this branch, some states are beginning to establish specialized business and high-tech courts to hear complex commercial disputes.

Landmark Case

INTERNATIONAL SHOE CO. V. STATE OF WASHINGTON

326 U.S. 310
Supreme Court of the United States, 1945

Facts: Although International Shoe manufactured footwear only in St. Louis, Missouri, it sold its products nationwide. It did not have offices or warehouses in Washington State, but it did send about a dozen salespeople there. The salespeople rented space in hotels and businesses, displayed sample products, and took orders. They were not authorized to collect payments from customers.

When Washington State sought contributions to the state's unemployment fund, International Shoe refused to pay. Washington sued. The company argued that it was not engaged in business in the state, and, therefore, that Washington courts had no jurisdiction over it.

The Supreme Court of Washington ruled that International Shoe did have sufficient contacts with the state to justify a lawsuit there. International Shoe appealed to the United States Supreme Court.

Issue: *Did International Shoe have sufficient minimum contacts in Washington State to permit jurisdiction there?*

Excerpts from Chief Justice Stone's Decision:
Appellant insists that its activities within the state were not sufficient to manifest its "presence" there and that in its absence, the state courts were without jurisdiction, that consequently, it was a denial of due process for the state to subject appellant to suit. Appellant [International Shoe] refers to those cases in which it was said that the mere solicitation of orders for the purchase of goods within a state, to be accepted without the state and filled by shipment of the purchased goods interstate, does not render the corporation seller amenable to suit within the state.

Historically the jurisdiction of courts to render judgment is grounded on their power over the defendant's person. Hence his presence within the territorial jurisdiction of a court was prerequisite to a judgment personally binding him. But now due process requires that [a defendant] have certain minimum contacts with it such that the maintenance of the suit does not offend "traditional notions of fair play and substantial justice."

Since the corporate personality is a fiction, its "presence" can be manifested only by those activities of the corporation's agent within the state which courts will deem to be sufficient to satisfy the demands of due process.

"Presence" in the state in this sense has never been doubted when the activities of the corporation there have not only been continuous and systematic, but also give rise to the liabilities sued on, even though no consent to be sued or authorization to an agent to accept service of process has been given. Conversely, it has been generally recognized that the casual presence of the corporate agent or even his conduct of single or isolated items of activities in a state in the corporation's behalf are not enough to subject it to suit on causes of action unconnected with the activities there. To require the corporation in such circumstances to defend the suit away from its home or other jurisdiction where it carries on more substantial activities has been thought to lay too great and unreasonable a burden on the corporation to comport with due process.

But to the extent that a corporation exercises the privilege of conducting activities within a state, it enjoys the benefits and protection of the laws of that state. The exercise of that privilege may give rise to obligations.

Applying these standards, the activities carried on in behalf of appellant in the State of Washington were neither irregular nor casual. They were systematic and continuous throughout the years in question. They resulted in a large volume of interstate business, in the course of which appellant received the benefits and protection of the laws of the state, including the right to resort to the courts for the enforcement of its rights. The obligation which is here sued upon arose out of those very activities. It is evident that these operations establish sufficient contacts or ties with the state of the forum to make it reasonable and just, according to our traditional conception of fair play and substantial justice, to permit the state to enforce the obligations which appellant has incurred there.

The state may maintain the present suit to collect the tax.

Affirmed.

Appellate Courts

Appellate courts are entirely different from trial courts. Three or more judges hear the case. There are no juries, ever. These courts do not hear witnesses or take new evidence. They hear appeals of cases already tried below. **Appeals courts** generally accept the facts given to them by trial courts and review the trial record to see if the court made errors of law.

Higher courts generally defer to lower courts on factual findings. Juries and trial court judges see all evidence as it is presented, and they are in the best position to evaluate it. An appeals court will accept a factual finding unless there was *no evidence at all* to support it. If the jury decides that Tony Caruso committed suicide, the appeals court will normally accept that fact, even if the appeals judges consider the jury's conclusion dubious. On the other hand, if a jury concluded that Tony had been murdered, an appeals court would overturn that finding if neither side had introduced any evidence of murder during the trial.

An appeals court reviews the trial record to make sure that the lower court correctly applied the law to the facts. If the trial court made an **error of law**, the appeals court may require a new trial. Suppose the jury concludes that Tony Caruso committed suicide but votes to award Enviro-Vision $1 million because it feels sorry for Beth Smiles. That is an error of law: If Tony committed suicide, Beth is entitled to nothing. An appellate court will reverse the decision. Or suppose that the trial judge permitted a friend of Tony's to state that he was certain Tony would never commit suicide. Normally, such opinions are not permissible in trial, and it was a legal error for the judge to allow the jury to hear it.

Court of Appeals.   The party that loses at the trial court may appeal to the intermediate court of appeals. The party filing the appeal is the **appellant**. The party opposing the appeal (because it won at trial) is the **appellee**.

This court allows both sides to submit written arguments on the case, called **briefs**. Each side then appears for oral argument, usually before a panel of three judges. The appellant's lawyer has about 15 minutes to convince the judges that the trial court made serious errors of law, and that the decision should be **reversed**; that is, nullified. The appellee's lawyer has the same time to persuade the court that the trial court acted correctly, and that the result should be **affirmed**; that is, permitted to stand

State Supreme Court.   This is the highest court in the state, and it accepts some appeals from the court of appeals. In most states, there is no absolute right to appeal to the Supreme Court. If the high court regards a legal issue as important, it accepts the case. It then takes briefs and hears oral argument just as the appeals court did. If it considers the matter unimportant, it refuses to hear the case, meaning that the court of appeals' ruling is the final word on the case.[2]

In most states, seven judges, often called *justices*, sit on the Supreme Court. They have the final word on state law.

6-2b Federal Courts

As discussed in Chapter 1, federal courts are established by the U.S. Constitution, which limits what kinds of cases can be brought in any federal court. See Exhibit 6.2. For our purposes, two kinds of civil lawsuits are permitted in federal court: federal question cases and diversity cases.

---

[2]In some states with smaller populations, there is no intermediate appeals court. All appeals from trial courts go directly to the state supreme court.

Appeals courts
Higher courts that review the trial record to see if the court made errors of law

Error of law
Because of this, the appeals court may require a new trial.

Appellant
The party filing the appeal

Appellee
The party opposing the appeal

Briefs
Written arguments on the case

Reversed
Nullified

Affirmed
Permitted to stand

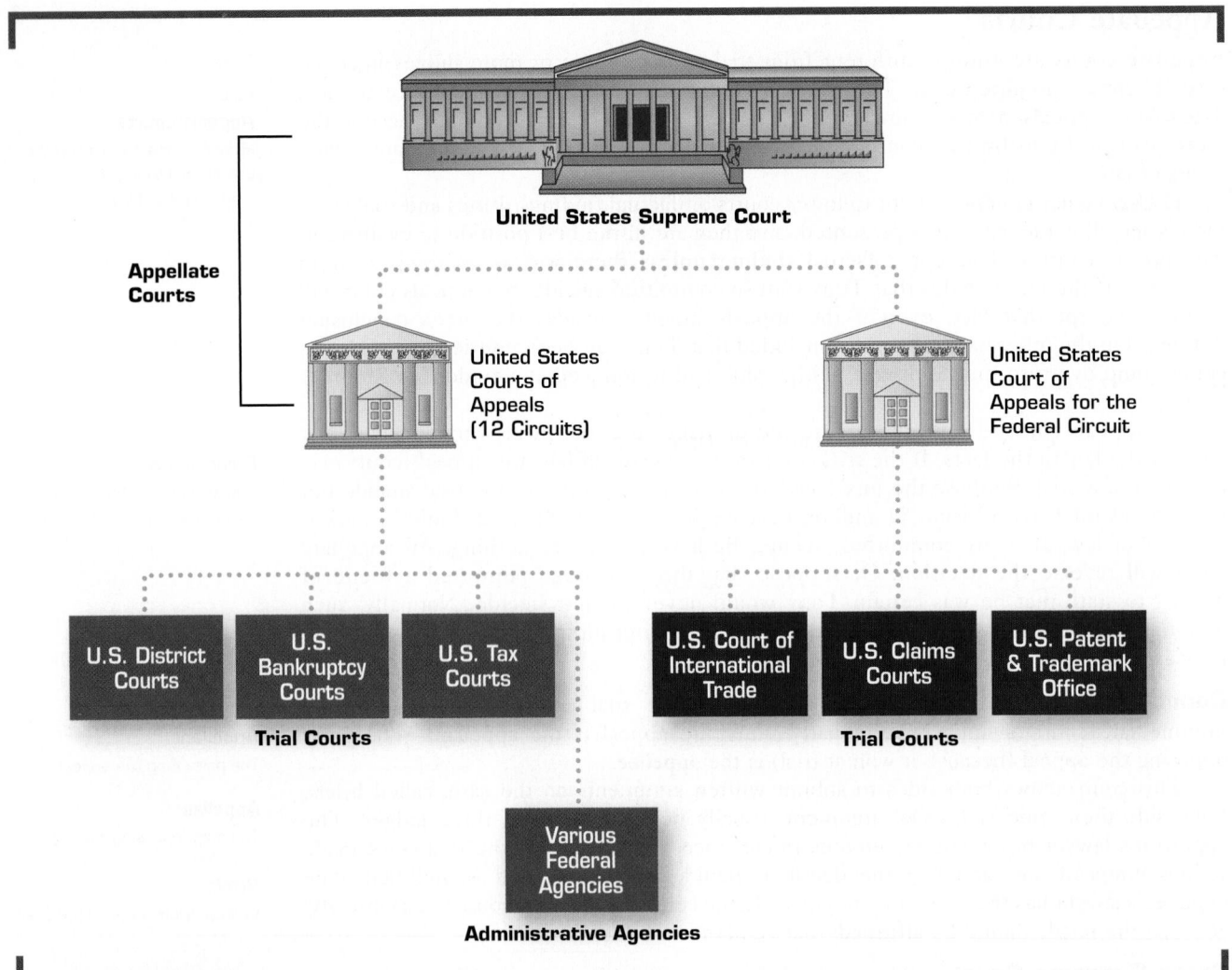

United States Supreme Court

Appellate Courts

United States Courts of Appeals (12 Circuits)

United States Court of Appeals for the Federal Circuit

U.S. District Courts

U.S. Bankruptcy Courts

U.S. Tax Courts

Trial Courts

U.S. Court of International Trade

U.S. Claims Courts

U.S. Patent & Trademark Office

Trial Courts

Various Federal Agencies

Administrative Agencies

EXHIBIT 6.2

Federal Question Cases

Federal question

A case in which the claim is based on the United States Constitution, a federal statute, or a federal treaty

A claim based on the U.S. Constitution, a federal statute, or a federal treaty is called a **federal question** case.[3] Federal courts have jurisdiction over these cases. If the Environmental Protection Agency (EPA), a part of the federal government, orders Logging Company not to cut in a particular forest, and Logging Company claims that the agency has wrongly deprived it of its property, that suit is based on a federal statute and is thus a federal question. If Little Retailer sues Mega Retailer, claiming that Mega has established a monopoly, that claim is also based on a statute—the Sherman Antitrust Act—and creates federal question jurisdiction. Enviro-Vision's potential suit merely concerns an insurance contract. The federal district court has no federal question jurisdiction over the case.

[3] 28 U.S.C. §1331 governs federal question jurisdiction and 28 U.S.C. §1332 covers diversity jurisdiction.

Diversity Cases

Even if no federal law is at issue, federal courts have **diversity jurisdiction** when (1) the plaintiff and defendant are citizens of different states *and* (2) the amount in dispute exceeds $75,000. The theory behind diversity jurisdiction is that courts of one state might be biased against citizens of another state. To ensure fairness, the parties have the option to use a federal court as a neutral playing field.

Enviro-Vision is located in Oregon and Coastal Insurance is incorporated in Georgia.[4] They are citizens of different states and the amount in dispute far exceeds $75,000. Janet could file this case in United States District Court based on diversity jurisdiction.

Diversity jurisdiction
Applies when (1) the plaintiff and defendant are citizens of different states and (2) the amount in dispute exceeds $75,000

Trial Courts

United States District Court. This is the primary trial court in the federal system. The nation is divided into about 94 districts, and each has a district court. States with smaller populations have one district. States with larger populations have several; Texas is divided geographically into four districts.

Other Trial Courts. There are other, specialized trial courts in the federal system. Bankruptcy Court, Tax Court, and the United States Court of International Trade all handle name-appropriate cases. The United States Claims Court hears cases brought against the United States, typically on contract disputes. The Foreign Intelligence Surveillance Court is a very specialized, secret court that oversees requests for surveillance warrants against suspected foreign agents.

Judges. The president of the United States nominates all federal court judges, from district court to Supreme Court. The nominees must be confirmed by the Senate. Once confirmed, federal judges serve for "life in good behavior." Many federal judges literally stay on the job for life. Judge Wesley Brown of Kansas holds the records as the oldest and the longest-serving federal judge. Appointed to the federal bench by president Kennedy at age 55, Brown had heard federal cases for almost 50 years at the time of his death at age 104.

Appellate Courts

United States Courts of Appeals. These are the intermediate courts of appeals. As the following map shows, they are divided into "circuits," which are geographical areas. There are 11 numbered circuits, hearing appeals from district courts. For example, an appeal from the Northern District of Illinois would go to the Court of Appeals for the Seventh Circuit.

A twelfth court, the Court of Appeals for the District of Columbia, hears appeals only from the district court of Washington, D.C. This court is particularly powerful because so many suits about federal statutes begin in the district court for the District of Columbia. Also in Washington is the Thirteenth Court of Appeals, known as the Federal Circuit. It hears appeals from specialized trial courts, as shown in Exhibit 6.2.

Within one circuit there are many circuit judges, up to about 50 judges in the largest circuit, the Ninth. When a case is appealed, three judges hear the appeal, taking briefs and hearing oral arguments.

---

[4]For diversity purposes, a corporation is a citizen of the state in which it is incorporated and the state in which it has its principal place of business.

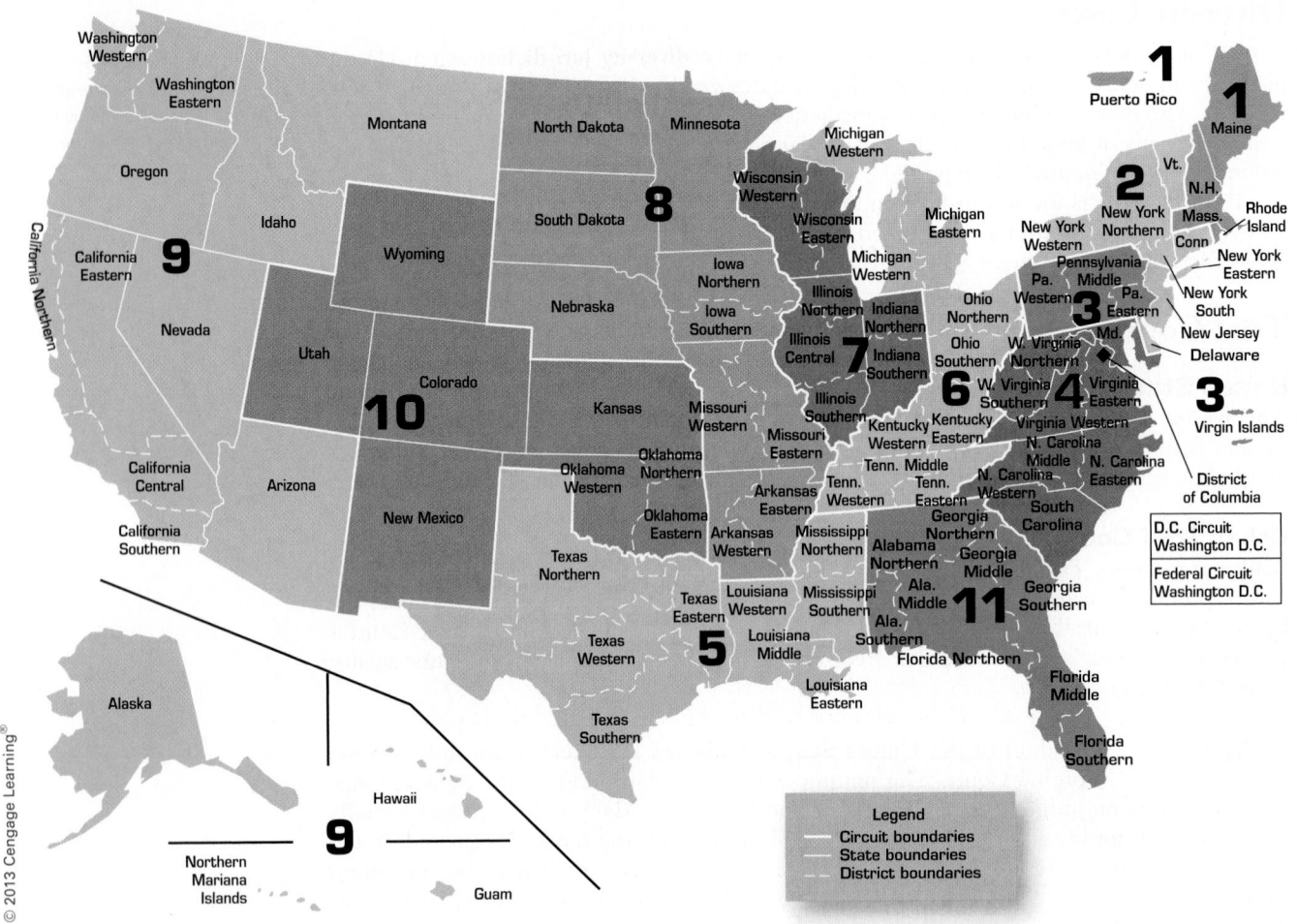

United States Supreme Court.   This is the highest court in the country. There are nine justices on the Court. One justice is the chief justice and the other eight are associate justices. When they decide a case, each justice casts an equal vote. The chief justice's special power comes from his authority to assign opinions to a given justice. The justice assigned to write an opinion has an opportunity to control the precise language and thus to influence the voting by other justices.

The Supreme Court has the power to hear appeals in any federal case, and in certain cases that began in state courts. Generally, it is up to the Court whether or not it will accept a case. A party that wants the Supreme Court to review a lower court ruling must file a petition for a **writ of** *certiorari*, asking the Court to hear the case. Four of the nine justices must vote in favor of hearing a case before a writ will be granted. The Court receives several thousand requests every year but usually accepts fewer than 100. Most cases accepted involve either an important issue of constitutional law or an interpretation of a major federal statute.

Writ of *certiorari*

A petition asking the Supreme Court to hear a case

EXAM Strategy

Question: Mark has sued Janelle, based on the state common law of negligence. He is testifying in court, explaining how Janelle backed a rented truck out of her driveway and slammed into his Lamborghini, causing $82,000 in damages. Where would this take place?

(a) State appeals court

(b) United States Court of Appeals

(c) State trial court

(d) federal district court

(e) Either state trial court or federal district court

Strategy: The question asks about trial and appellate courts, and also about state versus federal courts. One issue at a time, please. What are the different functions of trial and appellate courts? *Trial* courts use witnesses, and often juries, to resolve factual disputes. *Appellate* courts never hear witnesses and never have juries. Applying that distinction to these facts tells us whether we are in a trial or appeals court.

Next Issue: *State* trial courts may hear lawsuits on virtually any issue. *Federal District Courts* may only hear two kinds of cases: federal question (those involving a statute or constitutional provision), or diversity (where the parties are from different states *and* the amount at issue is $75,000 or higher). Apply what we know to the facts here.

Result: We are in a trial court because Mark is testifying. Could we be in Federal District Court? No. The suit is based on state common law. This is not a diversity case because the parties live in the same state. We are in a state trial court.

6-3 LITIGATION

Janet Booker decides to file the Enviro-Vision suit in the Oregon trial court. She thinks that a state court judge may take the issue more seriously than a federal district court judge.

6-3a Pleadings

The documents that begin a lawsuit are called the **pleadings**. These consist of the complaint, the answer, and sometimes a reply.

Complaint

The plaintiff files in court a **complaint**, which is a short, plain statement of the facts she is alleging and the legal claims she is making. The purpose of the complaint is to inform the defendant of the general nature of the claims and the need to come into court and protect his interests.

Janet Booker files the complaint, as shown below. Since Enviro-Vision is a partnership, she files the suit on behalf of Beth personally.

Pleadings

The documents that begin a lawsuit, consisting of the complaint, the answer, and sometimes a reply

Complaint

A short, plain statement of the facts alleged and the legal claims made

STATE OF OREGON
CIRCUIT COURT

Multnomah County   Civil Action No. _____

_____
Elizabeth Smiles,
Plaintiff
                                                            JURY TRIAL DEMANDED

v.

Coastal Insurance Company, Inc.,
Defendant

_____

COMPLAINT

Plaintiff Elizabeth Smiles states that:

1. She is a citizen of Multnomah County, Oregon.
2. Defendant Coastal Insurance Company, Inc., is incorporated under the laws of Georgia and has as its usual place of business 148 Thrift Street, Savannah, Georgia.
3. On or about July 5, 2015, plaintiff Smiles ("Smiles"), Defendant Coastal Insurance Co, Inc. ("Coastal") and Anthony Caruso entered into an insurance contract ("the contract"), a copy of which is annexed hereto as Exhibit "A." This contract was signed by all parties or their authorized agents, in Multnomah County, Oregon.
4. The contract obligates Coastal to pay to Smiles the sum of two million dollars ($2 million) if Anthony Caruso should die accidentally.
5. On or about September 20, 2015, Anthony Caruso accidentally drowned and died while swimming.
6. Coastal has refused to pay any sum pursuant to the contract.
7. Coastal has knowingly, willingly and unreasonably refused to honor its obligations under the contract.

WHEREFORE, plaintiff Elizabeth Smiles demands judgment against defendant Coastal for all monies due under the contract; demands triple damages for Coastal's knowing, willing, and unreasonable refusal to honor its obligations; and demands all costs and attorney's fees, with interest.
ELIZABETH SMILES,
By her attorney,
[Signed]
Janet Booker
Pruitt, Booker & Bother
983 Joy Avenue
Portland, OR
October 18, 2015

Service

When she files the complaint in court, Janet gets a summons, which is a paper ordering the defendant to answer the complaint within 20 days. A sheriff or constable then *serves* the two papers by delivering them to the defendant. Coastal's headquarters are in Georgia, so the state of Oregon has required Coastal to specify someone as its agent for receipt of service in Oregon.

Answer

Once the complaint and summons are served, Coastal has 20 days in which to file an answer. Coastal's answer, shown below, is a brief reply to each of the allegations in the complaint. The answer tells the court and the plaintiff exactly what issues are in dispute. Because Coastal admits that the parties entered into the contract that Beth claims they did, there is no need for her to prove that in court. The court can focus its attention on the disputed issue: whether Tony Caruso died accidentally.

```
                          STATE OF OREGON
                           CIRCUIT COURT

Multnomah County                              Civil Action No. 09-5626
_____
Elizabeth Smiles,
Plaintiff
v.
Coastal Insurance Company, Inc.,
Defendant
_____

                              ANSWER

Defendant Coastal Insurance Company, Inc., answers the complaint as follows:

    1. Admit.
    2. Admit.
    3. Admit.
    4. Admit.
    5. Deny.
    6. Admit.
    7. Deny.

COASTAL INSURANCE COMPANY, INC.,
By its attorney,
[Signed]
Richard B. Stewart
Kiley, Robbins, Stewart & Glote
333 Victory Boulevard
Portland, OR
October 30, 2015
```

If the defendant fails to answer in time, the plaintiff will ask for a **default judgment**. In granting a default judgment, the judge accepts every allegation in the complaint as true and renders a decision that the plaintiff wins without a trial.

Recently, two men sued PepsiCo, claiming that the company stole the idea for Aquafina water from them. They argued that they should receive a portion of the profits for every bottle of Aquafina ever sold.

PepsiCo failed to file a timely answer, and the judge entered a default judgment in the amount of $1.26 billion. On appeal, the default judgment was overturned and PepsiCo was able to escape paying the massive sum, but other defendants are sometimes not so lucky.

It is important to respond to courts on time.

Counterclaim

Sometimes a defendant does more than merely answer a complaint and files a **counterclaim**, meaning a second lawsuit by the defendant against the plaintiff. Suppose that after her complaint was filed in court, Beth had written a letter to the newspaper, calling Coastal a bunch of "thieves and scoundrels who spend their days mired in fraud and larceny." Coastal would not have found that amusing. The company's answer would have included a counterclaim against Beth for libel, claiming that she falsely accused the insurer of serious criminal acts. Coastal would have demanded money damages.

If Coastal counterclaimed, Beth would have to file a **reply**, which is simply an answer to a counterclaim. Beth's reply would be similar to Coastal's answer, admitting or denying the various allegations.

Default judgment
A decision that the plaintiff wins without trial because the defendant failed to answer in time

Counterclaim
A second lawsuit by the defendant against the plaintiff

Reply
An answer to a counterclaim

Class Actions

Class action

One plaintiff represents the entire group of plaintiffs, including those who are unaware of the lawsuit or even unaware they were harmed

Suppose Janet uncovers evidence that Coastal denies 80 percent of all life insurance claims, calling them suicide. She could ask the court to permit a **class action**. If the court granted her request, she would represent the entire group of plaintiffs, including those who are unaware of the lawsuit or even unaware they were harmed. Class actions can give the plaintiffs much greater leverage, because the defendant's potential liability is vastly increased. In the back of her mind, Janet has thoughts of a class action, *if* she can uncover evidence that Coastal has used a claim of suicide to deny coverage to a large number of claimants.

Notice how potent a class action can be. From his small town in Maine, Ernie decides to get rich quickly. On the Internet, he advertises "Energy Breakthrough! Cut your heating costs 15 percent for only $25." In response, 100,000 people send him their money, and they receive a photocopied graph, illustrating that if you wear two sweaters instead of one, you will feel 15 percent warmer. Ernie has deceitfully earned $2,500,000 in pure profit. What can the angry homeowners do? Under the laws of fraud and consumer protection, they have a legitimate claim to their $25, and perhaps even to treble damages ($75). But few will sue, because the time and effort required would be greater than the money recovered.

Economists analyze such legal issues in terms of *efficiency*. The laws against Ernie's fraud are clear and well intended, but they will not help in this case because it is too expensive for 100,000 people to litigate such a small claim. The effort would be hugely *inefficient*, both for the homeowners and for society generally. The economic reality may permit Ernie to evade the law's grasp.

That is one reason we have class actions. A dozen or so "heating plan" buyers can all hire the same lawyer. This attorney will file court papers in Maine on behalf of *everyone*, nationwide, who has been swindled by Ernie—including the 99,988 people who have yet to be notified that they are part of the case. Now the con artist, instead of facing a few harmless suits for $25, must respond to a multimillion-dollar claim being handled by an experienced lawyer. Treble damages become menacing: Three times $25 times 100,000 is no joke, even to a cynic like Ernie. He may also be forced to pay for the plaintiffs' attorney, as well as all costs of notifying class members and disbursing money to them. With one lawyer representing an entire class, the legal system has become fiercely efficient.

Judgment on the Pleadings

Motion

A formal request to the court that it take some step or issue some order.

Motion to dismiss

A request that the court terminate a case without permitting it to go further.

A party can ask the court for a judgment based simply on the pleadings themselves, by filing a motion to dismiss. A **motion** is a formal request to the court that it take some step or issue some order. During a lawsuit, the parties file many motions. A **motion to dismiss** is a request that the court terminate a case without permitting it to go further. Suppose that a state law requires claims on life insurance contracts to be filed within three years, and Beth files her claim four years after Tony's death. Coastal would move to dismiss based on this late filing. The court might well agree, and Beth would never get into court.

Discovery

Few cases are dismissed on the pleadings. Most proceed quickly to the next step.

The theory behind civil litigation is that the best outcome is a negotiated settlement and that parties will move toward agreement if they understand the opponent's case. That is likeliest to occur if both sides have an opportunity to examine most of the evidence the other side will bring to trial. Further, if a case does go all the way to trial, efficient and fair litigation cannot take place in a courtroom filled with surprises. On television dramas, witnesses say astonishing things that amaze the courtroom (and keep viewers hooked through the next commercial). In real trials, the lawyers know in advance the answers to practically all questions asked because discovery has allowed them to see the opponent's documents and question its witnesses. The following are the most important forms of discovery.

Interrogatories.   These are written questions that the opposing party must answer, in writing, under oath.

Depositions.   These provide a chance for one party's lawyer to question the other party, or a potential witness, under oath. The person being questioned is the **deponent**. Lawyers for both parties are present. During depositions, and in trial, good lawyers choose words carefully and ask questions calculated to advance their cause. A fine line separates ethical, probing questions from those that are tricky, and a similar line divides answers that are merely unhelpful from perjury.

Deponent
The person being questioned in a deposition

Production of Documents and Things.   Each side may ask the other side to produce relevant documents for inspection and copying; to produce physical objects, such as part of a car alleged to be defective; and for permission to enter on land to make an inspection, for example, at the scene of an accident.

Physical and Mental Examination.   A party may ask the court to order an examination of the other party, if his physical or mental condition is relevant, for example, in a case of medical malpractice.

Janet Booker begins her discovery with interrogatories. Her goal is to learn Coastal's basic position and factual evidence and then follow up with more detailed questioning during depositions. Her interrogatories ask for every fact Coastal relied on in denying the claim. She asks for the names of all witnesses, the identity of all documents, including electronic records and the description of all things or objects that they considered. She requests the names of all corporate officers who played any role in the decision and of any expert witnesses Coastal plans to call. Interrogatory No. 18 demands extensive information on all *other* claims in the past three years that Coastal has denied based on alleged suicide. Janet is looking for evidence that would support a class action.

Beth remarks on how thorough the interrogatories are. "This will tell us what their case is." Janet frowns and looks less optimistic: She has done this before.

Coastal has 30 days to answer Janet's interrogatories. Before it responds, Coastal mails to Janet a notice of deposition, stating its intention to depose Beth Smiles. Beth and Janet will go to the office of Coastal's lawyer, and Beth will answer questions under oath. But at the same time Coastal sends the first deposition notice, it also sends *25 other notices of deposition*. The company will depose Karen Caruso as soon as Beth's deposition is over. Coastal also plans to depose all seven employees of Enviro-Vision; three neighbors who lived near Tony and Karen's beach house; two policemen who participated in the search; the doctor and two nurses involved in the case; Tony's physician; Jerry Johnson, Tony's tennis partner; Craig Bergson, a college roommate; a couple who had dinner with Tony and Karen a week before his death; and several other people.

Beth is appalled. Janet explains that some of these people might have relevant information. But there may be another reason that Coastal is doing this: The company wants to make this litigation hurt. Janet will have to attend every one of these depositions. Costs will skyrocket.

Janet files a **motion for a protective order**. This is a request that the court limit Coastal's discovery by decreasing the number of depositions. Janet also calls Rich Stewart and suggests that they discuss what depositions are really necessary. Rich insists that all of the depositions are important. This is a $2 million case, and Coastal is entitled to protect itself. As both lawyers know, **the parties are entitled to discover anything that could reasonably lead to valid evidence.**

But there may be another reason that Coastal is doing this: The company wants to make this litigation hurt.

> But there may be another reason that Coastal is doing this: The company wants to make this litigation hurt.

Motion for a protective order
Request that the court limit discovery

Before Beth's deposition date arrives, Rich sends Coastal's answers to Enviro-Vision's interrogatories. The answers contain no useful information whatsoever. For example, Interrogatory No. 10 asked, "If you claim that Anthony Caruso committed suicide, describe every fact upon which you rely in reaching that conclusion." Coastal's answer simply says, "His state of mind, his poor business affairs, and the circumstances of his death all indicate suicide."

Janet calls Rich and complains that the interrogatory answers are a bad joke. Rich disagrees, saying that it is the best information they have so early in the case. After they debate it for 20 minutes, Rich offers to settle the case for $100,000. Janet refuses and makes no counteroffer.

Janet files a **motion to compel answers to interrogatories**, in other words, a formal request that the court order Coastal to supply more complete answers. Janet submits a **memorandum** with the motion, which is a supporting argument. Although it is only a few pages long, the memorandum takes several hours of online research and writing to prepare—more costs. Janet also informs Rich Stewart that Beth will not appear for the deposition because Coastal's interrogatory answers are inadequate.

Rich now files *his* motion to compel, asking the court to order Beth Smiles to appear for her deposition. The court hears all of the motions together. Janet argues that Coastal's interrogatory answers are hopelessly uninformative and defeat the whole purpose of discovery. She claims that Coastal's large number of depositions creates a huge and unfair expense for a small firm.

Rich claims that the interrogatory answers are the best that Coastal can do thus far and that Coastal will supplement the answers when more information becomes available. He argues against Interrogatory No. 18, the one in which Janet asked for the names of other policyholders whom Coastal considered suicides. He claims that Janet is engaging in a fishing expedition that would violate the privacy of Coastal's insurance customers and provide no information relevant to this case. He demands that Janet make Beth available for a deposition.

These discovery rulings are critical because they will color the entire lawsuit. A trial judge has to make many discovery decisions before a case reaches trial. At times, the judge must weigh the need of one party to see documents against the other side's need for privacy. One device a judge can use in reaching a discovery ruling is an **in camera inspection**, meaning that the judge views the requested documents alone, with no lawyers present, and decides whether the other side is entitled to view them.

E-Discovery.   The biggest change in litigation in the last decade is the explosive rise of electronic discovery. Companies send hundreds, or thousands, or millions of emails—every

day. Businesses large and small have vast amounts of data stored electronically. And many people post volumes of personal information on social media sites. All of this information is potentially subject to discovery.

It is enormously time-consuming and expensive for companies to locate all of the relevant material, separate it from irrelevant or confidential matter, and furnish it. A firm may be obligated to furnish *millions* of emails to the opposing party. In one case, a defendant had to pay 31 lawyers full-time, for six months, just to wade through the e-ocean of documents and figure out which had to be supplied and how to produce them. Not surprisingly, this data eruption has created a new industry: high-tech companies that assist law firms in finding, sorting, and delivering electronic data.

Who is to say what must be supplied? What if an email string contains individual emails that are clearly privileged (meaning a party need not divulge them), but others that are not privileged? May a company refuse to furnish the entire string? Many will try. However, some courts have ruled that companies seeking to protect email strings must create a log describing every individual email and allow the court to determine which ones are privileged.[5]

Social media further complicates discovery. When a Facebook profile or Twitter account is public, opposing parties are free to rummage through the treasure trove of personal information. One recent study found that the word "Facebook" occurred in one-third of all U.S. divorce filings—and more than 80 percent of divorce lawyers have used social media evidence in court. Likewise, many plaintiffs have lost their tort cases because of incriminating online photos of them engaged in activities that undermine their claims. (What, you claim you can never work at a desk again, but you can still waterski?)

But what about access to a *private* social media profile? To protect people's privacy, courts require parties to show that the discovery request is reasonably calculated to lead to relevant and admissible evidence. For example, one court denied a company's request that an employee supply a list of all of his time-stamped social media postings during a four-year period because the request was unreasonably burdensome and unlikely to show whether the worker had taken lunch breaks.[6]

Another court found that limited discovery of a plaintiff's Twitter and Facebook accounts was proper because her online activity would likely reveal information about whether or not she was experiencing the emotional distress her lawsuit claimed.[7]

Both sides in litigation sometimes use gamesmanship during discovery. For example, if an individual sues a large corporation, the company may deliberately make discovery so expensive that the plaintiff cannot afford the legal fees. And if a plaintiff has a bad case, he might intentionally try to make the discovery process more expensive for the defendant than his settlement offer.

In the following case, it was not just legends that were forever—discovery was, too. Was the plaintiff's failure to cooperate part of a calculated plan to tire Nike into settling or just a costly decision?

LEGENDS ARE FOREVER, INC. v. NIKE, INC.

2013 WL 6086461, 2013 U.S. Dist. LEXIS 164091
U.S. District Court, Northern District, New York, 2013

Facts: Legends are Forever, Inc. (Legends) trademarked the slogan "Legends are Forever." When Nike used the slogan in an ad campaign featuring basketball player Kobe Bryant, Legends sued Nike.

But, during discovery, Legends repeatedly failed to comply with Nike's reasonable requests. Ultimately, Nike was forced to file a motion to compel Legends to produce the requested documents and witnesses. So, Nike requested more than just discovery: It also asked the court for recovery of all of the costs and fees it incurred in litigating the motion to compel, totaling $25,186.91. This sum included Nike's attorney's fees (ranging from $250 to $450 per hour) and all the travel expenses incurred by the two Nike attorneys who attended the hearing on the motion to compel.

The court agreed with Nike, granting it both discovery and its fees. Legends challenged the order, arguing that a small company should not have to pay for Nike's high-priced attorneys.

---

[5]Universal Service Fund Telephone Billing Practices Litigation, 232 F.R.D. 669 (D. Kan. 2005).
[6]Jewell v. Aaron's Inc., 2013 WL 3770837 (N.D. Ga. 2013).
[7]Kear v. Kohl's Department Stores, Inc., 2013 WL 3088922 (D. Kan. 2013).

Issue: *What is a reasonable penalty for unacceptable behavior during discovery?*

Excerpts from Magistrate Judge Peebles's Decision:

Discovery in this case has proceeded at an unacceptably slow pace, and Nike has experienced considerable difficulties in obtaining compliance by plaintiff with legitimate discovery demands. An award of costs and attorney's fees is warranted.

Now the task of the court shifts to determining the appropriate amount to award. Fee awards are awarded by determining a reasonable fee, reached by multiplying a reasonable hourly rate by the number of reasonably expended hours.

When establishing a reasonable rate, courts consider the time and labor required, the novelty of the questions, and the level of skill required to perform the legal service properly [among other factors]. Attorney's fees awarded as sanctions are not intended only as compensation of reimbursement for legal services, but also serve to deter abusive litigation practices and, as such, district courts have discretion in determining the amount of an attorney's fee awarded as sanctions. I conclude that the court should apply the following rates: $350 to $250 per hour.

I have reduced the number of hours upon which fees will be awarded for two reasons. First, it appears that several of the entries are excessive, given the description of the work performed. As one example, Nike chose to send two attorneys to the hearing, apparently as a result of a strategic decision. The motion, however, was relatively straightforward and not particularly complex. While Nike certainly retains the prerogative to send multiple attorneys to such a hearing, I decline to award costs and attorney's fees based upon that duplication of effort. Based upon the foregoing, I am awarding attorney's fees in the amount of $11,146.25,

In addition to attorney's fees, Nike has also sought recovery of costs representing travel expenses incurred for the hearing. It is appropriate to award the expense associated with [only one of Nike's attorneys] travel to the hearing, in the amount of $1,186.57.

Plaintiff Legends now complains that, as a small corporation, it would be economically disadvantaged by the award. Nike, however, despite its size and prominence, having been sued, is entitled to the same discovery as any other litigant. When discovery is sought but not provided, it is fair and appropriate to award costs and attorney's fees, notwithstanding the disparity in size of the two parties involved.

Nike, Inc., is hereby awarded the sum of $12,332.82, representing reasonable costs and attorney's fees associated with having to bring and argue the recent motion to compel discovery.

In the Enviro-Vision case, the judge rules that Coastal must furnish more complete answers to the interrogatories, especially as to why the company denied the claim. However, he rules against Interrogatory No. 18, the one concerning other claims Coastal has denied. This simple ruling kills Janet's hope of making a class action of the case. He orders Beth to appear for the deposition. As to future depositions, Coastal may take any 10 but then may take additional depositions only by demonstrating to the court that the deponents have useful information.

Rich proceeds to take Beth's deposition. It takes two full days. He asks about Enviro-Vision's past and present. He learns that Tony appeared to have won their biggest contract ever from Rapid City, Oregon, but that he then lost it when he had a fight with Rapid City's mayor. He inquires into Tony's mood, learns that he was depressed, and probes in every direction he can to find evidence of suicidal motivation. Janet and Rich argue frequently over questions and whether Beth should have to answer them. At times, Janet is persuaded and permits Beth to answer; other times, she instructs Beth not to answer. For example, toward the end of the second day, Rich asks Beth whether she and Tony had been sexually involved. Janet instructs Beth not to answer. This fight necessitates another trip into court to determine whether Beth must answer. The judge rules that Beth must discuss Tony's romantic life only if Coastal has some evidence that he was involved with someone outside his marriage. The company lacks any such evidence.

Now limited to 10 depositions, Rich selects his nine other deponents carefully. For example, he decides to depose only one of the two nurses; he chooses to question Jerry Johnson, the tennis partner, but not Craig Bergson, the former roommate; and so forth. When we look at the many legal issues this case raises, his choices seem minor. In fact, unbeknownst to Rich or anyone else, his choices may determine the outcome of the case. As we will see later, Craig Bergson has evidence that is possibly crucial to the lawsuit. If Rich decides not to depose him, neither side will ever learn the evidence and the jury will never hear it. A jury can decide a case only based on the evidence presented to it. *Facts are elusive—and often controlling.*

In each deposition, Rich carefully probes with his questions, sometimes trying to learn what he actually does not know, sometimes trying to pin down the witness to a specific version of facts so that Rich knows how the witness will testify at trial. Neighbors at the beach testify that Tony seemed tense; one testifies about seeing Tony, unhappy, on the beach with his dog. Another testifies he had never before seen Blue tied up on the beach. Karen Caruso admits that Tony had been somewhat tense and unhappy the last couple of months. She reluctantly discusses their marriage, admitting there were problems.

Other Discovery.   Rich sends Requests to Produce Documents, seeking medical records about Tony. Once again, the parties fight over which records are relevant, but Rich gets most of what he wants. Janet does less discovery than Rich because most of the witnesses she will call are friendly witnesses. She can interview them privately without giving any information to Coastal. With the help of Beth and Karen, Janet builds her case just as carefully as Rich, choosing the witnesses who will bolster the view that Tony was in good spirits and died accidentally.

She deposes all the officers of Coastal who participated in the decision to deny insurance coverage. She is particularly aggressive in pinning them down as to the limited information they had when they denied Beth's claim.

Summary Judgment

When discovery is completed, both sides may consider seeking summary judgment. **Summary judgment** is a ruling by the court that no trial is necessary on a particular issue because the essential facts are not in dispute. The purpose of a trial is to determine the facts of the case; that is, to decide who did what to whom, why, when, and with what consequences. If there are no relevant facts in dispute, then there is no need for a trial.

In the following case, the defendant won summary judgment, meaning that the case never went to trial. And yet, this was only the beginning of trouble for that defendant, Bill Clinton.

Summary judgment
A ruling by the court that no trial is necessary because there are no essential facts in dispute

JONES V. CLINTON

990 F. Supp. 657
United States District Court for the Eastern District of Arkansas, 1998

Facts: In 1991, Bill Clinton was governor of Arkansas. Paula Jones worked for a state agency, the Arkansas Industrial Development Commission (AIDC). When Clinton became President, Jones sued him, claiming that he had sexually harassed her. She alleged that, in May 1991, the governor arranged for her to meet him in a hotel room in Little Rock, Arkansas. When they were alone, he put his hand on her leg and slid it toward her pelvis. She escaped from his grasp, exclaimed, "What are you doing?" and said she was "not that kind of girl." She was upset and confused, and sat on a sofa near the door. She claimed that Clinton approached her, "lowered his trousers and underwear, exposed his penis and told her to kiss it."

Jones was horrified, jumped up, and said she had to leave. Clinton responded by saying, "Well, I don't want to make you do anything you don't want to do," and pulled his pants up. He added that if she got in trouble for leaving work, Jones should "have Dave call me immediately and I'll take care of it." He also said, "You are smart. Let's keep this between ourselves." Jones remained at AIDC until February 1993, when she moved to California because of her husband's job transfer.

President Clinton denied all of the allegations. He also filed for summary judgment, claiming that Jones had not alleged facts that justified a trial. Jones opposed the motion for summary judgment.

Issue: *Was Clinton entitled to summary judgment, or was Jones entitled to a trial?*

Excerpts from Judge Wright's Decision: [To establish this type of a sexual harassment case, a plaintiff must show that her refusal to submit to unwelcome sexual advances resulted in a tangible job detriment, meaning that she suffered a specific loss. Jones claims that she was denied promotions, given a job with fewer responsibilities, isolated physically, required to sit at a workstation with no work to do, and singled out as the only female employee not to be given flowers on Secretary's Day.]

There is no record of plaintiff ever applying for another job within AIDC, however, and the record shows that not only was plaintiff never downgraded, her position was reclassified upward from a Grade 9 classification to a Grade 11 classification, thereby increasing her annual salary. Indeed, it is undisputed that plaintiff received every merit increase and cost-of-living allowance for which she was eligible during her nearly two-year tenure with the AIDC and consistently received satisfactory job evaluations.

Although plaintiff states that her job title upon returning from maternity leave was no longer that of purchasing assistant, her job duties prior to taking maternity leave and her job duties upon returning to work both involved data input. That being so, plaintiff cannot establish a tangible job detriment. A transfer that does not involve a demotion in form or substance and involves only minor changes in working conditions, with no reduction in pay or benefits, will not constitute an adverse employment action, otherwise every trivial personnel action that an irritable employee did not like would form the basis of a discrimination suit.

Finally, the Court rejects plaintiff's claim that she was subjected to hostile treatment having tangible effects when she was isolated physically, made to sit in a location from which she was constantly watched, made to sit at her workstation with no work to do, and singled out as the only female employee not to be given flowers on Secretary's Day. Plaintiff may well have perceived hostility and animus on the part of her supervisors, but these perceptions are merely conclusory in nature and do not, without more, constitute a tangible job detriment. Although it is not clear why plaintiff failed to receive flowers on Secretary's Day in 1992, such an omission does not give rise to a federal cause of action.

In sum, the Court finds that a showing of a tangible job detriment or adverse employment action is an essential element of plaintiff's sexual harassment claim and that plaintiff has not demonstrated any tangible job detriment or adverse employment action for her refusal to submit to the Governor's alleged advances. The President is therefore entitled to summary judgment [on this claim].

In other words, the court acknowledged that there were factual disputes, but concluded that even if Jones proved each of her allegations, she would *still* lose the case, because her allegations fell short of a legitimate case of sexual harassment. Jones appealed the case. Later the same year, as the appeal was pending and the House of Representatives was considering whether to impeach President Clinton, the parties settled the dispute. Clinton, without acknowledging any of the allegations, agreed to pay Jones $850,000 to drop the suit.

Janet and Rich each consider moving for summary judgment, but both correctly decide that they would lose. There is one major fact in dispute: Did Tony Caruso commit suicide? Only a jury may decide that issue. As long as there is *some evidence* supporting each side of a key factual dispute, the court may not grant summary judgment.

EXAM Strategy

Question: You are a judge. Mel has sued Kevin, claiming that while Kevin was drunk, he negligently drove his car down Mel's street and destroyed rare trees on a lot that Mel owns, next to his house. Mel's complaint stated that three witnesses at a bar saw Kevin take at least eight drinks less than an hour before the damage was done. In Kevin's answer, he denied causing the damage and denied being in the bar that night.

Kevin's lawyer has moved for summary judgment. He proves that three weeks before the alleged accident, Mel sold the lot to Tatiana.

Mel's lawyer opposes summary judgment. He produces a security camera tape proving that Kevin was in the bar, drinking beer, 34 minutes before the damage was done. He produces a signed statement from Sandy, a landscape gardener who lives across the street from the scene. Sandy states that she heard a crash, hurried to the windows, and saw Kevin's car weaving away from the damaged trees. She estimates the tree damage at $30,000 to $40,000. How should you rule on the motion?

Strategy: Do not be fooled by red herrings about Kevin's drinking or the value of the trees. Stick to the question: Should you grant summary judgment? Trials are necessary to resolve disputes about essential factual issues. Summary judgment is appropriate when there are no essential facts in dispute. Is there an essential fact not in dispute? Find it. Apply the rule. Being a judge is easy!

Result: It makes no difference whether Kevin was drunk or sober, whether he caused the harm or was at home in bed. Because Mel does not own the property, he cannot recover for the damage to it. He cannot win. You should grant Kevin's summary judgment motion.

Final Preparation

More than 90 percent of all lawsuits are settled before trial. But the parties in the Enviro-Vision dispute are unable to compromise, so each side gears up for trial. The attorneys make lists of all witnesses they will call. They then prepare each witness very carefully, rehearsing the questions they will ask. It is considered ethical and proper to rehearse the questions, provided the answers are honest and come from the witness. It is unethical and illegal for a lawyer to tell a witness what to say. It also makes for a weaker presentation of evidence—witnesses giving scripted answers are often easy to spot. The lawyers also have colleagues cross-examine each witness, so that the witnesses are ready for the questions the other side's lawyer will ask.

This preparation takes hours and hours, for many days. Beth is frustrated that she cannot do the work she needs to for Enviro-Vision because she is spending so much time preparing the case. Other employees have to prepare as well, especially for cross-examination by Rich Stewart, and it is a terrible drain on the small firm. More than a year after Janet filed her complaint, they are ready to begin trial.

6-4 TRIAL

6-4a Adversary System

Our system of justice assumes that the best way to bring out the truth is for the two contesting sides to present the strongest case possible to a neutral factfinder. Each side presents its witnesses and then the opponent has a chance to cross-examine. The adversary system presumes that by putting a witness on the stand and letting both lawyers question her, the truth will emerge.

The judge runs the trial. Each lawyer sits at a large table near the front. Beth, looking tense and unhappy, sits with Janet. Rich Stewart sits with a Coastal executive. In the back of the courtroom are benches for the public. On one bench sits Craig Bergson. He will watch the entire proceeding with intense interest and a strange feeling of unease. He is convinced he knows what really happened.

Janet has demanded a jury trial for Beth's case, and Judge Rowland announces that they will now impanel the jury.

6-4b Right to Jury Trial

Not all cases are tried to a jury. As a general rule, both plaintiff and defendant have a right to demand a jury trial when the lawsuit is one for money damages. For example, in a typical contract lawsuit, such as Beth's insurance claim, both plaintiff and defendant have a jury trial right whether they are in state or federal court. Even in such a case, though, the parties may *waive* the jury right, meaning they agree to try the case to a judge. Also, if the plaintiff is seeking an equitable remedy such as an injunction, there is no jury right for either party.

6-4c Voir Dire

Voir dire
The process of selecting a jury

The process of selecting a jury is called **voir dire**, which means "to speak the truth."[8] The court's goal is to select an impartial jury; the lawyers will each try to get a jury as favorable to their side as possible. A court sends letters to potential jurors who live in its county. Those who do not report for jury duty face significant consequences.

Challenges for cause
A claim that a juror has demonstrated probable bias.

Peremptory challenges
The right to excuse a juror for virtually any reason

When voir dire begins, potential jurors are questioned individually, sometimes by the judge and sometimes by the two lawyers, as each side tries to ferret out potential bias. Each lawyer may make any number of **challenges for cause**, claiming that a juror has demonstrated probable bias. For example, if a prospective juror in the Enviro-Vision case works for an insurance company, the judge will excuse her on the assumption that she would be biased in favor of Coastal. If the judge perceives no bias, the lawyer may still make a limited number of **peremptory challenges**, entitling him to excuse that juror for virtually any reason, which need not be stated in court. For example, if Rich Stewart believes that a juror seems hostile to him personally, he will use a peremptory challenge to excuse that juror, even if the judge sensed no animosity. The process continues until 14 jurors are seated. Twelve will comprise the jury; the other two are alternates who hear the case and remain available in the event one of the impaneled jurors becomes ill or otherwise cannot continue.

Although jury selection for a case can sometimes take many days, in the Enviro-Vision case, the first day of the hearing ends with the jury selected. In the hallway outside the court, Rich offers Janet $200,000 to settle. Janet reports the offer to Beth and they agree to reject it. Craig Bergson drives home, emotionally confused. Only three weeks before his death, Tony had accidentally met his old roommate and they had had several drinks. Craig believes that what Tony told him answers the riddle of this case.

---

[8]Students of French note that voir means "to see" and assume that voir dire should translate as "to see, to speak." However, the legal term is centuries old and derives not from modern French but from Old French, in which voir meant "truth."

PEREDA V. PARAJON

957 So.2d 1194
Florida Court of Appeals, 2007

Facts: Maria Parajon sued Diana Pereda for injuring her in a car accident. During voir dire, Parajon's lawyer asked the panel of prospective jurors these questions: "Is there anybody sitting on this panel now that has ever been under the care of a physician for personal injuries, whether you had a lawsuit or not? In other words, you may not have had any sort of lawsuit, but you slipped and fell—you had any accidents?"

Several of the prospective jurors raised their hands, allowing the lawyers to question more deeply into possible bias. However, Lisa Berg, a prospective juror who happened to be a lawyer, did not respond. Berg and others were seated as jurors, and ultimately awarded Parajon $450,000 for medical damages and pain and suffering.

After the trial, questioned in court by the judge, Berg admitted that three years earlier she had been injured in a car accident, hired a lawyer to sue, and settled out of court for $4,000. Asked about the settlement, Berg replied, "I think everyone always wants more money."

Parajon moved for a new trial but the judge denied the motion. Parajon appealed.

Issue: *Is Parajon entitled to a new trial based on Berg's failure to disclose her own personal injury lawsuit?*

Excerpts from Judge Rothenberg's Decision: To determine whether a juror's nondisclosure warrants a new trial, the complaining party must show that (1) the information is relevant and material to jury service in the case; (2) the juror concealed the information during questioning; and (3) the failure to disclose the information was not attributable to the complaining party's lack of diligence.

Both Parajon's and Pereda's respective counsels may indeed have been influenced to challenge Berg peremptorily had the facts of her personal injury litigation history been known. Berg's personal injury claim was not remote in time. Berg settled out of court at the urging of her parents in order to put the matter behind her. Her involvement in this matter may have affected her point of view in [this case]. Her nondisclosure, which precluded counsel's ability to question Berg about the experience and to fairly evaluate her as a prospective juror, was material.

It is clear from the record that Berg concealed her personal injury litigation history. She is a lawyer and an officer of the court. It is, therefore, difficult to imagine that she did not think the questions posed by Parajon's counsel applied to her.

The record evidence demonstrates that other prospective jurors, none of whom were lawyers, clearly understood what type of information Parajon's counsel was asking them to disclose. We find that Parajon's counsel made a diligent inquiry.

Reversed and remanded for a new trial.

6-4d Opening Statements

The next day, each attorney makes an opening statement to the jury, summarizing the proof he or she expects to offer, with the plaintiff going first. Janet focuses on Tony's successful life, his business and strong marriage, and the tragedy of his accidental death. [9]

Rich works hard to establish a friendly rapport with the jury. If members of the jury like him, they will tend to pay more attention to his presentation of evidence. He expresses regret about the death. Nonetheless, suicide is a clear exclusion from the policy. If insurance companies are forced to pay claims never bargained for, everyone's insurance rates will go up.

---

[9]Janet Booker has dropped her claim for triple damages against Coastal. To have any hope of such a verdict, she would have to show that Coastal had no legitimate reason at all for denying the claim. Discovery has convinced her that Coastal will demonstrate some rational reasons for what it did.

6-4e **Burden of Proof**

In civil cases, the plaintiff has the burden of proof. That means that the plaintiff must convince the jury that its version of the case is correct; the defendant is not obligated to disprove the allegations.

Preponderance of the evidence
The plaintiff's burden of proof in a civil lawsuit

Beyond a reasonable doubt
The government's burden of proof in a criminal prosecution

The plaintiff's burden in a civil lawsuit is to prove its case by a **preponderance of the evidence**. It must convince the jury that its version of the facts is at least *slightly more likely* than the defendant's version. Some courts describe this as a "51–49" persuasion; that is, that plaintiff's proof must "just tip" credibility in its favor. By contrast, in a criminal case, the prosecution must demonstrate **beyond a reasonable doubt** that the defendant is guilty. The burden of proof in a criminal case is much tougher because the likely consequences are, too. See Exhibit 6.3.

6-4f **Plaintiff's Case**

Because the plaintiff has the burden of proof, Janet puts in her case first. She wants to prove two things. First, that Tony died. That is easy because the death certificate clearly demonstrates it and Coastal does not seriously contest it. Second, in order to win double indemnity damages, she must show that the death was accidental. She will do this with the testimony of the witnesses she calls, one after the other. Her first witness is Beth. When a lawyer asks questions of her own witness, it is **direct examination**. Janet brings out all the evidence she wants the jury to hear: that the business was basically sound, though temporarily troubled, that Tony was a hard worker, why the company took out life insurance policies, and so forth.

Cross-examine
To ask questions of an opposing witness

Then Rich has a chance to **cross-examine** Beth, which means to ask questions of an opposing witness. He will try to create doubt in the jury's mind. He asks Beth only questions for which he is certain of the answers, based on discovery. Rich gets Beth to admit that the firm was not doing well the year of Tony's death; that Tony had lost the best client the firm ever had; that Beth had reduced salaries; and that Tony had been depressed about business.

6-4g **Rules of Evidence**

The lawyers are not free simply to ask any question they want. The **law of evidence** determines what questions a lawyer may ask and how the questions are to be phrased, what answers a witness may give, and what documents may be introduced. The goal is to

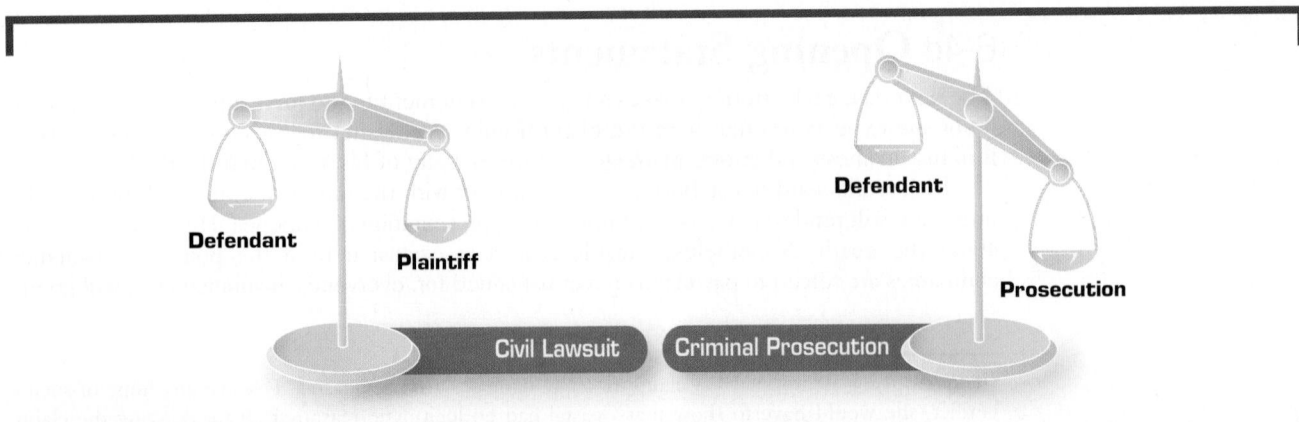

EXHIBIT 6.3   *Burden of Proof.* In a civil lawsuit, a plaintiff wins with a mere preponderance of the evidence. But the prosecution must persuade a jury beyond a reasonable doubt in order to win a criminal conviction.

get the best evidence possible before the jurors so they can decide what really happened. In general, witnesses may only testify about things they saw or heard.

These rules are complex, and a thorough look at them is beyond the scope of this chapter. However, they can be just as important in resolving a dispute as the underlying substantive law. Suppose that a plaintiff's case depends upon the jury hearing about a certain conversation, but the rules of evidence prevent the lawyer from asking about it. That conversation might just as well never have occurred.

Janet calls an expert witness, a marine geologist, who testifies about the tides and currents in the area where Tony's body was found. The expert testifies that even experienced swimmers can be overwhelmed by a sudden shift in currents.

Dave Porter/Alamy

Rich objects strenuously that this is irrelevant, because there is no testimony that there *was* such a current at the time of Tony's death. The judge permits the testimony.

Karen Caruso testifies that Tony was in "reasonably good" spirits the day of his death, and that he often took Blue for walks along the beach. Karen testifies that Blue was part Newfoundland. Rich objects that testimony about Blue's pedigree is irrelevant, but Janet insists it will show why Blue was tied up. The judge allows the testimony. Karen says that whenever Blue saw them swim, he would instinctively go into the water and pull them to shore. Does that explain why Blue was tied up? Only the jury can answer.

Cross-examination is grim for Karen. Rich slowly but methodically questions her about Tony's state of mind and brings out the problems with the company, his depression, and tension within the marriage. Janet's other witnesses testify essentially as they did during their depositions.

6-4h **Motion for Directed Verdict**

At the close of the plaintiff's case, Rich moves for a directed verdict; that is, a ruling that the plaintiff has entirely failed to prove some aspect of her case. Rich is seeking to win without even putting in his own case. He argues that it was Beth's burden to prove that Tony died accidentally and that she has entirely failed to do that.

A directed verdict is permissible only if the evidence so clearly favors the defendant that reasonable minds could not disagree on it. If reasonable minds could disagree, the motion must be denied. Here, Judge Rowland rules that the plaintiff has put in enough evidence of accidental death that a reasonable person could find in Beth's favor. The motion is denied.

There is no downside for Rich to ask for a directed verdict. The trial continues as if he had never made such a motion.

Directed verdict

A ruling that the plaintiff has entirely failed to prove some aspect of her case

6-4i **Defendant's Case**

Rich now puts in his case, exactly as Janet did, except that he happens to have fewer witnesses. He calls the examining doctor, who admits that Tony could have committed suicide by swimming out too far. On cross-examination, Janet gets the doctor to acknowledge that he has no idea whether Tony intentionally drowned. Rich also questions several neighbors as to how depressed Tony had seemed and how unusual it was that Blue was tied up. Some of the witnesses Rich deposed, such as the tennis partner Jerry Johnson, have nothing that will help Coastal's case, so he does not call them.

Craig Bergson, sitting in the back of the courtroom, thinks how different the trial would have been had he been called as a witness. When he and Tony had the fateful drink, Tony had been distraught: Business was terrible, he was involved in an extramarital affair that he could not end, and he saw no way out of his problems. He had no one to talk to and had been hugely relieved to speak with Craig. Several times Tony had said, "I just can't go on like this. I don't want to, anymore." Craig thought Tony seemed suicidal and urged him to see a therapist Craig knew and trusted. Tony had said that it was good advice, but Craig is unsure whether Tony sought any help.

This evidence would have affected the case. Had Rich Stewart known of the conversation, he would have deposed Craig and the therapist. Coastal's case would have been far stronger, perhaps overwhelming. But Craig's evidence will never be heard. Facts are critical. Rich's decision to depose other witnesses and omit Craig may influence the verdict more than any rule of law.

6-4j Closing Arguments

Both lawyers sum up their case to the jury, explaining how they hope the jury will interpret what they have heard. Janet summarizes the plaintiff's version of the facts, claiming that Blue was tied up so that Tony could swim without worrying about him. Rich claims that business and personal pressures had overwhelmed Tony. He tied up his dog, neatly folded his clothes, and took his own life.

6-4k Jury Instructions

Judge Rowland instructs the jury as to its duty. He tells them that they are to evaluate the case based only on the evidence they heard at trial, relying on their own experience and common sense.

He explains the law and the burden of proof, telling the jury that it is Beth's obligation to prove that Tony died. If Beth has proven that Tony died, she is entitled to $1 million; if she has proven that his death was accidental, she is entitled to $2 million. However, if Coastal has proven suicide, Beth receives nothing. Finally, he states that if they are unable to decide between accidental death and suicide, there is a legal presumption that it was accidental. Rich asks Judge Rowland to rephrase the "legal presumption" part, but the judge declines.

6-4l Verdict

The jury deliberates informally, with all jurors entitled to voice their opinion. Some deliberations take two hours; some take two weeks. Many states require a unanimous verdict; others require only, for example, a 10–2 vote in civil cases.

This case presents a close call. No one saw Tony die. Yet even though they cannot know with certainty, the jury's decision will probably be the final word on whether he took his own life. After a day and a half of deliberating, the jury notifies the judge that it has reached a verdict. Rich Stewart quickly makes a new offer: $350,000. (The two sides have the right to settle a case until the moment when the last appeal is decided.) Beth hesitates but turns it down.

The judge summons the lawyers to court, and Beth goes as well. The judge asks the foreman if the jury has reached a decision. He states that it has: The jury finds that Tony Caruso drowned accidentally, and awards Beth Smiles $2 million.

6-4m Motions after the Verdict

Judgment *non obstante veredicto*

A judgment notwithstanding the jury's verdict

Rich immediately moves for a **judgment *non obstante veredicto*** (JNOV), meaning a judgment notwithstanding the jury's verdict. He is asking the judge to overturn the jury's verdict. Rich argues that the jury's decision went against all of the evidence. He also claims that the judge's instructions were wrong and misled the jury.

Judge Rowland denies the JNOV. Rich immediately moves for a new trial, making the same claim, and the judge denies the motion. Beth is elated that the case is finally over—until Janet says she expects an appeal. Craig Bergson, leaving the courtroom, wonders if he did the right thing. He felt sympathy for Beth and none for Coastal. Yet now he is neither happy nor proud.

6-5 APPEALS

Two days later, Rich files an appeal to the court of appeals. The same day, he phones Janet and increases his settlement offer to $425,000. Beth is tempted but wants Janet's advice. Janet says the risks of an appeal are that the court will order a new trial, and they would start all over. But to accept this offer is to forfeit over $1.5 million. Beth is unsure what to do. The firm desperately needs cash now, and appeals may take years. Janet suggests they wait until oral argument, another eight months.

Rich files a brief arguing that there were two basic errors at the trial: first, that the jury's verdict is clearly contrary to the evidence; and second, that the judge gave the wrong instructions to the jury. Janet files a reply brief, opposing Rich on both issues. In her brief, Janet cites many cases that she claims are **precedent**: earlier decisions by the state appellate courts on similar or identical issues

Eight months later, the lawyers representing Coastal and Enviro-Vision appear in the court of appeals to argue their case. Rich, the appellant, goes first. The judges frequently interrupt his argument with questions. They show little sympathy for his claim that the verdict was against the facts. They seem more sympathetic with his second point, that the instructions were wrong.

When Janet argues, all of their questions concern the judge's instructions. It appears they believe the instructions were in error. The judges take the case under advisement, meaning they will decide some time in the future—maybe in two weeks, maybe in five months.

Precedent
Earlier decisions by the state appellate courts on similar or identical issues

6-5a Appeals Court Options

The court of appeals can **affirm** the trial court, allowing the decision to stand. The court may **modify** the decision, for example, by affirming that the plaintiff wins but decreasing the size of the award. (That is unlikely here; Beth is entitled to $2 million or nothing.) The court might **reverse and remand**, nullifying the lower court's decision and returning the case to the lower court for a new trial. Or it could simply **reverse**, turning the loser (Coastal) into the winner, with no new trial.

What will it do here? On the factual issue, it will probably rule in Beth's favor. There *was* evidence from which a jury could conclude that Tony died accidentally. It is true that there was also considerable evidence to support Coastal's position, but that is probably not enough to overturn the verdict. If reasonable people could disagree on what the evidence proves, an appellate court generally refuses to change the jury's factual findings. The court of appeals is likely to rule that a reasonable jury *could* have found accidental death, even if the appellate judges personally suspect that Tony may have killed himself.

The judge's instructions raise a more difficult problem. Some states would require a more complex statement about "presumptions."[10]

Affirm
To allow the decision to stand

Modify
To affirm the outcome but with changes

Reverse and remand
To nullify the lower decision and return the case for reconsideration or retrial

---

[10]Judge Rowland probably should have said, "The law presumes that death is accidental, not suicide. So if there were no evidence either way, the plaintiff would win because we presume accident. But if there is competing evidence, the presumption becomes irrelevant. If you think that Coastal Insurance has introduced some evidence of suicide, then forget the legal presumption. You must then decide what happened based on what you have seen and heard in court, and on any inferences you choose to draw." Note that the judge's instructions were different, though similar.

What does a court of appeals do if it decides the trial court's instructions were wrong? If it believes the error rendered the trial and verdict unfair, it will remand the case; that is, send it back to the lower court for a new trial. However, the court may conclude that the mistake was **harmless error**. A trial judge cannot do a perfect job, and not every error is fatal. The court may decide the verdict was fair in spite of the mistake.

harmless error

A mistake by the trial judge that was too minor to affect the outcome.

Janet and Beth talk. Beth is very anxious and wants to settle. She does not want to wait four or five months, only to learn that they must start all over. Janet urges that they wait a few weeks to hear from Rich: They don't want to seem too eager.

A week later, Rich telephones and offers $500,000. Janet turns it down, but says she will ask Beth if she wants to make a counteroffer. She and Beth talk. They agree that they will settle for $1 million. Janet then calls Rich and offers to settle for $1.7 million. Rich and Janet debate the merits of the case. Rich later calls back and offers $750,000, saying he doubts that he can go any higher. Janet counters with $1.4 million, saying she doubts she can go any lower. They argue, both predicting that they will win on appeal.

Rich calls, offers $900,000, and says, "That's it. No more." Janet argues for $1.2 million, expecting to nudge Rich up to $1 million. He doesn't nudge, instead saying, "Take it or leave it." Janet and Beth talk it over. Janet telephones Rich and accepts $900,000 to settle the case.

If they had waited for the court of appeals decision, would Beth have won? It is impossible to know. It is certain, though, that whoever lost would have appealed. Months would have passed waiting to learn if the state supreme court would accept the case. If that court had agreed to hear the appeal, Beth would have endured another year of waiting, brief writing, oral argument, and tense hoping. The high court has all of the options discussed: to affirm, modify, reverse and remand, or simply reverse.

6-6 ALTERNATIVE DISPUTE RESOLUTION

As we have seen in the previous section, trials can be trying. Lawsuits can cause prolonged periods of stress, significant legal bills, and general unpleasantness. Many people and companies prefer to settle cases out of court. Alternative dispute resolution (ADR) provides several semiformal methods of resolving conflicts. We will look at different types of ADR and analyze their strengths and weaknesses.

6-6a Negotiation

In most cases, the parties negotiate, whether personally or through lawyers. Fortunately, the great majority of disputes are resolved this way. Negotiation often begins as soon as a dispute arises and may last a few days or several years.

6-6b Mediation

Mediation is the fastest-growing method of dispute resolution in the United States. Here, a neutral person, called a *mediator*, attempts to guide the two disputing parties toward a voluntary settlement. (In some cases, there may be two or more mediators, but we will use the singular.) Generally, the two disputants voluntarily enter mediation, although some judges order the parties to try this form of ADR before allowing a case to go to trial.

A mediator does not render a decision in the dispute, but uses a variety of skills to move the parties toward agreement. Often a mediator will shuttle between the antagonists, hearing their arguments, sorting out the serious issues from the less important, prompting the parties and lawyers alike to consider new perspectives, and looking for areas of agreement. Mediators must earn the trust of both parties, listen closely, try to diffuse anger and fear, and build the will to settle. Good mediators do not need a law degree, but they must have a sense of humor and low blood pressure.

Mediation has several major advantages. Because the parties maintain control of the process, the two antagonists can speak freely. They need not fear conceding too much, because no settlement takes effect until both parties sign. All discussions are confidential, further encouraging candid talk. This is particularly helpful in cases involving proprietary information that might be revealed during a trial.

Of all forms of dispute resolution, mediation probably offers the strongest "win–win" potential. Because the goal is voluntary settlement, neither party needs to fear that it will end up the loser. This is in sharp contrast to litigation, where one party will lose. Removing the fear of defeat often encourages thinking and talking that are more open and realistic than negotiations held in the midst of a lawsuit. Studies show that more than 75 percent of mediated cases do reach a voluntary settlement. Such an agreement is particularly valuable to parties that wish to preserve a long-term relationship. Consider two companies that have done business successfully for 10 years but now are in the midst of a million-dollar trade dispute. A lawsuit could last three or more years and destroy any chance of future trade. However, if the parties mediate the disagreement, they might reach an amicable settlement within a month or two and could quickly resume their mutually profitable business.

6-6c **Arbitration**

In this form of ADR, the parties agree to bring in a neutral third party, but with a major difference: The arbitrator has the power to impose an award. The arbitrator allows each side equal time to present its case and, after deliberation, issues a binding decision, generally without giving reasons. Unlike mediation, arbitration ensures that there will be a final result, although the parties lose control of the outcome.

Judge Judy and similar TV court shows are examples of arbitration. Before the shows are taped, people involved in a real dispute sign a contract in which they give up the right to go to court over the incident and agree to be bound by the judge's decision.

Parties in arbitration give up many additional rights that litigants retain, including discovery and class action. In arbitration, as already discussed as applied to trials, *discovery* allows the two sides in a lawsuit to obtain documentary and other evidence from the opponent before the dispute is decided. Arbitration permits both sides to keep secret many files that would have to be divulged in a court case, potentially depriving the opposing side of valuable evidence. A party may have a stronger case than it realizes, and the absence of discovery may permanently deny it that knowledge. As discussed earlier in this chapter, a *class action* is a suit in which one injured party represents a large group of people who have suffered similar harm. Arbitration eliminates this possibility because injured employees face the employer one at a time. Finally, the fact that an arbitrator may not provide a written, public decision bars other plaintiffs, and society generally, from learning what happened.

Traditionally, parties sign arbitration agreements *after* some incident took place. A car accident would happen first, and the drivers would agree to arbitration second. But today, many parties agree *in advance* to arbitrate any disputes that may arise in the future. For example, a new employee may sign an agreement requiring arbitration of any future disputes with his employer; a customer opening an account with a stockbroker or bank— or health plan—may sign a similar form, often without realizing it. The good news is fewer lawsuits; the bad news is you might be the person kept out of court.

Assume that you live in Miami. Using the Internet, you order a $2,000 ThinkLite laptop computer, which arrives in a carton loaded with six fat instructional manuals and many small leaflets. You read some of the documents and ignore others. For four weeks, you struggle to make your computer work, to no avail. Finally, you call ThinkLite and demand a refund, but the company refuses. You file suit in your local court, at which time the company points out that buried among the hundreds of pages it mailed you was a *mandatory arbitration form*. This document prohibits you from filing suit against the company and states that if you have any complaint with the company, you must fly to Chicago, pay a $2,000 arbitrator's fee, plead your case before an arbitrator selected by the Laptop Trade Association of America, and, should you lose, pay ThinkLite's attorneys' fees, which could be several thousand dollars. Is that mandatory arbitration provision valid? The majority of the courts that have faced such clauses have enforced them.[11]

Chapter Conclusion

No one will ever know for sure whether Tony Caruso took his own life. Craig Bergson's evidence might have tipped the scales in favor of Coastal. But even that is uncertain, since the jury could have found him unpersuasive. After two years, the case ends with a settlement and uncertainty—both typical lawsuit results. The missing witness is less common but not extraordinary. The vaguely unsatisfying feeling about it all is only too common and indicates why most parties settle out of court.

EXAM REVIEW

1. **COURT SYSTEMS** There are many *systems* of courts, one federal and one in each state. A federal court will hear a case only if it involves a federal question or diversity jurisdiction.

2. **TRIAL AND APPELLATE COURTS** Trial courts determine facts and apply the law to the facts; appeals courts generally accept the facts found by the trial court and review the trial record for errors of law.

EXAM Strategy

Question: Jade sued Kim, claiming that Kim promised to hire her as an in-store model for $1,000 per week for eight weeks. Kim denied making the promise, and the jury was persuaded: Kim won. Jade has appealed, and now she offers Steve as a witness. Steve will testify to the appeals court that he saw Kim hire Jade as a model, exactly as Jade claimed. Will Jade win on appeal?

Strategy: Before you answer, make sure you know the difference between trial and appellate courts. What is the difference? Apply that distinction here. (See the "Result" at the end of this section.)

3. **PLEADINGS** A complaint and an answer are the two most important pleadings; that is, documents that start a lawsuit.

---

[11]See, e.g., Hill v. Gateway 2000, 105 F.3d 1147 (7th Cir. 1997), upholding a similar clause.

4. **DISCOVERY**   Discovery is the critical pre-trial opportunity for both parties to learn the strengths and weaknesses of the opponent's case. Important forms of discovery include interrogatories, depositions, production of documents and objects, physical and mental examinations, and requests for admission.

5. **MOTIONS**   A motion is a formal request to the court.

6. **SUMMARY JUDGMENT**   Summary judgment is a ruling by the court that no trial is necessary because there are no essential facts in dispute.

7. **JURY TRIALS**   Generally, both plaintiff and defendant may demand a jury in any lawsuit for money damages.

8. **VOIR DIRE**   Voir dire is the process of selecting jurors in order to obtain an impartial panel.

EXAM Strategy

Question: You are a lawyer, representing the plaintiff in a case of alleged employment discrimination. The court is selecting a jury. Based on questions you have asked, you believe that juror number 3 is biased against your client. You explain this to the judge, but she disagrees. Is there anything you can do?

Strategy: The question focuses on your rights during voir dire. If you believe that a juror will not be fair, you may make two different types of challenge. What are they? (See the "Result" at the end of this section.)

---

9. **BURDEN OF PROOF**   The plaintiff's burden of proof in a civil lawsuit is preponderance of the evidence, meaning that its version of the facts must be at least slightly more persuasive than the defendant's. In a criminal prosecution, the government must offer proof beyond a reasonable doubt in order to win a conviction.

10. **RULES OF EVIDENCE**   The rules of evidence determine what questions may be asked during trial, what testimony may be given, and what documents may be introduced.

11. **VERDICTS**   The verdict is the jury's decision in a case. The losing party may ask the trial judge to overturn the verdict, seeking a JNOV or a new trial. Judges seldom grant either.

12. **APPEALS**   An appeals court has many options. The court may affirm, upholding the lower court's decision; modify, changing the verdict but leaving the same party victorious; reverse, transforming the loser into the winner; and/or remand, sending the case back to the lower court.

13. **ADR**   Alternative dispute resolution is any formal or informal process to settle disputes without a trial. Mediation, arbitration, and other forms of ADR have grown in popularity.

2. Result: Trial courts use witnesses to help resolve fact disputes. Appellate courts review the record to see if there have been errors of law. Appellate courts never hear witnesses, and they will not hear Steve. Jade will lose her appeal.

8. Result: You have already made a *challenge for cause*, claiming bias, but the judge has rejected your challenge. If you have not used up all of your *peremptory challenges*, you may use one to excuse this juror, without giving any reason.

MULTIPLE-CHOICE QUESTIONS

1. The burden of proof in a civil trial is to prove a case ———————— .
The burden of proof rests with the ———————— .

   (a) beyond a reasonable doubt; plaintiff

   (b) by a preponderance of the evidence; plaintiff

   (c) beyond a reasonable doubt; defendant

   (d) by a preponderance of the evidence; defendant

2. Alice is suing Betty. After the discovery process, Alice believes that no relevant facts are in dispute, and that there is no need for a trial. She should move for ———————— .

   (a) a judgment on the pleadings

   (b) a directed verdict

   (c) a summary judgment

   (d) a JNOV

3. Glen lives in Illinois. He applies for a job with a Missouri company, and he is told, amazingly, that the job is open only to white applicants. He will now sue the Missouri company under the Civil Rights Act, a federal statute. Can Glen sue in federal court?

   (a) Yes, absolutely.

   (b) Yes, but only if he seeks damages of at least $75,000. Otherwise, he must sue in a state court.

   (c) Yes, but only if the Missouri company agrees. Otherwise, he must sue in a state court.

   (d) No, absolutely not. He must sue in a state court.

4. A default judgment can be entered if which of the following is true?

   (a) A plaintiff presents her evidence at trial and clearly fails to meet her burden of proof.

   (b) A defendant loses a lawsuit and does not pay a judgment within 180 days.

   (c) A defendant fails to file an answer to a plaintiff's complaint on time.

   (d) A citizen fails to obey an order to appear for jury duty.

5. Barry and Carl are next-door neighbors. Barry's dog digs under Carl's fence and does $500 worth of damage to Carl's garden. Barry refuses to pay for the damage, claiming that Carl's cats "have been digging up my yard for years."

The two argue repeatedly, and the relationship turns frosty. Of the following choices, which has no outside decision maker and is most likely to allow the neighbors to peacefully coexist after working out the dispute?

(a) Trial

(b) Arbitration

(c) Mediation

CASE QUESTIONS

1. You plan to open a store in Chicago, specializing in rugs imported from Turkey. You will work with a native Turk who will purchase and ship the rugs to your store. You are wise enough to insist on a contract establishing the rights and obligations of both parties and would prefer an ADR clause. But you do not want a clause that will alienate your overseas partner. What kind of ADR clause should you include, and why?

2. Which court(s) have jurisdiction over each of these lawsuits—state or federal? Explain your reasoning for each answer.

   • Pat wants to sue his next-door neighbor, Dorothy, claiming that Dorothy promised to sell him the house next door.

   • Paula, who lives in New York City, wants to sue Dizzy Movie Theatres, whose principal place of business is Dallas. She claims that while she was in Texas on holiday, she was injured by their negligent maintenance of a stairway. She claims damages of $30,000.

   • Phil lives in Tennessee. He wants to sue Dick, who lives in Ohio. Phil claims that Dick agreed to sell him 3,000 acres of farmland in Ohio, worth more than $2 million.

   • Pete, incarcerated in a federal prison in Kansas, wants to sue the United States government. He claims that his treatment by prison authorities violates three federal statutes.

3. British discovery practice differs from that in the United States. Most discovery in Britain concerns documents. The lawyers for the two sides, called *solicitors*, must deliver to the opposing side a list of all relevant documents in their possession. Each side may then request to look at and copy those it wishes. Depositions are rare. What advantages and disadvantages are there to the British practice?

4. Trial practice also is dramatically different in Britain. The parties' solicitors do not go into court. Courtroom work is done by different lawyers, called barristers. The barristers have very limited rights to interview witnesses before trial. They know the substance of what each witness intends to say but do not rehearse questions and answers, as in the United States. Which approach do you consider more effective? More ethical? What is the purpose of a trial? Of pre-trial preparation?

5. Claus Scherer worked for Rockwell International and was paid more than $300,000 per year. Rockwell fired Scherer for alleged sexual harassment of several workers, including his secretary, Terry Pendy. Scherer sued in United States District Court, alleging that Rockwell's real motive in firing him was his high salary.

Rockwell moved for summary judgment, offering deposition transcripts of various employees. Pendy's deposition detailed instances of harassment, including comments about her body, instances of unwelcome touching, and discussions of extramarital affairs. Another deposition, from a Rockwell employee who investigated the allegations, included complaints by other employees as to Scherer's harassment. In his own deposition, which he offered to oppose summary judgment, Scherer testified that he could not recall the incidents alleged by Pendy and others. He denied generally that he had sexually harassed anyone. The district court granted summary judgment for Rockwell. Was its ruling correct?

DISCUSSION QUESTIONS

1. In the Tony Caruso case described throughout this chapter, the defendant offers to settle the case at several stages. Knowing what you do now about litigation, would you have accepted any of the offers? If so, which one(s)? If not, why not?

2. The burden of proof in civil cases is fairly low. A plaintiff wins a lawsuit if he is 51 percent convincing, and then he collects 100 percent of his damages. Is this result reasonable? Should a plaintiff in a civil case be required to prove his case beyond a reasonable doubt? Or, if a plaintiff is only 51 percent convincing, should he get only 51 percent of his damages?

3. Large numbers of employees have signed mandatory arbitration agreements in employment contracts. Courts usually uphold these clauses. Imagine that you signed a contract with an arbitration agreement, that the company later mistreated you, and that you could not sue in court. Would you be upset? Or would you be relieved to go through the faster and cheaper process of arbitration?

4. Imagine a state law that allows for residents to sue "spammers"—those who send uninvited commercial messages through email—for $30. One particularly prolific spammer sends messages to hundreds of thousands of people.

John Smith, a lawyer, signs up 100,000 people to participate in a class-action lawsuit. According to the agreements with his many clients, Smith will keep one-third of any winnings. In the end, Smith wins a $3 million verdict and pockets $1 million. Each individual plaintiff receives a check for $20.

Is this lawsuit a reasonable use of the court's resources? Why or why not?

5. Higher courts are reluctant to review a lower court's *factual* findings. Should this be so? Would appeals be fairer if appellate courts reviewed *everything*?

Torts

CHAPTER 8

INTENTIONAL TORTS AND BUSINESS TORTS

They say politics can get ugly. *Doubt it?* Just ask John Vogel and Paul Grannis. Both men started off as candidates for public office in California—and then learned about defamation the hard way. They had no defense when mean and nasty statements were posted about them online. Here is their story.

Joseph Felice ran a website that listed "Top Ten Dumb Asses." Vogel and Grannis earned the honor of being number 1 and 2 on the list, respectively. The site also claimed that Vogel was "WANTED as a Dead Beat Dad" because he was behind on his child support payments. When users clicked on Vogel's name, they were led to another website—www.satan.com—that included a picture of him altered to look like a devil.

Grannis did not fare any better. Felice's site declared him "Bankrupt, Drunk & Chewin' Tobaccy." It stated that Grannis had "bankrupted many businesses throughout California." His name was hyperlinked to a website with the address www.olddrunk.com that accused him of criminal, fraudulent, and immoral conduct.

Understandably offended, Vogel and Grannis sued Felice for libel.[1] But they soon learned that filing such a lawsuit is easier than winning it.

> **They had no defense when mean and nasty statements were posted about them online.**

© biletskiy/Shutterstock.com

---

[1]Vogel v. Felice, 127 Cal. App. 4th 1006 (2005).

The odd word *tort* is borrowed from the French, meaning "wrong." And that is what it means in law: a wrong. More precisely, a **tort** is a violation of a duty imposed by the civil law. When a person breaks one of those duties and injures another, it is a tort. The injury could be to a person or her property. Libel, which the politicians in the opening scenario alleged, is one example of a tort. A surgeon who removes the wrong kidney from a patient commits a different kind of tort, called *negligence*. A business executive who deliberately steals a client away from a competitor, interfering with a valid contract, commits a tort called *interference with a contract*. A con artist who tricks you out of your money with a phony offer to sell you a boat commits *fraud*, yet another tort.

Because tort law is so broad, it takes a while—and two chapters—to understand its boundaries. To start with, we must distinguish torts from two other areas of law: criminal law and contract law.

It is a *crime* to steal a car, to embezzle money from a bank, to sell cocaine. As discussed in Chapter 1, society considers such behavior so threatening that the government itself will prosecute the wrongdoer, whether or not the car owner or bank president wants the case to go forward. A district attorney, who is paid by the government, will bring the case to court, seeking to send the defendant to prison, fine him, or both. If there is a fine, the money goes to the state, not to the victim.

In a tort case, it is up to the injured party to seek compensation. She must hire her own lawyer, who will file a lawsuit. Her lawyer must convince the court that the defendant breached some legal duty and ought to pay money damages to the plaintiff. The plaintiff has no power to send the defendant to jail. Bear in mind that a defendant's action might be both a crime and a tort. A man who punches you in the face for no reason commits the tort of battery. You may file a civil suit against him and will collect money damages if you can prove your case. He has also committed a crime, and the state may prosecute, seeking to imprison and fine him.

Tort

A violation of a duty imposed by the civil law

Differences between Contract, Tort, and Criminal Law

Type of Obligation	Contract	Tort	Criminal Law
How the obligation is created	The parties agree on a contract, which creates duties for both	The civil law imposes duties of conduct on all persons	The criminal law prohibits certain conduct
How the obligation is enforced	Suit by plaintiff	Suit by plaintiff	Prosecution by government
Possible result	Money damages for plaintiff	Money damages for plaintiff	Punishment for defendant, including prison and/or fine
Example	Raul contracts to sell Deirdre 5,000 pairs of sneakers at $50 per pair, but fails to deliver them. Deirdre buys the sneakers elsewhere for $60 per pair and receives $50,000, her extra expense	A newspaper falsely accuses a private citizen of being an alcoholic. The plaintiff sues and wins money damages to compensate for her injured reputation	Leo steals Kelly's car. The government prosecutes Leo for grand theft, and the judge sentences him to two years in prison. Kelly gets nothing

A tort is also different from a contract dispute. A contract case is based on an agreement two people have already made. For example, Deirdre claims that Raul promised to sell her 10,000 pairs of sneakers at a good price but has failed to deliver them. She files a contract lawsuit. In a tort case, there is usually no "deal" between the parties. John Vogel and Paul Grannis had never made any kind of contract with their online critic. The plaintiff in a tort case claims that the law itself creates a duty that the defendant has breached.

Intentional torts
Harm caused by a deliberate action

Tort law is divided into categories. In this chapter, we consider **intentional torts**, that is, harm caused by a deliberate action. When Paula hits Paul, she has committed the intentional tort of battery. In the next chapter, we examine negligence, strict liability, and product liability, which involve injuries and losses caused by neglect and oversight rather than by deliberate conduct.

A final introductory point: When we speak of intentional torts, we do not necessarily mean that the defendant intended to harm the plaintiff. If the defendant does something deliberately and it ends up injuring somebody, she is probably liable even if she meant no harm. For example, intentionally throwing a snowball at a friend is a deliberate act. If the snowball permanently damages his eye, the *harm* is unintended, but the defendant is liable for the intentional tort of battery because the *act* was intentional.

We look first at the most common intentional torts and then at the most important intentional torts that are related to business.

8-1 INTENTIONAL TORTS

8-1a **Defamation**

The First Amendment guarantees the right to free speech, a vital freedom that enables us to protect other rights. But that freedom is not absolute.

Libel
Written defamation

Slander
Oral defamation

The law of defamation concerns false statements that harm someone's reputation. Defamatory statements can be written or spoken. Written defamation is called **libel**. Suppose a newspaper accuses a local retail store of programming its cash registers to overcharge customers when the store has never done so. That is libel. Oral defamation is **slander**. If Professor Wisdom, in class, refers to Sally Student as a drug dealer although she has never sold drugs, he has slandered her.

There are four elements to a defamation case. An element is something that a plaintiff must prove to win a lawsuit. The plaintiff in any kind of lawsuit must prove *all* of the elements to prevail. The elements in a defamation case are:

- **Defamatory statement.** This is a factual statement that is likely to harm another person's reputation. Because opinions are not factual, they do not generally count as defamatory statements. In the case from the opening scenario, the judge found that "dumb ass" was not a defamatory statement. The court interpreted that slang phrase as a general expression of contempt, not a fact. On the other hand, the accusations that Vogel owed child support payments and Grannis was bankrupt *were* defamatory statements because they were facts that could be proven true or false.

- **Falsity.** The statement must be false. Felice, the website's author, was ultimately successful in his defense because he proved that Vogel did in fact fail to pay child support and Grannis had filed for bankruptcy. Making a true statement, no matter how mean, is not defamation.

- **Communicated.** The statement must be communicated to at least one person *other than the plaintiff*. It stands to reason: If no one else receives the defamatory message, there is no harm done. Defamation protects against injury to reputation, not hurt feelings.

- **Injury.** The plaintiff must show some injury, unless the case involves false statements about sexual behavior, crimes, contagious diseases, and professional abilities. In these cases, the law is willing to *assume* injury without requiring the plaintiff to prove it. Lies in these four categories amount to **slander per se** when they are spoken and **libel per se** when they are published.[2]

The following case involves libel per se, *The New York Times*, and alleged police brutality. Set in Alabama during the racially charged Sixties, this landmark Supreme Court decision changed the rules of the defamation game for all public personalities.

Slander per se

When oral statements relate to criminal or sexual conduct, contagious diseases, or professional abilities, they are assumed to be harmful to the subject's reputation.

Libel per se

When written statements relate to criminal or sexual conduct, contagious diseases, or professional abilities, they are assumed to be harmful to the subject's reputation.

---

[2]The courts consider defamation on radio and television to be libel, not slander, because of their vast audiences. As a result, plaintiffs in broadcasting cases generally do not have to prove damages.

Landmark Case

NEW YORK TIMES CO. V. SULLIVAN

376 U.S. 254
United States Supreme Court, 1964

Facts: In 1960, *The New York Times* ran a full-page advertisement paid for by civil rights activists. The ad described an "unprecedented wave of terror" by the police of Montgomery, Alabama, against civil rights protesters. It stated that the police had assaulted nonviolent protesters with shotguns and tear gas and had padlocked a dining hall to starve them into submission. The ad also accused the Montgomery police of bombing the home of Dr. Martin Luther King, Jr., and unjustly arresting him seven times. Most of the ad's statements were true, but a few were not.

L.B. Sullivan was Montgomery's police commissioner. Although the ad did not mention him by name, Sullivan argued that the accusations hurt his reputation because he was head of the police. He sued *The New York Times* under Alabama's law on libel per se.

An Alabama court agreed with Sullivan, awarding him damages of $500,000. The Supreme Court of Alabama affirmed. *The New York Times* appealed to the U.S. Supreme Court, arguing that the ad was protected by the First Amendment and the evidence did not support such an award.

Issue: *Does the First Amendment protect those who criticize public officials?*

Excerpts from Justice Brennan's Decision: We consider this case against the background of a profound national commitment to the principle that debate on public issues should be uninhibited, robust, and wide-open, and that it may well include vehement, caustic, and sometimes unpleasantly sharp attacks on government and public officials. The present advertisement, as an expression of grievance and protest on one of the major public issues of our time, would seem clearly to qualify for the constitutional protection. The question is whether it forfeits that protection by the falsity of some of its factual statements and by its alleged defamation of respondent.

First Amendment protection does not turn upon the truth, popularity, or social utility of the ideas and beliefs which are offered. Erroneous statement [are] inevitable in free debate, and must be protected. Whatever is added to the field of libel is taken from the field of free debate. Criticism of official conduct does not lose its constitutional protection merely because it diminishes official reputations.

A rule compelling the critic of official conduct to guarantee the truth of all his factual assertions leads to self-censorship. Under such a rule, would-be critics of official conduct may be deterred from voicing their criticism. The rule thus dampens the vigor and limits the variety of public debate. It is inconsistent with the First Amendment.

The constitutional guarantees require a federal rule that prohibits a public official from recovering damages for a defamatory falsehood relating to his official conduct unless he proves that the statement was made with "actual malice"—that is, with knowledge that it was false or with reckless disregard of whether it was false or not.

Applying these standards, we consider that the facts do not support a finding of actual malice as to the *Times*. The *Times* published the advertisement without checking its accuracy. We think the evidence against the *Times* supports at most a finding of negligence in failing to discover the misstatements, and is constitutionally insufficient to show the recklessness that is required for a finding of actual malice.

The judgment of the Supreme Court of Alabama is reversed and the case is remanded.

Now we see another reason why the politicians from our chapter opener lost their defamation case. **The rule from** *The New York Times* **case is that a public official can win a defamation case only by proving the defendant's actual malice, that is, that the defendant knew the statement was false or acted with reckless disregard of the truth.** As candidates for public office, the politicians had to prove their critic's malice—and they could not do so. The *New York Times* rule has been extended to all public figures, like actors, business leaders, and anyone else who assumes an influential and visible role in society.[3]

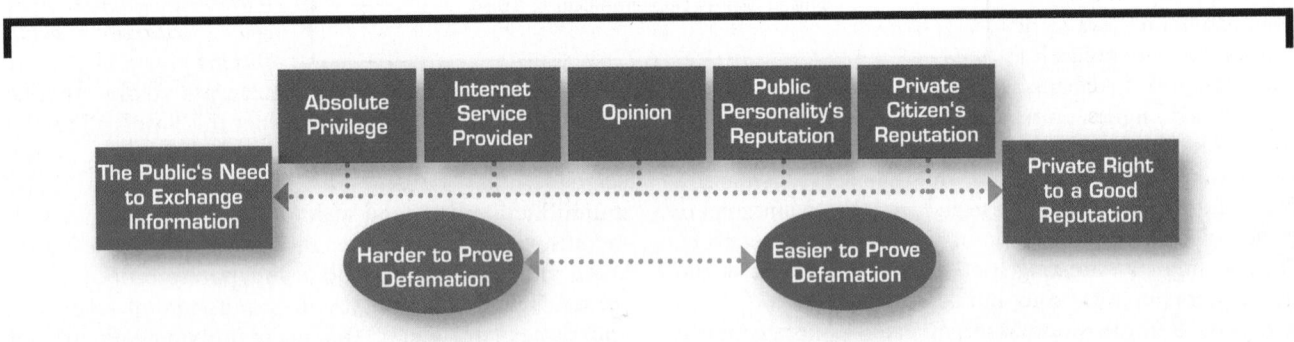

| EXHIBIT 8.1 | Defamation cases show a tension between the public's need for information and a citizen's right to protect his reputation. |

---

[3]Curtis Publishing Co. v. Butts, 388 U.S. 130 (1967); Associated Press v. Walker, 388 U.S. 130 (1967).

Privilege

Defendants receive additional protection from defamation cases when it is important for them to speak freely. **Absolute privilege** exists in courtrooms and legislative hearings. Anyone speaking there, such as a witness in court, can say anything at all and never be sued for defamation. (Deliberately false testimony would be *perjury*, but still not *slander*.)

Absolute privilege

A witness testifying in a court or legislature may never be sued for defamation.

8-1b False Imprisonment

False imprisonment is the intentional restraint of another person without reasonable cause and without consent. Suppose that a bank teller becomes seriously ill and wants to go to the doctor, but the bank will not permit her to leave until she makes a final tally of her accounts. Against her wishes, company officials physically bar her from leaving the bank. That is false imprisonment. The restraint was unreasonable because her accounts could have been verified later.[4]

False imprisonment cases most commonly arise in retail stores, which sometimes detain employees or customers for suspected theft. Most states now have statutes governing the detention of suspected shoplifters. **Generally, a store may detain a customer or worker for alleged shoplifting provided there is a reasonable basis for the suspicion and the detention is done reasonably.** To detain a customer in the manager's office for 20 minutes and question him about where he got an item is lawful. To chain that customer to a display counter for three hours and humiliate him in front of other customers is unreasonable and constitutes false imprisonment.

False imprisonment

The intentional restraint of another person without reasonable cause and without consent

8-1c Intentional Infliction of Emotional Distress

What should happen when a defendant's conduct hurts a plaintiff emotionally but not physically? Historically, not much did happen. Courts once refused to allow recovery, assuming that if they awarded damages for mere emotional injury, they would be inviting a floodgate of dubious claims. But gradually judges reexamined their thinking and reversed this tendency. Today, most courts allow a plaintiff to recover for emotional injury that a defendant intentionally caused.

The **intentional infliction of emotional distress** results from extreme and outrageous conduct that causes serious emotional harm. A credit officer was struggling vainly to locate Sheehan, who owed money on his car. The officer phoned Sheehan's mother, falsely identified herself as a hospital employee, and said she needed to find Sheehan because his children had been in a serious auto accident. The mother provided Sheehan's whereabouts, which enabled the company to seize his car. But Sheehan spent seven hours frantically trying to locate his supposedly injured children, who in fact were fine. The credit company was liable for the intentional infliction of emotional distress.[5]

By contrast, a muffler shop, trying to collect a debt from a customer, made six phone calls over three months, using abusive language. The customer testified that this caused her to be upset, to cry, and to have difficulty sleeping. The court ruled that the muffler shop's conduct was neither extreme nor outrageous.[6]

The following case arose in a setting that guarantees controversy—an abortion clinic.

Intentional infliction of emotional distress

An intentional tort in which the harm results from extreme and outrageous conduct that causes serious emotional harm

---

[4]Kanner v. First National Bank of South Miami, 287 So.2d 715 (Fla. Dist. Ct. App. 1974).
[5]Ford Motor Credit Co. v. Sheehan, 373 So.2d 956 (Fla. Dist. Ct. App. 1979).
[6]Midas Muffler Shop v. Ellison, 133 Ariz. 194 (Ariz. Ct. App. 1982).

JANE DOE AND NANCY ROE V. LYNN MILLS

212 Mich. App. 73
Michigan Court of Appeals, 1995

Facts: Late one night, an anti-abortion protestor named Robert Thomas climbed into a dumpster located behind the Women's Advisory Center, an abortion clinic. He found documents indicating that the plaintiffs were soon to have abortions at the clinic. Thomas gave the information to Lynn Mills. The next day, Mills and Sister Lois Mitoraj created signs, using the women's names, indicating that they were about to undergo abortions, and urging them not to "kill their babies."

Doe and Roe (not their real names) sued, claiming intentional infliction of emotional distress (as well as breach of privacy, discussed later in this chapter). The trial court dismissed the lawsuit, ruling that the defendants' conduct was not extreme and outrageous. The plaintiffs appealed.

Issue: *Have the plaintiffs made a valid claim of intentional infliction of emotional distress?*

Excerpts from the Court's *Per Curiam* Decision:
Liability for the intentional infliction of emotional distress has been found only where the conduct complained of has been so outrageous in character, and so extreme in degree, as to go beyond all possible bounds of decency, and to be regarded as atrocious and utterly intolerable in a civilized community. Liability does not extend to mere insults, indignities, threats, annoyances, petty oppressions, or other trivialities. It has been said that the case is generally one in which the recitation of the facts to an average member of the community would arouse his resentment against the actor, and lead him to exclaim, "Outrageous!"

The conduct in this case involved defendants identifying plaintiffs by name and publicizing the fact of their abortions by displaying such information on large signs that were held up for public view. In ruling that defendants'

conduct was not sufficiently extreme and outrageous so as to permit recovery, the trial court was influenced in part by its conclusion that the information disclosed did not concern a private matter, inasmuch as it was obtained from a document that had been discarded into the trash. [But the plaintiffs themselves never placed their names on the discarded papers, and even if they had, such an act would not have indicated consent to such publicity.] The trial court also observed that defendants have a constitutional right to "protest peaceably against abortion." However, the objectionable aspect of defendants' conduct does not relate to their views on abortion or their right to express those views, but, rather, to the fact that defendants gave unreasonable or unnecessary publicity to purely private matters involving plaintiffs. Finally, the trial court observed that there is no statute prohibiting the kind of activity engaged in by defendants. It is not necessary, however, that a defendant's conduct constitute a statutory violation in order for it to be found extreme and outrageous.

We are of the opinion that the trial court erred in granting the defendants' motion for summary disposition of plaintiffs' claim of intentional infliction of emotional distress. Defendants' conduct involved more than mere insults, indignities, threats, annoyances, or petty oppressions. We believe this is the type of case that might cause an average member of the community, upon learning of defendants' conduct, to exclaim, "Outrageous!" Because reasonable men may differ with regard to whether defendants' conduct may be considered sufficiently outrageous and extreme so as to subject them to liability for intentional infliction of emotional distress, this matter should be determined by the trier of fact.

Summary judgment for the defendants is reversed, and the case is remanded for trial.

8-1d **Battery and Assault**

Battery

An intentional touching of another person in a way that is harmful or offensive

Assault and battery are related, but not identical. **Battery** is an intentional touching of another person in a way that is harmful or offensive.

If an irate parent throws a chair at a referee during his daughter's basketball game, breaking the man's jaw, he has committed battery. But a parent who cheerfully slaps the winning coach on the back has not committed battery because a reasonable coach would not be offended.

As mentioned earlier, there need be no intention to hurt the plaintiff. If the defendant intended to do the physical act, and a reasonable plaintiff would be offended by it, battery has occurred. An executive who gives an unwanted sexual caress to a secretary also commits this tort, even if he assumed that any normal female would be ecstatic over his attentions. (This is also sexual harassment, discussed in Chapter 29, on employment law.)

Assault occurs when a defendant does some act that makes a plaintiff *fear* an imminent battery. This tort is based on apprehension—it does not matter whether a battery ever occurs. Suppose Ms. Wilson shouts "Think fast!" at her husband and hurls a toaster at him. He turns and sees it flying at him. His fear of being struck is enough to win a case of assault, even if the toaster misses. If the toaster happens to strike him, Ms. Wilson has also committed battery.

Recall the shoplifting problem. Assume that a store guard pulls an unloaded pistol on Sandra Shopper, suspecting her of theft. Sandra faints and strikes her head on a counter. When sued for assault, the store defends by claiming the guard never touched her and the gun was unloaded. Obviously, the store did not have the benefit of this law course. A reasonable shopper would have feared imminent battery, and the store is liable for assault.

Assault

An act that makes a person reasonably fear an imminent battery

EXAM Strategy

Question: Mark is furious because his girlfriend, Denise, just told him she is leaving him. He never saw it coming. On the sidewalk, he picks up a rock and hurls it at Denise's head. She *does* see it coming, and she ducks. The rock misses Denise but hits Terrance (who never saw it coming) in the back of his head. Denise and Terrance both sue Mark for assault and for battery. Outcomes?

Strategy: Separate the two plaintiffs. What injury did Denise suffer? She saw a rock flying at her and thought she would be struck. Now recall the elements of the two torts. Battery is an intentional touching that is offensive. Assault is an act that makes another person *fear* an imminent battery.

Result: Was Denise touched? No. Did she fear an imminent battery? Yes. Denise wins a suit for assault but loses one for battery. Now Terrance: Was he touched? Yes. Did he fear an imminent battery? No. Terrance wins a suit for battery but loses one for assault.

8-1e **Trespass, Conversion, and Fraud**

Trespass

Trespass is intentionally entering land that belongs to someone else or remaining on the land after being asked to leave. It is also trespass if you have some object, let's say a car, on someone else's property and refuse to remove it. "Intentionally" means that you deliberately walk onto the land. If you walk through a meadow, believing it to be a public park, and it belongs to a private owner, you have trespassed.

Trespass

Intentionally entering land that belongs to someone else or remaining on the land after being asked to leave

Conversion

Conversion is taking or using someone's personal property without consent. Personal property is any possession other than land or structures permanently attached to land, such as houses. Priceless jewels, ratty sneakers, and sailboats are all personal property. If Stormy sails away in Jib's sailboat and keeps it all summer, that is conversion. Stormy owes Jib the full value of the boat. This, of course, is similar to the crime of theft. The tort of conversion enables a plaintiff to pursue the case herself, without awaiting a criminal prosecution, and to obtain compensation.

Fraud

Fraud is injuring another person by deliberate deception. Later in this chapter, a plaintiff claims that for many years a cigarette manufacturer fraudulently suggested its product was safe, knowing its assurances were deadly lies. Fraud is a tort, but it typically occurs during the negotiation or performance of a contract, and it is discussed in detail in Unit 3, on contracts.

8-2 DAMAGES

8-2a Compensatory Damages

Mitchel Bien, who is deaf and mute, enters the George Grubbs Nissan dealership, where folks sell cars aggressively. Very aggressively. Maturelli, a salesman, and Bien communicate by writing messages back and forth. Maturelli takes Bien's own car keys, and the two then test-drive a 300ZX. Bien says he does not want the car, but Maturelli escorts him back inside and fills out a sales sheet. Bien repeatedly asks for his keys, but Maturelli only laughs, pressuring him to buy the new car. Minutes pass. Hours pass. Bien becomes frantic, writing a dozen notes, begging to leave, threatening to call the police. Maturelli mocks Bien and his physical disabilities. Finally, after four hours, the customer escapes.

> Bien becomes frantic, writing a dozen notes, begging to leave, threatening to call the police.

Bien sues for the intentional infliction of emotional distress. Two former salesmen from Grubbs testify they have witnessed customers cry, yell, and curse as a result of the aggressive tactics. Doctors state that the incident has traumatized Bien, dramatically reducing his confidence and self-esteem and preventing his return to work even three years later.

The jury awards Bien damages. But how does a jury calculate the money? For that matter, why should a jury even try? Money can never erase pain or undo a permanent injury. The answer is simple: Money, however inexact, is often the only thing a court has to give.

A successful plaintiff generally receives **compensatory damages**, meaning an amount of money that the court believes will restore him to the position he was in before the defendant's conduct caused injury. Here is how damages are calculated.

First, a plaintiff receives money for medical expenses that he has proven by producing bills from doctors, hospitals, physical therapists, and psychotherapists. Bien receives all the money he has paid. If a doctor testifies that he needs future treatment, Bien will offer evidence of how much that will cost. The **single recovery principle** requires a court to settle the matter once and for all, by awarding a lump sum for past *and future* expenses, if there will be any. A plaintiff may not return in a year and say, "Oh, by the way, there are some new bills."

Second, the defendants are liable for lost wages. The court takes the number of days or months that Bien missed work and multiplies that number times his salary. If Bien is currently unable to work, a doctor estimates how many more months he will miss work, and the court adds that to his damages.

Third, a plaintiff is paid for pain and suffering. Bien testifies about how traumatic the four hours were and how the experience has affected his life. He may state that he now fears shopping, suffers nightmares, and seldom socializes. To bolster the case, a plaintiff uses expert testimony, such as the psychiatrists who testified for Bien. Awards for pain and suffering vary enormously, from a few dollars to many millions, depending on the injury and depending on the jury. In some lawsuits, physical and psychological pains are momentary and insignificant; in other cases, the pain is the biggest part of the verdict. In this case, the jury awarded Bien $573,815, calculated as in the following table.[7]

Past medical	$ 70.00
Future medical	6,000.00
Past rehabilitation	3,205.00
Past lost earning capacity	112,910.00
Future lost earning capacity	34,650.00
Past physical symptoms and discomfort	50,000.00
Future physical symptoms and discomfort	50,000.00
Past emotional injury and mental anguish	101,980.00
Future emotional injury and mental anguish	200,000.00
Past loss of society and reduced ability to socially interact with family, former fiancée, friends, and hearing (i.e., nondeaf) people in general	10,000.00
Future loss of society and reduced ability to socially interact with family, former fiancée, friends, and hearing people	5,000.00
TOTAL	**$573,815.00**

[7]The compensatory damages are described in George Grubbs Enterprises v. Bien, 881 S.W.2d 843 (Tex. Ct. App. 1994). In addition to the compensatory damages described, the jury awarded $5 million in punitive damages. The Texas Supreme Court reversed the award of punitive damages, but not the compensatory. Id., 900 S.W.2d 337 (Tex. 1995). The high court did not dispute the appropriateness of punitive damages, but reversed because the trial court failed to instruct the jury properly as to how it should determine the assets actually under the defendants' control, an issue essential to punitive damages but not compensatory.

Awards for future harm (such as future pain and suffering) involve the court making its best estimate of the plaintiff's hardship in the years to come. This is not an exact science. If the judgment is reasonable, it will rarely be overturned. Ethel Flanzraich, age 78, fell on stairs that had been badly maintained. In addition to her medical expense, the court awarded her $150,000 for future pain and suffering. The day after the court gave its award, Ms. Flanzraich died of other causes. Did that mean her family must forfeit that money? No. The award was reasonable when made and had to be paid.[8]

8-2b Punitive Damages

Punitive damages

Damages that are intended to punish the defendant for conduct that is extreme and outrageous

Here we look at a different kind of award, one that is more controversial and potentially more powerful: punitive damages. The purpose is not to compensate the plaintiff for harm, because compensatory damages will have done that. **Punitive damages** are intended to punish the defendant for conduct that is extreme and outrageous. Courts award these damages in relatively few cases. The idea behind punitive damages is that certain behavior is so unacceptable that society must make an example of it. A large award of money should deter the defendant from repeating the mistake and others from ever making it. Some believe punitive damages represent the law at its most avaricious, while others attribute to them great social benefit.

Although a jury has wide discretion in awarding punitive damages, the Supreme Court has ruled that a verdict must be reasonable. Ira Gore purchased a new BMW automobile from an Alabama dealer and then discovered that the car had been repainted. He sued. At trial, BMW acknowledged a nationwide policy of not informing customers of predelivery repairs when the cost was less than 3 percent of the retail price. The company had sold about 1,000 repainted cars nationwide. The jury concluded that BMW had engaged in gross, malicious fraud and awarded Gore $4,000 in compensatory damages and $4 million in punitive damages. The Alabama Supreme Court reduced the award to $2 million, but the United States Supreme Court ruled that even that amount was grossly excessive. The Court held that in awarding punitive damages, a court must consider three "guideposts":

- The reprehensibility of the defendant's conduct;

- The ratio between the harm suffered and the award; and

- The difference between the punitive award and any civil penalties used in similar cases.

The Court concluded that BMW had shown no evil intent and that Gore's harm had been purely economic (as opposed to physical). Further, the Court found the ratio of 500 to 1, between punitive and compensatory damages, to be excessive, although it offered no definitive rule about a proper ratio. On remand, the Alabama Supreme Court reduced the punitive damages award to $50,000.[9]

The U.S. Supreme Court gave additional guidance on punitive damages in the following landmark case.

---

[8]Stinton v. Robin's Wood, 842 N.Y.S.2d 477 (N.Y. App. Div. 2007).
[9]BMW of North America, Inc. v. Gore, 517 U.S. 559 (1996).

Landmark Case

STATE FARM V. CAMPBELL

538 U.S. 408
Supreme Court of the United States, 2003

Facts: While attempting to pass several cars on a two-lane road, Campbell drove into oncoming traffic. An innocent driver swerved to avoid Campbell and died in a collision with a third driver. The family of the deceased driver and the surviving third driver both sued Campbell.

As Campbell's insurer, State Farm represented him in the lawsuit. It turned down an offer to settle the case for $50,000, the limit of Campbell's policy. The company had nothing to gain by settling because even if Campbell lost big at trial, State Farm's liability was capped at $50,000.

A jury returned a judgment against Campbell for $185,000. He was responsible for the $135,000 that exceeded his policy limit. He argued with State Farm, claiming that it should have settled the case. Eventually, State Farm paid the entire $185,000, but Campbell still sued the company, alleging fraud and intentional infliction of emotional distress.

His lawyers presented evidence that State Farm had deliberately acted in its own best interests rather than his. The jury was convinced, and in the end, Campbell won an award of $1 million in compensatory damages and $145 million in punitive damages. State Farm appealed.

Issue: *What is the limit on punitive damages?*

Excerpts from Justice Kennedy's Decision: We address whether an award of $145 million in punitive damages, where full compensatory damages are $1 million, is excessive and in violation of the Due Process Clause. The Utah Supreme Court relied upon testimony indicating that State Farm's actions, because of their clandestine nature, will be punished at most in 1 out of every 50,000 cases as a matter of statistical probability, and concluded that the ratio between punitive and compensatory damages was not unwarranted.

Compensatory damages are intended to redress the concrete loss that the plaintiff has suffered by reason of the defendant's wrongful conduct. By contrast, punitive damages serve a broader function; they are aimed at deterrence and retribution.

The Due Process Clause prohibits the imposition of grossly excessive or arbitrary punishments. The reason is that elementary notions of fairness dictate that a person receive fair notice not only of the conduct that will subject him to punishment, but also of the severity of the penalty that a State may impose. To the extent an award is grossly excessive, it furthers no legitimate purpose and constitutes an arbitrary deprivation of property. A defendant should be punished for the conduct that harmed the plaintiff, not for being an unsavory.

We decline to impose a bright-line ratio which a punitive damages award cannot exceed. Our jurisprudence and the principles it has now established demonstrate, however, that, in practice, few awards exceeding a single-digit ratio between punitive and compensatory damages, to a significant degree, will satisfy due process. Single-digit multipliers are more likely to comport with due process, while still achieving the State's goals of deterrence and retribution, than awards with ratios in the range of 145 to 1.

Nonetheless, because there are no rigid benchmarks that a punitive damages award may not surpass, ratios greater than those we have previously upheld may comport with due process where a particularly egregious act has resulted in only a small amount of economic damages. The precise award in any case must be based upon the facts and circumstances of the defendant's conduct and the harm to the plaintiff.

In sum, courts must ensure that the measure of punishment is both reasonable and proportionate to the amount of harm to the plaintiff and to the general damages recovered. In the context of this case, we have no doubt that there is a presumption against an award that has a 145-to-1 ratio. The compensatory award in this case was substantial; the Campbells were awarded $1 million for a year and a half of emotional distress. This was complete compensation. The harm arose from a transaction in the economic realm, not from some physical assault or trauma; there were no physical injuries; and State Farm paid the excess verdict before the complaint was filed, so the Campbells suffered only minor economic injuries.

The judgment of the Utah Supreme Court is reversed, and the case is remanded for proceedings not inconsistent with this opinion.

Dramatic cases may *still* lead to very large awards.

And so, the Supreme Court seeks to limit, but not completely prohibit, enormous punitive damages. A California Court of Appeals decided the following case two years after *State Farm v. Campbell*. How should it implement the Supreme Court's guidelines? You be the judge.

You be the Judge

BOEKEN V. PHILIP MORRIS, INCORPORATED

127 Cal. App.4th 1640
California Court of Appeals, 2005

Facts: In the mid-1950s, Richard Boeken began smoking Marlboro cigarettes at the age of 10. Countless advertisements, targeted at boys ages 10 to 18, convinced him and his friends that the "Marlboro man" was powerful, healthy, and manly. Eventually, Richard changed to "Marlboro Lite" cigarettes but continued smoking into the 1990s, when he was diagnosed with lung cancer. He filed suit against Philip Morris, the cigarette manufacturer, for fraud and other torts. He died of cancer before the case was concluded.

Evidence at trial demonstrated that by the mid-1950s, scientists uniformly accepted that cigarette smoking caused lung cancer. However, at about the same time, Philip Morris and other tobacco companies began a decades-long campaign to convince the public that there was substantial doubt about any link between smoking and illness. The plaintiffs also demonstrated that tobacco was physically addictive, and that Philip Morris added ingredients such as urea to its cigarettes to increase their addictive power. Boeken testified that in the late 1960s he saw the Surgeon General warnings about the risk of smoking but trusted the cigarette company's statements that smoking was safe. By the 1970s he tried many times, and many cures, to stop smoking but always failed. He finally quit just before surgery to remove part of his lung but resumed after the operation.

The jury found Philip Morris liable for fraudulently concealing that cigarettes were addictive and carcinogenic. It awarded Boeken $5.5 million in compensatory damages, and also assessed punitive damages—of $3 *billion*. The trial judge reduced the punitive award to $100 million. Philip Morris appealed.

You Be the Judge: *Was the punitive damage award too high, too low, or just right?*

Argument for Philip Morris: The court should substantially reduce the $100 million punitive award because it constitutes an "arbitrary deprivation of property." The Supreme Court has indicated that punitive awards should not exceed compensatory damages by more than a factor of nine. The jury awarded Mr. Boeken $5.5 million in compensatory damages, which means that punitive damages should absolutely not exceed $49.5 million. We argue that they should be even lower.

Cigarettes are a legal product, and our packages have displayed the Surgeon General's health warnings for decades. Mr. Boeken's death is tragic, but his cancer was not necessarily caused by Marlboro cigarettes. And even if cigarettes did contribute to his failing health, Mr. Boeken chose to smoke throughout his life, even after major surgery on one of his lungs.

Argument for Boeken: The Supreme Court says that "few" cases may exceed the 9-to-1 ratio, but that "the precise award in any case must be based upon the facts and circumstances of the defendant's conduct and the harm to the plaintiff." Phillip Morris created ads that targeted children, challenged clear scientific data that its products caused cancer, and added substances to its cigarettes to make them more addictive. Does it get worse than that?

As for harm to the plaintiff, he died a terrible death from cancer. Philip Morris cigarettes kill 200,000 American customers each year. The defendant's conduct could not be more reprehensible. Philip Morris's weekly profit is roughly $100 million. At a minimum, the court should keep the punitive award at that figure. But we ask that the court reinstate the jury's original $3 billion award.

8-2c **Tort Reform and the *Exxon Valdez***

Some people believe that jury awards are excessive and need statutory reform, while others argue that the evidence demonstrates excessive awards are rare and modest in size. About one-half of the states have passed limits. The laws vary, but many distinguish between **economic damage** and **noneconomic damages**. In such a state, a jury is permitted to award any amount for economic damages, meaning lost wages, medical expenses, and other measureable losses. However, noneconomic damages-pain and suffering and other losses that are difficult to measure—are capped at some level, such as $500,000. In some states, punitive awards have similar caps. These restrictions can drastically lower the total verdict.

In the famous *Exxon Valdez* case, the Supreme Court placed a severe limit on a certain type of punitive award. It is unclear how influential the decision will be because the case arises in the isolated area of maritime law, which governs ships at sea. Nonetheless, the justices wrote at length about punitive awards, and the decision may reverberate in future holdings. This is what happened.

Captain Joseph Hazelwood's negligence caused the *Exxon Valdez* to run aground off the coast of Alaska. The ship dumped 11 million gallons of oil into the sea, damaging 3,000 square miles of vulnerable ecosystem. The oil spill forced fishermen into bankruptcy, disrupted entire communities, and killed hundreds of thousands of birds and marine animals. A decade later, many of the damaged species had not recovered. The jury decided that Exxon had been reckless by allowing Hazelwood to pilot the ship when the company knew he was an alcoholic. The jury awarded compensatory damages to the plaintiffs, and punitive damages of $5 *billion*. Exxon appealed.

Almost two decades after the accident, the Supreme Court ruled. The justices discussed punitive damages in general, noting that much of the criticism of punitive awards appeared overstated. The court declared there had been no major increase in how frequently juries gave punitive damages. In the unusual cases where jurors made such awards, the sums were modest. The problem, declared the justices, was the unpredictability of punitive damages.

Until the 2010 Deepwater Horizon Oil Spill, the Exxon Valdez was the largest ever oil spill in U.S. waters.

Accent Alaska.com/Alamy

The court ruled that *in maritime cases*, the ratio should be no higher than 1:1. The court approved the jury's compensatory award of $507 million, and then reduced the punitive award from $5 billion to $507 million. Supporters of the court's decision stated that it would allow businesses to make plans based on predictable outcomes. Opponents said that the justices ignored the jury's finding of reckless behavior and calamitous environmental harm.[10]

---

[10]Exxon Shipping Co. v. Baker, 554 U.S. 471 (2008).

EXAM Strategy

Question: Patrick owns a fast-food restaurant, which is repeatedly painted with graffiti. He is convinced that 15-year-old John, a frequent customer, is the culprit. The next time John comes to the restaurant, Patrick locks the men's room door while John is inside. Patrick calls the police, but because of a misunderstanding, the police are very slow to arrive. John shouts and cries for help, banging on the door, but Patrick does not release him for two hours. John sues. He claims that he has suffered great psychological harm because of the incident; his psychiatrist asserts that John may have unpredictable suffering in the future. John sues for assault, battery, and false imprisonment. Will he win? May John return to court in the future to seek further damages?

Strategy: The question focuses on two issues: first, the distinction between several intentional torts; second, damages. Analyze one issue at a time. As to the intentional torts, what injury has John suffered? He was locked in the men's room and suffered psychological harm. Recall the elements of the three possible torts. Battery concerns an offensive touching. A defendant commits assault by causing an imminent fear of battery. False imprisonment: A store may detain someone if it does so reasonably.

As to damages, review the *single recovery principle*.

Result: Locking John up for two hours, based on an unproven suspicion, was clearly unreasonable. Patrick has committed false imprisonment. The single recovery principle forces John to recover now for all past and future harm. He may not return to court later and seek additional damages.

8-3 BUSINESS TORTS

In this section, we look at several intentional torts that occur almost exclusively in a commercial setting: interference with a contract, interference with a prospective advantage, and Lanham Act violations. Note that several business torts are discussed elsewhere in the book:

- Violations of the rights to privacy and publicity are examined in Chapter 10, on cyberlaw and privacy.

- Patents, copyrights, and trademarks are discussed in Chapter 41, on intellectual property.

- False advertising and other consumer issues are considered more broadly in Chapter 39, on consumer law.

8-3a **Tortious Interference with Business Relations**

Competition is the essence of business. Successful corporations compete aggressively, and the law permits and expects them to. But there are times when healthy competition becomes illegal interference. This is called *tortious interference with business relations*. It can take one of two closely related forms—interference with a contract or interference with a prospective advantage.

8-3b **Tortious Interference with a Contract**

Tortious interference with a contract exists if the plaintiff can establish the following four elements:

- There was a contract between the plaintiff and a third party;

- The defendant knew of the contract;

- The defendant improperly *induced* the third party to breach the contract or made performance of the contract impossible; and

- There was injury to the plaintiff.

Because businesses routinely compete for customers, employees, and market share, it is not always easy to identify tortious interference. There is nothing wrong with two companies bidding against each other to buy a parcel of land, and nothing wrong with one corporation doing everything possible to convince the seller to ignore all competitors. But once a company has signed a contract to buy the land, it is improper to induce the seller to break the deal. The most commonly disputed issues in these cases concern elements one and three: Was there a contract between the plaintiff and another party? Did the defendant improperly induce a party to breach it? Defendants will try to show that the plaintiff had no contract.

A defendant may also rely on the defense of **justification**, that is, a claim that special circumstances made its conduct fair. To establish justification, a defendant must show that:

- It was acting to protect an existing economic interest, such as its own contract with the third party;

- It was acting in the public interest, for example, by reporting to a government agency that a corporation was overbilling for government services; or

- The existing contract could be terminated at will by either party, meaning that although the plaintiff had a contract, the plaintiff had no long-term assurances because the other side could end it at any time.

Texaco v. Pennzoil

The jury returned an enormous verdict in a famous case of contract interference. *Texaco, Inc. v. Pennzoil Co.* illustrates the two key issues: Did a contract exist, and was the defendant's behavior improper? Pennzoil made an unsolicited bid to buy 20 percent of Getty Oil at $100 per share. This offer was too low to satisfy the Getty board of directors, but it got the parties talking. The price increased to $110 per share, and the two sides began to put together pieces of a complicated deal: Gordon Getty would control four-sevenths of the Getty Oil stock, and Pennzoil would control three-sevenths. The J. Paul Getty Museum, which owned 11.8 percent of Getty stock, agreed to sell its shares provided it was paid immediately. Talks continued, the price moved up to $112.50 a share, and finally the Getty board voted to approve the deal. A press release announced an agreement in principle between Pennzoil and Getty.

Before the lawyers for both sides could complete the paperwork for the deal, Texaco appeared and offered Getty stockholders $125 per share for the entire company and later upped that offer to $128 per share. Getty turned its attention to Texaco, leaving Pennzoil the jilted lover. This lover, though, decided to sue. In Texas state court, Pennzoil claimed that Texaco had maliciously interfered with a Pennzoil–Getty contract, costing Pennzoil vast amounts of money.

Texaco argued that it had acted in good faith, asserting that there was no binding contract between the other two. But the jury bought Pennzoil's argument, and they bought

Tortious interference with a contract

An intentional tort in which the defendant improperly induced a third party to breach a contract with the plaintiff

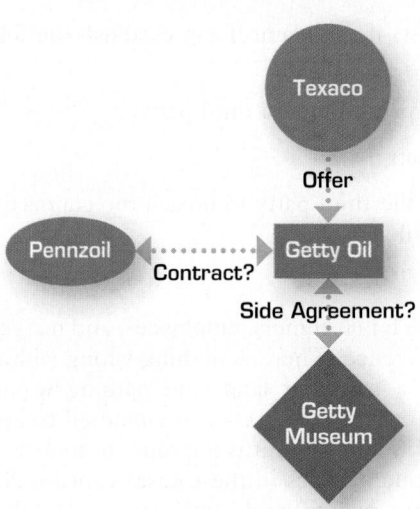

EXHIBIT 8.2   The $10 *billion* question. Texaco offered to pay $125 per share for Getty stock. The key issue was this: when Texaco made the offer, did a contract exist between Pennzoil and Getty? If, as the jury decided, there was a binding agreement, then Texaco committed tortious interference with a contract. If, however, Getty Corp. had a side agreement with the Getty Museum (one of its owners), then arguably there could be no contract between Getty and Pennzoil, and Texaco would have committed no tort at all.

it big: $7.53 billion in actual damages, plus $3 billion more in punitive damages. Texaco did not happen to have $10 billion it could spare, and the verdict threatened to destroy the oil company. Texaco appealed, but Texas appeals courts require a bond, in this case a $10 billion bond, meaning that the money must be paid into court while the appeal goes forward. Texaco filed for bankruptcy.

At the state supreme court, Texaco based its argument on an obscure rule of the Securities and Exchange Commission (SEC), Rule 10B-13. This rule prevents the parties in a takeover negotiation from arranging a "side deal" while an offer is pending. Texaco's argument thus became: Pennzoil's original $100 per share offer was still pending when the two sides came up with their $112.50 per share, "three-sevenths/four-sevenths" deal. That deal involved a side arrangement with the Getty Museum, which would get its money faster than any other shareholders would. Because it would get about $1 billion, early receipt was a major financial advantage. The deal violated Rule 10B-13 and was therefore invalid. There was no contract, and Texaco could not legally have interfered.

A $10 billion case would be decided on the classic "interference" issue of whether a contract existed. Then the SEC entered the case, filing a brief that appeared strongly to support Texaco's interpretation of the law. Pennzoil could sense that the tide was turning, and the companies settled: Texaco agreed to pay Pennzoil $3 billion as settlement for having wrongfully interfered with Pennzoil's agreement to buy Getty.

8-3c Tortious Interference with a Prospective Advantage

Tortious interference with a prospective advantage
Malicious interference with a developing economic relationship

Tortious interference with a prospective advantage is an awkward name for a tort that is simply a variation on interference with a contract. The difference is that, for this tort, there need be no contract; the plaintiff is claiming outside interference with an expected economic relationship. Obviously, the plaintiff must show more than just the hope of a profit. **A plaintiff who has a definite and reasonable expectation of obtaining an economic advantage may sue a corporation that maliciously interferes and prevents the relationship from developing.**

The defense of justification, discussed earlier, applies here as well. A typical example of justification is that the defendant is simply competing for the same business that the plaintiff seeks. There is nothing wrong with that.

To demonstrate interference with a prospective advantage, most courts require a plaintiff to show that the defendant's conduct was independently unlawful. Suppose Pink manufactures valves used in heart surgery. Pink is about to sign a deal for Rabbit to distribute the products. Zebra then says to Pink, "I want that deal. If you sign with Rabbit, I'll spread false rumors that the valves are unreliable." Pink gives in and signs a contract with Zebra. Zebra has committed interference with a prospective advantage because slander is independently illegal.[11]

The ice cream fight that follows demonstrates why plaintiffs often file but seldom win these cases.

CARVEL V. NOONAN

3 N.Y.3d 182
New York Court of Appeals, 2004

Facts: For decades, Carvel sold its ice cream only through franchised stores. However, a decline in revenues caused the company to begin selling its product in supermarkets. That effort expanded quickly, but many of the franchised stores (franchisees) went out of business. Franchisees filed suit, claiming tortious interference with a prospective advantage. In particular, the plaintiffs argued that Carvel undersold them in supermarkets and issued coupons only redeemable there. The case reached New York's highest court.

Issue: *Had Carvel committed tortious interference with a prospective advantage?*

Excerpts from Justice Smith's Decision: The franchisees' tort claim is that Carvel unlawfully interfered with the relationships between the franchisees and their customers. The franchisees do not claim that the customers had binding contracts that Carvel induced them to breach; they allege only that, by implementing its supermarket program, Carvel induced the customers not to buy Carvel products from the franchisees. The juries have found that Carvel did so induce customers, and the question for us is whether that inducement was tortious interference under New York law.

We have recognized that inducing breach of a binding agreement and interfering with a nonbinding "economic relation" can both be torts, but that the elements of the two torts are not the same. Where there has been no breach of an existing contract, but only interference with prospective contract rights, however, plaintiff must show more culpable conduct on the part of the defendant. The implication is that, as a general rule, the defendant's conduct must amount to a crime or an independent tort.

The franchisees claim that Carvel did use wrongful "economic pressure" but that argument is ill-founded for two independent reasons. First, it is ill-founded because the economic pressure that must be shown is not, as the franchisees assume, pressure on the franchisees, but on the franchisees' customers. Conduct constituting tortious interference with business relations is, by definition, conduct directed not at the plaintiff itself, but at the party with which the plaintiff has or seeks to have a relationship.

Here, all Carvel did to the franchisees' customers was to make Carvel goods available in supermarkets at attractive prices; this was not "pressure" on these third parties but

---

[11]For a more detailed explanation, see Wal-Mart Stores, Inc. v. Sturges, 52 S.W.3d 711 (Tex. 2001).

legitimate "persuasion," and thus tortious interference with economic relations was not established.

The franchisees' argument is also ill-founded because the Carvel activities they complain of do not amount to the sort of extreme and unfair "economic pressure" that might be "wrongful." The crux of the franchisees' complaint is that Carvel distributed its products through competitive channels, to an extent and in a way that was inconsistent with the franchisor–franchisee relationship. But the relationship between franchisors and franchisees is a complex one; while cooperative, it does not preclude all competition; and the extent to which competition is allowed should be determined by the contracts between the parties, not by courts or juries seeking after the fact to devise a code of conduct.

Apart from attacking the supermarket program in general as excessively and destructively competitive, the franchisees also attack the coupon-redemption element of that program as excessive "economic pressure." The essence of the coupon program was to give customers who used coupons a better price when they shopped in supermarkets. The mere institution of a coupon program was not "economic pressure" rising to the level of "wrongful" or "culpable" conduct.

Carvel's conduct was not tortious interference with a prospective advantage.

The Lanham Act

The Lanham Act provides broad protection against false statements intended to hurt another business. In order to win a case, a plaintiff must prove three things:

- That the defendants made false or misleading fact statements about the plaintiff's business. This could be a false comparative ad, showing the plaintiff's product to be worse than it is, or it could be a misleading ad, which, though literally accurate, is misleading about the defendant's own product.

- That the defendants used the statements in commercial advertising or promotion. In order to protect First Amendment rights of free speech, particularly political and social commentary, this act covers only commercial speech. A radio ad for beer could violate the Lanham Act; however, a radio ad urging that smoking be abolished in public places is not a commercial statement and cannot violate the act.

- That statements created the likelihood of harm to the plaintiff.[12]

"Knock It Off brand food supplement will help you lose weight and gain muscle faster than any competing supplement," shrieks the television commercial, offering an independent study as proof. However, a competitor sues and demonstrates that during the study, users of Knock It Off received free health club memberships and low-fat gourmet meals, distorting the results. Knock It Off has violated the Lanham Act. The court will order the company to knock it off and stop showing the commercial, and also to pay damages to the injured competitor.

Chapter Conclusion

This chapter has been a potpourri of misdeeds, a bubbling cauldron of conduct best avoided. Although tortious acts and their consequences are diverse, two generalities apply. First, the boundaries of intentional torts are imprecise, the outcome of a particular case depending to a considerable extent upon the factfinder who analyzes it. Second, thoughtful executives and careful citizens, aware of the shifting standards and potentially vast liability, will strive to ensure that their conduct never provides that factfinder an opportunity to give judgment.

---

[12]18 U.S.C §2511.

EXAM REVIEW

1. TORT   A tort is a violation of a duty imposed by the civil law.

Question: Keith is driving while intoxicated. He swerves into the wrong lane and causes an accident, seriously injuring Caroline. Which statement is true?

a. Caroline could sue Keith, who might be found guilty in her suit.

b. Caroline and the state could start separate criminal cases against Keith.

c. Caroline could sue Keith, and the state could prosecute Keith for drunk driving.

d. The state could sue Keith but only with Caroline's consent.

e. The state could prosecute Keith and sue him at the same time for drunk driving.

Strategy: What party prosecutes a criminal case? The government does, not the injured party. What is the result in a criminal case? Guilt or innocence. What about a tort lawsuit? The injured party brings a tort suit. The defendant may be found liable but never guilty. (See the "Result" at the end of this section.)

2. DEFAMATION   Defamation involves a defamatory statement that is false, uttered to a third person, and causes an injury. Opinion and privilege are valid defenses.

Question: Benzaquin had a radio talk show. On the program, he complained about an incident in which state trooper Fleming had stopped his car, apparently for lack of a proper license plate and safety sticker. Benzaquin explained that the license plate had been stolen and the sticker fallen onto the dashboard, but Fleming refused to let him drive away. Benzaquin and two young grandsons had to find other transportation. On the show, Benzaquin angrily recounted the incident, and then described Fleming and troopers generally: "we're not paying them to be dictators and Nazis"; "this man is an absolute barbarian, a lunkhead, a meathead." Fleming sued Benzaquin for defamation. Comment.

Strategy: Review the elements of defamation. Can these statements be proven true or false? If not, what is the result? Look at the defenses. Does one apply? (See the "Result" at the end of this section.)

3. MALICE   Public personalities can win a defamation suit only by proving actual malice.

4. FALSE IMPRISONMENT   False imprisonment is the intentional restraint of another person without reasonable cause and without consent.

5. EMOTIONAL DISTRESS   The intentional infliction of emotional distress involves extreme and outrageous conduct that causes serious emotional harm.

6. BATTERY   Battery is an intentional touching of another person in a way that is unwanted or offensive. Assault involves an act that makes the plaintiff fear an imminent battery.

EXAM Strategy

Question: Caudle worked at Betts Lincoln-Mercury dealer. During an office party, many of the employees, including president Betts, were playing with an electric auto condenser, which gave a slight shock when touched. Some employees played catch with it. Betts shocked Caudle on the back of his neck, and chased him around. The shock later caused Caudle to suffer headaches, pass out, feel numbness, and eventually to require nerve surgery. He sued Betts for battery. Betts defended by saying that it was all horseplay and that he had intended no harm. Please rule.

Strategy: Betts argues he intended no harm. Is intent to harm an element? (See the "Result" at the end of this section.)

7. **DAMAGES**   Compensatory damages are the normal remedy in a tort case. In unusual cases, the court may award punitive damages, not to compensate the plaintiff but to punish the defendant.

8. **TORTIOUS INTERFERENCE**   Tortious interference with business relations involves the defendant harming an existing contract or a prospective relationship that has a definite expectation of success.

9. **LANHAM ACT**   The Lanham Act prohibits false statements in commercial advertising or promotion.

> **1. Result:** Choice (a) is wrong because a defendant cannot be found guilty in a civil suit. (b) is wrong because a private party has no power to prosecute a criminal case. (c) is correct. (d) is wrong because the state will prosecute Keith, not sue him. (e) is wrong for the same reason.
>
> **2. Result:** The court ruled in favor of Benzaquin because a reasonable person would understand the words to be opinion and ridicule. They are not statements of fact because most of them could not be proven true or false. A statement like "dictators and Nazis" is not taken literally by anyone.[13]
>
> **6. Result:** The court held that it was irrelevant that Betts had shown no malice toward Caudle nor intended to hurt him. Betts *intended the physical contact* with Caudle, and even though he could not foresee everything that would happen, he is liable for all consequences of his intended physical action.[14]

MULTIPLE-CHOICE QUESTIONS

1. Jane writes an article for a newspaper reporting that Ann was arrested for stealing a car. The story is entirely false. Ann is not a public figure. Which of the following torts has Jane committed?

   (a) Ordinary slander

   (b) Slander per se

   (c) Libel

   (d) None of the above

---

[13]Fleming v. Benzaquin, 390 Mass. 175, 454 N.E.2d 95 (1983).
[14]Caudle v. Betts, 512 So.2d 389 (La. 1987).

2. Refer to question 1. If Ann decides to sue, she _____ have to show evidence that she suffered an injury. If she ultimately wins her case, a jury _____ have the option to award punitive damages.

(a) will; will

(b) will; will not

(c) will not; will

(d) will not; will not

3. Sam sneaks up on Tom, hits him with a baseball bat, and knocks him unconscious. Tom never saw Sam coming. He wakes up with a horrible headache. Which of the following torts has Sam committed?

(a) Assault

(b) Battery

(c) Both A and B

(d) None of the above

4. Imagine a case in which a jury awards compensatory damages of $1 million. In most cases, a jury would rarely be allowed to award more than _____ in punitive damages.

(a) $1 million

(b) $3 million

(c) $9 million

(d) $10 million

(e) $25 million

5. Al runs a red light and hits Carol's car. She later sues, claiming the following losses:

$10,000—car repairs

$10,000—medical expenses

$10,000—lost wages (she could not work for two months after the accident)

$10,000—pain and suffering

If the jury believes all of Carol's evidence and she wins her case, how much will she receive in *compensatory* damages?

(a) $40,000

(b) $30,000

(c) $20,000

(d) $10,000

(e) $0

CASE QUESTIONS

1. Lou DiBella was an executive responsible for programming boxing shows on HBO cable network. DiBella signed Bernard Hopkins, the then–middleweight world boxing champion, to participate in a fight televised by HBO. After DiBella's departure from the network, he and Hopkins entered into an agreement in which Hopkins paid $50,000 for DiBella's promotional services. Months later, Hopkins publicly accused DiBella of taking bribes and "selling" spots in HBO fights, calling him greedy, filthy, and unethical. DiBella sued Hopkins for libel. What did DiBella have to prove to be successful in his claim?

2. You are a vice-president in charge of personnel at a large manufacturing company. In-house detectives inform you that Gates, an employee, was seen stealing valuable computer equipment. Gates denies the theft, but you believe the detectives and fire him. The detectives suggest that you post notices around the company, informing all employees what happened to Gates and why, because it will discourage others from stealing. While you are considering that, a phone call from another company's personnel officer asks for a recommendation for Gates. Should you post the notices? What should you say to the other officer?

3. Caldwell was shopping in a K-Mart store, carrying a large purse. A security guard observed her looking at various small items such as stain, hinges, and antenna wire. On occasion, she bent down out of sight of the guard. The guard thought he saw Caldwell put something in her purse. Caldwell removed her glasses from her purse and returned them a few times. After she left, the guard approached her in the parking lot and said that he believed she had store merchandise in her pocketbook, but he could not say what he thought was put there. Caldwell opened the purse, and the guard testified that he saw no K-Mart merchandise in it. The guard then told Caldwell to return to the store with him. They walked around the store for approximately 15 minutes, while the guard said six or seven times that he saw her put something in her purse. Caldwell left the store after another store employee indicated she could go. Caldwell sued. What kind of suit did she file, and what should the outcome be?

4. Tata Consultancy of Bombay, India, is an international computer consulting firm. It spends considerable time and effort recruiting the best personnel from India's leading technical schools. Tata employees sign an initial three-year employment commitment, often work overseas, and agree to work for a specified additional time when they return to India. Desai worked for Tata, but then he quit and formed a competing company, which he called Syntel. His new company contacted Tata employees by phone, offering higher salaries, bonuses, and assistance in obtaining permanent resident visas in the United States if they would come work for Syntel. At least 16 former Tata employees left their jobs without completing their contractual obligations and went to work for Syntel. Tata sued. What did it claim, and what should be the result?

5. Pacific Express began operating as an airline in 1982. It had routes connecting western cities with Los Angeles and San Francisco, and by the summer of 1983, it was beginning to show a profit. In 1983, United Airlines tried to enter into a cooperative arrangement with Pacific in which United would provide Pacific with passengers for some routes so that United could concentrate on its longer routes. Negotiations failed. Later that year, United expanded its routes to include cities that only Pacific had

served. United also increased its service to cities in which the two airlines were already competing. By early 1984, Pacific Express was unable to compete and sought protection under bankruptcy laws. It also sued United, claiming interference with a prospective advantage. United moved for summary judgment. Comment.

Discussion Questions

1. The Supreme Court limits punitive damages in most cases to nine times the compensatory damages awarded in the same case. Is this a sensible guideline? If not, should it be higher or lower?

2. You have most likely heard of the *Liebeck v. McDonalds* case. Liebeck spilled hot McDonald's coffee in her lap and suffered third-degree burns. At trial, evidence showed that her cup of coffee was brewed at 190 degrees, and that, more typically, a restaurant's "hot coffee" is in the range of 140 to 160 degrees.

   A jury awarded Liebeck $160,000 in compensatory damages and $2.7 million in punitive damages. The judge reduced the punitive award to $480,000, or three times the compensatory award.

   Comment on the case and whether the result was reasonable.

3. With a national debt in the trillions, people are desensitized to "mere" billions. Stop for a moment and consider $1 billion. If you had that sum, invested it conservatively, and got a 5 percent return, you could spend roughly $1 million *a week* for the rest of your life *without reducing your principal*.

   This chapter described three lawsuits with jackpot punitive damage awards. The jury award was $10 billion in *Texaco v. Pennzoil*, $5 billion in the *Exxon Valdez* case, and $3 billion in *Boeken v. Philip Morris*. Is there any point at which the raw number of dollars awarded is just too large? Was the original jury award excessive in any of these cases? If so, which one(s)?

4. Many retailers have policies that instruct employees *not* to attempt to stop shoplifters. Some store owners fear false imprisonment lawsuits and possible injuries to workers more than losses related to stolen merchandise.

   Are these "don't be a hero" policies reasonable? Would you put one in place if you owned a retail store?

5. The Supreme Court has defined public figures as those who have "voluntarily exposed themselves to increased risk of injury by assuming an influential role in ordering society." When deciding whether someone is a public figure, courts look at whether this person has received press coverage, sought the public spotlight, and has the opportunity to publicly rebut the accusations. Some have argued that social media makes anyone with a public Facebook profile or a certain number of Twitter followers a public figure. Do you agree? Should the Court revisit the definition of "public figure" in light of social media?

CHAPTER 9

NEGLIGENCE, STRICT LIABILITY, AND PRODUCT LIABILITY

© biletskiy/Shutterstock.com

The story you are about to read is true; not even the names have been changed. The participants were the plaintiff and defendant in a tort case. Do not try this at home.

Connie was very depressed. She felt so "overburdened," she decided to end her life by locking herself inside the trunk of her 1973 Ford LTD.

Fortunately, Connie decided against committing suicide. Unfortunately, her decision occurred after she had already closed the trunk. The LTD did not have an internal release latch or other emergency opening mechanism. And these were the days before cell phones. Result? Connie was trapped in her trunk for *nine* days awaiting rescue.

> **Unfortunately, her decision occurred after she had already closed the trunk.**

This awful episode caused Connie serious psychological and physical injuries. She sued Ford for damages under negligence and strict liability. According to Connie, Ford was negligent because it had a duty to warn her that there was no latch; and the missing latch was a design defect for which Ford should pay.[1]

But whose fault was it? Was Ford's design defective? Was the car unreasonably dangerous? Or was Connie just unreasonable?

These are all practical questions and moral ones, as well. They are also typical issues in the law of negligence, strict liability, and product liability. In these contentious areas, courts continually face one question: *When someone is injured, who is responsible?*

---

[1]Based on Daniell v. Ford Motor Co., 581 F. Supp. 728 (D. Ct. N.M. 1984).

9-1 NEGLIGENCE

We might call negligence the "unintentional" tort because it concerns harm that arises by accident. Should a court impose liability?

Things go wrong all the time, and people are hurt in large ways and small. Society needs a means of analyzing negligence cases consistently and fairly. We cannot have each court that hears such a lawsuit extend or limit liability based on an emotional response to the facts. One of America's greatest judges, Benjamin Cardozo, offered an analysis more than 85 years ago. In a case called *Palsgraf v. Long Island Railroad*, he made a decision that still influences negligence thinking today.

Landmark Case

PALSGRAF V. LONG ISLAND RAILROAD

248 N.Y. 339
Court of Appeals of New York, 1928

Facts: Helen Palsgraf was waiting on a railroad platform. As a train began to leave the station, a man carrying a package ran to catch it. He jumped aboard but looked unsteady, so a guard on the car reached out to help him as another guard, on the platform, pushed from behind. The man dropped the package, which struck the tracks and exploded—because it was packed with fireworks. The shock knocked over some heavy scales at the far end of the platform, and one of them struck Palsgraf, who was injured as a result. She sued the railroad.

Issue: *Was the railroad liable for Palsgraf's injuries?*

Excerpts from Judge Cardozo's Decision: The conduct of the defendant's guard was not a wrong in its relation to the plaintiff, standing far away. Relatively to her, it was not negligence at all. Nothing in the situation gave notice that the falling package had in it the potency of peril to persons thus removed. Negligence is not actionable unless it involves the invasion of a legally protected interest, the violation of a right. Negligence is the absence of care, according to the circumstances.

If no hazard was apparent to the eye of ordinary vigilance, an act innocent and harmless, at least to outward seeming, with reference to her, did not take to itself the quality of a tort because it happened to be a wrong with reference to some one else. In every instance, before negligence can be predicated of a given act, back of the act must be sought and found a duty to the individual complaining."

What the plaintiff must show is "a wrong" to herself and not merely a wrong to someone else. We are told that one who drives at reckless speed through a crowded city street is guilty of a negligent act because the eye of vigilance perceives the risk of damage. The risk reasonably to be perceived defines the duty to be obeyed.

Here, by concession, there was nothing in the situation to suggest to the most cautious mind that the parcel wrapped in newspaper would spread wreckage through the station.

The law of causation, remote or proximate, is thus foreign to the case before us. If there is no tort to be redressed, there is no occasion to consider what damage might be recovered if there were a finding of a tort. The consequences to be followed must first be rooted in a wrong.

Judge Cardozo ruled that the guard's conduct might have been a wrong as to the passenger, but not as to Ms. Palsgraf, standing far away. Her negligence case failed. "Proof of negligence in the air, so to speak, will not do," declared the judge. Courts are still guided by Judge Cardozo's ruling.

To win a negligence case, a plaintiff must prove five elements. Much of the remainder of the chapter will examine them in detail. They are:

- *Duty of Due Care.* The defendant had a legal responsibility *to the plaintiff.* This is the point from the *Palsgraf* case.

- *Breach.* The defendant breached her duty of care or failed to meet her legal obligations.

- *Factual Cause.* The defendant's conduct actually caused the injury.

- *Proximate Cause.* It was *foreseeable* that conduct like the defendant's might cause *this type of harm.*

- *Damages.* The plaintiff has actually been hurt or has actually suffered a measureable loss.

To win a case, a plaintiff must prove all the elements listed previously. If a defendant eliminates only one item on the list, there is no liability.

9-1a Duty of Due Care

Each of us has a duty to behave as a reasonable person would under the circumstances. If you are driving a car, you have a duty to all the other people near you to drive like a reasonable person. If you drive while drunk, or send text messages while behind the wheel, then you fail to live up to your duty of care.

But how *far* does your duty extend? Most courts accept Cardozo's viewpoint in the *Palsgraf* case. Judges draw an imaginary line around the defendant and say that she owes a duty to the people within the circle, but not to those outside it. The test is generally "foreseeability." If the defendant could have foreseen injury to a particular person, she has a duty to him. Suppose that one of your friends posts a YouTube video of you texting behind the wheel and her father is so upset from watching it that he falls down the stairs. You would not be liable for the father's downfall because it was not foreseeable that he would be harmed by your texting.

Let us apply these principles to a case involving a fraternity party.

HERNANDEZ V. ARIZONA BOARD OF REGENTS

177 Ariz. 244
Arizona Supreme Court, 1994

Facts: At the University of Arizona, the Epsilon Epsilon chapter of Delta Tau Delta fraternity gave a welcoming party for new members. The fraternity's officers knew that the majority of its members were under the legal drinking age, but they permitted everyone to consume alcohol. John Rayner, who was under 21 years of age, left the party. He drove negligently and caused a collision with an auto driven by Ruben Hernandez. At the time of the accident, Rayner's blood alcohol level was .15, exceeding the legal limit. The crash left Hernandez blind and paralyzed.

Hernandez sued Rayner, who settled the case based on the amount of his insurance coverage. The victim also sued the fraternity, its officers and national organization, all fraternity members who contributed money to buy alcohol, the university, and others. The trial court granted summary judgment for all defendants and the court of appeals affirmed. Hernandez appealed to the Arizona Supreme Court.

Issue: *Did the fraternity and the other defendants have a duty of due care to Hernandez?*

Excerpts from Justice Feldman's Decision: Before 1983, this court arguably recognized the common-law rule of non-liability for tavern owners and, presumably, for social hosts. Traditional authority held that when "an able-bodied man" caused harm because of his intoxication, the act from which liability arose was the consuming not the furnishing of alcohol.

However, the common law also provides that:

One who supplies [a thing] for the use of another whom the supplier knows or has reason to know to be likely because of his youth, inexperience, or otherwise to use it in a manner involving unreasonable risk of physical harm to himself and others is subject to liability for physical harm resulting to them.

We perceive little difference in principle between liability for giving a car to an intoxicated youth and liability for giving drinks to a youth with a car. A growing number of cases have recognized that one of the very hazards that makes it negligent to furnish liquor to a minor is the foreseeable prospect that the [youthful] patron will become drunk and injure himself or others.

Accordingly, modern authority has increasingly recognized that one who furnishes liquor to a minor breaches a common-law duty owed to innocent third parties who may be injured.

Furnishing alcohol to underaged drinkers violates numerous statutes. The conduct in question violates well-established common-law principles that recognize a duty to avoid furnishing dangerous items to those known to have diminished capacity to use them safely. We join the majority of other states and conclude that as to Plaintiffs and the public in general, Defendants had a duty of care to avoid furnishing alcohol to underage consumers.

Arizona courts, therefore, will entertain an action for damages against [one] who negligently furnishes alcohol to those under the legal drinking age when that act is a cause of injury to a third person. [Reversed and remanded.]

In several circumstances, people have special duties to others. Three of them are outlined here.

Special Duty: Landowners

The common law applies special rules to a landowner for injuries occurring on her property. In most states, the owner's duty depends on the type of person injured.

Lowest Liability: Trespassing Adults. A **trespasser** is anyone on the property without consent. A landowner is liable to a trespasser only for intentionally injuring him or for some other gross misconduct. The landowner has no liability to a trespasser for mere negligence. Jake is not liable if a vagrant wanders onto his land and is burned by defective electrical wires.

Trespasser

A person on another's property without consent

Mid-level Liability: Trespassing Children. The law makes exceptions when the trespassers are **children**. If there is some manmade thing on the land *that may be reasonably expected to attract children*, the landowner is probably liable for any harm. Daphne lives next door to a day-care center and builds a treehouse on her property. Unless she has fenced off the dangerous area, she is probably liable if a small child wanders onto her property and injures himself when he falls from the rope ladder to the treehouse.

Higher Liability: Licensee. A **licensee** is anyone on the land for her own purposes but with the owner's permission. A social guest is a typical licensee. A licensee is entitled to a warning of hidden dangers that the owner knows about. If Juliet invites Romeo for a late supper on the balcony and fails to mention that the wooden railing is rotted, she is liable when her hero plunges to the courtyard.

But Juliet is liable only for injuries caused by *hidden* dangers—she has no duty to warn guests of obvious dangers. She need not say, "Romeo, oh Romeo, don't place thy hand in the toaster, Romeo."

Licensee

A person on another's land for her own purposes but with the owner's permission

Highest Liability: Invitee. An **invitee** is someone who has a right to be on the property because it is a public place or a business open to the public. The owner has a duty of reasonable care to an invitee. Perry is an invitee when he goes to the town beach.

Invitee

A person who has a right to enter another's property because it is a public place or a business open to the public

Can the owner of this trampoline be liable?

If riptides have existed for years and the town fails to post a warning, it is liable if Perry drowns. Perry is also an invitee when he goes to Dana's coffee shop. Dana is liable if she ignores spilled coffee that causes Perry to slip.

With social guests, you must have *actual knowledge* of some specific hidden danger to be liable. Not so with invitees. You are liable even if you had *no idea* that something on your property posed a hidden danger. Therefore, if you own a business, you must conduct inspections of your property on a regular basis to make sure that nothing is becoming dangerous.

However, you generally do not have an obligation to protect against the wrongdoing of a third person. When a gunman went on a shooting spree at Virginia Tech, students Erin Peterson and Julia Pryde were among the 32 killed. The victims' families sued the university for wrongful death, claiming that it should have warned its students that a killer was on the loose. The Virginia Supreme Court disagreed. It held that the university had no duty to warn its students about this third-party criminal act because it was not reasonably foreseeable that the gunman would continue on and kill others. At the time of the initial shootings, the university believed it was an isolated incident and that gunman had left the university grounds.[2]

Special Duty: Professionals

A person at work has a heightened duty of care. While on the job, she must act as a reasonable person *in her profession*. A taxi driver must drive as a reasonable taxi driver would. A heart surgeon must perform bypass surgery with the care of a trained specialist in that field.

Two medical cases illustrate the reasonable person standard. A doctor prescribes a powerful drug without asking his patient about other medicines she is currently taking. The patient suffers a serious drug reaction from the combined medications. The physician is liable for the harm. A reasonable doctor *always* checks current medicines before prescribing new ones.

On the other hand, assume that a patient dies on the operating table in an emergency room. The physician followed normal medical procedures at every step of the procedure and acted with reasonable speed. In fact, the man had a fatal stroke. The surgeon is not liable. A doctor must do a reasonable professional job, but she cannot guarantee a happy outcome.

9-1b Breach of Duty

The second element of a plaintiff's negligence case is **breach of duty**. If a legal duty of care exists, then a plaintiff must show that the defendant did not meet it. Did the defendant act as a reasonable person, or as a reasonable professional? Did he warn social guests of hidden dangers he knew to exist in her apartment?

Normally, a plaintiff proves this part of a negligence case by convincing a jury that they would not have behaved as the defendant did—indeed, that no reasonable person would.

---

[2]*Commonwealth of Virginia v. Peterson*, __S.E.2d __ (S. Ct. Va. 2013).

Negligence Per Se

In certain areas of life, courts are not free to decide what a "reasonable" person would have done because the state legislature has made the decision for them. **When a legislature sets a minimum standard of care for a particular activity, in order to protect a certain group of people, and a violation of the statute injures a member of that group, the defendant has committed negligence per se.** A plaintiff who can show negligence per se need not prove breach of duty.

In Minnesota, the state legislature became alarmed about children sniffing glue, which they could easily purchase in stores. The legislature passed a statute prohibiting the sale to a minor of any glue containing toluene or benzene. About one month later, 14-year-old Steven Zerby purchased Weldwood Contact Cement from the Coast-to-Coast Store in his hometown. The glue contained toluene. Steven inhaled the glue and died from injury to his central nervous system.

The store clerk had not realized that the glue was dangerous. Irrelevant: He was negligent per se because he violated the statute. Perhaps a reasonable person would have made the same error. Irrelevant. The legislature had passed the statute to protect children, the sale of the glue violated the law, and a child was injured. The store was automatically liable.

9-1c **Causation**

We have seen that a plaintiff must show that the defendant owed him a duty of care and that the defendant breached the duty. To win, the plaintiff must also show that the defendant's breach of duty *caused* the plaintiff's harm. Courts look at two separate causation issues: Was the defendant's behavior the *factual cause* of the harm? Was it the *proximate cause?*

Factual Cause

If the defendant's breach led to the ultimate harm, it is the factual cause. Suppose that Dom's Brake Shop tells a customer his brakes are now working fine, even though Dom knows that is false. The customer drives out of the shop, cannot stop at a red light, and hits a bicyclist crossing the intersection. Dom is liable to the cyclist. Dom's unreasonable behavior was the factual cause of the harm. Think of it as a row of dominoes. The first domino (Dom's behavior) knocked over the next one (failing brakes), which toppled the last one (the cyclist's injury).

Suppose, alternatively, that just as the customer is exiting the repair shop, the cyclist hits a pothole and tumbles off her cycle. Dom has breached his duty to his customer, but he is not liable to the cyclist—she would have been hurt anyway. This is a row of dominoes that veers off to the side, leaving the last domino (the cyclist's injury) untouched. No factual causation.

Proximate Cause

For the defendant to be liable, the *type of harm* must have been reasonably *foreseeable*. In the example just discussed, Dom could easily foresee that bad brakes would cause an automobile accident. He need not have foreseen *exactly* what happened. He did not know there would be a cyclist nearby. What he could foresee was this *general type* of harm involving defective brakes. Because the accident that occurred was of the type he could foresee, he is liable.

By contrast, assume the collision of car and bicycle produces a loud crash. Two blocks away, a pet pig, asleep on the window ledge of a twelfth-story apartment, is startled by the noise, awakens with a start, and plunges to the sidewalk, killing a veterinarian who was making a house call. If the vet's family sues Dom, should it win? Dom's negligence was the factual cause: It led to the collision, which startled the pig, which flattened the vet. Most courts would rule, though, that Dom is not liable. The type of harm is too bizarre. Dom could not reasonably foresee such an extraordinary chain of events, and it would be unfair to make him pay for it. See Exhibit 9.1. Another way of stating that Dom is not liable to the vet's family is by calling the falling pig a *superseding cause.* When one of the "dominoes" in

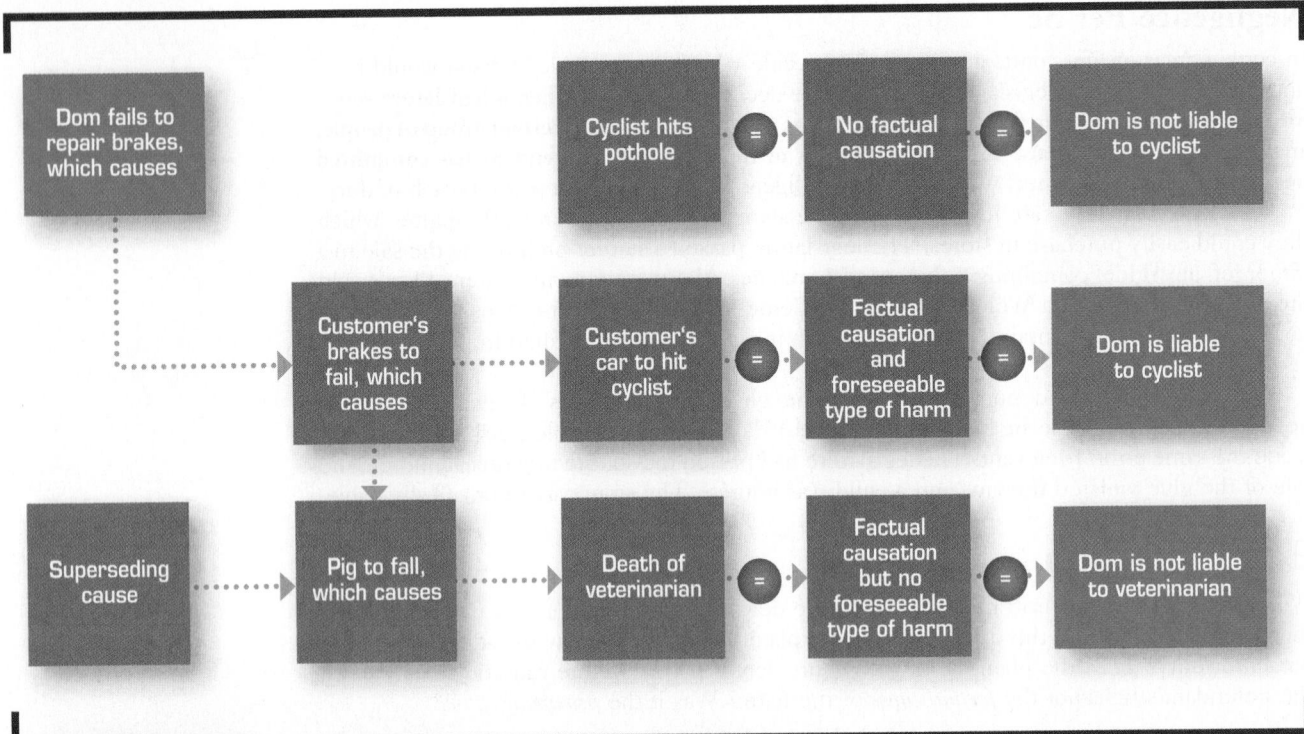

EXHIBIT 9.1

the row is entirely unforeseeable, courts will call that event a superseding cause, letting the defendant off the hook.

EXAM Strategy

Question: Jenny asked a neighbor, Tom, to water her flowers while she was on vacation. For three days, Tom did this without incident, but on the fourth day, when he touched the outside faucet, he received a violent electric shock that shot him through the air, melted his sneakers and glasses, set his clothes on fire, and seriously burned him. Tom sued, claiming that Jenny had caused his injuries by negligently repairing a second-floor toilet. Water from the steady leak had flooded through the walls, soaking wires and eventually causing the faucet to become electrified. You are Jenny's lawyer. Use one (and only one) element of negligence law to move for summary judgment.

Strategy: The four elements of negligence we have examined thus far are: duty to this plaintiff, breach, factual cause, and proximate cause. Which element seems to be most helpful to Jenny's defense? Why?

Result: Jenny is entitled to summary judgment because this was not a foreseeable type of injury. Even if she did a bad job of fixing the toilet, she could not reasonably have anticipated that her poor workmanship could cause *electrical* injuries to anyone.[3]

---

[3]Based on Hebert v. Enos, 60 Mass. App. Ct. 817 (Mass. Ct. App. 2004).

Res Ipsa Loquitur

Normally, a plaintiff must prove factual cause and foreseeable type of harm in order to establish negligence. But in a few cases, a court may be willing to *infer* that the defendant caused the harm under the doctrine of **res ipsa loquitur** ("the thing speaks for itself"). Suppose a pedestrian is walking along a sidewalk when an air conditioning unit falls on his head from a third-story window. The defendant, who owns the third-story apartment, denies any wrongdoing, and it may be difficult or impossible for the plaintiff to prove why the air conditioner fell. In such cases, many courts will apply *res ipsa loquitur* and declare that **the facts imply that the defendant's negligence caused the accident**. If a court uses this doctrine, then the defendant must come forward with evidence establishing that it did *not* cause the harm.

Because *res ipsa loquitur* dramatically shifts the burden of proof from plaintiff to defendant, it applies only when (1) the defendant had exclusive control of the thing that caused the harm, (2) the harm normally would not have occurred without negligence, and (3) the plaintiff had no role in causing the harm. In the air conditioner example, most states would apply the doctrine and force the defendant to prove she did nothing wrong. The following case applies *res ipsa loquitur* to a prickly problem.

res ipsa loquitur

The facts *imply* that the defendant's negligence caused the accident.

BRUMBERG v. CIPRIANI USA, INC.

2013 NY Slip Op 06759
Supreme Court of New York, 2013

Facts: Cornell professor Joan Jacobs Brumberg attended a university fundraiser catered by Cipriani. During the event, she feasted on fancy appetizers. About 30 minutes later, she felt intense abdominal pain, which did not go away. Weeks later, her doctors removed a 1 1/2-inch piece of wood from her digestive tract. The shard caused internal injuries, which took two surgeries to repair.

Brumberg's physician believed that her injuries were the result of eating wood at Cornell's cocktail party. On that day, she had eaten little else and had experienced no pain until the event, where she ate many appetizers, including shrimp on wood skewers. The doctor supposed that the wood moved through her digestive system for 30 minutes before becoming caught and causing the pain. But when experts compared Brumberg's shard with the wood in Cipriani's toothpicks and skewers, they found that the two were not the same material, eliminating direct evidence of causation.

Brumberg sued Cipriani USA, Inc. for negligence. A lower court dismissed her case on a motion for summary judgment, concluding there was not enough proof that Cipriani caused Brumberg's injury. The professor appealed, relying on the doctrine of *res ipsa loquitur*.

Issue: *Does* **res ipsa loquitur** *apply here?*

Excerpts from Judge Lahtinen's Decision: *Res ipsa loquitur* is neither a theory of liability nor a presumption of liability, but instead is simply a permitted inference—that the trier of fact may accept or reject—reflecting a common-sense application of the probative value of circumstantial evidence.

Criteria for *res ipsa loquitur* to apply are that (1) "the event must be of a kind which ordinarily does not occur in the absence of someone's negligence; (2) it must be caused by an agency or instrumentality within the exclusive control of the defendant; and (3) it must not have been due to any voluntary action or contribution on the part of the plaintiff."

The parties dispute the exclusive control element. Here, the event occurred at a banquet hall operated by Cipriani. Cipriani prepared and provided all of the food. Attendees were not permitted to bring food onto the premises. Individuals under Cipriani's control acted as captains, servers and bartenders. Cipriani thus exclusively prepared, provided, and served the food.

Although the shard possibly could have been present when the ingredients were purchased from suppliers, it was not so small as to have been concealed and not visible upon careful preparation.

Defendants point to the fact that other attendees had access to the hors d'oeuvres as reflecting a lack of exclusive control. Cipriani's personnel were present in the room serving the food both butler style and at stations, thus reducing the likelihood of some third party placing the shard unseen in food. There is sufficient proof under these circumstances to find ample control by defendants for purposes of *res ipsa loquitur*.

Defendants' further contention that *res ipsa loquitur* is foreclosed by their allegation of contributory negligence by plaintiff in not seeing the shard or discerning it while chewing the food in which it was located is without merit.

Plaintiffs' set forth ample proof to avoid summary judgment.

9-1d **Damages**

Finally, a plaintiff must prove that he has been injured, or that he has had some kind of measureable losses. In some cases, injury is obvious. For example, Ruben Hernandez suffered grievous harm when struck by the drunk driver. But in other cases, injury is unclear. **The plaintiff must persuade the court that he has suffered harm that is genuine, not speculative.**

Some cases raise tough questions. Among the most vexing are suits involving *future* harm. Exposure to toxins or trauma may lead to serious medical problems down the road— or it may not. A woman's knee is damaged in an auto accident, causing severe pain for two years. She is clearly entitled to compensation for her suffering. After two years, all pain may cease for a decade—or forever. Yet there is also a chance that in 15 or 20 years, the trauma will lead to painful arthritis. A court must decide today the full extent of present *and future* damages; the single recovery principle, discussed in Chapter 8, prevents a plaintiff from returning to court years later and demanding compensation for newly arisen ailments. The challenge to our courts is to weigh the possibilities and percentages of future suffering and decide whether to compensate a plaintiff for something that might never happen.

9-2 DEFENSES

9-2a **Contributory and Comparative Negligence**

Sixteen-year-old Michelle Wightman was out driving at night, with her friend Karrie Wieber in the passenger seat. They came to a railroad crossing, where the mechanical arm had descended and warning bells were sounding. They had been sounding for a long time. A Conrail train had suffered mechanical problems and was stopped 200 feet from the crossing, where it had stalled for roughly an hour. Michelle and Karrie saw several cars ahead of them go around the barrier and cross the tracks. Michelle had to decide whether she would do the same.

Long before Michelle made her decision, the train's engineer had seen the heavy Saturday night traffic crossing the tracks and realized the danger. The conductor and brakeman also understood the peril, but rather than posting a flagman, who could have stopped traffic when a train approached, they walked to the far end of their train to repair the mechanical problem. A police officer had come upon the scene, told his dispatcher to notify the train's parent company Conrail of the danger, and left.

Michelle decided to cross the tracks. She slowly followed the cars ahead of her. Seconds later, both girls were dead. A freight train traveling at 60 miles per hour struck the car broadside, killing both girls instantly.

Michelle's mother sued Conrail for negligence. The company claimed that it was Michelle's foolish risk that led to her death. Who wins when both parties are partly responsible? It depends on whether the state uses a legal theory called contributory negligence. Under contributory negligence, if the plaintiff is even slightly negligent, she recovers nothing. If Michelle's death occurred in a contributory negligence state, and the jury considered her even minimally responsible, her estate would receive no money.

Critics attacked this rule as unreasonable. A plaintiff who was 1 percent negligent could not recover from a defendant who was 99 percent responsible. So most states threw out the contributory negligence rule, replacing it with comparative negligence. In a comparative negligence state, a plaintiff may generally recover even if she is partially responsible. The jury will be asked to assess the relative negligence of the two parties.

Michelle died in Ohio, which is a comparative negligence state. The jury concluded that reasonable compensatory damages were $1 million. It also concluded that Conrail was 60 percent responsible for the tragedy and Michelle 40 percent. See Exhibit 9.2. The girl's mother received $600,000 in compensatory damages.

Today, most, but not all, states have adopted some form of comparative negligence. Critics claim that this principle rewards a careless plaintiff. If Michelle had obeyed the law, she would still be alive. In response to this complaint, many comparative negligence states do *not* permit a plaintiff to recover anything if he was more than 50 percent responsible for his own injury.

In the Conrail case, the jury decided that the rail company was extraordinarily negligent. Expert witnesses testified that similar tragedies occurred every year around the nation and the company knew it. Conrail could easily have prevented the loss of life by posting a flagman on the road. The jury awarded the estate $25 million in punitive damages. The trial judge reduced the verdict by 40 percent to $15 million. The state supreme court affirmed the award.[4]

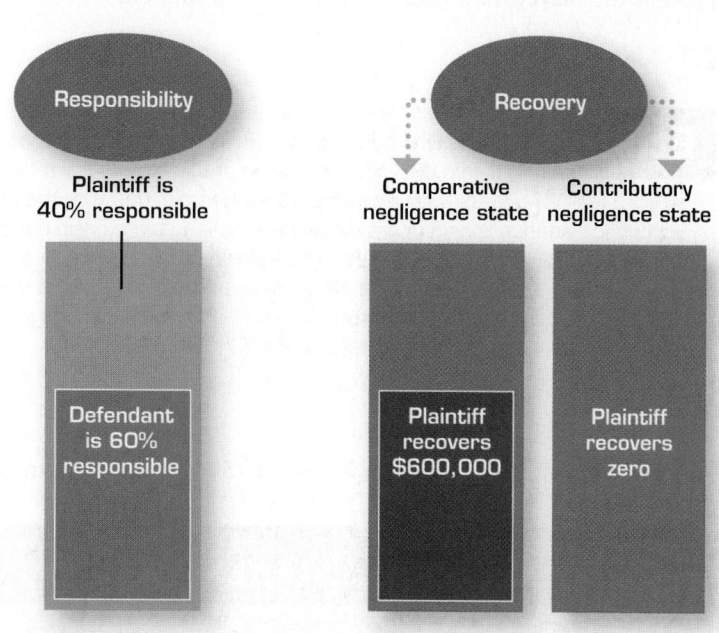

EXHIBIT 9.2   Defendant's negligence injures plaintiff, who suffers $1 million in damages.

[4]Wightman v. Consolidated Rail Corporation, 86 Ohio St. 3d 431(Ohio 1999).

Matt Sullivan/REUTERS

Do NFL players assume the risk of all on-field injuries?

9-2b Assumption of the Risk

Good Guys, a restaurant, holds an ice-fishing contest on a frozen lake to raise money for accident victims. Margie grabs a can full of worms and strolls to the middle of the lake to try her luck, but slips on the ice and suffers a concussion. If she sues Good Guys, how will she fare? She will fall a second time. Wherever there is an obvious hazard, a special rule applies. **Assumption of the risk: A person who voluntarily enters a situation that has an obvious danger cannot complain if she is injured.** Ice is slippery and we all know it. If you venture onto a frozen lake, any falls are your own tough luck.

However, the doctrine does not apply if someone is injured in a way that is not an inherent part of the dangerous activity. NFL players assume substantial risks each time they take the field, but some injuries fall outside the rule. In a game between the Jets and the Dolphins, a Jets assistant coach standing on the sideline tripped a Dolphins player during a punt return. The trip was not a "normal" part of a football game, and the "assumption of the risk" doctrine would not prevent the player from recovering damages if injured.

Ethics   Anyone who has watched an NFL game knows that football is a rough sport. But, did the NFL hide some of the sport's risks? In a negligence lawsuit, 4,500 football players with neurological injuries claimed that the NFL had decades of scientific evidence linking blows to the head to long-term brain damage, but it chose to bury these risks to make more money. A rougher sport makes for a better show—and more profit—the players argued. (The NFL makes approximately $10 billion in revenue per year.) Did the NFL owe a legal duty to the players or should the players just know better? What are the NFL's ethical duties to its players, if any?

The following case involves a lake, Jet Skis, and a great tragedy.

TRUONG V. NGUYEN

67 Cal. Rptr.3d 675
California Court of Appeals, 2007

Facts: On a warm California day, there were about 30 personal watercraft (Jet Skis) operating on Coyote Lake. The weather was fair and visibility good. Anthony Nguyen and Rachael Truong went for a ride on Anthony's Polaris watercraft. Cu Van Nguyen and Chuong Nguyen (neither of whom were related to Anthony) were both riding a Yamaha Waverunner. Both jet skis permitted a driver and passenger, each seated. The two watercraft collided near the middle of the lake. Rachael was killed, and the others all injured.

Rachael's parents sued Anthony, Cu Van, and Chuong, alleging that negligent operation of their watercraft caused their daughter's death. The defendants moved for summary judgment, claiming that assumption of the risk applies to jet skiing. The parents appealed, arguing that jet skiing was not a sport and Rachael never assumed any risk.

Issue: *Does assumption of the risk apply to jet skiing?*

Excerpts from Judge McAdams's Decision: In a sports context, [assumption of the risk] bars liability because the plaintiff is said to have assumed the particular risks inherent in a sport by choosing to participate. Thus, a court need not ask what risks a particular plaintiff subjectively knew of and chose to encounter, but instead must evaluate the fundamental nature of the sport and the defendant's role in or relationship to that sport.

In baseball, a batter is not supposed to carelessly throw the bat after getting a hit and starting to run to first base. However, assumption of risk recognizes that vigorous bat deployment is an integral part of the sport and a risk players assume when they choose to participate. A batter does not have a duty to another player to avoid carelessly throwing the bat after getting a hit.

Even when a participant's conduct violates a rule of the game and may subject the violator to internal sanctions prescribed by the sport itself, imposition of legal liability for such conduct might well alter fundamentally the nature of the sport by deterring participants from vigorously engaging in activity. Coparticipants' limited duty of care is to refrain from intentionally injuring one another or engaging in conduct that is so reckless as to be totally outside the range of the ordinary activity involved in the sport.

It appears that an activity falls within the meaning of 'sport' if the activity is done for enjoyment or thrill, requires physical exertion as well as elements of skill, and involves a challenge containing a potential risk of injury.

As a matter of common knowledge, jet skiing is an active sport involving physical skill and challenges that pose a significant risk of injury, particularly when it is done—as it often is—together with other jet skiers in order to add to the exhilaration of the sport by racing, jumping the wakes of the other jet skis or nearby boats, or in other respects making the sporting activity more challenging and entertaining. In response to the plaintiff's complaint that the trial court erroneously assumed that the litigants were contestants in some sort of consensual competition event and/or spectator sport, [we conclude] that the doctrine applies equally to competitive and non-competitive but active sports.

Plaintiffs urge [that] Rachael was merely a passenger on the Polaris and was not actively involved in the sport. The record supports the conclusion that riding as a passenger on a personal watercraft [is participating in a sport], because it is done for enjoyment or thrill, requires physical exertion as well as elements of skill, and involves a challenge containing a potential risk of injury. The vessel is open to the elements, with no hull or cabin. It is designed for high performance, speed, and quick turning maneuvers. The thrill of riding the vessel is shared by both the operator and the passenger. Obstacles in the environment such as spraying water, wakes to be crossed, and other watercraft are part of the thrill of the sport, both for the operator and the passenger.

The summary judgment is *affirmed*.

9-3 STRICT LIABILITY

Some activities are so naturally dangerous that the law places an especially high burden on anyone who engages in them. A corporation that produces toxic waste can foresee dire consequences from its business that a stationery store cannot. This higher burden is **strict liability**. There are two main areas of business that incur strict liability: *ultrahazardous activity* and *defective products*. Defective products are discussed in the following section, in the section on product liability.

Strict liability

A branch of tort law that imposes a much higher level of liability when harm results from ultrahazardous acts or defective products

9-3a **Ultrahazardous Activity**

Ultrahazardous activities include using harmful chemicals, operating explosives, keeping wild animals, bringing dangerous substances onto property, and a few similar activities where the danger to the general public is especially great. **A defendant engaging in an**

ultrahazardous activity is almost always liable for any harm that results. Plaintiffs do not have to prove duty or breach or foreseeable harm. Recall the deliberately bizarre case we posed earlier of the pig falling from a window ledge and killing a veterinarian. Dom, the mechanic whose negligence caused the car crash, could not be liable for the veterinarian's death because the plunging pig was a superseding cause.

But now imagine that the pig is jolted off the window ledge by a company engaged in an ultrahazardous activity. Sam's Blasting Co. sets off a perfectly lawful blast to clear ground for a new building down the street. When the pig is startled and falls, the blasting company is liable. Even if Sam took extraordinary care, it will do him no good at trial. The "reasonable person" rule is irrelevant in a strict liability case.

Because "strict liability" translates into "defendant is liable," parties in tort cases often fight over whether the defendant was engaged in an ultrahazardous activity. If the court rules that the activity was ultrahazardous, the plaintiff is assured of winning. If the court rules that it was not ultrahazardous, the plaintiff must prove all elements of negligence.

The line is often hazy. A lawful fireworks display does not incur strict liability, but crop dusting does. Cutting timber is generally not abnormally dangerous, but hauling logs might be. The enormous diversity of business activities in our nation ensures continual disputes over this important principle.

NEW JERSEY DEPARTMENT OF ENVIRONMENTAL PROTECTION v. ALDEN LEEDS, INC.

153 N.J. 272
Supreme Court of New Jersey, 1998

Facts: The Alden Leeds Company packages, stores, and ships swimming pool chemicals. The firm does most of its work at its facility in Kearns, New Jersey. At any given time, about 21 different hazardous chemicals are present.

The day before Easter, a fire of unknown origin broke out in "Building One" of the company's site, releasing chlorine gas and other potentially dangerous by-products into the air. There were no guards or other personnel on duty. The fire caused $9 million in damage to company property. Because of the potentially dangerous gas, the Department of Environmental Protection (DEP) closed the New Jersey Turnpike along with half a dozen other major highways, halted all commuter rail and train service in the area, and urged residents to stay indoors with windows closed. An unspecified number of residents went to local hospitals with respiratory problems.

Based on New Jersey's Air Pollution Control Act (APCA), the DEP imposed a civil fine on Alden Leeds for releasing the toxic chemicals. The appellate court reversed, finding that there was no evidence the company had caused the fire or the harm, and the case reached the state's high court.

Issue: *Did the company cause the harm?*

Excerpts from Justice Coleman's Decision: In 1962, this Court adopted the proposition that "an ultrahazardous activity which introduces an unusual danger into the community should pay its own way in the event it actually causes damage to others." In 1983, the Court expressly recognized "that the law of liability has evolved so that a landowner is strictly liable to others for harm caused by toxic wastes that are stored on his property and flow onto the property of others." The Court explained "that those who use, or permit others to use, land for the conduct of abnormally dangerous activities are strictly liable for resultant damages." The same rationale applies to pollution that is released into the air from chemicals stored at a chemical facility.

An actor who chooses to store dangerous chemicals should be responsible for the release of those chemicals into the air. That Alden Leeds lawfully and properly stored chemicals does not alter that conclusion. The risks attendant to the storage of dangerous substances counsel in favor of precautions to prevent their release. Alden Leeds took no such precautions. On the day of the fire, there was no one stationed at the plant to alert the authorities as soon as a fire or other unforeseen calamity erupted. Nor was there any other early warning system in place. A burglar or smoke alarm sounded, but there was no response to that alarm. The law imposes a duty upon those who store hazardous substances to ensure that the substances on their property do not escape in a manner harmful to the public. Alden Leeds failed to meet that burden.

Although Alden Leeds was not found responsible for the fire, the company's facility caused a release of air pollutants. The required nexus is satisfied by the knowing storage of hazardous chemicals. Regardless of what started the fire, it was the knowing storage of chemicals by Alden Leeds that caused the release of air contaminants once the fire reached the chemicals.

[Affirmed that the APCA is a strict liability statute and that there must be a causal nexus between the defendant and the harm. Reversed that the storing of hazardous chemicals by Alden Leeds does not satisfy that nexus. The DEP does *not* have to prove that the chemical operator started the fire.]

EXAM Strategy

Question: Ahmed plans to transport a 25-foot boa constrictor from one zoo to another. The snake is locked in a special cage in Ahmed's truck, approved by the American Zoo Society. Experts check the cage to be sure it is locked and entirely secure. Then Ahmed himself checks the cage. During the transport, his engine begins to fail. He pulls into the breakdown lane and sets up four flares, warning motorists of the stalled vehicle. Katy drives off the road and slams into Ahmed's truck. She is badly injured. Somehow the snake escapes and eats a champion show dog, worth $35,000. Katy and the dog's owner both sue Ahmed. What will be the result in each case?

Strategy: Ahmed's behavior seems reasonable throughout this incident. However, the two suits against him are governed by different rules: negligence in one case, strict liability in the other. Apply each rule to the correct case.

Result: The dog was killed by a dangerous snake. Transporting wild animals is an ultrahazardous activity, and Ahmed is strictly liable. His reasonable behavior will not save him. However, when he parked his truck in the breakdown lane, he did a reasonable job. Katy cannot prove that he breached his duty to her, and she loses.

9-4 PRODUCT LIABILITY

So far in this chapter, we have discussed how two tort theories—negligence and strict liability—apply when someone's action or inaction harms another. But sometimes products, not people, cause harm. When an exploding cola bottle, a flammable pajama, or a toxic cookie injures, who pays? Someone who is injured by a defective product may have claims in both negligence and strict liability.

9-4a Negligence

In negligence cases concerning goods, plaintiffs typically raise one or more of these claims:

- **Negligent design.** The buyer claims that the product injured her because the manufacturer designed it poorly. For example, company engineers placed the Ford Pinto's fuel tank behind the axle, making the car more likely to explode in a rear-end collision. Negligence law requires a manufacturer to design a product free of *unreasonable* risks. The product does not have to be absolutely safe. An automobile that nearly guaranteed a driver's safety could be made, in theory, but it would be prohibitively expensive. Reasonable safety features must be built in, if they can be included at a tolerable cost.

- **Negligent manufacture.** The buyer claims that the design was adequate but that failure to inspect or some other careless conduct caused a dangerous product to leave the plant. Peter Vamos got sick after gulping his Diet Coke—only to discover that there were two AA batteries in the bottle. Because he was able to prove that the batteries were in the bottle when it left the plant, Vamos recovered from the bottler for his injuries.[5]

- **Failure to warn.** A manufacturer is liable for failing to warn the purchaser or users about the dangers of normal use and also foreseeable misuse. However, there is no duty to warn about obvious dangers, a point evidently lost on some manufacturers. A Batman costume came with this statement: "For play only: cape does not enable user to fly."

In the following case, the plaintiffs raise issues of negligent design and failure to warn concerning a disposable lighter. Did the manufacturer breach its duty? You decide.

---

[5]Vamos v. The Coca-Cola Bottling Co. of New York, Inc., 627 N.Y.S.2d 265 (1995).
[6]198 Mich. App. 1 (Mich. Ct. App. 1993).

You be the Judge

BOUMELHEM V. BIC CORP.
211 Mich. App. 175
Michigan Court of Appeals, 1995

Facts: Ibrahim Boumelhem, aged four, began playing with a Bic disposable lighter that his parents had purchased. He started a fire that burned his legs and severely burned his six-month-old brother over 85 percent of his body. Ibrahim's father sued Bic, claiming that the lighter was negligently designed because it could have been childproof. He also claimed failure to warn because the lighter did not clearly warn of the danger to children.

The *Boumelhem* court considered evidence and analyses from several other cases against Bic. The court noted that consumers use over 500 million disposable lighters annually in the United States. Each lighter provides 1,000 to 2,000 lights. During one three-year period, children playing with disposable lighters started 8,100 fires annually, causing an average of 180 people to die every year, of whom 140 were children under five. Another 990 people were injured. The average annual cost of deaths, injuries, and property damage from child-play fires was estimated at $310 to $375 million, or 60 to 75 cents per lighter sold. Bic had acknowledged in earlier litigation that it was foreseeable lighters would get into children's hands and injure them. Bic had also agreed that it was feasible to make a more child-resistant lighter.

The trial court relied on a Michigan case. In *Adams v. Perry Furniture Co.*,[6] four minor children had died in a fire started when one of them was playing with a Bic lighter. The *Adams* court had found no negligent design and no failure to warn, and it dismissed all claims. The trial court in the present case followed *Adams* and dismissed Boumelhem's claims. He appealed.

You Be the Judge: *Did Bic negligently design its disposable lighter? Did Bic negligently fail to warn of the lighter's dangers?*

Argument for Boumelhem: Your honors, the Adams court decided the issues wrongly. There is a reason that new plaintiffs are back in this court, the year after Adams, raising related issues against Bic: The company is killing hundreds of children every year. In its efforts to maximize corporate profits, it is literally burning these children to death and injuring hundreds more. That's wrong.

Bic has acknowledged that its disposable lighters can and will get into the hands of children. Bic knows full well that its product will injure or kill a certain percentage of these children—very young children. Bic has admitted that it could design a childproof lighter, and it knows perfectly well how to include effective warnings on its lighters. But rather than improve product design and give effective warnings, Bic prefers to do business as usual and litigate liability for injured children.

We ask this court to rule that Bic breached its duty to design and manufacture a lighter that will keep our kids safe, and breached its duty to warn.

Argument for Bic: Your honors, the Bic Corp. is as horrified as anyone over the injuries to these children and the deaths of other kids. But Bic is not responsible. The children's parents are responsible. We sympathize with their grief, but not with their attempt to pass parental responsibility onto the shoulders of a corporation. There are several reasons Bic is not liable in this case.

First, the *Adams* court decided the matter, and that precedent is binding.

Second, Bic has no duty to design a different lighter. The test in design defect cases is whether the risks are unreasonable in light of the foreseeable injuries. Young children can hurt themselves in countless ways, from falls to poisonings to automobile injuries. There is one answer to these dangers, and it is called good parenting. The parents who bought this lighter purchased it because it could start a fire. The moment they purchased it, they assumed the obligation to keep it away from their children. These are useful products, which is why Bic sells hundreds of millions per year. Other consumers should not be forced to pay an outrageously high price for a simple tool, just because some parents fail to do their job.

The failure to warn argument is even weaker. The law imposes no failure to warn when the danger is obvious. Every adult knows that lighters are *potentially* dangerous, if misused, or if passed on to children. No one would be helped by a warning that said, "This lighter starts fires. Don't give it to children."

9-4b **Strict Liability for Defective Products**

The other tort claim that an injured person can bring against the manufacturer or seller of a product is strict liability. Like negligence, strict liability is a burden created by the law rather than by the parties. And, as with all torts, strict liability concerns claims of physical harm. But there is a key distinction between negligence and strict liability: in a negligence case, the injured buyer must demonstrate that the seller's conduct was unreasonable. Not so in strict liability.

In strict liability, the injured person need not prove that the defendant's conduct was unreasonable. The injured person must show only that the defendant manufactured or sold a product that was defective and that the defect caused harm. Almost all states permit such lawsuits, and most of them have adopted the following model:

1. One who sells any product in a defective condition unreasonably dangerous to the user or consumer or to his property is subject to liability for physical harm thereby caused to the ultimate user or consumer, or to his property, if

    a. the seller is engaged in the business of selling such a product, and

    b. it is expected to and does reach the user or consumer without substantial change in the condition in which it is sold.

2. The rule stated in Subsection (1) applies although

    a. the seller has exercised all possible care in the preparation and sale of his product, and

    b. the user or consumer has not bought the product from or entered into any contractual relation with the seller.[7]

---

[7]Restatement (Second) of Torts § 402A.

These are the key terms in subsection (1):

- *Defective condition unreasonably dangerous to the user.* The defendant is liable only if the product is defective when it leaves his hands. There must be something wrong with the goods. If they are reasonably safe and the buyer's mishandling of the goods causes the harm, there is no strict liability. If you attempt to open a soda bottle by knocking the cap against a counter, and the glass shatters and cuts you, the manufacturer owes nothing. A carving knife can produce a lethal wound, but everyone knows that, and a sharp knife is not unreasonably dangerous. On the other hand, prescription drugs may harm in ways that neither a layperson nor a doctor would anticipate. The manufacturer *must provide adequate warnings* of any dangers that are not apparent.

- *In the business of selling.* The seller is liable only if she normally sells this kind of product. Suppose your roommate makes you a peanut butter sandwich and, while eating it, you cut your mouth on a sliver of glass that was in the jar. The peanut butter manufacturer faces strict liability, as does the grocery store where your roommate bought the goods. But your roommate is not strictly liable because he is not in the food business.

- *Reaches the user without substantial change.* Obviously, if your roommate put the glass in the peanut butter thinking it was funny, neither the manufacturer nor the store is liable.

And here are the important phrases in subsection (2):

- *Has exercised all possible care.* This is the heart of strict liability, which makes it a potent claim for consumers. *It is no defense that the seller used reasonable care.* If the product is dangerously defective and injures the user, the seller is liable even if it took every precaution to design and manufacture the product safely. Suppose the peanut butter jar did in fact contain a glass sliver when it left the factory. The manufacturer proves that it uses extraordinary care in keeping foreign particles out of the jars and thoroughly inspects each container before it is shipped. The evidence is irrelevant. The manufacturer has shown that it was not *negligent* in packaging the food, but reasonable care is irrelevant in strict liability cases.

- *No contractual relation.* When two parties contract, they are in privity. Note that privity only exists between the user and the person from whom she actually bought the goods, but in strict liability cases, *privity is not required.* Suppose the manufacturer that made the peanut butter sold it to a distributor, which sold it to a wholesaler, which sold it to a grocery store, which sold it to your roommate. You may sue the manufacturer, distributor, wholesaler, and store, even though you had no privity with any of them.

As we have seen, an injured plaintiff may sue a manufacturer for both negligence and strict liability. Remember Connie from the chapter opener? Let's see how her story ended.

DANIELL V. FORD

581 F. Supp. 728
U.S. District Court, New Mexico 1984

Facts: See the chapter opener. Connie Daniell argued that Ford was both (1) negligent because it did not warn her that there was no opening mechanism in the trunk and (2) strictly liable for this design defect. Ford sought summary judgment.

Issue: *Was Ford negligent in failing to warn Connie of the missing latch? Was Ford strictly liable for a design defect?*

Excerpts from Judge Baldock's Decision: Under strict products liability or negligence, a manufacturer has a duty to consider only those risks of injury which are foreseeable. A risk is not foreseeable by a manufacturer where a product is used in a manner which could not reasonably be anticipated by the manufacturer and that use is the cause of the plaintiff's injury. The plaintiff's injury would not be foreseeable by the manufacturer.

The purposes of an automobile trunk are to transport, stow, and secure the automobile spare tire, luggage, and other goods and to protect those items from elements of the weather. The design features of an automobile trunk make it well near impossible that an adult intentionally would enter the trunk and close the lid. The dimensions of a trunk, the height of its sill and its load floor are among the design features which encourage closing and latching the trunk lid while standing outside the vehicle. The plaintiff's use of the trunk compartment as a means to attempt suicide was an unforeseeable use. Therefore, the manufacturer had no duty to design an internal release or opening mechanism that might have prevented this occurrence.

Nor did the manufacturer have a duty to warn the plaintiff of the danger of her conduct, given the plaintiff's unforeseeable use of the product. The risk is obvious. There is no duty to warn of known dangers in strict products liability or tort. Moreover, the potential efficacy of any warning, given the plaintiff's use of the automobile trunk compartment for a deliberate suicide attempt, is questionable.

The automobile trunk was not defective under these circumstances. The automobile trunk was not unreasonably dangerous within the contemplation of the ordinary consumer or user of such a trunk when used in the ordinary ways and for the ordinary purposes for which such a trunk is used.

The defendant's Motion for Summary Judgment is granted.

Contemporary Trends

If the steering wheel on a brand new car falls off, and the driver is injured, that is a clear case of defective manufacturing, and the company will be strictly liable. Those are the easy cases. But defective design cases have been more contentious. Suppose a vaccine that prevents serious childhood illnesses inevitably causes brain damage in a very small number of children because of the nature of the drug. Is the manufacturer liable? What if a racing sailboat, designed only for speed, is dangerously unstable in the hands of a less-experienced sailor? Is the boat's maker responsible for fatalities? Suppose an automobile made of lightweight metal uses less fuel but exposes its occupants to more serious injuries in an accident. How is a court to decide whether the design was defective? Often, these design cases also involve issues of warnings: Did the drug designer diligently detail dangers to doctors? Should a sailboat seller sell speedy sailboats solely to seasoned sailors?

Over the years, most courts have adopted one of two tests for design and warning cases. The first is *consumer expectation*. Here, a court finds the manufacturer liable for defective design if the product is less safe than a reasonable consumer would expect. If a smoke detector has a 3 percent failure rate and the average consumer has no way of anticipating that danger, effective cautions must be included, though the design may be defective anyway.

Many other states use a *risk-utility test*. Here, a court must weigh the benefits for society against the dangers that the product poses. Principal factors in the risk-utility test include:

- The *value* of the product,

- The *gravity*, or seriousness, of the danger,

- The *likelihood* that such danger will occur,

- The mechanical feasibility of a *safer alternative* design, and

- The *adverse consequences* of an alternative design.

9-4c **Tort Reform**

Some people believe that jury awards are excessive and need statutory reform. About two-thirds of the states have passed at least some limits on damages in tort actions. About one-third of states have created new rules for particular kinds of product liability. *Unavoidably unsafe* prescription drugs are an example. Suppose that a plaintiff proves that a prescription medicine caused her grievous, permanent harm, and that 1 percent of all users will suffer similar damage. If the pharmaceutical company can demonstrate that it is impossible to manufacture the drug to eliminate all danger, many states will deny the plaintiff any damages. These states have essentially decided that the benefits of that prescription medicine outweigh its risks. If the medicine is unavoidably unsafe—that is, it cannot be made safer—the company should not be held liable; large verdicts might drive pharmaceutical firms out of a business that has great social value.

Opponents consider tort reform dangerous to society. They argue that the real goal of the so-called reform is to free irresponsible corporations from any potential liability, enabling them to save money while injuring innocent people. They insist that giving the 12 average members of society on a jury a say in product safety benefits everyone.

9-4d **Time Limits: Statutes of Limitations and Statutes of Repose**

In tort cases, the passage of time provides a seller with two possible defenses: statutes of limitations and statutes of repose.

The statute of limitations requires that a lawsuit be brought within a specified period. These time limits vary from state to state, ranging from one year to five years, beginning when the defect is discovered or should have been discovered.

A statute of repose places an absolute limit on when a lawsuit may be filed, regardless of when the defect is discovered. Jeffrey Oats was riding in the back seat of a Nissan sports car when it was involved in an accident. Tragically, Oats suffered spinal cord injuries that left him a quadriplegic. Oats sued Nissan, based on defective design, claiming that the rear seat lacked adequate head and leg room and that the car's body panels lacked sufficient strength. He argued that these defects only became apparent in an accident. But the Idaho Supreme Court dismissed his claims because the car was 11 years old at the time of the accident. The Idaho statute of repose prohibits most product liability suits filed more than 10 years after the goods were sold, regardless of when the defects were discoverable.[8]

EXAM Strategy

Question: Stuart lives in a state that sets a three-year statute of limitations on tort claims. His state also has an eight-year statute of repose. Stuart bought a television on June 1, 2010. On July 1, 2017, a manufacturing defect causes the television to malfunction and cause an electrical fire. Stuart waits for a year and then files a lawsuit on July 1, 2018. Will he win, or will his case be dismissed?

Strategy: Because Stuart is a consumer, the court will not apply either the economic loss doctrine or the UCC's four-year statute of limitations. When does the state's three-year statute of limitations begin to run? What effect will the state's statute of repose have on Stuart's case?

---

[8]Oats v. Nissan Motor Corp., 126 Idaho 162 (1994).

Result: The statute of limitations' three-year period starts to run only when Stuart discovers the defect. Because he filed one year from the fire, the statute of limitations does not bar his recovery. But unfortunately, Stuart's lawsuit will fail because of the statute of repose. That eight-year limit begins to expire when Stuart buys the TV, and the lawsuit is not filed for eight years and one month from the time of the sale. Stuart loses.

Chapter Conclusion

Tort issues necessarily remain in flux, based on changing social values and concerns. There is no final word on what is an ultrahazardous activity, or whether a social host can be liable for the destruction caused by a guest. What is clear is that a working knowledge of these issues and pitfalls can help everyone—business executive and ordinary citizen alike.

EXAM REVIEW

1. **ELEMENTS** The five elements of negligence are duty of due care, breach, factual causation, proximate causation, and damage.

2. **DUTY** If the defendant could foresee that misconduct would injure a particular person, he probably has a duty to her. Special duties exist for people on the job, landowners, and employers.

EXAM Strategy

Question: A supervisor reprimanded an employee for eating in a restaurant when he should have been at work. Later, the employee showed up at the supervisor's office and shot him. Although the employee previously had been violent, management withheld this information from supervisory personnel. Is the company liable for the supervisor's injury?

Strategy: An employer must do a *reasonable* job of hiring and retaining employees. (See the "Result" at the end of this section.)

3. **BREACH OF DUTY** A defendant breaches his duty of due care by failing to meet his duty of care.

4. **NEGLIGENCE PER SE** If a legislature sets a minimum standard of care for a particular activity in order to protect a certain group of people, and a violation of the statute injures a member of that group, the defendant has committed negligence per se.

5. **FACTUAL CAUSE** If one event directly led to the ultimate harm, it is the factual cause.

6. **PROXIMATE CAUSE**   For the defendant to be liable, the type of harm must have been reasonably foreseeable.

7. **DAMAGE**   The plaintiff must persuade the court that he has suffered a harm that is genuine, not speculative. Damages for emotional distress, without a physical injury, are awarded only in select cases.

8. **CONTRIBUTORY AND COMPARATIVE NEGLIGENCE**   In a contributory negligence state, a plaintiff who is even slightly responsible for his own injury recovers nothing; in a comparative negligence state, the jury may apportion liability between plaintiff and defendant.

EXAM Strategy

Question: There is a collision between cars driven by Candy and Zeke. The evidence is that Candy is about 25 percent responsible, for failing to stop quickly enough, and Zeke about 75 percent responsible, for making a dangerous turn. Candy is most likely to win:

(a) A lawsuit for battery

(b) A lawsuit for negligence in a comparative negligence state

(c) A lawsuit for negligence in a contributory negligence state

(d) A lawsuit for strict liability

(e) A lawsuit for assault

Strategy: Battery and assault are intentional torts, irrelevant in a typical car accident. Are such collisions strict liability cases? No; therefore, the answer must be either (b) or (c). Apply the distinction between comparative and contributory negligence to the evidence here. (See the "Result" at the end of this section.)

9. **STRICT LIABILITY**   A defendant is strictly liable for harm caused by an ultrahazardous activity or a defective product. Strict liability means that if the defendant's conduct led to the harm, the defendant is liable, even if she exercises extraordinary care.

EXAM Strategy

Question: Marko owned a cat and allowed it to roam freely outside. In the three years he had owned the pet, the animal had never bitten anyone. The cat entered Romi's garage. When Romi attempted to move it outside, the cat bit her. Romi underwent four surgeries, was fitted with a plastic finger joint, and spent more than $39,000 in medical bills. She sued Marko, claiming both strict liability and ordinary negligence. Assume that state law allows a domestic cat to roam freely. Evaluate both of Romi's claims.

Strategy: Negligence requires proof that the defendant breached a duty to the plaintiff by behaving unreasonably, and that the resulting harm was foreseeable.

Was it? When would harm by a domestic cat be foreseeable? A defendant can be strictly liable for keeping a wild animal. Apply that rule as well. (See the "Result" at the end of this section.)

---

2. Result: This employer *may* have been liable for negligently hiring a previously violent employee, and it *certainly* did an unreasonable job in retaining him without advising his supervisor of the earlier violence. The assault was easily foreseeable, and the employer is liable.[9]

8. Result. In a contributory negligence state, a plaintiff even 1 percent responsible for the harm loses. Candy was 25 percent responsible. She can win *only* in a comparative negligence state.

9. Result: If Marko's cat had bitten or attacked people in the past, this harm was foreseeable and Marko is liable. If the cat had never done so, and state law allows domestic animals to roam, Romi probably loses her suit for negligence. Her strict liability case definitely fails: a housecat is not a wild animal.

MULTIPLE-CHOICE QUESTIONS

1. Two cars, driven by Fred and Barney, collide. At trial, the jury determines that the accident was 90 percent Fred's fault and 10 percent Barney's fault. Barney's losses total $100,000. If he lives in a state that uses contributory negligence, Barney will recover ———————.

   (a) $0

   (b) $10,000

   (c) $50,000

   (d) $90,000

   (e) $100,000

2. Assume the same facts as in Question 1, except now Barney lives in a state that follows comparative negligence. Now Barney will recover ———————.

   (a) $0

   (b) $10,000

   (c) $50,000

   (d) $90,000

   (e) $100,000

3. Zack lives in a state that prohibits factory laborers from working more than 12 hours in any 24-hour period. The state legislature passed the law to cut down on accidents caused by fatigued workers.

---

[9]Based on *Smith v. National R.R. Passenger Corp.*, 856 F.2d 467 (2d Cir. 1988).

Ignoring the law, Zack makes his factory employees put in 14-hour days. Eventually, a worker at the end of a long shift makes a mistake and severely injures a coworker. The injured worker sues Zack.

Which of the following terms will be most relevant to the case?

(a) *Res ipsa loquitur*

(b) Assumption of the risk

(c) Negligence per se

(d) Strict liability

4. Randy works for a vending machine company. One morning, he fills up an empty vending machine that is on the third floor of an office building. Later that day, Mark buys a can of Pepsi from that machine. He takes the full can to a nearby balcony and drops it three floors onto Carl, a coworker who recently started dating Mark's ex-girlfriend. Carl falls unconscious. Which of the following can be considered a factual cause of Carl's injuries?

(a) Randy

(b) Mark

(c) Both Randy and Mark

(d) None of the above

5. For this question, assume the same facts as in Question 4. Now determine which of the following can be considered a proximate cause of Carl's injuries.

(a) Randy

(b) Mark

(c) Both Randy and Mark

(d) None of the above

6. **CPA QUESTION** Which of the following factors is least important in determining whether a manufacturer is strictly liable in tort for a defective product?

(a) The negligence of the manufacturer

(b) The contributory negligence of the plaintiff

(c) Modifications to the product by the wholesaler

(d) Whether the product caused injuries

CASE QUESTIONS

1. At approximately 7:50 p.m, bells at the train station rang and red lights flashed, signaling an express train's approach. David Harris walked onto the tracks, ignoring a yellow line painted on the platform instructing people to stand back. Two men shouted to Harris, warning him to get off the tracks. The train's engineer saw him too late to stop the train, which was traveling at approximately 55 mph. The train struck and killed Harris as it passed through the station. Harris's widow sued the railroad, arguing that the railroad's negligence caused her husband's death. Evaluate her argument.

2. Ryder leased a truck to Florida Food Service; Powers, an employee, drove it to make deliveries. He noticed that the strap used to close the rear door was frayed, and he asked Ryder to fix it. Ryder failed to do so in spite of numerous requests. The strap broke, and Powers replaced it with a nylon rope. Later, when Powers was attempting to close the rear door, the nylon rope broke and he fell, sustaining severe injuries to his neck and back. He sued Ryder. The trial court found that Powers's attachment of the replacement rope was a superseding cause, relieving Ryder of any liability, and granted summary judgment for Ryder. Powers appealed. How should the appellate court rule?

3. A new truck, manufactured by General Motors Corp. (GMC), stalled in rush hour traffic on a busy interstate highway because of a defective alternator, which caused a complete failure of the truck's electrical system. The driver stood nearby and waved traffic around his stalled truck. A panel truck approached the GMC truck, and immediately behind the panel truck, Davis was driving a Volkswagen fastback. Because of the panel truck, Davis was unable to see the stalled GMC truck. The panel truck swerved out of the way of the GMC truck, and Davis drove straight into it. The accident killed him. Davis's widow sued GMC. GMC moved for summary judgment, alleging (1) no duty to Davis, (2) no factual causation, and (3) no foreseeable harm. Comment.

4. *YOU BE THE JUDGE* **WRITING PROBLEM**   When Thomas and Susan Tamplin were shopping at Star Lumber with their six-year-old daughter Ann Marie, a 150-pound roll of vinyl flooring fell on the girl, seriously injuring her head and pituitary gland. Ann was clearly entitled to recover for the physical harm, such as her fractured skull. The plaintiffs also sought recovery for potential future harm. Their medical expert was prepared to testify that although Ann would probably develop normally, he could not rule out the slight possibility that her pituitary injury might prevent her from sexually maturing. Is Ann entitled to damages for future harm? **Argument for Ann:** This was a major trauma, and it is impossible to know the full extent of the future harm. Sexual maturation is a fundamental part of life; if there is a possibility that Ann will not develop normally, she is entitled to present her case to a jury and receive damages. **Argument for Star Lumber:** A plaintiff may not recover for speculative harm. The "slight possibility" that Ann could fail to develop is not enough for her to take her case to the jury.

5. Texaco, Inc., and other oil companies sold mineral spirits in bulk to distributors, which then resold to retailers. Mineral spirits are used for cleaning. Texaco allegedly knew that the retailers, such as hardware stores, frequently packaged the mineral spirits (illegally) in used half-gallon milk containers and sold them to consumers, often with no warnings on the packages. Mineral spirits are harmful or fatal if swallowed. David Hunnings, aged 21 months, found a milk container in his home, swallowed the mineral spirits, and died. The Hunnings sued Texaco for negligence. The trial court dismissed the complaint, and the Hunnings appealed. What is the legal standard in a negligence case? Have the plaintiffs made out a valid case of negligence? Remember that at this stage, a court is not deciding who wins, but what standard a plaintiff must meet in order to take its case to a jury. Assume that Texaco knew about the repackaging and the grave risk but continued to sell in bulk because doing so was profitable. (If the plaintiffs cannot prove those facts, they will lose even if they *do* get to a jury.) Would that make you angry? Does that mean such a case should go to a jury? Or would you conclude that the fault still lies with the retailer, the parents, or both?

6. Boboli Co. wanted to promote its "California-style" pizza, which it sold in supermarkets. The company contracted with Highland Group, Inc., to produce 2 million recipe brochures, which would be inserted in the carton when the freshly baked pizza was still very hot. Highland contracted with Comark Merchandising to print the brochures. But when Comark asked for details concerning the pizza, the carton, and so forth, Highland refused to supply the information. Comark printed the first lot of 72,000 brochures, which Highland delivered to Boboli. Unfortunately, the hot bread caused the ink to run, and customers opening the carton often found red or blue splotches on their pizzas. Highland refused to accept additional brochures, and Comark sued for breach of contract. Highland defended by claiming that Comark had breached its warranty of merchantability. Please comment.

DISCUSSION QUESTIONS

1. Imagine an undefeated high school football team on which the average lineman weighs 300 pounds. Also, imagine an 0–10 team on which the average lineman weighs 170 pounds. The undefeated team sets out to hit as hard as they can on every play and to run up the score as much as possible. Before the game is over, 11 players from the lesser team have been carried off the field with significant injuries. All injuries were the result of "clean hits"—none of the plays resulted in a penalty. Even late in the game, when the score is 70–0, the undefeated team continues to deliver devastating hits that are far beyond what would be required to tackle and block. The assumption of the risk doctrine exempts the undefeated team from liability. Is this reasonable?

2. Should the law hold landowners to different standards of care for trespassers, social guests, and invitees? Or do the few states that say, "Just always be reasonable," have a better rule?

3. Are strict liability rules fair? Someone has to dispose of chemicals. Someone has to use dynamite if road projects are to be completed. Is it fair to say to those companies, "You are responsible for all harm caused by your activities, even if you are as careful as you can possibly be?"

4. People who serve alcohol to others take a risk. In some circumstances, they can be held legally responsible for the actions of the people they serve. Is this fair? Should an intoxicated person be the only one liable if harm results? If not, in what specific circumstances is it fair to stretch liability to other people?

5. In the near future, we will rely increasingly on robots in daily life. Honda has predicted that by the year 2020, it will sell as many personal robots as it does cars. It is likely that these robots will be capable of many household tasks, such as folding laundry and tidying rooms. How do these automated beings fit into existing tort law? When a robot malfunctions unforeseeably and causes harm, who should be at fault?

© biletskiy/Shutterstock.com

CYBERLAW AND PRIVACY

A Declaration of the Independence of Cyberspace
by
John Perry Barlow, 1996[1]

Governments of the Industrial World, you weary giants of flesh and steel, I come from Cyberspace, the new home of Mind. On behalf of the future, I ask you of the past to leave us alone. You are not welcome among us. You have no sovereignty where we gather.

We have no elected government, nor are we likely to have one, so I address you with no greater authority than that with which liberty itself always speaks. You have no moral right to rule us nor do you possess any methods of enforcement we have true reason to fear. Governance will arise according to the conditions of our world, not yours. Our world is different.

> ## Cyberspace … is different.

Governance will arise according to the conditions of our world, not yours. Our world is different.

Cyberspace consists of transactions, relationships, and thought itself, arrayed like a standing wave in the web of our communications. Ours is a world that is both everywhere and nowhere, but it is not where bodies live.

We are creating a world where anyone, anywhere may express his or her beliefs, no matter how singular, without fear of being coerced into silence or conformity.

Your legal concepts of property, expression, identity, movement, and context do not apply to us. They are all based on matter, and there is no matter here.

We will create a civilization of the Mind in Cyberspace. May it be more humane and fair than the world your governments have made before.

---

[1]Barlow is a cofounder of the Electronic Frontier Foundation, which is a leading nonprofit defending civil liberties online. You can learn more about it at www.eff.org. Barlow was also a lyricist for the Grateful Dead rock band.

The Internet and the World Wide Web comprise one of the great technological developments of modern times. The Internet has brought change to every aspect of our lives—how we do business, buy things, apply for jobs, keep in touch, obtain news, campaign for election, make new friends, and even start revolutions.

In his *Declaration of the Independence of Cyberspace*, John Perry Barlow, an early Internet activist, envisioned a digital world of ideas without government regulation. Although Barlow correctly foresaw the Internet as a tool for innovation, his idyllic cyberspace without rules never came to exist: Today's Internet is governed by many laws.

It stands to reason. Inevitably, new technologies create the need for new law. In the thirteenth century, England was one of the first countries to develop passable roads. Like the Internet, these roadways greatly enhanced communication, creating social and business opportunities, but also enabled new crimes. Good roads meant that bad guys could sneak out of town without paying their bills. Parliament responded with laws to facilitate the collection of out-of-town debts. Similarly, while the Internet has opened up enormous opportunities in both our business and personal lives, it has also created the need for new laws, both to pave the way for these opportunities and to limit their risks.

The process of lawmaking never stops. Judges sit and legislatures meet—all in an effort to create better rules and a better society. However, in an established area of law, such as contracts or employment, the basic structure changes little. Cyberlaw is constantly challenged by changing technologies. Not only are new laws being created almost daily, but whole areas of regulation are, as yet, unpaved roads.

Cyberlaw affects many areas of our lives. This chapter focuses on the business law issues that are unique to the digital world. We discuss three main topics: (1) regulation of the Internet itself (including net neutrality and user-generated content); (2) consumer protection; and (3) privacy in the digital world.

10-1 REGULATION OF THE INTERNET

The "Internet," a term derived from "interconnected network," began in the 1960s as a project to link military contractors and universities. Today, it is a giant network that connects smaller groups of linked computer networks. The World Wide Web, a subnetwork of the Internet, is a decentralized collection of documents containing text, pictures, and sound. Users can move from document to document using links that form a "web" of information.

10-1a Net Neutrality

Internet service providers (ISPs)

Companies that connect users to the Internet

Net neutrality

The principle that all information flows on the Internet must receive equal treatment

Internet service providers (ISPs) are companies like Verizon and Comcast that connect customers to the Internet. Some customers require more bandwidth than others: It takes much more capacity to watch movies and TV shows than to shop for clothing or download books or photos. ISPs would like to have the option of treating high-capacity users differently—either charging them more or slowing their access to the Internet.

This issue is subject to regulation by the Federal Communications Commission (FCC) because the Telecommunications Act of 1996 grants the agency the right to regulate broadband infrastructure. The FCC has adopted a policy of **net neutrality**: the principle that all information flows on the Internet must receive equal treatment. Net neutrality is highly controversial. Both those in favor and those opposed argue the same thing: that if their side wins, consumers and innovation will benefit. ISPs also argue that they should be able to control Internet traffic because some websites, like those that deliver telemedicine or emergency services, deserve priority access.

The following case confronts this issue: Can the FCC require net neutrality? Or do ISPs have the right to favor some users over others?

VERIZON V. FEDERAL COMMUNICATIONS COMMISSION

740 F.3d 623
United States Court of Appeals for the District of Columbia Circuit, 2014

Facts: Centuries ago, when travel was limited, businesses that provided travel services, such as inns and stage-coaches, had a virtual monopoly. There might be only one way to get to another town and only one place to stay when there. To protect consumers, the law imposed a set of so-called common carrier rules, which required these businesses to serve everyone equally and to charge fair prices.

In setting rules for Internet infrastructure, the FCC ruled that broadband ISPs are not common carriers and, therefore, not subject to rules that require equal treatment for all their customers. However, the Commission later became concerned that ISPs might disrupt the neutral flow of information on the Internet. It worried that an ISP like Comcast might, for example, limit access to the *USA Today* website if it wanted to spike traffic to its own news website, or it might degrade the quality of the connection to Bing if a competitor like Google paid for prioritized access.

To prevent such behavior, the FCC issued the Open Internet Order, which prohibited broadband ISPs from (1) blocking lawful content and services and (2) giving preferential treatment to some Internet content or traffic. But Verizon objected, arguing that (1) the Order would not safeguard the Internet and (2) the rules unfairly treated broadband ISPs as common carriers, even though the FCC had ruled that they were not.

Issue: *Could the FCC impose net neutrality rules on broadband ISPs?*

Excerpts from Judge Tatel's Decision: The Commission has reasonably interpreted [the Telecommunications Act] to empower it to promulgate rules governing broadband providers' treatment of Internet traffic, and its justification for the specific rules at issue here—that they will preserve and facilitate the "virtuous circle" of innovation that has driven the explosive growth of the Internet—is reasonable and supported by substantial evidence.

That said, even though the Commission has general authority to regulate in this arena, it may not impose requirements that contravene express statutory mandates. Given that the Commission has chosen to classify broadband providers in a manner that exempts them from treatment as common carriers, the Communications Act expressly prohibits the Commission from nonetheless regulating them as such. Because the Commission has failed to establish that the anti-discrimination and anti-blocking rules do not impose common carrier obligations, we vacate the Open Internet Order.

Within weeks of this decision, there were reports that Verizon had begun to limit bandwidth to some companies that provided cloud services (and, thus, were very heavy users). No company had, however, officially admitted to such a policy.

Although it might seem easy for the FCC simply to rule that broadband ISPs are common carriers, the process for making this change is not quick, easy, or definitive. Any change will certainly be challenged in the courts.

10-1b Regulation of User-Generated Content

Sir Tim Berners-Lee, creator of the World Wide Web, described his vision of the Web as "a collaborative medium, a place where we all meet and read and write." Berners-Lee was referring to **user-generated content**—everything from social media postings, blogs, comments, customer reviews, wikis, images, and videos—created by end users and shared publicly through the Web. But Berners-Lee also acknowledged that although the Web does not "inherently make people do good things, or bad things," bad things can happen online. One role of cyberlaw is to prevent these bad things.

User-generated content
Any content created and made publicly available by end users

The First Amendment

How would you like to be called a cockroach, mega-scumbag, and crook in front of thousands of people? Or be accused of having a fake medical degree, or poor hygiene? **The First Amendment to the Constitution protects free speech**, and that includes these postings—and worse—that have appeared on Internet message boards and blogs. As upsetting as they may be, they are protected as free speech under the First Amendment so long as the poster is not violating some other law. In these cases, the plaintiffs argued that the statements were defamatory but the courts disagreed, ruling that they were simply opinions.

Explaining its ruling in one of the cases, the court said:

> Users [of the Internet] are able to engage freely in informal debate and criticism, leading many to substitute gossip for accurate reporting and often to adopt a provocative, even combative tone. Hyperbole and exaggeration are common, and 'venting' is at least as common as careful and considered argumentation. Some commentators have likened cyberspace to a frontier society free from the conventions and constraints that limit discourse in the real world.

> It hardly need be said that this [court does not] condone [these] rude and childish posts; indeed, [the] intemperate, insulting, and often disgusting remarks understandably offended plaintiff and possibly many other readers. Nevertheless, the fact that society may find speech offensive is not a sufficient reason for suppressing it. Indeed, if it is the speaker's opinion that gives offense, that consequence is a reason for according it constitutional protection.[2]

In the following case, a teacher received hostile emails. Should the First Amendment protect the anonymous person who sent them?

---

[2]Krinsky v. Doe, 6159 Cal. App. 4th 1154 (2008).

You be the Judge

Facts: Juzwiak was a tenured teacher at Hightstown High School in New Jersey. He received three emails from someone who signed himself "Josh," with the address, "Josh Hartnett jharthat @yahoo. com." The teacher did not know anyone of that name. These emails said:

JUZWIAK V. JOHN/JANE DOE
415 N.J. Super. 442
Superior Court of New Jersey,
Appellate Division, 2010

1. Subject line: "Hopefully you will be gone permanently"

   Text: "We are all praying for that. Josh"

2. Subject line: "I hear Friday is 'D' day for you"

   Text: "I certainly hope so. You don't deserve to be allowed to teach anymore. Not just in Hightstown but anywhere. If Hightstown bids you farewell I will make it my lifes [sic] work to ensure that wherever you look for work they know what you have done."

3. Subject line: "Mr. Juzwiak in the Hightstown/East Windsor School System."

   Text: It has been brought to my attention and I am sure many of you know that Mr. J is reapplying for his position as a teacher in this town. It has further been pointed out that certain people are soliciting supporters for him. This is tantamount to supporting the devil himself. I am not asking anyone to speak out against Mr. J but I urge you to then be silent as we can not continue to allow the children of this school system nor the parents to be subjected to his evil ways. Thank you. Josh

It seems that this third email was sent to other people, but it was not clear to whom.

Because Juzwiak did not know who "Josh" was, he filed a complaint against "John/Jane Doe," seeking damages for intentional infliction of emotional distress. As part of the lawsuit, he served a subpoena on Yahoo!, asking it to reveal "Josh's" identity. When Yahoo! notified "Josh" of the lawsuit, he asked the court not to issue the subpoena.

In a court hearing, Juzwiak testified that the threatening emails had severely disrupted his life, causing deep anger and depression as well as insomnia that had impaired his ability to concentrate and function effectively. In addition, this emotional stress had exacerbated his back problems and caused him to lose 20 pounds. Although he had already been taking antidepressants, a psychiatrist prescribed four additional drugs for depression, anxiety, and insomnia, which were not effective in reducing his symptoms. Juzwiak also stated that he had thoughts of hurting himself and the entire episode had consumed his life for several months.

When the trial court refused to issue the subpoena against Yahoo!, Juzwiak appealed.

You Be the Judge: Should the trial court have issued the subpoena? Which interest is more important: "Josh's" First Amendment right to free speech or Juzwiak's protection from harassing emails?

Argument for "Josh": Free speech is the first, and most important, right in the Bill of Rights. To ensure a vibrant marketplace of ideas, the First Amendment protects not only open but also anonymous speech. Sometimes speakers must be allowed to withhold their identities to protect themselves from harassment and persecution.

Nothing in these messages was a realistic threat to the teacher's safety. "Hopefully you will be gone permanently" could easily mean "Hope you will move out of town." Juzwiak reported these emails to the police, but they took no action. Presumably they would have done so if there had been any real threat.

Nor did these emails constitute an intentional infliction of emotional distress. They were not so extreme and outrageous as to be utterly intolerable in a civilized community. "Josh" did not accuse Juzwiak of vile or criminal acts. The language was not obscene or profane. In short, if Juzwiak is going to teach high school, he needs to develop a thicker skin and a better sense of humor.

Argument for Juzwiak: The right to speak anonymously is not absolute. *"Josh"* requires protection from harassment? That is an absurd argument.

These emails contained death threats: "Hopefully you will be gone permanently" and "I hear Friday is 'D' day for you." Juzwiak was frightened enough to go to the police. He suffered serious physical and emotional harm. These emails are not entitled to the protection of the First Amendment.

Furthermore, the emails constituted intentional infliction of emotional distress. They were extreme and outrageous conduct designed to cause harm. They achieved their goal.

In balancing the rights in this case, why would the court protect "Josh," who has deliberately caused harm, rather than the innocent teacher?

The Communications Decency Act of 1996

The Internet is an enormously powerful tool for disseminating information. But what if some of this information happens to be false or in violation of our privacy rights? Is an ISP liable for transmitting it to the world?

Congress reasoned that if ISPs faced the threat of a lawsuit for every problematic posting, the companies would severely restrict content, and the development of the Internet. To prevent his result, Congress passed the **Communications Decency Act of 1996 (CDA)**, which created broad immunity for ISPs and websites.

Under the CDA, end users and anyone who simply provides a neutral forum for information (such as ISPs and website operators) are not liable for content that is provided by someone else. Only content providers are liable.[3] But to avoid liability, the ISP or website must not write, edit, encourage, or influence the content. When a minor was sexually assaulted by a man she met on MySpace, her family sued the website, claiming it did not have proper safety measures to prevent the girl from meeting her attacker. The court rejected this claim, reasoning that MySpace was immune because it had not provided the content.[4]

Communications Decency Act of 1996 (CDA)

Provides ISPs immunity from liability when information was provided by an end user

[3] 47 U.S.C. §230.
[4] Doe v. MySpace, 528 F.3d 413 (5th Cir. 2008).

The following case lays out the arguments in favor of the CDA, but also illustrates some of the costs of the statute (and of the Internet).

CARAFANO V. METROSPLASH.COM, INC.

339 F.3d 1119
United States Court of Appeals for the Ninth Circuit, 2003

Facts: Matchmaker.com[5] was an Internet dating service that permitted members to post their profiles and to view the profiles of others. Matchmaker reviewed photos for impropriety before posting them but did not examine the profiles.

Christianne Carafano was an actor who used the stage name Chase Masterson. She appeared in numerous films and television shows, such as *General Hospital*. Without her knowledge, someone in Berlin posted a profile of her in the Los Angeles section of Matchmaker. In answer to the question "Main source of current events?" the poster wrote "*Playboy Playgirl*" and for "Why did you call?" responded "Looking for a one-night stand." In addition, the essays indicated that she was looking for a "hard and dominant" man with "a strong sexual appetite" and that she "liked sort of being controlled by a man, in and out of bed." Pictures of the actor taken off the Internet were included with the profile. The profile also provided her home address and an email address, which, when contacted, produced an automatic email reply stating, "You think you are the right one? Proof it!!" [sic], and providing Carafano's home address and telephone number.

Unaware of the improper posting, Carafano began receiving sexually explicit and threatening messages at her home. She received numerous phone calls, letters, and email from male fans, expressing concern that she had given out her address and phone number (but simultaneously indicating an interest in meeting her). Feeling unsafe, Carafano and her son moved out of their home.

A week or two after the false profile was first posted, Carafano's assistant, Siouxzan Perry, learned of it through a message from "Jeff." Acting on Carafano's instructions, Perry contacted Matchmaker, demanding that the profile be removed immediately. The Matchmaker employee did not remove it then because Perry herself had not posted it, but two days later, the company blocked the profile from public view and then deleted it the following day.

Carafano filed suit against Matchmaker alleging invasion of privacy, defamation, and negligence. The district court rejected Matchmaker's argument for immunity under the CDA on the grounds that the company provided part of the profile content.

Issue: *Does the CDA protect Matchmaker from liability?*

Excerpts from Judge Thomas's Decision: Interactive computer services have millions of users. It would be impossible for service providers to screen each of their millions of postings for possible problems. Faced with potential liability for each message republished by their services, interactive computer service providers might choose to severely restrict the number and type of messages posted. Congress considered the weight of the speech interests implicated and chose to immunize service providers to avoid any such restrictive effect. Under [the CDA], therefore, so long as a third party willingly provides the essential published content, the interactive service provider receives full immunity regardless of the specific editing or selection process.

The fact that some of the content [in Carafano's fake profile] was formulated in response to Matchmaker's questionnaire does not [make Matchmaker liable]. Doubtless, the questionnaire facilitated the expression of information by individual users. However, the selection of the content was left exclusively to the user. Matchmaker cannot be considered an "information content provider" under the statute because no profile has any content until a user actively creates it.

Further, even assuming Matchmaker could be considered an information content provider, the statute would still bar Carafano's claims unless Matchmaker created or developed the particular information at issue. In this case, critical information about Carafano's home address and the email address that revealed her phone number were transmitted unaltered to profile viewers. Thus, Matchmaker did not play a significant role in creating, developing, or "transforming" the relevant information.

Thus, despite the serious and utterly deplorable consequences that occurred in this case, we conclude that Congress intended that service providers such as Matchmaker be afforded immunity from suit.

---

[5]Matchmaker.com, Inc., changed its legal name to Metrosplash.com, Inc., but continued to do business as Matchmaker.com.

Note that the CDA does not protect web hosts or ISPs that engage in crimes or infringe intellectual property rights (for more on intellectual property, see Chapter 41). Bright Builders, Inc., hosted Copycatclubs.com, a website that, as you might guess, sold counterfeit golf clubs. The court held that Bright Builders was liable despite the CDA because it participated in the design, building, marketing, and support of Copycatclubs.com. It even helped locate the counterfeit clubs that the website sold.[6] Ultimately, a jury returned a verdict of $770,750 against Bright Builders.

Website operators are also liable for their broken contracts and promises. After Cynthia Barnes broke up with her boyfriend, he created a profile of her on a Yahoo! website. He then spitefully posted nude photos of the two of them taken without her knowledge, together with her addresses and phone numbers at home and at work. He also suggested that she was interested in sex with random strangers. Many men were willing to oblige. For months, Yahoo! did not even respond to Barnes's request to remove the profile. Not until a TV show prepared to run a story about the incident did Yahoo! contact Barnes to promise that the profile would be removed immediately. But two months later the company had taken no action, so Barnes sued. The appeals court ruled that Barnes could bring a contract claim against Yahoo! under a theory of promissory estoppel—that she had relied on the company's promise.[7]

Ethics   JuicyCampus.com was a website where college students could anonymously gossip about their schools. To encourage users to "dish dirt," the site promised total anonymity: It did not require a login or username; its slogan was "Always anonymous … Always juicy"; and it assured its users that it was impossible "for anyone to find out who you are and where you are located." The site also instructed users on how to download IP-cloaking software to further ensure anonymity. As a result, most of the Juicy Campus posts were more than just juicy: They ranged from shocking accusations to harassment and revenge. These rumors tarnished reputations, hurt feelings, and tore apart college communities. Women, minorities, and gay students were disproportionately affected. Whether or not it is legally liable, does JuicyCampus.com have an ethical duty to its users? What Life Principles are at stake?

EXAM Strategy

Question: Someone posted an anonymous review on TripAdvisor.com alleging that the owner of a restaurant had entertained a prostitute there. The allegation was false. TripAdvisor refused to investigate or remove the review. Does the restaurant owner have a valid claim against the website?

Strategy: Remember that web hosts are liable only if they have engaged in wrongdoing.

Result: As a web host, TripAdvisor is not liable for content. It would be liable only if it promised to take down the review and then did not.

---

[6] Roger Cleveland Golf Co. v. Price, 2010 U.S. Dist. LEXIS 128044, 2010 WL 5019260 (D.S.C. 2010).
[7] Barnes v. Yahoo, Inc., 570 F.3d 1096 (9th Cir. 2008). Promissory estoppel is discussed in Chapter 11.

10-2 CONSUMER PROTECTION

The Federal Trade Commission Act authorizes the Federal Trade Commission (FTC) to protect consumers and prevent unfair competition. The FTC's regulatory activities are discussed in greater detail in Chapter 38 on antitrust and Chapter 39 on consumer protection. Here we focus on its regulation of the Internet marketplace.

10-2a **The FTC Act**

Section 5 of the FTC Act prohibits unfair and deceptive acts or practices. The FTC applies this statute to online privacy policies. It does not require websites to have a privacy policy, but if they do have one, they must comply with it, and it cannot be deceptive.

Sears paid consumers who visited sears.com and kmart.com websites $10 to become members of the "My SHC Community" and participate in "exciting, engaging, and on-going interactions—always on your terms and always by your choice." As part of this process, consumers downloaded "research" software that tracked their online browsing. Only at the end of a lengthy user agreement did Sears reveal the full extent of the data collected, that it could include the contents of shopping carts, online bank statements, drug prescription records, DVD rental records, and some personal email information. In a consent decree with the FTC, Sears agreed to stop collecting data from consumers who downloaded the software and to destroy all data it had previously collected.

The FTC also brought action against Twitter after hackers gained access to its users' accounts through its administrative system. Twitter had allowed any employee access to its system, which was protected by an easy-to-guess password (1234, maybe?). The hackers reset passwords and sent fake tweets. For example, an unauthorized person sent a tweet from Barack Obama's Twitter account offering free gasoline to users who took an Internet poll (which seems benign compared with what the hacker could have done). The FTC found that Twitter had engaged in deceptive acts because its faulty security violated the company's promise to users that it would protect their information from unauthorized access. As part of the settlement, Twitter agreed to strengthen its security practices.

One more FTC issue: Imagine that you are reading a blog that favorably reviews a new Microsoft product. Before clicking on the Buy button, would you want to know that Microsoft had given the blogger a free computer? The FTC thinks you should. Under FTC rules, bloggers face fines as high as $1,000 if they do not disclose all compensation they receive (either in cash or free products) for writing product reviews. Moreover, celebrities must disclose their relationships with advertisers when making endorsements outside of traditional ads, such as on talk shows or in social media.

10-2b **Spam**

Spam
Unsolicited commercial email

Spam is officially known as unsolicited commercial email (UCE) or unsolicited bulk email (UBE). Whatever it is called, it is one of the most annoying aspects of email. It has been estimated that 90 percent of email is spam. And roughly half of these messages were fraudulent—either in content (promoting a scam) or in packaging (the headers or return address are false). Aside from the annoyance factor, bulk email adds to the cost of connecting to the Internet as ISPs increase server capacity to handle the millions of spam emails.

The Controlling the Assault of Non-Solicited Pornography and Marketing Act (CAN-SPAM) is a federal statute that regulates spam, but does not prohibit it. This statute applies to virtually all promotional emails, whether or not the sender has a preexisting relationship with the recipient. **Under this statute, commercial email:**

- May not have deceptive headings (From, To, Reply To, Subject)

- Must offer an opt-out system permitting the recipient to unsubscribe (and must honor those requests promptly)

- Must clearly indicate that the email is an advertisement

- Must provide a valid physical return address (not a post office box) and

- Must clearly indicate the nature of pornographic messages

A company can avoid these requirements by obtaining advance permission from the recipients.

CAN-SPAM seems to have had little impact on the quantity of spam (although it has made opt-out provisions more common in legitimate commercial emails). More effective have been the tools developed by online security firms and governments that prevent as much as 98 percent of spam from reaching your email inbox.

But spammers have found other outlets. They post messages in the comment sections of websites and on Facebook and Twitter. Their goal is to entice you to click on a link that may take you to a website that sells foolproof "investments" or that simply steals bank information from your computer. If that link seems to come from a Facebook friend or someone whom you follow on Twitter, it seems more reliable. One study found that 8 percent of links sent via Twitter are fraudulent, but they are 20 times more likely to be clicked than those in spam email.[8]

EXAM Strategy

Question: Cruise.com operated a website selling cruise vacations. It sent unsolicited email advertisements—dubbed "E-deals"—to prospective customers. Eleven of these "E-deals" went to inbox@webguy.net. Each message offered the recipient an opportunity to be removed from the mailing list by clicking on a line of text or by writing to a specific postal address. Has Cruise.com violated the CAN-SPAM Act?

Strategy: Remember that this act does not prohibit all unsolicited emails.

Result: Cruise.com was not in violation because it offered the recipients a way to unsubscribe. Also, it provided a valid physical return address.

10-3 PRIVACY IN A DIGITAL WORLD

The Internet has vastly increased our ability to communicate quickly and widely. But it also provides a very large window through which the government, employers, businesses, and other invisible audiences can find out more than they should about you and your money, habits, beliefs, and health—so a discussion of privacy is more important than ever.

Issues of privacy occur in many areas of the law, including, in this book, crime (Chapter 7) and employment law (Chapter 29). In this chapter, we focus on privacy in cyberspace, including laws specifically tailored to the Internet and others that have been adapted for this use.

10-3a How We Lose Our Privacy Online

Sometimes we voluntarily give up our privacy without considering the consequences; in other cases, it is taken from us without our knowledge.

---

[8]"Long Life Spam," *The Economist*, November 20, 2010, p. 67.

Social Media

The ability to share our opinions, relationship status, and location on social media sites like Facebook, Twitter, and Instagram has transformed the concept of privacy and sharing. Not unlike the physical world, *oversharing* carries consequences—and these are not limited to the young and naïve.

- An Arkansas judge campaigning for a seat on the state Court of Appeals was caught after he posted his racist and sexist opinions under an alias on a Louisiana State University fan site. The judge also disclosed confidential information about pending cases, including one involving actress Charlize Theron. While it may not come as a surprise that he was forced to end his judicial campaign, you may be shocked to hear that in his apology statement, he asked for ... privacy.[9]

- After her father confidentially settled an age discrimination lawsuit with his former employer (which happened to be the prep school she attended), a college posted the following on her Facebook page: "Mama and Papa won the case against [my high school]. [The school] is now officially paying for my vacation to Europe this summer. SUCK IT." A Florida appeals court held that the posting violated the confidentiality agreement—and revoked the Snay's $80,000 settlement.[10]

But many victims of social media privacy breaches are entirely blameless, especially those whose information is collected and shared without their knowledge or consent. At its most extreme, people have used social media to harass, bully, and exact revenge on their victims. One woman committed suicide after a disgruntled ex-boyfriend posted revenge porn, or naked pictures of her, on Facebook.[11]

Data Mining and Behavioral Marketing

Consumers enter the most personal data—credit card numbers, bank accounts, lists of friends, medical information, product preferences—on the Internet, where it is accessed much more extensively than they may realize. The 50 most popular websites in America (which account for 40 percent of all page views) install thousands of **tracking tools** on the computers of people who visit their sites. These tools not only collect data on *all* the websites someone visits, but they also record keystrokes to keep track of whatever information the consumer has entered online. These tools are placed on computers without notice or warning to the consumer.

Collecting information allows websites to offer convenience and personalization: Shopping habits are remembered, and sites may even suggest a book you are likely to enjoy. Consumers who give their personal data also benefit from discounts and frequent shopper programs.

But websites are not collecting these data just to provide a better shopping experience. Consumer information is very valuable: U.S. firms spend $2 billion a year on personal data collection.[12] The nation's leading data broker has an estimated 500 million consumer profiles with an average of 1,500 data points per person, mined from 50 trillion data

Tracking tool

A computer program that tracks information about Internet users

---

[9]Joe Patrice, "Judge Caught Making Racist, Sexist, Comments on Internet Board," *Above the Law*, March 2, 2014.

[10]Gulliver Schools v. Patrick Snay, 2014 Fla. App. LEXIS 2595, 2014 WL 769030, Fla. App. 3 Dist. (2014).

[11]*The Huffington Post*, "Emma Jones, British Teacher, Killed Herself After Naked Photos Posted on Facebook," October 8, 2013.

[12]Stephane Armour, "Data Brokers Come Under Fresh Scrutiny," *The Wall Street Journal*, February 12, 2014.

transactions per year.[13] Why is this information so valuable? Because companies can use data-mining tools to find out a lot of information about … well … you. Credit card companies discovered that people who buy anti-scuff pads for their furniture are less likely to default on debts.[14]

Data mining also leads to **behavioral marketing**, or **behavioral targeting**. Behavioral marketing is a widespread practice that involves inferring needs and preferences from a consumer's online behavior and then targeting related advertisements to them. If you look at a sweater on the J.Crew website, but do not buy it, you may find that you are repeatedly shown ads for it—and for other items that people who bought that sweater also purchased. Target has found that shoppers who buy cocoa-butter lotion and large purses are likely to be pregnant.[15] That information is hugely important because the birth of a baby is one of the few times that consumers change their shopping habits. If Target can lure an expectant mother into their store, it may have a customer for life.

The most troubling aspect of massive information collection is that consumers are often unaware of who has access to what personal information, how it is being used, and with what consequences. When Target sent coupons for baby items to one teenager who bought cocoa-butter, it caused family strife by revealing her pregnancy before she told her parents.[16] A Gmail user reported receiving ads for funeral services after emailing family members about his mother's fatal illness.

In short, Internet users are inadvertently providing intensely personal data to unknown people for unknown uses. And the problem is likely to grow with technology. Imagine the price of an airplane ticket increasing *just for you* because airlines know you are flying to your honeymoon—or losing job opportunities because potential employers obtain medical information about you.

Behavioral Marketing, or Behavioral Targeting

The practice of aiming certain advertisements at consumers based on their online behavior

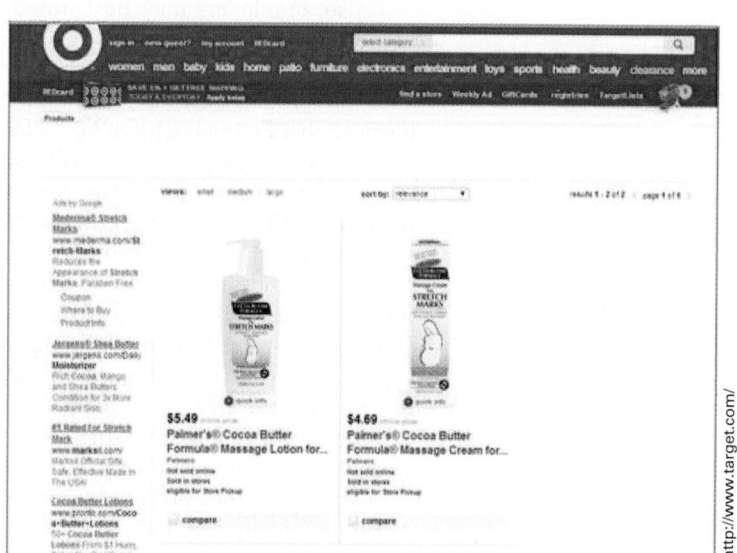

http://www.target.com/

Does buying this lotion indicate that you are pregnant? Target thinks so.

Ethics   Some companies have launched marketplaces for personal data. One firm offers users $8 a month in return for unrestricted access to their social media accounts and credit card transactions. Critics argue that privacy is an important component of human dignity and that it is wrong to cheapen it by turning it into a commodity —like a car or a cheeseburger. They also contend that these companies are exploiting people, who can never really know how their information may be used against them. Is it ethical to buy people's privacy? Under what conditions? What personal data would you be willing to sell? To whom? For how much?

---

[13]Natasha Singer, "Mapping, and Sharing, the Consumer Genome," *The New York Times*, June 16, 2012.
[14]Jonathan Shaw, "Why 'Big Data' Is a Big Deal," *Harvard Magazine*, March–April 2014.
[15]Charles Duhigg, "How Companies Learn Your Secrets," *The New Times Magazine*, February 16, 2012.
[16]Kashmir Hill, "How Target Figured Out a Teen Girl Was Pregnant Before Her Father Did," *Forbes*, February 16, 2012.

Workplace Privacy

The Internet and social media have affected the way employers and employees interact—and what employers can learn about their workers. Technology allows employers to monitor what their employees and job applicants do and say on the job and in their spare time. Many companies monitor employee use of electronic equipment in the workplace: telephone calls, voicemail, email, and Internet usage.

But employers have compelling business reasons to monitor workers' and applicants' online activities. Besides measuring employee productivity and performance, firms have a vested interest in learning about their present and future employees. Helpful hint: It is never a good idea to post hostile tweets about a job interview or a current boss.

Also, employers may be harmed by their workers' online activity. One company was found liable for failing to act against an employee who used a company computer to post nude photographs of his stepdaughter.[17] Domino's Pizza faced a public-relations nightmare after one of its cooks posted a prank YouTube video showing him putting pizza cheese up his nose in a Domino's kitchen.[18] Not surprisingly, about one-third of companies have fired a worker over inappropriate email or Internet use.

The Supreme Court has recognized that employers have a legitimate interest in monitoring their employees, especially for reasonable work-related reasons.[19]

Employer intrusion into an employee's personal life may lead to discriminatory practices. One study found that 45 percent of employers snooped around in candidates' social media profiles before hiring. More than a third of these employers reported having found content that caused them not to hire the applicants. When this content points to illegality or fraud, employers are within their rights to reject applicants. But what if the employer refuses to hire the candidate because her Facebook page reveals she is religious, married, or planning to have children? In those cases, the illegal discrimination may be damaging, yet virtually impossible to prove.

Critics say that privacy is outdated—or even overrated—and point to the fact that if consumers really cared about it, they would share less information online. One tech CEO commented: "You have zero privacy … Get over it."[20] Facebook founder Mark Zuckerberg has said that privacy is an outdated social norm.

But people who care about privacy should be worried. Without updated laws and oversight, it could well be obliterated.

10-3b Regulation of Online Privacy

The following sections discuss the most important laws and regulations that protect online privacy.

The Fourth Amendment

The Fourth Amendment to the Constitution prohibits unreasonable searches and seizures by the government. As we saw in Chapter 7 on crime, the Fourth Amendment protects the privacy rights of criminal defendants. But these same protections extend to the relationship between the government and certain of its citizens, including government workers and public school students.

---

[17]Doe v. XYC Corp., 887 A.2d 1156 (N.J. Super. Ct. 2005).
[18]Stephanie Clifford, "Video Prank at Domino's Taints Brand," *The New York Times*, April 16, 2009, p. B1.
[19]O'Connor v. Ortega, 480 U.S. 709 (1987).
[20]Polly Sprenger, "Sun on Privacy: 'Get Over It,'" *Wired.com*, January 26, 1999.

In enforcing this provision of the Constitution, the courts ask whether a person had a **reasonable expectation of privacy**. The two requirements for establishing a "reasonable expectation of privacy" are:

1. **The person had an actual, subjective expectation of privacy.** Most people expect privacy in restrooms, even at work. Some people might expect that no one will rummage through their desk drawers in their cubicle; others might think that the personal emails they send on the company computers are private. These examples are subjective expectations of privacy.

2. **Society accepts the person's expectation of privacy as reasonable.** Everyone agrees that a bathroom stall is private. (Note to employers: Two-way mirrors in an employee bathroom are a bad idea.) However, the privacy of a cubicle or personal emails *depends* on the circumstances. Did the person know the area might be searched? Did others have access to it? The answers to questions like these help courts determine what people in society would think.

Courts have generally held that employees do not have a reasonable expectation of privacy in the workplace, especially if using hardware provided by the employer,[21] **or if the employee handbook says they may be monitored.**[22] When a police officer persistently exceeded his monthly quota of short message service (SMS) messages, his superior reviewed his texts to determine if they were work related. It turned out that they were mostly sexts (sexual texts) sent to the married officer's mistress. After the officer was disciplined, he filed suit alleging that the department had violated his Fourth Amendment rights. The Supreme Court held that a government employer has the right to review its employee's electronic communications for a work-related purpose, if the search was "justified at its inception" and if "the measures adopted are reasonably related to the objectives of the search and not excessively intrusive in light of the circumstances giving rise to the search."[23]

The Fourth Amendment also protects public school students. In the following case, a bikini-clad teenager claimed she had a reasonable expectation of privacy in her Facebook picture. (Sexts. Bikinis. Who said privacy is boring?)

> **Reasonable expectation of privacy**
>
> The test to analyze whether privacy should be protected

CHELSEA CHANEY V. FAYETTE COUNTY PUBLIC SCHOOL DISTRICT

2013 U.S. Dist. LEXIS 143030; 2013 WL 5486829
U.S. District Court for the Northern District of Georgia, 2013

Facts: Chelsea Chaney was a seventeen-year-old high school student in Fayette County, Georgia. At a county-wide Internet safety seminar, Curtis Cearley, the District's technology director, presented a PowerPoint slideshow to illustrate the permanent and often-embarrassing nature of social media postings.

Cearley's first slide was a cartoon depicting a scene in the future: A curious daughter discovers her mother's old Facebook page, listing her hobbies as "body art, bad boys, and jello shooters." The following slide, entitled "Once It's There—It's There to Stay," featured a picture of Chaney in a bikini posing with a life-size cutout of rapper

---

[21]See, e.g., Bohach v. City of Reno, 932 F. Supp. 1232 (D. Nev. 1996).
[22]See, e.g., Muick v. Glenayre Elec., 280 F.3d 741, 743 (7th Cir. 2002).
[23]City of Ontario v. Quon, 560 U.S. 746 (S. Ct. 2010).

Snoop Dogg. The slide included Chaney's full name. Cearley distributed copies of the presentation to the hundreds of students and parents in attendance.

Cearley had found Chaney's photo while searching Facebook for materials to use in his presentation. Her page had a semi-private setting that allowed her Facebook "friends" and "friends of friends" to view her page. Neither Chaney nor her parents consented to the use of her picture.

Chaney was embarrassed and humiliated. In her view, Cearley had publicly implied that she was a sexually promiscuous abuser of alcohol who should be more careful about her Internet postings. In fact, she contended, the picture was taken on a family vacation that did not involve sex or alcohol.

Chaney sued, claiming that Cearley and the District violated her constitutional right to privacy under the Fourth Amendment. The District filed a motion to dismiss.

Issue: *Did Chaney have a reasonable expectation of privacy in her bikini Facebook picture?*

Excerpts from Judge Batten's Decision: Chaney argues that she had a reasonable expectation in the privacy of her Facebook picture, and that the District violated this expectation when Cearley used her photo in his presentation.

In establishing a reasonable expectation of privacy, a person must show that she had a subjective expectation of privacy and must show a willingness of society to recognize that expectation as legitimate. Even if she had a subjective expectation of privacy in her Facebook photos, Chaney cannot show that her expectation is legitimate.

Chaney contends that her privacy-setting choice of "friends and friends of friends" was "semi-private" and that her Facebook page was accessible "only to those people she had specifically approved." However, Chaney fails to acknowledge the lack of privacy afforded her by her selected Facebook setting. While Chaney may select her Facebook friends, she cannot select her Facebook friends' friends. By intentionally selecting the broadest privacy setting available to her at that time, Chaney made her page available to potentially hundreds, if not thousands, of people whom she did not know (i.e., the friends of her Facebook friends).

The Supreme Court consistently has held that a person has no legitimate expectation of privacy in information he voluntarily turns over to third parties. Chaney not only voluntarily turned over the picture to her Facebook friends, but she also chose to share the picture with an additional audience of unknown size, likely comprised of people Chaney did not know, subject to continuous expansion without Chaney's approval.

When an individual shares a photograph with his friends on Facebook, that individual has no justifiable expectation that his 'friends' would keep his profile private. Chaney shared her Facebook page, which includes her pictures, not only with her friends but their friends, too. By doing so, Chaney surrendered any reasonable expectation of privacy. Thus, Chaney cannot show that society would be willing to recognize her expectation of privacy as legitimate.

The fact that the photo was of Chaney in a bikini does not require a different result. People have a reasonable expectation not to be unclothed involuntarily and/or not to be observed unclothed. However, this case involves Chaney voluntarily posting a picture of herself in a bikini and sharing that picture on a social media website with the broadest audience possible for a Facebook user her age.

Because Chaney cannot show a violation of her Fourth Amendment rights, the Court will grant Defendants' motion on this claim.

Although the Fourth Amendment does not govern private-sector employers, the reasonable expectation of privacy analysis is a guide to judges and lawmakers in every area of privacy law, including the privacy torts, which we discuss next.

Privacy Torts

Society was more voyeuristic than ever, curious about every detail of other people's lives. Paparazzi and the nosy press were everywhere, using a new and intrusive technology to pry. Sound familiar? The year was 1890. A new technology called "photography" so angered soon-to-be Supreme Court Justice Louis Brandeis that it inspired him and his law partner, Samuel Warren, to write the most influential law review article in history. Titled "The Right to Privacy," this article advocated the creation of a new right protecting an individual's personal space from intrusion and disclosure.[24] Based on the authors' famous arguments,

---

[24]Samuel D. Warren and Louis D. Brandeis, "The Right to Privacy," 4 *Harvard Law Review*, Vol. 193, 1890.

courts created two new torts to protect against violations of privacy: public disclosure of private facts and intrusion.

Public Disclosure of Private Facts.

The tort of public disclosure of private facts applies when people spill the beans: It prohibits the unjustifiable revelation of truthful, but secret, information. **The public disclosure tort requires the plaintiff to show all of the following:**[25]

- **The defendant made public disclosure.** The defendant must have divulged the secret information to a number of people, not just one other person.

- **The disclosed facts had been private.** The person seeking privacy must prove that she had a reasonable expectation of privacy in the information. But courts have held that people cannot have a reasonable expectation of privacy in information that is generally visible or available. When Ralph Nader, a consumers' rights activist, criticized General Motors publicly, GM sent agents to dig up some dirt on Nader.[26] In an effort to embarrass Nader, GM interviewed his friends (*some* friends) about his racial and religious views, his personal and sexual habits, and his political beliefs. Nader sued GM for public disclosure of private facts, but GM won because the gathered information was not technically secret since Nader had already revealed it to many of his acquaintances.

- **The facts were not of legitimate concern to the public.** The First Amendment protects free speech and, therefore, sometimes undermines privacy rights. To protect their privacy, plaintiffs must prove that the revealed secret was not of public concern, that is, that the public was not entitled to know about it. A Florida newspaper mistakenly revealed a rape victim's name, which it had obtained from a public police report. The Supreme Court held that it was unconstitutional to prohibit the publication of truthful and legitimately obtained information about an issue of legitimate public interest such as crime.[27]

- **The disclosure is highly offensive to a reasonable person.** Privacy is somewhat subjective. One person's secret is another's reality show. For this reason, defendants must prove that most reasonable people would be offended if the secret was revealed.

After Calvin Green died of a gunshot wound, his mother, Laura, spoke to him in his hospital room, telling him how much she loved him. Reporters from the *Chicago Tribune* were in the hospital reporting on a story about Chicago's homicide rate. They overheard Laura's words to Calvin, which they then printed in the newspaper. When Laura sued, the court ruled that she had stated a claim under the public disclosure tort because the newspaper had (1) printed the information in the newspaper, (2) Calvin's hospital room had been private, (3) the facts were not of legitimate concern to the public, and (4) the disclosure of information about this extraordinarily painful incident was highly offensive.[28]

Public disclosure of private facts
A tort providing redress to victims of unauthorized and embarrassing disclosures

---

[25]Restatement (Second) of Torts §652D (1977).
[26]Nader v. Gen. Motors Corp., 255 N.E.2d 765 (N.Y. 1970).
[27]The Florida Star v. B.J.F. 491 U.S. 524 (S. Ct. 1989).
[28]Green v. Chicago Tribune Co., 286 Ill. App. 3d 1 (Ill. App. Ct. 1st Dist. 1996).

EXAM Strategy

Question: A group of college bullies made a flyer with a fellow student's picture, email address, and phone number—all information found on the university's website. The flyer, posted all around the university campus and online, falsely advertised that he was seeking a male romantic partner. The humiliated victim sued the bullies for public disclosure of private facts—not his sexual orientation but his contact information. What result?

Strategy: Remember that defendants are liable only if they have disclosed secret information.

Result: The bullies committed a horrible act, but they are not liable under the public disclosure tort. The victim's contact information and picture were accessible to all students and faculty via the university's website, so they were not private facts.

Ron Galella/Getty Images

Jacqueline Kennedy Onassis was a frequent target of the paparazzi.

Intrusion. **Intrusion into someone's private life is a tort if a reasonable person would find it offensive.** Peeping through someone's windows or wiretapping his telephone is an obvious example of intrusion. In a famous case involving a "paparazzo" photographer and Jacqueline Kennedy Onassis, the court found that the photographer had invaded her privacy by making a career out of photographing her. He had bribed doormen to gain access to hotels and restaurants she visited, had jumped out of bushes to photograph her young children, and had driven power boats dangerously close to her. The court ordered him to stop. Nine years later the paparazzo was found in contempt of court for again taking photographs too close to Ms. Onassis. He agreed to stop once and for all—in exchange for a suspended contempt sentence.

The tort of intrusion requires the plaintiff to show that the defendant (1) intentionally intruded, physically or otherwise, (2) upon the solitude or seclusion of another or on his private affairs or concerns, (3) in a manner highly offensive to a reasonable person.[29] A company had an explicit policy stating that emails were confidential and would not be intercepted or used against an employee. Yet the firm fired two workers who exchanged (they claimed) joking emails threatening violence to sales managers. They sued under the tort of intrusion, but the court ruled for the company on the grounds that a reasonable person would not consider the interception of those emails to have been a highly offensive invasion of privacy.[30]

In the following case, a nurse was offended when her supervisor snooped on her Facebook postings. But would her Facebook wall be strong enough to protect her privacy?

---

[29]Restatement (Second) of Torts §652B (1977).
[30]Smyth v. Pillsbury Co., 914 F. Supp. 97 (E.D. Pa. 1996).

EHLING V. MONMOUTH-OCEAN HOSP. SERV. CORP

872 F. Supp. 2d 369
United States District Court for the District of New Jersey, 2012

Facts: Deborah Ehling was a registered nurse and paramedic who worked at the Monmouth-Ocean Hospital Service Corporation (MONOC). The privacy settings on Ehling's Facebook page limited access to just her "friends." Many of her coworkers, but no members of management, were Facebook friends.

A hospital supervisor summoned one of Ehling's coworker Facebook friends into an office where she forced him to access his account so that she could view Ehling's Facebook wall. The supervisor copied Ehling's postings, including the following one, which was reacting to a shooting:

> An 88 yr old sociopath white supremacist opened fire in the Wash D.C. Holocaust Museum this morning and killed an innocent guard (leaving children). Other guards opened fire. The 88 yr old was shot. He survived. I blame the DC paramedics. I want to say 2 things to the DC medics. 1. WHAT WERE YOU THINKING? and 2. This was your opportunity to really make a difference! WTF!!!! And to the other guards go to target practice.

MONOC sent letters with this posting to the boards that regulate nursing and paramedics in New Jersey. MONOC told the boards that it was concerned that this posting showed a disregard for patient safety.

Ehling alleged that these letters were sent in a malicious attempt to damage her reputation and possibly cause her to lose her license. She filed suit against MONOC, alleging a violation of the tort of intrusion. The hospital filed a motion to dismiss, arguing that she did not have a reasonable expectation of privacy in her Facebook posting.

Issue: *Did Ehling have a reasonable expectation of privacy in her Facebook comment?*

Excerpts from Judge Martini's Decision: Under New Jersey law, to state a claim for intrusion, a plaintiff must allege sufficient facts to demonstrate that (1) her solitude, seclusion, or private affairs were intentionally infringed upon, and that (2) this infringement would highly offend a reasonable person. Expectations of privacy are established by general social norms and must be objectively reasonable—a plaintiff's subjective belief that something is private is irrelevant.

Although most courts hold that a communication is not necessarily public just because it is accessible to a number of people, courts differ dramatically in how far they think this theory extends. [M]ost courts have adopted the concept of "limited privacy," which is the idea that when an individual reveals private information about herself to one or more persons, she may retain a reasonable expectation that the recipients of the information will not disseminate it further. [In one case,] plaintiff's disclosure of facts to sixty people did not render them public, [but in another,] plaintiff's disclosure of facts to two coworkers deprived her of a reasonable expectation of privacy.

What is clear is that privacy determinations are made on a case-by-case basis, in light of all the facts presented. In this case, Plaintiff argues that she had a reasonable expectation of privacy in her Facebook posting because her comment was disclosed to a limited number of people who she had individually invited to view a restricted access webpage. Defendants argue that Plaintiff cannot have a reasonable expectation of privacy because the comment was disclosed to dozens, if not hundreds, of people.

The Court finds that Plaintiff has stated a plausible claim for invasion of privacy, considering that she actively took steps to protect her Facebook page from public viewing. More importantly, however, the question of the reasonableness of the Plaintiffs' expectations of privacy is a question of fact for the jury to decide. Accordingly, the motion to dismiss the Complaint is denied.

Fair Information Practices

In the 1960s and 1970s, the increasing use of computers to collect and store personal information began to give rise to widespread concerns about privacy. As a result, the Department of Housing, Education, and Welfare issued a highly influential report recommending the establishment of a Code of Fair Information Practices (FIPS). In the late 1990s, the FTC adapted the FIPS to the Internet marketplace. **The core principles of the FIPS are:**

- **Notice/Awareness.** Notice should be given before any personal information is collected.

- **Choice/Consent.** People should be able to control the use and destination of their information.

- **Access/Participation.** People should have the ability to view, correct, or amend any personally identifiable record about them.

- **Integrity/Security.** Information collectors must take reasonable precautions to ensure that the data they collect are accurate and secure.

Note that FIPS are recommendations, not law.[31] However, they are often the basis for online privacy policies and have guided the creation of the statutes we will now discuss.

Federal Privacy Statutes

As the *Declaration of the Independence of Cyberspace* at the beginning of this chapter suggested, the Internet was initially viewed as a relatively lawless land. In its early days, it was often compared to the "Wild West." Little by little, in response to growing concerns and online threats, lawmakers reacted in a piecemeal way.

Today, instead of having a single comprehensive data privacy law, the United States has a collection of federal privacy laws that apply to particular types of personal data. Different federal laws apply to your consumer credit information (discussed in Chapter 39 on consumer protection), your medical data, and even the movies you rent. Diverse laws also apply to the way information is collected and from whom. We will focus on laws covering electronic communications, children, and spies.

Electronic Communications Privacy Act

A federal statute prohibiting unauthorized interception of, access to, or disclosure of wire and electronic communications

Electronic Communications Privacy Act of 1986.   The Electronic Communications Privacy Act of 1986 (ECPA) is a federal statute that prohibits unauthorized interception of, access to, or disclosure of wire and electronic communications. The definition of electronic communication includes email, cell phones, and social media. Violators are subject to both criminal and civil penalties. An action does not violate the ECPA if it is unintentional or if either party consents. **Under the ECPA:**

- **Any intended recipient of an electronic communication has the right to disclose it.** Thus, if you sound off in an email to a friend about your boss, the (former) friend may legally forward that email to the boss or anyone else.

- **ISPs are generally prohibited from disclosing electronic messages to anyone other than the addressee**, unless this disclosure is necessary for the performance of their service or for the protection of their own rights or property.

- **An employer has the right to monitor workers' electronic communications if (1) the employee consents, (2) the monitoring occurs in the ordinary course of business, or (3) in the case of email, if the employer provides the computer system.**

Thus, an employer has the right to monitor electronic communication even if it does not relate to work activities. This monitoring may include an employee's social media activities. **But one thing employers cannot do is access an employee's social media profile by trickery or coercion.** As we saw earlier in the *Ehling* case, coercion may constitute an invasion of privacy. It may also violate the ECPA. Restaurant employee Brian Pietrylo created a password-protected MySpace group to vent about work-related topics. The forum contained references to illegal drug use and violence, sexual remarks about management, and disparaging comments about customers. When the restaurant managers began suspecting trouble, they wanted to see the postings for themselves. To gain access, they coerced another employee into giving them

---

[31]U.S. Federal Trade Commission. *Privacy Online: Fair Information Practices in the Electronic Marketplace: A Report to Congress.* May 2000.

her login information and password. The restaurant fired Pietrylo, who then accused the employer of violating the ECPA. Because the worker who provided her password did not act voluntarily, the court found that the employer accessed the electronic communication without authorization in violation of the ECPA.[32]

Some states also have laws regulating social media access. In short, the law is evolving, subtle, and varies by state, so employees should err on the side of caution and remember that the law often does not protect their electronic lives from employer prying. **You should consider anything you publish on the Internet to be public. As for companies, it makes sense to establish policies providing that:**

- Employees should never reveal their company's name on a personal blog or social media. Nor should they reveal confidential or proprietary information.

- Personal blogs should contain a disclaimer that "All postings are my opinion and not those of my employer, who has neither vetted nor approved them."

- Online behavior should never be offensive, impolite, or reflect badly on the employer.

Children's Online Privacy Protection Act of 1998.
The Children's Online Privacy Protection Act of 1998 (COPPA) prohibits Internet operators from collecting information from children under 13 without parental permission. It also requires sites to disclose how they will use any information they acquire. Enforcement is in the hands of the FTC. Path Inc. had a mobile app that allowed users to create a daily journal and share it with friends. This app permitted children to register without parental permission. Each time a user posted a "thought" on the app, they were invited to reveal their location through the geo-tracking feature as well as the names of friends who were with them. When challenged by the FTC, Path agreed to stop this practice and pay a fine of $800,000.[33]

Children's Online Privacy Protection Act (COPPA)
Federal statute regulating children's privacy online

Foreign Intelligence Surveillance Act.
Former National Security Agency (NSA) contractor Edward Snowden set off an international furor when he leaked information revealing the extent of U.S. surveillance on everyone from world leaders to international charities and even U.S. citizens. Angela Merkel, Chancellor of Germany and a U.S. ally, was furious to learn that the NSA had been listening in on her cell phone. Snowden reported that, as an NSA agent, he could, sitting at his desk, "wiretap anyone, from you or your accountant, to a federal judge or even the president, if I had a personal email." According to Snowden, the U.S. government was reading emails, mapping cell phone locations, reviewing browser histories, and monitoring just about everything that anyone does online. Is there a law against this?

The **Foreign Intelligence Surveillance Act (FISA)** sets out the rules for the use of electronic surveillance to collect foreign intelligence (otherwise known as spying) within the United States. FISA was enacted in 1978 after decades of abuses in the name of national security. However, in the aftermath of the 9/11 terrorist attacks, FISA's provisions were weakened. **Now, the FISA provides that:**

Foreign Intelligence Surveillance Act (FISA)
Federal statute governing the government's collection of foreign intelligence in the United States

- To spy on people located in the United States who are communicating abroad, the government does not need a warrant but it must obtain permission from a secret Foreign Intelligence Surveillance Court (FISC). To obtain this permission, the government need only demonstrate that the surveillance (1) targets "persons reasonably believed to be located outside the United States" and (2) seeks "foreign intelligence information." This standard gives the government broad powers to collect emails, phone calls, and other electronic communications between people in the U.S. and anyone abroad.

[32]Pietrylo v. Hillstone Rest. Grp., 2009 WL 3128420, 2009 U.S. Dist. LEXIS 88702 (D.N.J.2009).
[33]United States of America v. Path, Inc. FTC Matter/File Number: 122 3158.

- Government agencies must delete irrelevant and personally identifying data before providing it to other agencies.

- The government must notify defendants if the evidence being used against them in court was gathered in FISA surveillance.

State Regulation

An exhaustive list of state laws is beyond the scope of this book, but be aware that many states have passed their own online privacy laws. Here are some recent examples:

- California requires any website that collects personal information from California residents to post a privacy policy conspicuously and then abide by its terms. Companies, including mobile apps, collecting information from Californians must disclose their consumer software tracking policies.[34]

- Connecticut, Nebraska, and Pennsylvania regulate online privacy policies and some require ISPs to obtain their customers' consent before sharing their information.

- Delaware and Connecticut require employers to notify their workers before monitoring emails or Internet usage.

- Twelve states now ban employers from requesting job candidates' social media login information during the hiring process.[35]

- Some states, such as New Jersey and California, have laws making revenge porn a crime. Although many states already criminalize taking another person's nude picture without consent, these new laws apply to pictures taken consensually, but later posted online for the purpose of intentionally harassing or causing emotional distress.

European Privacy Law

It is important to keep in mind that other countries regulate privacy very differently. Europeans have long considered the privacy of personal information to be a fundamental right. The European Convention on Human Rights declares, "Everyone has the right to respect for his private and family life, his home, and his correspondence."[36] This fundamental right to privacy has been incorporated into the laws of EU member states.

EU Privacy Directive

Sets out the privacy rights of all Europeans, especially online

The EU Privacy Directive establishes data protection for Europeans in all their commercial transactions worldwide. The Directive requires an opt-in system, under which tracking tools cannot be employed unless the consumer is told how the tools will be used and then specifically grants permission for their use.

European courts have recognized that privacy can exist in public places. When model Naomi Campbell was photographed leaving a Narcotics Anonymous meeting, she sued for breach of privacy and won, even though she was in public.[37] And the Supreme Court of France has held employees have a right to private communications, even on an employer's computer.[38]

---

[34]Cal. Bus. & Prof. Code, §§22575–22579.

[35]Oregon, Arkansas, California, Colorado, Illinois, Maryland, Michigan, Nevada, New Jersey, New Mexico, Utah, and Washington are among those states with social media privacy laws.

[36]European Convention on Human Rights. art. 8, Nov. 4, 1950, 213 U.N.T.S. 221.

[37]Stuart Goldberg, "The Contest for a New Law of Privacy: A Battle Won, a War Lost?" Campbell v. Mirror Group Newspapers Limited, 9 Comm. L. 122 (2004).

[38]Arret 4164, Cour de Cassation—Chambre Sociale, 2001.

Chapter Conclusion

The Internet is a thriving ecosystem of knowledge and communication. It can be used for great social benefit and innovation, but also presents challenges. Although the law rushes to address some of these challenges, technology usually wins the race. Many of the laws that apply to today's Internet were written in the time before cyberspace was part of our daily lives. Courts can apply some of these old laws in new ways, but as legislators and courts learn from experience, new laws and novel problem-solving approaches will be needed.

EXAM REVIEW

1. **NET NEUTRALITY** The principle that all Internet content and traffic should receive equal treatment.

2. **THE FIRST AMENDMENT** The First Amendment to the Constitution protects speech on the Internet so long as the speech does not violate some other law.

3. **COMMUNICATIONS DECENCY ACT OF 1996 (CDA)** Under the CDA, ISPs and web hosts are not liable for information that is provided by someone else.

EXAM Strategy

Question: Ton Cremers was the director of security at Amsterdam's famous Rijksmuseum and the operator of the Museum Security Network (the Network) website. Robert Smith, a handyman working for Ellen Batzel in North Carolina, sent an email to the Network alleging that Batzel was the granddaughter of Heinrich Himmler (one of Hitler's henchmen) and that she had art that Himmler had stolen. These allegations were completely untrue. Cremers posted Smith's email on the Network's website and sent it to the Network's subscribers. Cremers exercised some editorial discretion in choosing which emails to send to subscribers, generally omitting any that were unrelated to stolen art. Is Cremers liable to Batzel for the harm that this inaccurate information caused?

Strategy: Cremers is liable only if he is a content provider. (See the "Result" at the end of this section.)

4. **THE FTC ACT** Section 5 of the FTC Act prohibits unfair and deceptive practices. The FTC does not require websites to have a privacy policy, but if they do have one, it cannot be deceptive and they must comply with it.

5. **THE CONTROLLING THE ASSAULT OF NON-SOLICITED PORNOGRAPHY AND MARKETING ACT (CAN-SPAM)** CAN-SPAM is a federal statute that does not prohibit spam but instead regulates it. Under this statute, commercial email:

- May not have deceptive headings (From, To, Reply To, Subject)

- Must offer an opt-out system permitting the recipient to unsubscribe (and must honor those requests promptly)

- Must clearly indicate that the email is an advertisement

- Must provide a valid physical return address (not a post office box) and

- Must clearly indicate the nature of pornographic messages

6. **THE FOURTH AMENDMENT** The Fourth Amendment to the Constitution prohibits unreasonable searches and seizures by the government. This provision applies to computers.

7. **REASONABLE EXPECTATION OF PRIVACY** There is a reasonable expectation of privacy if (1) the person had a subjective expectation of privacy and (2) society accepts that expectation as reasonable.

8. **PUBLIC DISCLOSURE OF PRIVATE FACTS** It is a violation of tort law to disclose secret information if disclosure would be highly offensive to a reasonable person and the information is not of legitimate public concern.

9. **INTRUSION** Intrusion into someone's private life is a tort if a reasonable person would find it offensive.

EXAM Strategy

Question: Every time Dave logs on to his company computer, he clicks "I agree" to the firm's computer usage policy, which states that the employer can monitor everything he does online. On his lunch break, Dave logs on to his Facebook account from his company computer to upload some pictures from his weekend's activities. Can Dave's employer snoop?

Strategy: Does Dave have a subjective expectation of privacy? Given the circumstances, is Dave's expectation of privacy accepted by society? (See the "Result" at the end of this section.)

10. **THE FAIR INFORMATION PRACTICES (FIPS)** The FIPs include Notice/Awareness, Choice/Consent, Access/Participation, and Integrity/Security. Although the FIPs are not law, they have had great influence on privacy laws and policy.

11. **THE ELECTRONIC COMMUNICATIONS PRIVACY ACT OF 1986 (ECPA)** THE ECPA is a federal statute that prohibits unauthorized interception or disclosure of wire and electronic communications. However, it permits an employer to monitor workers' electronic communications if (1) the employee consents, (2) the monitoring occurs in the ordinary course of business, or (3) the employer provides the computer system (in the case of email).

EXAM Strategy

Question: Dr. Norman Scott was the head of the orthopedics department at a hospital. His contract with the hospital provided for $14 million in severance pay if he was fired without cause. When the hospital fired him, he filed suit seeking his $14 million. He used the hospital's email system to send emails to his lawyer. The hospital notified him that it had copies of these emails, which it planned to read. He said that, because the emails were protected by the attorney–client privilege, the hospital did not have this right.

Strategy: What does the ECPA provide? Is there an exception for the attorney–client privilege? Should there be? (See the "Result" at the end of this section.)

12. **THE CHILDREN'S ONLINE PRIVACY PROTECTION ACT OF 1998 (COPPA)** COPPA prohibits Internet operators from collecting information from children under 13 without parental permission. It also requires sites to disclose how they will use any information they acquire.

13. **THE FOREIGN INTELLIGENCE SURVEILLANCE ACT (FISA)** FISA provides the rules for the government's collection of foreign intelligence within the United States.

14. **EU PRIVACY DIRECTIVE** The European Union's Privacy Directive requires an opt-in system under which tracking tools cannot be used unless the consumer is told how the tools will be used and then specifically grants permission for their use.

3. **Result:** The court found that Cremers was not liable under the CDA.

9. **Result:** Dave does not have a reasonable expectation of privacy on his work computer, even if he is on break and on his private Facebook page. He consented to employer surveillance when he logged in.

11. **Result:** The court ruled that the hospital could read the emails. If the doctor wanted the content of these emails to be protected under the attorney–client privilege, he should not have sent them over the hospital email system.

MULTIPLE-CHOICE QUESTIONS

1. The following agency is charged with the regulation of electronic communications:
   (a) National Security Agency
   (b) Federal Trade Commission
   (c) Federal Communications Commission
   (d) None of the above

2. Because Blaine Blogger reviews movies on his blog, cinemas allow him in for free. Nellie Newspaper Reporter also gets free admission to movies.

Blaine _____ disclose on his blog that he receives free tickets.
Nellie _____ disclose in her articles that she receives free tickets.

(a) must, must

(b) need not, need not

(c) must, need not

(d) need not, must

3. An employer has the right to monitor workers' electronic communications if

(a) The employee consents.

(b) The monitoring occurs in the ordinary course of business.

(c) The employer provides the computer system.

(d) All of the above

(e) None of the above

4. Spiro Spammer sends millions of emails a day asking people to donate to his college tuition fund. Oddly enough, many people do. Everything in the emails is accurate (including his 1.9 GPA). Which of the following statements is true?

(a) Spiro has violated the CAN-SPAM Act because he has sent unsolicited commercial emails.

(b) Spiro has violated the CAN-SPAM Act if he has not offered recipients an opportunity to unsubscribe.

(c) Spiro has violated the CAN-SPAM Act because he is asking for money.

(d) Spiro has violated the CAN-SPAM Act unless the recipients have granted permission to him to send these emails.

5. Sushila suspects that her boyfriend Plum is being unfaithful. While he is asleep, she takes his iPod out from under his pillow and goes through all his playlists. Then she finds what she has been looking for: Plum's Playlist. It is full of romantic songs. Sushila sends Plum an email that says, "You are the most evil person in the universe!" Which law has Sushila violated?

(a) The First Amendment

(b) The CDA

(c) The ECPA

(d) The CFAA

(e) None

CASE QUESTIONS

1. ETHICS Chitika, Inc., provided online tracking tools on websites. When consumers clicked the "opt-out" button, indicating that they did not want to be tracked, they were not—for 10 days. After that, the software would resume tracking. Is there a legal problem with Chitika's system? An ethical problem? What Life Principles were operating here?

2. ***YOU BE THE JUDGE* WRITING PROBLEM** Jerome Schneider wrote several books on how to avoid taxes. These books were sold on Amazon.com. Amazon permits visitors to post comments about items for sale. Amazon's policy suggests that these comments should be civil (e.g., no profanity or spiteful remarks). The comments about Schneider's books were not so kind. One person alleged Schneider was a felon. When Schneider complained, an Amazon representative agreed that some of the postings violated its guidelines and promised that they would be removed within one to two business days. Two days later, the posting had not been removed. Schneider filed suit. **Argument for Schneider:** Amazon has editorial discretion over the posted comments. It both establishes guidelines and then monitors the comments to ensure that they comply with the guidelines. These activities make Amazon an information content provider, not protected by the Communications Decency Act. Also, Amazon violated its promise to take down the content. **Argument for Amazon:** The right to edit material is not the same thing as creating the material in the first place.

3. Over the course of 10 months, Joseph Melle sent more than 60 million unsolicited email advertisements to AOL members. What charges could be brought against him? Would you need more information before deciding?

4. Roommates.com operated a website designed to match people renting spare rooms with those looking for a place to live. Before subscribers could search listings or post housing opportunities on Roommate's website, they had to create profiles, a process that required them to answer a series of questions that included the subscriber's sex, sexual orientation, and whether he would bring children to a household. The site also encouraged subscribers to provide "Additional Comments," describing themselves and their desired roommate in an open-ended essay. Here are some typical ads:

- "I am not looking for Muslims."

- "Not acceptable: freaks, geeks, prostitutes (male or female), druggies, pet cobras, drama queens, or mortgage brokers."

- "Must be a black gay male!"

- We are 3 Christian females who Love our Lord Jesus Christ…. We have weekly bible studies and bi-weekly times of fellowship."

Many of the ads violated the Fair Housing Act. Is Roommates.com liable?

5. Barrow was a government employee. Because he shared his office computer with another worker, he brought in his personal computer from home to use for office work. No other employee accessed it, but it was connected to the office network. The computer was not password protected, nor was it regularly turned off. When another networked computer was reported to be running slowly, an employee looked at Barrow's machine to see if it was the source of the problem. He found material that led to Barrow's termination. Had Barrow's Fourth Amendment rights been violated?

DISCUSSION QUESTIONS

1. Marina Stengart used her company laptop to communicate with her lawyer via her personal, password-protected, web-based email account. The company's policy stated:

   > E-mail and voice mail messages, Internet use and communication, and computer files are considered part of the company's business and client records. Such communications are not to be considered private or personal to any individual employee. Occasional personal use is permitted; however, the system should not be used to solicit for outside business ventures, charitable organizations, or for any political or religious purpose, unless authorized by the Director of Human Resources.

   After she filed an employment lawsuit against her employer, the company hired an expert to access her emails that had been automatically stored on the laptop. Are these emails private?

2. Eric Schmidt, former CEO of Google, has written:

   > The communication technologies we use today are invasive by design, collecting our photos, comments and friends into giant databases that are searchable and, in the absence of outside regulation, fair game for employers, university admissions personnel and town gossips. We are what we tweet.

   Do you consider this a problem? If so, can the law fix it?

3. **ETHICS** Matt Drudge published a report on his website (http://www.drudgereport .com) that White House aide Sidney Blumenthal "has a spousal abuse past that has been effectively covered up…. There are court records of Blumenthal's violence against his wife." The *Drudge Report* is an electronic publication focusing on Hollywood and Washington gossip. AOL paid Drudge $3,000 a month to make the *Drudge Report* available to AOL subscribers. Drudge emailed his reports to AOL, which then posted them. Before posting, however, AOL had the right to edit content. Drudge ultimately retracted his allegations against Blumenthal, who sued AOL. He alleged that under the Communications Decency Act of 1996, AOL was a "content provider" because it paid Drudge and edited what he wrote. Do you agree? Putting liability aside, what moral obligation did AOL have to its members? To Blumenthal? Should AOL be liable for content it bought and provided to its members?

4. The European Union has created a "right to be forgotten" online. This right allows Europeans to request that websites take down their personal information, as long as it is not in the public interest. For example, a person would be able to request that Facebook delete her unflattering photograph, if it is outdated and is not newsworthy. Is this law a good idea? Would U.S. lawmakers ever consider a law like this? Why or why not?

5. Tracking tools give consumers many benefits, but they also carry risks. Should Congress regulate them? If so, what should the law provide?

Contracts

CHAPTER 11

INTRODUCTION TO CONTRACTS

Chris always planned to propose to his girlfriend, Alissa, at Chez Luc, their favorite ritzy restaurant. When he was ready to pop the question, Chris went on Chez Luc's website to reserve a special table. But the website would not grant him a seating time unless he clicked the box that said: "No one in my party will use a cell phone at Chez Luc." Chris agreed and was issued a booking at his waterfront table of choice.

After Alissa's exuberant "yes" during the appetizer course, the newly engaged couple could not contain their excitement. First they posted selfies on both their Facebook pages. Then they called their parents to share the good news ... only to be confronted by the angry maître d', who escorted the couple out of the dining room for breaching their contract with the restaurant.

© Honza Krej/Shutterstock.com

The angry maitre d' escorted the couple out of the dining room.

We make promises and agreements all the time—from the casual "I'll call you later" to more formal business contracts. These agreements may be long or short, written or oral, negotiable or not. But they are not necessarily enforceable through the legal system. One of the aims of contract law is to determine which agreements are "worthy" of legal enforcement. How do we know if an agreement is "worthy"?

Contract law is based on the notion that you are the best judge of your own welfare. By and large, you are free to make whatever agreements you want, subject to whatever rules you choose, and the law will support you. However, this freedom is not limitless: The law does impose seven requirements, which we will analyze in detail in upcoming chapters.

Contract law is a story of freedom and power, rules and relationships—with drama to spare. It is important to study this story to avoid your own contract drama. Let's start with an introduction to contracts.

11-1 CONTRACTS

11-1a Elements of a Contract

A contract is a legally enforceable agreement. People regularly make promises, but only some of them are enforceable. For a contract to be enforceable, seven key characteristics *must* be present. We will study this "checklist" at length in the next several chapters.

> **Contracts Checklist**
> ☐ Offer
> ☐ Acceptance
> ☐ Consideration
> ☐ Legality
> ☐ Capacity
> ☐ Consent
> ☐ Writing

- *Offer.* All contracts begin when a person or a company proposes a deal. It might involve buying something, selling something, doing a job, or anything else. But only proposals made in certain ways amount to a legally recognized offer.

- *Acceptance.* Once a party receives an offer, he must respond to it in a certain way. We will examine the requirements of both offers and acceptances in the next chapter.

- *Consideration.* There has to be bargaining that leads to an *exchange* between the parties. Contracts cannot be a one-way street; both sides must receive some measureable benefit.

- *Legality.* The contract must be for a lawful purpose. Courts will not enforce agreements to sell cocaine, for example.

- *Capacity.* The parties must be adults of sound mind.

- *Consent.* Certain kinds of trickery and force can prevent the formation of a contract.

- *Writing.* While verbal agreements are often contracts, some types of contracts must be in writing to be enforceable.

11-1b Other Important Issues

Once we have examined the essential parts of contracts, the unit will turn to other important issues:

- *Third-Party Interests.* If Jerome and Tara have a contract, and if the deal falls apart, can Kevin sue to enforce the agreement? It depends.

- *Performance and Discharge.* If a party fully accomplishes what the contract requires, his duties are discharged. But what if his obligations are performed poorly, or not at all?

- *Remedies.* A court will award money or other relief to a party injured by a breach of contract.

Let's apply these principles to the opening scenario.

Is the "contract" between Chris and Chez Luc legally binding? Can Chez Luc kick out—or even *sue*—Chris for using his phone? In deciding this issue, a judge would consider whether the parties intentionally made an agreement, which included:

- A *valid offer and acceptance.* The restaurant's website set forth its terms, which was an offer. Chris accepted when he clicked the box.

- *Consideration.* A judge would then carefully examine whether the parties exchanged something of value that proved that they both meant to be bound by this agreement. And there was. The restaurant gave up a coveted reservation time in exchange for Chris's promise to stay away from his phone.

- *Capacity and Legality.* A judge would also verify that the parties were adults of sound mind and that the subject matter of the contract was legal. It seems that Chris understood what he was doing and was of legal age (we certainly hope so, since he was getting engaged).

- *Consent.* There was no fraud or trickery on the part of the restaurant (the terms were clear, not buried so that Chris was unaware of them).

- *Writing.* The terms were in writing (although they did not have to be.)

Therefore, the agreement was valid and enforceable. Whether kicking out a newly engaged couple is good business practice for a restaurant … now, that's a different story!

11-1c All Shapes and Sizes

Some contracts—like those in the opener—are small. But contracts can also be large. Lockheed Martin and Boeing spent years of work and millions of dollars competing for a U.S. Defense Department aircraft contract. Why the fierce effort? The deal was potentially good for 25 years and *$200 billion.* Lockheed won. The company earned the right to build the next generation of fighter jets—3,000 planes, with different varieties of the aircraft to be used by each of the American defense services and some allied forces as well.

Many contracts involve public issues. The Lockheed agreement concerns government agencies deciding how to spend taxpayer money for national defense. Other contracts concern intensely private matters. Mary Beth Whitehead signed a contract with William and Elizabeth Stern of New Jersey. For a fee of $10,000, Whitehead agreed to act as a surrogate mother, and then deliver the baby to the Sterns for adoption after she carried it to term. But when little Melissa was born, Whitehead changed her mind and fled to Florida with the baby. The Sterns sued for breach of contract. Surrogacy contracts now lead to hundreds of births per year. Are the contracts immoral? Should they be illegal? Are there limits to what one person may pay another to do? The New Jersey Supreme Court, the first to rule on the issue, declared the contract illegal and void. The court nonetheless awarded Melissa to the Sterns, saying that it was in the child's best interest to live with them. Inevitably, legislators disagree about this emotional issue. Some states have passed statutes permitting surrogacy, while others prohibit it.

At times, we even enter contracts without knowing it. We make contracts each time we download an app, purchase software, and order from a restaurant menu. We even form legally enforceable agreements when we buy a bag of chips from a vending machine.

11-1d Contracts Defined

Contract

A legally enforceable agreement

We have seen that a **contract** is a promise that the law will enforce. As we look more closely at the elements of contract law, we will encounter some intricate issues. This is partly because we live in a complex society, which conducts its business in a wide variety of ways.

Remember, though, that we are usually interested in answering three basic questions, all relating to promises:

- Is it certain that the defendant promised to do something?

- If she did promise, is it fair to make her honor her word?

- If she did not promise, are there unusual reasons to hold her liable anyway?

11-1e Development of Contract Law

Courts have not always assumed that promises are legally significant. In the twelfth and thirteenth centuries, promises were not binding unless a person made them *in writing and affixed a seal* to the document. This was seldom done, and therefore most promises were unenforceable.

The common law changed very slowly, but by the fifteenth century, courts began to allow some suits based on a broken promise. There were still major limitations. Suppose a merchant hired a carpenter to build a new shop, and the carpenter failed to start the job on time. Now courts would permit the suit, but only if the merchant had paid some money to the carpenter. If the merchant made a 10 percent down payment, the contract would be enforceable. But if the merchant merely *promised* to pay when the building was done, and the carpenter never began work, the merchant could recover nothing.

In 1602, English courts began to enforce mutual *promises;* that is, deals in which neither party gave anything to the other but both promised to do something in the future. Thus, if a farmer promised to deliver a certain quantity of wheat to a merchant and the merchant agreed on the price, both parties were now bound by their promise, even though there had been no down payment. This was a huge step forward in the development of contract law, but many issues remained. Consider the following employment case from 1792, which raises issues of public policy that still challenge courts today.

DAVIS v. MASON

Michaelmas Term, 33d George III, p. 118
Court of King's Bench, 1792

Facts: Mason was a surgeon/apothecary in the English town of Thetford. Davis wished to apprentice himself to Mason. The two agreed that Davis would work for Mason and learn his profession. They further agreed that if Davis left Mason's practice, he would not set up a competing establishment within 10 miles of Thetford at any time within 14 years. Davis promised to pay £200 if he violated the agreement not to compete.

Davis began working for Mason in July 1789. In August 1791, Mason dismissed Davis, claiming misconduct, although Davis denied it. Davis then established his own practice within 10 miles of Thetford. Mason sued for the £200.

Davis admitted promising to pay the money. But he claimed that the agreement should be declared illegal and unenforceable. He argued that 14 years was unreasonably long to restrict him from the town of Thetford and that 10 miles was too great a distance. (In those days, 10 miles might take the better part of a day to travel.) He added an additional policy argument, saying that it was harmful to the public health to restrict a doctor from practicing his profession: If the people needed his service, they should have it. Finally, he said that his "consideration" was too great for this deal. In other words, it was unfair that he should pay £200 because he did not receive anything of that value from Mason.

Issue: *Was the contract too unreasonable to enforce?*

Excerpts from Lord Kenyon's Decision: Here, the plaintiff being established in business as a surgeon at

Thetford, the defendant wished to act as his assistant with a view of deriving a degree of credit from that situation; on which the former stipulated that the defendant should not come to live there under his auspices and steal away his patients: this seems to be a fair consideration. Then it was objected that the limits within which the defendant engaged not to practise are unreasonable: but I do not see that they are necessarily unreasonable, nor do I know how to draw the line. Neither are the public likely to be injured by an agreement of this kind, since every other person is at liberty to practise as a surgeon in this town.

Judgment for the Plaintiff.

Noncompetition agreement

A contract in which one party agrees not to compete with another

The contract between Davis and Mason is called a **noncompetition agreement**. Today they are more common than ever, and frequently litigated. The policy issues that Davis raised have never gone away. You may well be asked to sign a noncompetition agreement sometime in your professional life. We look at the issue in detail in Chapter 13, on consideration. That outcome was typical of contract cases for the next 100 years. Courts took a *laissez-faire* approach, declaring that parties had *freedom to contract* and would have to live with the consequences. Lord Kenyon saw Davis and Mason as equals, entering a bargain that made basic sense, and he had no intention of rewriting it. After 500 years of evolution, courts had come to regard promises as almost sacred. The law had gone from ignoring most promises to enforcing nearly all.

By the early twentieth century, bargaining power in business deals had changed dramatically. Farms and small businesses were yielding place to huge corporations in a trend that accelerated throughout the century. In the twenty-first century, multinational corporations span many continents, wielding larger budgets and more power than many of the nations in which they do business. When such a corporation contracts with a small company or an individual consumer, the latter may have little or no leverage. Courts increasingly looked at the basic fairness of contracts. Noncompetition agreements are no longer automatically enforced. Courts may alter them or ignore them entirely because the parties have such unequal power and because the public may have an interest in letting the employee go on to compete. Davis's argument—that the public is entitled to as many doctors as it needs—is frequently more successful in court today than it was in the days of Lord Kenyon.

Legislatures and the courts limit the effect of promises in other ways. Suppose you purchase a lawn mower with an attached tag, warning you that the manufacturer is not responsible in the event of any malfunction or injury. You are required to sign a form acknowledging that the manufacturer has no liability of any kind. That agreement is clear enough—but a court will not enforce it. The law holds that the manufacturer *has* warranted the product to be good for normal purposes, regardless of any language included in the sales agreement. If the blade flies off and injures a child, the manufacturer is liable. This is socially responsible, even though it interferes with a private agreement.

The law has not come full circle back to the early days of the common law. Courts still enforce the great majority of contracts. But the possibility that a court will ignore an agreement means that any contract is a little less certain than it would have been a century ago.

11-2 TYPES OF CONTRACTS

Before undertaking a study of contracts, you need to familiarize yourself with some important vocabulary. This section will present five sets of terms.

11-2a Bilateral and Unilateral Contracts

Bilateral contract

A promise made in exchange for another promise

In a **bilateral contract**, both parties make a promise. A producer says to Gloria, "I'll pay you $2 million to star in my new romantic comedy, which we are shooting three months from now in Santa Fe." Gloria says, "It's a deal." That is a bilateral contract. Each party has made a promise to do something. The producer is now bound to pay Gloria $2 million, and Gloria is obligated to show up on time and act in the movie. The vast majority of contracts are bilateral contracts. They can be for services, such as this acting contract; they can be for the sale of goods, such as 1,000 tons of steel, or for almost any other purpose. When the bargain is a promise for a promise, it is a bilateral agreement.

In a unilateral contract, one party makes a promise that the other party can accept only by *actually doing* **something.** These contracts are less common. Suppose the movie producer tacks a sign to a community bulletin board. It has a picture of a dog with a phone number, and it reads, "I'll pay $100 to anyone who returns my lost dog." If Leo sees the sign, finds the producer, and merely promises to find the dog, he has not created a contract. Because of the terms on the sign, Leo must actually find and return the dog to stake a claim to the $100.

11-2b Executory and Executed Contracts

A contract is **executory** when it has been made, but one or more parties has not yet fulfilled its obligations. Recall Gloria, who agrees to act in the producer's film beginning in three months. The moment Gloria and the producer strike their bargain, they have an executory bilateral express contract.

A contract is **executed** when all parties have fulfilled their obligations. When Gloria finishes acting in the movie and the producer pays her final fee, their contract will be fully executed.

Executory contract
An agreement in which one or more parties has not yet fulfilled its obligations

Executed contract
An agreement in which all parties have fulfilled their obligations

---

EXAM Strategy

Question: Abby has long coveted Nicola's designer handbag because she saw one of them in a movie. Finally, Nicola offers to sell her friend the bag for $350 in cash. "I don't have the money right now," Abby replies, "but I'll have it a week from Friday. Is it a deal?" Nicola agrees to sell the bag. Use two terms to describe the contract.

Strategy: In a bilateral contract, both parties make a promise, but in a unilateral agreement, only one side does so. An executory contract is one with unfulfilled obligations, while an executed agreement is one with nothing left to be done.

Result: Nicola promised to sell the bag for $350 cash, and Abby agreed to pay. Because both parties made a promise, a bilateral agreement resulted. The deal is not yet completed, meaning that they have an executory contract.

11-2c Valid, Unenforceable, Voidable, and Void Agreements

A **valid contract** is one that satisfies all of the law's requirements. It has no problems in any of the seven areas listed at the beginning of this chapter, and a court will enforce it. The contract between Gloria and the producer is a valid contract, and if the producer fails to pay Gloria, she will win a lawsuit to collect the unpaid fee.

An **unenforceable agreement** occurs when the parties intend to form a valid bargain, but a court declares that some rule of law prevents enforcing it. Suppose Gloria and the producer orally agree that she will star in his movie, which he will start filming in 18 months. The law, as we will see in Chapter 16, requires that this contract be in writing because it cannot be completed within one year. If the producer signs up another actress two months later, Gloria has no claim against him.

A **voidable contract** occurs when the law permits one party to terminate the agreement. This happens, for example, when an agreement is signed under duress or a party commits

Voidable contract
An agreement that may be terminated by one of the parties

fraud. Suppose that, during negotiations, the producer lies to Gloria, telling her that Steven Spielberg has signed on to be the film's director. That is a major reason why she accepts the contract. As we will learn in Chapter 14, this fraudulent agreement is voidable at Gloria's option. If she later decides that another director is acceptable, she may choose to stay in the contract. But if she wants to cancel the agreement and sue, she can do that as well.

A **void agreement** is one that neither party can enforce, usually because the purpose of the deal is illegal or because one of the parties had no legal authority to make a contract.

The following case illustrates the difference between voidable and void agreements.

Void agreement

A contract that neither party can enforce, because the bargain is illegal or one of the parties had no legal authority to make it

MR. W FIREWORKS, INC. V. OZUNA

No. 04-08-00820-
CVCourt of Appeals of Texas, San Antonio, 2009

Facts: Mr. W sells fireworks. Under Texas law, retailers may sell fireworks to the public only during the two weeks immediately before the Fourth of July and during two weeks immediately before New Year's Day. And so, fireworks sellers like Mr. W tend to lease property.

Mr. W leased a portion of Ozuna's land. The lease contract contained two key terms:

"In the event the sale of fireworks on the aforementioned property is or shall become unlawful during the period of this lease and the term granted, this lease shall become void.

"Lessor(s) agree not to sell or lease any part of said property, including any adjoining, adjacent, or contiguous property, to any person(s) or corporation for the purpose of selling fireworks in competition to the Lessee during the term of this lease, *and for a period of ten years after lease is terminated*." (Emphasis added.)

A longstanding San Antonio city ordinance bans the sale of fireworks inside city limits, and also within 5,000 feet of city limits. Like all growing cities, San Antonio sometimes annexes new land, and its city limits change. One annexation caused the Ozuna property to fall within 5,000 feet of the new city limits, and it became illegal to sell fireworks from the property. Mr. W stopped selling fireworks and paying rent on Ozuna's land.

Two years later, San Antonio's border shifted again. This time, the city *disannexed* some property and *shrank*. The new city limits placed Ozuna's property just beyond the 5,000-foot no-fireworks zone. Ozuna then leased a part of his land to Alamo Fireworks, a competitor of Mr. W.

Mr. W sued for breach of contract, arguing that Ozuna had no right to lease to a competitor for a period of 10 years. The trial court granted Ozuna's motion for summary judgment. Mr. W appealed.

Issue: *Did Ozuna breach his contract with Mr. W by leasing his land to a competitor?*

Excerpts from Judge Angelini's Decision: The property owners [argue] that when the city ordinance made the sale of fireworks illegal on the subject properties, the leases became void, resulting in the property owners and Mr. W no longer having an enforceable agreement. Mr. W argues that the provision restricting the property owners from leasing to competitors survived the agreement. This is inconsistent with the meaning of "voidable" contracts. For example, when a minor enters into a contract, that contract is not void, but is voidable at the election of the minor. This means that the minor may set aside the entire contract at his option, but he *is not entitled to enforce portions that are favorable to him and at the same time disaffirm other provisions that he finds burdensome*. He is not permitted to retain the benefits of a contract while repudiating its obligations.

Could Ozuna declare independence from contractual obligations?

Here, while Mr. W is arguing that the illegalization of the sale of fireworks made the contract "voidable," it is still seeking to enforce the provision of the contract prohibiting the property owners from leasing to competitors. We decline to adopt such an interpretation.

Further, contracts requiring an illegal act are void. We therefore hold that the illegalization of the sale of the fireworks on the respective properties did not trigger the provision in the leases prohibiting the property owners from leasing to competitors of Mr. W.

We affirm the judgment of the trial court.

11-2d Express and Implied Contracts

In an **express contract**, the two parties explicitly state all the important terms of their agreement. The vast majority of contracts are express contracts. The contract between the producer and Gloria is an express contract because the parties explicitly state what Gloria will do, where and when she will do it, and how much she will be paid. Some express contracts are oral, as that one was, and some are written. They might be bilateral express contracts, as Gloria's was, or unilateral express contracts, as Leo's was. Obviously, it is wise to make express contracts, and to put them in writing. We emphasize, however, that many oral contracts are fully enforceable.

In an implied contract, the words and conduct of the parties indicate that they intended an agreement. Suppose every Friday, for two months, the producer asks Lance to mow his lawn, and loyal Lance does so each weekend. Then, for three more weekends, Lance simply shows up without the producer asking, and the producer continues to pay for the work done. But on the 12th weekend, when Lance rings the doorbell to collect, the producer suddenly says, "I never asked you to mow it. Scram." The producer is correct that there was no express contract because the parties had not spoken for several weeks. But a court will probably rule that the conduct of the parties has *implied* a contract. Not only did Lance mow the lawn every weekend, but the producer even paid on three weekends when they had not spoken. It was reasonable for Lance to assume that he had a weekly deal to mow and be paid.

Today, the hottest disputes about implied contracts continue to arise in the employment setting. Many corporate employees have at-will relationships with their companies. This means that the employees are free to quit at any time and the company has the right to fire them, for virtually any reason. But often a company provides its workers with personnel manuals that lay out certain rights. Does a handbook create a contract guaranteeing those rights? What is your opinion?

Express contract
An agreement with all the important terms explicitly stated

You be the Judge

DEMASSE V. ITT CORPORATION
194 Ariz. 500
Supreme Court of Arizona, 1999

Facts: Roger DeMasse and five others were employees-at-will at ITT Corporation, where they started working at various times between 1960 and 1979. Each was paid an hourly wage.

ITT issued an employee handbook, which it revised four times over two decades.

The first four editions of the handbook stated that within each job classification, any layoffs would be made in reverse order of seniority. The fifth handbook made two important changes. First, the document stated that "nothing contained herein shall be construed as a guarantee of continued employment. ITT does not guarantee continued employment to employees and retains the right to terminate or lay off employees."

Second, the handbook stated that "ITT reserves the right to amend, modify, or cancel this handbook, as well as any or all of the various policies [or rules] outlined in it." Four years later, ITT notified its hourly employees that layoff guidelines for hourly employees would be based not on seniority, but on ability and performance. About 10 days later, the six employees were laid off, though less senior employees kept their jobs. The six employees sued.

You Be The Judge: *Did ITT have the right to unilaterally change the layoff policy?*

Argument for the workers: It is true that all of the plaintiffs were originally employees-at-will, subject to termination at the company's whim. However, things changed when the company issued the first handbook. ITT chose to include a promise that layoffs would be based on seniority. Long-term workers and new employees all understood the promise and relied on it. The company put it there to attract and retain good workers. The policy worked. Responsible employees understood that the longer they remained at ITT, the safer their job was. Company and employees worked together for many years with a common understanding, and that is a textbook definition of an implied contract.

Once a contract is formed, whether express or implied, it is binding on both sides. That is the whole point of a contract. If one side could simply change the terms of an agreement on its own, what value would any contract have? The company's legal argument is a perfect symbol of its arrogance: It believes that because these workers are mere hourly workers, they have no rights, even under contract law. The company is mistaken. Implied contracts are binding, and ITT should not make promises it does not intend to keep.

Argument for ITT: Once an at-will employee, always one. ITT had the right to fire any of its employees at any time—just as the workers had the right to quit whenever they wished. That never changed, and in case any workers forgot it, the company reiterated the point in its most recent handbook. If the plaintiffs thought layoffs would happen in any particular order, that is their error, not ours.

All workers were bound by the terms of whichever handbook was then in place. For many years, the company had made a seniority-[based]-layoff promise. Had we fired a senior worker during that period, he or she would have had a legitimate complaint—and that is why we did not do it. Instead, we gave everyone four years' notice that things would change. Any workers unhappy with the new policies should have left to find more congenial work.

Why should an employee be allowed to say, "I prefer to rely on the old, outdated handbooks, not the new one"? The plaintiffs' position would mean that no company is ever free to change its general work policies and rules. Since when does an at-will employee have the right to dictate company policy? That would be disastrous for the whole economy—but fortunately it is not the law.

11-2e Promissory Estoppel and Quasi-Contracts

Now we turn away from "true" contracts and consider two unusual circumstances. Sometimes, courts will enforce agreements even if they fail to meet the usual requirement of a contract. We emphasize that these remedies are uncommon exceptions to the general rules. Most of the agreements that courts enforce are the express contracts that we have already studied. Nonetheless, the next two remedies are still pivotal in some lawsuits. In each case, a sympathetic plaintiff can demonstrate an injury but *there is no contract*. The plaintiff cannot claim that the defendant breached a contract, because none ever existed. The plaintiff must hope for more "creative" relief.

The two remedies can be confusingly similar. The best way to distinguish them is this:

- In promissory estoppel cases, the defendant made a promise that the plaintiff relied on.

- In quasi-contract cases, the defendant received a *benefit* from the plaintiff.

Promissory Estoppel

A fierce fire swept through Dana and Derek Andreason's house in Utah, seriously damaging it. The good news was that agents for Aetna Casualty promptly visited the Andreasons and helped them through the crisis. The agents reassured the couple that all of the damage was covered by their insurance, instructed them on which things to throw out and replace, and helped them choose materials for repairing other items. The bad news was that the agents were wrong: The Andreasons' policy had expired six weeks before the fire. When Derek Andreason presented a bill for $41,957 worth of meticulously itemized work that he had done under the agents' supervision, Aetna refused to pay.

The Andreasons sued—but not for breach of contract. There *was* no contract—they allowed their policy to expire. They sued Aetna under the legal theory of promissory estoppel: even when there is no contract, a plaintiff may use **promissory estoppel** to enforce the defendant's promise if he can show that:

- The defendant made a promise knowing that the plaintiff would likely rely on it;

- The plaintiff did rely on the promise; and

- The only way to avoid injustice is to enforce the promise.

Promissory estoppel

A *possible* remedy for an injured plaintiff in a case with no valid contract, when the plaintiff can show a promise, reasonable reliance, and injustice.

Aetna made a promise to the Andreasons—namely, its assurance that all of the damage was covered by insurance. The company knew that the Andreasons would rely on that promise, which they did by ripping up a floor that might have been salvaged, throwing out some furniture, and buying materials to repair the house. Is enforcing the promise the only way to avoid injustice? Yes, ruled the Utah Court of Appeals.[1] The Andreasons' conduct was reasonable and based entirely on what the Aetna agents told them. Under promissory estoppel, the Andreasons received virtually the same amount they would have obtained had the insurance contract been valid.

> **Is enforcing the promise the only way to avoid injustice?**

Many promissory estoppel cases involve employment law—bosses make promises that they fail to keep. The following case illustrates what can happen when you bet on the wrong promise.

Donald L. Harmon v. Delaware Harness Racing Commission

62 A.3d 1198
Supreme Court of Delaware, 2013

Facts: The Delaware Harness Racing Commission hired Donald Harmon to be the Presiding Judge of harness racing (charged with enforcing racetrack rules). After years on the job, Harmon was arrested for improperly changing a judging sheet to favor a horse. The Commission suspended him without pay pending the outcome of the criminal case.

© Jeff Schultes/Shutterstock.com

Quasi-contract may require compensation even when no contract exists.

John Wayne (yes, his name was John Wayne) was the executive officer of the Commission. During his suspension, Harmon asked Wayne to find out from the Commission whether it would reinstate him he if he was acquitted. When Wayne asked the commissioners this question they looked at each other and then said "Yes." The commissioners told Wayne he could relay that message to Harmon. Based on this promise, Harmon decided not to look for other jobs.

Immediately after his acquittal, Harmon asked for his job back. After some time, the Commission refused to reinstate him as promised. Harmon sued the Commission, claiming promissory estoppel. A trial court sided with Harmon and awarded him $102,273, representing the wages he would have earned if the Commission had kept its promise. But the Superior Court reversed the decision, so Harmon appealed to the Supreme Court of Delaware.

Issue: *Was the commissioners' promise to Harmon enforceable?*

Excerpts from Justice Berger's Decision: To prevail on a promissory estoppel claim, a plaintiff must establish

[1] Andreason v. Aetna Casualty & Surety Co.,1993 Utah App. (1993).

that: (i) a promise was made; (ii) it was the reasonable expectation of the promisor to induce action or forbearance on the part of the promisee; (iii) the promisee reasonably relied on the promise and took action to his detriment; and (iv) such promise is binding because injustice can be avoided only by enforcement of the promise.

The first element is a promise. The trial court reasoned that [because] no [formal] vote was taken before the members said "Yes," Wayne could not have reasonably believed that the Commission wanted him to commit to reinstate Harmon. But the fact that the Commission members all looked at each other before answering Wayne's question could be construed as a vote, albeit an informal one. Second, the Commission did not address all matters by vote. It was not hiring or reinstating Harmon at the time Wayne conveyed its position to Harmon. The Commission was only promising to take action in the future. In short, there was evidence that the promise was made.

The second element is that the Commission reasonably expected Harmon to rely on Wayne's representations. Wayne had authority to transmit the Commission's decision to Harmon. If Wayne's testimony is credited, there is no real dispute about this point.

The third element is that Harmon reasonably relied on the Commission's promise and took action to his detriment. But for the Commission's promise to reinstate him, [Harmon] would have looked for other work. He was offered several horse training opportunities, but he could not pursue them because, if he did, he would not be allowed to return to his position as a judge. This testimony satisfies Harmon's burden of showing reliance to his detriment.

The final element of a promissory estoppel claim is a finding that the promise must be enforced to avoid injustice. That is another way of saying that it would be unjust not to enforce the Commission's promise because Harmon suffered damages by relying on it. During the time that he was waiting to be reinstated, Harmon could not accept another job, and suffered lost income as a result. That lost income constitutes damages.

Based on the foregoing, the judgment of the Superior Court is reversed.

Why have we chosen to illustrate an important point of law—promissory estoppel—with a case that fails? Because that is the typical outcome. Plaintiffs allege promissory estoppel very frequently, but seldom succeed. They do occasionally win, as the Andreasons demonstrated earlier, but courts are skeptical of these claims. The lesson is clear: Before you rely on a promise, negotiate a binding contract.

Quasi-Contract

Don Easterwood leased over 5,000 acres of farmland in Jackson County, Texas, from PIC Realty for one year. The next year, he obtained a second one-year lease. During each year, Easterwood farmed the land, harvested the crops, and prepared the land for the following year's planting. Toward the end of the second lease, after Easterwood had harvested his crop, he and PIC began discussing the terms of another lease. While they negotiated, Easterwood prepared the land for the following year, cutting and plowing the soil. But the negotiations for a new lease failed, and Easterwood moved off the land. He sued PIC Realty for the value of his work preparing the soil.

Easterwood had neither an express nor an implied contract for the value of his work. How could he make any legal claim? By relying on the legal theory of a quasi-contract: Even when there is no contract, a court may use **quasi-contract** to compensate a plaintiff who can show that:

Quasi-contract

A *possible* remedy for an injured plaintiff in a case with no valid contract, when the plaintiff can show benefit to the defendant, reasonable expectation of payment, and unjust enrichment.

- The plaintiff gave some benefit to the defendant;

- The plaintiff reasonably expected to be paid for the benefit and the defendant knew this; and

- The defendant would be unjustly enriched if he did not pay.

If a court finds all of these elements present, it will generally award the value of the goods or services that the plaintiff has conferred. The damages awarded are called *quantum meruit*, meaning that the plaintiff gets "as much as he deserves." The court is awarding money that it believes the plaintiff *morally ought to have*, even though there was no valid contract entitling her to it. This again is judicial activism, with the courts inventing a "quasi" contract where no true contract exists. The purpose is justice, the term is contradictory.

Don Easterwood testified that in Jackson County, it was quite common for a tenant farmer to prepare the soil for the following year but then be unable to farm the land. In those cases, he claimed, the landowner compensated the farmer for the work done. Other witnesses agreed that this was the local custom. The court ruled that indeed there was no contract, but that all elements of quasi-contract had been satisfied. Easterwood gave a benefit to PIC because the land was ready for planting. Jackson County custom caused Easterwood to assume he would be paid, and PIC Realty knew it. Finally, said the court, it would be unjust to let PIC benefit without paying anything. The court ordered PIC to pay the fair market value of Easterwood's labors.

Quantum meruit

"As much as he deserves"—the damages awarded in a quasi-contract case

FOUR THEORIES OF RECOVERY

Theory	Did the Defendant Make a Promise?	Is There a Contract?	Description
Express Contract	Yes	Yes	The parties intend to contract and agree on explicit terms.
Implied Contract	Not explicitly	Yes	The parties do not formally agree, but their words and conduct indicate an intention to create a contract.
Promissory Estoppel	Yes	No	There is no contract, but the defendant makes a promise that she can foresee will induce reliance; the plaintiff relies on it; and it would be unjust not to enforce the promise.
Quasi-Contract	No	No	There is no intention to contract, but the plaintiff gives some benefit to the defendant, who knows that the plaintiff expects compensation; it would be unjust not to award the plaintiff damages.

EXAM Strategy

Question: The preceding table lists the different theories a plaintiff may use to recover damages in a contract dispute. In the following examples, which one will each plaintiff use in trying to win the case?

1. Company pays all employees 10 percent commission on new business they develop. Company compensates each employee when the new customer pays its first bill. After Leandro obtains three new clients, Company fires him. When the new customers pay their bill, Company refuses to pay Leandro a commission because he is no longer an employee. Leandro sues.

2. Burt agrees in writing to sell Red 100 lobsters for $15 each, payable by credit card, in exactly 30 days. When the lobsters fail to arrive, Red sues.

3. Company handbook, given to all new hires, states that no employee will be fired without a hearing and an appeal. Company fires Delores without a hearing or appeal. She sues.

Strategy: In (1), the Company never promised to pay a commission to nonemployees, so there is no contract. However, the Company *benefited* from Leandro's work. In (2), the parties have *clearly stated all terms* to a simple sales agreement. In (3), the Company and Delores never negotiated termination, but *the handbook suggests* that all employees have certain rights.

Result: (1) is a case of quasi-contract because the company benefited and should reasonably expect to pay. (2) is an express contract because all terms are clearly stated. (3) is an implied contract, similar to the *DeMasse* case, based on the handbook.

11-3 SOURCES OF CONTRACT LAW

11-3a Common Law

We have seen the evolution of contract law from the twelfth century to the present. Express and implied contracts, promissory estoppel, and quasi-contract were all crafted, over centuries, by courts deciding one contract lawsuit at a time. Many contract lawsuits continue to be decided using common-law principles developed by courts.

11-3b Uniform Commercial Code

Business methods changed quickly during the first half of the last century. Transportation speeded up. Corporations routinely conducted business across state borders and around the world. These developments presented a problem. Common-law principles, whether related to contracts, torts, or anything else, sometimes vary from one state to another. New York and California courts often reach similar conclusions when presented with similar cases, but they are under no obligation to do so. Business leaders became frustrated that, to do business across the country, their companies had to deal with many different sets of common-law rules.

Executives, lawyers, and judges wanted a body of law for business transactions that reflected modern commercial methods and provided uniformity throughout the United States. It would be much easier, they thought, if some parts of contract law were the same in every state. That desire gave birth to the Uniform Commercial Code (UCC), created in 1952. The drafters intended the UCC to facilitate the easy formation and enforcement of contracts in a fast-paced world. The Code governs many aspects of commerce, including the sale and leasing of goods, negotiable instruments, bank deposits, letters of credit, investment securities, secured transactions, and other commercial matters. Every state has adopted at least part of the UCC to govern commercial transactions within that state. For our purposes in studying contracts, the most important part of the Code is Article 2, which governs the sale of goods. **"Goods" means anything movable, except for money, securities, and certain legal rights.** Goods include pencils, commercial aircraft, books, and Christmas trees. Goods do not include land or a house because neither is movable, nor do they include a stock certificate. A contract for the sale of 10,000 sneakers is governed by the UCC; a contract for the sale of a condominium in Marina del Rey is governed by the California common law.

When analyzing any contract problem as a student or businessperson, you must note whether the agreement concerns the sale of goods. For many issues, the common law and the UCC are reasonably similar. But sometimes, the law is quite different under the two sets of rules.

And so, the UCC governs contracts for a sale of goods, while common-law principles govern contracts for sales of services and everything else. Most of the time, it will be clear whether the UCC or the common law applies. But what if a contract involves both goods and services? When you get your oil changed, you are paying in part for the new oil and oil filter (goods) and in part for the labor required to do the job (services). In a mixed contract, Article 2 governs only if the *primary purpose* was the sale of goods. In the following case, the court had to decide the primary purpose.

FALLSVIEW GLATT KOSHER CATERERS, INC. v. ROSENFELD

794 N.Y.S. 2d 790
Civil Court, City of New York, 2005

Facts: During the Jewish holidays, Fallsview Glatt Kosher Caterers organized programs at Kutcher's Country Club, where it provided all accommodations, food, and entertainment.

Fallsview sued Willie Rosenfeld, alleging that he had requested accommodations for 15 members of his family, agreeing to pay $24,050, and then failed to appear or pay.

Rosenfeld moved to dismiss, claiming that even if there had been an agreement, it was never put in writing. Under UCC §2-201, any contract for the sale of goods worth $500 or more can be enforced only if it is in writing and signed. Fallsview argued that the agreement was not for the sale of goods, but for services. The company claimed that because the contract was not governed by the UCC, it should be enforced even with no writing.

Issue: *Was the agreement one for the sale of goods, requiring a writing, or for services, enforceable with no writing?*

Excerpts from Judge Battaglia's Decision: Mr. Rosenfeld contends that the "predominant purpose" and "main objective" of the agreement alleged by Fallsview was the "service of Kosher food," while the hotel accommodations

and entertainment were merely "incidental or collateral" services.

Defendant's contention that the "predominant purpose" of the alleged agreement is the sale of food is said to be compelled by the very nature of the Passover holiday. [He argues that] "the essential religious obligation during this eight-day period and the principal reason why people attend events similar to the Program sponsored by plaintiff is in order to facilitate their fulfillment of the requirement to eat only food which is prepared in strict accordance with the mandate of Jewish law for Passover, i.e., food which is 'Kosher for Passover.' It is the desire to obtain these 'goods' and not the urge for 'entertainment' or 'accommodations' that motivates customers to subscribe to such 'Programs.' "

[Fallsview submitted] ten sheets, designated "Kutcher's Country Club Daily Activities" for Sunday, April 4, through Tuesday, April 13, 2004. The activities possible include tennis, racquetball, swimming, Swedish massage, "make over face lift show," "trivia time," aerobics, bingo, ice skating, dancing, "showtime," "power walk," arts and crafts, day camp, ping-pong, Yiddish theater, board games, horse racing, horseback riding, wine tasting, and indoor baci and that is only through Wednesday. These activities are provided, together with accommodations and food, for an "all inclusive" price that is apparently determined by the size and location of the room(s) and the numbers and ages of the persons in each party.

A review of the characteristics of the "program," which is the subject matter of the alleged agreement, leads the Court to conclude that the "essence" of the family and communal "experience" is defined primarily by "services" and not by "goods."

The intended scope of UCC section 2-201 is also indicated by its provision that "[a]writing is not insufficient because it omits or incorrectly states a term agreed upon but the contract is not enforceable under this paragraph beyond the quantity of goods shown in the writing." For the Code, quantity is even more important than price.

A contract of the type involved here would rarely, if ever, specify the "quantity" of the "goods" to be provided. Nor would, for example, a contract for a week's stay at a weight-loss spa, or a zen-vegetarian retreat, or a cruise of the islands.

Plaintiff argues that "Defendant's proposition that a hotel reservation is a sale of goods would render all reservations made via telephone or the Internet unenforceable and would leave hotels in a precarious economic position." That may or may not be true, but the argument does highlight the importance of ensuring that a Statute of Frauds structured and outfitted by the Legislature for a particular transactional context not be casually applied to a very different commercial segment and model. The structure and terms of section 2-201 tell us that it was not intended to cover the agreement alleged in this Complaint.

Defendant's motion to dismiss is denied.

EXAM Strategy

Question: Leila agrees to pay Kendrick $35,000 to repair windmills. Confident of this cash, Kendrick contracts to buy Derrick's used Porsche for $33,000. Then Leila informs Kendrick she does not need his help and will not pay him. Kendrick tells Derrick that he no longer wants the Porsche. Derrick sues Kendrick, and Kendrick files suit against Leila. What law or laws govern these lawsuits?

Strategy: Always be conscious of whether a contract is for services or the sale of goods. Different laws govern. To make that distinction, you must understand the term "goods." If you are clear about that, the question is answered easily.

Result: *Goods* means anything movable, and a Porsche is movable—one might say "super-movable." The UCC will control Derrick's suit. Repairing windmills is primarily a service. Kendrick's lawsuit is governed by the common law of contracts.

Chapter Conclusion

Contracts govern countless areas of our lives, from intimate family issues to multibillion-dollar corporate deals. Understanding contract principles is essential for a successful business or professional career and is invaluable in private life. This knowledge is especially important because courts no longer rubber-stamp any agreement that two parties have made. If we know the issues that courts scrutinize, the agreement we draft is likelier to be enforced. We thus achieve greater control over our affairs—the very purpose of a contract.

EXAM REVIEW

1. **CONTRACTS: DEFINITION AND ELEMENTS** A contract is a legally enforceable promise. Analyzing whether a contract exists involves inquiring into these issues: offer, acceptance, consideration, capacity, legal purpose, consent, and sometimes, whether the deal is in writing.

2. **DEVELOPMENT** The development of contract law stretches into the distant past. Before the fifteenth century, courts rarely enforced promises at all. By the 1600s, courts enforced many mutual promises, and by 1900, most promises containing the seven elements of a contract were strictly enforced.

3. **UNILATERAL AND BILATERAL CONTRACTS** In bilateral contracts, the parties exchange promises. In a unilateral contract, only one party makes a promise, and the other must take some action—his return promise is insufficient to form a contract.

4. **EXECUTORY AND EXECUTED CONTRACTS** In an executory contract, one or both of the parties have not yet have not done everything that they promised to do. In an executed contract, all parties have fully performed.

5. **ENFORCEABILITY**

   - Valid contracts are fully enforceable.

   - An unenforceable agreement is one with a legal defect.

   - A voidable contract occurs when one party has an option to cancel the agreement.

   - A void agreement means that the law will ignore the deal regardless of what the parties want.

Question: Yasmine is negotiating to buy Stewart's house. She asks him what condition the roof is in.

"Excellent," he replies. "It is only 2 years old, and should last 25 more." In fact, Stewart knows that the roof is 26 years old and has had a series of leaks. The parties sign a sales contract for $600,000. A week before Yasmine is to pay for the house and take possession, she discovers the leaks and learns that the mandatory new roof will cost $35,000. At the same time, she learns that the house has increased in value by $60,000 since she signed the agreement. What options does Yasmine have?

Strategy: You know intuitively that Stewart's conduct is as shabby as his roof. What is the legal term for his deception? Fraud. Does fraud make an agreement void or voidable? Does it matter? (See the "Result" at the end of this section.)

---

6. **EXPRESS AND IMPLIED CONTRACTS** If the parties formally agreed and stated explicit terms, there is probably an express contract. If the parties did not formally agree but their conduct, words, or past dealings indicate they intended a binding agreement, there may be an implied contract.

7. OTHER REMEDIES   If there is no contract, are there other reasons to give the plaintiff damages?

- A claim of promissory estoppel requires that the defendant made a promise knowing that the plaintiff would likely *rely,* and the plaintiff did so. It would be wrong to deny recovery.

- A claim of quasi-contract requires that the defendant received a benefit, knowing that the plaintiff would expect compensation, and it would be unjust not to grant it.

EXAM Strategy

Question: The Hoffmans owned and operated a successful small bakery and grocery store. They spoke with Lukowitz, an agent of Red Owl Stores, who told them that for $18,000, Red Owl would build a store and fully stock it for them. The Hoffmans sold their bakery and grocery store and purchased a lot on which Red Owl was to build the store. Lukowitz then told Hoffman that the price had gone up to $26,000. The Hoffmans borrowed the extra money from relatives, but then Lukowitz informed them that the cost would be $34,000. Negotiations broke off, and the Hoffmans sued. The court determined that there was no contract because too many details had not been worked out—the size of the store, its design, and the cost of constructing it. Can the Hoffmans recover any money?

Strategy: Because there is no contract, the Hoffmans must rely on either promissory estoppel or quasi-contract. Promissory estoppel focuses on the defendant's promise and the plaintiff's reliance. Those suing in quasi-contract must show that the defendant received a benefit for which it should reasonably expect to pay. Does either fit here? (See the "Result" at the end of this section.)

8. SOURCES OF CONTRACT LAW   If a contract is for the sale of goods, the UCC is the relevant body of law. For anything else, the common law governs. If a contract involves both goods and services, a court will determine the agreement's primary purpose.

EXAM Strategy

Question: Honeywell, Inc., and Minolta Camera Co. had a contract providing that Honeywell would give to Minolta various technical information on the design of a specialized camera lens. Minolta would have the right to use the information in its cameras, provided that Minolta also used certain Honeywell parts in its cameras. Honeywell delivered to Minolta numerous technical documents, computer software, and test equipment, and Honeywell engineers met with Minolta engineers at least 20 times to discuss the equipment. Several years later, Honeywell sued, claiming that Minolta had taken the design information but failed to use Honeywell parts in its cameras. Minolta moved to dismiss, claiming that the UCC required lawsuits concerning the sale of goods to be filed within four years of the breach and that this lawsuit was too late. Honeywell answered that the UCC did not apply, and that therefore, Minnesota's six-year statute of limitations governed. Who is right?

Strategy: Like many contracts, this one involves both goods, which are governed by the UCC, and services, controlled by the common law. We decide which of those two laws governs by using the predominant purpose test. Was this contract primarily about selling goods or about providing services? (See the "Result" at the end of this section.)

---

5. Result: Indeed, it does matter. Stewart's fraud makes the contract voidable by Yasmine. She has the right to terminate the agreement and pay nothing. However, she may go through with the contract if she prefers. The choice is hers—but not Stewart's.

7. Result: Red Owl received no benefit from the Hoffmans' sale of their store or purchase of the lot. However, Red Owl did make a promise and expected the Hoffmans to rely on it, which they did. The Hoffmans won their claim of promissory estoppel.

8. Result: The primary purpose of this agreement was not the sale of goods, but rather the exchange of technical data, ideas, designs, and so forth. The common law governs the contract, and Honeywell's suit may go forward.

MULTIPLE-CHOICE QUESTIONS

1. A sitcom actor, exhausted after his 10-hour workweek, agrees to buy a briefcase full of cocaine from Lewis for $12,000. Lewis and the actor have a(n) _____ contract.

   (a) valid

   (b) unenforceable

   (c) voidable

   (d) void

2. Carol says, "Pam, you're my best friend in the world. I just inherited a million bucks, and I want you to have some of it. Come with me to the bank tomorrow, and I'll give you $10,000." "Sweet!" Pam replies. Later that day, Carol has a change of heart. She is allowed to do so. Examine the list of the elements of a contract, and cite the correct reason.

   (a) The agreement was not put into writing.

   (b) The agreement lacks a legal purpose.

   (c) Pam did not give consideration.

   (d) Pam does not have the capacity to make a contract.

3. On the first day of the baseball season, Dean orders a new Cardinals hat from Amazon. At the moment he submits his order, Dean and Amazon have an _____ contract. Two days later, Amazon delivers the hat to Dean's house. At this point, Dean and Amazon have an _____ contract.

(a)   executory; executory

(b)   executory; executed

(c)   executed; executory

(d)   executed; executed

4. Linda goes to an electronics store and buys a high-definition TV. Lauren hires a company to clean her swimming pool once a week. The _____ governs Linda's contract with the store, and the _____ governs Lauren's contract with the cleaning company.

(a)   common law; common law

(b)   common law; UCC

(c)   UCC; common law

(d)   UCC; UCC

5. Consider the following scenarios:

I.   Madison says to a group of students, "I'll pay $35 to the first one of you who shows up at my house and mows my lawn."

II. Lea posts a flyer around town that reads, "Reward: $500 for information about the person who keyed my truck last Saturday night in the Wag-a-Bag parking lot. Call Lea at 555-5309."

Which of these proposes a *unilateral* contract?

(a)   I only

(b)   II only

(c)   Both I and II

(d)   None of the above

CASE QUESTIONS

1. Gail Norton began dating Russell Hoyt under the mistaken impression that he was single. She later learned that he was married, but he repeatedly assured her he was getting a divorce. Six years later, Hoyt convinced Norton to quit her job so that they could travel together. He promised that he would "take care of her for life." The couple lived lavishly all over the world. Hoyt rented Norton an apartment, bought her cars, and repeated his promises to divorce his wife and marry her. He did neither. After 23 years, Hoyt ended the relationship with Norton. On what theory could Norton sue Hoyt? Is she likely to win?

2. Central Maine Power Co. made a promotional offer in which it promised to pay a substantial sum to any homeowner or builder who constructed new housing heated with electricity. Motel Services, Inc., which was building a small housing project for the city of Waterville, Maine, decided to install electrical heat in the units in order to qualify for the offer. It built the units and requested payment for the full amount of the promotional offer. Is Central Maine obligated to pay? Why or why not?

3. Interactive Data Corp. hired Daniel Foley as an assistant product manager at a starting salary of $18,500. Over the next six years, Interactive steadily promoted Foley until he became Los Angeles branch manager at a salary of $56,116. Interactive's officers repeatedly told Foley that he would have his job as long as his performance was adequate. In addition, Interactive distributed an employee handbook that specified "termination guidelines," including a mandatory seven-step pre-termination procedure. Two years later, Foley learned that his recently hired supervisor, Robert Kuhne, was under investigation by the FBI for embezzlement at his previous job. Foley reported this to Interactive officers. Shortly thereafter, Interactive fired Foley. He sued, claiming that Interactive could fire him only for good cause, after the seven-step procedure. What kind of a claim is he making? Should he succeed?

4. **ETHICS** You want to lease your automobile to a friend for the summer but do not want to pay a lawyer to draw up the lease. Joanna, a neighbor, is in law school. She is not licensed to practice law. She offers to draft a lease for you for $100, and you unwisely accept. Later, you refuse to pay her fee, and she sues to collect. Who will win the lawsuit, and why? Apart from the law, was it morally right for the law student to try to help you by drafting the lease? Was she acting helpfully or foolishly or fraudulently? Is it just for you to agree to her fee and then refuse to pay it? What is society's interest in this dispute? Should a court be more concerned with the ethical issue raised by the conduct of the two parties or with the social consequences of this agreement?

5. *YOU BE THE JUDGE* **WRITING PROBLEM** John Stevens owned a dilapidated apartment that he rented to James and Cora Chesney for a low rent. The Chesneys began to remodel and rehabilitate the unit. Over a four-year period, they installed two new bathrooms, carpeted the floors, installed new septic and heating systems, and rewired, replumbed, and painted the apartment. Stevens periodically stopped by and saw the work in progress. The Chesneys transformed the unit into a respectable apartment. Three years after their work was done, Stevens served the Chesneys with an eviction notice. The Chesneys counterclaimed, seeking the value of the work they had done. Are they entitled to it? **Argument for Stevens:** Mr. Stevens is willing to pay the Chesneys exactly the amount he agreed to pay: nothing. The parties never contracted for the Chesneys to fix up the apartment. In fact, they never even discussed such an agreement. The Chesneys are making the absurd argument that anyone who chooses to perform certain work, without ever discussing it with another party, can finish the job and then charge it to the other person. If the Chesneys expected to get paid, obviously they should have said so. If the court were to allow this claim, it would be inviting other tenants to make improvements and then bill the landlord. The law has never been so foolish. **Argument for the Chesneys:** The law of quasi-contract was crafted for cases exactly like this. The Chesneys have given an enormous benefit to Stevens by transforming the apartment and enabling him to rent it at greater profit for many years to come. Stevens saw the work being done and understood that the Chesneys expected some compensation for these major renovations. If Stevens never intended to pay the fair value of the work, he should have stopped the couple from doing the work or notified them that there would be no compensation. It would be unjust to allow the landlord to seize the value of the work, evict the tenants who did it, and pay nothing.

DISCUSSION QUESTIONS

1. Have you ever made an agreement that mattered to you, only to have the other person refuse to follow through on the deal? Looking at the list of elements in the chapter, did your agreement amount to a contract? If not, which element did it lack?

2. Consider promissory estoppel and quasi-contracts. Do you like the fact that these doctrines exist? Should courts have "wiggle room" to enforce deals that fail to meet formal contract requirements? Or, should the rule be "If it's not an actual contract, too bad. No deal."

3. Is it sensible to have two different sets of contract rules—one for sales of goods and another for everything else? Would it be better to have a single set of rules for all contracts?

4. Have you read your apartment lease lately? How about your cellular service agreement? One study found that 67% of consumers do not read the contracts they sign. But notice that a contract is still enforceable, whether or not you read it. Which contracts should you read? iTunes terms and conditions? Your mortgage? An employment agreement?

5. Some states give consumers the right to cancel certain contracts for any reason within a short period of time after entering into them. For example, consumers in California can get out of gym membership contracts by sending the gym a cancellation notice within five business days of joining. Similar statutes cover insurance, weight loss services, door-to-door sales, and home repair contracts. If these agreements meet all of the requirements for a contract, why would a state allow people to get out of them so easily? Is this good policy? Alternatively, if consumers can cancel these contracts, why not allow everyone to cancel any contract within a few days?

CHAPTER 12

© Honza Krej/Shutterstock.com

THE AGREEMENT: OFFERS AND ACCEPTANCES

Interior. A glitzy café, New York. Evening. Bob, a famous director, and Katrina, a glamorous actress, sit at a table, near a wall of glass looking onto a New York sidewalk that is filled with life and motion. Bob sips a margarita while carefully eyeing Katrina. Katrina stares at her wineglass.

I should talk with my agent. I'd need something in writing about the nude scene…

BOB *(smiling confidently): Body Work* is going to be huge—for the right actress. I know a film that's gonna gross a hundred million when I'm holding one. I'm holding one.

KATRINA *(perking up at the mention of money)*: It is quirky. It's fun. And she's very strong, very real.

BOB: She's you. That's why we're sitting here. We start shooting in seven months.

KATRINA *(edging away from the table)*: I have a few questions. That nude scene.

BOB: The one on the toboggan run?

KATRINA: *That* one was OK. But the one in the poultry factory—very explicit. I don't work nude.

BOB: It's not really nude. Think of all those feathers fluttering around.

KATRINA: It's nude.

BOB: We'll work it out. This is a romantic comedy, not tawdry exploitation. Katrina, we're talking $2.5 million. A little accommodation, please. We'll give you $600,000 up front, and the rest deferred, the usual percentages.

KATRINA: Bob, my fee is $3 million. As you know. That hasn't changed.

Katrina picks up her drink, doesn't sip it, places it on the coaster, using both hands to center it perfectly. He waits, as she stares silently at her glass.

BOB: We're shooting in Santa Fe, the weather will be perfect. You have a suite at the Excelsior, plus a trailer on location.

KATRINA: I should talk with my agent. I'd need something in writing about the nude scene, the fee, percentages—all the business stuff. I never sign without talking to her.

BOB: Shrugs and sits back.

KATRINA: *(made anxious by the silence)*: I love the character, I really do.

BOB: You and several others love her. *(That jolts her.)* Agents can wait. I have to put this together fast. We can get you the details you want in writing. *Body Work* is going to be bigger than *Game of Thrones*.

That one hooks her. She looks at Bob. He nods reassuringly. Bob sticks out his hand, smiling. Katrina hesitates, lets go of her drink, and SHAKES HANDS, looking unsure. Bob signals for the check.

Do Bob and Katrina have a deal? *They* seem to think so. But is her fee $2.5 million or $3 million? What if Katrina demands that all nude scenes be taken out, and Bob refuses? Must she still act in the film? Or suppose her agent convinces her that *Body Work* is no good even with changes. Has Katrina committed herself? What if Bob auditions another actress the next day, likes her, and signs her? Does he owe Katrina her fee? Or suppose Bob learns that the funding has fallen apart and there will be no film. Is Katrina entitled to her money?

Bob and Katrina have acted out a classic problem in *agreement,* one of the basic issues in contract law. Their lack of clarity means that disputes are likely and lawsuits possible. Similar bargaining goes on every day around the country and around the world, and the problems created are too frequently resolved in court. Some negotiating is done in person; more is done over the phone, by fax, by email—or all of them combined. This chapter highlights the most common sources of misunderstanding and litigation so that you can avoid making contracts you never intended—or deals that you cannot enforce.

There almost certainly is no contract between Bob and Katrina. Bob's offer was unclear. Even if it was valid, Katrina counteroffered. When they shook hands, it is impossible to know what terms each had in mind.

Contracts Checklist
- ☑ Offer
- ☑ Acceptance
- ☐ Consideration
- ☐ Legality
- ☐ Capacity
- ☐ Consent
- ☐ Writing

12-1 MEETING OF THE MINDS

Remember from the last chapter that contracts have seven key characteristics. Agreements that have a problem in any of the areas do not amount to valid contracts. In this chapter, we examine the first two items on the checklist.

Parties form a contract only if they have a meeting of the minds. For this to happen, one side must make an **offer** and the other must make an **acceptance**. An offer proposes definite terms, and an acceptance unconditionally agrees to them.

Throughout the chapter, keep in mind that courts make *objective* assessments when evaluating offers and acceptances. A court will not try to get inside Katrina's head and decide what she was thinking as she shook hands. It will look at the handshake *objectively*, deciding how a reasonable person would interpret her words and conduct. Katrina may honestly have meant to conclude a deal for $3 million with no nude scenes, while Bob might in good faith have believed he was committing himself to $2.5 million and absolute control of the script. Neither belief will control the outcome.

12-2 OFFER

Bargaining begins with an offer. The person who makes an offer is the **offeror**. The person to whom he makes that offer is the **offeree**. The terms are annoying but inescapable because, like handcuffs, all courts use them.

Two questions determine whether a statement is an offer:

- Do the offeror's words and actions indicate an *intention* to make a bargain?

- Are the terms of the offer reasonably definite?

Zachary says to Sharon, "Come work in my English language center as a teacher. I'll pay you $800 per week for a 35-hour week, for six months starting Monday." This is a valid offer. Zachary's words seem to indicate that he intends to make a bargain and his offer is definite. If Sharon accepts, the parties have a contract that either one can enforce.

In the following section, we present several categories of statements that are generally *not* valid offers.

12-2a Statements that Usually Do Not Amount to Offers

Invitations to Bargain

An invitation to bargain is not an offer. Suppose Martha telephones Joe and leaves a message on his answering machine, asking if Joe would consider selling his vacation condo on Lake Michigan. Joe faxes a signed letter to Martha saying, "There is no way I could sell the condo for less than $150,000." Martha promptly sends Joe a cashier's check for that amount. Does she own the condo? No. Joe's fax was not an offer. It is merely an invitation to negotiate. Joe is indicating that he might well be happy to receive an offer from Martha, but he is not promising to sell the condo for $150,000 or for any amount.

Price Quotes

A price quote is generally not an offer. If Imperial Textile sends a list of fabric prices for the new year to its regular customers, the list is not an offer. Once again, the law regards it merely as a solicitation of offers. Suppose Ralph orders 1,000 yards of fabric, quoted in the list at $40 per yard. *Ralph* is making the offer, and Imperial may decline to sell at $40, or at any price, for that matter.

This can be an expensive point to learn. Leviton Manufacturing makes electrical fixtures and switches. Litton Microwave manufactures ovens. Leviton sent a price list to Litton, stating what it would charge for specially modified switches for use in Litton's microwaves. The price letter included a statement greatly limiting Leviton's liability in the event of any problem with the switches. Litton purchased thousands of the switches and used them in manufacturing its microwaves. But consumers reported fires due to defects in the switches. Leviton claimed that under the contract it had no liability. But the court held that the price letter was not an offer.

Offer

An act or statement that proposes definite terms and permits the other party to create a contract by accepting those terms

Offeror

The person who makes an offer

Offeree

The person to whom an offer is made

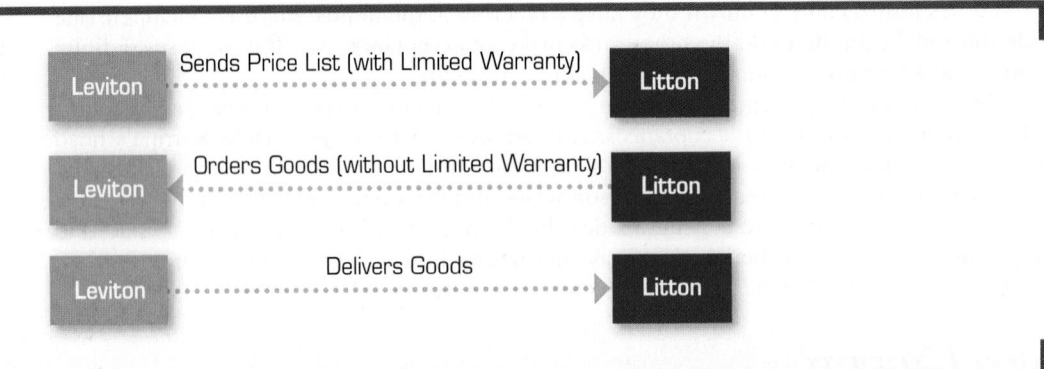

The Litton case demonstrates why it is important to distinguish a valid offer from a mere price quote. Leviton's price list (including a limited warranty) was *not* an offer. When Litton ordered goods (with no limit to the warranty), it was making an offer, which Leviton accepted by delivering the goods. The resulting contract did not contain the limited warranty that Leviton wanted, costing that company a $4 million judgment.

It was a request to receive an offer. Thus, the contract ultimately formed did not include Leviton's liability exclusion. Litton won over $4 million.[1] See Exhibit 12.1.

Letters of Intent

Letter of intent
A letter that summarizes negotiating progress

In complex business negotiations, the parties may spend months bargaining over dozens of interrelated issues. Because each party wants to protect itself during the discussions, ensuring that the other side is serious without binding itself to premature commitments, it may be tempting during the negotiations to draft a **letter of intent**. The letter *might* help distinguish a serious party from one with a casual interest, summarize the progress made thus far, and assist the parties in securing necessary financing. Usually, letters of intent do not create any legal obligation. They merely state what the parties are considering, not what they have actually agreed to. But note that is possible for a letter of intent to bind the parties if its language indicates that the parties *intended* to be bound.

Advertisements

Mary Mesaros received a notice from the United States Bureau of the Mint, announcing a new $5 gold coin to commemorate the Statue of Liberty. The notice contained an order form stating:

VERY IMPORTANT—PLEASE READ: YES, Please accept my order for the U.S. Liberty Coins I have indicated. I understand that all sales are final and not subject to refund. Verification of my order will be made by the Department of the Treasury, U.S. Mint. If my order is received by December 31, I will be entitled to purchase the coins at the Pre-Issue Discount price shown.

Mesaros ordered almost $2,000 worth of the coins. But the Mint was inundated with so many requests for the coin that the supply was soon exhausted. Mesaros and thousands of others never got their coins. This was particularly disappointing because the market value of the coins doubled shortly after their issue. Mesaros sued on behalf of the entire class of disappointed purchasers. Like most who sue based on an advertisement, she lost.[2] **An advertisement is generally not an offer.** An advertisement is merely a request for offers. The consumer makes the offer, whether by mail, like Mesaros, or by arriving at a merchant's

[1]Litton Microwave Cooking Products v. Leviton Manufacturing Co., Inc., 15 F.3d 790 (8th Cir. 1994).
[2]Mesaros v. United States, 845 F.2d 1576 (Fed. Cir. 1988).

store ready to buy. The seller is free to reject the offer. Advertisers should be careful, however, not to be too specific in their ads. Some ads do count as offers, as the following case illustrates.

Landmark Case

CARLILL V. CARBOLIC SMOKE BALL COMPANY
1 QB 256 Court of Appeal, 1892

Facts: In the early 1890s, English citizens greatly feared the Russian flu. The Carbolic Smoke Ball Company ran a newspaper ad that contained two key passages:

"£100 reward will be paid by the Carbolic Smoke Ball Company to any person who contracts the influenza after having used the ball three times daily for two weeks according to the printed directions supplied with each ball.

"£1000 is deposited with the Alliance Bank, shewing our sincerity in the matter."

The product was a ball that contained carbolic acid. Users would inhale vapors from the ball through a long tube.

Carlill purchased a smoke ball and used it as directed for two months. She then caught the flu. She sued, arguing that because her response to the ad had created a contract with the company, she was entitled to £100.

The trial court agreed, awarding Carlill the money. The company appealed.

Issues: *Did the advertisement amount to an offer? If so, was the offer accepted?*

Excerpts from Lord Justice Lindley's Decision: The first observation I will make is that we are dealing with an express promise to pay £100 in certain events. Read the advertisement how you will, and twist it about as you will, here is a distinct promise expressed in language which is perfectly unmistakable.

We must first consider whether this was intended to be a promise at all. The deposit is called by the advertiser as proof of his sincerity in the matter—that is, the sincerity of his promise to pay this £100 in the event which he has specified. I say there is the promise, as plain as words can make it.

Then it is contended that it is not binding. In the first place, the performance of the conditions is the acceptance of the offer. Unquestionably, as a general proposition, when an offer is made, it is necessary that the acceptance should be notified. But is that so in cases of this kind? I think that in a case of this kind that the person who makes the [offer] shews by his language and from the nature of the transaction that he does not expect and does not require notice of the acceptance apart from notice of the performance.

We, therefore, find here all the elements which are necessary to form a binding contract enforceable in point of law.

It appears to me, therefore, that the defendants must perform their promise, and, if they have been so unwary as to expose themselves to a great many actions, so much the worse for them. Appeal dismissed.

Carlill lived 50 years more, dying at the age of 96—of the flu.

This case serves as a cautionary tale. Running a "normal" ad, which describes a product, its features, and its price, does not amount to an offer. But, if a company proposes to take an action—such as pay $100 to customers who take certain, specific actions—then it may find itself contractually obligated to follow through on its promises. The acceptance of the offer makes a unilateral contract.

Note also that, regardless of whether an ad counts as an offer, consumers have protection from those shopkeepers who are intent upon deceit. Almost every state has some form of **consumer protection statute**, which outlaws false advertising. For example, an automobile dealer who advertises a remarkably low price but then has only one automobile at that price has probably violated a consumer protection statute because the ad was published in bad faith, to trick consumers into coming to the dealership. In the *Mesaros* case, the United

Consumer protection statute

Laws protecting consumers from fraud

You have the high bid—but you may not win.

AP Images/Seth Wenig

States Mint did not violate any consumer protection statute because it acted in good faith and simply ran out of coins.

Auctions

It is the property you have always dreamed of owning—and it is up for auction! You arrive bright and early, stand in front, bid early, bid often, bid higher, bid highest of all—it's yours! For five seconds. Then, to your horror, the auctioneer announces that none of the bids were juicy enough and he is withdrawing the property. Robbery! Surely he cannot do that? But he can. Auctions are exciting and useful, but you must understand the rules.

Every day, auctions are used to sell exquisite works of art, real estate, and many other things. **Placing an item up for auction is *not* an offer—it is merely a request for an offer.** The *bids* are the offers. If and when the hammer falls, the auctioneer has accepted the offer.

The important thing to know about a particular auction is whether it is conducted with or without reserve. Most auctions are *with reserve*, meaning that the items for sale have a minimum price. The law assumes that an auction is with reserve unless the auctioneer clearly states otherwise. The auctioneer will not sell anything for less than its reserve (minimum price). So when the bidding for your property failed to reach the reserve, the auctioneer was free to withdraw it.

The rules are different in an auction *without reserve*. Here, there is no minimum. Once the first bid is received, the auctioneer *must* sell the merchandise to the highest bidder.

EXAM Strategy

Question: Ahn and Chet are both unhappy. (1) Ahn, an interior designer, is working on a hotel project. In the annual catalog of a furniture wholesaler, she sees that sofa beds cost $3,000. Based on the catalog, she sends an order for 100 sofa beds to the wholesaler. The wholesaler notifies Ahn that the price has gone up to $4,000. (2) At an estate auction, held without reserve, Chet is high bidder on a rare violin. The seller considers Chet's bid too low and refuses to sell. Both Ahn and Chet sue, but only one will win. Which plaintiff will win, and why?

Strategy: (1) A contract requires an offer and an acceptance. When the furniture wholesaler sent out its catalog, did it make an offer that Ahn could accept? (2) Chet was high bidder. At some auctions, the high bidder is merely making an offer, but at others, he wins the item. Which kind of auction was this?

Result: (1) A price quote is generally not an offer. Ahn's order for 100 sofas was the offer, and the company was free to reject it. Ahn loses. (2) Most auctions are with reserve, meaning that the high bidder is merely making an offer. However, this one was without reserve. Chet gets the violin.

12-2b **Problems with Definiteness**

It is not enough that the offeror indicates that she intends to enter into an agreement. **The terms of the offer must also be definite.** If they are vague, then even if the offeree agrees to the deal, a court does not have enough information to enforce it and there is no contract.

You want a friend to work in your store for the holiday season. This is a definite offer: "I offer you a job as a sales clerk in the store from November 1 through December 29, 40 hours per week at $10 per hour." But suppose, by contrast, you say: "I offer you a job as a sales clerk in the store during the holiday season. We will work out a fair wage once we see how busy things get." Your friend replies, "That's fine with me." This offer is indefinite, and there is no contract. What is a fair wage? $15 per hour? Or $20 per hour? What is the "holiday season"? How will the determinations be made? There is no binding agreement.

The following case, which concerns a famous television show, presents a problem with definiteness.

BAER v. CHASE

392 F.3d 609
Third Circuit Court of Appeals, 2004

Facts: David Chase was a television writer-producer with many credits, including a detective series called *The Rockford Files*. He became interested in a new program, set in New Jersey, about a "mob boss in therapy," a concept he eventually developed into *The Sopranos*. Robert Baer was a prosecutor in New Jersey who wanted to write for television. He submitted a *Rockford Files* script to Chase, who agreed to meet with Baer.

When they met, Baer pitched a different idea, concerning "a film or television series about the New Jersey Mafia." He did not realize Chase was already working on such an idea. Later that year, Chase visited New Jersey. Baer arranged meetings for Chase with local detectives and prosecutors, who provided the producer with information, material, and personal stories about their experiences with organized crime. Detective Thomas Koczur drove Chase and Baer to various New Jersey locations and introduced Chase to Tony Spirito. Spirito shared stories about loan sharking, power struggles between family members connected with the mob, and two colorful individuals known as Big Pussy and Little Pussy, both of whom later became characters on the show.

Back in Los Angeles, Chase wrote and sent to Baer a draft of the first *Sopranos* teleplay. Baer called Chase and commented on the script. The two spoke at least four times that year, and Baer sent Chase a letter about the script.

When *The Sopranos* became a hit television show, Baer sued Chase. He alleged that on three separate occasions Chase had agreed that if the program succeeded, Chase would "take care of" Baer, and would "remunerate Baer in a manner commensurate to the true value of his services." This happened twice on the phone, Baer claimed, and once during Chase's visit to New Jersey. The understanding was that if the show failed, Chase would owe nothing. Chase never paid Baer anything.

The district court dismissed the case, holding that the alleged promises were too vague to be enforced. Baer appealed.

Issue: *Was Chase's promise definite enough to be enforced?*

Excerpts from Judge Greenberg's Decision: A contract arises from offer and acceptance, and must be sufficiently definite so that the performance to be rendered by each party can be ascertained with reasonable certainty. Therefore parties create an enforceable contract when they agree on its essential terms and manifest an intent that the terms bind them. If parties to an agreement do not agree on one or more essential terms of the purported agreement courts generally hold it to be unenforceable.

New Jersey law deems the price term, that is, the amount of compensation, an essential term of any contract. An agreement lacking definiteness of price, however, is not unenforceable if the parties specify a practicable method by which they can determine the amount. However, in the absence of an agreement as to the manner or method of determining compensation the purported agreement is invalid. Additionally, the duration of the contract is deemed an essential term and therefore any agreement must be sufficiently definitive to allow a court to determine the agreed upon length of the contractual relationship.

Baer premises his argument on his view that New Jersey should disregard the well-established requirement of definiteness in its contract law when the subject-matter of the contract is an "idea submission." [However,] New Jersey precedent does not support Baer's attempt to carve out an exception to traditional principles of contract law for submission-of-idea cases. The New Jersey courts have not provided even the slightest indication that they intend to depart from their well-established

requirement that enforceability of a contract requires definiteness with respect to the essential terms of that contract.

Nothing in the record indicates that the parties agreed on how, how much, where, or for what period Chase would compensate Baer. The parties did not discuss who would determine the "true value" of Baer's services, when the "true value" would be calculated, or what variables would go into such a calculation. There was no discussion or agreement as to the meaning of "success" of *The Sopranos*. There was no discussion how "profits" were to be defined. There was no contemplation of dates of commencement or termination of the contract. And again, nothing in Baer's or Chase's conduct, or the surrounding circumstances of the relationship, shed light on, or answers, any of these questions.

Affirmed.

"I'll take care of you." You probably have a sense of what this statement meant to Baer when he heard it from Chase: a reliable assurance that he would be paid. However, it was not enough to be a legally enforceable promise. Recall that courts only make *objective* assessments when evaluating offers and acceptances. Judges cannot—and will not—guess what the parties *meant to do* or analyze what was in their heads.

In the following case, the court asked whether a reasonable person would consider a syllabus to be a contract. You be the (objective) judge.

You be the Judge

GABRIEL V. ALBANY COLLEGE OF PHARMACY AND HEALTH SERVICES

No. 2:12-cv 14
United States District Court for
the District of Vermont, 2013

Facts: Matthew Gabriel was a student in Professor Pumo's immunology class. Professor Pumo's syllabus outlined course requirements and stated that "plagiarism will not be tolerated." After grading the first assignment, Professor Pumo realized that many papers had sentences copied from other sources without citations. Instead of reporting everyone for plagiarism, Professor Pumo said she would give students a *free pass* on one copied sentence. But Gabriel's paper contained many plagiarized sentences, so he received a failing grade for the assignment.

Gabriel sued the professor for breach of contract. He argued that the syllabus was a contract and that the "free pass" policy broke it—because that term was not part of their original agreement. According to Gabriel, since the professor breached the contract, he was no

longer obligated to refrain from plagiarizing, and so should not be punished.

You Be the Judge: *Was the professor's syllabus an offer whose acceptance formed an enforceable contract?*

Argument for Gabriel: A syllabus is a contract. On the first day of class, the professor presents the syllabus as an offer and students agree by staying in the course. Who has not chosen a class because of its particular workload or assignments? The terms in the syllabus are promises upon which students rely. Professor Pumo unilaterally changed the written "rules of the game." Once she broke her promise, there was no longer a "deal." Students should not be held to her arbitrary rules.

Argument for Professor: Professors do not intend to make an offer when they hand out a syllabus—much less be legally bound! The syllabus is merely an announcement that provides general information about course requirements, grading policies, and behavior guidelines. Reasonable people do not expect a syllabus to be enforceable in court. It was not a contract—Professor Pumo had the right to change the class rules, make additional assignments, or even kick Gabriel out at any time. Even if the syllabus were a contract, the phrase "plagiarism will not be tolerated" is too indefinite to be a valid offer. Gabriel is not immune from the plagiarism rules.

12-2c The UCC and Open Terms

In the last chapter, we introduced the Uniform Commercial Code (UCC). Article 2 of the UCC governs contracts when the primary purpose is a sale of goods. Remember that goods are moveable, tangible objects. Usually, UCC provisions are not significantly different from common-law rules. But on occasion, the UCC modifies the common-law rule in some major way. In such cases, we will present a separate description of the key UCC provision. The UCC as a whole is covered in Unit 3. Depending on the class time available, some instructors prefer to discuss the UCC separately, while others like to include it in the general discussion of contracts. This book is designed to work with either approach.

We have just seen that, under the common law, the terms of an offer must be definite. But under the UCC, many indefinite contracts are allowed to stand. Throughout this unit, we witness how the Uniform Commercial Code makes the law of sales more flexible. There are several areas of contract law where imperfect negotiations may still create a binding agreement under the Code, even though the same negotiations under the common law would have yielded no contract. "Open terms" is one such area.

Yuma County Corp. produced natural gas. Yuma wanted a long-term contract to sell its gas so that it could be certain of recouping the expenses of exploration and drilling. Northwest Central Pipeline, which operated an interstate pipeline, also wanted a deal for 10 or more years so it could make its own distribution contracts, knowing it would have a steady supply of natural gas in a competitive market. But neither Yuma nor Northwest wanted to make a long-term *price* commitment, because over a period of years the price of natural gas could double—or crash. Each party wanted a binding agreement without a definitive price. If their negotiations had been governed by the common law, they would have run smack into the requirement of definiteness—no price, no contract. But because this was a sale of goods, it was governed by the UCC.

Under UCC §2-204(3), even though one or more terms are left open, a contract does not fail for indefiniteness if the parties have intended to make a contract and there is a reasonably certain basis for giving an appropriate remedy. Thus, a contract for the sale of goods may be enforced when a key term is missing. Business executives may have many reasons to leave open a delivery date, a price, or some other term. But note that the parties must still have *intended* to create a contract. The UCC will not create a contract where the parties never intended one.

In some cases, the contract will state how the missing term is to be determined. Yuma County and Northwest drafted a contract with alternative methods of determining the price. In the event that the price of natural gas was regulated by the Federal Energy Regulatory Commission (FERC), the price would be the highest allowed by the FERC. If the FERC deregulated the price (as it ultimately did), the contract price would be the average of the two highest prices paid by different gas producers in a specified geographic area.

Gap-Filler Provisions

Even if a UCC contract lacks a specific method for determining missing terms, the Code itself contains **gap-filler provisions**, which are rules for *supplying* missing terms. Some of the most important gap-filler provisions of the Code follow.

Gap-filler provisions
UCC rules for supplying missing terms

Open Price.   In general, if the parties do not settle on a price, the Code establishes that the goods will be sold for a reasonable price. This will usually be the market value or a price established by a neutral expert or agency.[3]

Output and Requirements Provisions.   An **output contract** obligates the seller to sell all of his output to the buyer, who agrees to accept it. For example, a cotton grower might agree to sell all of his next crop to a textile firm. A **requirements contract** obligates a buyer to obtain all of his needed goods from the seller. A vineyard might agree to buy all of its wine bottles from one supplier. Output and requirements contracts are by definition incomplete, since the exact quantity of the goods is unspecified. The Code requires that in carrying out such contracts, both parties act in good faith. Neither party may suddenly demand a quantity of goods (or offer a quantity of goods) that is disproportionate to their past dealings or their reasonable estimates.[4]

Output contract
Obligates the seller to sell all of his output to the buyer, who agrees to accept it

Requirements contract
Obligates a buyer to obtain all of his needed goods from the seller

12-2d **Termination of Offers**

Once an offer has been made, it faces only two possible fates—it can be terminated or accepted. If an offer is terminated, it can never be accepted. If it is accepted, and if there are no problems with any of the five remaining elements on the Contracts Checklist, then a valid contract is created. Offers can be terminated in four ways: revocation, rejection, expiration, and by operation of law.

Termination by Revocation

An offer is **revoked** when the offeror "takes it back" before the offeree accepts. In general, the offeror may revoke the offer any time before it has been accepted. Imagine that I call you and say, "I'm going out of town this weekend. I'll sell you my ticket to this weekend's football game for $75." You tell me that you'll think it over and call me back. An hour later, my plans change. I call you a second time and say, "Sorry, but the deal's off—I'm going to the game after all." I have revoked my offer, and you can no longer accept it.

Making Contracts Temporarily Irrevocable

Some offers cannot be revoked, at least for a time. Often, people and businesses need time to evaluate offers. If a car dealer offers you a green sedan for $25,000, you may want to shop around for a few days to try to find a better price. In the meantime, you may want to make sure that the green sedan is still available if you decide to return. Can you legally prevent the car dealer from selling the car to anyone else while you ponder the offer? In some circumstances, yes.

Option Contract (All types of contracts).   With an option contract, an interested purchaser *buys* the right to have the offer held open. **The offeror may not revoke an offer during the option period.** Suppose you pay the car dealer $250 to hold open its offer until February 2. Later that day, the dealership notifies you that it is selling to someone else. Result? You can enforce *your* contract. The car dealer had no power to revoke because you purchased an option.

---

[3]UCC §2-305
[4]UCC §2-306

Firm Offers (UCC contracts only).   Once again, the UCC has changed the law on the sale of goods. If a promise made in writing is signed by a *merchant*, and if it agrees to hold open an offer for a stated period, then an offer may not be revoked. The open period may not exceed three months. So, if the car dealer gives you a piece of paper that reads, "The offer on the green sedan is open at $25,000 until Friday at noon," he cannot revoke the offer before Friday at noon, even though you have not paid him anything.[5]

Termination by Rejection

If an offeree clearly indicates that he does not want to take the offer, then he has **rejected** it. **If an offeree rejects an offer, the rejection immediately terminates the offer.** Suppose a major accounting firm telephones you and offers a job, starting at $80,000. You respond, "Nah. I'm gonna work on my surfing for a year or two." The next day, you come to your senses and write the firm, accepting its offer. No contract. Your rejection terminated the offer and ended your power to accept it.

Counteroffer.   A party makes a **counteroffer** when it responds to an offer with a new and different proposal. Frederick faxes Kim, offering to sell a 50 percent interest in the Fab Hotel in New York for only $135 million. Kim faxes back and says, "That's too much, but I'll pay $115 million." Moments later, Kim's business partner convinces her that Frederick's offer was a bargain, and she faxes an acceptance of his $135 million offer. Does Kim have a binding deal? No. **A counteroffer is a rejection.** When Kim offered $115 million, she rejected Frederick's offer. Her original fax created a new offer, for $115 million, which Frederick never accepted. The parties have no contract at any price.

Counteroffer
A different proposal made in response to an original offer

Termination by Expiration

An offeror may set a time limit. Quentin calls you and offers you a job in his next motion picture. He tells you, "I've got to know by tomorrow night." If you call him in three days to accept, you are out of the picture. **When an offer specifies a time limit for acceptance, that period is binding.**

If the offer specifies no time limit, the offeree has a *reasonable* period in which to accept. A reasonable period varies, depending upon the type of offer, previous dealings between the parties, and any normal trade usage or customary practices in a particular industry.

Termination by Operation of Law

In some circumstances, the law itself terminates an offer. **If an offeror dies or becomes mentally incapacitated, the offer terminates automatically and immediately.** Arnie offers you a job as an assistant in his hot-air balloon business. Before you can even accept, Arnie tumbles out of a balloon at 3,000 feet. The offer terminates along with Arnie.

Destruction of the subject matter terminates the offer. A car dealer offers to sell you a rare 1938 Bugatti for $7,500,000 if you bring cash the next day. You arrive, suitcase stuffed with cash, just in time to see Arnie drop 3,000 feet through the air and crush the Bugatti. The dealer's offer is terminated.

12-3 ACCEPTANCE

As we have seen, when there is a valid offer outstanding, it remains effective until it is terminated or accepted. An offeree accepts by saying or doing something that a reasonable person would understand to mean that he definitely wants to take the offer. Assume that

---

[5]UCC §2-205

Ellie offers to sell Gene her old iPod for $50. If Gene says, "I accept your offer," then he has indeed accepted, but there is no need to be so formal. He can accept the offer by saying, "It's a deal," or, "I'll take it," or any number of things. He need not even speak. If he hands her a $50 bill, he also accepts the offer.

It is worth noting that **the offeree must say or do** *something* **to accept.** Marge telephones Vick and leaves a message on his answering machine: "I'll pay $75 for your business law textbook from last semester. I'm desperate to get a copy, so I will assume you agree unless I hear from you by 6:00 tonight." Marge hears nothing by the deadline and assumes she has a deal. She is mistaken. Vick neither said nor did anything to indicate that he accepted.

12-3a **Mirror Image Rule**

Was it sensible to deny the professor a job over a mere 14-day difference? Sensible or not, that is the law.

If only he had known! A splendid university, an excellent position as department chair—gone. And all because of the mirror image rule.

Ohio State University wrote to Philip Foster offering him an appointment as a professor and chair of the art history department. His position was to begin July 1, and he had until June 2 to accept the job. On June 2, Foster telephoned the dean and left a message accepting the position, *effective July 15.* Later, Foster thought better of it and wrote the university, accepting the school's starting date of July 1. Too late! Professor Foster never did occupy that chair at Ohio State. The court held that since his acceptance varied the starting date, it was a counteroffer. And a counteroffer, as we know, is a rejection.[6]

Was it sensible to deny the professor a job over a mere 14-day difference? Sensible or not, that is the law. The common-law **mirror image rule** requires that acceptance be on *precisely* the same terms as the offer. If the acceptance contains terms that add or contradict the offer, even in minor ways, courts generally consider it a counteroffer. The rule worked reasonably well in the nineteenth century, when parties would write an original contract and exchange it, penciling in any changes. But now that businesses use standardized forms to purchase most goods and services, the rule creates enormous difficulties. Sellers use forms they have prepared, with all conditions stated to their advantage, and buyers employ their own forms, with terms they prefer. The forms are exchanged in the mail or electronically, with neither side clearly agreeing to the other party's terms.

The problem is known as the "battle of forms." Once again, the UCC has entered the fray, attempting to provide flexibility and common sense for those contracts involving the sale of goods. But for contracts governed by the common law, such as Professor Foster's, the mirror image rule is still the law.

Mirror image rule

Requires that acceptance be on precisely the same terms as the offer

12-3b **UCC and the Battle of Forms**

UCC §2-207 dramatically modifies the mirror image rule for the sale of goods. Under this provision, an acceptance that adds additional or different terms often will create a contract.

Additional or Different Terms

One basic principle of the common law of contracts remains unchanged: the key to creation of a contract is a valid offer that the offeree *intends* to accept. If there is no intent to accept, there is no contract. The big change brought about by UCC §2-207 is this: **An offeree who**

---

[6]Foster v. Ohio State University, 41 Ohio App. 3d 86 (1987).

accepts may include in the acceptance terms that are additional to or different from those in the offer. Thus, even with additional or different terms, the acceptance may well create a contract.

Example A. Wholesaler writes to Manufacturer, offering to buy "10,000 wheelbarrows at $50 per unit. Payable on delivery, 30 days from today's date." Manufacturer writes back, "We accept your offer of 10,000 wheelbarrows at $50 per unit, payable on delivery. *Interest at normal trade rates for unpaid balances.*" Manufacturer clearly intends to form a contract. The company has added a new term, but there is still a valid contract.

However, if the offeree states that her acceptance is *conditioned on the offeror's assent* to the new terms, there is no contract.

Example B. Same offer as above. Manufacturer adds the interest rate clause and states, "Our acceptance is conditional upon your agreement to this interest rate." Manufacturer has made a counteroffer. There is no contract, yet. If Wholesaler accepts the counteroffer, there is a contract; if Wholesaler does not accept it, there is no contract.

Additional terms are those that bring up *new* issues, such as interest rates, not contained in the original offer. Additional terms in the acceptance are considered proposals to add to the contract. Assuming that both parties are merchants, the additional terms *will generally become part of the contract.* Thus, in Example A, the interest rate will become a part of the binding deal. If Wholesaler is late in paying, it must pay whatever interest rate is current.

In three circumstances, the additional terms in the acceptance *do not* become part of the contract:

- If the original offeror *insisted on its own terms.* In other words, if Wholesaler wrote, "I offer to buy them on the following terms and *no other terms*," then Manufacturer is not free to make additions.

- If the additional terms *materially alter* the original offer. Suppose Manufacturer wrote back, "We accept your offer for 10,000 wheelbarrows. Delivery will be made within 180 days, unless we notify you of late delivery." Manufacturer has changed the time from 30 days to 180 days, with a possible extension beyond that. That is a material alteration, and it will not become part of the contract. By contrast, Manufacturer's new language concerning "interest at normal trade rates" was not a material alteration, and therefore that interest rate becomes part of the contract.

- If the offeror receives the additional terms and *promptly objects* to them.

Different terms are those that contradict terms in the offer. For example, if the seller's form clearly states that no warranty is included, and the buyer's form says the seller warrants all goods for three years, the acceptance contains different terms. An acceptance may contain different terms and still create a contract. But in these cases, courts have struggled to decide what the terms of the contract are. **The majority of states hold that different (contradictory) terms cancel each other out.** Neither term is included in the contract. Instead, the neutral terms from the Code itself are "read into" the contract. These are the gap-filler terms discussed earlier. If, for example, the forms had contradictory warranty clauses (as they almost always do), the different terms would cancel each other out, and the warranty clauses from the UCC would be substituted.[7]

---

[7]Not all states follow this rule, however. Some courts have held that when the acceptance contains terms that contradict those in the offer, the language in the offer should be final. A few courts have ruled that the terms in the acceptance should control.

EXAM Strategy

Question: Elaine faxes an offer to Raoul. Raoul writes, "I accept. Please note, I will charge 2 percent interest per month for any unpaid money." He signs the document and faxes it back to Elaine. Do the two have a binding contract?

Strategy: Slow down, this is trickier than it seems. Raoul has added a term to Elaine's offer. We must take two steps to decide whether there is a contract. In a contract for services, acceptance must mirror the offer, but not so in an agreement for the sale of goods.

Result: If this is an agreement for services, there is no contract. However, if this agreement is for goods, the additional term *may* become part of an enforceable contract.

Question: Assume that Elaine's offer concerns goods. Is there an agreement?

Strategy: Under UCC §2-207, an additional term will become part of a binding agreement for goods except in three instances. What are the three exceptions?

Result: Raoul's extra term will be incorporated in a binding contract unless (1) Elaine's offer made clear she would accept no other terms, (2) Raoul's interest rate is a material alteration of the offer (almost never the case for interest rates), or (3) Elaine promptly rejects the interest rate.

12-3c Clickwraps and Shrinkwraps

You want to purchase Attila brand software and download it to your computer. You type in your credit card number and other information, agreeing to pay $99. Attila also requires that you "read and agree to" all of the company's terms. You click "I agree," without having read one word of the terms. Three frustrating weeks later, tired of trying to operate defective Attilaware, you demand a refund and threaten to sue. The company replies that you are barred from suing because the terms you agreed to included an arbitration clause. To resolve any disputes, you must travel to Attila's hometown, halfway across the nation, use an arbitrator that the company chooses, pay one-half the arbitrator's fee, and also pay Attila's legal bills if you should lose. The agreement makes it financially impossible for you to get your money back. Is that contract enforceable?

You have entered into a "clickwrap" agreement. Similar agreements, called "shrinkwraps," are packaged inside many electronic products. A shrinkwrap notice might require that before inserting a purchased CD into your computer, you must read and agree to all terms in the brochure. Clickwraps and shrinkwraps often include arbitration clauses. They frequently limit the seller's liability if anything goes wrong, saying that the manufacturer's maximum responsibility is to refund the purchase price (even if the software destroys your hard drive).

Many courts that have analyzed these issues have ruled that clickwrap and shrinkwrap agreements are indeed binding, even against consumers. The courts have emphasized that sellers are entitled to offer a product on any terms they wish, and that shrinkwrap and clickwrap are the most efficient methods of including complicated terms in a small space. Think before you click![8]

---

[8]ProCD, Inc. v. Zeidenberg, 86 F.3d 1447 (7th Cir. 1996), is the leading case to enforce shrinkwrap agreements (and, by extension, clickwraps).

However, some courts have *refused* to enforce such contracts against a consumer, stating that the buyer never understood or agreed to the shrinkwrapped terms. The court in the following case works hard to balance the competing interests, and in the process demonstrates that this new area of law is very much in flux.

SPECHT V. NETSCAPE COMMUNICATIONS CORPORATION

306 F.3d 17
Second Circuit Court of Appeals, 2002

Facts: A group of plaintiffs sued Netscape, claiming that two of the company's products illegally captured private information about files that they downloaded from the Internet. The plaintiffs alleged that this was electronic eavesdropping, in violation of two federal statutes.

From Netscape's web page, the plaintiffs had downloaded SmartDownload, a software plug-in that enabled them to download the company's Communicator software. The Web page advertised the benefits of SmartDownload, and near the bottom of the screen was a tinted button labeled "Download." The plaintiffs clicked to download. If, instead of downloading, they had scrolled further down, they would have seen an invitation to "review and agree to the terms of the Netscape Smart-Download software license agreement." By clicking the appropriate button, they would have been sent to a series of linked pages, and finally arrived at a license agreement. Among the terms was an agreement to arbitrate any dispute. In other words, a consumer downloading Smart-Download was in theory giving up the right to file suit if anything went wrong, and agreeing to settle the dispute by arbitration. However, the plaintiffs never reviewed the license terms.

In the district court, Netscape moved to dismiss the case and compel arbitration. Netscape claimed that the plaintiffs had forfeited any right to sue based on the license agreement. The district court denied the company's motion, ruling that the plaintiffs had not agreed to the terms of the license. Netscape appealed.

Issue: *Had the plaintiffs agreed to arbitrate their claims?*

Excerpts from Judge Sotomayor's Decision: Defendants argue that plaintiffs must be held to a standard of reasonable prudence and that, because notice of the existence of SmartDownload license terms was on the next scrollable screen, plaintiffs were on "inquiry notice" of those terms. We disagree with the proposition that a reasonably prudent offeree in plaintiffs' position would necessarily have known or learned of the existence of the SmartDownload license agreement prior to acting, so that plaintiffs may be held to

have assented to that agreement with constructive notice of its terms.

Receipt of a physical document containing contract terms or notice thereof is frequently deemed, in the world of paper transactions, a sufficient circumstance to place the offeree on inquiry notice of those terms. These principles apply equally to the emergent world of online product delivery, pop-up screens, hyperlinked pages, clickwrap licensing, scrollable documents, and urgent admonitions to "Download Now!" What plaintiffs saw when they were being invited by defendants to download this fast, free plug-in called SmartDownload was a screen containing praise for the product and, at the very bottom of the screen, a "Download" button. Defendants argue that a fair and prudent person using ordinary care would have been on inquiry notice of SmartDownload's license terms.

We are not persuaded that a reasonably prudent offeree in these circumstances would have known of the existence of license terms. Plaintiffs were responding to an offer that did not carry an immediately visible notice of the existence of license terms or require unambiguous manifestation of assent to those terms. Thus, plaintiffs' apparent manifestation of consent was to terms contained in a document whose contractual nature was not obvious. Moreover, the fact that, given the position of the scroll bar on their computer screens, plaintiffs may have been aware that an unexplored portion of the Netscape Web page remained below the download button does not mean that they reasonably should have concluded that this portion contained a notice of license terms.

We conclude that in circumstances such as these, where consumers are urged to download free software at the immediate click of a button, a reference to the existence of license terms on a submerged screen is not sufficient to place consumers on inquiry or constructive notice of those terms. There is no reason to assume that viewers will scroll down to subsequent screens simply because screens are there.

For the foregoing reasons, we affirm the district court's denial of defendants' motion to compel arbitration and to stay court proceedings.

The plaintiffs in *Specht* won because they knew nothing about the arbitration clause and were unlikely to discover it on the company's website. Notice what happens when a user *does* know about terms posted online. Register.com was a registrar of Internet domain names, meaning that it issued domain names to people and companies establishing a new website. The company was legally obligated to make available to the public, for free, the names and contact information of its customers. Register was also in the business of assisting owners, for a fee, to develop their websites.

Verio, Inc. competed in the site development business. Verio's automated software program (robot) would search Register.com daily, seeking information about new sites. *After* Verio obtained contact information, a notice would appear on the Register site, stating:

> By submitting a query, you agree that under no circumstances will you use this data to support the transmission of mass unsolicited, commercial advertising or solicitation via email.

In fact, though, Verio used the contact information for exactly that purpose, sending mass emailings to owners of new websites, soliciting their development business. Register sued. Verio defended by stating it was not bound by the notice because the notice did not appear until after it had obtained the information. Verio argued that when it sent the queries, it was unaware of any restrictions on use of the data. The court was unpersuaded, and explained its reasoning with a simple but telling metaphor:

> The situation might be compared to one in which plaintiff P maintains a roadside fruit stand displaying bins of apples. A visitor, defendant D, takes an apple and bites into it. As D turns to leave, D sees a sign, visible only as one turns to exit, which says "Apples—50 cents apiece." D does not pay for the apple. D believes he has no obligation to pay because he had no notice when he bit into the apple that 50 cents was expected in return. D's view is that he never agreed to pay for the apple. Thereafter, each day, several times a day, D revisits the stand, takes an apple, and eats it. D never leaves money.
>
> P sues D in contract for the price of the apples taken. D defends on the ground that on no occasion did he see P's price notice until after he had bitten into the apples. D may well prevail as to the first apple taken. D had no reason to understand upon taking it that P was demanding the payment. In our view, however, D cannot continue on a daily basis to take apples for free, knowing full well that P is offering them only in exchange for 50 cents in compensation, merely because the sign demanding payment is so placed that on each occasion D does not see it until he has bitten into the apple.

Register.com won its case. Verio was prohibited from using the contact information for mass emailings because it had actual knowledge of the restrictions placed on its use.[9]

Ethics   Imagine browsing for an airline ticket online, only to discover that the first class fare from New York to India is $1, round trip. Would you rush to purchase it? Airlines regularly make programming mistakes resulting in mispriced online fares. Brian Kelly found a United Airlines first class ticket from New York to Hong Kong—which usually costs about $11,000—for $43 and immediately bought it on the company's online ticketing system.[10] Kelly, who runs a website for frequent flyers, advised his readers to take advantage of the glitch before United discovered it. And many did.

Are these "mistake fares"—which are obviously "too good to be true"—enforceable as contracts? Is there a valid offer and acceptance? Ethically speaking, would you take advantage of this deal? Why or why not?

---

[9]Register.Com v. Verio, Inc., 353 F.3d 393 (2d Cir. 2004).
[10]Tim Hume, *Too good to be true: New York to Hong Kong for $43*, CNN.com (July 23, 2012).

12-3d **Communication of Acceptance**

The offeree must communicate his acceptance for it to be effective. The questions that typically arise concern the method, the manner, and the time of acceptance.

Method and Manner of Acceptance

The term *method* refers to whether acceptance is done in person or by mail, telephone, email, or fax. The term *manner* refers to whether the offeree accepts by promising, by making a down payment, by performing, and so forth. **If an offer demands acceptance in a particular method or manner, the offeree must follow those requirements.** An offer might specify that it be accepted in writing, or in person, or before midnight on June 23. An offeror can set any requirements she wishes. Omri might say to Oliver, "I'll sell you my bike for $200. You must accept my offer by standing on a chair in the lunchroom tomorrow and reciting a poem about a cow." Oliver can only accept the offer in the exact manner specified if he wants to form a contract.

If the offer does not specify a type of acceptance, the offeree may accept in any reasonable manner and method. An offer generally may be accepted by performance or by a promise, unless it specifies a particular method. The same freedom applies to the method. If Masako faxes Eric an offer to sell 1,000 acres in Montana for $800,000, Eric may accept by mail or fax. Both are routinely used in real estate transactions, and either is reasonable.

Time of Acceptance: The Mailbox Rule

An acceptance is generally effective upon dispatch, meaning the moment it is out of the offeree's control. Terminations, on the other hand, are effective when received. When Masako faxes her offer to sell land to Eric, and he mails his acceptance, the contract is binding the moment he puts the letter into the mail. In most cases, this **mailbox rule** is just a detail. But it becomes important when the offeror revokes her offer at about the same time the offeree accepts. Who wins? Suppose Masako's offer has one twist:

> **Mailbox rule**
> Acceptance is generally effective upon dispatch. Terminations are effective when received.

- On Monday morning, Masako faxes her offer to Eric.

- On Monday afternoon, Eric writes, "I accept" on the fax, and Masako mails a revocation of her offer.

- On Tuesday morning, Eric mails his acceptance.

- On Thursday morning, Masako's revocation arrives at Eric's office.

- On Friday morning, Eric's acceptance arrives at Masako's office.

Outcome? Eric has an enforceable contract. Masako's offer was effective when it reached Eric. His acceptance was effective on Tuesday morning, when he mailed it. Nothing that happens later can "undo" the contract.

SOLDAU V. ORGANON, INC.

860 F.2d 355
United States Court of Appeals for the Ninth Circuit, 1988

Facts: Organon fired John Soldau. Then the company sent to him a letter offering to pay him double the normal severance pay, provided Soldau would sign a full release, that is, a document giving up any and all claims he might have against Organon. The release was included with the letter. Soldau signed it, dated it, and took it to the nearest post office, where he deposited it in the mailbox. When he returned home, Soldau discovered in the mail a check from Organon for the double severance pay. He hustled back to the post office, where he persuaded a postal clerk to open the mailbox and retrieve the release he had posted. He then cashed Organon's check and finally filed a suit against the company, alleging that his firing was age discrimination.

The federal district court gave summary judgment for Organon, ruling that Soldau's acceptance of the proposed release was effective when he mailed it, creating a contract. He appealed.

Issue: *Did Soldau create a contract by mailing the release?*

Excerpts from the *Per Curiam* Decision: The district court was clearly correct under California law. Soldau does not argue to the contrary. Instead, he contends that the formation and validity of the release are governed by federal law, and would not have been effective unless and until it had been received by Organon. We need not decide which body of law controls. Under federal as well as California law, Soldau's acceptance was effective when it was mailed.

The so-called mailbox or effective when mailed rule was adopted and followed as federal common law by the Supreme Court [at the beginning of the 20th century]. We could not change the rule, and there is no reason to believe the Supreme Court would be inclined to do so. It is almost universally accepted in the common law world. It is enshrined in the Restatement (Second) of Contracts and endorsed by the major contract treatises.

Commentators are also virtually unanimous in [supporting the "effective upon dispatch" rule,] pointing to the long history of the rule; its importance in creating certainty for contracting parties; its essential soundness, on balance, as a means of allocating the risk during the period between the making of the offer and the communication of the acceptance or rejection to the offeror; and the inadequacy of the rationale offered by the Court of Claims for the change.

Since Soldau's contractual obligation to release Organon in return for Organon's obligation to make the enhanced severance payment arose when Soldau deposited his acceptance in the post office mailbox, his subsequent withdrawal of the acceptance was ineffectual. *Affirmed*.

Chapter Conclusion

The law of offer and acceptance can be complex. Yet for all its faults, the law is not the principal source of dispute between parties unhappy with negotiations. Most litigation concerning offer and acceptance comes from *lack of clarity* on the part of the people negotiating. The many examples discussed are all understandable given the speed and fluidity of the real world of business. But the executive who insists on clarity is likelier in the long run to spend more time doing business and less time in court.

EXAM REVIEW

1. **MEETING OF THE MINDS** The parties can form a contract only if they have a meeting of the minds, which requires that they understand each other and show that they intend to reach an agreement.

EXAM Strategy

Question: Norv owned a Ford dealership and wanted to expand by obtaining a BMW outlet. He spoke with Jackson and other BMW executives on several occasions. Norv now claims that those discussions resulted in an oral contract that requires BMW to grant him a franchise, but the company disagrees. Norv's strongest evidence of a contract is the fact that Jackson gave him forms on which to order BMWs. Jackson answered that it was his standard practice to give such forms to prospective dealers, so that if the franchise were approved, car orders could be processed quickly. Norv states that he was "shocked" when BMW refused to go through with the deal. Is there a contract?

> **Strategy:** A court makes an *objective* assessment of what the parties did and said to determine whether they had a meeting of the minds and intended to form a contract. Norv's "shock" is irrelevant. Do the order forms indicate a meeting of the minds? Was there additional evidence that the parties had reached an agreement? (See the "Result" at the end of this section.)

2. **OFFER**   An offer is an act or statement that proposes definite terms and permits the other party to create a contract by accepting those terms.

3. **OTHER STATEMENTS**   Invitations to bargain, price quotes, letters of intent, and advertisements are generally not offers. However, an ad in which a company proposes to take a specific action when a customer takes a specific action can amount to an offer. And letters of intent that indicate the parties intended to be bound can also count as offers.

> **Question:** "Huge selection of Guernsey sweaters," reads a newspaper ad from Stuffed Shirt, a clothing retailer. "Regularly $135, today only $65." Waldo arrives at Stuffed Shirt at 4:00 that afternoon, but the shop clerk says there are no more sweaters. He shows Waldo a newly arrived Shetland sweater that sells for $145. Waldo sues, claiming breach of contract and violation of a consumer protection statute. Who will prevail?
>
> (a)   Waldo will win the breach of contract suit and the consumer protection suit.
>
> (b)   Waldo will lose the breach of contract suit but might win the consumer protection suit.
>
> (c)   Waldo will lose the consumer protection suit but should win the breach of contract suit.
>
> (d)   Waldo will win the consumer protection suit only if he wins the contract case.
>
> (e)   Waldo will lose both the breach of contract suit and the consumer protection suit.
>
> **Strategy:** Waldo assumes that he is accepting the store's offer. But did Stuffed Shirt make an offer? If not, there cannot be a contract. Does the consumer protection statute help him? (See the "Result" at the end of this section.)

4. **DEFINITENESS**   The terms of the offer must be definite, although under the UCC the parties may create a contract that has open terms.

5. **TERMINATION**   An offer may be terminated by revocation, rejection, expiration, or operation of law.

Question: Rick is selling his Espresso Coffee Maker. He sends Tamara an email, offering to sell the machine for $350. Tamara promptly emails back, offering to buy the item for $300. She hears nothing from Rick, so an hour later Tamara stops by his apartment, where she learns that he just sold the machine to his roommate for $250. She sues Rick. Outcome?

(a) Tamara will win because her offer was higher than the roommate's.

(b) Tamara will win because Rick never responded to her offer.

(c) Tamara will win because both parties made clear offers, in writing.

(d) Tamara will lose because she rejected Rick's offer.

(e) Tamara will lose because her offer was not definite.

Strategy: A valid contract requires a definite offer and acceptance. Rick made a valid offer. When Tamara said she would buy the machine for a lower amount, was that acceptance? If not, what was it? (See the "Result" at the end of this section.)

6. **MIRROR IMAGE RULE AND UCC §2-207**   The common-law mirror image rule requires acceptance on precisely the same terms as the offer. Under the UCC, an offeree may often create a contract even when the acceptance includes terms that are additional to or different from those in the offer.

7. **CLICKWRAP AGREEMENTS**   Clickwrap and shrinkwrap agreements are generally enforceable.

8. **MANNER OF ACCEPTANCE**   If an offer demands acceptance in a particular method or manner, the offeree must follow those requirements. If the offer does not specify a type of acceptance, the offeree may accept in any reasonable manner and medium.

9. **MAILBOX RULE**   An acceptance is generally effective upon dispatch, meaning from the moment it is out of the offeree's control. Terminations usually are not effective until received.

1. Result: The order forms are neither an offer nor an acceptance. Norv has offered no evidence that the parties agreed on price, date of performance, or any other key terms. There is no contract. Norv allowed eagerness and optimism to replace common sense.

3. Result: An advertisement is usually not an offer, but merely a solicitation of one. It is Waldo who is making the offer, which the store may reject. Waldo loses his contract case, but he may win under the consumer protection statute. The correct answer is B. If Stuffed Shirt proclaimed "huge selection" when there were only five sweaters, the store was deliberately misleading consumers, and Waldo wins. However, if there was indeed a large selection, and Waldo arrived too late, he is out of luck.

5. Result: Tamara made a counteroffer of $300. A counteroffer is a rejection. Tamara rejected Rick's offer and simultaneously offered to buy the coffee maker at a lower price. Rick was under no obligation to sell to Tamara at any price. He will win Tamara's suit.

MULTIPLE-CHOICE QUESTIONS

1. Rebecca, in Honolulu, faxes a job offer to Spike, in Pittsburgh, saying, "We can pay you $55,000 per year, starting June 1." Spike faxes a reply, saying, "Thank you! I accept your generous offer, though I will also need $3,000 in relocation money. See you June 1. Can't wait!" On June 1, Spike arrives, to find that his position is filled by Gus. He sues Rebecca.

    (a) Spike wins $55,000.

    (b) Spike wins $58,000.

    (c) Spike wins $3,000.

    (d) Spike wins restitution.

    (e) Spike wins nothing.

2. Arturo hires Kate to work in his new sporting goods store. "Look," he explains, "I can only pay you $9.00 an hour. But if business is good a year from now, and you're still here, I'm sure I can pay you a healthy bonus." Four months later, Arturo terminates Kate. She sues.

    (a) Kate will win her job back, plus the year's pay and the bonus.

    (b) Kate will win the year's pay and the bonus.

    (c) Kate will win only the bonus.

    (d) Kate will win only her job back.

    (e) Kate will win nothing.

3. Manny offers to sell Gina his TV for $100 on January 1. On January 2, Gina writes out a letter of acceptance. On January 3, Gina drops the letter in a mailbox. On January 4, a postal worker gets the letter out of the mailbox and takes it to the post office. On January 5, the letter arrives in Manny's mailbox. When (if ever) was a contract formed?

    (a) January 2

    (b) January 3

    (c) January 4

    (d) January 5

    (e) None of the above—a contract has not been formed.

4. Frank, an accountant, says to Missy, "I'll sell you my laptop for $100." Missy asks, "Will you give me until tomorrow to make up my mind?" "Sure," Frank replies. Which of the following is true?

    (a) Frank cannot revoke his offer, no matter what.

    (b) Frank cannot revoke his offer, but only if Missy pays him to keep the offer open until tomorrow.

    (c) Frank can revoke his offer no matter what, because he is not a merchant.

    (d) Frank can revoke his offer no matter what, because he did not promise Missy anything in writing.

5. Which of the following amounts to an offer?

    (a) Ed says to Carmen, "I offer to sell you my pen for $1."

    (b) Ed says to Carmen, "I'll sell you my pen for $1."

    (c) Ed writes, "I'll sell you my pen for $1," and gives the note to Carmen.

    (d) All of the above

    (e) A and C only

CASE QUESTIONS

1. The town of Sanford, Maine, decided to auction off a lot it owned. The town advertised that it would accept bids through the mail, up to a specified date. Arthur and Arline Chevalier mailed in a bid that turned out to be the highest. When the town refused to sell them the lot, they sued. Result?

2. The Tufte family leased a 260-acre farm from the Travelers Insurance Co. Toward the end of the lease, Travelers mailed the Tuftes an option to renew the lease. The option arrived at the Tuftes' house on March 30, and gave them until April 14 to accept. On April 13, the Tuftes signed and mailed their acceptance, which Travelers received on April 19. Travelers claimed there was no lease and attempted to evict the Tuftes from the farm. May they stay?

3. Consolidated Edison Co. of New York (Con Ed) sought bids from General Electric Co. (GE) and others to supply it with two huge transformers. Con Ed required that the bids be held open for 90 days. GE submitted a written bid and included a clause holding the bid open for 90 days. During that period, Con Ed accepted GE's bid, but GE refused to honor it. Is there a contract?

4. Niels owned three adjoining parcels of land in Arizona. Hannah wanted to buy one. Over dinner, the two sketched and signed this agreement: "Binding Contract: Niels agrees to sell one of his three Arizona lots to Hannah. Within 14 days, the parties will meet on the land, decide which lot Hannah is buying, and settle on a price. If they cannot agree on a price, they will decide a fair method of doing so. Both parties agree to be bound by this contract." Later, Niels refused to sell any land, and Hannah sued. What will happen?

5. When a Tom Cat Bakery delivery van struck Elizabeth Nadel, she suffered significant injuries, Nadel filed suit. Before the trial, Tom Cat's attorney offered a $100,000 settlement, which Nadel refused. While the jury was deliberating, the bakery's lawyer again offered Nadel the $100,000 settlement. She decided to think about it during lunch. Later that day, the jury sent a note to the judge. The bakery owner told her lawyer that if the note indicated the jury had reached a verdict, he should revoke the settlement offer. Back in the courtroom, the bakery's lawyer said, "If the note is a verdict, my client wants to take the verdict." Nadel's lawyer then said, "My client will take the settlement." The trial court judge allowed the forewoman to read the verdict, which awarded Nadel—nothing. Did Nadel's lawyer accept the settlement offer in time?

DISCUSSION QUESTIONS

1. Each time employees at BizCorp enter their work computers, the following alert appears: "You are attempting to access the BizCorp network. By logging in, you agree to BizCorp's Computer Usage Policy and certify that your use of this computer is strictly for business purposes. Any activities conducted on this system may be monitored for any reason at the discretion of BizCorp." Once an employee has logged in, have the parties formed a valid contract? Discuss.

2. Case law tells us that a course syllabus is not a binding contract—but how about your school's honor code? Under what conditions could an honor code be a contract?

3. The day after Thanksgiving, known as Black Friday, is the biggest shopping day of the year. One major retailer advertised a "Black Friday only" laptop for $150. On Thanksgiving night, hundreds of people waited for the store to open to take advantage of the laptop deal—only to learn that the store only had two units for sale at the discounted price. Did the retailer breach its contract with the hundreds of consumers who sought the deal? What obligation, if any, does the retailer have to its consumers?

4. Someone offers to sell you a concert ticket for $50, and you reply, "I'll give you $40," The seller refuses to sell at the lower price, and you say, "OK, OK, I'll pay you $50." Clearly, no contract has been formed, because you made a counteroffer. If the seller has changed her mind and no longer wants to sell for $50, she doesn't have to. But is this fair? If it is all part of the same conversation, should you be able to accept the $50 offer and get the ticket?

5. If you click an "I agree" box, odds are that its terms are binding on you, even if the box contains dozens or even hundreds of lines of dense text. Is this fair? Should the law change to limit the enforceability of clickwraps?

6. Courts stick to objective (reasonable person) standards when evaluating offers and acceptances. Juries are not asked to "get inside someone's head," they are instructed to determine what a reasonable person would think of offerors' and offereees' statements. Is this practice reasonable? Would it be better if the law directly considered whether people *wanted* to make contracts?

CHAPTER 13

CONSIDERATION

Have you ever rented a movie that you did not want every one of your friends to know about? Cathryn Harris did. Imagine her shock when she rented a movie online from Blockbuster, only to find out that this news was automatically transmitted to her Facebook page and then broadcast to all her "friends." Just think how bad that could be.

Harris sued Blockbuster for this violation of her privacy, only to find out she had clicked away her right to sue. To rent the movie, she clicked that little box saying she agreed to all the terms and conditions. And one of those terms and conditions was an agreement to arbitrate, not litigate. Can Blockbuster get away with this?

It turns out that this movie has a happy ending. The court ruled that the contract between Harris and Blockbuster was unenforceable because there was no *consideration*.

© Honza Krej/Shutterstock.com

To rent the movie, she had to click that little box saying she agreed to all the terms and conditions.

Consideration is our next step on the road to understanding contracts. In the Chapter 12, we learned what it takes to create an agreement. But an agreement is not necessarily a legally enforceable contract.

This is the first of four chapters that will examine problems that can prevent an agreement from becoming a contract. A lack of consideration is one of them. Without it, a promise is "just a promise" and nothing more.

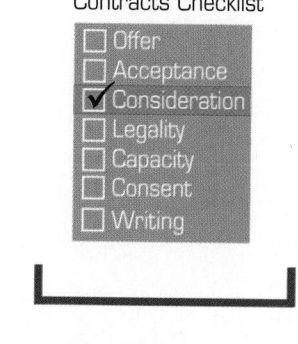

Contracts Checklist
- ☐ Offer
- ☐ Acceptance
- ☑ Consideration
- ☐ Legality
- ☐ Capacity
- ☐ Consent
- ☐ Writing

13-1 WHAT IS CONSIDERATION?

In early English law, courts would not enforce contracts unless they were under formal seal.[1]

It soon became evident that many other types of mutual promises should be recognized as contracts, regardless of their form. But how would judges know which promises were worth enforcing? How would they distinguish between mere gifts and legally binding commitments?

The answer is **consideration. Consideration is the inducement, price, or promise that causes a person to enter into a contract and forms the basis for the parties' exchange.** The central idea of consideration is simple: Contracts must be a two-way street. If one side gets all the benefit and the other side gets nothing, then an agreement lacks consideration and is not an enforceable contract. Consideration is proof that the parties intended to be bound to their promises.

There are two basic elements of consideration:

1. **Value** Consideration requires legal benefit to the promisor or legal detriment to the promisee. Legal benefit means receiving something of *measureable value.* That thing can be money, groceries, insurance, a promise not to sue, or anything else of value to the promisee.

2. **Bargained-for Exchange** According to Supreme Court Justice Oliver Wendell Holmes, Jr., the essence of consideration is that "the promise must induce the detriment and the detriment must induce the promise."[2] Consideration involves reciprocity. The parties must have *bargained for* whatever was exchanged and struck a deal: "If you do this, I'll do that." If you just decide to deliver a cake to your neighbor's house without her knowing, that may be something of value, but since you two did not bargain for it, there is no contract and she does not owe you the price of the cake.

Let's take an example: Sally's Shoe Store and Baker Boots agree that Sally's will pay $20,000 for 100 pairs of boots. As to the $20,000, Sally's is the promisor (because it has committed to paying) and Baker the promisee (because it is the recipient). Regarding the boots, Baker is the promisor, and Sally's the promisee. Both parties get a legal benefit that is of value—Sally gets the boots, Baker gets the money. Also, each incurs a detriment—Sally gives up the money, Baker parts with the boots. Note that a contract is

Consideration
The inducement, price, or promise that causes a person to enter into a contract and forms the basis for the parties' exchange.

For Holmes, consideration required a reciprocal bargain.

Time Life Pictures/Library of Congress/Time Life Pictures/Getty Images

---

[1]It was once common to authenticate contracts with a seal, an instrument that creates an impression on paper or wax. This practice is rare today.
[2]*Wisconsin & Michigan Ry. v. Powers,* 191 U.S. 379 (1903).

formed at the moment when the promises are made because a promise to give something of value counts. The two have bargained for this deal, so there is valid consideration.

Now for an example where there is no consideration. Marvin works at Sally's. At 9 a.m., he is in a good mood and promises to buy his coworker a Starbucks latte during the lunch hour. The delighted coworker agrees. Later that morning, the coworker is rude to Marvin, who then changes his mind about buying the coffee. He is free to do so. His promise was a one-way street: The coworker stood to receive all the benefit of the agreement, while Marvin got nothing. Because Marvin received no value, there is no contract.

13-1a **What Is Value?**

As we have seen, an essential part of consideration is that both parties must get something of value. That item of value can be either an "act," a "forbearance," or a promise to do either of these.

Act

A party commits an **act** when she does something she was not legally required to do in the first place. She might do a job, deliver an item, or pay money, for example. An act does not count if the party was simply complying with the law or fulfilling her obligations under an existing contract. Suppose that your professor tells the university that she will not post final grades unless she is paid an extra $5,000. Even if the university agrees to this outrageous demand, that agreement is not a valid contract because the professor is already under an obligation to post final grades.

Forbearance

A **forbearance** is, in essence, the opposite of an act. A person forbears if he agrees *not* to do something he had a legal right to do. An entrepreneur might promise a competitor *not* to open a competing business, or an elderly driver (with a valid driver's license) might promise concerned family members that he will not drive at night.

Promise to Act or Forbear

A promise to do (or not do) something in the future counts as consideration. When evaluating whether consideration exists, the *promise* to mow someone's lawn next week is the equivalent of actually *doing* the yardwork.

Let's apply these ideas to the most famous of all consideration lawsuits. Our story begins in 1869, when a well-meaning uncle made a promise to his nephew. Ever since *Hamer v. Sidway* appeared, generations of U.S. law students have dutifully inhaled the facts and sworn by its wisdom; now you, too, may drink it in.

Act
Any action that a party was not legally required to take in the first place

Forbearance
Refraining from doing something that one has a legal right to do

Landmark Case

HAMER V. SIDWAY
124 N.Y. 538
New York Court of Appeals, 1891

Facts: This is a story with two Stories. William Story wanted his nephew to grow up healthy and prosperous. In 1869, he promised the 15-year-old boy (who was also named William Story) $5,000 if the lad would refrain from drinking liquor, using tobacco, swearing, and playing cards or billiards for money until his twenty-first birthday. (In that wild era—can you believe it?—the nephew had a legal right to do all those things.) The nephew agreed and, what is more, he kept his word. When he reached his twenty-first birthday, the nephew notified his uncle that he had honored the agreement. The uncle congratulated the young man and promised to give him the money but said he would wait a few more years before handing over the cash, until the nephew was mature enough to handle such a large sum. The uncle died in 1887 without having paid, and his estate refused to honor the promise. Because the nephew had transferred his rights in the money, it was a man named Hamer who eventually sought to collect from the uncle's estate. The estate argued that since the nephew had given no consideration for the uncle's promise, there was no enforceable contract. The trial court found for the plaintiff, and the uncle's estate appealed.

Issue: *Did the nephew give consideration for the uncle's promise?*

Excerpts from Justice Parker's Decision: The defendant contends that the contract was without consideration to support it, and therefore invalid. He asserts that the promisee, by refraining from the use of liquor and tobacco, was not harmed, but benefited; that that which he did was best for him to do, independently of his uncle's promise, and insists that it follows that, unless the promisor was benefited, the contract was without consideration, a contention which, if well founded, would seem to leave open for controversy in many cases whether that which the promisee did or omitted to do was in fact of such benefit to him as to leave no consideration to support the enforcement of the promisor's agreement. Such a rule could not be tolerated, and is without foundation in the law. Courts will not ask whether the thing which forms the consideration does in fact benefit the promisee or a third party, or is of any substantial value to anyone. It is enough that something is promised, done, forborne, or suffered by the party to whom the promise is made as consideration for the promise made to him.

Now applying this rule to the facts before us, the promisee used tobacco, occasionally drank liquor, and he had a legal right to do so. That right he abandoned for a period of years upon the strength of the promise of the testator [that is, the uncle] that for such forbearance he would give him $5,000. We need not speculate on the effort which may have been required to give up the use of those stimulants. It is sufficient that he restricted his lawful freedom of action within certain prescribed limits upon the faith of his uncle's agreement, and now, having fully performed the conditions imposed, it is of no moment whether such performance actually proved a benefit to the promisor, and the court will not inquire into it.

The issue of value in a contract is an important one, so let's look at another case. In the movies, when a character wants to get serious about keeping a promise—*really* serious—he sometimes signs an agreement in blood. As it turns out, this kind of thing actually happens in real life. In the following case, did the promise of forbearance have value? Did a contract signed in blood count? You be the judge.

You be the Judge

Facts: Stephen Son was a part owner and operator of two corporations. Because the businesses were corporations, Son was not personally liable for the debts of either one.

Jinsoo Kim invested a total of about $170,000 in the companies. Eventually, both of them failed, and Kim lost his investment. Son felt guilty over Kim's losses.

Later, Son and Kim met in a sushi restaurant and drank heroic quantities of alcohol. At one point, Son pricked his finger with a safety pin and wrote the following in his own

> ### KIM V. SON
> 2009 Cal. App. LEXIS 2011, 2009 WL 597232
> Court of Appeal of California, 2009

blood: "Sir, please forgive me. Because of my deeds, you have suffered financially. I will repay you to the best of my ability." In return, Kim agreed not to sue him for the money owed.

Son later refused to honor the bloody document and pay Kim the money. Kim filed suit to enforce their contract.

The judge determined that the promise did not create a contract because there had been no consideration.

You Be the Judge: *Was there consideration?*

Argument for Kim: As a part of the deal made at the sushi restaurant, Kim agreed not to sue Son. What could be more of a forbearance than that? Kim had a right to sue at any time, and he gave the right up. Even if Kim was unlikely to win, Son would still prefer not to be sued.

Besides, the fact that Son signed the agreement in blood indicates how seriously he took the obligation to repay his loyal investor. At a minimum, Son eased his guilty conscience by making the agreement, and surely that is worth something.

Argument for Son: Who among you has not at one point or another become intoxicated, experienced emotions more powerful than usual, and regretted them the next morning? Whether calling an ex-girlfriend and professing endless love or writing out an agreement in your own blood, it is all the same.

A promise not to file a meritless lawsuit has no value at all. It did not matter to Son whether or not Kim filed suit because Kim could not possibly win. If this promise counts as value, then the concept of consideration is meaningless because anyone can promise not to sue anytime. Son had no obligation to pay Kim. And the bloody napkin does not change that fact because it was made without consideration of any kind. It is an ordinary promise, not a contract that creates any legal obligation.

13-1b **What Is a Bargained-for Exchange?**

Bargained for

When something is sought by the promisor and given by the promise in exchange for their promises

The parties must bargain for the consideration. Something is **Bargained for** if it is sought by the promisor and given by the promisee in exchange for their respective promises. Eliza hires Joe to be her public relations manager for $15,000 a year. Both Eliza and Joe have made promises to induce the other's action. But what if the going rate for a PR manager with Joe's experience is $65,000?

Joe made a bad deal, but that does not mean it lacked consideration. **Courts do not analyze the economic terms of an exchange to determine whether consideration was adequate.** For consideration to be adequate in the eyes of the law, it must provide some benefit to the promisor or some detriment to the promisee, but these need not amount to much. Law professors often call this the "peppercorn rule," a reference to a Civil War–era case in which a judge mused, "What is a valuable consideration? A peppercorn."[3] Here, both Eliza and Joe are promisor and promisee; each receives a benefit and incurs a detriment.

Gold can make people crazy. At the turn of the 20th century, John Tuppela joined the gold rush to Alaska. He bought a mine, but sadly, his prospecting proved futile. In 1914, a court declared him insane and locked him in an institution. Four years later, Tuppela emerged and learned to his ecstasy that gold had been discovered in his mine, now valued at over half a million dollars. Then the bad news hit: A court-appointed guardian had sold the mine for pennies while Tuppela was institutionalized. Destitute and forlorn, Tuppela turned to his lifelong friend, Embola, saying, "If you will give me $50 so I can go to Alaska and get my property back, I will pay you $10,000 when I win my property." After Tuppela won back his mine, his court-appointed guardian refused to pay Embola, arguing that $50 was not enough consideration to support Tuppela's $10,000 promise. The court disagreed. Embola and Tuppela freely bargained for those terms.

Although the difference between Embola's $50 and Tuppela's $10,000 was staggering, it was not for the court to judge whether it was an intelligent bargain. Both parties knew what they were doing, Embola undertook a risk, and his $50 was valid consideration. The question of adequacy is for the parties as they bargain, not for the courts.

---

[3] Hobbs v. Duff, 23 Cal. 596 (1863).

EXAM Strategy

Question: 50 Cent has been rapping all day, and he is very thirsty. He pulls his Ferrari into the parking lot of a convenience store. The store turns out to be closed, but luckily for him, a soda machine sits outside. While walking over to it, he realizes that he has left his wallet at home. Frustrated, he whistles to a 10-year-old kid who is walking by. "Hey kid!" he shouts. "I need to borrow fifty cents!" "I know you are!" the kid replies. Fiddy tries again. "No, no, I need to *borrow* fifty cents!" The kid walks over. "Well, I'm not going to just give you my last fifty cents. But maybe you can sell me something." 50 Cent cannot believe it, but he really is very thirsty. He takes off a Rolex, which is his least expensive bling. "How about this?" "Deal," the kid says, handing over two quarters. Is the kid entitled to keep the luxury watch?

Strategy: Even in extreme cases, courts rarely take an interest in *how much* consideration is given, or whether everyone got a "good deal." Even though the Rolex is worth thousands of times more than the quarters, the quarters still count under the peppercorn rule.

Result: After this transaction, 50 Cent may have second thoughts, but they will be too late. The kid committed an act by handing over his money—he was under no legal obligation to do so. And 50 Cent received something of small but measureable value. So there is consideration to support this deal, and 50 Cent would not get his watch back.

13-2 WHAT CONSIDERATION IS NOT

For centuries, scholars and judges have tried unsuccessfully to craft a single, simple rule of consideration but a rigid application of these rules would sometimes interfere with legitimate business goals or, in the worst case, lead to an unfair outcome. As a result, **courts have created three exceptions to the basic rule of consideration: illusory promises, preexisting duties, and past consideration.** Of course, exceptions are the spice of law, and these consideration rules provide us with a rackful. Why, in some cases, we have exceptions to the exception.

> Of course, exceptions are the spice of law, and these consideration rules provide us with a rackful.

13-2a **Illusory Promises**

Annabel calls Jim and says, "I'll sell you my bicycle for 325 bucks. Interested?" Jim says, "I'll look at it tonight in the bike rack. If I like what I see, I'll pay you in the morning." At sunrise, Jim shows up with the $325, but Annabel refuses to sell. Can Jim enforce their deal? No. He said he would buy the bicycle *if he liked it*, keeping for himself the power to get out of the agreement for any reason at all. He is not *committing* himself to do anything, and the law considers his promise illusory—that is, not really a promise at all. **An illusory promise is not consideration.** Because he has given no consideration, there is no contract, and *neither party* can enforce the deal.

Let's revisit the Blockbuster case from the opening scenario. Blockbuster's clickwrap box read, in part:

> "Blockbuster may at any time, and at its sole discretion, modify these Terms and Conditions of Use, including without limitation the Privacy Policy, with or without notice. Such modifications will be effective immediately upon posting."

Because Blockbuster had the ability to change the rules at any time for any reason, the court determined that the contract was illusory and that Harris was not bound by Blockbuster's arbitration clause.[4]

Exception: Requirements and Output Contracts under the UCC

Requirements contract
Contract in which a buyer agrees to purchase all of her goods from one seller

Output contract
Contract in which the seller guarantees to sell all of its output to one buyer, and the buyer agrees to accept the entire quantity

In a **requirements contract**, the buyer agrees to purchase 100 percent of her goods from one seller. The seller agrees to sell the buyer whatever quantity she reasonably needs. The quantity is not stated in the contract, though it may be estimated based on previous years or best calculations. In an **output contract**, the seller guarantees to sell 100 percent of its output to one buyer, and the buyer agrees to accept the entire quantity. For example, a vineyard might agree to sell all of its wine to a chain restaurant.

The common law frowned on requirements and output contracts because the promisors are making no real commitment, and hence are giving no consideration. In the view of common-law courts, these were illusory contracts.

The problem with the common-law rule was that many merchants valued these contracts. Consider the utility of requirements contracts. From the buyer's viewpoint, a requirements contract provides flexibility. The buyer can adjust purchases based on consumer demands. The agreement also guarantees her a source of goods in a competitive market. For a seller, the requirements agreement will ensure him at least this one outlet and will prevent competitors from selling to this buyer. The contract should enable the seller to spend less on marketing and may enable him to predict sales more accurately. Output contracts have similar value.

The UCC responded in a forthright fashion: **Section 2-306 expressly allows output and requirements contracts in the sale of goods.**[5] However, the Code places one limitation on how much the buyer may demand (or the seller may offer):

> A term which measures the quantity by the output of the seller or the requirements of the buyer means such actual output or requirements as may occur *in good faith*, ...

The "good faith" phrase is critical. In requirements contracts, courts have ruled that it is the "good faith" that a buyer brings to the deal that represents her consideration.[6] In other words, by agreeing to act in good faith, she actually is limiting her options. Because she is obligating herself, the deal becomes binding. Beware that this is not just wordplay. A buyer *must make its requirement demands in good faith*, based on the expectations the parties had when they signed the deal.

Suppose that you operate a T-shirt business. You and a wholesaler agree on a two-year requirements contract with a fixed price of $3 per T-shirt and an estimate of 150 T-shirts per

---

[4]Harris v. Blockbuster Inc., 622 F. Supp. 2d 396 (N.D. Tex. 2009).
[5]UCC §2-306(2) permits a related type of contract, the exclusive dealing agreement. Here, either a buyer or a seller of goods agrees to deal exclusively with the other party. The results are similar to an output or requirements agreement. Once again, one party is receiving a guarantee in exchange for a promise that the common law would have considered illusory. Under the Code, such a deal is enforceable.
[6]Famous Brands, Inc. v. David Sherman Corp., 814 F.2d 517 (8th Cir. 1987).

week. If business is slow the first two months, you are permitted to purchase only 25 T-shirts per week if that is all you are selling. Should sales suddenly boom and you need 200 per week, you may also require that many. Both of those demands are made in good faith. But suppose the price of cotton skyrockets and the wholesale cost of T-shirts everywhere suddenly doubles. You have a two-year guaranteed price of $3 per T-shirt. Could you demand 2,000 T-shirts per week, knowing that you will be able to resell the shirts to other retailers for a big profit? No. That is not acting in good faith based on the original expectations of the parties. The wholesaler is free to ignore your exorbitant demand. The legal requirement has come full circle: Your good faith is valid consideration and makes the deal enforceable—but it is binding on you, too.

EXAM Strategy

Question: Will bought simple wood furniture and custom-painted it for sale to interior designers. He entered into a written agreement to buy all the furniture he needed, for two years, from Wood Knot, Inc. Wood Knot agreed to supply Will with all the furniture he requested. During the second year, Will's business grew, and he requested 28 percent more furniture than in the first year. Wood Knot would not deliver unless Will would pay a higher price per unit, which Will would not. Will sued. What kind of a contract was this? Will Will win? Why or why not?

Strategy: Because this agreement did not specify the quantity of goods being sold, we know that it was either a requirements contract or an output contract. Review the difference between the two. Which was this agreement? These contracts are now legal, with one major limitation. What is that limitation? Apply it here.

Result: This was a requirements contract because Will agreed to purchase all his furniture from Wood Knot. Under the UCC, requirements contracts are enforceable, provided the buyer makes his demands in good faith. Will's increased order was a result of his booming business. Indeed, he entered into this agreement to protect his ability to grow his company. He made the request in good faith, the contract is enforceable, and yes—Will will win.

13-2b Preexisting Duty

Imagine yourself at the beach right now (in our dreams). Into the water you go, where an undertow grabs you and carries you out into deep water. The lifeguard leaps from her chair and runs to the water's edge. But instead of jumping in, she yells to you, "I won't get my hair wet unless you pay me $100." Helplessly, you signal your assent. Once you are safely back on shore, do you owe the lifeguard anything?

You may be relieved to hear that the answer is no. **If someone provides a service that she is already obligated to do, that act does not count as consideration.** A lifeguard who saves people cannot receive additional money for her rescues because, well, that is what lifeguards are supposed to do. A police officer who apprehends a criminal in the line of duty cannot collect the posted reward. A banker cannot get a bonus for upholding the law. In these cases, consideration does not induce their actions, duty does. Since they already have the duty to perform, they suffer no legal detriment when they do their job.

In the following Landmark Case, many fishy things occurred. There was a catch. But was it sufficient consideration?

Landmark Case

ALASKA PACKERS' ASS'N V. DOMENICO

117 F. 99
United States Court of Appeals for the Ninth Circuit,
1902

Facts: Twenty-one seamen entered into a written contract with the Alaska Packer's Association (APA) to sail from San Francisco to Pyramid Harbor, Alaska, where they would work as fisherman and sailors during the salmon-fishing season. The workers agreed to perform "regular ship's duty, both up and down, discharging and loading; and to do any other work whatsoever when requested to do so by the captain." In return, the APA was to pay each worker $50 for the season, and two cents for each red salmon he caught.

A few days after arriving at Pyramid Harbor, the men collectively stopped working and demanded an additional $50—or else they would return to San Francisco. At that point, it was impossible for the APA to replace them, so after several days of unproductive negotiations, the APA's superintendent in Alaska yielded to their demands—and agreed to double their pay.

When they returned to San Francisco at the close of the fishing season, the seamen demanded their $100, but the APA refused, claiming that the Alaska agreement failed for lack of consideration. The lower court agreed with the seamen, but the APA appealed.

Issue: *Was there consideration for the promise to pay more money?*

Excerpts from Judge Ross's Decision:[7] The seamen agreed in writing, for certain stated compensation, to render their services to the APA in remote waters where the season for conducting fishing operations is extremely short, and in which enterprise the APA had a large amount of money invested; and, after having entered upon the discharge of their contract, and at a time when it was impossible for APA to secure other men in their places, the seamen, without any valid cause, absolutely refused to continue the services they were under contract to perform unless the APA would consent to pay them more money.

Consent to such a demand, under such circumstances, if given, was, in our opinion, without consideration, for the reason that it was based solely upon the seamen's agreement to render the exact services, and none other, that they were already under contract to render. The case shows that they willfully and arbitrarily broke that obligation.

No astute reasoning can change the plain fact that the party who refuses to perform, and thereby coerces a promise from the other party to the contract to pay him an increased compensation for doing that which he is legally bound to do, takes an unjustifiable advantage of the necessities of the other party. Surely it would be a travesty on justice to hold that the party so making the promise for extra pay was estopped from asserting that the promise was without consideration. A party cannot lay the foundation of an estoppel by his own wrong, where the promise is simply a repetition of a subsisting legal promise.

There can be no consideration for the promise of the other party, and there is no warrant for inferring that the parties have voluntarily rescinded or modified their contract. The promise cannot be legally enforced, although the other party has completed his contract in reliance upon it.

The judgment must be reversed. It is so ordered.

Exception: Additional Work

When a party agrees to do something above and beyond what he is obligated to do, his promise is generally valid consideration. If the seamen had agreed to work overtime or commit to a longer fishing season in exchange for the increased pay, the court would have upheld their second contract. The APA would have been obligated to pay because the seamen's extra work would have been valid consideration.

---

[7]For readability, the authors have inserted "APA" and "seamen" instead of "appellant" and "libelants."

Exception: Modification

Under the common law, additional consideration is necessary for a modification of contract terms because it is unfair for one party to get something more, while the other does not. As we saw in the *Alaska Packers* case, if one side unfairly coerces the other into the changes, the modification is invalid.

Once again, the UCC has changed the common law, making it easier for merchants to modify agreements for the sale of goods. **UCC §2-209 provides:**

- An agreement modifying a contract within this Article needs no consideration to be binding.

- A signed agreement which excludes modification or rescission except by a signed writing cannot be otherwise modified or rescinded.

Here is how these two provisions work together. Mike's Magic Mania (MMM) agrees to deliver 500 rabbits and 500 top hats to State University for the school's Sleight of Hand 101 course. The goods, including 100 cages and 1,000 pounds of rabbit food, are to arrive no later than September 1, in time for the new semester, with payment on delivery. By September 20, no rabbits have appeared, in or out of hats. The university buys similar products from another supply house at a 25 percent steeper price and sues MMM for the difference. Mike claims that in early September, the dean had orally agreed to permit delivery in October. The dean is on sabbatical in Tahiti and cannot be reached for comment. Is the alleged modification valid?

Under the common law, the modification would have been void because MMM gave no consideration for the extended delivery date. However, this is a sale of goods, and under UCC §2-209, an oral modification may be valid even without consideration. Unfortunately for Mike, though, the original agreement included a clause forbidding oral modification. Any changes had to be in writing, signed by both parties. Mike never obtained such a document. Even if the dean did make the oral agreement, the university wins.

If both parties agree that a modification is necessary, the surest way to accomplish that result is to rescind the original contract and draft a new one. To **rescind** means to cancel. Thus, if neither party has completed its obligations, the agreement to rescind will terminate each party's rights and obligations under the old contract. This should be done in writing. Then the parties sign the new agreement. Courts will *generally* enforce a rescission and modification provided both parties voluntarily entered into it, in good faith.

Rescind
To cancel

EXAM Strategy

Question: Star Struck, a Hollywood talent agency, employs Puneet as one of its young agents and Max as a part-time delivery boy. Puneet's contract is for one year. She earns $5,000 per month, payable on the last day of each month. After she has worked at the firm for four months, a Star Struck executive says to her, "We are having cash flow problems. We cannot pay you this month, and will probably fall about two months behind. However, if you will agree to do Max's job for the next few months, we can pay you on time." Puneet cheerfully agrees to the deal. However, after a few weeks of the extra labor, Puneet confesses that she is overwhelmed and can no longer do Max's job. Star Struck fires her. Puneet sues. Was there a binding agreement for Puneet to do Max's work?

Strategy: Star Struck made an offer to Puneet and she accepted it. But a contract needs more than offer and acceptance. Both parties must give consideration. Had they done more than they were required to do under their preexisting duty?

Result: A promise to do what a party is already obligated to do is not consideration. Star Struck was required to pay Puneet every month, so its "offer" included no consideration. Without consideration, there can be no agreement. Puneet was not obligated to do Max's job, and she will win this lawsuit.

Exception: Unforeseen Circumstances

Hugo has a deal to repair major highways. Hugo hires Hal's Hauling to cart soil and debris. Hal's trucks begin work, but after crossing the work site several times, they sink to their axles in sinister, sucking slime. Hal demands an additional 35 percent payment from Hugo to complete the job, pointing out that the surface was dry and cracked and that neither Hal nor Hugo was aware of the subsurface water. Hal howls that he must use different trucks with different tires and work more slowly to permit the soil to dry. Hugo hems and haws and finally agrees. But when the hauling is finished, Hugo refuses to pay the extra money. Is Hugo liable?

Yes. When unforeseen circumstances cause a party to make a promise regarding an unfinished project, that promise is generally valid consideration. Even though Hal is only promising to finish what he was already obligated to do, his promise is valid consideration because neither party knew of the subsoil mud. Hal was facing a situation quite different from what the parties anticipated. It is almost as though he were undertaking a new project. Hal has given consideration, and Hugo is bound by his promise to pay extra money

13-2c Past Consideration

A completed act cannot be the basis for consideration. When they learn that their son earned an "A" in Advanced Business Law, Pablo's doting parents promise to buy him a car. This star student will surely know that the generous promise is unenforceable in court. It lacks consideration because it is based on something Pablo has already done. However, if early in the semester, Pablo's parents make the same promise, consideration is present. Pablo's detriment is his future work, which is induced by the promise of a reward.

Exception: Parties Agree in Advance

Moore was psychic. She foresaw that Elmer was going to die before a certain date. In gratitude and amazement, Elmer gave her a signed letter stating that if what she said proved true, he would pay off her mortgage. Apparently, Moore was clairvoyant: Elmer died before her predicted date. What happened next is not difficult to predict. Moore's heirs refused to pay her, claiming his promise lacked consideration.

The court agreed. Although Moore argued that the promise was payment for her services, she had voluntarily offered the information and after that, Elmer gave her the note. Had the parties agreed in advance that he would pay her if her predictions proved true, the court would have foreseen a different outcome: **Past consideration is valid consideration when the parties agree that it will be *in advance*.**

Exception: Promissory Estoppel

As we saw in Chapter 11, promissory estoppel is a theory courts use to enforce promises that are not contracts. It applies when a defendant makes a promise, which the plaintiff reasonably relied on, and enforcing that promise is the only way to avoid injustice.

Courts sometimes use promissory estoppel to validate promises based on past consideration. Feinberg had been a loyal employee for 37 years. She was so beloved that, in gratitude for her service, her employer's board of directors elected to pay her $200 a month for the rest of her life, once she retired. Two years later, she retired in reliance on her monthly pension, which she enjoyed—until new management decided to revoke it. By this time, she was ill, unemployable, and wholly dependent on the pension. The court held for Feinberg, even though the promise was based on past consideration. Because she justifiably relied on the board's offer, Feinberg's pension was upheld under promissory estoppel.

13-3 SPECIAL CONSIDERATION CASES

We have seen what consideration is and what it is not. Now we will look at some special cases that involve two very familiar four-letter words: debt and work.

13-3a Settlement of Debts

You claim that your friend Felicity owes you $90,000, but she refuses to pay. Finally, when you are desperate, Felicity offers you a cashier's check for $60,000—provided you accept it as full settlement. To get your hands on some money, you agree and cash the check. The next day, you sue Felicity for $30,000. Who wins? It will depend principally upon one major issue: Was Felicity's debt liquidated or unliquidated?

Liquidated Debt

A **liquidated debt** is one in which there is no dispute about the amount owed. A loan is a typical example. If a bank lends you $10,000, and the note obligates you to repay that amount on June 1 of the following year, you clearly owe that sum. The debt is liquidated.

One famous jurist commented that a creditor may accept anything—"a horse, hawk, or robe"—in satisfaction of a liquidated debt.[8]

But the one thing he may not accept? Less than one hundred cents on the dollar. **In cases of liquidated debt, if the creditor agrees to take less than the full amount as full payment, her agreement is not binding.** The debtor has given no consideration to support the creditor's promise to accept a reduced payment, and therefore the creditor is not bound by her word. The reasoning is simply that the debtor is already obligated to pay the full amount, so no bargaining could reasonably cause the creditor to accept less. If Felicity's debt to you is liquidated, your agreement to accept $60,000 is not binding, and you will successfully sue for the balance.

> **Liquidated debt**
> A debt in which there is no dispute about the amount owed

> But the one thing he may not accept? Less than one hundred cents on the dollar.

Exception: Different Performance.   There is one important exception to this rule. If the debtor offers a *different performance* to settle the liquidated debt, and the creditor agrees to take it as full settlement, the agreement is binding. Suppose that Felicity, instead of paying $60,000, offers you five acres in Alaska, and you accept. When you accept the deed to the land, you have given up your entire claim, regardless of the land's precise value.

Unliquidated Debt: Accord and Satisfaction

A debt is **unliquidated** for either of two reasons: (1) The parties dispute whether any money is owed, or (2) the parties agree that some money is owed but dispute how much. When a debt is unliquidated for either reason, the parties may enter into a binding agreement to settle for less than what the creditor demands.

> **Unliquidated**
> A debt that is disputed because the parties disagree over its existence or amount

[8]Birdsall v. Saucier, 1992 WL 33731 (Conn. Super. Ct. 1992).

If there is no doubt about the amount owed, that debt is liquidated.

Such a compromise will be enforced if:

- The debt is unliquidated;

- The parties agree that the creditor will accept as full payment a sum less than she has claimed; and

- The debtor pays the amount agreed upon.

This agreement is called an **accord and satisfaction**. The accord is the agreement to settle for less than the creditor claims. The satisfaction is the actual payment of that compromised sum. An accord and satisfaction is valid consideration to support the creditor's agreement to drop all claims. Each party is giving up something: the creditor gives up her full claim, and the debtor gives up his assertion that he owed little or nothing.

Accord and satisfaction

A completed agreement to settle a debt for less than the sum claimed

Accord and Satisfaction by Check.   Most accord and satisfaction agreements involve payment by check. UCC §3-311 governs these agreements, using the same common-law rules described earlier.[9] The Code specifies that when the debtor writes "full settlement" on the check, a creditor who cashes the check generally has entered into an accord and satisfaction. If Felicity's debt is unliquidated, and she gives you a check with "full payment of all debts" written on the face in bold letters, the moment you deposit the check, you lose any claim to more money. What happens if the debtor makes such a notation but the creditor changes it? A massage therapist learned the answer and felt sore for days.

HENCHES V. TAYLOR

138 Wash. App. 1026
Washington Court of Appeals, 2007

Facts: Jim Henches, a licensed massage therapist, treated Benjamin Taylor after he was injured in a car accident. When all treatments were finished, Henches billed Taylor for more than $7,000. Taylor's insurance company claimed the bill was exorbitant and paid only $2,625, for 24 massage treatments.

Henches continued to send bills to Taylor, not only for the balance due but for additional time spent consulting with Taylor's other health care providers, preparing to testify in

Taylor's personal injury lawsuit, and attempting to collect his debts. In response to a bill for $11,945.86, Taylor's lawyer, James Harris, sent Henches a letter, stating:

I have reviewed your billing statements and am having a difficult time understanding a number of charges you included. By my calculations, the amount owed to you is approximately $5,243.45. I have enclosed a check for that amount as payment in full to settle Mr. Taylor's account with you.

---

[9]A check is legally an instrument, which is why this section comes from Article 3 of the Code. For a full discussion of instruments, see Chapters 25–26.

The letter was accompanied by a check with "final payment" written on the notation line. Henches filed suit, seeking the full balance. Then he wrote "attorney/fee" on the check, over the word "final," and deposited the check.

The trial court gave summary judgment to Taylor, ruling that deposit of the check constituted accord and satisfaction. Henches appealed.

Issue: *Was there an accord and satisfaction, discharging the debt?*

Excerpts from Judge Ellington's Decision: A debt is discharged by accord and satisfaction when the debtor and creditor agree to settle a claim by some performance other than that which is claimed due, and the creditor accepts the substituted performance as full satisfaction of the claim. Accord and satisfaction requires a bona fide dispute, an agreement to settle the dispute for a certain sum, and performance of the agreement.

Taylor easily satisfied the first element of accord and satisfaction. The parties' contracts did not establish a liquidated amount for the services provided, and the letter that accompanied Taylor's check to Henches demonstrates a good faith dispute over the amount owed.

As with any contract, an accord and satisfaction cannot be formed without a meeting of the minds. But the required intent is shown when payment is offered in full satisfaction and is accompanied by conduct from which the creditor cannot fail to understand that payment is tendered on condition its acceptance constitutes satisfaction.

Given the undisputed facts here, Henches could not fail to understand that the check was offered on condition of full settlement. Henches' alteration of the "final payment" language is further demonstration that he read and understood the notation. Taylor tendered a check in final payment and Henches deposited the check, thereby accepting that payment.

A creditor can accept payment and avoid formation of an accord only where both parties understand before payment is accepted that the payment will not settle the claim. Henches contends his alteration of the check prevents accord and satisfaction. But a creditor cannot prevent formation of an accord by making a unilateral change to a draft tendered in full payment, even if the creditor endorses the check with the words accepted as partial payment and not as payment in full and not as an accord and satisfaction of the known full amount legally due and owing.

Where the amount due is in dispute, and the debtor sends cash or check for less than the amount claimed, clearly expressing his intention that it is sent as a settlement in full, and not on account or in part payment, the retention and use of the money or the cashing of the check is almost always held to be an acceptance of the offer operating as full satisfaction, even though the creditor may assert or send word to the debtor that the sum is received only in part payment.

Henches' alteration of the check was a unilateral act not communicated to Taylor. Accord and satisfaction discharged Taylor's debts to Henches. We affirm the trial court's summary judgment dismissal of Henches' suit.

UCC Exceptions. The Code creates two exceptions for accord and satisfaction cases involving checks. The first exception concerns "organizations," which typically are businesses. The general rule of §3-311 is potentially calamitous to them because a company that receives thousands of checks every day is unlikely to inspect all notations. A consumer who owes $12,000 on a credit card might write "full settlement" on a $200 check, potentially extinguishing the entire debt through accord and satisfaction. Under the exception, if an organization notifies a debtor that any offers to settle for less than the debt claimed must be made to a particular official, and the check is sent to anyone else in the organization, depositing the check generally does *not* create an accord and satisfaction. Thus, a clerk who deposits 900 checks daily for payment of MasterCard debts will not have inadvertently entered into dozens of accord and satisfaction agreements.

The second exception allows a way out to most creditors who have inadvertently created an accord and satisfaction. If, within 90 days of cashing a "full payment" check, the creditor offers repayment of the same amount to the debtor, there is no accord and satisfaction. Homer claims that Virgil owes him $7 million but foolishly cashes Virgil's check for $3 million, without understanding that "paid in full" means just what it says. Homer has created an accord and satisfaction. But if he promptly sends Virgil a check for $3 million, he has undone the agreement and may sue for the full amount.

13-3b Employment Agreements

In a noncompete agreement, an employee promises not to work for a competitor for some time after leaving the company. It used to be that these covenants were rare and reserved for top officers, but they have now become commonplace throughout many organizations. We will talk about them more in the next chapter, but often these covenants raise an issue of consideration: What consideration does the employee receive for signing a covenant not to compete? After all, the company is already under an obligation to pay the employee for working. What additional value does the employee receive in return for signing the agreement?

The following case reflects the current majority view. Sometimes consideration issues can drive you nuts.

SNIDER BOLT & SCREW V. QUALITY SCREW & NUT

2009 U.S. Dist. LEXIS 50797, 2009 WL 1657549
United States District Court for the Western District of Kentucky, 2009

Facts: James Scott signed a covenant not to compete when he went to work for Snider Bolt & Screw. The agreement prohibited him from taking a job with a competitor for one year after leaving Snider. Three years later, Scott quit his job at Snider and immediately went to work for Quality Screw & Nut (QSN).

Snider obtained a temporary restraining order that banned Scott from working at his new job. QSN argued that the covenant not to compete was void for lack of consideration. It asked the court to lift the temporary restraining order.

Issue: *Did the covenant not to compete lack consideration?*

Excerpt from Judge Heyburn's Decision: Snider says that when Scott signed his covenant not to compete, he did so based upon an implied promise that Snider would continue his employment. Indeed, Snider did maintain Scott's employment until Scott himself left his job. Kentucky courts have found quite specifically that "where an employer has fulfilled an implied promise to continue the employee's employment, that promise is sufficient consideration [to] support enforcement of the employee's promise not to compete." The Kentucky Supreme Court subsequently held that even continued at-will employment would be sufficient consideration. Here, Scott worked for another three years and left on his own accord to join QSN. These circumstances fit within the rule and the Court finds that the Covenant is supported by adequate consideration.

Consequently, the Court has no basis for sustaining QSN's motion.

13-4 MORAL CONSIDERATION

Some promises should not be broken. No one wants to live in a society where donors to charity go back on their word or promises to widows and orphans are ignored. These are commitments whose obligation is moral, not necessarily legal, in nature. Under some circumstances, courts will uphold agreements with "moral consideration."

Consider a pledge to charity. If Dave promises to give $25,000 to "Save the Mexican Spotted Owl" and then fails to make the donation, there is no consideration because he has received nothing in return. If the nonprofit sues to enforce the promise, it cannot show that it gave anything up in return for Dave's promise, so there is no consideration.[10]

Nevertheless, some courts will force donors like Dave to make good on their pledges anyway. If, based on Dave's promise, the charity funded a bird-watching program or began construction on a sanctuary, it can prove reliance. As we have seen, judges can use the doctrine of promissory estoppel to enforce promises if there has been reliance and a great injustice would otherwise result.

Other courts have dispensed with the reliance requirement, requiring promisors to pay if breaching would simply be unjust. Especially in the case of large donations, courts will often cite the "grave injustices" that can follow from breaking a promise. "If you don't give 'Save the Mexican Spotted Owl' the $25,000 you've pledged, then the bird will become extinct," a judge might say.

It is unwise to make charitable pledges, especially large pledges, unless you intend to follow through.

Ethics   What is a "moral obligation" and when should it be enforced? Courts are divided on this issue. Two cases illustrate the leading schools of thought:

In an Alabama case, Webb saved McGowin's life by preventing a 75 lb. block of wood from falling on his head. Webb was permanently disabled in the accident and was never able to work again. Later, McGowin promised to give Webb money every two weeks for the rest of his life. McGowin made the payments for a while but then stopped. Webb sued. The court found that "moral consideration" was present because McGowin received a material benefit. Webb was entitled to the payments to prevent substantial injustice.[11]

A famous Massachusetts case reaches the opposite conclusion. Twenty-five-year-old Levi Wyman contracted an illness while at sea. Mills nursed Wyman during his sickness. After Wyman's death, his parents promised to repay Mills for the expenses incurred in caring for their son. Later, Wyman refused to pay, so Mills filed suit. The court sided with Wyman, holding that a moral obligation was not enough to constitute consideration.[12]

Mills v. Wyman is the majority rule; *Webb v. McGowin* is the minority rule. But some commentators have argued that this discrepancy serves another moral purpose: It allows judges the leeway to enforce promises when they feel enforcement is just. Do you agree? How else can these cases be reconciled? Is it possible to formulate a single rule applying to every case of moral obligation?

It is important to note that applications of promissory estoppel and similar doctrines are rare. Ordinarily, if there is no consideration, then there is no contract. However, in extreme cases, it is possible for a court to enforce a deal even without consideration. But this is not something you can count on.

---

[10]An exception to this, of course, would be if the charity agreed to give Dave something at the time he made the pledge. As a "fix" for consideration problems, many charities send donors something of trivial value when pledges are made—maybe a water bottle or a tote bag. Under the peppercorn rule, even something of small value counts as a legal act, and it converts a mere promise of a donation into an enforceable contract.

[11]Webb v. McGowin, 168 So. 196 (Ala. 1935).

[12]Mills v. Wyman 20 Mass. (3 Pick.) 207 (Mass. Sup. Jud. Ct. 1825).

Chapter Conclusion

This ancient doctrine of consideration is simple to state but subtle to apply. The parties must bargain and enter into an exchange of promises or actions. If they do not, there is no consideration and the courts are unlikely to enforce any promise made. A variety of exceptions modify the law, but a party wishing to render its future more predictable—the purpose of a contract—will rely on a solid bargain and exchange.

EXAM REVIEW

1. **CONSIDERATION**   There are two basic rules of consideration:

   - Value: Both parties must get something of *measureable value* from the contract.
   - Bargained for Exchange: The two parties must have *bargained for* whatever was exchanged.

2. **ACT, FORBEARANCE, OR PROMISE**   The item of value can be either an act or a forbearance.

EXAM Strategy

Question: An aunt saw her eight-year-old nephew enter the room, remarked what a nice boy he was, and said, "I would like to take care of him now." She promptly wrote a note, promising to pay the boy $3,000 upon her death. Her estate refused to pay. Is it obligated to do so?

Strategy: A contract is enforceable only if the parties have given consideration. The consideration might be an act or a forbearance. Did the nephew give consideration? (See the "Result" at the end of this section.)

3. **ADEQUACY**   The courts examine whether consideration exists, but will seldom inquire if it was enough consideration or a smart financial deal. This is the "peppercorn rule."

4. **ILLUSORY PROMISES**   An illusory promise is not consideration.

EXAM Strategy

Question: Eagle ran convenience stores. He entered into an agreement with Commercial Movie in which Commercial would provide Eagle with DVDs for rental. Eagle would pay Commercial 50 percent of the rental revenues. If Eagle stopped using Commercial's service, Eagle could not use a competitor's services for 18 months. The agreement also provided: "Commercial shall not be liable for compensation or damages of any kind, whether on account of the loss by Eagle of profits, sales or expenditures, or on account of any other event or cause whatsoever." Eagle complied with the agreement for two years but then began using a competitor's service, and Commercial sued. Eagle claimed that the agreement was unenforceable for lack of consideration. Please rule.

Strategy: In this case, both parties seem to have given consideration. But there is a flaw in the "promise" that Commercial made. Commercial can never be liable to Eagle—no matter what happens. (See the "Result" at the end of this section.)

5. **REQUIREMENT AND OUTPUT CONTRACTS** Under sales law, requirement and output contracts are valid. Although one side controls the quantity, its agreement to make demands *in good faith* is consideration.

6. **PREEXISTING DUTY** Under the doctrine of preexisting duty, a promise to do something that the party is already legally obligated to perform is generally not consideration.

7. **LIQUIDATED DEBT** A liquidated debt is one in which there is no dispute about the amount owed. For a liquidated debt, a creditor's promise to accept less than the full amount is not binding.

8. **UNLIQUIDATED DEBT** For an unliquidated debt, if the parties agree that the creditor will accept less than the full amount claimed and the debtor performs, there is an accord and satisfaction and the creditor may not claim any balance.

9. **"FULL PAYMENT" NOTATIONS** In most states, payment by a check that has a "full payment" notation will create an accord and satisfaction unless the creditor is an organization that has notified the debtor that full payment offers must go to a certain officer.

EXAM Strategy

Question: When White's wife died, he filed a claim with Boston Mutual for $10,000 death benefits under her insurance policy. The insurer rejected the claim, saying that his wife had misrepresented her medical condition in the application form. The company sent White a check for $478.75, which it said represented "a full refund of all applicable premiums paid" for the coverage. White deposited the check. Had the parties reached an accord and satisfaction?

Strategy: The UCC permits parties to enter into an accord and satisfaction by check. The debtor must make clear that the check is offered in full payment of a disputed debt. Debtors generally do that by writing "Final Settlement," "Accepted as Full Payment of All Debts," or some similar notation on the check. Had the insurance company complied with that requirement? (See the "Result" at the end of this section.)

10. **PROMISSORY ESTOPPEL** Sometimes, to prevent injustice, courts will enforce agreements even if no consideration is present. These deals are still not formal contracts, but the courts will enforce a promise nonetheless.

EXAM Strategy

Question: Phil Philanthropist called PBS during a fund drive and pledged to donate $100,000. PBS then planned and began to produce a Fourth of July *Sesame Street* special, counting on the large donation to fund it. Later, Phil changed his mind and said he had decided not to donate the money after all. PBS sued because without the money, it would not be able to complete the show. Will PBS win the lawsuit?

Strategy: Analyze the promise to donate the $100,000. Does it contain consideration? If not, is there any other legal possibility? (See the "Result" at the end of this section.)

2. Result: The nephew gave no consideration. He did not promise to do anything. He committed no act or forbearance. Without consideration, there is no enforceable contract. The estate wins.

4. Result: Commercial's promise was illusory. The company was free to walk away from the deal at any time. Commercial could never be held liable. Commercial gave no consideration, and there was no binding contract for either party to enforce.

9. Result: The insurer merely stated that its check was a refund of premiums. Nowhere did the company indicate that the check was full payment of its disputed obligation. The company should have made it clear that it would not pay any benefits and that this payment was all that it would offer. There was no accord and satisfaction.

10. Result: There is no "regular" consideration here because Phil received no measureable benefit and PBS did not act or forbear. But PBS can likely make a strong case that a great injustice will be done if the money is not paid. A judge might well decide to apply the doctrine of promissory estoppel and require Phil to make the donation.

MULTIPLE-CHOICE QUESTIONS

1. For consideration to exist, there must be:
   (a) A bargained-for exchange
   (b) A manifestation of mutual assent
   (c) Genuineness of assent
   (d) Substantially equal economic benefits to both parties

2. Which of the following requires consideration in order to be binding on the parties?

(a) Modification of a contract involving the sale of real estate

(b) Modification of a sale of goods contract under the UCC

(c) Both A and B

(d) None of the above

3. Ted's wallet is as empty as his bank account, and he needs $3,500 immediately. Fortunately, he has three gold coins that he inherited from his grandfather. Each is worth $2,500, but it is Sunday, and the local rare coins store is closed. When approached, Ted's neighbor Andrea agrees to buy the first coin for $2,300. Another neighbor, Cami, agrees to buy the second for $1,100. A final neighbor, Lorne, offers "all the money I have on me"—$100—for the last coin. Desperate, Ted agrees to the proposal. Which of the deals is supported by consideration?

(a) Ted's agreement with Andrea only

(b) Ted's agreements with Andrea and Cami only

(c) All three of the agreements

(d) None of the agreements

4. In a(n) _____ contract, the seller guarantees to sell 100 percent of its output to one buyer, and the buyer agrees to accept the entire quantity. This kind of arrangement _____ acceptable under the UCC.

(a) output; is

(b) output; is not

(c) requirements; is

(d) requirements; is not

5. Noncompete agreements are common features of employment contracts. Currently, courts _____ enforce these clauses.

(a) always

(b) usually

(c) rarely

(d) never

CASE QUESTIONS

1. American Bakeries had a fleet of over 3,000 delivery trucks. Because of the increasing cost of gasoline, the company was interested in converting the trucks to propane fuel. It signed a requirements contract with Empire Gas, in which Empire would convert "approximately 3,000" trucks to propane fuel, as American Bakeries requested, and would then sell all the required propane fuel to run the trucks. But American Bakeries changed its mind and never requested a single conversion. Empire sued for lost profits. Who won?

2. CeCe Hylton and Edward Meztista, partners in a small advertising firm, agreed to terminate the business and split assets evenly. Meztista gave Hylton a two-page document showing assets, liabilities, and a bottom line of $35,235.67, with half due to each partner. Hylton questioned the accounting and asked to see the books. Meztista did not permit Hylton to see any records and refused to answer her phone calls. Instead, he gave her a check in the amount of $17,617.83, on which he wrote "Final payment/payment in full." Hylton cashed the check, but she wrote on it, "Under protest—cashing this check does not constitute my acceptance of this amount as payment in full." Hylton then filed suit, demanding additional monies. Meztista claimed that the parties had made an accord and satisfaction. What is the best argument for each party? Who should win?

3. **ETHICS** Melnick built a house for Gintzler, but the foundation was defective. Gintzler agreed to accept the foundation if Melnick guaranteed to make future repairs caused by the defects. Melnick agreed but later refused to make any repairs. Melnick argued that his promise to make future repairs was unsupported by consideration. Who will win the suit? Is either party acting unethically? Which one, and why?

4. Sami walks into a restaurant. She is given a menu, which indicates that lobster is $30. Sami orders the lobster. It arrives, and Sami thinks it is very tasty. When the bill arrives, Sami tries to execute a clever ploy she learned about in her business law class. She writes a check to the restaurant for $20 and writes "full settlement" across the top. The waiter accepts the check without looking at it, and the restaurant manager later deposits it in the restaurant's bank account. Is this a liquidated or an unliquidated debt? Is Sami off the hook for the last $10?

5. In the bleachers …

"You're a prince, George!" Mike exclaimed. "Who else would give me a ticket to the big game?"

"No one, Mike, no one."

"Let me offer my thanks. I'll buy you a beer!"

"Ah," George said. "A large beer would hit the spot right now."

"Small. Let me buy you a small beer."

"Ah, well, good enough."

Mike stood and took his wallet from his pocket. He was distressed to find a very small number of bills inside. "There's bad news, George!" he said.

"What's that?"

"I can't buy you the beer, George."

George considered that for a moment. "I'll tell you what, Mike," he said. "If you march to the concession stand right this minute and get me my beer, I won't punch you in the face."

"It's a deal!" Mike said.

Discuss the consideration issues raised by this exchange.

6. Jack Tallas came to the United States from Greece in 1914. He lived in Salt Lake City for nearly 70 years, achieving great success in insurance and real estate. During the last 14 years of his life, his friend Peter Dementas helped him with numerous personal and business chores. Two months before his death, Tallas dictated a memorandum to Dementas, in Greek, stating:

PETER K. DEMENTAS is my best friend I have in this country, and since he came to the United States, he treats me like a father and I think of him as my own son. He takes me in his car grocery shopping. He drives me to the doctor and also takes me every week to Bingham to pick up my mail, collect the rents, and manage my properties. For all the services Peter has given me all these years, I owe to him the amount of $50,000 (Fifty Thousand Dollars). I will shortly change my will to include him as my heir.

Tallas signed the memorandum, but he did not in fact alter his will to include Dementas. The estate refused to pay, and Dementas sued. Was there consideration? Please rule.

DISCUSSION QUESTIONS

Apply the following material to the next two questions.

Some view consideration as a technicality that allows people to make promises and then back out of them. Perhaps all promises should be enforced. In Japan, for example, promises to give gifts are enforceable without consideration.[13]

In the United States, if I promise to give you a gift merely because I feel like being nice, I can freely change my mind as far as contract law is concerned. A court will not make me follow through because there is no consideration.

In Japan, I would be obligated to buy the gift if all other elements of a contract were present—an offer, an acceptance, and so forth.

1. When it comes to giving gifts, which is better—the Japanese or American rule?

2. Are there any specific types of agreements (perhaps high-value, long-term, extremely time-consuming ones) that should definitely require consideration?

3. Albert and Luis, lifelong friends, had a tradition. Every Friday, they took turns going to the corner store and buying what they called a "package"—some vodka and a lottery ticket. One lucky Friday, Albert purchased the package, but Luis scratched off the lottery ticket, only to learn that it was a $20,000 winner. Luis refused to share. Albert sued, claiming the former friends had an enforceable contract supported by valid consideration. Rule.

4. The consideration doctrine is controversial. Critics argue that it is a remnant of a bygone era, lacking any reasonable modern purpose and that it undermines the purpose of contract law, which is to enforce the intention of the parties to an agreement. Should consideration be abolished?

5. Amber Williams and Frederick Ormsby were lovers, embroiled in a turbulent romantic relationship. After knowing each other for a short time, Frederick moved into Amber's house and paid off her $310,000 mortgage. She then gave him title to the house. But their happiness was not to last. The couple canceled their plans to marry and Amber moved out of the house. Two months later, Frederick sought reconciliation. Amber refused to get back together unless Frederick gave her half ownership of the house. Frederick agreed. After the couple split up for the last time, Amber sued for her half of the house. Frederick argued that his promise was not supported by adequate consideration. Was it?

---

[13]See Japan's Civil Code, Article 549.

CHAPTER 14

LEGALITY

Soheil Sadri, a California resident, did some serious gambling at Caesar's Tahoe casino in Nevada. And lost. To keep gambling, he wrote checks to Caesar's and then signed two memoranda pledging to repay all money advanced. After two days, with his losses totaling more than $22,000, he went home. Back in California, Sadri stopped payment on the checks and refused to pay any of the money he owed Caesar's. The casino sued. In defense, Sadri claimed that California law considered his agreements illegal and unenforceable. He was unquestionably correct about one thing: A contract that is illegal is void and unenforceable.

© Honza Krej/Shutterstock.com

A contract that is illegal is void and unenforceable.

14-1 CONTRACTS THAT VIOLATE A STATUTE

In this chapter, we examine a variety of contracts that may be void, or unenforceable. Illegal agreements fall into two groups: those that violate a statute, and those that violate public policy.

14-1a Wagers

Gambling is big business. Almost all states now permit some form of wagering, from casinos to racetracks to lotteries, and they eagerly collect the billions of dollars in revenue generated. Supporters urge that casinos create jobs and steady income, boost state coffers, and take business away from organized crime. Critics argue that naive citizens inevitably lose money they can ill afford to forfeit, and that addicted gamblers destroy their families and weaken the fabric of communities. With citizens and states divided over the ethics of gambling, it is inevitable that we have conflicts such as the dispute between Sadri and Caesar's. The basic rule, however, is clear: **A gambling contract is illegal unless it is a type of wagering *specifically authorized* by state statute.**

In California, as in many states, gambling on credit is not allowed. In other words, it is illegal to lend money to help someone wager. But in Nevada, gambling on credit is legal, and debt memoranda such as Sadri's are enforceable contracts. Caesar's sued Sadri in California (where he lived). The result? The court admitted that California's attitude toward gambling had changed, and that bingo, poker clubs, and lotteries were common. Nonetheless, the court denied that the new tolerance extended to wagering on credit:

> There is a special reason for treating gambling on credit differently from gambling itself. Having lost his or her cash, the pathological gambler will continue to play on credit, if extended, in an attempt to win back the losses. This is why enforcement of gambling debts has always been against public policy in California and should remain so, regardless of shifting public attitudes about gambling itself. If Californians want to play, so be it. But the law should not invite them to play themselves into debt. The judiciary cannot protect pathological gamblers from themselves, but we can refuse to participate in their financial ruin.[1]

Caesar's lost and Sadri kept his money. However, do not become too excited at the prospect of risk-free wagering. Casinos responded to cases like *Sadri* by changing their practices. Most now extend credit only to a gambler who agrees that disputes about repayment will be settled in *Nevada* courts. Because such contracts are legal in that state, the casino is able to obtain a judgment against a defaulting debtor and—yes— enforce that judgment in the gambler's home state.

Despite these more restrictive casino practices, Sadri's dispute is a useful starting place from which to examine contract legality because it illustrates two important themes.

First, morality is a significant part of contract legality. In refusing to enforce an obligation that Sadri undeniably had made, the California court relied on the human and social consequences of gambling and on the ethics of judicial enforcement of gambling debts. Second, "void" really means just that: A court will not intercede to assist either party to an illegal agreement, even if its refusal leaves one party shortchanged.

The gambling may be legal—but what about a gambling contract?

---

[1]Metropolitan Creditors Service of Sacramento v. Sadri, 15 Cal. App. 4th 1821 (Cal. Ct. App. 1993).

14-1b **Insurance**

Another market in which "wagering" unexpectedly pops up is that of insurance. You may certainly insure your own life for any sum you choose. But may you insure someone else's life? **Anyone taking out a policy on the life of another must have an insurable interest in that person.** The most common insurable interest is family connection, such as spouses or parents. Other valid interests include creditor-debtor status (the creditor wants payment if the debtor dies) and business association (an executive in the company is so valuable that the firm will need compensation if something happens to him). If there is no insurable interest, there is generally no contract.

EXAM Strategy

Question: Jimenez sold Breton a used motorcycle for $5,500, payable in weekly installments. Jimenez then purchased an insurance policy on Breton's life, worth $320,000 if Breton died in an accident. Breton promptly died in a collision with an automobile. The insurance company offered only $5,500, representing the balance due on the motorcycle. Jimenez sued, demanding $320,000. Make an argument that the insurance company should win.

Strategy: The issue is whether Jimenez had an insurable interest in Breton's life. If he had no interest, he cannot collect on an insurance policy. If he had an interest, what was it? For how much money?

Result: Jimenez had an interest in Breton's life to insure payment of the motorcycle debt—$5,500. Beyond that, this policy represented a wager by Jimenez that Breton was going to die. Contracts for such wagers are unenforceable. Jimenez is entitled only to $5,500.[2]

14-2 LICENSING STATUTES

You sue your next-door neighbor in small claims court, charging that he keeps a kangaroo in his backyard and that the beast has disrupted your family barbecues by leaping over the fence, demanding salad, and even kicking your cousin in the ear. Your friend Foster, a graduate student from Melbourne, offers to help you prepare the case, and you agree to pay him 10 percent of anything you recover. Foster proves surprisingly adept at organizing documents and arguments. You win $1,200, and Foster demands $120. Must you pay? The answer is determined by the law of licensing.

States require licenses for anyone who practices a profession, such as law or medicine, works as a contractor or plumber, and for many other kinds of work. These licenses are required in order to protect the public. States demand that an electrician be licensed because the work is potentially dangerous to a homeowner: The person doing the work must know an amp from a watt. **When a licensing requirement is designed to protect the public, any contract made by an unlicensed worker is unenforceable.** Your friend Foster is unlicensed to practice law. Even though Foster did a fine job with your small claims case, he cannot enforce his contract for $120.

---

[2]Jimenez v. Protective Life Insurance Co., 8 Cal. App. 4th 528 (Cal. App. 1992).

States use other licenses simply to raise money. For example, most states require a license to open certain kinds of retail stores. This requirement does not protect the public because the state will not investigate the store owner the way it will examine a prospective lawyer or electrician. The state is simply raising money. **When a licensing requirement is designed merely to raise revenue, a contract made by an unlicensed person is generally enforceable.** Thus, if you open a stationery store and forget to pay the state's licensing fee, you can still enforce a contract to buy 10,000 envelopes from a wholesaler at a bargain price.

Many cases, such as the following one, involve contractors seeking to recover money for work they did without a license.

AUTHENTIC HOME IMPROVEMENTS V. MAYO

2006 WL 2687533
District of Columbia Superior Court, 2006

Facts: Authentic Home Improvements (Authentic) performed work on Diane Mayo's home, but she sued for return of the money she had paid. In court, Authentic's owner acknowledged that he had no contractor's license when it began the work, but he expected to obtain it soon. The court ordered Authentic to refund Mayo the entire sum she had paid, and the company agreed. Later, however, Authentic returned to court, stating that things had changed. The license had in fact been issued soon after work began. Authentic argued that it should not be obligated to return Mayo's money and was in fact entitled to its full fee for the work accomplished.

Issue: *Did the new license entitle Authentic to its home improvement fee?*

Excerpts from Judge Goodbread's Decision: This is not a matter of a trial judge doggedly cleaving to his original ruling—one that he frankly wishes he could modify under these circumstances. To use the words of Proteus, "My duty pricks me on to utter that which else no worldly good should draw from me." Shakespeare, "The Two Gentlemen of Verona." Not that it makes any difference to anyone, but the undersigned, a carpenter's son dwelling at this end of the Judicial Food Chain, disagrees with the harsh general rule in these cases and [believes that exceptions to the licensing requirement should be made in deserving cases]. Nevertheless, the undersigned is bound by the repeated rulings of the Court of Appeals.

As early as 1974, our Court of Appeals noted the high incidence of complaints emanating from the home improvement industry, noting that, even then, it was estimated that fraudulent practices in the industry cost consumers from 500 million to 1 billion dollars annually (this would amount to over $4.3 billion in today's dollars). A simple search of the Internet for the term "home improvement fraud" brings up over two million sites.

Not only is it immaterial that the parties may be in equal fault in the home improvement contract matter, but it has also been held that the unlicensed contractor may not recover even in instances wherein the homeowner *already knew* at all times relevant that the contractor was not licensed and impliedly or expressly "waived" that requirement in return for the work being done promptly. Moreover—turning the purpose of the rule inside out—even where it was the contractor who was the "victim" and the home owner herself who knew in advance that the contract would be invalid and unenforceable, yet still benefitted unfairly from the contractor's good work, the homeowner was allowed to prevail, despite what might be termed "malice aforethought."

The unique defense of a "retroactive" license presented in this case does not vitiate the rule. [Authentic's owner argues that he] had every reasonable *expectation* of receiving a license and that, in fact, he *did* receive the license within a reasonable time of beginning work. Yet the requirement to have *already* had issued, and in hand, a license or permit to conduct or perform the act at issue is not a difficult concept to grasp and one need go no further than the common driver's permit or license tags to understand it. No one could legally drive a vehicle in *anticipation* of the license and the plates that had already been approved, on the premise that they would eventually arrive in the mail in due course, and that it would be all right to drive until they do.

The Court's original ruling in this case must stand.

14-2a **Usury**

It pays to understand usury.

Henry Paper and Anthony Pugliese were real estate developers. They bought property in Florida, intending to erect an office building. Walter Gross, another developer, agreed to lend them $200,000 at 15 percent interest. Gross knew the partners were desperate for the money, so at the loan closing, he demanded 15 percent equity (ownership) in the partnership, in addition to the interest. Paper and Pugliese had no choice but to sign the agreement. The two partners never repaid the loan, and when Gross sued, the court ruled that they need never pay a cent.

Usury laws prohibit charging excess interest on loans. Some states, such as New York, set very strict limits. Others, like Utah, allow for virtually any rate. A lender who charges a usurious rate of interest may forfeit the illegal interest, all interest, or, in some states, the entire loan.

Florida law requires a lender who exceeds 25 percent interest to forfeit the entire debt. Where was the usury in Gross's case? Just here: When Gross insisted on a 15 percent share of the partnership, he was simply extracting additional interest and disguising it as partnership equity. The Paper-Pugliese partnership had equity assets of $600,000. A 15 percent equity, plus interest payments of 15 percent over 18 months, was the equivalent of a per annum interest rate of 45 percent. Gross probably thought he had made a deal that was too good to be true. And in the state of Florida, it was. He lost the entire debt.[3]

Credit Card Debt

Many consumers are desperate to obtain credit cards on any terms. When First Premier Bank launched a credit card with a 79.9 percent rate of interest, 700,000 people applied for it within the next two years. How can such a rate exist?

Even if a state's usury statute applies to credit cards, savvy lenders can often avoid limits on interest rates. The Supreme Court has ruled that when national banks issue a credit card, they can use the rate of their own state or of that of the consumer, whichever is higher. Also, many card issuers require borrowers to sign contracts that say the laws of a lender-friendly state will be applied to all future disputes. New York customers might agree to live by Utah laws, for example.

Most courts continue to enforce these contracts that impose high out-of-state rates. But since the financial meltdown of 2008, some courts have started to express distaste for this practice. In the following case, a New York court addressed the issue.

AMERICAN EXPRESS TRAVEL RELATED SERVICES COMPANY, INC. v. ASSIH

893 N.Y.S.2d 438
Civil Court of the City of New York, Richmond County, 2009

Facts: American Express Travel Related Services (American Express) alleged that New York resident Titus Assih missed a credit card payment. His interest rate ballooned from 12.24 percent to 21 percent, and eventually to 27.99 percent. Assih made small payments for a time, but soon he stopped paying altogether.

American Express sued Assih. The company sought to enforce this provision of its agreement: "This Agreement is governed by Utah law and applicable federal law." The agreement's only connection to Utah was that American Express assigned its interest to a one-branch bank in Utah.

[3]Jersey Palm-Gross, Inc. v. Paper, 639 So.2d 664 (Fla. Ct. App. 1994).

Assih argued that New York law, which sets strict limits on maximum rates of credit card interest, should apply instead.

Issues: *Should New York or Utah law apply? Did the increased rates violate usury statutes?*

Excerpts from Judge Straniere's Opinion: Having dealt with thousands of consumer credit cases over the years, the court is sometimes caused to wonder if the regulations governing this industry originated in the Wonderful Land of Oz. For example, the scene where Dorothy and friends approach the gates of the Emerald City and ring the bell seeking entrance seems to present a number of the issues arising in debt collection litigation.

> Guardian: Well, that's more like it! Now state your business!
> Dorothy and Friends: We want to see the Wizard!
> Guardian: The Wizard? But nobody can see the Great Oz! Nobody's ever seen the Great Oz! Even I've never seen him!
> Dorothy: Well, then how do you know there is one?

Like the Land of Oz, run by a Wizard who no one has ever seen, the Land of Credit Cards permits consumers to be bound by agreements they never sign, agreements they may have never received, subject to change without notice and the laws of a state other than those existing where they reside.

The Utah usury statute provides: The parties to a lawful contract may agree upon any rate of interest for the loan that is the subject of their contract.

Is it any wonder that credit card issuers, such as plaintiff, make their agreements subject to Utah law? An interest rate is not usurious so long as the parties "agree upon any rate of interest." If Nathan Detroit had known he could make loans charging 100 percent interest a day by reducing them to writing, signed and subject to Utah law, he would not have had to seek a living running the "oldest, established, permanent floating crap game in

New York." Incredibly, courts are expected to enforce these agreements against unsophisticated, unrepresented consumers who reside in states such as New York, which does not have similar statutes, and who have no idea that their agreement is subject to Utah law.

Is New York required to apply the Utah usury statute to credit card interest charges that far exceed the legal rate in New York? New York follows the "substantial relationship" approach, which provides:

> The law of the state chosen by the parties to govern their contractual rights and duties will be applied.... unless the chosen state has no substantial relationship to the parties.

The corporate plaintiff is incorporated in New York and its principal place of business is in New York. Defendant resides in New York. Most of the transactions charged to the credit card took place in New York. Payments on the credit card are mailed to a New York address. Utah has no substantial relationship to the parties.

Taking all of the above into account, it is clear that New York has the most significant contacts to the parties and New York law will apply to the Agreement.

The legal rate of interest in New York in general obligations [is] sixteen per cent. New York still retains a criminal usury statute for interest rates which exceed twenty-five per cent. Except for the initial interest rate charged on defendant's account by plaintiff of 12.24%, all other interest charges assessed by plaintiff violated the New York civil usury statutes. The last billings on this account in fact exceeded the criminal usury rate of 25% when they reached 27.99%.

Under New York law, all usurious contracts are void and the lender forfeits both principal and interest.

The Wizard in *The Wizard of Oz* warned Dorothy and friends, "Do not arouse the wrath of the great and powerful Oz." I am sure the court will likewise be arousing the wrath of the plaintiff.

Plaintiff's cause of action is dismissed.

14-3 CONTRACTS THAT VIOLATE PUBLIC POLICY

A judge may declare a contract void even if it does not violate a statute. Contracts that promote immorality or illegality are unenforceable. One court refused to enforce a contract for the sale of a company because its main business was the manufacture of marijuana bongs.[4] It reasoned that hearing about such a contract would have a negative

---

[4]Bovard v. American Horse Enterprises, Inc. 201 Cal. App. 3d 832 (1988).

impact on society. In this section, we examine cases in which a *public policy* prohibits certain contracts. In other words, we focus primarily on common law rules.

14-3a Restraint of Trade: Noncompete Agreements

Free trade is the basis of the U.S. economy, and any bargain that restricts it is suspect. Most restraint of free trade is barred by antitrust law. But it is the common law that still regulates one restriction on trade: agreements to refrain from competition. Some of these agreements are legal, and some are void.

Recall that a noncompete agreement is a contract in which one party agrees not to compete with another in a stated type of business. For example, an anchorwoman for an NBC news affiliate in Miami might agree that she will not anchor any other Miami station's news for one year after she leaves her present employer. Noncompetes are often valid, but the common law places some restrictions on them.

To be valid, an agreement not to compete must be ancillary to a legitimate bargain. "Ancillary" means that the noncompetition agreement must be part of a larger agreement. Suppose Cliff sells his gasoline station to Mina, and the two agree that Cliff will not open a competing gas station within 5 miles anytime during the next two years. Cliff's agreement not to compete is ancillary to the sale of his service station. His noncompetition promise is enforceable. But suppose that Cliff and Mina already had the only two gas stations within 35 miles. They agree between themselves not to hire each other's workers. Their agreement might be profitable to them because each could now keep wages artificially low. But their deal is ancillary to no legitimate bargain, and it is therefore void. Mina is free to hire Cliff's mechanic despite her agreement with Cliff.

The two most common settings for legitimate noncompetition agreements are the sale of a business and an employment relationship.

Sale of a Business

Kory has operated a real estate office, Hearth Attack, in a small city for 35 years, building an excellent reputation and many ties with the community. She offers to sell you the business and its goodwill for $300,000. But you need assurance that Kory will not take your money and promptly open a competing office across the street. With her reputation and connections, she would ruin your chances of success. You insist on a noncompete clause in the sale contract. In this clause, Kory promises that for one year, she will not open a new real estate office or go to work for a competing company within a 10-mile radius of Hearth Attack. Suppose, six months after selling you the business, Kory goes to work for a competing real estate agency two blocks away. You seek an injunction to prevent her from working. Who wins?

> With her reputation and connections, she would ruin your chances of success.

When a noncompete agreement is ancillary to the sale of a business, it is enforceable if reasonable in time, geographic area, and scope of activity. In other words, a court will not enforce a noncompete agreement that lasts an unreasonably long time, covers an unfairly large area, or prohibits the seller of the business from doing a type of work that she never had done before. Measured by this test, Kory is almost certainly bound by her agreement. One year is a reasonable time to allow you to get your new business started. A 10-mile radius is probably about the area that Hearth Attack covers, and realty is obviously a fair business from which to prohibit Kory. A court will probably grant the injunction, barring Kory from her new job.

If, on the other hand, the noncompetition agreement had prevented Kory from working anywhere within 200 miles of Hearth Attack, and she started working 50 miles away, a court would refuse to enforce the contract. That geographic restriction would be unreasonable since Kory never previously did business 50 miles away, and Hearth Attack is unlikely to be affected if she works there now. An overly broad restriction would make for bad public policy, and it would lack a legal purpose.

Employment

When you sign an employment contract, the document may well contain a noncompete clause. Employers have legitimate worries that employees might go to a competitor and take with them trade secrets or other proprietary information. Some employers, though, attempt to place harsh restrictions on their employees, perhaps demanding a blanket agreement that the employee will never go to work for a competitor.

Noncompetes limit an individual's right to make a living and choose their work. For this reason, about one-third of states have restrictions on the enforceability of employment-related noncompetes. California prohibits them altogether, except when they are tied to the sale of a business or a verifiable trade secret.[5] In other states, employment restrictions are highly scrutinized for fairness. **Generally, a noncompete clause in an employment contract is enforceable only if it is essential to the employer, fair to the employee, and harmless to the general public.**

Judges usually enforce these agreements to protect trade secrets and confidential information. They may protect customer lists that have been expensive to produce. Courts rarely restrain an employee simply because he wants to work for a competitor, and they disfavor agreements that last too long or apply in a very wide area. The following chart summarizes the factors that courts look at in all types of noncompetition agreements.

The Legality of Noncompetition Clauses (Noncompetes)

Type of Noncompetition Agreement	When Enforceable	
Not ancillary to a sale of business or employment	Never	
Ancillary to a sale of business	If reasonable in time, geography, and scope of activity	
Ancillary to employment	Contract is *more* likely to be enforced when it involves:	Contract is *less* likely to be enforced when it involves:
	• Trade secrets or confidential information: these are almost always protected	• Employee who already had the skills when he arrived, or merely developed general skills on the job
	• Customer lists developed over extended period of time and carefully protected	• Customer lists that can be derived from public sources
	• Limited time and geographical scope	• Excessive time or geographical scope
	• Terms essential to protect the employer's business	• Terms that are unduly harsh on the employee or contrary to public interest

---

[5]Edwards v. Arthur Andersen LLP, 44 Cal,.4th 937 (S. Ct. Cal. 2008).

Suppose that Gina, an engineer, goes to work for Fission Chips, a silicon chip manufacturer that specializes in defense work. She signs a noncompete agreement promising never to work for a competitor. Over a period of three years, Gina learns some of Fission's proprietary methods of etching information onto the chips. She acquires a great deal of new expertise about chips generally. Also, she periodically deals with Fission Chip's customers, all of whom are well-known software and hardware manufacturers. Gina accepts an offer from WriteSmall, a competitor. Fission Chips races to court, seeking an injunction that would prevent Gina from (1) working for WriteSmall, (2) working for any other competitor, (3) revealing any of Fission's trade secrets, (4) using any of the general expertise she acquired at Fission Chips, and (5) contacting any of Fission's customers.

This injunction threatens Gina's career. If she cannot work for a competitor or use her general engineering skills, what *will* she do? And for exactly that reason, no court will grant such a broad order. The court will allow Gina to work for competitors, including WriteSmall. It will order her not to use or reveal any trade secrets belonging to Fission. She will, however, be permitted to use the general expertise she has acquired, and she may contact former customers since anyone could get their names from the yellow pages.

Was the noncompete in the following case styled fairly, or was the employee clipped?

KING V. HEAD START FAMILY HAIR SALONS, INC.

886 So.2d 769
Supreme Court of Alabama, 2004

Facts: Kathy King was a single mother supporting a college-age daughter. For 25 years, she had worked as a hair stylist. For the most recent 16 years, she had worked at Head Start, which provided haircuts, coloring, and styling for men and women. King was primarily a stylist, though she had also managed one of the Head Start facilities.

King quit Head Start and began working as manager of a Sport Clips shop, located in the same mall as the store she just left. Sport Clips offered only haircuts and primarily served men and boys. Head Start filed suit, claiming that King was violating the noncompetition agreement that she had signed. The agreement prohibited King from working at a competing business within a 2-mile radius of any Head Start facility for 12 months after leaving the company. The trial court issued an injunction enforcing the noncompete. King appealed.

Issue: *Was the noncompetition agreement valid?*

Excerpts from Justice Lyons's Decision: King's most persuasive argument is that the geographic restriction contained in the noncompetition agreement imposes an undue hardship on her. King has been in the hair-care industry for 25 years, and it is the only industry in which she is skilled and the only industry in which she can find employment. Head Start has 30 locations throughout the Jefferson County and Shelby County area, making it virtually impossible for her to find employment in the hair-care industry at a facility that does not violate the terms of the noncompetition agreement. According to King, the geographic restriction constitutes a blanket prohibition on practicing her trade.

It cannot reasonably be argued that King, at the age of 40 and having spent more than half of her life as a hair stylist, can learn a new job skill that would allow her to be gainfully employed and meet her needs and the needs of her daughter. Under the circumstances presented here, enforcement of the noncompetition agreement works an undue hardship upon King. The noncompetition agreement cannot so burden King that it would result in her impoverishment.

Head Start is nevertheless entitled to some of the protection it sought in the noncompetition agreement. Head Start has a valid concern that King would be able to attract many of her former Head Start customers if she is allowed to provide hair-care services unencumbered by any limitations. To prevent an undue burden on King and to afford some protection to Head Start, the trial court should enforce a more reasonable geographic restriction—such as one prohibiting King from providing hair-care services within a 2-mile radius of the location of the Head Start facility at which she was formerly employed or imposing some other limitation that does not unreasonably interfere with King's right to gainful employment while, at the same time, protecting Head Start's interest in preventing King from unreasonably competing with it during the one-year period following her resignation.

Reversed and remanded.

EXAM Strategy

Question: Caf-Fiend is an expanding chain of coffeehouses. The company offers to buy Bessie's Coffee Shop, in St. Louis, on these terms: Bessie will manage the store, as Caf-Fiend's employee, for one year after the sale. For four years after the sale, Bessie will not open a competing restaurant anywhere within 12 miles. For the same four years, she will not work anywhere in the United States for a competing coffee retailer. Are the last two terms enforceable against Bessie?

Strategy: This contract includes two noncompete clauses. In the first, Bessie agrees not to open a competing business. Courts generally enforce such clauses if they are reasonable in time, geography, and scope of activity. Is this clause reasonable? The second clause involves employment. Courts take a dimmer view of these agreements. Is this clause essential to protect the company's business? Is it unduly harsh for Bessie?

Result: The first restriction is reasonable. Caf-Fiend is entitled to prevent Bessie from opening her own coffeehouse around the corner and drawing her old customers. The second clause is unfair to Bessie. If she wants to move from St. Louis to San Diego and work as a store manager, she is prohibited. It is impossible to see how such employment would harm Caf-Fiend—but it certainly takes away Bessie's career options. The first restriction is valid, the second one unenforceable.

14-3b **Exculpatory Clauses**

You decide to capitalize on your expert ability as a skier and open a ski and snowboarding school in Colorado, "Pike's Pique." But you realize that skiing and snowboarding sometimes cause injuries, so you require anyone signing up for lessons to sign this form:

> I agree to hold Pike's Pique and its employees entirely harmless in the event that I am injured in any way or for any reason or cause, including but not limited to any acts, whether negligent or otherwise, of Pike's Pique or any employee or agent thereof.

The day your school opens, Sara Beth, an instructor, deliberately pushes Toby over a cliff because Toby criticized her clothes. Eddie, a beginning student, "blows out" his knee attempting an advanced racing turn, and Maureen, another student, reaches the bottom of a steep run and slams into a snowmobile that Sara Beth parked there. Maureen, Eddie, and Toby's families all sue Pike's Pique. You defend based on the form you had them sign. Does it save the day?

The form on which you are relying is an **exculpatory clause**, that is, one that attempts to release you from liability in the event of injury to another party. Exculpatory clauses are common. Ski and snowboarding schools use them, and so do parking lots, landlords, warehouses, sports franchises, fitness centers, and day-care centers. All manner of businesses hope to avoid large tort judgments by requiring their customers to give up any right to recover. Is such a clause valid? Sometimes. Courts frequently—but do not always—ignore exculpatory clauses, finding that one party was forcing the other party to give up legal rights that no one should be forced to surrender.

An exculpatory clause is generally unenforceable when it attempts to exclude an intentional tort or gross negligence. When Sara Beth pushes Toby over a cliff, that is the intentional tort of battery. A court will not enforce the exculpatory clause. Sara Beth is clearly liable.[6] As to the

Exculpatory clause
A contract provision that attempts to release one party from liability in the event the other is injured

---

[6]Note that Pike's Pique is probably not liable under agency law principles that preclude an employer's liability for an employee's intentional tort.

Exculpatory clauses are important to the operators of businesses that involve some risk, such as ski and snowboarding resorts.

snowmobile at the bottom of the run, if a court determines that was gross negligence (carelessness far greater than ordinary negligence), then the exculpatory clause will again be ignored. If, however, it was ordinary negligence, then we must continue the analysis.

An exculpatory clause is usually unenforceable when the affected activity is in the public interest, such as medical care, public transportation, or some essential service. Suppose Eddie goes to a doctor for surgery on his damaged knee, and the doctor requires him to sign an exculpatory clause. The doctor negligently performs the surgery, accidentally leaving his cuff links in Eddie's left knee. The exculpatory clause will not protect the doctor. Medical care is an essential service, and the public cannot give up its right to demand reasonable work.

But what about Eddie's suit against Pike's Pique? Eddie claims that he should never have been allowed to attempt an advanced maneuver. His suit is for ordinary negligence, and the exculpatory clause probably *does* bar him from recovery. Skiing and snowboarding are recreational activities. No one is obligated to do them, and there is no strong public interest in ensuring that we have access to ski slopes.

An exculpatory clause is generally unenforceable when the parties have greatly unequal bargaining power. When Maureen flies to Colorado, suppose that the airline requires her to sign a form contract with an exculpatory clause. Because the airline almost certainly has much greater bargaining power, it can afford to offer a "take it or leave it" contract. The bargaining power is so unequal, though, that the clause is probably unenforceable. Does Pike's Pique have a similar advantage? Probably not. Ski and snowboarding schools are not essential and are much smaller enterprises. A dissatisfied customer might refuse to sign such an agreement and take her business elsewhere. A court probably will not see the parties as *grossly* unequal.

An exculpatory clause is generally unenforceable unless the clause is clearly written and readily visible. If Pike's Pique gave all ski and snowboarding students an eight-page contract, and the exculpatory clause was at the bottom of page seven in small print, the average customer would never notice it. The clause would be void.

In the following case, the court focused on the public policy concerns of exculpatory clauses used in a very common setting. Should the exculpatory clause stop the tenant from suing the landlord? You be the judge.

You be the **Judge**

Facts: Barbara Richards leased an apartment at Twin Lakes, a complex owned by Lenna Ransburg. The written lease declared that:

- Twin Lakes would "gratuitously" maintain the common areas.

RANSBURG V. RICHARDS
770 N.E.2d 393
Indiana Court of Appeals, 2002

- Richards's use of the facilities would be "at her own risk."

- Twin Lakes was not responsible for any harm to the tenant or her guests, anywhere on the property (including the parking lot), even if the damage was caused by Twin Lakes' negligence.

It snowed. As Richards walked across the parking lot to her car, she slipped and fell on snow-covered ice. Richards sued Ransburg, who moved for summary judgment based on the exculpatory clause. The trial court denied Ransburg's motion, and she appealed.

You Be the Judge: *Was the exculpatory clause valid?*

Argument for Tenant: An exculpatory clause in a contract for an essential service violates public policy. When an ill person seeks medical care, his doctor cannot require him to sign an exculpatory clause. In the same way, a person has to live somewhere. Her landlord cannot force her to sign a waiver.

Landlords tend to be wealthy and powerful. There is generally no equality of bargaining power between them. The tenants are not freely agreeing to the exculpatory language.

Moreover, if a landlord fails to maintain property, not just the tenant is at risk. Visitors, the mail carrier, and the general public could all walk through the Twin Lakes parking lot. The public's interest is served when landlords maintain their properties. They must be held liable when they negligently fail to maintain common areas and injuries result.

Argument for Landlord: Ms. Richards does indeed have to live somewhere, but she does not have to live on the plaintiff's property. Surely there are many dozens of properties nearby. If Richards had been dissatisfied with any part of the proposed lease—excessive rent, strict rules, or an exculpatory clause—she was free to take her business to another landlord.

Landlords may generally be wealthier than their tenants, but that fact alone does not mean that a landlord is so powerful that leases are offered on a "take it or leave it" basis. Here, the landlord stated the exculpatory clause plainly. This is a clear contract between adults, and it should stand in its entirety.

Bailment Cases

Exculpatory clauses are very common in bailment cases. **Bailment** means giving possession and control of personal property to another person. The person giving up possession is the **bailor**, and the one accepting possession is the **bailee**. When you leave your laptop computer with a dealer to be repaired, you create a bailment. The same is true when you check your coat at a restaurant or lend your Matisse to a museum. Bailees often try to limit their liability for damage to property by using an exculpatory clause.

Judges are slightly more apt to enforce an exculpatory clause in a bailment case because any harm is to *property* and not persons. But courts will still look at many of the same criteria we have just examined to decide whether a bailment contract is enforceable. In particular, when the bailee is engaged in an important public service, a court is once again likely to ignore the exculpatory clause. The following contrasting cases illustrate this.

In *Weiss v. Freeman*,[7] Weiss stored personal goods in Freeman's self-storage facility. Freeman's contract included an exculpatory clause relieving it of any and all liability. Weiss's goods were damaged by mildew, and she sued. The court held the exculpatory clause valid. The court considered self-storage to be a significant business, but not as vital as medical care or housing. It pointed out that a storage facility would not know what each customer stored and therefore could not anticipate the harm that might occur. Freedom of contract should prevail, the clause was enforceable, and Weiss got no money.

Bailment
Giving possession and control of personal property to another person

Bailor
One who creates a bailment by delivering goods to another

Bailee
A person who rightfully possesses goods belonging to another

---

[7] 1994 Tenn. App. LEXIS 393 (Tenn. Ct. App. 1993).

But in *Gardner v. Downtown Porsche Audi*,[8] Gardner left his Porsche 911 at Downtown for repairs. He signed an exculpatory clause saying that Downtown was "Not Responsible for Loss or Damage to Cars or Articles Left in Cars in Case of Fire, Theft, or Any Other Cause Beyond Our Control." Due to Downtown's negligence, Gardner's Porsche was stolen. The court held the exculpatory clause void. It ruled that contemporary society is utterly dependent upon automobile transportation and Downtown was therefore in a business of great public importance. No repair shop should be able to contract away liability, and Gardner won. (This case also illustrates that using seventeen capitalized words in one sentence does not guarantee legal victory.)

EXAM Strategy

Facts: Shauna flew a World War II fighter aircraft as a member of an exhibition flight team. While the team was performing in a delta formation, another plane collided with Shauna's aircraft, causing her to crash-land and leaving her permanently disabled. Shauna sued the other pilot and the team. The defendants moved to dismiss based on an exculpatory clause that Shauna had signed. The clause was one paragraph long, and it stated that Shauna knew team flying was inherently dangerous and could result in injury or death. She agreed not to hold the team or any members liable in case of an accident. Shauna argued that the clause should not be enforced against her if she could prove the other pilot was negligent. Please rule.

Strategy: The issue is whether the exculpatory clause is valid. Courts are likely to declare such clauses void if they concern vital activities like medical care, exclude an intentional tort or gross negligence, or if the parties had unequal bargaining power.

Result: This is a clear, short clause, between parties with equal bargaining power, and does not exclude an intentional tort or gross negligence. The activity is unimportant to the public welfare. The clause is valid. Even if the other pilot was negligent, Shauna will lose, meaning the court should dismiss her lawsuit.

14-3c Unconscionable Contracts

An unconscionable contract is one that a court refuses to enforce because of fundamental unfairness. Even if a contract does not violate any specific statute or public policy, it may still be void if it "shocks the conscience" of the court.

Historically, a contract was considered unconscionable if it was "such as no man in his senses and not under delusion would make on the one hand, and as no honest and fair man would accept on the other."[9]

But that standard was unhelpfully vague. Further, anytime a court rejects a contract as unconscionable, it diminishes freedom of contract. If one party can escape a deal based on something as hard to define as unconscionability, then no one can rely as confidently on any agreement. As an English jurist said in 1824, "public policy is a very unruly horse, and when once you get astride it, you never know where it will carry you."[10]

The following historic case provides a classic example of unconscionability.

---

[8]180 Cal. App. 3d 713 (Cal. Ct. App. 1986).
[9]Hume v. United States, 132 U.S. 406 (1889), quoting Earl of Chesterfield v. Janssen, 38 Eng. Rep. 82, 100 (Ch. 1750).
[10]Richardson v. Mellish, 2 Bing. 229 (1824).

Landmark Case

WILLIAMS V. WALKER-THOMAS FURNITURE CO.

350 F.2d 445
United States Court of Appeals for the DC Circuit, 1965

Facts: Walker-Thomas Furniture Company operated a retail furniture store in an economically disadvantaged DC neighborhood. The store's standard boilerplate contract provided, in fine print, that when a purchaser bought more than one item, any payment she made would be applied equally to everything she had purchased. In this way, the purchaser would not actually own any item until she had paid for everything in full. As a result, when customers missed a payment, Walker-Thomas would repossess every item they ever bought.

Ora Williams was a single mother raising seven children on a $218 monthly welfare check. Despite this knowledge, Walker-Thomas sold Williams fourteen household items totaling $1,800 from 1957 to 1962. Williams dutifully made her monthly payments. In 1962, Williams bought a stereo valued at $514.95. At the time of this purchase, she still owed $164 from her prior purchases. When Williams defaulted on her payment, Walker-Thomas sought to repossess every item she had ever purchased.

With the help of a legal aid society, Williams and other Walker-Thomas customers sued the company, arguing the contract was void for unconscionability. Lower courts sided with Walker-Thomas, and the customers appealed.

Issue: *Is an unconscionable contract unenforceable?*

Excerpts from Judge Skelly Wright's Decision:
Unconscionability has generally been recognized to include an absence of meaningful choice on the part of one of the parties together with contract terms which are unreasonably favorable to the other party. Whether a meaningful choice is present in a particular case can only be determined by consideration of all the circumstances surrounding the transaction. In many cases the meaningfulness of the choice is negated by a gross inequality of bargaining power.

The manner in which the contract was entered is also relevant to this consideration. Did each party to the contract, considering his obvious education or lack of it, have a reasonable opportunity to understand the terms of the contract, or were the important terms hidden in a maze of fine print and minimized by deceptive sales practices? Ordinarily, one who signs an agreement without full knowledge of its terms might be held to assume the risk that he has entered a one-sided bargain. But when a party of little bargaining power, and hence little real choice, signs a commercially unreasonable contract with little or no knowledge of its terms, it is hardly likely that his consent, or even an objective manifestation of his consent, was ever given to all the terms. In such a case the usual rule that the terms of the agreement are not to be questioned should be abandoned and the court should consider whether the terms of the contract are so unfair that enforcement should be withheld.

The test [of unconscionability] is not simple, nor can it be mechanically applied. The terms are to be considered in the light of the general commercial background and the commercial needs of the particular trade or case. The test [is] whether the terms are 'so extreme as to appear unconscionable according to the mores and business practices of the time and place.'

[Now that this court has established the test for determining "unconscionability" the case is remanded to the trial court to decide if this contract meets the test.]

Today, plaintiffs claiming unconscionability must prove two elements: procedural and substantive unconscionability:

- **Procedural unconscionability** focuses on oppression or unfair surprise. Oppression exists when the stronger party forces an unfavorable contract on the weaker one, often by taking advantage of their lack of education. Unfair surprise means the

Procedural Unconscionability
One party uses its superior power to force a contract on the weaker party.

weaker part did not fully understand the consequences of the agreement because the terms were hidden in the fine print.

Substantive Unconscionability

A contract with extremely one-sided and unfair terms

- **Substantive unconscionability** refers to contract terms that are overly harsh or unfairly one-sided.

Paula desperately needed a job. When her prospective employer asked her to sign an employment contract, she did not hesitate. (After all, she thought, it would not bode well for her career if she haggled over the fine print.) The agreement contained an arbitration clause, which provided that Paula would give up her right to litigate in the event of breach. Although such clauses are generally favored as fair and efficient, this one contained a twist: If Paula wanted to arbitrate, she would have to pay $10,000 to bring a claim, a requirement that did not apply to her employer. This sneaky term made it difficult (if not impossible) for an employee to bring a claim, but easy for an employer to do so.[11] Courts have found that disparity in bargaining power, together with fine print and unequal terms, render a contract void for unconscionability.

Adhesion Contracts

Adhesion contracts

Standard form contracts prepared by one party and presented to the other on a "take it or leave it" basis

A related issue concerns **adhesion contracts**, which are standard form contracts prepared by one party and given to the other on a "take it or leave it" basis. We have all encountered them many times when purchasing goods or services. Adhesion contracts are generally enforced, but they are subject to greater scrutiny and unconscionability challenges.

The UCC: Unconscionability and Sales Law

With the creation of the Uniform Commercial Code (UCC), the law of unconscionability got a boost. The Code explicitly adopts unconscionability as a reason to reject a contract.[12] Although the Code directly applies only to the sale of goods, its unconscionability section has proven to be influential in other cases as well, and courts today are more receptive than they were 100 years ago to a contract defense of fundamental unfairness.

The drafters of the UCC reinforced the principle of unconscionability by including it in §2-302:

> If the court as a matter of law finds the contract or any clause of the contract to have been unconscionable at the time it was made the court may refuse to enforce the contract, or it may enforce the remainder of the contract without the unconscionable clause, or it may so limit the application of any unconscionable clause as to avoid any unconscionable result.

In Code cases, the issue of unconscionability often arises when a company attempts to limit the normal contract law remedies. Yet the Code itself allows such limitations, provided they are reasonable.

Section 2-719 provides in part:

> [A contract] may provide for remedies in addition to or in substitution for those provided [by the Code itself] *and may limit or alter the measure of damages recoverable* … as by limiting the buyer's remedies to return of the goods and repayment of the price….

In other words, the Code includes two potentially competing sections: §2-719 permits a seller to insist that the buyer's only remedy for defective goods is return of the purchase price, but §2-302 says that *any unconscionable* provision is unenforceable. In lawsuits concerning defective goods, the seller often argues that the buyer's only remedies are those stated in the agreement, and the buyer responds that the contract limitation is unconscionable.

---

[11]See Sonic-Calabasas A Inc. v. Moreno, 57 Cal. 4th 1109 (S. Ct. Cal. 2013).
[12]UCC §2-302.

Electronic Data Systems (EDS) agreed to create complex software for Chubb Life America at a cost of $21 million. Chubb agreed to make staggered payments over many months as the work proceeded. The contract included a limitation on remedies, stating that if EDS became liable to Chubb, its maximum liability would be equal to two monthly payments.

EDS's work was woefully late and unusable, forcing Chubb to obtain its software elsewhere. Chubb sued, claiming $40 million in damages based on the money paid to EDS and additional funds spent purchasing alternative goods. EDS argued that the contract limited its liability to two monthly payments, a fraction of Chubb's damage. Chubb, of course, responded that the limitation was unconscionable.

The court noted that both parties were large, sophisticated corporations. As they negotiated the agreement, the companies both used experienced attorneys and independent consultants. This was no contract of adhesion presented to a meek consumer, but an allocation of risk resulting from hard bargaining. The court declared that the clause was valid, and EDS owed no more than two monthly payments.[13]

Chapter Conclusion

It is not enough to bargain effectively and obtain a contract that gives you exactly what you want. You must also be sure that the contract is legal. What appears to be an insurance contract might legally be an invalid wager. Unintentionally forgetting to obtain a state license to perform a certain job could mean you will never be paid for it. Bargaining a contract with a noncompete or exculpatory clause that is too one-sided may lead a court to ignore it. Legality is multifaceted, sometimes nuanced, and always important.

EXAM REVIEW

Illegal contracts are void and unenforceable. Illegality most often arises in these settings:

1. **WAGERING**   A purely speculative contract—whether for gambling or insurance— is likely to be unenforceable.

2. **LICENSING**   When the licensing statute is designed to protect the public, a contract by an unlicensed plaintiff is generally unenforceable. When such a statute is designed merely to raise revenue, a contract by an unlicensed plaintiff is generally enforceable.

EXAM Strategy

Question: James Wagner agreed to build a house for Nancy Graham. Wagner was not licensed as a contractor, and Graham knew it. When the house was finished, Graham refused to pay the final $23,000, and Wagner sued. Who will prevail?

[13]Colonial Life Insurance Co. v. Electronic Data Systems Corp., 817 F. Supp. 235 (D.N.H. 1993).

Strategy: A licensing statute designed to protect the public is strictly enforced, but that is not true for one intended only to raise revenue. What was the purpose of this statute? (See the "Result" at the end of this section.)

3. **USURY**   Excessive interest is generally unenforceable and may be fatal to the entire debt. Credit card debt is often exempt from usury laws.

EXAM Strategy

Question: McElroy owned 104 acres worth about $230,000. He got into financial difficulties and approached Grisham, asking to borrow $100,000. Grisham refused, but ultimately the two reached this agreement: McElroy would sell Grisham his property for $80,000, and the contract would include a clause allowing McElroy to repurchase the land within two years for $120,000. McElroy later claimed the contract was void. Is he right?

Strategy: Loans involving usury do not always include a clearly visible interest rate. You may have to do some simple math to see the interest being charged. McElroy wanted to borrow $100,000, but instead sold his property, with the right to repurchase. If he did repurchase, how much interest would he have effectively paid? (See the "Result" at the end of this section.)

4. **NONCOMPETE**   A noncompete clause in the sale of a business must be limited to a reasonable time, geographic area, and scope of activity. In an employment contract, such a clause is considered reasonable—and enforceable—only to protect trade secrets, confidential information, and customer lists.

EXAM Strategy

Question: The purchaser of a business insisted on putting this clause in the sales contract: The seller would not compete, for five years, "anywhere in the United States, the continent of North America, or anywhere else on Earth." What danger does that contract represent *to the purchaser?*

Strategy: This is a noncompete clause based on the sale of a business. Such clauses are valid if reasonable. Is this clause reasonable? If it is unreasonable, what might a court do? (See the "Result" at the end of this section.)

5. **EXCULPATORY CLAUSES**   These clauses are generally void if the activity involved is in the public interest, the parties are greatly unequal in bargaining power, or the clause is unclear. In other cases, they are generally enforced.

6. **PROCEDURAL UNCONSCIONABILITY** Oppression and surprise may create an unconscionable bargain. An adhesion contract is especially suspect when it is imposed by a corporation on a consumer or small company. Under the UCC, a limitation of liability is less likely to be unconscionable when both parties are sophisticated corporations.

7. **SUBSTANTIVE UNCONSIONABILITY** When contract terms are unfairly one-sided at the time of contracting, the contract may be substantively unconscionable.

> **2. Result:** This statute was designed to protect the public. Wagner was unlicensed and cannot enforce the contract. Graham wins.
>
> **3. Result:** By selling at $80,000 and repurchasing at $120,000, McElroy would be paying $40,000 in interest on an $80,000 loan. The 50 percent rate is usurious. The court prohibited Graham from collecting the interest.
>
> **4. Result:** "Anywhere else on Earth"? This is almost certainly unreasonable. It is hard to imagine a purchaser who would legitimately need such wide-ranging protection. In some states, a court might rewrite the clause, limiting the effect to the seller's state, or some reasonable area. However, in other states, a court finding a clause unreasonable will declare it void in its entirety—enabling the seller to open a competing business next door.

MULTIPLE-CHOICE QUESTIONS

1. At a fraternity party, George mentions that he is going to learn to hang glide during spring break. Vicki, a casual friend, overhears him, and the next day she purchases a $100,000 life insurance policy on George's life. George has a happy week of hang gliding. But on the way home, he is bitten by a parrot and dies of a rare tropical illness. Vicki files a claim for $100,000. The insurance company refuses to pay.

    (a) Vicki will win $100,000, but only if she mentioned animal bites to the insurance agent.

    (b) Vicki will win $100,000 regardless of whether she mentioned animal bites to the insurance agent.

    (c) Vicki will win $50,000.

    (d) Vicki will win nothing.

2. Now assume that Vicki has loaned George $50,000. George again mentions that he is going to learn to hang glide during spring break, so Vicki purchases the $100,000 life insurance policy on George's life. If George dies and the insurance company refuses to pay …

    (a) Vicki will win $100,000, but only if she mentioned animal bites to the insurance agent.

    (b) Vicki will win $100,000 regardless of whether she mentioned animal bites to the insurance agent.

    (c) Vicki will win $50,000.

    (d) Vicki will win nothing.

3. KwikFix, a Fortune 500 company, contracts with Allied Rocket, another huge company, to provide the software for Allied's new Jupiter Probe rocket for $14 million. The software is negligently designed, and when the rocket blasts off from Cape Kennedy, it travels only as far as Fort Lauderdale before crashing to Earth. Allied Rocket sues for $200 million and proves that as a result of the disaster, it lost a huge government contract, worth at least that much, which KwikFix was aware of. KwikFix responds that its contract with Allied included a clause limiting its liability to the value of the contract. Is the contract clause valid?

   (a) The clause is unenforceable because it is unconscionable.

   (b) The clause is unenforceable because it is exculpatory.

   (c) The clause is enforceable because both parties are sophisticated corporations.

   (d) The clause is enforceable because $200 million is an unconscionable claim.

4. Ricki goes to a baseball game. The back of her ticket clearly reads: "Fan agrees to hold team blameless for all injuries—pay attention to the game at all times for your own safety!" In the first inning, a foul ball hits Ricki in the elbow. She _____ sue the team over the foul ball. Ricki spends the next several innings riding the opposing team's first baseman. The *nicest* thing she says to him is, "You suck, Franklin!" In the eighth inning, Franklin has had enough. He grabs the ballboy's chair and throws it into the stands, injuring Ricki's other elbow.
   Ricki _____ sue the team over the thrown chair.

   (a) can; can

   (b) can; cannot

   (c) cannot; can

   (d) cannot; cannot

5. Jim, about to start a pickup soccer game, asks Desiree if she will hold his wallet while he plays. Desiree, a law student, says, "Sure, if you'll sign this exculpatory clause holding me blameless for negligence." Jim is very surprised, but he signs the paper that Desiree holds out for him. A bailment _____ been created. If Desiree is careless and loses the wallet, she _____ be liable to Jim.

   (a) has; will

   (b) has; will not

   (c) has not; will

   (d) has not; will not

CASE QUESTIONS

1. For 20 years, Art's Flower Shop relied almost exclusively on advertising in the yellow pages to bring business to its shop in a small West Virginia town. One year, the yellow pages printer accidentally did not print Art's ad, and Art's suffered an enormous drop in business. Art's sued for negligence and won a judgment of $50,000 from the jury, but the printing company appealed, claiming that under an exculpatory clause in the contract, the company could not be liable to Art's for more than the cost of the ad, about $910. Art's claimed that the exculpatory clause was unconscionable. Please rule.

2. Brockwell left his boat to be repaired at Lake Gaston Sales. The boat contained electronic equipment and other personal items. Brockwell signed a form stating that Lake Gaston had no responsibility for any loss to any property in or on the boat. Brockwell's electronic equipment was stolen and other personal items were damaged, and he sued. Is the exculpatory clause enforceable?

3. Guyan Machinery, a West Virginia manufacturing corporation, hired Albert Voorhees as a salesman and required him to sign a contract stating that if he left Guyan, he would not work for a competing corporation anywhere within 250 miles of West Virginia for a two-year period. Later, Voorhees left Guyan and began working at Polydeck Corp., another West Virginia manufacturer. The only product Polydeck made was urethane screens, which comprised half of 1 percent of Guyan's business. Is Guyan entitled to enforce its noncompete clause?

4. 810 Associates owned a 42-story skyscraper in midtown Manhattan. The building had a central station fire alarm system, which was monitored by Holmes Protection. A fire broke out and Holmes received the signal. But Holmes's inexperienced dispatcher misunderstood the signal and failed to summon the fire department for about nine minutes, permitting tremendous damage. 810 sued Holmes, which defended based on an exculpatory clause that relieved Holmes of any liability caused in any way. Holmes's dispatcher was negligent. Does it matter *how* negligent he was?

5. *YOU BE THE JUDGE* **WRITING PROBLEM** Oasis Waterpark, located in Palm Springs, California, sought out Hydrotech Systems, Inc., a New York corporation, to design and construct a surfing pool. Hydrotech replied that it could design the pool and sell all the necessary equipment to Oasis, but it could not build the pool because it was not licensed in California. Oasis insisted that Hydrotech do the construction work because Hydrotech had unique expertise in these pools. Oasis promised to arrange for a licensed California contractor to "work with" Hydrotech on the construction; Oasis also assured Hydrotech that it would pay the full contract price of $850,000, regardless of any licensing issues. Hydrotech designed and installed the pool as ordered. But Oasis failed to make the final payment of $110,000. Hydrotech sued. Can Hydrotech sue for either breach of contract or fraud (trickery)? **Argument for Oasis:** The licensing law protects the public from incompetence and dishonesty. The legislature made the section strict: no license, no payment. If the court were to start picking and choosing which unlicensed contractors could win a suit, it would be inviting incompetent workers to endanger the public and then come into court and try their luck. That is precisely the danger the legislature seeks to avoid. **Argument for Hydrotech:** This is not the kind of case the legislature was worried about. Hydrotech has never solicited work in California. Hydrotech went out of its way to avoid doing any contracting work, informing Oasis that it was unlicensed in the state. Oasis insisted on bringing Hydrotech into the state to do work. If Oasis has its way, word will go out that any owner can get free work done by hiring an *unlicensed* builder. Make any promises you want, get the work done to your satisfaction, and then stiff the contractor—you'll never have to pay.

DISCUSSION QUESTIONS

1. **ETHICS** Richard and Michelle Kommit traveled to New Jersey to have fun in the casinos. While in Atlantic City, they used their MasterCard to withdraw cash from an ATM conveniently located in the "pit"—the gambling area of a casino. They ran up debts of $5,500 on the credit card and did not pay. The Connecticut National Bank sued for the money. Law aside, who has the moral high ground? Is it acceptable for the casino to offer ATM services in the gambling pit? If a credit card company allows customers to withdraw cash in a casino, is it encouraging them to lose money? Do the Kommits have any ethical right to use the ATM, attempt to win money by gambling, and then seek to avoid liability?

2. The Justice Department shut down three of the most popular online poker websites (Poker Stars, Absolute Poker, and Full Tilt Poker). State agencies take countless actions each year to stop illegal gaming operations. Do you believe that gambling by adults *should* be regulated? If so, which types? Rate the following types of gambling from most acceptable to least acceptable:

> – online poker   – state lotteries   – horse racing
> – casino gambling   – bets on pro sports   – bets on college sports

3. Van hires Terri to add an electrical outlet to his living room for his new HDTV. Terri does an excellent job, and the new outlet works perfectly. She presents Van with a bill for $200. But Terri is not a licensed electrician. Her state sets licensing standards in the profession to protect the public. And so, Van can refuse to pay Terri's bill. Is this reasonable? *Should* he be able to avoid payment?

4. Imagine that you are starting your own company in your hyper-competitive industry: You are putting your life savings, your professional contacts, and your innovative ideas on the line. As you begin to hire a sales force, you consider binding new employees to noncompete agreements. Outline the ideal terms of your employees' noncompetes. What is its duration? What is its geographical radius? Are these terms appropriate for your industry? When you are done, pass your proposed terms to classmates and discuss its enforceability.

5. When Ruth Klopp was injured in a serious accident with an uninsured motorist, she filed a claim under her own policy with Worldwide Insurance. Her policy contained an arbitration provision, stating that if the arbitrators awarded more than $15,000, either side could appeal to the courts, but a low award could not be appealed. The arbitrators awarded Klopp $90,000, and Worldwide demanded a full trial. Klopp claimed that the appeal provision was unconscionable. What was the result?

6. **ETHICS** Some commentators argue that Walker-Thomas Furniture was providing a valuable service to Mrs. Williams and that the litigation ultimately harmed her community. No other business of the time was willing to offer credit to people of such limited means, much less to African Americans. As a result of that landmark case, Walker-Thomas went out of business and an entire group of people lost access to essential household items. Comment.

CHAPTER 15

© Honza Krej/Shutterstock.com

VOIDABLE CONTRACTS: CAPACITY AND CONSENT

As the sole heiress to a copper fortune, Mrs. Clark knew unimaginable luxury—a palatial 42-room home on Fifth Avenue and a vast collection of rare art, antiques, and expensive dolls with custom clothes by the House of Dior. But Mrs. Clark was also a recluse: For 40 years, she lived alone, malnourished, and dehydrated amidst her opulence and her dolls, whom she considered her closest friends.

At 85, she was admitted to Beth Israel Medical Center for routine surgery. And there she stayed for 20 years, despite being in reasonably good health. She passed her days watching *The Smurfs* cartoons and tending to her dolls. Finally, she died at the hospital, aged 105.

After her death, peculiar tales surfaced. Over the years, she had given her doctor over $900,000. The hospital aggressively courted her for money. Memos from the hospital's president revealed that he was only too happy to house his wealthy (but healthy) tenant. Ultimately, in addition to the $1,200 per day charged for her stay, Mrs. Clark gave a prized Manet painting and many millions of dollars to Beth Israel.[1]

> **Huguette Clark had no family or human friends, but she *did* have over $300 million to her name—which tended to draw people to her.**

---

[1]Bill Dedman, *Empty Mansions* (Ballantine Books, 2013); Anemona Hartocollis, "Hospital Caring for an Heiress Pressed Her to Give Lavishly," *The New York Times*, May 29, 2013.

Clark's estate sued Beth Israel and her doctor, claiming they took advantage of the heiress to extract lavish gifts. Although this case is still pending as of this writing, this true story leads us to examine two issues that interfere with valid contract formation: capacity and consent.

Capacity means the legal ability of a party to enter a contract in the first place. Someone may lack capacity because of youth or mental infirmity. **Consent** refers to whether a contracting party truly understood the terms of the contract and whether she made the agreement voluntarily. Consent issues arise in cases of fraud, mistake, duress, and undue influence.

Problems with capacity and consent make a contract **voidable**. When a contract is voidable, one party has the option either to enforce or terminate the agreement. If her estate can prove that Clark did not understand her promises or was defrauded, mistaken, or coerced, it can terminate the contracts.

15-1 CAPACITY

Capacity is the legal ability to enter into a contract. An adult of sound mind has capacity. Generally, any deal she enters into will be enforced if all elements on the Contracts Checklist—agreement, consideration, and so forth—are present. But two groups of people usually lack legal capacity: minors and those with a mental impairment.

15-1a **Minors**

In contract law, a minor is someone under the age of 18. **Because a minor lacks legal capacity, she normally can create only a voidable contract.** A voidable contract may be canceled by the party who lacks capacity. Notice that *only the party lacking capacity* may cancel the agreement. So a minor who enters into a contract generally may choose between enforcing the agreement or negating it. The other party—an adult, or perhaps a store—has no such right. Voidable contracts are very different from those that are void, which we examined in Chapter 14, on legality. A *void* contract is illegal from the beginning and may not be enforced by either party. A *voidable* contract is legal but permits one party to escape, if she so wishes.

Disaffirmance

A minor who wishes to escape from a contract generally may **disaffirm** it; that is, he may notify the other party that he refuses to be bound by the agreement. There are several ways a minor may disaffirm a contract. He may simply tell the other party, orally or in writing, that he will not honor the deal. Or he may disaffirm a contract by refusing to perform his obligations under it. A minor may go further—he can undo a contract that has already been completed by filing a suit to **rescind** the contract; that is, to have a court formally cancel it.

Kevin Green was 16 when he signed a contract with Star Chevrolet to buy a used Camaro. Because he was a minor, the deal was voidable. When the Camaro blew a gasket and Kevin informed Star Chevrolet that he wanted his money back, he was disaffirming the contract. He happened to do it because the car suddenly seemed a poor buy, but he could have disaffirmed for any reason at all, such as deciding that he no longer liked Camaros. When Kevin disaffirmed the contract, he was entitled to his money back.

Restitution

A minor who disaffirms a contract must return the consideration he has received, to the extent he is able. Restoring the other party to its original position is called **restitution**. The consideration that Kevin Green received in the contract was, of course, the Camaro.

What happens if the minor is not able to return the consideration because he no longer has it or it has been destroyed? Most states hold that the minor is *still* entitled to his money back. A

Voidable contract

When a contract is voidable, the injured party may choose to terminate it.

Contracts Checklist
- ☐ Offer
- ☐ Acceptance
- ☐ Consideration
- ☐ Legality
- ☑ Capacity
- ☐ Consent
- ☐ Writing

Disaffirm

To give notice of refusal to be bound by an agreement

Rescind

To cancel a contract

Restitution

Restoring an injured party to its original position

minority of states follow the status quo rule, which provides that, if a minor cannot return the consideration, the adult or store is only required to return its *profit margin* to the minor.

Assume that Kevin's Camaro was totaled, not just in need of repair. He had originally bought the Camaro for $7,000. Star Chevrolet had paid $5,000 for the used car at auction and then marked it up $2,000.

In most states, Kevin would be entitled to the full $7,000 purchase price, even though the car is now worthless. The dealer would simply have to absorb the loss. But, if Kevin lives in a state with the status quo rule, then the dealer would have to refund only $2,000 to Kevin. It is permitted to keep the other $5,000 so that it breaks even on the transaction, or is "returned to the status quo."

Ethics   The rule permitting a minor to disaffirm a contract is designed to discourage adults from making deals with innocent children, and it is centuries old. Is this rule still workable in our modern consumer society? There are entire industries devoted to (and dependent upon) minors. Think of children's films, breakfast cereal, and gaming apps. Does this rule imperil retailers? Is it *right* to give a 17-year-old high school senior so much power to cancel agreements? Is it *right* for a 17-year-old high school senior to take advantage of this rule?

Timing of Disaffirmance/Ratification

A minor may disaffirm a contract anytime before she reaches age 18. She also may disaffirm within a reasonable time *after* turning 18. Suppose that 17-year-old Bret signs a contract to buy a $3,000 3-D television. The following week, he picks up the TV and pays for it in full. Four months later, he turns 18, and two months after that—after his Super Bowl party—he disaffirms the contract. His disaffirmance is effective. In most states, he gets 100 percent of his money back. In some cases, minors have been entitled to disaffirm a contract several *years* after turning 18. But the minor's right to disaffirm ends if he ratifies the contract.

Ratification is made by any words or action indicating an intention to be bound by the contract. Suppose Bret, age 17, buys his TV on credit, promising to pay $150 per month. He has made only four payments by the time he turns 18, but after reaching his majority, he continues to pay every month for six more months. He then attempts to disaffirm the contract. Too late. His actions—payment of the monthly bill for six months as an adult—ratified the contract he entered into as a minor. He is now fully obligated to pay the entire $3,000, on the agreed-upon schedule. Hope the party was worth it.

Ratification
Words or actions indicating an intention to be bound by a contract

Exception: Necessaries

A necessary is something essential to a minor's life and welfare. Food, clothing, housing, and medical care are necessaries. In some circumstances, courts have considered less essential items, like legal advice, automobiles, and tuition, to be necessaries.

On a contract for necessaries, a minor must pay for the value of the benefit received. In other words, the minor may still disaffirm the contract and return whatever is unused. But he is liable to pay for whatever benefit he obtained from the goods while he had them. Thus, the 16-year-old who buys and eats a 99-cent cheeseburger and later disaffirms his contract with Burger Central is only liable for what the burger is *reasonably* worth, which is less than the 99-cent purchase price. (And, no, he does not have to return the burger.)

> In some circumstances, courts have considered less essential items, like legal advice, automobiles, and tuition, to be necessaries.

Exception: Misrepresentation of Age

The rules change somewhat if a minor lies about his age. Sixteen-year-old Dan is delighted to learn from his friend Bret that a minor can buy a fancy TV, use it for a year or so, and then get his money back. Dan drops into SoundBlast and asks to buy a $4,000 surround-sound system. The store clerk says that the store no longer sells expensive systems to underage customers. Dan produces a fake driver's license indicating that he is 18, and the gullible clerk sells him the system. A year later, Dan drives up to SoundBlast and unloads the system, now in shambles. He asks for his $4,000 back. Is he still permitted to disaffirm?

States have been troubled by this problem, and there is no clear rule. A few states will still permit Dan to disaffirm the contract entirely. The theory is that a minor must be saved from his own poor judgment, including his foolish lie. Many states, though, will prohibit Dan from disaffirming the contract. They take the reasonable position that the law was intended to protect childhood innocence, not calculated deceit.

15-1b Mentally Impaired Persons

You are a trial court judge. Don wants you to rule that his father, Cedric, is mentally incompetent and, on behalf of Cedric, to terminate a contract he signed. Here is the evidence:

Cedric is a 75-year-old millionaire who keeps $300,000 stuffed in pillow cases in the attic. He lives in a filthy house with a parrot whom he calls the Bishop, an iguana named Orlando, and a tortoise known as Mrs. Sedgely. All of the pets have small beds in Cedric's grungy bedroom, and each one eats at the dining table with its master. Cedric pays college students $50 an hour to read poetry to the animals, but he forbids the reading of sonnets, which he regards as "the devil's handiwork."

Don has been worried about Cedric's bizarre behavior for several years and has urged his father to enter a nursing home. Last week, when Don stopped in to visit, Cedric became angry at him, accusing his son of disrespecting the Bishop and Mrs. Sedgely, who were enjoying a fifteenth-century Castilian poem that Jane, a college student, was reading. Don then blurted out that Cedric was no longer able to take care of himself. Cedric snapped back, "I'll show you how capable I am." On the back of a 40-year-old menu, he scratched out a contract promising to give Jane "$100,000 today and $200,000 one year from today if she agrees to feed, house, and care for the Bishop, Orlando, and Mrs. Sedgely for the rest of their long lives." Jane *quickly* signed the agreement. Don urges that the court, on Cedric's behalf, declare the contract void. How will you rule? Courts often struggle when deciding cases of mental competence.

A person suffers from a mental impairment if, by reason of mental illness or defect, he is unable to understand the nature and consequences of the transaction.[2] The mental impairment can be due to some mental illness, such as schizophrenia, or to mental retardation, brain injury, senility, or any other cause that renders the person unable to understand the nature and consequences of the contract.

A party suffering a mental impairment usually creates only a voidable contract. The impaired person has the right to disaffirm the contract just as a minor does. But again, the contract is voidable, not void. The mentally impaired party generally has the right to full performance if she wishes.

The law creates an exception: If a person has been adjudicated incompetent, then all of his future agreements are void. "Adjudicated incompetent" means that a judge has made a formal finding that a person is mentally incompetent and has assigned the person a guardian by court order.

---

[2]For a similar case, see *Harwell v. Garrett*, 239 Ark. 551 (1965).

How will a court evaluate Cedric's mental status? Of course, if there had already been a judicial determination that he was insane, any contract he signed would be void. Since no judge has issued such a ruling about Cedric, the court will listen to doctors or therapists who have evaluated him and to anyone else who can testify about Cedric's recent conduct. The court may also choose to look at the contract itself, to see if it is so lopsided that no competent person would agree to it.

How will Don fare in seeking to preserve Cedric's wealth? Poorly. Unless Don has more evidence than we have heard thus far, he is destined to eat canned tuna while Jane and the Bishop dine on caviar. Cedric is decidedly eccentric, and perhaps unwise. But those characteristics do not prove mental impairment. Neither does leaving a fortune to a poetry reader. If Don could produce evidence from a psychiatrist that Cedric, for example, was generally delusional or could not distinguish a parrot from a religious leader, that would persuade a court of mental impairment. But on the evidence presented thus far, Mrs. Sedgely and friends will be living well.[3]

Intoxication

Similar rules apply in cases of drug or alcohol intoxication. **When one party is so intoxicated that he cannot understand the nature and consequences of the transaction, the contract is voidable.**

We wish to stress that courts are *highly* skeptical of intoxication arguments. If you go out drinking and make a foolish agreement, you are probably stuck with it. Even if you are too drunk to drive, you are probably not nearly too drunk to make a contract. If your blood alcohol level is, say, .08, your coordination and judgment are poor. Driving in such a condition is dangerous, but you probably have a fairly clear awareness of what is going on around you.

To back out of a contract on the grounds of intoxication, you must be able to provide evidence that you did not understand the "nature of the agreement," or the basic deal that you made.

The following Landmark Case is a rare exception, where the defendant was able to escape the deal.

Landmark Case

BABCOCK V. ENGEL

58 Mont. 597
Supreme Court of Montana, 1920

Facts: While Charles Engel's wife was out of town, he sat home alone, drinking mightily. During this period, he made an agreement with G. M. Babcock to trade a 320-acre farm and $2,000 worth of personal property for a hotel. Engel's property was worth approximately twice the value of the hotel. Engel later refused to honor the deal on the grounds that he had been intoxicated when he made the agreement.

Babcock sued, but the jury sided with Engel and dismissed the complaint. Babcock appealed.

Issue: *Was Engel so intoxicated that his agreement with Babcock became voidable?*

Excerpts from Justice Holloway's Decision: If, as a matter of fact, Engel was so far under the influence of intoxicating liquor when he signed the contract that he was incapable of giving his assent, it would be

---

[3]Barbara's Sales, Inc. v. Intel Corp., 879 N.E.2d 910 (Ill. 2007).

voidable at the election of Engel when he became sober.

[T]he jury answered that on November 22, Engel was "so under the influence of intoxicating liquors as to deprive him of his powers of reasoning and render him unable to comprehend the consequences of his act in executing said agreement."

Engel himself testified to the effect that, availing himself of his wife's absence from home, he had been indulging greatly to excess and had been drunk on November 21; that he drank heavily of whisky which he had at his home on the morning of November 22; that immediately upon his arrival in the town, he had four or five drinks of whisky and blackberry before he entered upon the negotiations with Babcock.

Four other witnesses, each apparently disinterested, testified that at the time in question, Engel was intoxicated, could not comprehend the nature of his acts, in other words, that he was not qualified to transact business. The jury determined upon the credibility of the witnesses.

Intoxication is not made a defense by the Codes, and there was a time in the history of our jurisprudence when courts refused to lend their aid to relieve one from the consequences of his own voluntary intemperance, but the doctrine has long since been abandoned. The courts do not now concern themselves so much with the question of intoxication as with the question of contractual capacity, and if in fact either party is not mentally capable of giving his free consent to the terms disclosed by the writing, it is altogether immaterial by what cause his incapacity was produced. The courts have simply recognized the fact that intoxication, among other things, may render a person incapable of making a binding contract.

The test approved by the great majority of the decisions is the same which is applied in other forms of mental derangement, namely, that the deed or contract will be voidable if the person, at the time of its execution, was so far under the influence of intoxicants as to be unable to understand the nature and consequences of his act, and unable to bring to bear upon the business in hand any degree of intelligent choice and purpose.

Affirmed.

Restitution

A mentally infirm party who seeks to void a contract must make restitution. If a party succeeds with a claim of mental impairment, the court will normally void the contract but will require the impaired party to give back whatever she got. Suppose that Danielle buys a Rolls-Royce and promises in writing to pay $5,000 per month for five years. Three weeks later, she seeks to void the contract on the grounds of mental impairment. She must return the Rolls. If the car has depreciated, Danielle normally will have to pay for the decrease in value. What happens if restitution is impossible? Generally, courts require a mentally infirm person to make full restitution if the contract is to be rescinded. If restitution is impossible, the court will not rescind the agreement unless the infirm party can show bad faith by the other party. This is because, unlike minority, which is generally easy to establish, mental competence may not be apparent to the other person negotiating.

Contracts Checklist
- [ ] Offer
- [ ] Acceptance
- [ ] Consideration
- [ ] Legality
- [ ] Capacity
- [✓] Consent
- [ ] Writing

15-2 REALITY OF CONSENT

Smiley offers to sell you his house for $300,000, and you agree in writing to buy it. After you move in, you discover that the house is sinking into the earth at the rate of 6 inches per week. In twelve months, your only access to the house may be through the chimney. You sue, seeking to rescind. You argue that when you signed the contract, you did not truly consent because you lacked essential information. In this section, we look at four claims that parties make in an effort to rescind a contract based on lack of valid consent: (1) fraud, (2) mistake, (3) duress, and (4) undue influence.

15-2a **Fraud**

Fraud begins when a party to a contract represents something that is factually wrong. "This house has no termites," says a homeowner to a prospective buyer. If the house is swarming with the nasty pests, the statement is a misrepresentation. But does it amount to fraud? An injured person must show the following:

1. The defendant knew that his statement was false, or that he made the statement recklessly and without knowledge of whether it was false;

2. The false statement was material; and

3. The injured party justifiably relied on the statement.

Element One: Intentional or Reckless Misrepresentation of Fact

The injured party must show a false statement of fact. Notice that this does not mean the statement was a necessarily a "lie." If a homeowner says that the famous architect Stanford White designed her house, but Bozo Loco actually did the work, it is a false statement.

Now, if the owner knows that Loco designed the house, she has committed the first element of fraud. If she has no idea who designed the house, her assertion that it was "Stanford White" also meets the first element.

But the owner might have a good reason for the error. Perhaps a local history book identifies the house as a Stanford White. If she makes the statement with a reasonable belief that she is telling the truth, she has made an innocent misrepresentation (discussed in the next section) and not fraud.

Opinions and "puffery" do not amount to fraud. An opinion is not a statement of fact. A seller says, "I think land values around here will be going up 20 or 30 percent for the foreseeable future." That statement is pretty enticing to a buyer, but it is not a false statement of fact. The maker is clearly stating her own opinion, and the buyer who relies on it does so at his peril. A close relative of opinion is something called "puffery."

Get ready for one of the most astonishing experiences you've ever had! This section on puffery is going to be the finest section of any textbook you have ever read! You're going to find the issue intriguing, the writing dazzling, and the legal summary unforgettable!

"But what happens," you might wonder, "if this section fails to astonish? What if I find the issue dull, the writing mediocre, and the legal summary incomprehensible? Can I sue for fraud?" No. The promises we made were mere puffery. A statement is puffery when a reasonable person would realize that it is a sales pitch, representing the exaggerated opinion of the seller. Puffery is not a statement of fact. Because puffery is not factual, it is never a basis for rescission.

Consumers filed a class action against Intel Corporation, claiming fraud. They asserted that Intel advertised its Pentium 4 computer chip as the "best" in the market when in fact it was no faster than the Pentium III chip. The Illinois Supreme Court dismissed the claims, asserting that no reasonable consumer would make a purchase relying solely on the name Pentium 4. Even if the consumers could show that Intel plotted to persuade the market that the Pentium 4 was the finest processor, they are demonstrating nothing but puffery because "best" could mean the chip is anything from the cheapest to the newest compared to other processors.[4]

Courts have found many similar phrases to be puffery, including "high-quality," "expert workmanship," and "you're in good hands with us."

---

[4]*Laidlaw v. Organ*, 15 U.S. 178 (1817).

Element Two: Materiality

The injured party must demonstrate that the statement was material, or important. A minor misstatement does not meet this second element of fraud. Was the misstatement likely to influence the decision of the misled party significantly? If so, it was material.

Imagine a farmer selling a piece of his land. He measures the acres himself and calculates a total of 200 acres. If the actual acreage is 199, he has almost certainly not made a *material* misstatement. But if the actual acreage is 150, he has.

Element Three: Justifiable Reliance

The injured party also must show that she actually did rely on the false statement and that her reliance was reasonable. Suppose the seller of a gas station lies through his teeth about the structural soundness of the building. The buyer believes what he hears but does not much care because he plans to demolish the building and construct a day-care center. There was a material misstatement but no reliance, and the buyer may not rescind.

The reliance must be justifiable—that is, reasonable. If the seller of wilderness land tells Lewis that the area is untouched by pollution, but Lewis can see a large lake on the property covered with 6 inches of oily red scum, Lewis is not justified in relying on the seller's statements. If he goes forward with the purchase, he may not rescind.

No Duty to Investigate.   In the previous example, Lewis must act reasonably and keep his eyes open if he walks around the "wilderness" property. But he has no duty to undertake an investigation of what he is told. In other words, if the seller states that the countryside is pure and the lake looks crystal clear, Lewis is not obligated to take water samples and have them tested by a laboratory. A party to a contract has no obligation to investigate the other party's factual statements.

Plaintiff's Remedies for Fraud

In the case of fraud, the injured party generally has a choice of rescinding the contract or suing for damages or, in some cases, doing both. The contract is voidable, which means that injured party is not *forced* to rescind the deal but may if he wants. Fraud *permits* the injured party to cancel. Alternatively, the injured party can sue for damages—the difference between what the contract promised and what it delivered.

Nancy learns that the building she bought has a terrible heating system. A new one will cost $12,000. If the seller told her the system was "like new," Nancy may rescind the deal, but it may be economically harmful for her to do so. She might have sold her old house, hired a mover, taken a new job, and so forth. What are her other remedies? She could move into the new house and sue for the difference between what she got and what was promised, which is $12,000, the cost of replacing the heating system.

In some states, a party injured by fraud may both rescind *and* sue for damages. In these states, Nancy could rescind her contract, get her deposit back, and then sue the seller for any damages she has suffered. Her damages might be, for example, a lost opportunity to buy another house or wasted moving expenses.

In fact, this last option—rescinding and still suing for damages—is available in all states when a contract is for the sale of goods. **UCC §2-721 permits a party to rescind a contract and then sue for damages when fraud is committed.**

Innocent Misrepresentation

If all elements of fraud are present except the misrepresentation of fact was not made intentionally or recklessly, then **innocent misrepresentation** has occurred. So, if a person misstates a material fact and induces reliance, but he had good reason to believe that his statement was true, then he has not committed fraud. Most states allow rescission of a contract, but not damages, in such a case.

Special Problem: Silence

We know that a party negotiating a contract may not misrepresent a material fact. The house seller may not say that "the roof is in great shape" when she sleeps under an umbrella to avoid rain. But what about silence? Suppose that the seller knows the roof is in dreadful condition but the buyer never asks. Does the seller have an affirmative legal obligation to disclose what she knows?

In 1817, the United States Supreme Court laid down the general rule that a party had no duty to disclose, even when he knew that the other person was negotiating under a mistake.[5] In other words, the Court was reinforcing the old rule of *caveat emptor,* "let the buyer beware." But social attitudes about fairness have changed. Today, a seller who knows something that the buyer does not know is often required to divulge it.

Nondisclosure of a fact amounts to misrepresentation in these four cases: (1) where disclosure is necessary to *correct a previous assertion,* (2) where disclosure would correct a *basic mistaken assumption* that the other party is relying on, (3) where disclosure would correct the other party's *mistaken understanding about a writing,* or (4) where there is *a relationship of trust* between the two parties.[5]

To Correct a Previous Assertion. During the course of negotiations, one party's perception of the facts may change. When an earlier statement later appears inaccurate, the change generally must be reported.

W. R. Grace & Co. wanted to buy a natural-gas field in Mississippi. An engineer's report indicated the presence of large gas reserves. On the basis of the engineering report, the Continental Illinois National Bank committed to a $75 million nonrecourse production loan. A "nonrecourse loan" meant that Continental would be repaid only with revenues from the gas field. After Continental committed, but before it had closed on the loan, Grace had an exploratory well drilled and struck it rich—with water. The land would never produce any gas. Without informing Continental of the news, Grace closed the $75 million loan. When Grace failed to repay, Continental sued and won. A party who learns new information indicating that a previous statement is inaccurate must disclose the bad news.[6]

To Correct a Basic Mistaken Assumption. When one party knows that the other is negotiating with a mistaken assumption about an important fact, the party who knows of the error must correct it. Jeffrey Stambovsky agreed to buy Helen Ackley's house in Nyack, New York, for $650,000. Stambovsky signed a contract and made a $32,500 down payment. Before completing the deal, he learned that in several newspaper articles, Ackley had publicized the house as being haunted. Ackley had also permitted the house to be featured in a walking tour of the neighborhood as "a riverfront Victorian (*with ghost*)." Stambovsky refused to go through with the deal and sued to rescind. He won. The court ruled that Ackley sold the house knowing Stambovsky was ignorant of the alleged ghosts. She also knew that a reasonable buyer might avoid a haunted house, fearing grisly events—or diminished resale value. Stambovsky could not have discovered the apparitions himself, and Ackley's failure to warn permitted him to rescind the deal.[7]

What if the defect is ... a ghost?

---

[5]Restatement (Second) of Contracts §161.
[6]FDIC v. W.R. Grace & Co., 877 F.2d 614 (7th Cir. 1989).
[7]Stambovsky v. Ackley, 169 A.D.2d 254 (N.Y. App. Div. 1991).

A seller generally must report any latent defect he knows about that the buyer should not be expected to discover himself. As social awareness of the environment increases, a buyer potentially worries about more and more problems. We now know that underground toxic waste, carelessly dumped in earlier decades, can be dangerous or even lethal. Accordingly, any property seller who realizes that there is toxic waste underground, or any other hidden hazard, must reveal that fact.

To Correct a Mistaken Understanding about a Writing. Suppose the potential buyer of a vacation property has a town map showing that the land he wants to buy has a legal right of way to a beautiful lake. If the seller of the land knows that the town map is out of date and that there is no such right of way, she must disclose her information.

A Relationship of Trust. Maria is planning to sell her restaurant to her brother Ricardo. Maria has a greater duty to reveal problems in the business because Ricardo assumes she will be honest. **When one party naturally expects openness and honesty, based on a close relationship, the other party must act accordingly.** If the building's owner has told Maria he will not renew her lease, she must pass that information on to Ricardo.

What happens if an owner, rather than disclosing hidden defects, sells the property "as is"? The following case provides insight.

HESS V. CHASE MANHATTAN BANK, USA, N.A.

220 S.W.3d 758
Missouri Supreme Court, 2007

Facts: Billy Stevens owned a paint company. On several occasions, he ordered employees to load a trailer with 55-gallon paint drums and pallets of old paint cans and then dump them on property he owned. This illegal dumping saved Stevens the cost of proper disposal. Later, employees notified the Environmental Protection Agency (EPA) of what Stevens had done, and the EPA began an investigation. (Stevens later served time for environmental crimes.)

Stevens defaulted on his mortgage to the land. While Chase Manhattan Bank was in the process of foreclosing, it learned that the EPA was investigating the property for contamination. Chase foreclosed and put the property up for sale "as is." Several buyers expressed interest. The bank did not inform any of them of the ongoing EPA investigation. Dennis Hess bought the property for $52,000.

After Hess bought the land, he discovered the illegal waste and sued Chase for failing to disclose the EPA's investigation. The jury awarded Hess $52,000 and Chase appealed.

Issue: *Did Chase have a duty to disclose to Hess the ongoing investigation?*

Excerpts from Judge Stith's Decision: The buyer has a right to rely on the seller to disclose where the undisclosed

material information would not be discoverable through ordinary diligence. Chase learned that the EPA was investigating the property before Chase completed its foreclosure of the mortgage. Even with superior knowledge, a duty to disclose will be imposed only if the material facts would not be discovered through the exercise of ordinary diligence. Chase asserts that a reasonable inspection of the property by Hess would have disclosed the presence of the paint cans near the old barn foundation. Chase's argument misapprehends the factual basis of Hess's fraudulent nondisclosure claim. It is the *EPA investigation* into hazardous waste dumping on the property that is the material fact that Hess asserts Chase had a duty to disclose, not the presence (or absence) of paint cans.

Hess presented evidence that two potential buyers who did discover the paint cans each still made an offer to purchase the property. Both testified that the presence of paint cans did not give them notice that the EPA was investigating and that, had they known of its investigation, they would not have made offers for the property. From this evidence, the jury could have found that even had Hess further inspected the property and discovered the paint cans, this would not have put him on notice that the EPA had an ongoing investigation into hazardous waste dumping on the property.

Chase asserts that in spite of the evidence of its knowledge and Hess's inability to discover the EPA investigation, a duty to disclose should not be imposed because the contract specified that Chase was making "no representations, guaranties, or warranties, either written or implied, regarding the property" and that "the property is being sold in AS-IS condition with no express or implied representations or warranties by the seller or its agents." It claims that through these provisions, it bargained for the right to remain silent and no duty to speak ever arose.

What Chase misapprehends is that Hess alleges *fraud in the inducement* to contract, not fraud in the terms of the contract. Missouri law holds that a party may not, by disclaimer or otherwise, contractually exclude liability for fraud in inducing that contract. Each of the individuals who made an offer to purchase this property did so without knowledge that it was under EPA investigation. They all testified that, had they known, they would not have made an offer to purchase this property and would not, therefore, have "bargained for" Chase's silence. Chase's duty to speak arose from its superior knowledge prior to the execution of this contract. The presence of a clause disclaiming warranties in a contract does not negate a pre-contractual duty to speak.

Affirmed.

EXAM Strategy

Question: Mako is selling his country house for $400,000. Guppy, an interested buyer, asks whether there is sufficient water from the property's well. Mako replies, "Are you kidding? Watch this." He turns on the tap, and the water flows bountifully. Mako then shows Guppy the well, which is full. Guppy buys the property, but two weeks later, the well runs dry. In fact, Mako knew the water supply was inadequate, and he had the well filled by a tanker truck while the property was being sold. A hydrologist tells Guppy it will cost $100,000 to dig a better well, with no guarantee of success. Guppy sues Mako. What remedy should Guppy seek? Who will win?

Strategy: Is this a case of innocent misrepresentation or fraud? Fraud. Therefore, Guppy may seek two remedies: damages or rescission. Make sure that you understand the difference. To win, Guppy must show he relied on a fact that was both false and material.

Result: When Mako responded to Guppy's question by demonstrating the apparent abundance of water, he made a false statement. This was fraud (not innocent misrepresentation), because Mako knew the well was inadequate. That was a material fact. Guppy reasonably relied on the demonstration. Guppy will win. He can elect to rescind the contract (return the property to Mako and get his money back) or choose damages (the cost of digging a proper well). Given the uncertain nature of well digging, he would be wise to rescind.

15-2b Mistake

When she heard she was going to lose her job, Laura became very upset, so of course, she went shopping. She bought a pair of $1,345 orange stiletto heels, on final sale for $941.50. The shoes consoled Laura for about two hours, after which she realized she had made a big mistake: She could neither return the impractical shoes nor pay her credit card bill. Despite Laura's retail regret, contract law will not fix her mistake. Nor does it excuse her when she signs a contract without reading it. Generally, contract law forces parties to suffer the consequences of their folly. But in some cases, such as when one party seeks to profit unreasonably from another's error, rescission may be warranted on the grounds of mistake.

Not all mistakes are created equal: Some mistakes lead to voidable contracts; others create enforceable (if unfortunate) deals. How can we know the difference? First, we must ask who was mistaken because different rules apply to unilateral and **mutual mistakes**. We must also examine the character of the mistake to see if its circumstances warrant rescission.

Unilateral Mistake

Unilateral mistake

Occurs when only one party enters a contract under a mistaken assumption

A **unilateral mistake** occurs when one party enters a contract under a mistaken assumption; the other is not mistaken. It is not easy for the mistaken party to rescind a contract—the more astute party may simply have made a better bargain. So, to rescind a contract, a mistaken party must show something more than just a regrettable deal.

To rescind for unilateral mistake, the mistaken party must demonstrate that he entered the contract because of a basic factual error and that:

- the nonmistaken party knew or had reason to know of the error, or

- the mistake is mathematical or mechanical alone, or

- enforcing the contract would be unconscionable.

Knowledge of the Error.   Every market has information asymmetries. That is, some contracting parties know more than others, which helps them secure favorable deals. The law of unilateral mistake draws the line where one party takes *unfair* advantage of what he knows to be another's error. **If the nonmistaken party knows or has reason to know of the other party's error, courts will not allow him to profit by snapping it up.**

Fernando is an art dealer who specializes in nineteenth-century French painting. At Fiona's flea market stall, he sees a painting that he suspects is by Gustave Courbet. Knowing the painting could be worth millions, Fernando offers Fiona $10 for it. She accepts his offer because she thinks the painting is, at best, by one of Courbet's students. Fernando then does further research, which confirms his guess. He ultimately auctions the masterpiece for $2.4 million. For Fiona to be able to rescind the contract, she must show that Fernando's hunch was much more than a lucky guess, that he had known certainly that the painting was by Courbet. Practically speaking, cases like these are difficult for plaintiffs to win because they must prove that the nonmistaken party knew and that the parties had not assumed the risk of the error.

Mathematical and Mechanical Errors.

Two plus two is four; but what happens when it is accidentally forty? Whether the mistake is due to bad math or a typographical error, courts generally allow the nonmistaken party to undo the faulty agreement, if there is clear and convincing evidence that the term was a mistake. A town obtains five bids for construction of a new municipal swimming pool. Four are between $100,000 and $111,000. Fred's bid is for $82,000. His offer includes a figure of $2,000 for excavation work, while all the others have allotted about $20,000 for that work. It is obvious that Fred has inadvertently dropped a zero, resulting in a bid that is $18,000 too low. Town officials are quick to accept Fred's offer. When he sues to rescind, Fred wins. Town

AP Images/Art Institute of Chicago

What would you do if you saw this painting in a flea market for $6?

officials knew that the work could not be done that cheaply, and it would be unfair to hold Fred to a mathematical error.[8]

Unconscionability. When enforcing the contract would result in exploitation or unfairness, contracts are voidable. St. Mary's School conducts an annual fundraising raffle, whose grand prize is free school tuition for a year. Accidentally, a machine prints multiple raffle tickets with the same number. As a result, ten people hold winning tickets and claim the tuition award. Since enforcing these ten agreements would likely bankrupt the school, a court will look kindly upon St. Mary's (even though the ten winners might not).

In the following case, an automobile dealer made a mistake in the customer's favor— how often does this happen?

Donovan v. RRL Corporation

26 Cal.4th 261
Supreme Court of California, 2001

Facts: Brian Donovan was in the market for a used car. As he scanned the Costa Mesa *Daily Pilot*, he came upon a "Pre-Owned Coup-A-Rama Sale!" at Lexus of Westminster. Of the 16 cars listed in the ad (with vehicle identification numbers), one was a sapphire-blue Jaguar XJ6 Vanden Plas, priced at $25,995.

Brian drove to a Jaguar dealership to do some comparison shopping. Jaguars of the same year and mileage cost about $8,000 to $10,000 more than the auto at the Lexus agency. The next day, Brian and his wife hurried over to the Coup-A-Rama event, spotted the Jaguar and asked a salesperson why it had such a good price. The salesperson responded that, as a Lexus dealership, it could offer better prices than Jaguar and suggested that the Donovans test drive it. Pleased with the ride, Brian said to the salesman, "O.K. We will take it at your price, $26,000." This figure startled the sales representative, who glanced at the newspaper ad Brian showed him, and responded, "That's a mistake."

As indeed it was. The Lexus agency had paid $35,000 for the Jaguar and intended to sell it for about $37,000. Brian was adamant. "No, I want to buy it at your advertised price, and I will write you a check right now." The sales manager was called in, and he refused to sell the car for less than $37,000.

It turned out that the *Daily Pilot*'s typographical and proofreading errors had caused the mistake, although the Lexus dealership had failed to review the proof sheet, which would have revealed the error before the ad went to press.

Brian sued. The trial court found that unilateral mistake prevented enforcement of the contract. The appellate court reversed the decision, and Donovan appealed to the state's highest court.

The state supreme court first ruled that there *was* in fact a contract between the parties. (Generally, a newspaper advertisement is merely a solicitation for an offer, but a California statute generally holds *automobile dealers* to the terms of their offers.) The court then went on to examine the mistake to determine if the contract was enforceable.

Issue: *Did the Lexus dealer's mistake entitle it to rescind the contract?*

Excerpts from Justice George's Decision: A significant error in the price term of a contract constitutes a mistake regarding a basic assumption upon which the contract is made, and such a mistake ordinarily has a material effect adverse to the mistaken party. The defendant must show that the resulting imbalance in the agreed exchange is so severe that it would be unfair to require the defendant to perform.

Measured against this standard, defendant's mistake in the contract for the sale of the Jaguar automobile constitutes a material mistake regarding a basic assumption upon which it made the contract. Enforcing the contract with the mistaken price of $25,995 would require defendant to sell the vehicle to plaintiff for $12,000 less than the intended advertised price of $37,995—an error amounting to 32 percent of the price defendant intended. The exchange of performances would be substantially less desirable for defendant and more desirable for plaintiff.

The mere fact that a mistaken party could have avoided the mistake by the exercise of reasonable care

---

[8]Restatement (Second) of Contracts §153.

does not preclude avoidance on the ground of mistake. Indeed, since a party can often avoid a mistake by the exercise of such care, the availability of relief would be severely circumscribed if he were to be barred by his negligence. Nevertheless, in *extreme cases*, the mistaken party's fault is a proper ground for denying him relief for a mistake that he otherwise could have avoided.

If we were to accept plaintiff's position that that the dealer always must be held to the strict terms of a contract arising from an advertisement, we would be holding that the dealer intended to assume the risk of all typographical errors in advertisements, no matter how serious the error and regardless of the circumstances in which the error was made. For example, if an automobile dealer proofread an advertisement but, through carelessness, failed to detect a typographical error listing a $75,000 automobile for sale at $75, the defense of mistake would be unavailable to the dealer.

No evidence presented at trial suggested that defendant knew of the mistake before plaintiff attempted to purchase the automobile, that defendant intended to mislead customers, or that it had adopted a practice of deliberate indifference regarding errors in advertisements. The uncontradicted evidence established that the *Daily Pilot* made the proofreading error resulting in defendant's mistake.

We conclude that the municipal court correctly entered judgment in defendant's favor.

Mutual Mistake

A mutual mistake **occurs when both contracting parties share the same mistake. If the contract is based on a fundamental factual error by both parties, the contract is voidable by either one.**

But what types of errors are important enough to warrant rescission? Generally, when the parties are mistaken as to the existence or the identity of the contract's subject matter, the contract is voidable. Believing himself the rightful owner, Arthur contracts to sell a parcel of land to James. When it is later discovered that the land never belonged to Arthur, James can rescind the contract. Both parties were mistaken as to the existence of Arthur's land.

Farnsworth believes he is selling Corbin a topaz, and Corbin thinks he is buying a topaz. In fact, both are wrong: The stone turns out to be a diamond. Since the parties made a material error as to the subject of their contract, there was no valid assent and either one can rescind.

The following case is read by every U.S. law student. It illustrates a basic factual mistake as to the subject matter of a contract. When is a cow more than a cow? Answer: When it is two.

Landmark Case

SHERWOOD V. WALKER
66 Mich. 568
Supreme Court of Michigan, 1887

Facts: Rose 2d of Aberlone was a gentle, 1,420 lb. cow that lived in Michigan in 1886. Rose's owner, Hiram Walker & Sons, was a cattle breeder who bought her for $850. After a few years, Walker concluded that Rose could have no calves. As a barren cow, she was worth much less than $850, so Walker agreed to sell her for beef to T. C. Sherwood. Walker told Sherwood that Rose was "probably barren, and would not breed." After some negotiation, Walker agreed to sell Rose for "five and one-half cents per pound, live weight, fifty pounds shrinkage," or $80.

But when Sherwood came to collect Rose, the parties realized that (surprise!) she was pregnant. As a confirmed breeder, Rose was now worth about $1,000. Walker refused to part with the happy mother, and Sherwood sued for breach of contract. Walker defended, claiming that both parties had made a *mistake* and that the contract was voidable. After the lower court ruled the contract was enforceable, Walker appealed.

Issue: *Does a mutual mistake of fact render a contract voidable?*

Excerpts from Justice Morse's Decision: A party who has given an apparent consent to a contract of sale may refuse to execute it, or he may avoid it after it has been completed, if the assent was founded, or the contract made, upon the mistake of a material fact—such as the subject matter of the sale, the price, or some collateral fact materially inducing the agreement; and this can be done when the mistake is mutual.

If there is a difference as to the substance of the thing bargained for, then there is no contract; but if it be only a difference in some quality or accident, the contract remains binding.

The mistake of the parties went to the whole substance of the agreement. The parties would not have made the contract of sale except upon the understanding and belief that she was incapable of breeding, and of no use as a cow. A barren cow is substantially a different creature than a breeding one. There is as much difference between them for all purposes of use as there is between an ox and a cow that is capable of breeding and giving milk. The mistake affected the character of the animal for all time, and for its present and ultimate use. She was not in fact the animal, or the kind of animal, the defendants intended to sell or the plaintiff to buy.

The mistake affected the substance of the whole consideration, and it must be considered that there was no contract to sell or sale of the cow as she actually was. The thing sold and bought had in fact no existence. Defendants had a right to rescind, and to refuse to deliver, and the verdict should be in their favor.

The defense of mistake is not a cure-all for all bad deals. Courts will not rescind contracts on the basis of a prediction error, a mistaken value, or where the parties assume the risk of error.

Prediction Error. Sherwood and Walker were both wrong about Rose's reproductive ability, and the error was basic enough to cause a tenfold difference in price. Walker, the injured party, was entitled to rescind the contract. Note that the error must be *factual.* Suppose Walker sold Rose thinking that the price of beef was going to drop, when in fact the price rose 60 percent in five months. That would be simply a *prediction* that proved wrong, and Walker would have no right to rescind.

Mistake of Value. Here is one case in which it pays to know less. Suppose that Fiona the flea market vendor sold the nineteenth-century masterpiece for $100 to Marguerite, a financial analyst with no inkling of its real worth. Both Fiona and Marguerite shared the same mistake in their estimate of the painting's market value. Sadly for Fiona, Marguerite will reap the benefit of her bargain, because a mistaken value alone is not enough to take back a deal.

Conscious Uncertainty. No rescission is permitted where one of the parties knows he is taking on a risk; that is, he realizes there is uncertainty about the quality of the thing being exchanged. Rufus offers 10 acres of mountainous land to Priscilla. "I can't promise you anything about this land," he says, "but they've found gold on every adjoining parcel." Priscilla, eager for gold, buys the land, digs long and hard, and discovers—mud. She may not rescind the contract. She understood the risk she was assuming, and there was no mutual mistake.

15-2c **Duress**

True consent is also lacking when one party agrees to a contract under **duress.** If kindly Uncle Hugo signs over the deed to the ranch because Niece Nelly is holding a gun to his head, Hugo has not consented in any real sense, and he will have the right to rescind the contract.

Duress

An improper threat made to force another party to enter into a contract

If one party makes an improper threat that causes the victim to enter into a contract, and the victim had no reasonable alternative, the contract is voidable.

On a Sunday morning, Bancroft Hall drove to pick up his daughter Sandra, who had slept at a friend's house. The Halls are black and the neighborhood was white. A suspicious neighbor called the police, who arrived, aggressively prevented the Halls from getting into their own car, and arrested the father. The Halls had not violated any law or otherwise done anything wrong. Later an officer told Hall that he could leave immediately if he signed a release relinquishing his right to sue the police, but that if he refused to sign it, he would be detained for a bail hearing. Hall signed the release but later filed suit. The police defended based on the release.

The court held that the release was voidable because Hall had signed it under duress. The threat to detain Hall for a bail hearing was clearly improper because he had committed no crime. He also had no reasonable alternative to signing. A jury awarded the Halls over half a million dollars.[9]

Can "improper threats" take other forms? Does *economic* intimidation count? Many plaintiffs have posed that question over the last half century, and courts have grudgingly yielded.

Today, in most states, economic duress *can* also be used to void a contract. But economic duress sounds perilously close to hard bargaining—in other words, business. The free market system is expected to produce tough competition. A smart, aggressive executive may bargain fiercely. How do we distinguish economic duress from legal, successful business tactics? Courts have created no single rule to answer the question, but they do focus on certain issues.

In analyzing a claim of economic duress, courts look at these factors:

- Acts that have no legitimate business purpose
- Greatly unequal bargaining power
- An unnaturally large gain for one party
- Financial distress to one party

Is the following case one of duress or hard bargaining?

---

[9]Halls v. Ochs, 817 F.2d 920 (1st Cir. 1987).

You be the Judge

Facts: Amy Maida sued her employer, RLS Legal Solutions, for various claims relating to her job. RLS asked that the case be dismissed because Maida had signed an arbitration agreement. Maida had in fact signed the contract while already working at RLS. However, she responded that the agreement should not be enforced because she had signed it under economic duress. At trial, she was asked whether she had found the agreement acceptable:

IN RE RLS LEGAL SOLUTIONS, L.L.C.
221 S.W.3d 629
Supreme Court of Texas, 2007

"I did not. The arbitration clause was going to allow me not to be able to be in a position that I needed to be in now, and that is, to have someone represent me to help me where I feel like the company did me wrong.

After I refused to agree to this arbitration clause, I was told that my payroll checks would not be direct deposited into my account until I signed the agreement and that I would not be paid until I signed the agreement. I had received my paychecks by direct deposit for three years. [RLS did in fact stop the direct deposit payment of Maida's salary.]

I needed my paycheck to meet my financial responsibilities since I am a single family income household provider. I had no way to pay my mortgage, vehicle note, car and homeowner's insurance as well as any household bills."

Maida testified that after signing and returning the agreement, she received a manual check. Maida said that when she asked why she had not been paid by direct deposit as usual, she was told her paycheck would be held until she signed the agreement.

RLS argued that Maida had eventually received every paycheck to which she was entitled, had suffered no losses, and was free to leave RLS at any time if she found her employment terms unacceptable.

The trial court refused to dismiss the case or order arbitration, and RLS appealed.

You Be the Judge: *Did Maida sign the arbitration under economic duress?*

Argument for RLS: Your honors, it is hard to take seriously a claim of economic duress when the plaintiff has not lost one cent and was never forced to sign anything. RLS runs a business, not a community center.

To stay competitive, we constantly revise our commercial practices, and this was one such change. We did not ask for a bizarre or inappropriate change: Arbitration is a widely favored method of settling disputes, quicker and cheaper *for all parties*. Maida signed. Yes, we stopped direct deposit of her check, but in the end, we paid her all she was due. We were not obligated to pay her in any particular fashion, or even to continue her employment. If she wanted to stay with us, she had to play by our rules.

Argument for Maida: The company could offer an arbitration contract to all workers. But that is distinct from forcing such agreements down employee throats, which is what they did here. RLS knows that its workers depend on prompt payment of payroll checks to avoid falling quickly into debt. The company offered Maida the arbitration agreement, she rejected it, and they responded by stopping direct deposit of her check. Knowing that she was the sole provider for her family, the firm intended to subject her to intolerable economic pressure. It worked. However, the court should have no part of this coercion. The two sides had hugely differing bargaining power, and RLS attempted to use financial distress to obtain what it could not by persuasion.

15-2d **Undue Influence**

Recall the hospital-bound Huguette Clark, who had penchants for the Smurfs and million-dollar gifts. If her estate can prove that Beth Israel and her physician preyed upon her vulnerability to get her money, it can rescind her agreements based on *undue influence*. Where one party has used undue influence, the contract is voidable at the option of the injured party. There are two elements to the plaintiff's case. **To prove undue influence, the injured party must demonstrate:**

- A relationship between the two parties either of trust or of domination, and

- Improper persuasion by the stronger party.[10]

Heiresses are not the only victims of undue influence. Eighty-year-old Agnes Seals owned a small building in New York City, but she was homebound and unable to care for herself or the property. A 35-year-old neighbor, David Aviles, seemingly came to her rescue. Promising to take care of her for the rest of her life, he earned her trust by bringing her groceries and ultimately convinced her to sell him her building at a deep discount. At the

---

[10]Restatement (Second) of Contracts §177.

closing, Mrs. Seals was represented by an attorney of David's choosing whom she had never met. The court ruled that David exploited Mrs. Seals for his own financial gain and that undue influence rendered the transactions voidable.[11]

Chapter Conclusion

Agreement alone may not be enough to make a contract enforceable. A minor or a mentally impaired person may generally disaffirm contracts. Even if both parties are adults of sound mind, courts will insist that consent be genuine. Misrepresentation, mistake, duress, and undue influence all indicate that at least one party did not truly consent. As the law evolves, it imposes an increasingly greater burden of *good faith negotiating* on the party in the stronger position.

EXAM REVIEW

1. **VOIDABLE CONTRACT**   Capacity and consent are different contract issues that can lead to the same result: a voidable contract. A voidable agreement is one that can be canceled by a party who lacks legal capacity or who did not give true consent.

2. **MINORS**   A minor (someone under the age of 18) generally may disaffirm any contract while she is still a minor or within a reasonable time after reaching age 18.

EXAM Strategy

Question: John Marshall and Kirsten Fletcher decided to live together. They leased an apartment, each agreeing to pay one-half of the rent. When he signed the lease, Marshall was 17. Shortly after signing the lease, Marshall turned 18, and two weeks later, he moved into the apartment. He paid his half of the rent for two months and then moved out because he and Fletcher were not getting along. Fletcher sued Marshall for one-half of the monthly rent for the remainder of the lease. Who wins?

Strategy: Marshall was clearly a minor when he signed the lease, and he could have rescinded the agreement at that time. However, after he turned 18, he moved in and began to pay rent. What effect did that have on his contract obligation? (See the "Result" at the end of this section.)

3. **MENTAL IMPAIRMENT**   A mentally impaired person may generally disaffirm a contract. In such a case, though, he generally must make restitution.

---

[11]Sepulveda v. Aviles, 762 N.Y.S.2d 358 (NY S. Ct. 2003).

4. INTOXICATION A person who is so intoxicated that he fails to understand the nature of an agreement may disaffirm a contract.

5. FRAUD Fraud is grounds for rescinding a contract. The injured party must prove all of the following:

a. A false statement of fact made intentionally or recklessly

b. Materiality

c. Justifiable reliance

6. INNOCENT MISREPRESENTATION Innocent misrepresentation also allows an injured party to rescind a contract, but it does not allow a plaintiff to sue for damages. It has the same elements as fraud, but it does not require intent or recklessness.

EXAM Strategy

Question: Ron buys 1,000 "Smudgy Dolls" for his toy store. Karen, the seller, tells him the dolls are in perfect condition, even though she knows their heads are defectively attached. Ron sells all of the products, but then he has to face 1,000 angry customers with headless dolls. Ron sues Karen seeking recission. What is the likely outcome?

a. This is fraud, and Ron will be able to rescind.

b. This is an innocent misrepresentation, and Ron will be able to rescind.

c. This is fraud, but Ron will not be able to rescind.

d. This is an innocent misrepresentation, but Ron will not be able to rescind.

e. This is neither fraud nor an innocent misrepresentation.

Strategy: Karen knew her statement was false, so this is a case of fraud if all elements can be met. Ron must prove a false statement of fact, materiality, and reliance. Can he do so? (See the "Result" at the end of this section.)

7. SILENCE Silence amounts to misrepresentation only in four instances:

- When disclosure is necessary to correct a previous assertion

- When disclosure would correct a basic mistaken assumption on which the other party is relying

- When disclosure would correct the other party's mistaken understanding about a writing

- Where there is a relationship of trust between the two parties.

8. UNILATERAL MISTAKE In a case of unilateral mistake, the injured party may rescind only upon a showing that the other party knew or had reason to know of the mistake, the mistake was solely mathematical or mechanical, or that enforcement would be unconscionable.

9. **MUTUAL MISTAKE.**   When both parties to a contract make the same fundamental factual error as to the existence or the identity of the contract's subject matter, either party may rescind.

10. **DURESS**   If one party makes an improper threat that causes the victim to enter into a contract, and the victim had no reasonable alternative, the contract is voidable.

EXAM Strategy

Question: Andreini's nerve problem diminished the use of his hands. Dr. Beck operated, but the problem grew worse. A nurse told the patient that Beck might have committed a serious error that exacerbated the problem. Andreini returned for a second operation, which Beck assured him would correct the problem. But after Andreini had been placed in a surgical gown, shaved, and prepared for surgery, the doctor insisted that he sign a release relieving Beck of liability for the first operation. Andreini did not want to sign it, but Beck refused to operate until he did. Later, Andreini sued Beck for malpractice. A trial court dismissed Andreini's suit based on the release. You are on the appeals court. Will you affirm the dismissal or reverse?

Strategy: Andreini is claiming physical duress. Did Beck act *improperly* in demanding a release? Did Andreini have a *realistic alternative?* (See the "Result" at the end of this section.)

11. **UNDUE INFLUENCE**   Once again the injured party may rescind a contract, but only upon a showing of a special relationship of trust and improper persuasion.

2. Result: A minor can disaffirm a contract. However, if he turns 18 and then ratifies the agreement, he is fully liable. When he paid the rent, Marshall ratified the contract, and thus he is fully liable.

6. Result: Karen made a false statement of fact, knowing it was wrong. It was material, and Ron reasonably relied on her. Karen has committed fraud. Ron is entitled to rescind the agreement. The correct answer is "a."

10. Result: The Utah Supreme Court reversed the trial court, so you probably should as well. Beck forced Andreini to sign under duress. The threat to withhold surgery was improper, and Andreini had no reasonable alternative.

MULTIPLE-CHOICE QUESTIONS

1. Kerry finds a big green ring in the street. She shows it to Leroy, who says, "Wow. That could be valuable." Neither Kerry nor Leroy knows what the ring is made of or whether it is valuable. Kerry sells the ring to Leroy for $100, saying, "Don't come griping if it turns out to be worth two dollars." Leroy takes the ring to a jeweler who

tells him it is an unusually perfect emerald, worth at least $75,000. Kerry sues to rescind.

(a) Kerry will win based on fraud.

(b) Kerry will win based on mutual mistake.

(c) Kerry will win based on unilateral mistake.

(d) Kerry will lose.

2. Veronica has a beer and then makes a contract. She continues drinking, and her blood alcohol level eventually rises to .09, which is just above her state's threshold for drunk driving. She makes a second contract while in this condition. Veronica's first contract is _____ , and her second contract is _____ .

(a) valid; valid

(b) valid; voidable

(c) voidable; voidable

(d) voidable; void

3. Jerry is so mentally ill that he is unable to understand the nature and consequences of his transactions, but he has not been adjudicated insane. Penny has been adjudicated insane, and has a court-appointed a guardian. Jerry's contracts are _____ , and Penny's contracts are _____ .

(a) valid; valid

(b) valid; voidable

(c) valid; void

(d) voidable; voidable

(e) voidable; void

4. Angela makes a material misstatement of fact to Lance, which he relies on when he signs Angela's contract. Fraud exists if Angela made the misstatement _____ .

(a) intentionally

(b) recklessly

(c) carelessly

(d) a and b only

(e) a, b, and c

5. Scarborough's Department Store opens for business on a busy shopping day just before Christmas. A hurried clerk places a sign in the middle of a table piled high with red cashmere sweaters. The sign reads, "SALE—100% Cashmere—$0.99 Each." The sign, of course, was supposed to read "$99 each."

This is a _____ mistake, and customers _____ be able to demand that Scarborough's sell the sweaters for 99 cents.

(a) unilateral; will

(b) unilateral; will not

(c) mutual; will

(d) mutual; will not

CASE QUESTIONS

1. Raymond Barrows owned a 17-acre parcel of undeveloped land in Seaford, Delaware. For most of his life, Mr. Barrows had been an astute and successful businessman, but by the time he was 85 years old, he had been diagnosed as "very senile and confused 90 percent of the time." Glenn Bowen offered to buy the land. Barrows had no idea of its value, so Bowen had it appraised by a friend, who said it was worth $50,000. Bowen drew up a contract, which Barrows signed. In the contract, Barrows agreed to sell the land for $45,000, of which Bowen would pay $100 at the time of closing; the remaining $44,900 was due whenever Bowen developed the land and sold it. There was no time limit on Bowen's right to develop the land nor any interest due on the second payment. Comment.

2. On television and in magazines, Maurine and Mamie Mason saw numerous advertisements for Chrysler Fifth Avenue automobiles. The ads described the car as "luxurious," "quality-engineered," and "reliable." When they went to inspect the car, the salesman told them the warranty was "the best ... comparable to Cadillacs and Lincolns." After the Masons bought a Fifth Avenue, they began to have many problems with it. Even after numerous repairs, the car was unsatisfactory and required more work. The Masons sued, seeking to rescind the contract based on the ads and the dealer's statement. Will they win?

3. The McAllisters had several serious problems with their house, including leaks in the ceiling, a buckling wall, and dampness throughout. They repaired the buckling wall by installing I-beams to support it. They never resolved the leaks and the dampness. When they decided to sell the house, they said nothing to prospective buyers about the problems. They stated that the I-beam had been added for reinforcement. The Silvas bought the house for $60,000. Soon afterward, they began to have problems with leaks, mildew, and dampness. Are the Silvas entitled to any money damages? Why or why not?

4. Roy Newburn borrowed money and bought a $49,000 truck from Treadwell Ford. A few months later, the truck developed transmission problems. Newburn learned that the truck had 170,000 more miles on it than the odometer indicated. The company admitted the mileage error and promised to install a new transmission for free. Treadwell did install the new transmission, but when Newburn came to pick up the truck, Treadwell demanded that he sign a general release absolving the dealership of any claims based on the inaccurate mileage. Treadwell refused to turn over the truck until Newburn finally signed. The truck broke down again, and delays cost Newburn so much income that he fell behind on his loan payments and lost the truck. He sued Treadwell, which defended based on the release. Is the release valid?

5. Morell bought a security guard business from Conley, including the property on which the business was located. Neither party knew that underground storage tanks were leaking and contaminating the property. After the sale, Morell discovered the tanks and sought to rescind the contract. Should he be allowed to do so?

DISCUSSION QUESTIONS

1. Sixteen-year-old Travis Mitchell brought his Pontiac GTO into M&M Precision Body and Paint for body work and a paint job. M&M did the work and charged $1,900, which Travis paid. When Travis later complained about the quality of the work, M&M did some touching up, but Travis was still dissatisfied. He demanded his $1,900 back, but M&M refused to refund it because all of the work was "in" the car and Travis could not return it to the shop. The state of Nebraska, where this occurred, follows the majority rule on this issue. Does Travis get his money? Is this a *fair* result?

2. Contract law gives minors substantial legal protection. But does a modern high school student *need* so much protection? Older teens may have been naive in the 1700s, but today, they are quite savvy. Should the law change so that only younger children—perhaps those aged 14 and under—have the ability to undo agreements? Or is the law reasonable the way it currently exists?

3. Ball-Mart, a baseball card store, had a 1968 Nolan Ryan rookie card in almost perfect condition for sale. Any baseball collector would have known that the card was worth at least $1,000; the published monthly price guide listed its market value at $1,200. Bryan was a twelve-year-old boy with a collection of over 40,000 baseball cards. When Bryan went to Ball-Mart, Kathleen, who knew nothing about cards, was filling in for the owner. The Ryan card was marked "1200," so Bryan asked Kathleen if this meant twelve dollars. She said yes and sold it to him for that amount. When Ball-Mart's owner realized the mix-up, he sued to rescind the contract. Who wins?

4. Paula was alone, pregnant, and confused. She needed help and support, which she found at Methodist Mission Home of Texas. In the days following her child's birth, representatives of Methodist Mission forcefully told her that she had no moral or legal right to keep her child: She had to place her baby for adoption. Paula signed the adoption papers, but days later, she decided she wanted to keep the baby after all. Was there any ground to rescind?

5. Do you have sympathy for intoxicated people who make agreements? Should the law ever let them back out of deals when they sober up? After all, no one forced them to get drunk. Should the law be more lenient, or is it reasonable as it currently exists?

6. When Steven Simkin and Laura Blank divorced in 2006, they agreed to split their $13.5 million fortune evenly. Two years later, it became evident that Simkin had a problem: His half was invested in Bernard Madoff's giant Ponzi scheme and he lost millions. Simkin asked Blank to revise their deal and she refused, so he sued to rescind their 2006 settlement based on mutual mistake of fact. He argued that the fatal mistake was that neither party knew that his half was invested in a fraud. Should a court invalidate the settlement for this mistake?

CHAPTER 16

WRITTEN CONTRACTS

Oliver and Perry were college roommates, two sophomores with contrasting personalities. They were sitting in the cafeteria with some friends, Oliver chatting away, Perry slumped on a plastic bench. Oliver suggested that they buy a lottery ticket, as the prize for that week's drawing was $13 million. Perry muttered, "Nah. You never win if you buy just one ticket." Oliver bubbled up, "OK, we'll buy a ticket every week. We'll keep buying them from now until we graduate. Come on, it'll be fun. This month, I'll buy the tickets. Next month, you will, and so on." Other students urged Perry to do it and, finally, he agreed.

The two friends carefully reviewed their deal. Each party was providing consideration—namely, the responsibility for purchasing tickets during his month. The amount of each purchase was clearly defined at one dollar. They would start that week and continue until graduation day, two and a half years down the road.

> **Perry moved out of their dorm room into a suite at the Ritz and refused to give Oliver one red cent.**

Finally, they would share equally any money won. As three witnesses looked on, they shook hands on the bargain. That month, Oliver bought a ticket every week, randomly choosing numbers, and won nothing. The next month, Perry bought a ticket with equally random numbers—and won $52 million. Perry moved out of their dorm room into a suite at the Ritz and refused to give Oliver one red cent. Oliver sued, seeking $26 million, and the return of his blue fleece hoodie. If the former friends had understood the Statute of Frauds, they would never have gotten into this mess.[1]

---

[1]Based loosely on Lydon v. Beauregard (Middlesex Sup. Ct., Mass., 1989), reported in Paul Langher, "Couple Lose Suit to Share $2.8M Prize," *Boston Globe*, December 23, 1989, p. 21.

The rule we examine in this chapter is not exactly news. Originally passed by the British Parliament in 1677, the Statute of Frauds has changed little over the centuries. The purpose was to prevent lying (fraud) in civil lawsuits. Jury trials of that era invited perjury. Neither the plaintiff nor the defendant was permitted to testify, meaning that the jury never heard from the people who really knew what had happened. Instead, the court heard testimony from people who claimed to have witnessed the contract being created. Knowing that he would never be subjected to aggressive cross-examination, a plaintiff might easily allege that a fake contract was real and then bribe witnesses to support his case. A powerful earl, seeking to acquire 300 acres of valuable land owned by a neighboring commoner, might claim that the neighbor had orally promised to sell his land. Although the claim was utterly false, the earl would win if he could bribe enough "reputable" witnesses to persuade the jury.

To provide juries with more reliable evidence that a contract did or did not exist, Parliament passed the Statute of Frauds. It required that in several types of cases, a contract would be enforced only if it were in writing. Contracts involving interests in land were first on the list.

In the days before the Revolutionary War, when Pennsylvania was still a British possession, the colony's supreme court heard the following case, which centered on the Statute of Frauds. Notice the case citation. This is very nearly the first case reported in U.S. history. Back then, rulings were expressed quite differently (and everything was capitalized), but you will be able to see Judge Coleman's point.

Landmark Case

THE LESSEE OF RICHARDSON V. CAMPBELL

1 U.S. 10
Supreme Court of Pennsylvania, 1764

Facts: A tenant had rented land from Richardson. However, Campbell claimed the leased property was really his. Unless the tenant could prove that Richardson owned the land, he would have no right to stay there.

Richardson's tenant offered a deed (which was then called a *patent*) to support his claim; Campbell provided receipts as evidence that he had bought the property.

To prove that the receipts were for the disputed property, Campbell wanted to introduce statements from an important person—Thomas Penn, whose father, William, had founded the Pennsylvania colony. Obviously, the tenant did not want that evidence admitted in court.

Issue: *Was oral evidence about the ownership of land admissible in court?*

Excerpts from Justice Coleman's Decision:
PLAINTIFF supported his Title by a Patent. The Defendant produced Receipts several Years prior to Plaintiff's Patent; but the Plaintiff contend[ed] that the Receipts were only for Money paid on an adjacent Tract; the Defendant produced a Witness to prove a parol Declaration of Mr. Thomas Penn that the Land in dispute was sold to Defendant.

This piece of Evidence was opposed by the Plaintiff, and refused BY THE COURT.

Almost all states of the United States have passed their own version of the Statute of Frauds. It is important to remember, as we examine the rules and exceptions, that Parliament and the state legislatures all had a commendable, straightforward purpose in passing their respective Statutes of Frauds: *to provide a court with the best possible evidence of whether the parties intended to make a contract.* Ironically, the British government has repealed the writing requirement for most contracts. Parliament concluded that the old statute, far from preventing wrongdoing, was helping people commit fraud. A wily negotiator could orally agree to terms and then, if the deal turned unprofitable, walk away from the contract, knowing it was unenforceable without written evidence.

Thus far, no state has entirely repealed its Statute of Frauds. Instead, courts have carved exceptions into the original statute to prevent unfairness. Some scholars have urged state legislatures to go further and repeal the law altogether. Other commentators defend the Statute of Frauds as a valuable tool for justice. They argue that, among other benefits, the requirement of a writing cautions people to be careful before making—or relying on—a promise. For now, the Statute of Frauds is a vital part of law. Sadly, Oliver from the opening scenario will learn this the hard way.

The Statute of Frauds: A plaintiff may not enforce any of the following agreements unless the agreement, or some memorandum of it, is in writing and signed by the defendant. The agreements that must be in writing are those:

- For any interest in **land;**

- That **cannot be performed within one year;**

- To pay the **debt of another;**

- Made by an **executor of an estate to pay the debt of the estate;**

- Made **in consideration of marriage;** and

- For the **sale of goods of $500 or more.**

In other words, when two parties make an agreement covered by any one of these six topics, it must be in writing to be enforceable. Oliver and Perry made a definite agreement to purchase lottery tickets during alternate months and share the proceeds of any winning ticket. But their agreement was to last two and a half years. As the second item on the list indicates, a contract must be in writing if it cannot be performed within one year. The good news is that Oliver gets back his fleece jacket. The bad news is he gets none of the lottery money. Even though three witnesses saw the deal made, it is unlikely to be enforced in any state. Perry will walk away with all $52 million.

Note that although the Oliver–Perry agreement is unenforceable, it is not void. Suppose that Perry does the right thing, agreeing to share the winnings with Oliver. Over the next 20 years, as he receives the winnings, Perry gives one-half to his friend. But then, having squandered his own fortune, Perry demands the money back from Oliver, claiming that the original contract violated the Statute of Frauds. Perry loses. **Once a contract is fully executed, it makes no difference that it was unwritten.** The Statute of Frauds prevents the enforcement of an executory contract; that is, one in which the parties have not fulfilled their obligations. But the contract is not *illegal.* Once both parties have fully performed, neither party may demand rescission. The Statute of Frauds allows a party to cancel future obligations but not to undo past actions.

Ethics The *law* permits Perry to keep all of the lottery money. But does Perry have a *moral* right to deny Oliver his half-share? Is the Statute of Frauds serving a useful purpose here? Remember that Parliament passed the original Statute of Frauds believing that a written document would be more reliable than the testimony of alleged witnesses. If we permitted Oliver to enforce the oral contract, based on his testimony and that of the witnesses, would we simply be inviting other plaintiffs to invent lottery "contracts" that had never been made?

16-1 COMMON LAW STATUTE OF FRAUDS: CONTRACTS THAT MUST BE IN WRITING

16-1a Agreements for an Interest in Land

A contract for the sale of any interest in land must be in writing to be enforceable. Notice the phrase "interest in land." This means *any legal right* regarding land. A house on a lot is an interest in land. A mortgage, an easement, and a leased apartment are all interests in land. As a general rule, leases must therefore be in writing, although most states have created an exception for short-term leases. A short-term lease is often one for a year or less, although the length varies from state to state.

Kary Presten and Ken Sailer were roommates in a rental apartment in New Jersey that had a view of the Manhattan skyline. The lease was in Sailer's name, but the two split all expenses. The building became a "cooperative," meaning that each tenant would have the option of buying the apartment.[2] Sailer learned he could buy his unit for only $55,800 if he promptly paid a $1,000 fee to maintain his rights. He mentioned to Presten that he planned to buy the unit, and Presten asked if he could become half-owner. Sailer agreed and borrowed the $1,000 from Presten to pay his initial fee. But as the time for closing on the purchase came nearer, Sailer realized that he could sell the apartment for a substantial profit. He placed an ad in a paper and promptly received a firm offer for $125,000. Sailer then told Presten that their deal was off, and that he, Sailer, would be buying the unit alone. He did exactly that, and Presten filed suit. Regrettably, the outcome of Presten's suit was only too easy to predict.

"Any interest in land" may sound obscure, but those who understand it are better off than those who do not.

A cooperative apartment is an interest in land, said the court. This agreement could be enforced only if put in writing and signed by Sailer. The parties had put nothing in writing, and therefore Presten was out of luck. He was entitled to his $1,000 back but nothing more. The apartment belonged to Sailer, who could live in it or sell it for a large, quick profit.[3]

Suppose that you are interested in buying five expensive acres in a fast-growing rural area. There is no water on the property, and the only way to bring public water to it is through land owned by the neighbor, Joanne, who agrees to sell you an easement through her property. An *easement* is a legal right that an owner gives to another person to make some use of the owner's land. In other words, Joanne will permit you to dig a 200-foot trench through her land and lay a water pipe there in exchange for $15,000. May you now safely purchase the 5 acres? Not until Joanne has signed the written easement. You might ignore this "technicality," since Joanne seems friendly and honest. But you could then

---

[2]Technically, the residents of a "co-op" do not own their apartments. They own a share of the corporation that owns the building. Along with their ownership shares, residents have a right to lease their unit for a modest fee.

[3]Presten v. Sailer, 225 N.J. Super. 178, 542 A.2d 7 (N.J. Super. Ct. App. Div. 1988).

spend $300,000 buying your property only to learn that Joanne has changed her mind. She might refuse to go through with the deal unless you pay $150,000 for the easement. Without her permission to lay the pipe, your new land is worthless. Avoid such nightmares: Get it in writing.

Exception: Full Performance by the Seller

If the seller completely performs her side of a contract for an interest in land, a court is likely to enforce the agreement even if it was oral. Adam orally agrees to sell his condominium to Maggie for $150,000. Adam delivers the deed to Maggie and expects his money a week later, but Maggie fails to pay. Most courts will allow Adam to enforce the oral contract and collect the full purchase price from Maggie.

Exception: Part Performance by the Buyer

The buyer of land may be able to enforce an oral contract if she paid part of the purchase price *and either* entered upon the land *or* made improvements to it. Suppose that Eloise sues Grover to enforce an alleged oral contract to sell a lot in Happydale. She claims they struck a bargain in January. Grover defends based on the Statute of Frauds, saying that, even if the two did reach an oral agreement, it is unenforceable. Eloise proves that she paid 10 percent of the purchase price, that she began excavating on the lot in February to build a house, and that Grover knew of the work. Eloise has established part performance and will be allowed to enforce her contract.

This exception makes sense if we recall the purpose of the Statute of Frauds: to provide the best possible evidence of the parties' intentions. The fact that Grover permitted Eloise to enter upon the land and begin building on it is compelling evidence that the two parties had reached an agreement. But be aware that most claims of part performance fail. Merely paying a deposit on a house is not part performance. A plaintiff seeking to rely on part performance must show partial payment *and* either entrance onto the land *or* physical improvements to it.

Exception: Promissory Estoppel

The other exception to the writing requirement is our old friend promissory estoppel. **If a promisor makes an oral promise that should reasonably cause the promisee to rely on it, and the promisee does rely, the promisee may be able to enforce the promise**, despite the Statute of Frauds, if that is the only way to avoid injustice. This exception potentially applies to any contract that must be written, such as those for land, those that cannot be performed within one year, and so forth.

Maureen Sullivan and James Rooney lived together for seven years, although they never married. They decided to buy a house. The two agreed that they would be equal owners, but Rooney told Sullivan that in order to obtain Veterans Administration financing, he would have to be the sole owner on the deed. They each contributed to the purchase and maintenance of the house, and Rooney repeatedly told Sullivan that he would change the deed to joint ownership. He never did. When the couple split up, Sullivan sued, seeking a 50 percent interest in the house. She won. The agreement was for an interest in land and should have been in writing, said the court. But Rooney had clearly promised Sullivan that she would be a half-owner, and she had relied by contributing to the purchase and maintenance. The Statute of Frauds was passed to *prevent* fraud, not to enable one person to mislead another and benefit at her expense.[4]

---

[4]*Sullivan v. Rooney,* 404 Mass. 160, 533 N.E.2d 1372 (1989).

EXAM Strategy

Question: Aditi and Danielle, MBA students, need an apartment for next September. They find a lovely two-bedroom unit that the owner is rehabbing. The students can see that the owner is honest, his workmanship excellent. The owner agrees to rent them the apartment beginning September 1, for $1,200 per month for one year. "Come back at the end of August. By then, my work will be done and I'll have the papers to sign." Aditi asks, "Should we sign something now, to be sure?" The landlord laughs and replies, "I trust you. You don't trust me?" They both trust him, and they shake hands on the deal. When the students return in August, the landlord has rented it to Danielle's former boyfriend for $1,400 per month. Aditi and Danielle sue. Who wins?

Strategy: Under the Statute of Frauds, a contract for the sale of any interest in land must be in writing to be enforceable. What does "any interest" mean? Does the Statute of Frauds apply to this case?

Result: An "interest" means any legal right. A lease is an interest in land, meaning that the students cannot enforce this agreement unless it is in writing, signed by the owner—and it is not. The students need to look for a different apartment.

16-1b Agreements That Cannot Be Performed within One Year

Contracts that cannot be performed within one year are unenforceable unless they are in writing. This one-year period begins on the date the parties make the agreement. The critical word here is "cannot." If a contract *could possibly* be completed within one year, it need not be in writing. Betty gets a job at Burger Brain, throwing fries in oil. Her boss tells her she can have Fridays off for as long as she works there. That oral contract is enforceable whether Betty stays one week or twenty years. "As long as she works there" *could* last for less than one year. Betty might quit the job after six months. Therefore, it does not need to be in writing.[5]

If an agreement will *necessarily* take longer than one year to finish, it must be in writing to be enforceable. If Betty is hired for a term of three years as manager of Burger Brain, the agreement is unenforceable unless put in writing. She cannot perform three years of work in one year.

Or, if you hire a band to play at your wedding 15 months from today, the agreement must be in writing. The gig may take only a single day, but that day will definitely not fall in the next 12 months.

The following case is not quite as old as the Statute of Frauds, but it is set in what now seems a distant time—the dark days before corporate executives knew about the Internet. Did the right to develop mtv.com need to be in writing?

---

[5]This is the majority rule. In most states, for example, if a company hires an employee "for life," the contract need not be in writing because the employee could die within one year. "Contracts of uncertain duration are simply excluded [from the Statute of Frauds]; the provision covers only those contracts whose performance cannot possibly be completed within a year." Restatement (Second) of Contracts §130, Comment a, at 328 (1981). See, e.g., Mackay v. Four Rivers Packing Co., 2008 WL 427789 (Id. 2008). However, a few states disagree. The Illinois Supreme Court ruled that a contract for lifetime employment is enforceable only if written. McInerney v. Charter Golf, Inc., 176 Ill. 2d 482 (Ill. 1997).

You be the Judge

MTV Networks v. Curry

867 F.Supp. 202

District Court for the Southern District of New York, 1994

Facts: Adam Curry was an MTV video disc jockey ("VJ") and host of the popular *Headbanger's Ball* and *MTV Top 20 Video Countdown*. In the early days of the Internet, when VJs had big hair and many major companies (including MTV) were not yet online, Curry dreamed up the idea of a website with the address "mtv.com."

In June, 1993, Curry met with MTV vice president Matthew Farber to discuss his idea and ask if MTV would become his partner. Farber told Curry that MTV was not interested in mtv.com, but that Curry was free to register and develop the site at his own expense. And he did. Many MTV employees, including senior executives, encouraged Curry's efforts, even giving him materials to upload to the site. Curry and other VJs advertised mtv.com on air.

In late 1993, MTV began exploring its own online presence. It formally requested that Curry cease use of the mtv.com address. But Curry continued his site, which had already been accessed by millions.

MTV sued Curry for trademark infringement, and Curry counterclaimed for breach of oral contract. MTV moved to dismiss Curry's contract suit, claiming that the promise between MTV and Curry required a writing because it could not be fully executed within one year.

You Be the Judge: *Did an agreement for rights to a web address require a writing?*

Argument for MTV: According to Curry, his contract with MTV provided that he would promote MTV programming on his mtv.com site in return for MTV's promise to give up its web address. Two problems. One, no executives in their right mind would give away a web address in such a casual way. Two, there is absolutely no possibility that this "contract" could be performed within one year. Curry was free to terminate his website at will, but MTV was giving up its rights to "mtv.com" forever. Curry's duties could be completed within a year, but MTV's obligations continue indefinitely. For this reason, this promise had to be in writing. The verbal assurances of MTV executives did not form a binding contract.

Argument for Curry: Your honor, we can all see what happened here. In 1993, MTV executives were blind to the commercial potential of the Internet, so they let Curry test the waters to see if mtv.com would be successful. And now that they have got with the program, they want mtv.com back. But they are too late—they have already contracted away mtv.com to Curry. The Statute of Frauds does not require this agreement to be in writing. Both parties' performances could have been completed within one year: Curry could have canceled development of the website at any time, which also means that MTV's promise to allow Curry to use mtv.com might have ended any time, too. The contract was enforceable and MTV has to pay Curry for its breach.

16-1c Promise to Pay the Debt of Another

When one person agrees to pay the debt of another as a favor to that debtor, it is called a collateral promise, and it must be in writing to be enforceable. D. R. Kemp was a young entrepreneur who wanted to build housing in Tuscaloosa, Alabama. He needed $25,000 to complete a project he was working on, so he went to his old college professor, Jim Hanks, for help. The professor said he would see what he could do about getting Kemp a loan. Professor Hanks spoke with his good friend Travis Chandler, telling him that Kemp was highly responsible and would be certain to repay any money loaned. Chandler trusted Professor Hanks but wanted to be sure of his money. Professor Hanks assured Chandler that if for any reason Kemp did not repay the loan, he, Hanks, would pay Chandler in full. With that assurance, Chandler wrote out a check for $25,000, payable to Kemp, never having met the young man.

Kemp, of course, never repaid the loan. (Thank goodness he did not; this textbook has no use for people who do what they are supposed to do.) Kemp exhausted the cash trying to sustain his business, which failed anyway, so he had nothing to give his creditor. Chandler approached Professor Hanks, who refused to pay, and Chandler sued. The outcome was easy to predict. Professor Hanks had agreed to repay Kemp's debt *as a favor to Kemp*, making it a collateral promise. Chandler had nothing in writing, and that is exactly what he got from his lawsuit—nothing.

Exception: The Leading Object Rule

There is one major exception to the collateral promise rule. **When the promisor guarantees to pay the debt of another and *the leading object of the promise is some benefit to the promisor himself*, then the contract will be enforceable even if unwritten.** In other words, if the promisor makes the guarantee not as a favor to the debtor, but primarily out of *self-interest*, the Statute of Frauds does not apply.

Robert Perry was a hog farmer in Ohio. He owed $26,000 to Sunrise Cooperative, a supplier of feed. Because Perry was in debt, Sunrise stopped giving him feed on credit and began selling him feed on a cash-only basis. Perry also owed money to Farm Credit Services, a loan agency. Perry promised Farm Credit he would repay his loans as soon as his hogs were big enough to sell. But Perry couldn't raise hogs without feed, which he lacked the money to purchase. Farm Credit was determined to bring home the bacon, so it asked Sunrise Cooperative to give Perry the feed on credit. Farm Credit orally promised to pay any debt that Perry did not take care of. When Perry defaulted on his payments to Sunrise, the feed supplier sued Farm Credit based on its oral guarantee. Farm Credit claimed the promise was unenforceable, based on the Statute of Frauds. But the court found in favor of Sunrise. The *leading object* of Farm Credit's promise to Sunrise was self-interest, and the oral promise was fully enforceable.[6]

16-1d Promise Made by an Executor of an Estate

This rule is merely a special application of the previous one, concerning the debt of another person. An executor is the person who is in charge of an estate after someone dies. The executor's job is to pay debts of the deceased, obtain money owed to him, and disburse the assets according to the will. In most cases, the executor will use only the estate's assets to pay those debts. The Statute of Frauds comes into play when an executor promises to pay an estate's debts with her own funds. **An executor's promise to use her own funds to pay a debt of the deceased must be in writing to be enforceable.**

Suppose Esmeralda dies penniless, owing Tina $35,000. Esmeralda's daughter, Sapphire, is the executor of her estate. Tina comes to Sapphire and demands her $35,000. Sapphire responds, "There is no money in mamma's estate, but don't worry, I'll make it up to you with my own money." Sapphire's oral promise is unenforceable. Tina should get it in writing while Sapphire is feeling generous.

16-1e Promise Made in Consideration of Marriage

This is not the stuff of fairy tales: Barney is a multimillionaire with the integrity of a gangster and the charm of a tax collector. He proposes to Li-Tsing, who promptly rejects him. Barney then pleads that if Li-Tsing will be his bride, he will give her an island he owns off the coast of California. Li-Tsing begins to see his good qualities and accepts. After they are married, Barney refuses to deliver the deed. Li-Tsing will get nothing from a court either, because **a promise made in consideration of marriage must be in writing to be enforceable.**

---

[6]Sunrise Cooperative v. Robert Perry, 1992 Ohio App. LEXIS 3913 (Ohio Ct. App. 1992).

16-2 THE COMMON LAW STATUTE OF FRAUDS: WHAT THE WRITING MUST CONTAIN

Each of the types of contract just described must be in writing in order to be enforceable. What must the writing contain? It may be a carefully typed contract, using precise legal terminology, or an informal memo scrawled on the back of a paper napkin at a business lunch. The writing may consist of more than one document, written at different times, with each document making a piece of the puzzle. But there are some general requirements: the writing

- **Must be signed by the defendant, and**

- **Must state with reasonable certainty the name of each party, the subject matter of the agreement, and all of the essential terms and promises.**[7]

16-2a **Signature**

A state's Statute of Frauds typically requires that the writing be "signed by the party to be charged therewith"; that is, the party who is resisting enforcement of the contract. Throughout this chapter, we refer to that person as the defendant, because when these cases go to court, it is the defendant who is disputing the existence of a contract.

Judges define "signature" very broadly. Using a pen to write one's name certainly counts, but it is not required. A secretary who stamps an executive's signature on a letter fulfills this requirement. In fact, any mark or logo placed on a document to indicate acceptance, even an "X," will generally satisfy the Statute of Frauds. And electronic commerce, as we discuss in the next section, creates new methods of signing.

16-2b **Reasonable Certainty**

Suppose Garfield and Hayes are having lunch, discussing the sale of Garfield's vacation condominium. They agree on a price and want to make some notation of the agreement even before their lawyers work out a detailed purchase and sales agreement. A perfectly adequate memorandum might say, "Garfield agrees to sell Hayes his condominium at 234 Baron Boulevard, Apartment 18, for $350,000 cash, payable on June 18, 2015, and Hayes promises to pay the sum on that day." They should make two copies of their agreement and sign both. Notice that although Garfield's memo is short, it is *certain* and *complete*. This is critical because problems of vagueness and incompleteness often doom informal memoranda.

Vagueness

Ella Hayden owned valuable commercial property on a highway called Route 9. She wrote a series of letters to her stepson Mark, promising that several of the children, including Mark, would share the property. One letter said: "We four shall fairly divide on the Route 9 property. [sic]" Other letters said: "When the Route 9 Plaza is sold, you can take a long vacation," and "The property will be sold. You and Dennis shall receive the same amount." Ella Hayden died without leaving Mark anything. He sued, but got nothing. The court ruled:

> The above passages written by Ms. Hayden do not recite the essential elements of the alleged contract with reasonable certainty. The writings do not state unequivocally or with sufficient

---

[7]Restatement (Second) of Contracts §131.

particularity the subject matter to which the writings relate, nor do they provide the terms and conditions of alleged promises made which constitute a contract. The alleged oral contract between Ms. Hayden and Mr. Hayden cannot be identified from the passages from Ms. Hayden's letters quoted above when applied to existing facts. In sum, Mr. Hayden's cause of action seeking an interest in the Route 9 property is foreclosed by the Statute of Frauds.[8]

Incompleteness

During Ronald McCoy's second interview with Spelman Memorial Hospital, the board of directors orally offered him a three-year job as assistant hospital administrator. McCoy accepted. Spelman's CEO, Gene Meyer, sent a letter confirming the offer, which said:

> To reconfirm the offer, it is as follows: 1. We will pay for your moving expenses. 2. I would like you to pursue your Master's Degree at an area program. We will pay 100 percent tuition reimbursement. 3. Effective September 26, you will be eligible for all benefits. 4. A starting salary of $48,000 annually with reviews and eligibility for increases at 6 months, 12 months, and annually thereafter. 5. We will pay for the expenses of 3 trips, if necessary, in order for you to find housing. 6. Vacation will be for 3 weeks a year after one year; however, we do allow for this to be taken earlier. [Signed] Gene Meyer.

Spelman Hospital fired McCoy less than a year after he started work, and McCoy sued. The hospital's letter seems clear, and it is signed by an authorized official. The problem is, it is incomplete. Can you spot the fatal omission? The court did.

McCoy wanted to hold the hospital's board to its spoken promise that he would have a job for a term of three years. To be enforceable, a contract for a term of over one year must be in writing under the Statute of Frauds.

To satisfy the Statute of Frauds, an employment contract—[or] its memorandum or note—must contain *all* essential terms, including *duration of the employment relationship.* Without a statement of duration, an employment-at-will arrangement is created, which is terminable at any time by either party with no liability for breach of contract. McCoy's argument that the letter constituted a memorandum of an oral contract fails because the letter does not state an essential element: duration. The letter did not state that Spelman was granting McCoy employment for any term—only that his salary would be reviewed at 6 months, 12 months, and "annually thereafter."[9]

The lawsuits in this section demonstrate the continuing force of the Statute of Frauds. If the promisor had truly wanted to make a binding commitment, he or she could have written the appropriate contract or memorandum in a matter of minutes. Great formality and expense are unnecessary. But the written document *must be clear and complete,* or it will fail.

EXAM Strategy

Question: Major Retailer and Owner negotiated a lease of a strip mall, the tenancy to begin August 1. Retailer's lawyer then drafted a lease accurately reflecting all terms agreed to, including the parties, exact premises, condition of the store, dates of the lease, and monthly rent of $18,000. Retailer signed the lease and delivered it to Owner on July 1. On July 20, Owner leased the same space to a different tenant for $23,000 per month. Retailer sued, claiming that the parties had a binding deal, and the Owner had breached his agreement in order to obtain higher rent. Who will win?

---

[8]Hayden v. Hayden, Mass. Lawyers Weekly No. 12-299-93 (Middlesex Sup. Ct. 1994).
[9]McCoy v. Spelman Memorial Hospital, 845 S.W.2d 727 (Mo. Ct. App. 1993).

Strategy: To comply with the Statute of Frauds, a writing must state all essential terms. This lease appears to do that. However, the writing must contain one other thing. What is it?

Result: The writing must be *signed* by the party claiming that there is no contract; that is, by the defendant. Owner never signed the lease. This lease does not comply with the Statute of Frauds, and the Retailer will lose his case.

16-2c Electronic Contracts and Signatures

Modern life has moved online: We can now buy everything from toothpaste to cars with the click of a mouse. What happens to the writing requirement, though, when there is no paper? The Statute of Frauds requires some sort of "signature" to prove that the defendant committed to the deal. Today, an "electronic signature" could mean a name typed (or automatically included) at the bottom of an email message, a retinal or vocal scan, or a name signed by electronic pen on a writing tablet, among others.

E-signatures are valid in all 50 states. Almost every state has adopted the Uniform Electronic Transactions Act (UETA), which makes *electronic* contracts and signatures as enforceable as those on paper.[10] In other words, the normal rules of contract formation apply, and neither party can avoid a deal merely because it originated electronically. A federal statute, the **Electronic Signatures in Global and National Commerce Act (E-SIGN)** extends UETA's principles to interstate and foreign commerce.

UETA and E-SIGN also require courts, when in doubt, to favor the validity of email contracts. This requirement means that parties must be careful to avoid entering into contracts *unintentionally*. Stevens was renegotiating his employment contract with his boss through several conversational rounds of email. At one point, Stevens wrote "I accept your proposal" on an email with his signature block. Before a formal contract was inked, Stevens changed his mind. But it was too late. A court ruled that the contract was enforceable the moment Stevens pressed "send" with an acceptance and a signature block. Stevens might have considered email to be an informal conversation, but in fact, it created a final, binding contract.[11]

Note that, in many states, certain documents still require a traditional (non-electronic) signature. Wills, adoptions, court orders, and notice of foreclosure are common exceptions. If in doubt, get a hard copy, signed in ink.

16-3 THE UCC'S STATUTE OF FRAUDS

We have reached another section dedicated to the Uniform Commercial Code. Remember that UCC rules govern only contracts involving a sale of goods. Because merchants can make many verbal contracts every day, the drafters of the UCC wanted to make the writing requirement less onerous for the sale of goods.

The UCC requires a writing for the sale of goods priced $500 or more. The Code's requirements are easier to meet than those of the common law. **UCC §2-201**, the Statute of Frauds section, has three important elements:

1. The basic rule

2. The merchants' exception

3. Special circumstances

---

[10]Note that while Illinois, New York, and Washington have not adopted UETA, they have adopted their own similar versions of it.
[11]Stevens v. Publicis, S.A. 50 AD3d 253 (N.Y. Sup. Ct. 2008).

16-3a UCC §2-201(1)—The Basic Rule

A contract for the sale of goods of $500 or more is not enforceable unless there is some writing, signed by the defendant, indicating that the parties reached an agreement. The key difference between the common-law rule and the UCC rule is that the Code does *not* require *all* of the terms of the agreement to be in writing. The Code looks for something simpler: *an indication that the parties reached an agreement.* Only two things are required: the signature of the defendant and the quantity of goods being sold. Suppose a short memorandum between textile dealers indicates that Seller will sell to Buyer "grade AA 100 percent cotton, white athletic socks." If the writing does not state the price, the parties can testify at court about what the market price was at the time of the deal. If the writing says nothing about the delivery date, the court will assume a reasonable delivery date, say, 60 days. But how many socks were to be delivered? 100 pairs or 100,000? The court will have no objective evidence, and so, the quantity must be written.

> The key difference between the common-law rule and the UCC rule is that the Code does *not* require *all* of the terms of the agreement to be in writing.

Writing	Result
"Confirming phone conversation today, I will send you 1,000 reams of paper for laser printing, usual quality & price. [Signed,] Seller."	This memorandum satisfies UCC §2-201(1), and the contract may be enforced against the seller. The buyer may testify as to the "usual" quality and price between the two parties, and both sides may rely on normal trade usage.
"Confirming phone conversation today, I will send you best quality paper for laser printing, $3.25 per ream, delivery date next Thursday. [Signed,] Seller."	This memorandum is not enforceable because it states no quantity.

The UCC's purpose is to make sales easier while still preventing fraud. Ultimately, courts seek to balance the formality of the writing requirement with their own common sense. They examine the situation as a whole to determine if there is enough evidence to show that the parties contracted. The following case involved an art auction, a wily buyer, and a precious Russian box worth, well, we do not know what it was worth, but definitely more than $500. The one thing lacking? A single document signed by the defendant.

WILLIAM J. JENACK ESTATE APPRAISERS AND AUCTIONEERS, INC. v. ALBERT RABIZADEH

2013 NY Slip Op 08373
Court of Appeals of New York, 2013

Facts: William J. Jenack Estate Appraisers and Auctioneers, Inc. sold fine art and antiques at public auctions. Albert Rabizadeh wanted to buy a nineteenth-century Russian silver and enamel box, with an estimated value of $4,000, that was to be sold at one of Jenack's auctions. Rabizadeh could not attend the auction, so he submitted an "absentee

William J. Jenack Estate Appraisers & Auctioneers

This rare Russian box measured only 1½ by 3⅝ inches, but was worth a fortune.

bidder form," in accordance with Jenack's online and telephone bidder policy. Rabizadeh signed the form and listed his name, email address, telephone numbers, fax number, address, credit card number, and the items that he intended to bid on. Jenack assigned Rabizadeh bidder number 305.

The rare Russian box garnered much excitement from collectors who believed it was worth much more than its initially appraised value of $4,000. During the frenzied auction, Rabizadeh beat out many other bidders with a telephone bid of $400,000. (Yes, that is two zeros more than $4,000—it was quite a box.) Jenack recorded Rabizadeh's winning bid on an official "clerking sheet," along with the item, its description, and bidder number 305. When he received Jenack's invoice, Rabizadeh decided he did not want it anymore and refused to pay.

Jenack sued Rabizadeh for breach of contract. Rabizadeh claimed that there was no contract because the sale was not in a signed writing, as required by the UCC for goods over $500. Jenack argued that the clerking sheet and related documents satisfied the writing requirement, because they contained all the necessary terms. The trial court agreed with Jenack and awarded it $402,398. A New York appeals court reversed the decision. Jenack appealed to New York's highest court.

Issue: *Did the clerking sheet and the absentee bidder form satisfy the Statute of Frauds?*

Excerpts from Judge Rivera's Decision: In general, a contract for the sale of goods at a price of $500 or more must comply with the signed writing requirement of the UCC. In the case of a public auction, a bid may satisfy the [UCC's] Statute of Frauds where there exists an appropriate writing "signed by the party against whom enforcement is sought to be charged" (*see* UCC 2-201). [New York law also permits] a memorandum specifying the nature and price of the item, the terms of sale, and the names of the parties.

It is well established that the writing need not be contained in one single document, but rather may be furnished by piecing together other, related writings. Therefore, a court may look to documents relevant to the bidding and the auction.

The clerking sheet, in isolation, does not satisfy the New York law because it requires the disclosure of the name of the buyer. We are unpersuaded by Jenack's arguments that this requirement can be satisfied by Jenack's insertion of numbers in place of those names. To allow for numbers, rather than names, would undermine the purpose of the Statute by increasing the possibility of fraud.

We must consider whether there are "related writings" that supply the required names, and which may be read, along with the clerking sheet, to provide the information necessary to constitute a memorandum. The absentee bidder form, along with the clerking sheet, provide the necessary information to establish the name of Rabizadeh as the buyer. This conclusion is inescapable given that each of the documents contained information pertaining to the terms of the sale. Both contain the item number, the bidder number, the auctioneer, and a detailed description of the item.

The Statute of Frauds was not enacted to afford persons a means of evading just obligations. [That] is precisely what Rabizadeh attempts to do here, but the law and the facts foreclose him from doing so. Rabizadeh took affirmative steps to participate in Jenack's auction, including executing an absentee bidder form with the required personal information. He then successfully won the bidding, closing out other interested bidders, with his $400,000 bid. He cannot seek to avoid the consequences of his actions by ignoring the existence of a documentary trail leading to him.

16-3b UCC §2-201(2)—The Merchants' Exception

When both parties are "merchants," that is, businesspeople who routinely deal in the goods being sold, the Code will accept an even more informal writing. **Within a reasonable time of making an oral contract, if a merchant sends a written confirmation to another, and if the confirmation is definite enough to bind the *sender herself*, then the merchant who receives the confirmation will *also* be bound by it unless he objects in writing within 10 days.** This exception dramatically changes the rules from the common law, but it applies only between two merchants. The UCC's drafters assumed that experienced merchants are able to take care of themselves in fast-moving negotiations. The critical difference is this: A writing may create a binding contract *even when it is not signed by the defendant.*

Madge manufactures "beanies," that is, silly caps with plastic propellers on top. Rachel, a retailer, telephones her, and they discuss the price of the beanies, shipping time, and other details. Madge then faxes Rachel a memo: "This confirms your order for 2,500 beanies at $12.25 per beanie. Colors: blue, green, black, orange, red. Delivery date: 10 days. [Signed] Madge." Rachel receives the fax, reads it while negotiating with another manufacturer, and throws it in the wastebasket. Rachel buys her beanies elsewhere, and Madge sues. Rachel defends, claiming there is no written contract because she, Rachel, never signed anything. Madge wins under UCC §2-201(2). Both parties were merchants because they routinely dealt in these goods. Madge signed and sent a confirming memo that could have been used to hold her, Madge, to the deal. When Rachel read it, she was not free to disregard it. Obviously, the intelligent business practice would have been to promptly fax a reply saying, "I disagree. We do not have any deal for beanies." Since Rachel failed to respond within 10 days, Madge has an enforceable contract.

16-3c UCC §2-201(3)—Special Circumstances

An oral contract *may* be enforceable, even without a written memorandum, if:

- **The seller is specially manufacturing the goods for the buyer, *or***
- **The defendant admits in court proceedings that there was a contract, *or***
- **The goods have been delivered or they have been paid for.**

Specially Manufactured Goods

If a seller, specially manufacturing goods for the buyer, begins work on them before the buyer cancels, and the goods cannot be sold elsewhere, the oral contract is binding. Bernice manufactures solar heating systems. She phones Jason and orders 75 special electrical converter units designed for her heating system, at $150 per unit. Jason begins manufacturing the units, but then Bernice phones again and says she no longer needs them. Bernice is bound by the contract. The goods are being manufactured for her and cannot be sold elsewhere. Jason had already begun work when she attempted to cancel. If the case goes to court, Jason will win.

Admissions in Court

When the defendant admits in court proceedings that the parties made an oral contract, the agreement is binding. Rex sues Sophie, alleging that she orally agreed to sell him five boa constrictors that have been trained to stand in a line and pass a full wineglass from one snake to the next. Sophie defends the lawsuit, but during a deposition, she says, "OK, we agreed verbally, but nothing was ever put in writing, and I knew I didn't have to go through with it. When I went home, the snakes made me feel really guilty, and I decided not to sell." Sophie's admission under oath dooms her defense.

Goods Delivered or Paid For

If the seller has delivered the goods, or the buyer has paid for them, the contract may be enforced even with nothing in writing. Malik orally agrees to sell 500 plastic chairs to a university for use in its cafeteria. Malik delivers 300 of the chairs, but then the university notifies him that it will not honor the deal. Malik is entitled to payment for the 300 chairs, although not for the other 200. Conversely, if the university had sent a check for one-half of the chairs, it would be entitled to 250 chairs.

EXAM Strategy

Question: Beasley is a commercial honey farmer. He orally agrees to sell 500,000 pounds of honey to Grizzly at $1 per pound. Grizzly immediately faxes Beasley a signed confirmation, summarizing the deal. Beasley receives the fax but ignores it, and he never responds to Grizzly. Five days later, Beasley sells his honey to Brown for $1.15 per pound. Grizzly sues Beasley for breach of contract. Beasley claims that he signed nothing and was free to sell his honey anywhere he wanted. Who will win?

Strategy: Honey is a movable thing, meaning that this contract is governed by the UCC. Under the Code, contracts for the sale of goods worth $500 or more must be in writing. However, the merchant exception changes things when both parties are merchants. Beasley and Grizzly are both merchants. Apply the merchant exception.

Result: Beasley breached the contract. Within a reasonable time after making the agreement, Grizzly sent a memo to Beasley confirming it. Beasley had 10 days either to object in writing or be held to the agreement. Beasley will lose this lawsuit because he ignored the faxed confirmation.

16-4 PAROL EVIDENCE

Tyrone agrees to buy Martha's house for $800,000. The contract obligates Tyrone to make a 10 percent down payment immediately and pay the remaining $720,000 in 45 days. As the two parties sign the deal, Tyrone discusses his need for financing. Unfortunately, at the end of 45 days, he has been unable to get a mortgage for the full amount. He claims that the parties orally agreed that he would get his deposit back if he could not obtain financing, but the written agreement says no such thing, and Martha disputes the claim. Who will win? Probably Martha, because of the parol evidence rule.

Parol evidence refers to anything (apart from the written contract itself) that was said, done, or written *before* the parties signed the agreement or *as they signed it*. Martha's conversation with Tyrone about financing the house was parol evidence because it occurred as they were signing the contract. Another important term is **integrated contract**, which means a writing that the parties intend as the final, complete expression of their agreement. Now for the rule.

Integrated contract

A writing that the parties intend as the final, complete expression of their agreement

The parol evidence rule: When two parties make an integrated contract, neither one may use parol evidence to contradict, vary, or add to its terms. Negotiations may last for hours, weeks, or even months. Almost no contract includes everything that the parties said. When parties consider their agreement integrated, any statements they made before or while signing are irrelevant. If a court determines that Martha and Tyrone intended their agreement to be integrated, it will prohibit testimony about Martha's oral promises. One way to avoid parol evidence disputes is to include an *integration clause*. That is a statement clearly proclaiming that this writing is the "full and final expression" of the parties' agreement, and that anything said before signing or while signing is irrelevant. In the following case, learned people learned about parol evidence the hard way.

MAYO v. NORTH CAROLINA STATE UNIVERSITY

168 N.C.App. 503
North Carolina Court of Appeals, 2005

Facts: Dr. Robert Mayo was a tenured faculty member of the engineering department at North Carolina State University (NCSU), and director of the school's nuclear engineering program. In July, he informed his department chair, Dr. Paul Turinsky, that he was leaving NCSU effective September 1. Turinsky accepted the resignation.

In October, after Mayo had departed, Phyllis Jennette, the university's payroll coordinator, informed him that he had been overpaid. She explained that for employees who worked 9 months but were paid over 12 months, the salary checks for July and August were in fact prepayments for the period beginning that September. Because Mayo had not worked after September 1, the checks for July and August were overpayment. When he refused to refund the money, NCSU sought to claim it in legal proceedings. The first step was a hearing before an administrative agency.

At the hearing, Turinsky and Brian Simet, the university's payroll director, explained that the "prepayment" rule was a basic part of every employee's contract. However, both acknowledged that the prepayment rule was not included in any of the documents that formed Mayo's contract, including his appointment letter, annual salary letter, and policies adopted by the university's trustees. The university officials used other evidence, outside the written documents, to establish the prepayment policy.

Based on the additional evidence, the agency ruled that NCSU was entitled to its money. However, Mayo appealed to court, and the trial judge declared that he owed nothing, ruling that the university was not permitted to rely on parol evidence to establish its policy. NCSU appealed.

Issue: *May NCSU rely on parol evidence to establish its prepayment rule?*

Excerpts from Judge Bryant's Decision: Here, the language of the employment agreement is clear and unambiguous—petitioner is to be paid in twelve monthly installments for his service as a nine-month, academic year, tenured faculty member.

The terms relied upon by NCSU were not expressly included in the employment agreement. Dr. Turinsky testified that petitioner's written employment agreement is comprised of terms found in petitioner's appointment letter, annual salary letter, and written policies adopted and amended by the UNC Board of Governors and the NCSU Board of Trustees. However, none of these documents forming the employment agreement set forth the compensation policies upon which NCSU bases its claim. Simet, Director of NCSU's Payroll Department, admitted at the agency hearing that the policies were "not stated anywhere specifically." Further, Dr. Turinsky testified he did not know of the existence of the terms until September, after petitioner left his employment with NCSU. NCSU, however, attempts to offer parol evidence to explain that payments made in July and August were prepayments for the following academic year.

The parol evidence rule prohibits the admission of parol evidence to vary, add to, or contradict a written instrument intended to be the final integration of the transaction. The rule is otherwise where it is shown that the writing is not a full integration of the terms of the contract, or when a contract is ambiguous, parol evidence is admissible to show and make certain the intention behind the contract.

Here Dr. Turinsky testified that petitioner's employment agreement consisted only of petitioner's appointment letter, his annual salary letter, and the policies adopted and amended by the UNC Board of Governors and by the NCSU Board of Trustees. It therefore appears the parties intended the above documents to be the final integration of the employment agreement. Additionally, we have already noted the language contained in the documents are unambiguous; thus, parol evidence may not be introduced to explain the terms of the agreement.

We hold petitioner does not owe a debt to NCSU as result of an alleged overpayment of salary.

[Affirmed.]

16-4a Exception: An Incomplete or Ambiguous Contract

If a court determines that a written contract is incomplete or ambiguous, it will permit parol evidence. Suppose that an employment contract states that the company will provide "full health coverage for Robert Watson and his family," but does not define *family*. Three years later, Watson divorces and remarries, acquiring three stepchildren, and a year later, his second wife has a baby. Watson now has two children by his first marriage and four by the second. The company refuses to insure Watson's first wife or his stepchildren. A court will probably find a key clause in his health care contract—"coverage for ... *his family*"—is ambiguous. A judge cannot determine exactly what the clause means from the contract itself, so the parties will be permitted to introduce parol evidence to prove whether or not the company must insure Watson's extended family.[12]

16-4b Fraud, Misrepresentation, or Duress

A court will permit parol evidence of fraud, misrepresentation, or duress. To encourage Annette to buy his house, Will assures her that no floodwaters from the nearby river have ever come within 2 miles of the house. Annette signs a contract that is silent about flooding and includes an integration clause stating that neither party is relying on any oral statements made during negotiations. When Annette moves in, she discovers that the foundation is collapsing due to earlier flooding and that Will knew of the flooding and the damage. Despite the integration clause, a court will probably allow Annette to testify about Will's misrepresentations.[13]

Chapter Conclusion

Some contracts must be in writing to be enforceable, and the writing must be clear and unambiguous. Drafting the contract need not be arduous. The disputes illustrated in this chapter could all have been prevented with a few carefully crafted sentences. It is worth the time and effort to write them.

EXAM REVIEW

1. **THE STATUTE OF FRAUDS**   Several types of contract are enforceable only if written:

   - **LAND**   The sale of any interest in land.

   - **ONE YEAR**   An agreement that *cannot* be performed within one year.

---

[12]See, for example, Eure v. Norfolk Shipbuilding & Drydock Corp., Inc., 561 S.E.2d 663 (Va. 2002).
[13]Lindberg v. Roseth, 137 Idaho 222 (Idaho 2002).

CPA Question: Able hired Carr to restore Able's antique car for $800. The terms of their oral agreement provided that Carr had 18 months to complete the work. Actually, the work could be completed within one year. The agreement is:

(a) Unenforceable because it covers services with a value in excess of $500

(b) Unenforceable because it covers a time period in excess of one year

(c) Enforceable because personal service contracts are exempt from the Statute of Frauds

(d) Enforceable because the work could be completed within one year

Strategy: This is a subtle question. Notice that the contract is for a sum greater than $500. But that is a red herring. Why? The contract also might take 18 months to perform. But it *could* be finished in less than a year. (See the "Result" at the end of this section.)

- **DEBT OF ANOTHER** A promise to pay the debt of another, including promises made by executors to pay an estate's debts.

Question: Donald Waide had a contracting business. He bought most of his supplies from Paul Bingham's supply center. Waide fell behind on his bills, and Bingham told Waide that he would extend no more credit to him. That same day, Donald's father, Elmer Waide, came to Bingham's store, and said to Bingham that he would "stand good" for any sales to Donald made on credit. Based on Elmer's statement, Bingham again gave Donald credit, and Donald ran up $10,000 in goods before Bingham sued Donald and Elmer. What defense did Elmer make, and what was the outcome?

Strategy: This was an oral agreement, so the issue is whether the promise had to be in writing to be enforceable. Review the list of six contracts that must be in writing. Is this agreement there? (See the "Result" at the end of this section.)

- **EXECUTORS** A promise made by an executor of an estate to pay for the estate's debts.
- **MARRIAGE** A promise made in consideration of marriage.
- **GOODS** The sale of goods of $500 or more.

Question: James River-Norwalk, Inc., was a paper and textile company that needed a constant supply of wood. James River orally contracted with Gary Futch to supply wood for the company, and Futch did so for several years. The deal was worth many thousands of dollars, but nothing was put in writing. Futch actually purchased the wood for his own account and then resold it to James River. After a few years, James River refused to do more business with Futch. Did the parties have a binding contract?

> **Strategy:** If this is a contract for services, it is enforceable without anything in writing. However, if it is one for the sale of goods, it must be in writing. Clearly what James River wanted was the wood, and it did not care where Futch found it. (See the "Result" at the end of this section.)

2. **CONTENTS**   The writing must be signed by the defendant and must state the name of all parties, the subject matter of the agreement, and all essential terms and promises. Electronic signatures usually are valid.

3. **UNIFORM COMMERCIAL CODE (UCC)**   A contract or memorandum for the sale of goods may be less complete than those required by the common law.

   - The basic UCC rule requires only a memorandum signed by the defendant, indicating that the parties reached an agreement and specifying the quantity of goods.

   - Between merchants, even less is required. If one merchant sends written confirmation of a contract, the merchant who receives the document must object within 10 days or be bound by the writing.

   - In the following special circumstances, no writing may be required: the goods are specially manufactured, one party admits in litigation that there was a contract, or one party pays for part of the goods or delivers some of the goods.

4. **PAROL EVIDENCE**   When an integrated contract exists, neither party may generally use parol evidence to contradict, vary, or add to its terms. Parol evidence refers to anything (apart from the written contract itself) that was said, done, or written before the parties signed the agreement or as they signed it.

> **1. "One Year" Result:** (d) A contract for the sale of goods worth $500 or more must be in writing—but this is a contract for *services*, not the sale of goods, so the $800 price is irrelevant. The contract *can* be completed within one year, and thus it falls outside the Statute of Frauds. This is an enforceable agreement.
>
> **1. "Debt of Another" Result:** Elmer made a promise to pay the debt of another. He did so as a favor to his son. This is a collateral promise. Elmer never signed any such promise, and the agreement cannot be enforced against him.
>
> **1. "Goods" Result:** James River was buying wood, and this is a contract for the sale of goods. With nothing in writing, signed by James River, Futch has no enforceable agreement.

MULTIPLE-CHOICE QUESTIONS

1. *CPA QUESTION*   Two individuals signed a contract that was intended to be their entire agreement. The parol evidence rule will prevent the admission of evidence offered to:

   (a) Explain the meaning of an ambiguity in the written contract.

   (b) Establish that fraud had been committed in the formation of the contract.

(c) Prove the existence of a contemporaneous oral agreement modifying the contract.

(d) Prove the existence of a subsequent oral agreement modifying the contract.

2. Rafaella wants to plant a garden, and she agrees to buy a small piece of land for $300. Later, she agrees to buy a table for $300. Neither agreement is put in writing. The agreement to buy the land _____ enforceable, and the agreement to buy the table _____ enforceable.

(a) is; is

(b) is; is not

(c) is not; is

(d) is not; is not

3. The common-law Statute of Frauds requires that to be "in writing," an agreement must be signed by:

(a) the plaintiff

(b) the defendant

(c) both a and b

(d) none of the above

4. Mandy verbally tells a motorcycle dealer that she will make her son's motorcycle payments if he falls behind on them. Will Mandy be legally required to live up to this agreement?

(a) Yes, absolutely.

(b) Yes, if her son is under 18.

(c) Yes, if Mandy will be the primary driver of the motorcycle.

(d) Yes, if the motorcycle is worth less than $500.

(e) No, absolutely not.

5. In December 2012, Eric hires a band to play at a huge graduation party he is planning to hold in May, 2014. The deal is never put into writing. In January 2014, if he wanted to cancel the job, Eric _____ be able to do so. If he does not cancel, and if the band shows up and plays at the party in May 2014, Eric _____ have to pay them.

(a) will; will

(b) will; will not

(c) will not; will

(d) will not; will not

CASE QUESTIONS

1. Richard Griffin and three other men owned a grain company, called Bearhouse, Inc., which needed to borrow money. First National Bank was willing to loan $490,000, but it insisted that the four men sign personal guarantees on the loan, committing themselves to repaying up to 25 percent of the loan each if Bearhouse defaulted. Bearhouse went bankrupt. The bank was able to collect some of its money from

Bearhouse's assets, but it sued Griffin for the balance. At trial, Griffin wanted to testify that before he signed his guaranty, a bank officer assured him that he would only owe 25 percent of *whatever balance was unpaid,* not 25 percent of the total loan. How will the court decide whether Griffin is entitled to testify about the conversation?

2. When Deana Byers married Steven Byers, she was pregnant with another man's child. Shortly after the marriage, Deana gave birth. The marriage lasted only two months, and the couple separated. In divorce proceedings, Deana sought child support. She claimed that Steven had orally promised to support the child if Deana would marry him. Steven claims he never made the promise. Comment on the outcome.

3. Lonnie Hippen moved to Long Island, Kansas, to work in an insurance company owned by Griffiths. After he moved there, Griffiths offered to sell Hippen a house he owned, and Hippen agreed in writing to buy it. He did buy the house and moved in, but two years later, Hippen left the insurance company. He then claimed that at the time of the sale, Griffiths had orally promised to buy back his house at the selling price if Hippen should happen to leave the company. Griffiths defended based on the Statute of Frauds. Hippen argued that the Statute of Frauds did not apply because the repurchase of the house was essentially part of his employment with Griffiths. Comment.

4. Landlord owned a clothing store and agreed in writing to lease the store's basement to another retailer. The written lease, which both parties signed, (1) described the premises exactly, (2) identified the parties, and (3) stated the monthly rent clearly. But an appeals court held that the lease did not satisfy the Statute of Frauds. Why not?

5. *YOU BE THE JUDGE* **WRITING PROBLEM**   Because of his success in a big case, a lawyer named Melbourne promised his assistant, Barbara, a large bonus. After the case settled, Melbourne met with Barbara to discuss when and how much he would pay her. In the conversation that she secretly recorded, Melbourne agreed to pay Barbara $1 million, plus $65,000 for a luxury automobile. Payments were to be made in monthly installments of $10,000, for 10 years. Melbourne also agreed to sign a document confirming his promise. Barbara's lawyer drafted the writing, but Melbourne never signed it. He did pay nine monthly installments, along with an extra payment of $100,000. Did Melbourne and Barbara have a valid contract? Argument for Barbara: The Statute of Frauds exists to prevent fraud. The fear that a plaintiff would lie about a contract is not an issue here. We know what Melbourne agreed to do because we *heard* him. Argument for Melbourne: If there was an agreement, it could not have been performed in one year because it had ten years' worth of installment payments.

Discussion Questions

1. **ETHICS** Jacob Deutsch owned commercial property. He orally agreed to rent it for six years to Budget Rent A Car. Budget took possession, began paying monthly rent, and, over a period of several months, expended about $6,000 in upgrading the property. Deutsch was aware of the repairs. After a year, Deutsch attempted to evict Budget. Budget claimed it had a six-year oral lease, but Deutsch claimed that such a lease was worthless. Please rule. Is it ethical for Deutsch to use the Statute of Frauds

in attempting to defeat the lease? Assume that, as landlord, you had orally agreed to rent premises to a tenant, but then for business reasons, you preferred not to carry out the deal. Would you evict a tenant if you thought the Statute of Frauds would enable you to do so? How should you analyze the problem? What values are most important to you?

2. Mast Industries and Bazak International were two textile firms. Mast verbally offered to sell certain textiles to Bazak for $103,000. Mast promised to send documents confirming the agreement, but it never did. Finally, Bazak sent a memorandum to Mast confirming the agreement, describing the goods, and specifying their quantity and the price. Bazak's officer signed the memo. Mast received the memo but never agreed to it in writing. When Mast failed to deliver the goods, Bazak sued. Who will win? Why?

3. A disc jockey named Z-Trip made a remix of a Beastie Boys song with the hip-hop group's permission. Monster Energy (ME), an energy drink company, wanted to use the remix as part of a video promotion. ME sent an email asking Z-Trip to approve the video. In an email, Z-Trip responded "Dope!" When the Beastie Boys sued ME for copyright infringement, ME claimed that Z-Trip's reply was a contract granting it approval to use the remix. Is there an enforceable contract between Z-Trip and ME?

4. Does the coverage of the Statute of Frauds make sense as it currently stands? Would it be better to expand the law and require that all contracts be in writing? Or should the law be done away with altogether?

5. Compare the common-law Statute of Frauds to the UCC version. What are the specific differences? Which is more reasonable? Why?

CHAPTER 17

THIRD PARTIES

First, Ronald Schmalfeldt got his teeth knocked out … and then he got his wind knocked out by his dental bills. Here is what happened.

Schmalfeldt was at the Elite Bar playing a pick-up game of pool with another bar patron, whom he did not know. A heated argument ensued. Schmalfeldt tried to walk away but was struck in the face by the other player, who then fled—never to be heard from again. The brawl caused Schmalfeldt extensive dental damage, to the tune of $1,921. He asked the owner of the Elite Bar to pay his dental expenses, but the owner refused. Schmalfeldt was left with his teeth—and his dental bills—in his hands.

Schmalfeldt sought payment directly from North Pointe, which had issued a commercial liability insurance policy to the owner of the Elite Bar. He claimed that, as a pool-playing bar patron, he had a right to medical benefits under the policy. In its contract with Elite, North Pointe had agreed to pay up to $5,000 for medical expenses for a bodily injury caused by an accident occurring on Elite's premises, regardless of fault. When North Pointe refused to pay, Schmalfeldt sued. Could Schmalfeldt enforce the bar's contract rights, or did he have to put his money where his mouth was?[1]

© Honza Krej/Shutterstock.com

> **Schmalfeldt was left with his teeth—and his dental bills—in his hands.**

---
[1]Schmalfeldt v. North Pointe Ins. Co. 469 Mich. 422 (2003).

Chapters 13 through 16 examined the Contracts Checklist, so you now know all the elements that must be present for a valid contract to exist. In this chapter and Chapters 18 and 19, we turn our attention to other contract issues.

17-1 THIRD-PARTY BENEFICIARY

The two parties who make a contract always intend to gain some benefit for themselves. Often, though, their bargain will also benefit *someone else*. **A third-party beneficiary is someone who was not a party to the contract but stands to benefit from it.** Many contracts are clear in their intent to create third-party beneficiaries—and some even mention these lucky people by name. Sometimes, however, unnamed third parties want to enforce others' contracts. In that case, courts must analyze the particulars of the deal to see who is entitled to recover. In the case from the opening scenario, the Michigan Supreme Court held that since the insurance contract was intended to benefit the insured (the bar) and made no mention of patrons, Schmalfeldt was not a third-party beneficiary and, therefore, could not recover his damages.

As another example, suppose a major league baseball team contracts to purchase from Seller 20 acres of an abandoned industrial site to be used for a new stadium. The owner of a pizza parlor on the edge of Seller's land might benefit enormously, since 40,000 hungry fans in the neighborhood for 81 home games every season could turn her once-marginal operation into a gold mine of cheese and pepperoni.

But what if the contract falls apart? What if the team backs out of the land deal? Seller can certainly sue because it is a party to the contract. But what about the pizza parlor owner? Can she sue to enforce the deal and recover lost profits for unsold sausage and green pepper?

The outcome in cases like these depends upon the intentions of the two contracting parties. If they *intended* to benefit the third party, she will probably be permitted to enforce their contract. If they did not intend to benefit her, she probably has no power to enforce the agreement.

17-1a **Intended Beneficiaries**

A person is an **intended beneficiary** and may enforce a contract if the parties intended her to benefit and if either (a) enforcing the promise will satisfy a *duty* of the promisee to the beneficiary, or (b) the promisee intended to make a *gift* to the beneficiary. (The **promisor** is the one who makes the promise that the third-party beneficiary is seeking to enforce. The **promisee** is the other party to the contract.)

In other words, a third-party beneficiary must show two things in order to enforce a contract that two other people created. First, she must show that the two contracting parties were aware of her situation and knew that she would receive something of value from their deal. Second, she must show that the promisee wanted to benefit her for one of two reasons: either to satisfy some duty owed or to make her a gift.

If the promisee is fulfilling some duty, the third-party beneficiary is called a **creditor beneficiary**. Most often, the duty that a promisee will be fulfilling is a debt already owed to the beneficiary. If the promisee is making a gift, the third party is a **donee beneficiary**.[2] As long as the third party is either a creditor or a donee beneficiary, she may enforce the contract. If she is only an incidental beneficiary, she may not.

John's father, Clarence, has an overgrown lawn. So, John enters into a contract with Billy Goat Landscapers for it to mow Clarence's lawn every week. Billy Goat is the promisor and John, the promisee. Although Clarence was not a party to the contract, he is the beneficiary—it is his lawn being cut. John did not owe his father a legal duty but simply

Intended beneficiary

Someone who may enforce a contract made between two other parties

Promisor

Makes the promise that a third party seeks to enforce

Promisee

The contract party *to whom* a promise is made

---

[2]"Donee" comes from the word *donate*.

intended to make him a gift, so, Clarence is an intended, donee beneficiary, and he can sue the landscaping company to enforce the contract himself.

By contrast, the pizza parlor owner will surely lose. A stadium is a multimillion-dollar investment, and it is most unlikely that the baseball team and the seller of the land were even aware of the owner's existence, let alone that they intended to benefit her. She probably cannot prove either the first element or the second element, and certainly not both.

In the following case, an unlikely plaintiff sues for breach of a state contract. Was the prison inmate an intended beneficiary or was his argument just smoke in mirrors? Who is entitled to sue?

RATHKE V. CORRECTIONS CORPORATION OF AMERICA, INC.

153 P.3d 303
Supreme Court of Alaska, 2007

Facts: The state of Alaska entered into a contract with Corrections Corporation of America (CCA), a private company, to house Alaska's inmates. The contract required CCA to abide by the terms of a settlement agreement between the state and its inmates known as the Cleary FSA. This agreement listed Alaska's duties to its prisoners and also provided a list of permissible disciplinary procedures.

Gus Rathke was an Alaska inmate at a CCA prison located in Arizona. A routine drug test revealed marijuana in his system. Rathke's level of marijuana was within the limit allowed by the Cleary FSA (50 ng/ml) but exceeded Arizona's limit (20 ng/ml). CCA applied the more stringent Arizona standard. As a result, Rathke spent thirty days in punitive segregation and lost his prison job.

Rathke sued CCA, seeking lost wages and an apology. He claimed that CCA breached its contract with Alaska when it punished him according to the stricter marijuana standard. Rathke argued that as an Alaska inmate, he was an intended third-party beneficiary of the contract between Alaska and CCA.

The trial court disagreed with Rathke. It held that, even though he was entitled to certain rights under the Cleary FSA, he was not a third-party beneficiary of the CCA/Alaska contract. It reasoned that the Clearly FSA duties were only between Alaska and the inmates, while the duties in the CCA/Alaska contract were only between CCA and the state. Rathke appealed to Alaska's Supreme Court.

Issue: *Was Rathke an intended beneficiary of the contract between the state of Alaska and CCA?*

Excerpts from Justice Carpeneti's Decision: In determining whether a third party is an intended beneficiary of a contract, we refer to the Restatement (Second) of Contracts. According to §302, "a beneficiary of a promise is an intended beneficiary if the circumstances indicate that the promisee intends to give the beneficiary the benefit of the promised performance."

When applying these provisions, the motives of the parties in executing a contract—especially the promisee—are determinative. As a general rule, if the promised performance is rendered directly to the beneficiary, the intent to benefit the third party will be clearly manifested.

The state owes legal duties to all Alaska inmates, including those housed like Rathke at the CCA's Arizona facility. These duties are detailed in the Cleary FSA, which is an enforceable contract between Alaska inmates and the state.

We disagree with the [lower] court's analysis. First, the Cleary settlement is incorporated by reference into the state/CCA contract. Even more, many of its provisions are repeated virtually word for word in the contract. For example, portions of the discipline section of the state/CCA contract, allegedly breached in Rathke's case are virtually identical to the Cleary FSA.

Given this identity of provisions between the FSA and the state/CCA contract, we conclude that the prisoners are intended third-party beneficiaries of the portions of the contract which are taken directly from the FSA.

Accordingly, we hold that inmates have the right to sue CCA for violations of the Cleary FSA provisions contained in the CCA's contract with the state.

EXAM Strategy

Question: Mr. Inspector examines houses and gives its reports to potential buyers. Mr. Inspector contracts with Greenlawn, a real estate agent, to furnish reports on houses that Greenlawn is selling. The agreement allows the agent to give the reports to potential buyers. Greenlawn gives Molly one of Mr. Inspector's reports and, relying upon it, she buys a house. Although the report states that the house is structurally sound, it turns out that chronic roof leaks have caused water to seep into the walls. Molly sues Mr. Inspector. The inspector requests summary judgment, claiming that he had no contract with Molly.

Strategy: Mr. Inspector is right in saying he had no agreement with Molly. To prevail, Molly must demonstrate she is a third-party beneficiary of the contract between the other two. A third-party beneficiary may enforce a contract if the parties intended to benefit her and either (a) enforcing the promise will satisfy a duty of the promisee to the beneficiary or (b) the promisee intended to make a gift to the beneficiary.

Result: Greenlawn used the inspection summaries as sales tools. When Greenlawn assured a potential buyer that she could rely upon a report, the real estate agent took on a duty to deliver reliable information. Mr. Inspector understood that. The two parties intended to benefit Greenlawn's buyers. Molly may sue Mr. Inspector for breach of his contract with the agent. Mr. Inspector's motion for summary judgment is denied.

17-1b Incidental Beneficiaries

A person who fails to qualify as a donee beneficiary or a creditor beneficiary is merely an **incidental beneficiary** and may not enforce the contract. The pizza parlor owner is an incidental beneficiary.

In an effort to persuade courts, many plaintiffs make creative arguments that they are intended beneficiaries with enforcement rights. Is every taxpayer an intended beneficiary of a government contract? Do labor unions have rights if a contract refers to them in general terms? Or are these plaintiffs incidental beneficiaries? The following case answers these questions.

Incidental beneficiary
Someone who might have benefited from a contract between two others but has no right to enforce that agreement

UNITE HERE LOCAL 30 v. CALIFORNIA DEPARTMENT OF PARKS AND RECREATION

2011 Cal. App. LEXIS 510
Court of Appeal of California, 2011

Facts: The California Department of Parks and Recreation (DPR) and Delaware North Companies (DNC) entered into a contract giving DNC the right to operate a concession stand at a state park in San Diego for 10 years. Four years into the contract, DNC assigned its rights to operate the stand to another company.

DNC fired many of its employees, and the new operator did not rehire them. Some of these workers were members of the union Unite Here Local 30. Local 30

sued to block the assignment. It was joined in the suit by Bridgette Browning, who lived in the area and seemed to care who provided her hot dogs.

The trial court rejected the plaintiff's claims, and the plaintiffs appealed.

Issue: *Were the plaintiffs incidental or donee beneficiaries?*

Excerpts from Judge Hull's Decision: Paragraph 37(a) of the contract limits assignments and reads: "No assignment shall be made unless first consented to in writing by State." Before State considers such assignment, the proposed assignment must comply with applicable law. DPR reviewed the evidence submitted by Delaware North and determined that the proposed assignment met the requirements under paragraph 37(a).

Plaintiffs contend a third party who is within the class of those for whose benefit a contract is made have standing to sue for breach of that contract. They further argue, Local 30 and the employees it represents are clearly intended beneficiaries of the original contract.

The test for determining whether a contract was made for the benefit of a third person is whether an intent to benefit a third person appears from the terms of the contract. Under the intent test, it is not enough that the third party would incidentally have benefited from performance. On the other hand, the third person need not be named or identified individually. A third party may enforce a contract where he shows that he is a member of a class of persons for whose benefit it was made.

Plaintiffs contend Bridgette Browning has a right to sue as a taxpayer of California. They point out that paragraph 37 procedures are intended to eliminate favoritism, fraud, corruption, and misuse of public funds. Thus, plaintiffs argue, can be said to have the intent to benefit the general public

and the taxpayer. Of course, any contract entered into by the state would presumably be for the benefit of the state's residents and taxpayers, just as a contract entered into by a corporation would presumably be for the benefit of the corporation's shareholders. However, the fact that members of the public derive a benefit from the contract does not make them intended beneficiaries. A person is a donee beneficiary only if the promisee's contractual intent is to make a gift to him. Browning is no more than an incidental beneficiary who benefits merely because the state as a whole benefits.

Likewise, Local 30 is no more than an incidental beneficiary. Plaintiffs argue that because the Concession Contract contains a neutrality agreement regarding union organizing, Local 30 and the employees it represents are clearly intended beneficiaries of the original contract. The neutrality agreement states, in part, "Concessionaire shall not use the Premises to hold a meeting if the purpose is to promote or deter union organizing." This provision hardly reveals an intent to confer a benefit on Local 30, or any union for that matter. At best, it shows an intent not to provide either a benefit or a detriment to union organizing.

We conclude the trial court correctly determined plaintiffs are not third party beneficiaries and therefore lack standing to sue on that basis.

The judgment is affirmed.

17-2 ASSIGNMENT AND DELEGATION

After a contract is made, one or both parties may wish to substitute someone else for themselves. Six months before Maria's lease expires, an out-of-town company offers her a new job at a substantial increase in pay. After taking the job, she wants to sublease her apartment to her friend Sarah.

Assignment
Transferring contract *rights*

Delegation
Transferring contract *duties*

A contracting party may transfer his rights under the contract, which is called an **assignment** of rights. Or a party may transfer her obligations under the contract, which is a **delegation** of duties. Frequently, a party will make an assignment and delegation simultaneously, transferring both rights (such as the right to inhabit an apartment) and duties (like the obligation to pay monthly rent) to a third party.

17-2a Assignment

Lydia needs 500 bottles of champagne. Bruno agrees to sell them to her for $10,000, payable 30 days after delivery. He transports the wine to her.

Bruno owes Doug $8,000 from a previous deal. He says to Doug, "I don't have your money, but I'll give you my claim to Lydia's $10,000." Doug agrees. Bruno then *assigns* to Doug his rights to Lydia's money, and in exchange Doug gives up his claim against Bruno for $8,000. Bruno is the assignor, the one making an assignment, and Doug is the assignee, the one receiving an assignment.

Why would Bruno offer $10,000 when he owed Doug only $8,000? Because all he has is a *claim* to Lydia's money. Cash in hand is often more valuable. Doug, however, is willing to assume some risk for a potential $2,000 gain.

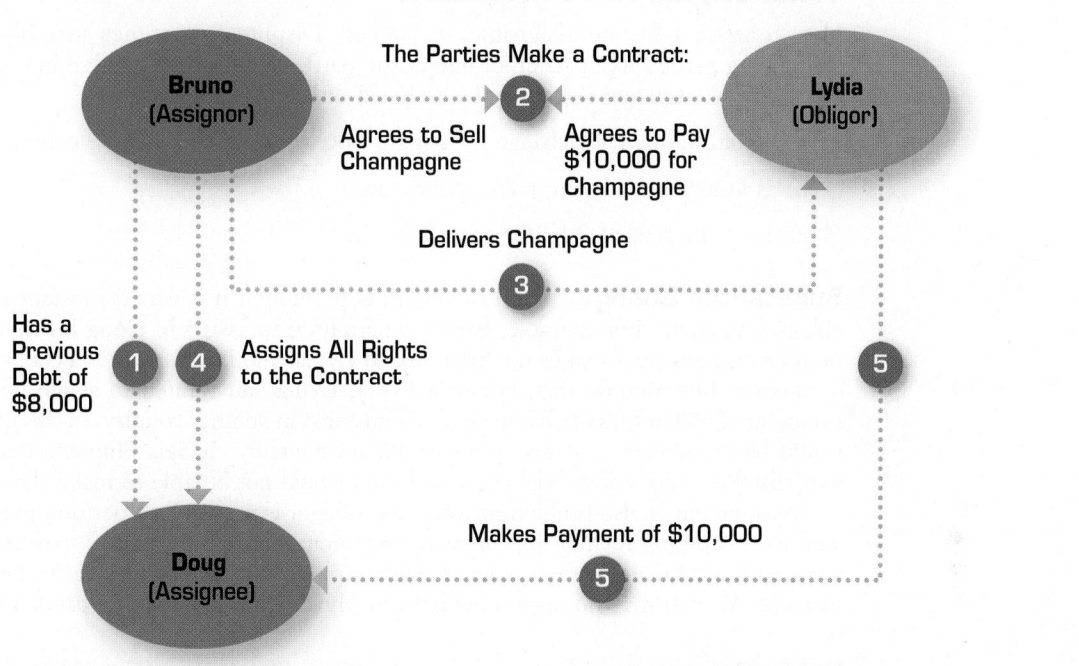

The Parties Make a Contract:

Bruno
(Assignor)

Agrees to Sell
Champagne

2

Agrees to Pay
$10,000 for
Champagne

Lydia
(Obligor)

Delivers Champagne
3

Has a
Previous
Debt of
$8,000

1 4 Assigns All Rights
to the Contract

5

Doug
(Assignee)

Makes Payment of $10,000
5

EXHIBIT 17.1

Bruno notifies Lydia of the assignment. Lydia, who owes the money, is called the **obligor**; that is, the one obligated to do something. At the end of 30 days, Doug arrives at Lydia's doorstep, asks for his money, and gets it, since Lydia is obligated to him. Bruno has no claim to any payment. See Exhibit 17.1.

Obligor

The party obligated to do something

EXAM Strategy

Question: Hasannah, an art dealer, signs a contract with Jason. Hasannah will deliver a David Hockney painting to Jason's house. Jason may keep it for 30 days and then either return it or pay Hasannah $2 million. Hasannah delivers the painting. Hasannah finds a better building to house her gallery and agrees to buy it from Shannon. She and Shannon sign a contract allowing Shannon to receive Jason's payment if he keeps the picture. Hasannah then notifies Jason to pay Shannon the $2 million. Identify the obligor, the assignor, and the assignee.

Strategy: The obligor is the one obligated to do something. The assignor makes an assignment and the assignee receives it.

Result: Jason is obligated either to return the picture or pay $2 million for it. He is the obligor. Hasannah is entitled to the money, but she assigns her right to Shannon. Hasannah is the assignor and Shannon the assignee.

What Rights Are Assignable?

Most contract rights are assignable, but not all. Disputes sometimes arise between the two contracting parties about whether one of the parties could legally assign her rights to a third party. Any **contractual right may be assigned unless assignment**

   (a) would substantially change the obligor's rights or duties under the contract;

   (b) is forbidden by law or public policy; or

   (c) is validly precluded by the contract itself.[3]

Substantial Change.   An assignment is prohibited if it would substantially change the obligor's situation. For example, Bruno is permitted to assign to Doug his rights to payment from Lydia because it makes no difference to Lydia whether she writes a check to one person or another. But suppose that, before delivery, Lydia had wanted to assign her rights to the shipment of 500 bottles of champagne to a business in another country. In this example, Bruno would be the obligor, and his duties would substantially change. Shipping heavy items over long distances adds substantial costs, so Lydia would not be able to make the assignment.

Assignment is also prohibited when the obligor is agreeing to perform personal services. The close working relationship in such agreements makes it unfair to expect the obligor to work with a stranger. Warner, a candidate for public office, hires Mayer to be his campaign manager. Warner may not assign his right to Mayer's work to another candidate.

Public Policy.   Some assignments are prohibited by public policy. For example, someone who has suffered a personal injury may not assign her claim to a third person. Vladimir is playing the piano on his roof deck when the instrument rolls over the balustrade and drops 35 stories before smashing Wanda's foot. Wanda has a valid tort claim against Vladimir, but she may not assign the claim to anyone else. As a matter of public policy, all states have decided that the sale of personal injury claims could create an unseemly and unethical marketplace.

Contract Prohibition.   Finally, one of the contracting parties may try to prohibit assignment in the agreement itself. For example, most landlords include in the written lease a clause prohibiting the tenant from assigning the tenancy without the landlord's written permission.

Subleasing disputes between landlord and tenant are common. How much leeway does a landlord have in rejecting a proposed assignment? The following case provides the answer.

TENET HEALTHSYSTEM SURGICAL, L.L.C. v. JEFFERSON PARISH HOSPITAL SERVICE DISTRICT NO. 1

426 F.3d 738
Fifth Circuit Court of Appeals, 2005

Facts: MSC, Inc. owned the Marrero Shopping Center, and leased space to Tenet Healthsystem for use in out-patient surgery and general medical practice. The lease allowed Tenet to assign the lease with MSC's consent, and stated that consent would not be unreasonably withheld.

Two years later, MSC sold the shopping center to West Jefferson Medical Center, which owned an adjacent hospital and wanted the space for expansion. A few months after that, Tenet requested permission from West Jefferson to assign its lease to Pelican Medical, which

---

[3]Restatement (Second) of Contracts §317(2). And note that UCC §2-210 is, for our purposes, nearly identical.

intended to use the space for an occupational medical clinic. West Jefferson denied permission, stating that Pelican would be performing work not permitted under the original lease, and also because Pelican would compete with West Jefferson.

Tenet sued, claiming that West Jefferson was unreasonably withholding permission to assign. The trial court granted summary judgment for West Jefferson. Tenet appealed.

Issue: *Did West Jefferson unreasonably withhold permission to assign the lease?*

Excerpts from Judge Davis's Decision: West Jefferson asserts that Pelican's contemplated uses of the facility exceed those permitted under the lease [and also argues] that its refusal was reasonable because the proposed use of the facility poses more competition to its adjacent hospital.

Tenet used the facility for an outpatient surgery center. Pelican planned to use the facility for an occupational medical clinic. The services offered by an occupational medicine practice are quite comprehensive, from physical examinations and drug screening to low acuity emergencies. The clinic can treat patients with depression, lacerations, broken bones [and] pneumonia, and provides related lab and x-ray services. Nothing in this description takes the proposed practice outside the limits of a "general medical and physician's offices, including related uses," a permitted use under the lease.

West Jefferson also opposes the lease assignment from Tenet to Pelican on the basis that Pelican's broadened scope of operations would include new areas of competition with its hospital. When determining the reasonableness of a landlord's refusal to consent to an assignment of a lease, the standard is that of a reasonable prudent man.

In determining whether a landlord's refusal to consent was reasonable in a commercial context, only factors that relate to the landlord's interest in preserving the leased property or in having the terms of prime lease performed should be considered. Among factors a landlord can consider are the financial responsibility of the proposed subtenant, the legality and suitability of proposed use and nature of the occupancy. A landlord's personal taste or convenience is not properly considered. Rather the landlord's objection must relate to ownership and operation of leased property, not lessor's general economic interest. Under this standard, West Jefferson's refusal to consent to the assignment of the Tenet lease because Pelican would be a new competitor relates not to the ownership and operation of the leased property, but to West Jefferson's general economic interest.

West Jefferson's reason for denying consent to the assignment to Pelican based on increased competition is wholly personal to West Jefferson and does not relate in any way to an objective evaluation of Pelican as a tenant. Further, allowing West Jefferson to deny consent on a basis personal to it, a successor owner who took subject to the existing lease, would expand West Jefferson's rights under the lease to the detriment of the lessee in a manner not bargained for in the lease itself. Accordingly, we conclude that West Jefferson's refusal of consent to the assignment of the lease on the basis of increased competition was unreasonable.

Reversed and remanded.

How Rights Are Assigned

Writing. In general, an assignment may be written or oral, and no particular formalities are required. However, when someone wants to assign rights governed by the Statute of Frauds, she must do it in writing. Suppose City contracts with Seller to buy Seller's land and then brings in Investor to complete the project. If City wants to assign to Investor its rights to the land, it must do so in writing.

Consideration. An assignment can be valid with or without consideration, but the lack of consideration may have consequences. Two examples should clarify this. Recall Bruno, who sells champagne to Lydia and then assigns to Doug his right to payment. In that case, there *is* consideration for the assignment. Bruno assigns his rights only because Doug cancels the old debt, and his agreement to do that is valid consideration. **An assignment for consideration is irrevocable.** Once the two men agree, Bruno may not telephone Doug and say, "I've changed my mind, I want Lydia to pay me after all." Lydia's $10,000 now belongs to Doug.

Gratuitous assignment
One made as a gift, for no consideration

But suppose that Bruno assigns his contract rights to his sister Brunhilde as a birthday present. This is a **gratuitous assignment**; that is, one made as a gift, for no consideration. **A gratuitous assignment is generally revocable if it is oral and generally irrevocable if it is written.** If Bruno verbally assigns his rights to Brunhilde, but then changes his mind, telephones Lydia, and says, "I want you to pay me after all," that revocation is effective and Brunhilde gets nothing. But if Bruno puts his assignment in writing and Brunhilde receives it, Bruno has given up his right to receive Lydia's payment.

If you assign your rights under a contract, inform the obligor immediately.

Notice to Obligor. The assignment is valid from the moment it is made, regardless of whether the assignor notifies the obligor. But an assignor with common sense will immediately inform the obligor of the assignment. Suppose that Maude has a contract with Nelson, who is obligated to deliver 700 live frogs to her shop. If Maude (assignor) assigns her rights to Obie (assignee), Maude should notify Nelson (obligor) the same day. If she fails to inform Nelson, he may deliver the frogs to Maude. Nelson will have no further obligations under the contract, and Maude will owe Obie 700 frogs.

Rights of the Parties after Assignment

Once the assignment is made and the obligor notified, the assignee may enforce her contractual rights against the obligor. If Lydia fails to pay Doug for the champagne she gets from Bruno, Doug may sue to enforce the agreement. The law will treat Doug as though he had entered into the contract with Lydia.

But if a lawsuit arises, the reverse is also true. **The obligor may generally raise all defenses against the assignee that she could have raised against the assignor.** Suppose that Lydia opens the first bottle of champagne—silently. "Where's the pop?" she wonders. There is no pop because all 500 bottles have gone flat. Bruno has failed to perform his part of the contract, and Lydia may use Bruno's nonperformance as a defense against Doug. If the champagne was indeed worthless, Lydia owes Doug nothing.

Assignor's Warranty. The law implies certain warranties, or assurances, on the part of the assignor. Unless the parties expressly agree to exclude them, the assignor warrants that (1) the rights he is assigning actually do exist, and (2) there are no defenses to the rights other than those that would be obvious, such as nonperformance. But the assignor *does not* warrant that the obligor is solvent. Bruno is by implication warranting to Doug that Lydia has no defenses to the contract, but he is not guaranteeing Doug that she has the money to pay, or that she will pay.

Special Issue: The Uniform Commercial Code and Assignments of Security Interests

The provisions of the Uniform Commercial Code regarding assignments in contracts for the sale of goods are very similar to common-law rules.[4] However, Article 9 of the UCC has special rules about the assignment of **security interests**, which are the legal rights in personal property that ensure payment. When an automobile dealer sells you a new car on credit, the

Security interests
Rights in personal property that assure payment or the performance of some obligation

———————————

[4] UCC §2-210.

dealer will keep a security interest in your car. If you do not make your monthly payments, the dealer retains a right to repossess the vehicle. That authority is called a *security interest*. (See Chapter 25 for a full discussion.)

Companies that sell goods often prefer to assign their security interests to some other firm, such as a bank or finance company. The bank is the assignee. Just as we saw with the common law, the assignee of a security interest generally has all of the rights that the assignor had. And the obligor (the buyer) may also raise all of the defenses against the assignee that she could have raised against the assignor.

Under UCC §9-404, the obligor on a sales contract may generally assert any defenses against the assignee that arise from the contract, and any other defenses that arose before notice of assignment. The Code's reference to any defenses that arise from the contract means that if the assignor breached his part of the deal, the obligor may raise that as a defense. Suppose that a dealer sells you a new Porsche on credit, retaining a security interest. He assigns the security interest to the bank. The car is great for the first few weeks, but then the roof slides onto the street and both doors fall off. You refuse to make any more monthly payments. When the bank sues you, you may raise the automobile's defects as a defense, just as you could have raised them against the dealer itself. Where the Code talks about other defenses that arose before notice of assignment, it refers, for example, to fraud. Suppose that the dealer knew that before you bought the Porsche, it had been smashed up and rebuilt. If the dealer told you it was brand new, that was fraud, and you could raise the defense against the bank.

A contract may prohibit an obligor from raising certain defenses against an assignee. Sometimes a seller of goods will require the buyer to sign a contract that permits the seller to assign *and* prohibits the buyer from raising defenses against the assignee that he could have raised against the seller. University wants to buy a computer system on credit from Leland for $85,000. Leland agrees to the deal but insists that the contract permit him to assign his rights to anyone he chooses. He also wants this clause: "University agrees that it will not raise against an assignee any defenses that it may have had against Leland." This clause is sometimes called a *waiver clause* because the obligor is waiving (giving up) rights. Courts may also refer to it as an *exclusion clause* since the parties are excluding potential defenses. Leland wants a waiver clause because it makes his contract more valuable. As soon as University signs the agreement, Leland can take his contract to Krushem Collections, a finance company. Krushem might offer Leland $70,000 cash for the contract. Leland can argue, "You have to pay $85,000 for this. You are guaranteed payment by University since they cannot raise any defenses against you, even if the computer system collapses in the first half-hour." Leland gets cash and need not worry about collecting payments. Krushem receives the full value of the contract, with interest, spread out over several years.

Under UCC §9-403, an agreement by a buyer (or lessee) that he will not assert against an assignee any claim or defense that he may have against the seller (or lessor) is generally enforceable by the assignee if he took the assignment in good faith, for value, without notice of the potential defenses. In other words, Leland's waiver clause with University is enforceable. If Leland assigns the contract to Krushem Collections and the system proves worthless, Krushem is still entitled to its monthly payments from University. The school must seek its damages against Leland—a far more arduous step than simply withholding payment.

These waiver clauses are generally *not* valid in consumer contracts. If Leland sold a computer system to a consumer (an individual purchasing it for her personal use), the waiver would generally be unenforceable.

In the following case, one side pushes the waiver rule to its extreme. Can an assignee recover for money advanced … when the money was never advanced? You be the judge.

You be the Judge

Facts: Michael Brooks desperately needed financing for his company, BrooksAmerica, so he agreed to a sale-leaseback agreement with Terminal Marketing Company. Terminal would pay Brooks America $250,000, and in exchange it would obtain title to BrooksAmerica's computers and office equipment. BrooksAmerica would then lease the equipment for three years, for $353,000. The equipment would never leave BrooksAmerica's offices.

The contract included a "hell or high water clause" stating that BrooksAmerica's obligation to pay was "absolute and unconditional." Another clause permitted Terminal to assign its rights without notice to BrooksAmerica and stated that the assignee took its rights "free from all defenses, setoffs, or counterclaims."

Brooks also signed a "Delivery and Acceptance Certificate" stating that BrooksAmerica had received the $250,000 (even though no money had yet changed hands) and reaffirming BrooksAmerica's absolute obligation to pay an assignee, despite any defenses BrooksAmerica might have.

Terminal assigned its rights to Wells Fargo, which had taken about 2,000 other equipment leases from Terminal. Terminal never paid any portion of the promised $250,000. Brooks refused to make the required payments (about $10,000 per month) and Wells Fargo sued. Brooks acknowledged that Wells Fargo paid Terminal for the assignment.

Both parties moved for summary judgment. The trial court ruled in favor of Wells Fargo, and Brooks appealed.

You Be the Judge: *Is Wells Fargo entitled to its monthly lease payments despite the fact that BrooksAmerica never received financing?*

Argument for BrooksAmerica: We acknowledge the general validity of UCC §9-403. However, in this case,

---

WELLS FARGO BANK MINNESOTA V. BROOKSAMERICA MORTGAGE CORPORATION

419 F.3d 107
Second Circuit Court of Appeals, 2005

---

owed to BrooksAmerica. "Good faith" required Wells Fargo to make sure that Terminal had performed. A simple inquiry would have informed Wells Fargo that Terminal was entitled to no money. This entire transaction is a sham, and §9-403 was never drafted to encourage financial swindles.

The trial court *penalized* BrooksAmerica for acting in good faith. Mr. Brooks signed the Delivery Certificate assuming that any reasonable company would promptly deliver the money it had promised. Unfortunately, Terminal does not operate at the same ethical level—a fact that Wells Fargo should know from its earlier assignments.

Argument for Wells Fargo: Under UCC §9-403, an assignee such as Wells Fargo may enforce a waiver of defenses clause if the assignment was taken in good faith, for value, and free of knowledge of any claims or defenses. Wells Fargo meets that test.

The "simple inquiry" argument has two flaws. First, §9-403 does not require one. The UCC requires good faith, not an investigation. Second, Wells Fargo *did* investigate by checking the contract and the Delivery Certificate. We have done more than required. We have taken thousands of equipment leases as assignees. In this case, we examined the contract and the Delivery Certificate, and assumed that BrooksAmerica had received its money. If Terminal had not paid, why did Mr. Brooks sign a certificate stating he had received his cash? We are entitled to payment. Any dispute between BrooksAmerica and Terminal is for those parties to resolve.

Wells Fargo makes an absurd argument. Neither Terminal nor any assignee has a right to enforce a financing contract when Terminal failed to deliver the financing. There is no valid contract to enforce here because Terminal never paid the $250,000

17-2b Delegation of Duties

Garret has always dreamed of racing stock cars. He borrows $250,000 from his sister, Maybelle, in order to buy a car and begin racing. He signs a promissory note, which is a document guaranteeing that he will repay Maybelle the full amount, plus interest, on a monthly basis over 10 years. Regrettably, during his first race, Garret discovers that he has a speed phobia and quits the business. Garret transfers the car and all of his equipment to Brady, who agrees in writing to pay all money owed to Maybelle. Brady sends a check for a few months, but then the payments stop. Maybelle sues Garret, who defends based on the transfer to Brady. Will his defense work?

Garret has assigned his rights in the car and business to Brady, and that is entirely legal. But more important, he has *delegated his duties* to Brady. Garret was the **delegator** and Brady was the **delegatee**. In other words, the promissory note he signed was a contract, and the agreement imposed certain *duties* on Garret, primarily the obligation to pay Maybelle $250,000 plus interest. Garret had a right to delegate his duties to Brady, but delegating those duties did not relieve Garret of *his own* obligation to perform them. When Maybelle sues, she will win. Garret, like many debtors, would have preferred to wash his hands of his debt, but the law is not so obliging.

Most duties are delegable. But delegation does not by itself relieve the delegator of his own liability to perform the contract.

Garret's delegation to Brady was typical in that it included an assignment at the same time. If he had merely transferred ownership, that would have been only an assignment. If he had convinced Brady to pay off the loan without getting the car, that would have been merely a delegation. He did both at once. See Exhibit 17.2.

What Duties Are Delegable?

The rules concerning what duties may be delegated mirror those about the assignment of rights. And once again, the common law agrees with the UCC. An obligor may delegate his duties unless

1. delegation would violate public policy, or

2. the original contract prohibits delegation, or

3. the obligee has a substantial interest in personal performance by the obligor.[5]

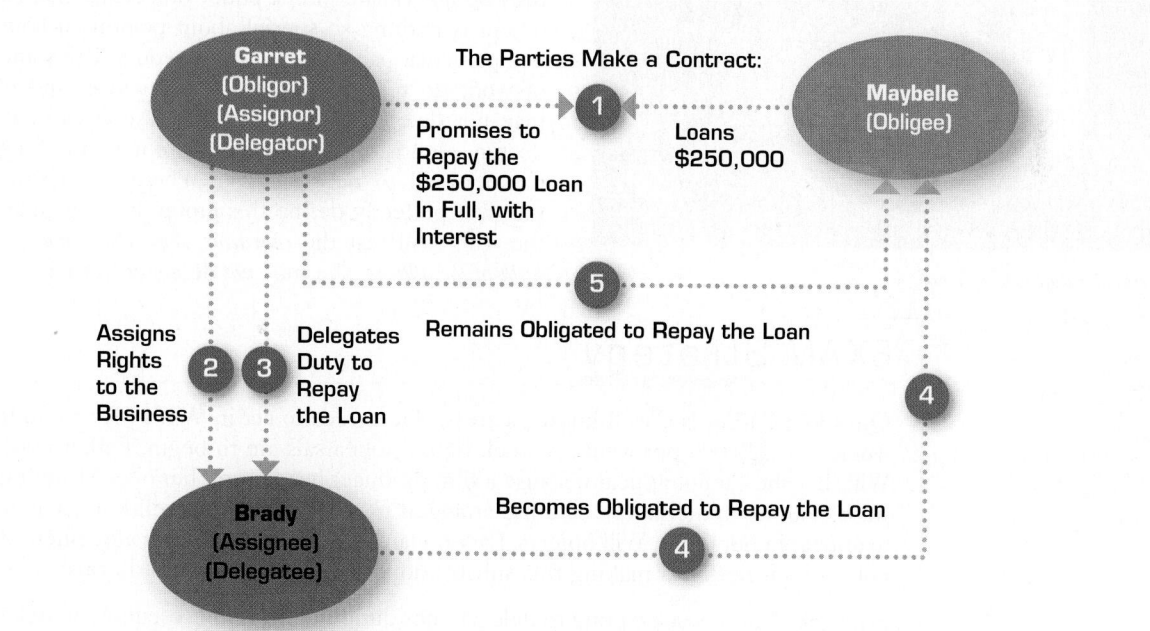

EXHIBIT 17.2

---

[5]Restatement (Second) of Contracts §318. And see UCC §2-210, establishing similar limits.

One may delegate and one may not.

Public Policy.   Delegation may violate public policy, such as in a public works contract. If City hires Builder to construct a subway system, state law may prohibit Builder from delegating his duties to Beginner. The theory is that a public agency should not have to work with parties that it never agreed to hire.

Contract Prohibition.   It is very common for a contract to prohibit delegation. We saw in the "Assignment" section that courts may refuse to enforce a clause that limits one party's ability to assign its contract rights. That does not hold true with delegation. The parties may forbid almost any delegation, and the courts will enforce the agreement. Hammer, a contractor, is building a house and hires Spot as his painter, including in his contract a clause prohibiting delegation. Just before the house is ready for painting, Spot gets a better job elsewhere and wants to delegate his duties to Brush. Hammer may refuse the delegation, even if Brush is equally qualified.

Substantial   Interest   in   Personal Performance.   Suppose Hammer had omitted the "nondelegation" clause from his contract with Spot. Could Hammer still refuse the delegation on the grounds that he has a substantial interest in having Spot do the work? No. Most duties are delegable, as long as they do not violate public policy or a clause in a contract. There is nothing so special about painting a house that one particular painter is required to do it. But some kinds of work do require personal performance, and obligors may not delegate these tasks. The services of lawyers, doctors, dentists, artists, and performers are considered too personal to be delegated. There is no single test that will perfectly define this group, but generally when the work will test the *character, skill, discretion, and good faith of the obligor,* she may *not* delegate her job.

EXAM Strategy

Question: Parker is a well-known actress. She agrees to act in Will's play for four weeks, for $30,000 per week. A week before rehearsals are to begin, Parker notifies Will that she cannot appear because a film producer has offered her over $1 million to start shooting immediately. She has arranged for Claire, another well-known actress, to appear in her place. Will objects. Parker claims, correctly, that their agreement does not prohibit her from making this substitution. Is Parker allowed to do this?

Strategy: Parker is attempting to delegate her duties. Under the Restatement, delegation is allowed unless (1) it would violate public policy, (2) it is prohibited by the contract, or (3) the obligee has a substantial interest in the obligor's personal performance.

Result: This is hardly a matter of public concern, and the contract does not speak to the issue. However, acting is a very personal kind of work. The actor must be right for the part, interact smoothly with other cast members, work well with the director, and help draw the audience. Will is entitled to have Parker perform the work, and she may not delegate her role.

Improper Delegation and Repudiation.   Sometimes parties delegate duties they should not. Suppose Spot, having agreed not to delegate his painting job, is so tempted by the higher offer from another contractor that he delegates the work anyway. Hammer informs Spot he will not allow Brush on the job site. If Spot still refuses to work, he has **repudiated** the agreement; in other words, he has formally notified the other side that he will not perform his side of the contract. Hammer will probably sue him. On the other hand, if Hammer allows Brush up the ladder and Brush completes the job, Hammer has no claim against anybody.

Novation

As we have seen, a delegator does not automatically get rid of his duties merely by delegating them. But there is one way a delegator *can* do so. A **novation** is a three-way agreement in which the obligor transfers all rights and duties to a third party. The obligee agrees to look only to that third party for performance.

Recall Garret, the forlorn race car driver. When he wanted to get out of his obligations to Maybelle, he should have proposed a novation. Were one created, he would assign all rights and delegate all duties to Brady, and Maybelle would agree that *only Brady* was obligated by the promissory note, releasing Garret from his responsibility to repay. Why would Maybelle do this? She might conclude that Brady was a better bet than Garret and that this was the best way to get her money. Maybelle would prefer to have both people liable. But Garret might refuse to bring Brady into the deal until Maybelle permits a novation. In the example given, Garret failed to obtain a novation, and hence he and Brady were *both* liable on the promissory note.

Since a novation has the critical effect of releasing the obligor from liability, you will not be surprised to learn that two parties to a contract sometimes fight over whether some event was a simple delegation of duties or a novation. Here is one such contest.

It appears that Mary Pratt, moving to Arizona, honestly thought she was not only out of the ice cream business but relieved of any debt to the Rosenbergs. This lawsuit undoubtedly came as a cold shock. What should she have done to avoid the dispute?

Novation

A three-way agreement in which the obligor transfers all rights and duties to a third party

ROSENBERG V. SON, INC.

491 N.W.2d 71
Supreme Court of North Dakota, 1992

Facts: The Rosenbergs owned a Dairy Queen in Grand Forks, North Dakota. They agreed in writing to sell the Dairy Queen to Mary Pratt. The contract required her to pay $10,000 down and $52,000 over 15 years, at 10 percent interest. Two years later, Pratt assigned her rights and delegated her duties under the sales contract to Son, Inc. The agreement between Pratt and Son contained a "Consent to Assignment" clause, which the Rosenbergs signed. Pratt then moved to Arizona and

had nothing further to do with the Dairy Queen. The Rosenbergs never received full payment for the Dairy Queen. They sued Mary Pratt.

The trial court gave summary judgment for Pratt, finding that she was no longer obligated on the original contract. The Rosenbergs appealed.

Issue: *Did Pratt obtain a novation relieving her of her duties under the original sales contract?*

Excerpts from Chief Justice Erickstad's Decision: It is a well-established principle in the law of contracts that a contracting party cannot escape its liability on the contract by merely assigning its duties and rights under the contract to a third party.

It is evident from the express language of the assignment agreement between Pratt and Son, Inc., that only an assignment was intended, not a novation. The agreement made no mention of discharging Pratt from any further liability on the contract.

Furthermore, the agreement was between Pratt and Son, Inc.; they were the parties signing the agreement,

not the Rosenbergs. An agreement between Pratt and Son, Inc., cannot unilaterally affect the Rosenbergs' rights under the contract. As mentioned earlier, the Rosenbergs did sign a consent to the assignment at the bottom of the agreement. However, by merely consenting to the assignment, the Rosenbergs did not consent to a discharge of the principal obligor—Pratt. Nothing in the language of the consent clause supports such an allegation. A creditor is free to consent to an assignment without releasing the original obligor.

We *reverse* the summary judgment and *remand* for further proceedings.

Chapter Conclusion

A moment's caution! It is important to remember that the parties to a contract may not have the right to substitute someone else into the contract. The parties to a contract always have legal rights themselves, but when outsiders enter the picture, subtle differences in key areas determine whether additional rights exist.

EXAM REVIEW

1. **THIRD-PARTY BENEFICIARY** A third-party beneficiary may enforce a contract if the parties intended her to benefit from the agreement and if either (1) enforcing the promise will satisfy a debt of the promisee to the beneficiary, or (2) the promisee intended to make a gift to the beneficiary. The intended beneficiary described in (1) is a creditor beneficiary, while (2) describes a donee beneficiary. Any beneficiary who meets neither description is an incidental beneficiary and has no right to enforce the contract.

2. **ASSIGNMENT AND DELEGATION** An assignment transfers the assignor's contract rights to the assignee. A delegation transfers the delegator's duties to the delegatee.

3. **RIGHTS ASSIGNABLE** A party generally may assign contract rights unless doing so would substantially change the obligor's rights or duties, is forbidden by law, or is validly precluded by the contract.

Question: Angelo Zavarella and Yvette Rodrigues were injured in an automobile accident allegedly caused by a vehicle belonging to Truck Equipment of Boston. Travelers Insurance Co. paid insurance benefits to Zavarella and Rodrigues, who then assigned to Travelers their claims against Truck Equipment. Travelers sued Truck Equipment, which moved to dismiss. What is Truck Equipment's claim that the case should be dismissed, and how would you rule?

Strategy: Travelers is claiming to be the assignee of the plaintiffs' claims. Any contractual right may be assigned except in the three instances listed. Does one of those prohibitions apply? (See the "Result" at the end of this section.)

4. **ENFORCEMENT** Once the assignment is made and the obligor notified, the assignee may enforce her contractual rights against the obligor. The obligor, in turn, may generally raise all defenses against the assignee that she could have raised against the assignor.

5. **THE UCC AND SECURITY INTERESTS:** Article 9 of the UCC governs security interests, which are the legal rights to personal property that assure payment of a debt. Under Article 9, obligors may assert defenses against assignees that arise from contracts, and agreements not to enforce such defenses are generally valid.

6. **DUTIES DELEGABLE** Duties are delegable unless delegation would violate public policy, the contract prohibits delegation, or the obligee has a substantial interest in personal performance by the obligor.

Question: Pizza of Gaithersburg, Maryland, owned five pizza shops. Pizza arranged with Virginia Coffee Service to install soft drink machines in each of its stores and maintain them. The contract made no mention of the rights of either party to delegate. Virginia Coffee delegated its duties to the Macke Co., leading to litigation between Pizza and Macke. Pizza claimed that Virginia Coffee was barred from delegating because Pizza had a close working relationship with the president of Virginia Coffee, who personally kept the machines in working order. Was the delegation legal?

Strategy: Any contractual duty may be delegated except in the three instances listed. Does one of those prohibitions apply? (See the "Result" at the end of this section.)

7. **DISCHARGE** Unless the obligee agrees otherwise, delegation does not discharge the delegator's duty to perform.

8. **NOVATION** A novation is a three-way agreement in which the obligor delegates all duties to the delegatee and the obligee agrees to hold only the delegatee responsible.

EXAM Strategy

Question: Mardy, a general contractor, is building a house. He contracts with Plumbco to do all plumbing work for $120,000. Before Plumbco begins the work, it notifies Mardy in writing that Leo will be doing the work instead. Mardy does not respond. When Leo fails to perform, Mardy sues Plumbco. Plumbco is

(a) Liable

(b) Liable only if Plumbco agreed to remain responsible for the job

(c) Not liable because Mardy failed to repudiate the delegation

(d) Not liable because Plumbco validly delegated its duties

(e) Not liable because the parties entered into a novation

Strategy: Delegation does not by itself relieve the delegator of his own liability to perform the contract. In a novation, the obligee agrees to look only to the third party for performance. Was this a delegation or a novation? (See the "Result" at the end of this section.)

---

3. Result: Truck Equipment's winning argument was one sentence long: Claims for personal injury may not be assigned. Such assignments would transform accident claims into commercial commodities and encourage assignees to exaggerate the gravity of the harm.

6. Result: There is no public policy issue involved. The contract is silent as to delegation. And Pizza's only legitimate interest was in seeing that installation and maintenance were adequate. There is no reason to believe that Virginia Coffee would perform the work better than others. The duty was delegable, and Virginia Coffee wins.

8. Result: When Plumbco announced that Leo would do the work, Mardy did not respond. Mardy certainly did not agree to look exclusively to Leo for performance. There has not been a novation, and Plumbco remains liable on the contract. The correct answer is (a).

MULTIPLE-CHOICE QUESTIONS

1. *CPA QUESTION* Yost contracted with Egan for Yost to buy certain real property. If the contract is otherwise silent, Yost's rights under the contract are:
   (a) Assignable only with Egan's consent
   (b) Nonassignable because they are personal to Yost
   (c) Nonassignable as a matter of law
   (d) Generally assignable

2. *CPA QUESTION* One of the criteria for a valid assignment of a sales contract to a third party is that the assignment must:
   (a) Not materially increase the other party's risk or duty
   (b) Not be revocable by the assignor
   (c) Be supported by adequate consideration from the assignee
   (d) Be in writing and signed by the assignor

3. Amanda agrees to pay Jennifer $300 for a pair of tickets to see Jerry Seinfeld. "Seinfeld is my boyfriend Octavio's favorite comedian, and the tickets will be a great birthday present for him," she tells Jennifer. Amanda pays up and tells a delighted Octavio about the tickets, but Jennifer never delivers them. Octavio is a (n) _____ beneficiary of the agreement, and as such, he _____ have a right to enforce the contract himself.

   (a) donee; does

   (b) donee; does not

   (c) incidental; does

   (d) incidental; does not

4. A novation completely releases an _____ from any further liability. To be effective, it _____ require the agreement of both the obligor and obligee.

   (a) obligor; does

   (b) obligor; does not

   (c) obligee; does

   (d) obligee; does not

5. Will misses three straight payments on his SUV, and his bank repossesses it. The right to repossess _____ a security interest. Security interests are governed by Article _____ of the Uniform Commercial Code.

   (a) is; 2

   (b) is; 9

   (c) is not; 2

   (d) is not; 9

CASE QUESTIONS

1. Intercontinental Metals Corp. (IMC) contracted with the accounting firm of Cherry, Bekaert, & Holland to perform an audit. Cherry issued its opinion about IMC, giving all copies of its report directly to the company. IMC later permitted Dun & Bradstreet to examine the statements, and Raritan River Steel Co. saw a report published by Dun & Bradstreet. Relying on the audit, Raritan sold IMC $2.2 million worth of steel on credit, but IMC promptly went bankrupt. Raritan sued Cherry, claiming that IMC was not as sound as Cherry had reported and that the accounting firm had breached its contract with IMC. Comment on Raritan's suit.

2. Woodson Walker and Associates leased computer equipment from Park Ryan Leasing. The lease said nothing about assignment. Park Ryan then assigned the lease to TCB as security for a loan. Park Ryan defaulted on its loan, and Walker failed to make several payments on the lease. TCB sued Walker for the lease payments. Was the assignment valid, given the fact that the original lease made no mention of it? If the assignment was valid, may Walker raise defenses against TCB that it could have raised against Park Ryan?

3. Darin bought his fiancée Sarah a 3-carat diamond ring for $43,121 from Mandarin Gems. Later, Mandarin supplied Erstad with a written appraisal valuing the engagement ring at $45,500. Years later, the couple divorced and Sarah kept the ring. When she had the ring reappraised, another gemologist assessed its value at only $20,000. Sarah sued Mandarin for breach of contract, but the jeweller defended by saying that it had never made a contract with her. Does Sarah have contract rights against Mandarin?

4. *YOU BE THE JUDGE* **WRITING PROBLEM** David Ricupero suspected his wife Polly of having an affair, so he taped her phone conversations and, based on what he heard, sued for divorce. David's lawyer, William Wuliger, had the recorded conversations transcribed for use at trial. The parties settled the divorce out of court and signed an agreement that included this clause:

> Except as herein otherwise provided, each party hereto completely and forever releases the other and his attorneys from any and all rights each has or may have … to any property, privileges, or benefits accruing to either by virtue of their marriage, or conferred by the Statutory or Common Law of Ohio or the United States of America.

After the divorce was final, Polly sued William Wuliger for invasion of privacy and violation of federal wiretapping law. Wuliger moved to dismiss the case based on the clause quoted. Polly argued that Wuliger was not a party to the divorce settlement and had no right to enforce it. May Wuliger enforce the waiver clause from the Ricuperos' divorce settlement? **Argument for Wuliger:** The contract language demonstrates that the parties intended to release one another and their attorneys from any claims. That makes Wuliger an intended third-party beneficiary, and he is entitled to enforce the agreement. If Polly did not want to release Wuliger from such claims, she was free not to sign the agreement. **Argument for Polly Ricupero:** A divorce agreement settles the affairs between the couple. That is all it is ever intended to do, and the parties here never intended to benefit a lawyer. Wuliger is only an incidental beneficiary and cannot use this contract to paper over his violation of federal wiretapping law.

5. Judith and John Brooks hired Wayne Hayes to build a house. The contract required Hayes to "provide all necessary labor and materials and perform all work of every nature whatsoever to be done in the erection of the residence." Hayes hired subcontractors to do all of the work. One of Hayes's employees checked on the work site daily, but neither Hayes nor any of his employees actively supervised the building. The Brookses were aware of this working arrangement and consented to it. The mason negligently installed the fireplace, ultimately leading to a serious fire. The Brookses sued Hayes for breach of contract. Hayes contended that, when the Brookses approved of his hiring of subcontractors to do all work, that created a novation relieving him of any liability. Discuss.

DISCUSSION QUESTIONS

1. A century and a half ago, an English judge stated: "All painters do not paint portraits like Sir Joshua Reynolds, nor landscapes like Claude Lorraine, nor do all writers write dramas like Shakespeare or fiction like Dickens. Rare genius and extraordinary skill are not transferable." What legal doctrine is the judge describing? What is the ethical basis of this rule?

2. Nationwide Discount Furniture hired Rampart Security to install an alarm in its warehouse. A fire would set off an alarm in Rampart's office, and the security company was then supposed to notify Nationwide immediately. A fire did break out, but Rampart allegedly failed to notify Nationwide, causing the fire to spread next door and damage a building owned by Gasket Materials Corp. Gasket sued Rampart for breach of contract, and Rampart moved for summary judgment. Comment.

3. If a person promises to give you a gift, there is usually no consideration. The person can change his mind and decide not to give you the present, and there is nothing you can do about it. But if a person makes a contract with *someone else* and intends that you will receive a gift under the agreement, you are a donee beneficiary and you *do* have rights to enforce the deal. Are these rules unacceptably inconsistent? If so, which rule should change?

4. In response to the subprime mortgage crisis, the federal government created the Home Affordable Modification Program (HAMP) to help struggling homeowners refinance their mortgage debt, thereby reducing the foreclosure rate. HAMP facilitates contracts between the U.S. Treasury and mortgage lenders, who modify eligible homeowners' mortgage loans in return for incentive payments. The Mackenzies applied for a HAMP modification of their home. Although they were eligible, Flagstar bank foreclosed on their Massachusetts home. The Mackenzies sued Flagstar for breach of contract, claiming they were intended third-party beneficiaries of the lender's contract with the government. Will the Mackenzies succeed on this theory?

5. In our society, a person can buy and sell almost anything. But as this chapter describes, you cannot sell personal injury claims. Should you be able to? Imagine that you are injured in a car wreck. You are told that you might win $100,000 in a lawsuit eventually, but that you might not receive payment for years, and you might also lose the case and recover nothing. If someone is willing to pay you $20,000 cash-on-the-barrelhead today for the rights to your claim, is it fair that public policy concerns prohibit you from taking the money?

CHAPTER 18

PERFORMANCE, BREACH, AND DISCHARGE

© Honza Krej/Shutterstock.com

Polly was elated. It was the grand opening of her new restaurant, Polly's Folly, and everything was bubbling. The waitstaff hustled, and Caesar, the chef, churned out succulent dishes. Polly had signed a contract promising him $1,500 per week for one year, "provided Polly is personally satisfied with his cooking." Polly was determined that her restaurant would be glorious. Her three-year lease would cost $6,000 per month, and she had signed an advertising deal with Billboard Bonanza for the same period. Polly had also promised Eddie, a publicity agent, a substantial monthly fee, to begin as soon as the restaurant was 80 percent booked for one month. Tonight, with candles flickering at packed tables, Polly beamed.

> **Polly disliked a veal dish and gagged on one of Caesar's soups. She fired her chef.**

After a week, Polly's smiles were a bit forced. Some of Caesar's new dishes had been failures, including a grilled swordfish that was hard to pierce and shrimp jambalaya that was too spicy. The restaurant was only 60 percent full, and the publicity agent yelled at Caesar for costing him money. Later that month, Polly disliked a veal dish and gagged on one of Caesar's soups. She fired her chef.

Then troubles gushed forth—literally. A water main burst in front of Polly's restaurant, flooding the street. The city embarked on a two-month repair job that ultimately took four times that long. The street was closed to traffic, and no one could park within blocks of Polly's restaurant. Patronage dropped steadily as hungry customers refused to deal with the bad parking and construction noise. After several months, behind on the rent and in debt to everyone, Polly closed her doors for good.

Shortly, the court doors swung open, offering a full menu of litigation. Polly's landlord sued for three years' rent, and Billboard Bonanza demanded its money for the same period. Caesar claimed his year's pay. Eddie, the agent, insisted on some money for his hard work. Polly defended vigorously, seeking to be *discharged* from her various contracts.

If a party is **discharged**, she is "finished," and has no more duties under a contract. In each lawsuit, Polly asked a court to declare that her obligations were terminated and that she owed no money.

Most contracts are discharged by full performance. In other words, the parties generally do what they promise. Suppose, before the restaurant opened, Walter had promised to deliver 100 sets of cutlery to Polly and she had promised to pay $20 per set. Walter delivered the goods on time, and Polly paid $2,000 on delivery. The parties got what they expected, and that contract was fully discharged.

Sometimes the parties discharge a contract by agreement. For example, the parties may agree to **rescind** their contract, meaning that they terminate it by mutual agreement.[1] If Polly's landlord believed he could get more rent from a new tenant, he might agree to rescind her lease. But he was dubious about the rental market and refused to rescind.

At times, a court may discharge a party who has not performed. When things have gone amiss, a judge must interpret the contract and issues of public policy to determine who in fairness should suffer the loss. In the lawsuits brought by the landlord and Billboard Bonanza, Polly argued a defense called "commercial impracticability," claiming that she should not be forced to rent space that was useless to her or buy advertising for a restaurant that had closed. From Polly's point of view, the claim was understandable. But we can also respect the arguments made by the landlord and the advertiser, that they did not cause the burst water main. Claims of commercial impracticability are difficult to win, and Polly lost against both of these opponents. Though she was making no money at all from the restaurant, the court found her liable in full for the lease and the advertising contract.[2]

Polly's argument against Caesar raised another issue of discharge. Caesar claimed that his cooking was good professional work and that all chefs have occasional disasters, especially in a new restaurant. But Polly responded that they had a "personal satisfaction" contract. Under such contracts, "good" work may not suffice if it fails to please the promisee. Polly won this argument, and Caesar recovered nothing.

As to Eddie's suit, Polly raised a defense called "condition precedent," meaning that some event had to occur before she was obligated to pay. Polly claimed that she owed Eddie money only if and when the restaurant was 80 percent full for a month, and that had never happened. The court agreed and discharged Polly on Eddie's claim.

We will analyze each of these issues, and begin with a look at conditions.

Discharge
A party is discharged when she has no more duties under the contract.

Rescind
To terminate a contract by mutual agreement

18-1 CONDITIONS

Parties often put conditions in a contract. A **condition** is an event that must occur before a party becomes obligated under a contract. "I'll agree to do something, but only if something else happens first." Polly agreed to pay Eddie, the agent, a percentage of her profits, but with an important condition: 80 percent of the tables had to be booked for a month. Unless and until those tables were occupied, Polly owed Eddie nothing. That never happened, or, in contract language, the *condition failed*, and so Polly was discharged.

Condition
An event that must occur before a party becomes obligated under a contract

---

[1] The parties could also decide that one party's duties will be performed by someone else, a modification called a novation. Alternatively, they could create an accord and satisfaction, in which they agree that one party will substitute a new kind of performance in place of his contract obligations. See Chapter 17, on third parties, and Chapter 13, on consideration.
[2] Based on Luminous Neon v. Parscale, 17 Kan. App. 2d 241 (Kan. Ct. App. 1992).

Conditions can take many forms. Alex would like to buy Kevin's empty lot and build a movie theater on it, but the city's zoning law will not permit that kind of business in that location. Alex signs a contract to buy Kevin's empty lot in 120 days, *provided that* within 100 days, the city rezones the area to permit a movie theater. If the city fails to rezone the area by day 100, Alex is discharged and need not complete the deal.

Another example: Friendly Insurance issues a policy covering Vivian's house, promising to pay for any loss due to fire, but only if Vivian furnishes proof of her losses within 60 days of the damage. If the house burns down, Friendly becomes liable to pay. But if Vivian arrives with her proof 70 days after the fire, she collects nothing. Friendly, though it briefly had a duty to pay, was discharged when Vivian failed to furnish the necessary information on time.

18-1a How Conditions Are Created

Express Conditions

The parties may expressly state a condition. Alex's contract with Kevin expressly discharged all obligations if the city failed to rezone within the stated period. Notice that **no special language is necessary to create the condition**. Phrases such as "provided that" frequently indicate a condition, but neither those nor any other specific words are essential. As long as the contract's language indicates that the parties *intended* to create a condition, a court will enforce it.

Because informal language can create a condition, the parties may dispute whether they intended one or not. Sand Creek Country Club, in Indiana, was eager to expand its club-house facilities and awarded the design work to CSO Architects. The club wanted the work done quickly but had not secured financing. The architects sent a letter confirming their agreement:

> It was our intent to allow Mr. Dan Moriarty of our office to start work on your project as early as possible in order to allow you to meet the goals that you have set for next fall. Also, it was the intent of CSO to begin work on your project and delay any billings to you until your financing is in place. As I explained to you earlier, we will continue on this course until we reach a point where we can no longer continue without receiving some payment.

The club gave CSO the go-ahead to begin design work, and the architects did their work and billed Sand Creek for $33,000. But the club, unable to obtain financing, refused to pay. Sand Creek claimed that CSO's letter created a *condition* in their agreement, namely, that the club would have to pay only if and when it obtained financing. The court was unpersuaded and ruled that the parties had never intended to create an express condition. The architects were merely delaying their billing as a convenience to the club. It would be absurd, said the court, to assume that CSO intended to perform $33,000 worth of work for free.[3]

Professional sports contracts are often full of conditions. Assume that the San Francisco Giants want to sign Tony Fleet to play center field. The club considers him a fine defensive player but a dubious offensive performer. The many conditional clauses in his contract reflect hard bargaining over an athlete who may or may not become a star. The Giants guarantee Fleet only $500,000, a very modest salary by Major League Baseball standards.

---

[3]Sand Creek Country Club, Ltd. v. CSO Architects, Inc., 582 N.E.2d 872 (Ind. Ct. App. 1991).

If the speedy outfielder appears in at least 120 games, his pay increases to $1 million. Winning a Gold Glove award is worth an extra $200,000 to him. The Giants insist on a team option to re-sign Fleet for the following season at a salary of $800,000, but if the center fielder plays in fewer than 100 games, the team loses that right, leaving Fleet free to negotiate for higher pay with other teams.

Implied Conditions

At other times, the parties say nothing about a condition, but it is clear from their agreement that they have implied one. Charlotte orally rents an apartment to Hakan for one year and promises to fix any problems in the unit. It is an implied condition that Hakan will promptly notify Charlotte of anything needing repair. Although the parties have not said anything about notice, it is only common sense that Hakan must inform his landlord of defects since she will have no other way to learn of them.

18-1b **Types of Conditions**

Courts divide conditional clauses into three categories: (1) condition precedent, (2) condition subsequent, and (3) concurrent conditions.[4] But what they have in common is more important than any of their differences. The key to all conditional clauses is this: **If the condition does not occur, one party will probably be discharged without having to perform his obligations under a contract.**

Condition Precedent

In this kind of condition, an event must occur *before* a duty arises. Polly's contract with Eddie concerned a condition precedent. Polly had no obligation to pay Eddie anything *unless and until* the restaurant was 80 percent full for a month. Since that never happened, she was discharged. If the parties agreed to a condition precedent, the *plaintiff* has the burden to prove that the condition happened and that the defendant was obligated to perform.

Contracts for the sale of real estate often have conditions precedent. Buyers commonly make purchase offers contingent on events like obtaining a mortgage or an acceptable property inspection. In these cases, the buyer has no duty to pay until the conditions are met.

Condition Subsequent

This type of condition must occur *after* a particular duty arises. If the condition does not occur, the duty is discharged. Vivian's policy with Friendly Insurance contains a condition subsequent. As soon as the fire broke out, Friendly became obligated to pay for the damage. But if Vivian failed to produce her proof of loss on time, Friendly's obligation ended—it was discharged. Note that, with a condition subsequent, it is the *defendant* who must prove that the condition occurred, relieving him of any obligation.

---

[4]The Restatement (Second) of Contracts has officially abandoned the terms *condition precedent* and *condition subsequent*. See Restatement §§224 et seq. But courts routinely use the terms, so it is difficult to avoid the old distinctions.

CONDITION PRECEDENT AND CONDITION SUBSEQUENT COMPARED

	Condition Created	Does Condition Occur?	Duty Is Determined	Result
Condition Precedent	"Fee to be paid when restaurant is filled to 80% capacity for one month."	Condition DOES occur: restaurant is packed.	Duty arises: Polly owes Eddie his fee.	Polly pays the fee.
		Condition DOES NOT occur: restaurant is empty.	Duty never arises: Polly is discharged.	Polly pays nothing.

	Condition Created	Duty Is Determined	Does Condition Occur?	Result
Condition Subsequent	"Vivian must give proof of loss within 60 days."	Fire damages property, and Friendly Insurance becomes obligated to pay Vivian.	Condition DOES occur: Vivian proves her losses within 60 days.	Friendly pays Vivian for her losses.
			Condition DOES NOT occur: Vivian fails to prove her losses within 60 days.	Friendly is discharged and owes nothing.

Concurrent Conditions

Here, both parties have a duty to perform *simultaneously*. Renee agrees to sell her condominium to Tim on July 5. Renee agrees to furnish a valid deed and clear title to the property on that date, and Tim promises to present a cashier's check for $200,000. The parties have agreed to concurrent conditions. Each performance is the condition for the other's performance. If Renee arrives at the Registry of Deeds and can say only, "Don't worry. I'm totally sure I own this property," Tim need not present his check; similarly, if Tim arrives with only an "IOU" scribbled on the back of a candy wrapper, Renee has no duty to hand over a valid deed.

EXAM Strategy

Question: Roberto wants to buy Naomi's house for $350,000 and is willing to make a 20 percent down payment, which satisfies Naomi. However, he needs a $280,000 mortgage in order to complete the purchase, and he is not certain he can obtain one. Naomi is worried that Roberto might change his mind about buying the house and then use alleged financing problems to skip out of the deal. How can the two parties protect themselves?

Strategy: Both parties should use conditional clauses in the sales agreement. Naomi must force Roberto to do his best to obtain a mortgage. How? Roberto's clause should protect him if he cannot obtain a sufficient mortgage. How?

Result: Naomi should demand the 20 percent down payment. Further, her conditional clause should state that Roberto forfeits the down payment unless he demonstrates that, within two weeks, he has applied in good faith for a mortgage to at least three banks. Roberto should insist that if he promptly and fully applies to three banks but fails to obtain a mortgage, his down payment is refunded.

Public Policy

At times, a court will refuse to enforce an express condition on the grounds that it is unfair and harmful to the general public. In other words, a court might agree that the parties created a conditional clause but conclude that permitting its enforcement would hurt society. Did the insurance contract in the following case harm society? You be the judge.

You be the Judge

ANDERSON V. COUNTRY LIFE INSURANCE CO.
180 Ariz. 625
Arizona Court of Appeals, 1994

Facts: On November 26, a Country Life Insurance agent went to the house of Donald and Anna Mae Anderson. He persuaded the Andersons to buy a life insurance policy and accepted a check for $1,600. He gave the Andersons a "conditional receipt for medical policy," dated that day. The form stated that the Andersons would have a valid life insurance policy with Country Life, effective November 26, but only when all conditions were met. The most important of these conditions was that the Country Life home office accepts the Andersons as medical risks. The Andersons were pleased with the new policy and glad that it was effective that same day.

It was not. Donald Anderson died of a heart attack a few weeks later. Country Life declined the Andersons as medical risks and refused to issue a policy. Anna Mae Anderson sued. Country Life pointed out that medical approval was a condition precedent. In other words, the company argued that the policy would be effective as of November 26, but only if it later decided to make the policy effective. Based on this argument, the trial court gave summary judgment for Country Life. Ms. Anderson appealed, claiming that the conditional clause was a violation of public policy.

You Be the Judge: *Did the conditional clause violate public policy?*

Argument for Ms. Anderson: Your honors, this policy is a scam. This so-called "conditional receipt for medical policy" is designed to trick customers and then steal their money. The company leads people to believe they are covered as of the day they write the check. But they aren't covered until *much later*, when the insurer gets around to deciding the applicant's medical status.

The company gets the customer's money right away and gives nothing in exchange. If the company, after taking its time, decides the applicant is not medically fit, it returns the money, having used it for weeks or even months to earn interest. If, on the other hand, the insurance company decides the applicant is a good bet, it then issues the policy effective for weeks or months *in the past, when coverage is of no use*. No one can die retroactively, your honors. The company is being paid for a period during which it had no risk. This is a fraud and a disgrace, and the company should pay the benefits it owes.

Argument for Country Life: Your honors, is Country Life supposed to issue life insurance policies without doing a medical check? That is the road to bankruptcy and would mean that no one could obtain this valuable coverage. Of course, we do a medical inquiry, as quickly as possible. It's in our interest to get the policy decided one way or the other.

The policy clearly stated that coverage was effective *only when approved by the home office*, after all inquiries were made. The Andersons knew that as well as the agent. If they were covered immediately, why would the company do a medical check? Country Life resents suggestions that this policy is a scam, when in reality it is Ms. Anderson who is trying to profit from a tragedy that the company had nothing to do with.

The facts of this case are unusual. Obviously, most insureds do not die between application and acceptance. It would be disastrous for society to rewrite every insurance policy in this state based on one very sad fact pattern. The contract was clear and it should be enforced as written.

18-2 PERFORMANCE

Caitlin has an architect draw up plans for a monumental new house, and Daniel agrees to build it by September 1. Caitlin promises to pay $900,000 on that date. The house is ready on time, but Caitlin has some complaints. The living room was supposed to be 18 feet high, but it is only 17 feet; the pool was to be azure, yet it is aquamarine; the maid's room was not supposed to be wired for cable television, but it is. Caitlin refuses to pay anything for the house. Is she justified? Of course not, it would be absurd to give her a magnificent house for free when it has only tiny defects. But in this easy answer lurks a danger. Technically, Daniel did breach the contract, and yet the law allows him to recover the full contract price, or virtually all of it. Once that principle is established, how far will a court stretch it? Suppose the living room is only 14 feet high, or 12 feet, or 5 feet? What if the foundation has a small crack? A vast and dangerous split? What if Daniel finishes the house a month late? Six months late? Three years late? At some point, a court will conclude that Daniel has so thoroughly botched the job that he deserves little or no money. But where, exactly, is that point? This is a question that businesses—and judges—face often.

The more complex a contract, the more certain that at least one party will perform imperfectly. Nearly every house ever built has at least some small defects. A delivery of a thousand bushels of apples is sure to include a few rotten ones. A custom-designed computer system for a huge airline is likely to have some glitches. The cases raise several related doctrines, all concerning *how well* a party performed its contractual obligations.

18-2a Strict Performance and Substantial Performance

Strict Performance

Strict performance

Requires one party to perform its obligations precisely, with no deviation from the contract terms

When Daniel built Caitlin's house with three minor defects, she refused to pay, arguing that he had not *strictly performed* his obligations. Her assertion was correct, yet she lost anyway. Courts dislike strict performance because it enables one party to benefit without paying and sends the other one home empty-handed. A party is generally not required to render **strict performance** unless the contract expressly demands it *and* such a demand is reasonable. Caitlin's contract never suggested that Daniel would forfeit all payment if there were minor problems. Even if Caitlin had insisted on such a clause, few courts would have enforced it because the requirement would be unreasonable for a project as complicated as the construction of a $900,000 home.

There are some cases where strict performance does make sense. Marshall agrees to deliver 500 sweaters to Leo's store, and Leo promises to pay $20,000 cash on delivery. If Leo has only $19,000 cash and a promissory note for $1,000, he has failed to perform, and Marshall need not give him the sweaters. Leo's payment represents 95 percent of what he promised, but there is a big difference between getting the last $1,000 in cash and receiving a promissory note for that amount.

Substantial Performance

Substantial performance

Occurs when one party fulfills enough of its contract obligations to warrant payment

Daniel, the house builder, won his case against Caitlin because he fulfilled *most* of his obligations, even though he did an imperfect job. Courts often rely on the substantial performance doctrine, especially in cases involving services as opposed to those concerning the sale of goods or land. In a contract for services, a party that **substantially performs** its obligations will generally receive the full contract price, minus the value of any defects. Daniel receives $900,000, the contract price, minus the value of a ceiling that is 1 foot too low, a pool the wrong color, and so forth. It will be for the trial court to decide how much those defects are worth. If the court decides the low ceiling is a $10,000 defect, the pool color is worth $5,000, and the cable television wiring error is worth $500, then Daniel receives $884,500.

On the other hand, a **party that fails to perform substantially receives nothing on the contract itself and will recover only the value of the work, if any.** If the foundation cracks in Caitlin's house and the walls collapse, Daniel will not receive his $900,000. In such a case, he collects only the market value of the work he has done, which, since the house is a pile of rubble, is probably zero.

When is performance substantial? There is no perfect test, but courts look at these issues:

- How much benefit has the promisee received?

- If it is a construction contract, can the owner use the thing for its intended purpose?

- Can the promisee be compensated with money damages for any defects?

- Did the promisor act in good faith?

Substantial performance is vital, unless you enjoy working for free.

EXAM Strategy

Question: Jade owns a straight track used for drag racing. She hires Trevor to resurface it, for $180,000, paying $90,000 down. When the project is completed, Jade refuses to pay the balance and sues Trevor for her down payment. He counterclaims for the $90,000 still due. At trial, Trevor proves that all of the required materials were applied by trained workers in an expert fashion, the dimensions were perfect, and his profit margin very modest. The head of the national drag racing association testifies that his group considers the strip unsafe. He noticed puddles in both asphalt lanes, found the concrete starting pads unsafe, and believed the racing surface needed to be ground off and reapplied. His organization refuses to sanction races at the track until repairs are made. Who wins the suit?

Strategy: When one party has performed imperfectly, we have an issue of substantial performance. To decide whether Trevor is entitled to his money, we apply four factors: (1) How much benefit did Jade receive? (2) Can she use the racing strip for its intended purpose? (3) Can Jade be compensated for defects? (4) Did Trevor act in good faith?

Result: Jade has received no benefit whatsoever. She cannot use her drag strip for racing. Compensation will not help Jade—she needs a new strip. Trevor's work must be ripped up and replaced. Trevor may have acted in good faith, but he failed to deliver what Jade bargained for. Jade wins all of the money she paid. (As we will see in the Chapter 19, she may also win additional sums for her lost profits.)

18-2b **Personal Satisfaction Contracts**

Sujata, president of a public relations firm, hires Ben to design a huge multimedia project for her company, involving computer software, music, and live actors, all designed to sell frozen bologna sandwiches to supermarkets. His contract guarantees him two years' employment, provided all of his work "is acceptable in the sole judgment of Sujata." Ben's immediate supervisor is delighted with his work and his colleagues are impressed, but Sujata is not. Three months later, she fires him, claiming that his work is "uninspired." Does she have the right to do that?

Personal satisfaction contract

Permit the promisee to make subjective evaluations of the promisor's performance

This is a **personal satisfaction contract**, in which the promisee makes a personal, subjective evaluation of the promisor's performance. Employment contracts may require personal satisfaction of the employer; agreements for the sale of goods may demand that the buyer be personally satisfied with the product; and deals involving a credit analysis of one party may insist that his finances be satisfactory to the other party. In resolving disputes like Ben and Sujata's, judges must decide: When is it *fair* for the promisee to claim that she is not satisfied? May she make that decision for any reason at all, even on a whim?

Personal Satisfaction Clauses

A court applies a subjective standard only if assessing the work involves personal feelings, taste, or judgment and the contract explicitly demanded personal satisfaction. A "subjective standard" means that the promisee's personal views will greatly influence her judgment, even if her decision is foolish and unfair. Artistic or creative work, or highly specialized tasks designed for a particular employer, may involve subtle issues of quality and personal preference. Ben's work combines several media and revolves around his judgment. Accordingly, the law applies a subjective standard to Sujata's decision. Since she concludes that his work is uninspired, she may legally fire him, even if her decision is irrational.

A woman offered to restore this mural for a church in Spain. The original mural is seen on the left. The mural before restoration is shown in the middle. The result of the restoration was the painting on the right. What would happen if the parties did not have a personal satisfaction clause?

Note that the promisee, Sujata, has to show two things: that assessing Ben's work involves her personal judgment *and* that their contract explicitly demands personal satisfaction. If the contract were vague on this point, Sujata would lose. Had the agreement merely said, "Ben will at all times make his best efforts," Sujata could not fire him.

In all other cases, a court applies an *objective* standard to the promisee's decision. In other words, the objective standard will be used if assessing the work does not involve personal judgment *or* if the contract failed to explicitly demand personal satisfaction. An objective standard means that the promisee's judgment of the work must be reasonable. Suppose Sujata hires Leila to install an alarm system for her company, and the contract requires that Sujata be "personally satisfied." Leila's system passes all tests, but Sujata claims, "It just doesn't make me feel secure. I know that someday it's going to break down." May Sujata refuse to pay? No.

Even though the contract used the phrase "personally satisfied," a mechanical alarm system does not involve personal judgment and taste. Either the system works or it does not. A reasonable person would find that Leila's system is just fine and, therefore, under the objective standard, Sujata must pay. The law strongly favors the objective standard because the subjective standard gives unlimited power to the promisee.

> **Either the system works or it does not.**

18-2c Good Faith

The parties to a contract must carry out their obligations in good faith. The difficulty, of course, is applying this general rule to the wide variety of problems that may arise when people or companies do business. How far must one side go to meet its good faith burden? Marvin Shuster was a physician in Florida. Three patients sued him for alleged malpractice. Shuster denied any wrongdoing and asked his insurer to defend the claims. But the insurance company settled all three claims without defending and with a minimum of investigation. Shuster paid nothing out of his own pocket, but he sued the insurance company, claiming that it acted in bad faith. The doctor argued that the company's failure to defend him caused emotional suffering and meant that it would be impossible for him to obtain new malpractice insurance. The Florida Supreme Court found that the insurer acted in good faith. The contract clearly gave all control of malpractice cases to the company. It could settle or defend as it saw fit. Here, the company considered it more economical to settle quickly, and Shuster should have known, from the contract language, that the insurer might choose to do so.[5]

In the following case, one party to a contract played its cards very close to its chest. Too close?

BRUNSWICK HILLS RACQUET CLUB INC. v. ROUTE 18 SHOPPING CENTER ASSOCIATES

182 N.J. 210
Supreme Court of New Jersey, 2005

Facts: Brunswick Hills Racquet Club (Brunswick) owned a tennis club on property that it leased from Route 18 Shopping Center Associates (Route 18). The lease ran for 25 years, and Brunswick had spent about $1 million in capital improvements. The lease expired, and Brunswick had the option of either buying the property or purchasing a 99-year lease, both on very favorable terms. To exercise its option, Brunswick had to notify Route 18 no later than September 30 and had to pay the option price of $150,000. If Brunswick failed to exercise its options, the existing lease automatically renewed as of September 30, for 25 more years, but at more than triple the current rent.

Brunswick's lawyer wrote to Rosen Associates, the company that managed Route 18, nineteen months before the option deadline, stating that Brunswick intended to exercise the option for a 99-year lease. He requested that

the lease be sent well in advance so that he could review it. He did not make the required payment of $150,000. Rosen replied that it had forwarded Spector's letter to its attorney, who would be in touch. In April, Spector again wrote, asking for a reply from Rosen or its lawyer.

Over the next six months, the lawyer continually asked for a copy of the lease or further information, but neither Route 18's lawyer nor anyone else provided any data. Eventually, the September deadline passed.

Route 18's lawyer notified Brunswick that it could not exercise its option to lease because it had failed to pay the $150,000 by September 30.

Brunswick sued, claiming that Route 18 had breached its duty of good faith and fair dealing. The trial court found that Route 18 had no duty to notify Brunswick of impending deadlines, and it gave summary judgment for

[5] *Shuster v. South Broward Hospital Dist. Physicians' Prof. Liability Ins. Trust,* 591 So. 2d 174 (Fla. 1992).

Route 18. The appellate court affirmed, and Brunswick appealed to the state supreme court.

Issue: *Did Route 18 breach its duty of good faith and fair dealing?*

Excerpts from Justice Albin's Decision: Courts generally should not tinker with a finely drawn and precise contract entered into by experienced business people that regulates their financial affairs. [However,] every party to a contract is bound by a duty of good faith and fair dealing in both the performance and enforcement of the contract. Good faith is a concept that defies precise definition. Good faith conduct is conduct that does not violate community standards of decency, fairness, or reasonableness. The covenant of good faith and fair dealing calls for parties to a contract to refrain from doing anything which will have the effect of destroying or injuring the right of the other party to receive the benefits of the contract.

Our review of the undisputed facts of this case leads us to the inescapable conclusion that defendant breached the covenant of good faith and fair dealing. Nineteen months in advance of the option deadline, plaintiff notified defendant in writing of its intent to exercise the option to purchase the 99-year lease. Plaintiff mistakenly believed that the purchase price was not due until the time of closing.

During a 19-month period, defendant, through its agents, engaged in a pattern of evasion, sidestepping every request by plaintiff to discuss the option and ignoring plaintiff's repeated written and verbal entreaties to move forward on closing the 99-year lease despite the impending option deadline and obvious potential harm to plaintiff.

Defendant never requested the purchase price of the lease. Indeed, as defendant's attorney candidly admitted at oral argument, defendant did not want the purchase price because the successful exercise of the option was not in defendant's economic interest.

Ordinarily, we are content to let experienced commercial parties fend for themselves and do not seek to introduce intolerable uncertainty into a carefully structured contractual relationship by balancing equities. But there are ethical norms that apply even to the harsh and sometimes cutthroat world of commercial transactions. We do not expect a landlord or even an attorney to act as his brother's keeper in a commercial transaction. We do expect, however, that they will act in good faith and deal fairly with an opposing party. Plaintiff's repeated letters and telephone calls to defendant concerning the exercise of the option and the closing of the 99-year lease obliged defendant to respond, and to respond truthfully.

[Plaintiff is entitled to exercise the 99-year lease.]

EXAM Strategy

Question: Sun operates an upscale sandwich shop in New Jersey, in a storefront that she leases from Ricky for $18,000 per month. The lease, which expires soon, allows Sun to renew for five years at $22,000 per month. Ricky knows, but Sun does not, that in a year, Prada will open a store on the same block. The dramatic increase in pedestrian traffic will render Sun's space more valuable. Ricky says nothing about Prada, Sun declines to renew, and Ricky leases the space for $40,000 a month. Sun sues Ricky, claiming he breached his duty of good faith and fair dealing. Based on the *Brunswick Hills* case, how would the New Jersey Supreme Court rule?

Strategy: In the *Brunswick Hills* case, the court, on the one hand, criticized the defendant for cynically evading the plaintiff's efforts to renew. However, the court also said, "We do not expect a landlord or even an attorney to act as his brother's keeper in a commercial transaction." Using those opposing themes as guidelines, examine the court's decision and predict the ruling in Sun's suit.

Result: *Brunswick Hills* begins: "Courts generally should not tinker with a finely drawn and precise contract entered into by experienced business people." Sun's lease imposes no responsibility on Ricky to report on neighborhood changes or forecast profitability. Further, Sun made no requests to Ricky about the area's future. Sun is asking Ricky to be "her brother's keeper," and neither this court nor any other will do that. She loses.

18-2d **Time of the Essence Clauses**

Go, sir, gallop, and don't forget that the world was made in six days. You can ask me for anything you like, except time.

Napoleon, to an aide, 1803

Generals are not the only ones who place a premium on time. Ask Gene LaSalle. The Seabreeze Restaurant agreed to sell him all of its assets. The parties signed a contract stating the price and closing date. Seabreeze insisted on a clause saying, "Seabreeze considers that time is of the essence in consummating the proposed transaction." Such clauses are common in real estate transactions and in any other agreement where a delay would cause serious damage to one party. LaSalle was unable to close on the date specified and asked for an extension. Seabreeze refused and sold its assets elsewhere. A Florida court affirmed that Seabreeze acted legally.

A **time is of the essence clause** will generally make contract deadlines strictly enforceable. Seabreeze regarded a timely sale as important, and LaSalle agreed to the provision. There was nothing unreasonable about the clause, and LaSalle suffered the consequences of his delay.[6]

Suppose that the contract had named a closing date but included no time of the essence clause. If LaSalle offered to close three days late, could Seabreeze sell elsewhere? No. **Merely including a date for performance does not make time of the essence.** Courts dislike time of the essence arguments because even a short delay may mean that one party forfeits everything it expected to gain from the bargain. If the parties do not *clearly* state that prompt performance is essential, then both are entitled to reasonable delays.

> **Time is of the essence clause**
> Generally make contract dates strictly enforceable

18-3 BREACH

When one party breaches a contract, the other party is discharged. The discharged party has no obligation to perform and may sue for damages. Edwin promises that on July 1, he will deliver 20 tuxedos, tailored to fit male chimpanzees, to Bubba's circus for $300 per suit. After weeks of delay, Edwin concedes he hasn't a cummerbund to his name. Bubba is discharged and owes nothing. In addition, he may sue Edwin for damages.

18-3a **Material Breach**

As we know, parties frequently perform their contract duties imperfectly, which is why courts accept substantial performance rather than strict performance, particularly in contracts involving services. In a more general sense, **courts will discharge a contract only if a party committed a *material* breach.** A material breach is one that substantially harms the innocent party and for which it would be hard to compensate without discharging the contract. Suppose Edwin fails to show up with the tuxedos on June 1 but calls to say they will arrive under the big top the next day. He has breached the agreement. Is his breach material? No. This is a trivial breach, and Bubba is not discharged. When the tuxedos arrive, he must pay.

The following case raises the issue in the context of a major college sports program.

---

[6]Seabreeze Restaurant, Inc. v. Paumgardhen, 639 So.2d 69 (Fla. Dist. Ct. App. 1994).

O'BRIEN V. OHIO STATE UNIVERSITY

2007-Ohio-4833
Court of Appeals of Ohio, 2007

Facts: Ohio State University (OSU), experiencing a drought in its men's basketball program, brought in Coach Jim O'Brien to turn things around. The plan was successful. In only his second year, he guided the team to its best record ever. The team advanced to the Final Four, and O'Brien was named national coach of the year. OSU's athletic director promptly offered the coach a new, multiyear contract worth about $800,000 per year.

Section 5.1 of the contract included termination provisions. The university could fire O'Brien *for cause* if (a) there was a material breach of the contract by the coach or (b) O'Brien's conduct subjected the school to NCAA sanctions. OSU could also terminate O'Brien *without cause*, but in that case, it had to pay him the full salary owed.

O'Brien began recruiting a talented 21-year-old Serbian player named Alex Radojevic. While getting to know the young man, O'Brien discovered two things. First, it appeared that Radojevic had been paid to play briefly for a Yugoslavian team, meaning that he was ineligible to play college basketball. Second, it was clear that Radojevic's family had suffered terribly during the strife in his homeland.

O'Brien concluded that Radojevic would never play for OSU or any major college. He also decided to loan Radojevic's mother some money. Any such loan would violate an NCAA rule if done to recruit a player, but O'Brien believed the loan was legal since Radojevic could not play in the NCAA anyway. Several years later, the university learned of the loan and realized that O'Brien had never reported it. Hoping to avoid trouble with the NCAA, OSU imposed sanctions on itself. The university also fired the coach, claiming he had lied, destroyed the possibility of postseason play, and harmed the school's reputation.

O'Brien sued, claiming he had not materially breached the contract. The trial court awarded the coach $2.5 million, and the university appealed.

Issue: *Did O'Brien materially breach the contract?*

Excerpts from Judge Tyack's Decision: OSU argued that it was substantially injured by the self-imposed sanctions, which included a ban from post-season and NCAA tournament play [during the current season],

and relinquishing two basketball scholarships from the [next] recruiting class. Contrary to OSU's argument, however, the trial court found these sanctions to be insubstantial. [Athletic Director] Geiger announced the one-year post-season ban in December, and it appears from the timing of that announcement that Geiger made the decision based on the fact that the team was unlikely to be invited to a post-season tournament in the first place.

The second alleged harm was harm to OSU's reputation. The trial court found that any reputational harm was similarly exaggerated, at least as it specifically related to the Radojevic matter. Radojevic never enrolled at OSU, and never played a single second for OSU's basketball team.

NCAA violations happen all the time. It's the nature of the beast. Also relevant to the issue of OSU's allegedly damaged reputation is the fact that almost immediately after firing O'Brien, OSU was able to lure one of the nation's top coaching prospects, [Thad Matta], to assume O'Brien's former position. Shortly thereafter, Matta successfully recruited possibly the best recruiting class ever. Based on this evidence, the trial court could reasonably find the Radojevic loan did not cause serious harm to OSU.

OSU argues that O'Brien acted in bad faith by covering up his misconduct for several years. In the words of OSU's counsel at oral argument: *"If lying to your employer for four years is not a material breach, it's hard to imagine what would be!"* Although the premise for counsel's argument is sound, it is unsound in application because it assumes facts not in evidence. Counsel for OSU assumes for the purposes of the argument that O'Brien systematically either denied allegations about the Radojevic loan, or took affirmative steps to conceal it from OSU. The evidence does not support such a conclusion. After Radojevic was drafted by the NBA, there is not a single inference that can be drawn from the record to suggest that O'Brien even thought about the loan. In O'Brien's own mind, he did not believe he had done anything wrong; thus, he would not have had a motive to conceal what he had done.

[There was no material breach.]

Affirmed.

18-3b **Anticipatory Breach**

Sally will receive her bachelor's degree in May and already has a job lined up for September. She has signed a two-year contract to work as window display designer for Surebet Department Store. The morning of graduation, she reads in the paper that Surebet is going out of business that very day. Surebet has told Sally nothing about her status. Sally need not wait until September to learn her fate. Surebet has committed an **anticipatory breach by making it unmistakably clear that it will not honor the contract.** Sometimes a promisor will actually inform the promisee that it will not perform its duties. At other times, as here, the promisor takes some step that makes the breach evident. Sally is discharged and may immediately seek other work. She is also entitled to file suit for breach of contract. The court will treat Surebet's anticipatory breach just as though the store had actually refused to perform on September 1.

18-3c **Statute of Limitations**

A party injured by a breach of contract should act promptly. A **statute of limitations** begins to run at the time of injury and will limit the time within which the injured party may file suit. These laws set time limits for filing lawsuits. Statutes of limitation vary from state to state and from issue to issue within a state. Failure to file suit within the time limits discharges the party who breached the contract. Always consult a lawyer promptly in the case of a legal injury.

Statute of limitations
A statutory time limit within which an injured party must file suit

18-4 IMPOSSIBILITY

"Your honor, my client wanted to honor the contract. He just couldn't. *Honest.*" This plea often echoes around courtrooms as one party seeks discharge without fulfilling his contract obligations. Does the argument work? It depends. If performing a contract was truly impossible, a court will discharge the agreement. But if honoring the deal merely imposed a financial burden, the law will generally enforce the contract.

18-4a **True Impossibility**

These cases are easy—and rare. **True impossibility means that something has happened making it literally impossible to do what the promisor said he would do.** Francoise owns a vineyard that produces Beaujolais Nouveau wine. She agrees to ship 1,000 cases of her wine to Tyrone, a New York importer, as soon as this year's vintage is ready. Tyrone will pay $50 per case. But a fungus wipes out her entire vineyard. Francoise is discharged. It is theoretically impossible for Francoise to deliver wine from her vineyard, and she owes Tyrone nothing.

Meanwhile, though, Tyrone has a contract with Jackson, a retailer, to sell 1,000 cases of Beaujolais Nouveau wine at $70 per case. Tyrone has no wine from Francoise, and the only other Beaujolais Nouveau available will cost him $85 per case. Instead of earning $20 per case, Tyrone will lose $15. Does this discharge Tyrone's contract with Jackson? No. It is possible for him to perform—it's just more expensive. He must fulfill his agreement.

True impossibility is generally limited to these three causes:

- *Destruction of the Subject Matter.* This is what happened with Francoise's vineyard.

- *Death of the Promisor in a Personal Services Contract.* When the promisor agrees personally to render a service that cannot be transferred to someone else, her death discharges the contract. Producer hires Josephine to write the lyrics for a new Broadway musical, but Josephine dies after writing only two words: "Act One."

The contract was personal to Josephine and is now discharged. Neither Josephine's estate nor Producer has any obligation to the other. But notice that most contracts are not for personal services. Suppose that Tyrone, the wine importer, dies. His contract to sell wine to Jackson is not discharged because anyone can deliver the required wine. Tyrone's estate remains liable on the deal with Jackson.

- *Illegality.* Chet, a Silicon Valley entrepreneur, wants to capitalize on his computer expertise. He contracts with Construction Co. to build a factory in Iran that will manufacture computers for sale in that country. Construction Co. fails to build the factory on time, and Chet sues. Construction Co. defends by pointing out that the president of the United States has issued an executive order barring trade between the United States and Iran. Construction Co. wins; the executive order discharged the contract.

18-4b Commercial Impracticability and Frustration of Purpose

It is rare for contract performance to be truly impossible but very common for it to become a financial burden to one party. Suppose Bradshaw Steel in Pittsburgh agrees to deliver 1,000 tons of steel beams to Rice Construction in Saudi Arabia at a given price, but a week later, the cost of raw ore increases 30 percent. A contract once lucrative to the manufacturer is suddenly a major liability. Does that change discharge Bradshaw? Absolutely not. Rice signed the deal *precisely to protect itself against price increases.* As we have seen, the primary purpose of contracts is to enable the parties to control their future.

Yet there may be times when a change in circumstances is so extreme that it would be unfair to enforce a deal. What if a strike made it impossible for Bradshaw to ship the steel to Saudi Arabia, and the only way to deliver would be by air, at *five times* the sea cost? Must Bradshaw fulfill its deal? What if a new war meant that any ships or planes delivering the goods might be fired upon? Other changes could make the contract undesirable for *Rice.* Suppose the builder wanted steel for a major public building in Riyadh, but the Saudi government decided not to go forward with the construction. The steel would then be worthless to Rice. Must the company still accept it?

None of these hypotheticals involves true impossibility. It is physically possible for Bradshaw to deliver the goods and for Rice to receive. But in some cases, it may be so dangerous, costly, or pointless to enforce a bargain that a court will discharge it instead. Courts use the related doctrines of commercial impracticability and frustration of purpose to decide when a change in circumstances should permit one side to escape its duties.

Commercial impracticability means some event has occurred that neither party anticipated and *fulfilling the contract would now be extraordinarily difficult and unfair to one party.* If a shipping strike forces Bradshaw to ship by air, the company will argue that neither side expected the strike and that Bradshaw should not suffer a fivefold increase in shipping costs. Bradshaw will probably win the argument.

Frustration of purpose means some event has occurred that neither party anticipated and *the contract now has no value for one party.* If Rice's building project is canceled, Rice will argue that the steel now is useless to the company. Frustration cases are hard to predict. Some states would agree with Rice, but others would hold that it was Rice's obligation to protect itself with a government guarantee that the project would be completed. Courts consider the following factors in deciding impracticability and frustration claims:

- *Mere financial difficulties will never suffice to discharge a contract.* Barbara and Michael Luber divorced, and Michael agreed to pay alimony. He stopped making payments and claimed that it was impracticable for him to do so because he had hit hard times and simply did not have the money. The court dismissed his argument, noting that commercial impracticability requires some objective event that neither party anticipated, not merely the financial deterioration of one party.[7]

- *The event must have been truly unexpected.* Wayne Carpenter bought land from the state of Alaska, intending to farm it and agreeing to make monthly payments. The sales contract stated that Alaska did not guarantee the land for agriculture or any other purpose. Carpenter struggled to farm the land but failed; as soon as the ground thawed, the water table rose too high for crops. Carpenter abandoned the land and stopped making payments. Alaska sued and won. The high court rejected Carpenter's claim of impracticability since the "event"—bad soil—was not unexpected. Alaska had warned that the land might prove unworkable, and Carpenter had no claim for commercial impracticability.[8]

- *If the promisor must use a different means to accomplish her task, at a greatly increased cost, she probably does have a valid claim of impracticability.* If a shipping strike forces Bradshaw to use a different means of delivery—say, air—and this multiplies its costs several times, the company is probably discharged. But a mere increase in the cost of raw materials, such as a 30 percent rise in the price of ore, will almost never discharge the promisor.

- A force majeure *clause is significant but not necessarily dispositive.* To protect themselves from unexpected events, companies sometimes include a *force majeure* clause, allowing cancellation of the agreement in case of certain listed extraordinary and unexpected events. A typical clause might permit the seller of goods to delay or cancel delivery in the event of "acts of God, fire, labor disputes, accidents, or transportation difficulties." A court will always consider a *force majeure* clause, but it may not enforce it if one party is trying to escape from routine financial problems.

The following case involves risky business, complex financial instruments, and a lot of excuses. Does a global credit meltdown excuse a party's duty to pay?

HOOSIER ENERGY RURAL ELECTRIC COOPERATIVE, INC. v. JOHN HANCOCK LIFE INSURANCE CO.

582 F.3d 721
United States Court of Appeals for Seventh Circuit, 2009

Facts: John Hancock Life Insurance Co. receives lots of cash in premium payments, which it then invests so that it will have enough funds to pay claims from its policy holders. To this end, it entered into a leveraged lease with Hoosier Energy. This transaction was highly complex and only profitable because of convoluted provisions of the tax code. (You definitely do not want to try this at home.) In short, Hancock paid Hoosier $300 million to lease a power plant for 63 years, which Hoosier then leased back for 30 years.

But Hancock foresaw some risks: What if the power station became unprofitable? What if Hoosier stopped paying rent? (What would Hancock do if it was stuck with a power plant?) To mitigate these risks, it asked to Hoosier to

---

[7]Luber v. Luber, 418 Pa. Super. 542, 614 A.2d 771 (Pa. Super. Ct. 1992).
[8]State v. Carpenter, 869 P.2d 1181 (Alaska 1994).

secure a credit-default swap (CDS). A CDS is a financial contract that acts as insurance against a loan default and other contingencies. Ambac Assurance Corporation, the CDS provider, agreed to pay Hancock if certain events occurred. One of those triggering events was a decline in Ambac's own credit rating below a certain level. In that case, Hoosier had to find a replacement swap partner. If Hoosier was unsuccessful, Ambac would pay Hancock $120 million.

And then came 2008—and a global financial crisis. Ambac's credit rating plummeted, along with pretty much everyone else's. Hancock demanded that Hoosier find a replacement, but Hoosier stalled. If it replaced Ambac, it would have to pay big money—enough to send Hoosier into bankruptcy. So Hoosier sued, requesting an injunction to suspend its duty to find a swap partner. It claimed that the global financial crisis rendered its performance impossible—or at the very least, "temporarily impracticable" until the economy improved. The lower court sympathized with Hoosier and granted the injunction. Hancock appealed.

Issue: *Did the global credit crisis render performance impossible?*

Excerpts from Judge Easterbrook's Decision: Like other states, New York recognizes the doctrine of impossibility—but even then only the kind of impossibility that the parties could not have anticipated. Here, the parties anticipated the possibility that Hoosier, Ambac, or both might get into financial distress and provided what was to happen.

Suppose that Hoosier had an in-the-money option to purchase the Indianapolis Colts, and that as a result of the reduced availability of credit it was unable to find a lender to finance the transaction. That would not make performance "impossible." The "impossibility" doctrine never justifies failure to make a payment, because financial distress differs from impossibility.

It is hard to see why Hoosier should be able to stiff John Hancock, just because the very risk specified in the contract has occurred. Hoosier did not expect an economic downturn. Downturns are types of things that happen, and against which contracts can be designed. When they do happen, the contractual risk allocation must be enforced rather than set aside.

The district court called the credit crunch of 2008 a "once-in-a-century" event. That's an overstatement (the Great Depression occurred within the last 100 years, and the 20th Century also saw financial crunches in 1973 and 1987), and also irrelevant. An insurer that sells hurricane or flood insurance against a "once in a century" catastrophe, or earthquake insurance in a city that rarely experiences tremblors, can't refuse to pay on the ground that, when a natural event devastates a city, its very improbability makes the contract unenforceable.

The defense works only if some unexpected event upsets all parties' expectations; it is not enough that the unexpected event puts one side in a bind. Financial distress could be and was foreseen; that's what the credit-default swap is all about.

Chapter Conclusion

Negotiate carefully. A casually written letter may imply a condition precedent that the author never intended. The term *personal satisfaction* should be defined so that both parties know whether one party may fire the other on a whim. Never assume that mere inconvenience, financial distress—or even a global recession—will discharge contractual duties.

Exam Review

1. **CONDITION** A condition is an event that must occur before a party becomes obligated. It may be stated expressly or implied, and no formal language is necessary to create one.

Question: Stephen Krogness, a real estate broker, agreed to act as an agent for Best Buy Co., which wanted to sell several of its stores. The contract provided that Best Buy would pay Krogness a commission of 2 percent for "a sale to any prospect submitted directly to Best Buy by Krogness." Krogness introduced Corporate Realty Capital (CRC) to Best Buy, and the parties negotiated but could not reach agreement. CRC then introduced Best Buy to BB Properties (BB). Best Buy sold several properties to BB for $46 million. CRC acted as the broker. Krogness sought a commission of $528,000. Is he entitled to it?

Strategy: This contract contains a conditional clause. What is it? What must occur before Best Buy is obligated to pay Krogness? Did that event happen? (See the "Result" at the end of this section.)

2. **SUBSTANTIAL PERFORMANCE** Strict performance, which requires one party to fulfill its duties perfectly, is unusual. In construction and service contracts, substantial performance is generally sufficient to entitle the promisor to the contract price, minus the cost of defects in the work.

3. **PERSONAL SATISFACTION** Personal satisfaction contracts are interpreted under an objective standard, requiring reasonable ground for dissatisfaction, unless the work involves personal judgment *and* the parties intended a subjective standard.

4. **GOOD FAITH** Good faith performance is required in all contracts.

5. **TIME OF THE ESSENCE** Time of the essence clauses result in strict enforcement of contract deadlines.

Question: Colony Park Associates signed a contract to buy 44 acres of residential land from John Gall. The contract stated that closing would take place exactly one year later. The delay was to enable Colony Park to obtain building permits to develop condominiums. Colony Park worked diligently to obtain all permits, but delays in sewer permits forced Colony Park to notify Gall it could not close on the agreed date. Colony Park suggested a date exactly one month later. Gall refused the new date and declined to sell. Colony Park sued. Gall argued that since the parties specified a date, time was of the essence and Colony Park's failure to buy on time discharged Gall. Please rule.

Strategy: A time of the essence clause generally makes a contract date strictly enforceable. Was there one in this agreement? (See the "Result" at the end of this section.)

6. **MATERIAL BREACH** A material breach is the only kind that will discharge a contract; a trivial breach will not.

7. **IMPOSSIBILITY** True impossibility means that some event has made it impossible to perform an agreement. It is typically caused by destruction of the subject matter, the death of an essential promisor, or intervening illegality.

Question: Omega Concrete had a gravel pit and factory. Access was difficult, so Omega contracted with Union Pacific Railroad (UP) for the right to use a private road that crossed UP property and tracks. The contract stated that use of the road was solely for Omega employees and that Omega would be responsible for closing a gate that UP planned to build where the private road joined a public highway. In fact, UP never constructed the gate; Omega had no authority to construct the gate. Mathew Rogers, an Omega employee, was killed by a train while using the private road. Rogers's family sued Omega, claiming that Omega failed to keep the gate closed as the contract required. Is Omega liable?

Strategy: True impossibility means that the promisor cannot do what he promised to do. Is this such a case? (See the "Result" at the end of this section.)

8. **COMMERCIAL IMPRACTICABILITY** Commercial impracticability means that some unexpected event has made it extraordinarily difficult and unfair for one party to perform its obligations.

9. **FRUSTRATION OF PURPOSE** Frustration of purpose may occur when an unexpected event renders a contract completely useless to one party.

---

1. Result: The conditional clause requires Best Buy to pay a commission for "a sale to any prospect submitted directly to Best Buy by Krogness." Krogness did not in fact introduce BB Properties to Best Buy. The condition has not occurred, and Best Buy is under no obligation to pay.

5. Result: Merely including a date for performance does not make time of the essence. A party that considers a date critical must make that clear. This contract did not indicate that the closing date was vital to either party, so a short delay was reasonable. Gail was ordered to convey the land to Colony Park.

7. Result: There was no gate, and Omega had no right to build one. This is a case of true impossibility. Omega was not liable.

MULTIPLE-CHOICE QUESTIONS

1. ***CPA QUESTION*** Nagel and Fields entered into a contract in which Nagel was obligated to deliver certain goods by September 10. On September 3, Nagel told Fields that he had no intention of delivering the goods. Prior to September 10, Fields may successfully sue Nagel under the doctrine of:

   (a) promissory estoppel

   (b) accord and satisfaction

   (c) anticipatory breach

   (d) substantial performance

2. Most contracts are discharged by:

(a) agreement of the parties

(b) full performance

(c) failure of conditions

(d) commercial impracticability

(e) a material breach

3. If a contract contains a condition precedent, the _____ has the burden of proving that the condition actually happened. If a condition subsequent exists, the _____ has the burden of showing that the condition occurred.

(a) plaintiff; plaintiff

(b) plaintiff; defendant

(c) defendant; plaintiff

(d) defendant; defendant

4. Big Co., a construction company, builds a grocery store. The contract calls for a final price of $5 million. Big Co. incurred $4.5 million in costs and stands to make a profit of $500,000. On a final inspection, the grocery store owner is upset. His blueprints called for 24 skylights, but the finished building has only 12. Installing the additional skylights would cost $100,000. Big Co. made no other errors. How much must the grocery store owner pay Big Co.?

(a) $5,000,000

(b) $4,900,000

(c) $4,500,000

(d) $0

5. Lenny makes K2, a synthetic form of marijuana, in his basement. He signs an agreement with the Super Smoke Shop to deliver 1,000 cans of K2 for $10,000. After the contract is signed, but before the delivery, Super Smoke Shop's state legislature makes the sale of K2 illegal. Lenny's contract will be discharged because of _____ .

(a) true impossibility

(b) commercial impracticability

(c) frustration of purpose

(d) none of the above

CASE QUESTIONS

1. ETHICS Commercial Union Insurance Co. (CU) insured Redux, Ltd. The contract made CU liable for fire damage but stated that the insurer would not pay for harm caused by criminal acts of any Redux employees. Fire destroyed Redux's property. CU claimed that the "criminal acts" clause was a condition precedent, but Redux asserted it was a condition subsequent. What difference does it make, and who is legally right? Does the insurance company's position raise any ethical issues? Who drafted the contract? How clear were its terms?

2. Stephen Muka owned U.S. Robotics. He hired his brother Chris to work in the company. His letter promised Chris $1 million worth of Robotics stock at the end of one year, "provided you work reasonably hard & smart at things in the next year." (We should all have such brothers.) Chris arrived at Robotics and worked the full year, but toward the end of the year, Stephen died. His estate refused to give Chris the stock, claiming their agreement was a personal satisfaction contract and only Stephen could decide whether Chris had earned the reward. Comment.

3. Ken Ward was an Illinois farmer who worked land owned by his father-in-law, Frank Ruda. To finance his operation, he frequently borrowed money from Watseka First National Bank, paying back the loans with farming profits. But Ward fell deeper and deeper into debt, and Watseka became concerned. When Ward sought additional loans, Watseka insisted that Ruda become a guarantor on all of the outstanding debt, and the father-in-law agreed. The new loans had an acceleration clause, permitting the bank to demand payment of the entire debt if it believed itself "insecure"; that is, at risk of a default. Unfortunately, just as Ward's debts reached more than $120,000, Illinois suffered a severe drought, and Ward's crops failed. Watseka asked Ruda to sell some of the land he owned to pay back part of the indebtedness. Ruda reluctantly agreed but never did so. Meanwhile, Ward decreased his payments to the bank because of the terrible crop. Watseka then "accelerated" the loan, demanding that Ruda pay off the entire debt. Ruda defended by claiming that Watseka's acceleration at such a difficult time was bad faith. Who should win?

4. Loehmann's clothing stores, a nationwide chain with headquarters in New York, was the anchor tenant in the Lincoln View Plaza Shopping Center in Phoenix, Arizona, with a 20-year lease from the landlord, Foundation Development, beginning in 1978. Loehmann's was obligated to pay rent the first of every month and to pay common-area charges four times a year. The lease stated that if Loehmann's failed to pay on time, Foundation could send a notice of default, and that if the store failed to pay all money due within 10 days, Foundation could evict. On February 23, 1987, Foundation sent to Loehmann's the common-area charges for the quarter ending January 31, 1987. The balance due was $3,500. Loehmann's believed the bill was in error and sent an inquiry on March 18, 1987. On April 10, 1987, Foundation insisted on payment of the full amount within 10 days. Foundation sent the letter to the Loehmann's store in Phoenix. On April 13, 1987, the Loehmann's store received the bill and, since it was not responsible for payments, forwarded it to the New York office. Because the company had moved offices in New York, a Loehmann's officer did not see the bill until April 20. Loehmann's issued a check for the full amount on April 24 and mailed it the following day. On April 28, Foundation sued to evict; on April 29, the company received Loehmann's check. Please rule.

5. *YOU BE THE JUDGE* **WRITING PROBLEM** Kuhn Farm Machinery, a European company, signed an agreement with Scottsdale Plaza Resort, of Arizona, to use the resort for its North American dealers' convention during March 1991. Kuhn agreed to rent 190 guest rooms and spend several thousand dollars on food and beverages. Kuhn invited its top 200 independent dealers from the United States and Canada and about 25 of its own employees from the United States, Europe, and Australia, although it never mentioned those plans to Scottsdale.

On August 2, 1990, Iraq invaded Kuwait, and on January 16, 1991, the United States and allied forces were at war with Iraq. Saddam Hussein and other Iraqi leaders threatened terrorist acts against the United States and its allies. Kuhn became concerned about the safety of those traveling to Arizona, especially its European employees. By mid-February, 11 of the top 50 dealers with expense-paid trips had either canceled their plans to attend or failed to sign up. Kuhn postponed the convention. The resort sued. The trial court discharged the contract under the doctrines of commercial impracticability and frustration of purpose. The resort appealed. Did commercial impracticability or frustration of purpose discharge the contract? **Argument for Scottsdale Plaza Resort:** The resort had no way of knowing that Kuhn anticipated bringing executives from Europe, and even less reason to expect that if anything interfered with their travel, the entire convention would become pointless. Most of the dealers could have attended the convention, and the resort stood ready to serve them. **Argument for Kuhn:** The parties never anticipated the threat of terrorism. Kuhn wanted this convention so that its European executives, among others, could meet top North American dealers. That is now impossible. No company would risk employee lives for a meeting. As a result, the contract has no value at all to Kuhn, and its obligations should be discharged by law.

DISCUSSION QUESTIONS

1. Evans built a house for Sandra Dyer, but the house had some problems. The garage ceiling was too low. Load-bearing beams in the "great room" cracked and appeared to be steadily weakening. The patio did not drain properly. Pipes froze. Evans wanted the money promised for the job, but Dyer refused to pay. Comment.

2. Krug International, an Ohio corporation, had a contract with Iraqi Airways to build aeromedical equipment for training pilots. Krug then contracted for Power Engineering, an Iowa corporation, to build the specialized gearbox to be used in the training equipment for $150,000. Power did not know that Krug planned to resell the gearbox to Iraqi Airways. When Power had almost completed the gearbox, the Gulf War broke out and the United Nations declared an embargo on all shipments to Iraq. Krug notified Power that it no longer wanted the gearbox. Power sued. Please rule.

3. Westinghouse sold uranium in long-term contracts at fixed prices, betting that market prices would be stable or fall (as they had been). But this was a bad bet: Uranium prices skyrocketed as a result of a cartel. Faced with large losses if it had to fulfill its contracts, Westinghouse argued that the unanticipated spike in uranium prices made its performance impossible. Should Westinghouse be freed of its contractual duties to sell uranium at a loss?

4. Jacobs Builders entered into a contract with Kent to build him a home. The agreement stated that Jacobs would use only certain brand-name materials. Upon completion of the home, Kent discovered that Jacobs had installed high-quality, but not brand-name, pipes throughout the house. This was an oversight, which even the architect failed to catch. Kent asked Jacobs to replace all the pipes, but this meant destroying all of the floors and walls in the house. Should Kent have to rebuild the house to get paid?

5. Franklin J. Moneypenny hires Angela to paint his portrait. She is to be paid $50,000 if the painting is acceptable "in Franklin's sole judgment." At the big unveiling, 99 of 100 attendees think that Angela has done a masterful job. Franklin disagrees. He thinks the painting makes him look like a toad. (He does in fact look like a toad, but he does not like to contemplate this fact.) Franklin refuses to pay, and, because he signed a personal satisfaction contract, Angela gets nothing. Is this fair? Should the law allow personal satisfaction contracts?

CHAPTER 19

REMEDIES

© Honza Krej/Shutterstock.com

Margot had great expectations—the dating service, that is. She signed a contract in which she paid $3,790 to Great Expectations dating service. For this fee, the service promised to introduce her to at least 12 eligible bachelors who matched her requirements. Great Expectations would also provide high-quality photo shoots, dating advice, and invitations to members-only events. Representatives assured Margot that she would feel like "a kid in a candy store," with online access to over 175,000 Great Expectation members nationwide. They also told her that their location alone had had over 300 marriages in the last year.

As it turned out, Margot's experience was far from great. The company did not introduce her to anyone. (One man approached her after seeing her profile, but he was no prize.) Her photos were terrible, and the dating advice she received was useless because she had no dates. In fact, Great Expectations had greatly exaggerated their numbers of members and matches.[1]

Forlorn and angry, Margot sued the dating service. What did she *really* want? Margot did not want her money back: She wanted a date—many dates with many handsome, intelligent, and well-adjusted men of her age. She wanted them to swoon over her picture and tend to her every need. She wanted to get married. And she wanted to take back the three years she wasted with Great Expectations. But what could a court give her?

> **Margot sued the dating service. What did she really want? Margot did not want her money back: She wanted a date.**

---

[1]Adapted from Doe v. Great Expectations 10 Misc.3d 618 (N.Y. City Civ. Ct. 2005) and various states' attorneys general complaints against the company.

19-1 IDENTIFYING THE "INTEREST" TO BE PROTECTED

Remedy

A court's compensation to the injured party

Interest

A legal right in something

Someone breaches a contract when he fails to perform a duty without a valid excuse. Great Expectations breached its contract with Margot when it failed to deliver 12 dates. But what can Margot do about this breach? In other words, what is her *remedy?* **A remedy is the method a court uses to compensate an injured party.**

The first step that a court takes in choosing a remedy is to decide what interest it is trying to protect. An **interest** is a legal right in something. Someone can have an interest in property, for example, by owning it, or renting it to a tenant, or lending money so someone else may buy it. He can have an interest in a *contract* if the agreement gives him some benefit. There are four principal contract interests that a court may seek to protect:

- *Expectation interest.* This interest is what the injured party reasonably thought she would get from the contract. The goal is to put her in the position she would have been in if both parties had fully performed their obligations. Margot's great expectation was to find a mate, but a court cannot require the defendant to produce a husband. Typically, an expectation interest is the profit the plaintiff would have earned under a contract.

- *Reliance interest.* Even if the injured party has not shown an expectation interest, he can still recover damages if he proves that he *spent money* in reliance on the agreement and that, in fairness, he should receive compensation. If Margot had spent money flying to another city to meet a date who, it turned out, was a serial killer just released after 30 years in prison, she might have a reliance interest.

- *Restitution interest.* The injured party may be unable to show an expectation interest or reliance. But perhaps she has conferred a benefit *on the other party*. Here, the objective is to restore to the injured party the benefit she has provided. Margot provided the service with a benefit—money. Her best argument is in restitution. A court will not get her a date, but it can return her money.

- *Equitable interest.* In some cases, money damages will not suffice to help the injured party. Something more is needed, such as an order for the breaching party to perform (specific performance) or an order forcing it to stop doing something (an injunction). If a party who has promised to sell land ultimately refuses to do so, a court may order specific performance or may injoin the defendant from selling the property to someone else. As we will see, these actions are not always available to injured plaintiffs like Margot.

In this chapter, we look at all four interests.

Ethics

Although a court may have several alternative remedies available, it is important to note that most have one thing in common: The focus is on compensating the injured party rather than punishing the party in breach.

Some critics argue that someone who willfully breaches a contract should pay a penalty. Margot and other Great Expectations members were duped by its false promises and inflated numbers. Should a remedy reflect morality? In this chapter, we will see very few instances in which a court *punishes* unethical conduct. Is this right? Should contract law exact a price for bad behavior? Should it try to prevent the same thing from happening to others? What would Kant and Mill say?

19-2 EXPECTATION INTEREST

This is the most common remedy that the law provides for a party injured by a breach of contract. **The expectation interest is designed to put the injured party in the position she would have been in had both sides fully performed their obligations.** A court tries to give the injured party the money she would have made from the contract. If accurately calculated, this should take into account all the gains she reasonably expected and all the expenses and losses she would have incurred. The injured party should not end up better off than she would have been under the agreement, nor should she suffer a loss.

If you ever go to law school, you will almost certainly encounter the following case during your first week of classes. It has been used to introduce the concept of damages in contract lawsuits for generations. Enjoy the famous "case of the hairy hand."

Landmark Case

HAWKINS V. MCGEE

84 N.H. 114
Supreme Court of New Hampshire, 1929

Facts: Hawkins suffered a severe electrical burn on the palm of his right hand. After years of living with disfiguring scars, he went to visit Dr. McGee, who was well known for his early attempts at skin-grafting surgery. The doctor told Hawkins "I will guarantee to make the hand a hundred percent perfect." Hawkins hired him to perform the operation.

McGee cut a patch of healthy skin from Hawkins's chest and grafted it over the scar tissue on Hawkins' palm. Unfortunately, the chest hair on the skin graft was very thick, and it continued to grow after the surgery. The operation resulted in a hairy palm for Hawkins. Feeling rather … embarrassed … Hawkins sued Dr. McGee.

The trial court judge instructed the jury to calculate damages in this way: "If you find the plaintiff entitled to anything, he is entitled to recover for what pain and suffering he has been made to endure and what injury he has sustained over and above the injury that he had before."

The jury awarded Hawkins $3,000, but the court reduced the award to $500. Dissatisfied, Hawkins appealed.

Issue: *How should Hawkins' damages be calculated?*

Excerpts from Justice Branch's Decision: The jury was permitted to consider two elements of damage, (1) pain and suffering due to the operation, and (2) positive ill effects of the operation upon the plaintiff's hand. [T]he foregoing instruction was erroneous.

By damages as that term is used in the law of contracts, is intended compensation to put the plaintiff in as good a position as he would have been in had the defendant kept his contract. The measure of recovery is what the defendant should have given the plaintiff, not what the plaintiff has given the defendant or otherwise expended.

We conclude that the true measure of the plaintiff's damage in the present case is the difference between the value to him of a perfect hand and the value of his hand in its present condition, including any incidental consequences fairly within the contemplation of the parties when they made their contract.

The extent of the plaintiff's suffering does not measure this difference in value. The pain necessarily incident to a serious surgical operation was a part of the contribution which the plaintiff was willing to make to his joint undertaking with the defendant to produce a good hand. It furnished no test of the difference between the value of the hand which the defendant promised and the one which resulted from the operation.

[Remanded for a] new trial.

When a contract is broken, what kind of interest is harmed?

Now let's consider a more modern example.

William Colby was a former director of the CIA. He wanted to write a book about his 15 years in Vietnam. He paid James McCarger $5,000 for help in writing an early draft and promised McCarger another $5,000 if the book was published. He then hired Alexander Burnham to co-write the book. Colby's agent secured a contract with Contemporary Books, which included a $100,000 advance. But Burnham was hopelessly late with the manuscript and Colby missed his publication date. Colby fired Burnham and finished the book without him. Contemporary published *Lost Victory* several years late, and the book flopped, earning no significant revenue. Because the book was so late, Contemporary paid Colby a total of only $17,000. Colby sued Burnham for his lost expectation interest. The court awarded him $23,000, calculated as follows:

	$100,000	Advance, the only money Colby was promised
	–10,000	Agent's fee
	= 90,000	Fee for the two authors, combined
Divided by 2	= 45,000	Colby's fee (The other half went to the coauthor.)
	– 5,000	Owed to McCarger under the earlier agreement
	= 40,000	Colby's expectation interest
	– 17,000	Fee Colby eventually received from Contemporary
	= 23,000	Colby's **expectation damages**; that is, the additional amount he would have received had Burnham finished on time

Expectation damages

The money required to put one party in the position she would have been in had the other side performed the contract

The *Colby* case presented a relatively easy calculation of damages.[2] Other contracts are complex. Courts typically divide the expectation damages into three parts: (1) direct (or "compensatory") damages, which represent harm that flowed directly from the contract's breach; (2) consequential (or "special") damages, which represent harm caused by the injured party's unique situation; and (3) incidental damages, which are minor costs such as storing or returning defective goods, advertising for alternative goods, and so forth. The first two, direct and consequential, are the important ones.

Note that punitive damages are absent from our list. The golden rule in contracts cases is to give successful plaintiffs "the benefit of the bargain" and not to punish defendants. Punitive damages are occasionally awarded in lawsuits that involve both a contract *and* either an intentional tort (such as fraud) or a breach of fiduciary duty, but they are not available in "simple" cases involving only a breach of contract.

19-2a **Direct Damages**

Direct damages are those that flow directly from the contract. They are the most common monetary award for the expectation interest. These are the damages that inevitably result from the breach. Suppose that Ace Productions hires Reina to star in its new movie, *Inside Straight*. Ace promises Reina $3 million, providing she shows up June 1 and works until the film is finished. But in late May, Joker Entertainment offers Reina $6 million to star in its

[2]Colby v. Burnham, 31 Conn. App. 707 (Conn. App. Ct. 1993).

new feature, and on June 1, Reina informs Ace that she will not appear. Reina has breached her contract, and Ace should recover direct damages.

What are the damages that flow directly from the contract? Ace has to replace Reina. If Ace hires Kayla as its star and pays her a fee of $4 million, Ace is entitled to the difference between what it expected to pay ($3 million) and what the breach forced it to pay ($4 million), or $1 million in direct damages.

19-2b Consequential Damages

In addition to direct damages, the injured party may seek **consequential damages** or, as they are also known, "special damages." Consequential damages reimburse for harm that results from the *particular* circumstances of the plaintiff. These damages are only available if they are a *foreseeable consequence* of the breach. Suppose, for example, that Raould breaches two contracts—he is late picking both Sharon and Paul up for a taxi ride. His breach is the same for both parties, but the consequences are very different. Sharon misses her flight to San Francisco and incurs a substantial fee to rebook the flight. Paul is simply late for the barber, who manages to fit him in anyway. Thus, Raould's damages would be different for these two contracts. The rule concerning this remedy comes from a famous 1854 case, *Hadley v. Baxendale*. This is another case that all American law students read. Now it is your turn.

Consequential damages
Are those resulting from the unique circumstances of this injured party

Landmark Case

HADLEY V. BAXENDALE
9 Ex. 341
Court of Exchequer, 1854

Facts: The Hadleys operated a flour mill in Gloucester. The crankshaft broke, causing the mill to grind to a halt. The Hadleys employed Baxendale to cart the damaged part to a foundry in Greenwich, where a new one could be manufactured. Baxendale promised to make the delivery in one day, but he was late transporting the shaft, and as a result, the Hadleys' mill was shut for five extra days. They sued, and the jury awarded damages based in part on their lost profits. Baxendale appealed.

Issue: *Should the defendant be liable for profits lost because of his delay in delivering the shaft?*

Excerpts from Judge Alderson's Decision: Where two parties have made a contract which one of them has broken, the damages which the other party ought to receive in respect of such breach of contract should be such as may fairly and reasonably be considered either arising naturally, i.e. according to the usual course of things, from such breach of contract itself, or such as may reasonably be supposed to have been in the contemplation of both parties, at the time they made the contract, as the probable result of the breach of it. Now, if the special circumstances under which the contract was actually made were communicated by the plaintiffs to the defendants, and thus known to both parties, the damages resulting from the breach of such a contract, which they would reasonably contemplate, would be the amount of injury which would ordinarily follow from a breach of contract under these special circumstances so known and communicated. But, on the other hand, if these special circumstances were wholly unknown to the party breaking the contract, he, at the most, could only be supposed to have had in his contemplation the amount of injury which would arise generally, and in the great multitude of cases not affected by any special circumstances, from such a breach of contract.

Now, in the present case, if we are to apply the principles above laid down, we find that the only circumstances here communicated by the plaintiffs to the defendants at the time the contract was made, were that the article to be carried was the broken shaft of a mill, and that the plaintiffs were the millers of that mill. But how do these circumstances show reasonably that the profits of the mill must be stopped by an unreasonable delay in the delivery of the broken shaft by the carrier to the third person? Suppose the plaintiffs had another shaft in their possession put up or putting up at the time, and that they only wished to send back the broken shaft to the engineer who made it; it is clear that this would be quite consistent with the above circumstances, and yet the unreasonable delay in the delivery would have no effect upon the intermediate profits of the mill. It follows, therefore, that the loss of profits here cannot reasonably be considered such a consequence of the breach of contract as could have been fairly and reasonably contemplated by both the parties when they made this contract.

[The court ordered a new trial, in which the jury would *not* be allowed to consider the plaintiffs' lost profits.]

The rule from *Hadley v. Baxendale* has been unchanged ever since: **The injured party may recover consequential damages only if the *breaching party* should have *foreseen* them when the two sides formed the contract.**

Let us return briefly to *Inside Straight.* Suppose that, long before shooting began, Ace had sold the film's soundtrack rights to Spinem Sound for $2 million. Spinem believed it would make a profit only if Reina appeared in the film, so it demanded the right to discharge the agreement if Reina dropped out. When Reina quit, Spinem terminated the contract. Now, when Ace sues Reina, it will also seek $2 million in consequential damages for the lost music revenue.

The $2 million is not a direct damage. The contract between Reina and Act has nothing directly to do with selling soundtrack rights. But the loss is nonetheless a consequence of Reina bailing out on the project. So, if Reina knew about Ace's contract with Spinem when she signed to do the film, the loss would be foreseeable to her, and she would be liable for $2 million. If she never realized she was an essential part of the music contract, and if a jury determines that she had no reason to expect the $2 million loss, she owes nothing for the lost soundtrack profits.

Injured plaintiffs often try to recover lost profits. Courts will generally award these damages if (1) the lost profits were foreseeable and (2) the plaintiff provides enough information so that the factfinder can reasonably estimate a fair amount. The calculation need not be done with mathematical precision. In the following case, the plaintiffs lost not only profits—but their entire business. Can they recover for harm that is so extensive? You decide.

You be the Judge

Facts: Bi-Economy Market was a family-owned meat market in Rochester, New York. The company was insured by Harleysville Insurance. The "Deluxe Business Owner's" policy provided replacement cost for damage to buildings and inventory. Coverage also included "business interruption insurance" for one year, meaning the loss of pretax profit plus normal operating expenses, including payroll.

The company suffered a disastrous fire, which destroyed its building and all inventory. Bi-Economy immediately filed

BI-ECONOMY MARKET, INC. v. HARLEYSVILLE INS. CO. OF NEW YORK
2008 N.Y. Slip Op. 01418
New York Court of Appeals, 2008

a claim with Harleysville, but the insurer responded slowly. Harleysville eventually offered a settlement of $163,000. A year later, an arbitrator awarded the Market $407,000. During that year, Harleysville paid for seven months of lost income but declined to pay more. The company never recovered or reopened.

Bi-Economy sued, claiming that Harleysville's slow, inadequate payments destroyed the company. The company also sought consequential damages for the permanent destruction of its business. Harleysville claimed that it was only responsible for damages specified in the contract: the building, inventory, and lost income. The trial court granted summary judgment for Harleysville. The appellate court affirmed, claiming that when they entered into the contract, the parties did not contemplate damages for termination of the business. Bi-Economy appealed to the state's highest court.

You Be the Judge: *Is Bi-Economy entitled to consequential damages for the destruction of its business?*

Argument for Bi-Economy: Bi-Economy is a small, family business. We paid for business interruption insurance for an obvious reason: In the event of a disaster, we lacked the resources to keep going while buildings were constructed and inventory purchased. We knew that in such a calamity, we would need prompt reimbursement—compensation covering the immediate damage and our ongoing lost income. Why else would we pay the premiums?

At the time we entered into the contract, Harleysville could easily foresee that if it responded slowly, with insufficient payments, we could not survive. They knew that is what we wanted to avoid—and it is just what happened. The insurer's bad faith offer of a low figure, and its payment of only seven months' lost income, ruined a fine family business. When the insurance company agreed to business interruption coverage, it was declaring that it would act fast and fairly to sustain a small firm in crisis. The insurer should now pay for the full harm it has wrought.

Argument for Harleysville: We contracted to insure the Market for three losses: its building, inventory, and lost income. After the fire, we performed a reasonable, careful evaluation and made an offer we considered fair. An arbitrator later awarded Bi-Market additional money, which we paid. However it is absurd to suggest that in addition to that, we are liable for an open-ended commitment for permanent destruction of the business.

Consequential damages are appropriate in cases where a plaintiff suffers a loss that was not covered in the contract. In this case, though, the parties bargained over exactly what Harleysville would pay in the event of a major fire. If the insurer has underpaid for lost income, let the court award a fair sum. However, the parties never contemplated an additional, enormous payment for cessation of the business. There is almost no limit as to what that obligation could be. If Bi-Market was concerned that a fire might put the company permanently out of business, it should have said so at the time of negotiating for insurance. The premium would have been dramatically higher.

Neither Bi-Market nor Harleysville ever imagined such an open-ended insurance obligation, and the insurer should not pay an extra cent.

19-2c Incidental Damages

Incidental damages are the relatively minor costs that the injured party suffers when *responding to* the breach. When Reina, the actress, breaches the film contract, the producers may have to leave the set and fly back to Los Angeles to hire a new actress. The travel cost is an incidental damage. In another setting, suppose Maud, a manufacturer, has produced 5,000 pairs of running shoes for Foot The Bill, a retail chain, but Foot The Bill breaches the agreement and refuses to accept the goods. Maud will have to store the shoes and advertise for alternate buyers. The storage and advertising costs are incidental expenses, and Maud will recover them.

Incidental damages
Relatively minor costs that the injured party suffers when responding to the breach

19-2d The UCC and Damages

Under the Uniform Commercial Code (UCC), remedies for breach of contract in the sale of goods are similar to the general rules discussed throughout this chapter. UCC §§2-703 through 2-715 govern the remedies available to buyers and sellers.[3]

---

[3]We discuss these remedies in greater detail in Unit 3, on commercial transactions.

Seller's Remedies

If a buyer breaches a sale of goods contract, the seller generally has at least two remedies. She may resell the goods elsewhere. If she acts in good faith, she will be awarded **the difference between the original contract price and the price she was able to obtain in the open market.** Assume that Maud, the manufacturer, had a contract to sell her shoes to Foot The Bill for $55 per pair and Foot The Bill's breach forces her to sell them on the open market, where she gets only $48 per pair. Maud will win $7 per pair times 5,000 pairs, or $35,000, from Foot The Bill.

Alternatively, the buyer may choose not to resell and settle for the difference between the contract price and the market value of the goods. Maud, in other words, may choose to keep the shoes. If she can prove that their market value is $48 per pair, for example, by showing what other retailers would have paid her for them, she will still get her $7 each, representing the difference between what the contract promised her and what the market would support. In either case, the money represents direct damages. Maud is also entitled to incidental damages, such as the storage and advertising expenses described. But there is one significant difference under the UCC: **Most courts hold that the seller of goods is *not* entitled to consequential damages.** Suppose Maud hired two extra workers to inspect, pack, and ship the shoes for Foot The Bill. Those are consequential damages, but Maud will not recover them because she is the seller and the contract is for the sale of goods.

Buyer's Remedies

Cover

To make a good faith purchase of goods similar to those in the contract

The buyer's remedies in sale of goods contracts (which are, as always, governed by the UCC) are similar to those we have already considered. She typically has two options. First, the buyer can "cover" by purchasing substitute goods. To **cover** means to make a good faith purchase of goods similar to those in the contract. The buyer may then obtain **the difference between the original contract price and her cover price.** Alternatively, if the buyer chooses not to cover, she is entitled to the difference between the original contract price and the market value of the goods.

Suppose Mary has contracted to buy one thousand 6-foot Christmas trees at $25 per tree from Elmo. The market suddenly rises, and not feeling the spirit of the season, Elmo breaches his deal and sells the trees elsewhere. If Mary makes a good faith effort to cover but is forced to pay $40 per tree, she may recover the difference from Elmo, meaning $15 per tree times 1,000 trees, or $15,000. Similarly, if she chooses not to cover but can prove that $40 is now the market value of the trees, she is entitled to her $15 per tree.

Under the UCC, **the buyer *is* entitled to consequential damages, provided that the seller could reasonably have foreseen them.** If Mary tells Elmo, when they sign their deal, that she has a dozen contracts to resell the trees for an average price of $50 per tree, she may recover $25 per tree, representing the difference between her contract price with Elmo and the value of the tree *to her*, based on her other contracts.[4] If she failed to inform Elmo of the other contracts, she would not receive any money based on them. The buyer is also entitled to whatever incidental damages may have accrued.

EXAM Strategy

Question: Chloe is a fashion designer. Her recent collection of silk-velvet evening gowns was gobbled up by high-end retailers, who now clamor for more. Chloe needs 300 yards of the same fabric by August 15. Mill House, which has supplied fabric to Chloe for many years, agrees to sell her 300 yards at $100 per yard, delivered on August 15. The market value of the fabric is $125, but Mill House gives Chloe a break because she is a major customer.

---

[4]As we discuss in the section on mitigation later in the chapter, Mary will get only her consequential damages if she attempts to cover.

Chloe contracts with high-end retailers Barneys and Neiman Marcus to sell a total of 50 dresses, at an *additional* profit to Chloe of $800 per dress. On August 15, Mill House delivers defective fabric. Chloe cannot make her dresses in time, and the retailers cancel their orders. Chloe sues Mill House and wins—but what are her damages?

Strategy: To determine damages, first ask whether the contract is governed by the common law or the UCC. This agreement concerns goods, so the Code applies. The UCC permits a buyer to recover damages for the difference between the contract price and the market value of the goods. The Code also allows consequential damages if the seller could have foreseen them. Apply those standards.

Result: Because Chloe's contract enabled her to save $25 per yard for 300 yards, she is entitled to $7,500. Chloe has also lost profits of $40,000. Mill House could easily have foreseen those losses because the supplier knew that Chloe was a designer who fabricated and sold dresses. Chloe is entitled to $47,500.

We turn now to cases where the injured party cannot prove expectation damages.

19-3 RELIANCE INTEREST

To win expectation damages, the injured party must prove the breach of contract caused damages that can be *quantified with reasonable certainty*. This rule sometimes presents plaintiffs with a problem.

George plans to manufacture and sell silk scarves during the holiday season. In the summer, he contracts with Cecily, the owner of a shopping mall, to rent a high-visibility stall for $100 per day. George then buys hundreds of yards of costly silk and gets to work cutting and sewing. But in September, Cecily refuses to honor the contract. George sues and proves Cecily breached a valid contract. But what is his remedy?

George cannot establish an expectation interest in his scarf business. He *hoped* to sell each scarf for a $40 gross profit. He *planned* on making $2,000 per day. But how much would he *actually* have earned? Enough to retire on? Enough to buy a salami sandwich for lunch? He has no way of proving his profits, and a court cannot give him his expectation interest.

Instead, George will ask for *reliance damages*. The **reliance interest** is designed to put an injured party in the position he would have been in had the parties never entered into a contract. This remedy focuses on the time and money the injured party spent performing his part of the agreement.

Reliance interest
Puts the injured party in the position he would have been in had the parties never entered into a contract

George should be able to recover reliance damages from Cecily. Assuming he is unable to sell the scarves to a retail store, which is probable since retailers will have made purchases long ago, George should be able to recover the cost of the silk fabric he bought and perhaps something for the hours of labor he spent cutting and sewing. But reliance damages can be difficult to win because *they are harder to quantify*. Courts prefer to compute damages using the numbers provided in a contract. If a contract states a price of $25 per Christmas tree and one party breaches, the arithmetic is easy. Judges can become uncomfortable when asked to base damages on vague calculations. How much was George's time worth in making the scarves? How good was his work? How likely were the scarves to sell? If George has a track record in the industry, he will be able to show a market price for his services. Without such a record, his reliance claim becomes a tough battle.

19-3a Promissory Estoppel

We have seen in earlier chapters that a plaintiff may sometimes recover damages based on promissory estoppel even when there is no valid contract. The plaintiff must show that the defendant made a promise knowing that the plaintiff would likely rely on it, that the plaintiff did rely, and that the only way to avoid injustice is to enforce the promise. **In promissory estoppel cases, a court will generally award *reliance damages*.** It would be unfair to give expectation damages for the full benefit of the bargain when, legally speaking, there has been no bargain.

In the following case, the victorious plaintiff demonstrates how unreliable reliance damages are and how winning can be hard to distinguish from losing.

TOSCANO V. GREENE MUSIC

124 Ca. App. 4th 685
Court of Appeal of California, 2004

Facts: Joseph Toscano was the general manager of Fields Pianos (Fields) in Santa Ana, California. He was unhappy with his job and decided to seek other employment. Toscano contacted Michael Greene, who owned similar stores. In July, Greene offered Toscano a sales management job starting September 1. Relying on that offer, Toscano resigned from Fields on August 1. However, in mid-August, Greene withdrew his employment offer. Toscano later found lower-paying jobs in other cities.

Toscano sued Greene for breach of contract and promissory estoppel. Greene argued that Toscano was not entitled to any expectation damages because his employment with Greene would have been at will, meaning he could lose the job at any time. Greene also urged that because Toscano was an at-will employee at Fields, he could recover at most one month's lost wage.

The trial court ruled that Toscano was entitled to reliance damages for all lost wages at Fields, starting from the day he resigned, going forward until his anticipated retirement in 2017. Toscano's expert accountant calculated his past losses (until the time of trial) at $119,061, and his future lost earnings at $417,772. The trial court awarded Toscano $536,833, and Greene appealed.

Issue: *Was Toscano entitled to reliance damages?*

Excerpts from Judge O'Rourke's Decision: Given the equitable underpinnings of the promissory estoppel doctrine, we hold that a plaintiff such as Toscano, who relinquished his job in reliance on an unfulfilled promise of employment, may on an appropriate showing recover the lost wages he would have expected to earn from his former employer but for the defendant's promise. Such a damage measure is in keeping with the equitable nature of promissory estoppel. The object of equity is to do right and justice.

Our holding necessarily rejects the notion that the at-will nature of Toscano's former employment with Fields (undisputed by the parties here) is a strict impediment to recovery of future wages that Toscano would have earned at Fields had he not relied on Greene's promise.

[However,] we conclude that even drawing all inferences in Toscano's favor, the evidence was too speculative to lend support to the trial court's award of Toscano's lost future earnings from September 1 to his retirement.

Roberta Spoon, Toscano's damages expert, testified that in calculating Toscano's lost wages for the remainder of his career, "[a]ll I have done is arithmetic. I have simply analyzed the numbers." She testified she was not aware that Toscano's employment with Fields called for any specific tenure. Indeed, Spoon admitted Toscano could have quit or been fired from that job from the time he resigned to the present. She simply assumed Toscano would have continued employment with Fields or another employer at a comparable salary, observing that he had never in the past changed employers for anything other than a pay increase.

Spoon's testimony does not establish Toscano had a definite expectation of continued employment with Fields for any particular period of time. It is evident her supposition was based only on Toscano's history of remaining with his employers until offered new employment. However, *Toscano's* intentions or practices are not relevant to whether he could expect to remain with Fields until his retirement. Evidence of Toscano's intentions does not establish with any reasonable certainty that Fields, an at-will employer who had the right to terminate Toscano at any time for any reason, had some different understanding of the terms of Toscano's employment, or that it would have continued to employ him until the end of his career. Neither party presented testimony from Jerry Goldman, Toscano's boss at Fields. An expert's opinion must not be based upon speculative or conjectural data.

The award of future earnings calculated from [the day he quit] to the date of Toscano's retirement in 2017 is vacated and the matter remanded for a new trial on the issue of damages only. The judgment is otherwise affirmed.

Notice that the court never even mentions that Toscano acted in good faith, relying on Greene's promise, while the latter offered no excuse for suddenly withdrawing his offer. Is it fair to permit Greene to escape all liability? This court, like most, simply will not award significant damages where there is no contract permitting a clear calculation of losses.

The judges, though, have not entirely closed the door on Toscano. What is the purpose of the remand? What might Toscano demonstrate on remand? What practical difficulties will he encounter?

19-4 RESTITUTION INTEREST

Restitution means giving back. The **restitution interest** is designed to return to the injured party a benefit that he has conferred on the other party, which it would be unjust to leave with that person. In the opening scenario, Margot suffered many damages. Unfortunately for her, the only remedy a court will afford her is restitution. Great Expectations misrepresented its network of singles and breached the contract. But Margot cannot prove expectation damages (no matter how *Great*) or reliance damages, so she will have to settle for getting her money back.

Restitution is awarded in three types of cases. First, the law allows restitution when a contract is breached or discharged. As you will recall, a contract is breached when one party fails to perform. A contract is said to be discharged when it is terminated by the nonoccurrence of a condition, impossibility, or another excuse. In such cases, a court may choose restitution because no other remedy is available or because no other remedy would be as fair. Second, judges allow restitution when the injured party to a voidable contract rescinds the agreement. Third, courts may award restitution in cases of quasi-contract, which we examined in Chapter 11. In quasi-contract cases, the parties never made a contract, but one side did benefit the other. We consider each kind of restitution interest in turn.

> **Restitution interest**
>
> Designed to return to the injured party a benefit he has conferred on the other party

19-4a Restitution in Cases of Contract Breach or Discharge

When one party breaches a contract, the other may be entitled to recoup what he put in. Lillian and Harold Toews signed a contract to sell 1,500 acres of Idaho farmland to Elmer Funk. (No, not him—the Bugs Bunny character you are thinking of is Elmer Fudd.) He was to take possession immediately, but he would not receive the deed until he finished paying for the property, in 10 years. This arrangement enabled him to enroll in a government program that would pay him "set-asides" for *not* farming. Funk kept most aspects of his agreement. He did move onto the land and did receive $76,000 from the government for a year's worth of inactivity. (Nice work if you can get it.) The only part of the bargain Funk did not keep was his promise to pay. The Toews sued. Funk had clearly breached the deal. But what was the remedy?

The couple still owned the land, so they did not need to recover it. Funk had no money to pay for the farm, so they would never get their expectation interest. And they had expended almost no money complying with the deal, so they had no reliance interest. What they had done, though, was to *confer a benefit* on Funk. They had enabled him to obtain $76,000 in government money. The Toews wanted restitution. They argued that they had bestowed a $76,000 benefit on Funk and that it was unfair for him to keep it. The Idaho Court of Appeals agreed. It ruled that the couple had a restitution interest in the government set-aside and ordered Funk to pay them the money.[5]

> He did move onto the land and did receive $76,000 from the government for a year's worth of inactivity. (Nice work if you can get it.)

---

[5]Toews v. Funk, 129 Idaho 316 (Idaho Ct. App. 1994).

In the following case, both parties breached the contract. Could the famous football player get restitution even if he dropped the ball?

ADDIE AND TAYLOR V. KJAER

737 F.3d 854
United States Court of Appeals for the Third Circuit, 2013

Facts: Christian Kjaer and his relatives (Sellers) owned a small island off the coast of St. Thomas, U.S. Virgin Islands. Some investors, led by Miami Dolphins football player Jason Taylor agreed to buy it for $21 million.

Marc Serota/Getty Images

Under the contract, Taylor paid a $1 million deposit and promised to close within 60 days. The contract allowed him to extend the closing date by paying an additional $500,000 nonrefundable deposit, which he did. The buyers' only other duty was to pay the remaining purchase price at closing. The Sellers committed to delivering clear title to the property, along with all of the island's permits.

According to the contract, if Taylor breached the contract, he would forfeit the deposits; if the Sellers breached, they would return the deposits. The contract did not say what would happen to the deposit it both parties breached.

On the closing date, the sale was not consummated; the Sellers delivered expired permits and did not convey clear title. Taylor and his partners did not pay. But the Sellers refused to return Taylor's deposit.

Taylor sued for restitution. The Sellers asserted they were entitled to the $1.5 million because Taylor breached the contract. Taylor argued that the Buyer's failure to deliver valid title discharged his obligation to close—and that allowing the Sellers to keep the money would unjustly enrich them. The district court found that since Taylor breached the valid contract, he could not recoup the deposit. Taylor challenged the lower court's call.

Issue: *Was Taylor entitled to restitution?*

Excerpts from Judge Roth's Decision: Agreements concerning an exchange of promises require performance to be exchanged simultaneously whenever possible, unless the agreement indicates otherwise. This simultaneous exchange of performances creates concurrent conditions, under which performance by one party creates a condition precedent for performance by the other party.

Here, the Sellers were required to convey Clear and Marketable title and assignments of all permits, leases, and licenses necessary. Because the Contract of Sale did not indicate otherwise, the performance of each obligation was to occur simultaneously. Therefore, fulfillment of each obligation was a concurrent condition to the other.

With regard to awarding restitution in cases involving valid contracts, we look to the Restatement (Second) of Contracts:

> A party whose duty of performance does not arise or is discharged as a result of nonoccurrence of a condition is entitled to restitution for any benefit that he has conferred on the other party by way of part performance or reliance.[6]

For example, the Restatement illustrates: "A contracts to sell a tract of land to B for $100,000. After B has made a part payment of $20,000, A wrongfully refuses to transfer title. B can recover the $20,000 in restitution."

In applying the Restatement (Second) of Contracts, it is clear that restitution is in order. Taylor provided a deposit of $1.5 million to the Sellers with the intent to purchase the property. However, all of the parties failed to perform within the timeframe specified in the contracts, and their respective duties were discharged. Thus, as the Restatement instructs, Taylor is entitled to restitution for the benefit of the deposit that he conferred to the Sellers.

For the foregoing reasons, we will reverse the District Court and order the return of the deposit to Taylor.

---

[6]Restatement (Second) of Contracts § 377 (1981).

19-4b Restitution in Cases of a Voidable Contract

Restitution is a common remedy in contracts involving fraud, misrepresentation, mistake, and duress. In these cases, restitution often goes hand in hand with **rescission**, which means to undo a contract and put the parties where they were before they made the agreement. Courtney sells her favorite sculpture to Adam for $95,000, both parties believing the work to be a valuable original by Barbara Hepworth. Two months later, Adam learns that the sculpture is a mere copy, worth very little. A court will permit Adam to rescind the contract on the ground of mutual mistake. At the same time, Adam is entitled to restitution of the purchase price. Courtney gets the worthless carving, and Adam receives his money back.

Rescission
To "undo" a contract and put the parties where they were before they made the agreement

19-4c Restitution in Cases of a Quasi-Contract

George Anderson owned a valuable 1936 Plymouth. He took it to Ronald Schwegel's repair shop, and the two orally agreed that Schwegel would restore the car for $6,000. Unfortunately, they never agreed on the meaning of the word *restore*. Anderson thought the term meant complete restoration, including body work and engine repairs, whereas Schwegel intended body work but no engine repairs. After doing some of the work, Schwegel told Anderson that the car needed substantial engine work, and he asked for Anderson's permission to allow an engine shop to do it. Anderson agreed, believing the cost was included in the original estimate. When the car was finished and running smoothly, Schwegel demanded $9,800. Anderson refused to pay more than the $6,000 agreed price, and Schwegel sued.

The court held that there was no valid contract between the parties. A contract requires a meeting of the minds. Here, said the court, there was no meeting of the minds on what *restore* included, and hence Schwegel could not recover either his expectation or his reliance interest since both require an enforceable agreement. Schwegel then argued that a quasi-contract existed. In other words, he claimed that even if there had been no valid agreement, he had performed a service for Anderson and that it would be unjust for Anderson to keep it without paying. **A court may award restitution, even in the absence of a contract, when one party has conferred a benefit on another and it would be unjust for the other party to retain the benefit.** The court ruled that Schwegel was entitled to the full $3,800 above and beyond the agreed price because that was the fair market value of the additional work. Anderson had asked for the repairs and now had an auto that was substantially improved. It would be unjust, ruled the court, to permit him to keep that benefit for free.[7]

19-5 OTHER REMEDIES

In contract lawsuits, plaintiffs are occasionally awarded the remedies of **specific performance**, injunction, and reformation.

Specific performance
Forces both parties to complete the deal

[7]Anderson v. Schwegel, 118 Idaho 362 (Idaho Ct. App. 1990).

19-5a Specific Performance

Leona Claussen owned Iowa farmland. She sold some of it to her sister-in-law, Evelyn Claussen, and, along with the land, granted Evelyn an option to buy additional property at $800 per acre. Evelyn could exercise her option anytime during Leona's lifetime or within six months of Leona's death. When Leona died, Evelyn informed the estate's executor that she was exercising her option. But other relatives wanted the property, and the executor refused to sell. Evelyn sued and asked for *specific performance*. She did not want an award of damages; she wanted *the land itself*. The remedy of specific performance forces the two parties to perform their contract.

A court will award specific performance, ordering the parties to perform the contract, only in cases involving the sale of land or some other asset that is considered "unique." Courts use this remedy when money damages would be inadequate to compensate an injured party. If the subject is unique and irreplaceable, money damages will not put the injured party in the same position she would have been in had the agreement been kept. So a court will order the seller to convey the rare object and the buyer to pay for it.

Historically, every parcel of land has been regarded as unique, and therefore **specific performance is always available in real estate contracts.** Family heirlooms and works of art are also often considered unique. Evelyn Claussen won specific performance. The Iowa Supreme Court ordered Leona's estate to convey the land to Evelyn for $800 per acre.[8] Generally, either the seller or the buyer may be granted specific performance. One limitation in land sales is that a buyer may obtain specific performance only if she was ready, willing, and able to purchase the property on time. If Evelyn had lacked the money to buy Leona's property for $800 per acre within the six-month time limit, the court would have declined to order the sale.

EXAM Strategy

Question: The Monroes, a retired couple who live in Illinois, want to move to Arizona to escape the northern winter. In May, the Monroes contract in writing to sell their house to the Temples for $450,000. Closing is to take place June 30. The Temples pay a deposit of $90,000. However, in early June, the Monroes travel through Arizona and discover it is too hot for them. They promptly notify the Temples they are no longer willing to sell, and return the $90,000, with interest. The Temples sue, seeking the house. In response, the Monroes offer evidence that the value of the house has dropped from about $450,000 to about $400,000. They claim that the Temples have suffered no loss. Who will win?

Strategy: Most contract lawsuits are for money damages, but not this one. The Temples want the house. Because they want the house itself, and not money damages, the drop in value is irrelevant. What legal remedy are the Temples seeking? They are suing for specific performance. When will a court grant specific performance? Should it do so here?

Result: In cases involving the sale of land or some other unique asset, a court will grant specific performance, ordering the parties to perform the agreement. All houses are regarded as unique. The court will force the Monroes to sell their house, provided the Temples have sufficient money to pay for it.

Other unique items, for which a court will order specific performance, include such things as secret formulas, patents, and shares in a closely held corporation. Money damages would be inadequate for all these things since the injured party, even if she got the cash,

---

[8]In re Estate of Claussen, 482 N.W.2d 381 (Iowa 1992).

could not go out and buy a substitute item. By contrast, a contract for a new Cadillac Escalade is not enforceable by specific performance. If the seller breaches, the buyer is entitled to the difference between the contract price and the market value of the car. The buyer can take his money elsewhere and purchase a virtually identical SUV.

19-5b Injunction

An **injunction** is a court order that requires someone to refrain from doing something.

In the increasingly litigious world of professional sports, injunctions are commonplace. In the following basketball case, the trial court issued a **preliminary injunction**; that is, an order issued early in a lawsuit prohibiting a party from doing something *during the course of the lawsuit*. The court attempts to protect the interests of the plaintiff immediately. If, after trial, it appears that the plaintiff has been injured and is entitled to an injunction, the trial court will make its order a **permanent injunction**. If it appears that the preliminary injunction should never have been issued, the court will terminate the order.

Injunction

A court order that requires someone to do something or refrain from doing something

MILICIC v. BASKETBALL MARKETING COMPANY, INC.

2004 Pa.A Super. 333
Superior Court of Pennsylvania, 2004

Facts: The Basketball Marketing Company (BMC) markets, distributes, and sells basketball apparel and related products. BMC signed a long-term endorsement contract with a 16-year-old Serbian player, Darko Milicic, who was virtually unknown in the United States. Two years later, Milicic became the second pick in the National Basketball Association draft, making him an immensely marketable athlete.

Four days after his 18th birthday, Milicic made a buy-out offer to BMC, seeking release from his contract so that he could arrange a more lucrative one elsewhere. BMC refused to release him. A week later, Milicic notified BMC in writing that he was disaffirming the contract, and he returned all money and goods he had received from the company. BMC again refused to release Milicic.

Believing that Milicic was negotiating an endorsement deal with either Reebok or Adidas, BMC sent both companies letters informing them it had an enforceable endorsement deal with Milicic that was valid for several more years. Because of BMC's letter, Adidas ceased negotiating with Milicic just short of signing a contract. Milicic sued BMC, seeking a preliminary injunction that would prohibit BMC from sending such letters to competitors. The trial court granted the preliminary injunction, and BMC appealed.

Issue: *Is Milicic entitled to a preliminary injunction?*

Excerpts from Judge McCaffery's Decision:[9] BMC argues that the trial court erred by concluding that Milicic had proven the four essential prerequisites necessary for injunctive relief. However, Milicic did meet these four requirements.

1. Milicic had a strong likelihood of success on the merits.

   Pennsylvania law recognizes, except as to necessities, the contract of a minor is voidable if the minor disaffirms it at any reasonable time after the minor attains majority. Just 11 days after his 18th birthday, Milicic sent BMC a letter withdrawing from the agreement. This letter was sent within a reasonable time after Milicic's reaching the age of majority and stated his unequivocal revocation and voidance of the agreement. There exists more than a reasonable probability that Milicic will succeed in [nullifying the contract with BMC].

2. Injunctive relief was necessary to prevent immediate and irreparable harm that could not be adequately compensated by the awarding of monetary damages.

   Top N.B.A. draft picks generally solicit, negotiate, and secure endorsement contracts within a short time after the draft to take advantage of the

---

[9]The authors have substituted "BMC" for "appellant" and "Milicic" for "appellee."

publicity, excitement, and attendant marketability associated with the promotion. BMC blocked Milicic's efforts to enter into such an endorsement agreement. After being contacted by BMC, advanced negotiations between Milicic and Adidas were suspended. These business opportunity and market advantage losses may aptly be characterized as irreparable injury for purposes of equitable relief.

3. Greater injury would have occurred from denying the injunction than from granting the injunction.

BMC's refusal to acknowledge Milicic's ability to disaffirm the contract is at odds with public policy. Because infants are not competent to contract, the ability to disaffirm protects them from their own immaturity and lack of discretion. It is established practice in Pennsylvania to petition the court to appoint a guardian for the child, to protect the interests of both parties. It confounds the Court that BMC, a corporation of great magnitude, whose business may be said to be based in contract law, failed to have a guardian appointed for Milicic. Harm to the public is an additional consideration. The public policy consideration underlying the rule which allows a child to disaffirm a contract within a reasonable time after reaching the age of majority is that minors should not be bound by mistakes resulting from their immaturity or the overbearance of unscrupulous adults.

4. The preliminary injunction restored the parties to the status quo that existed prior to the wrongful conduct:

Enjoining BMC from further interfering with Milicic's ability to contract will place the parties where they were prior to BMC's wrongful conduct. As all four of the essential prerequisites have been satisfied in this case, the Court properly granted injunctive relief.

Order affirmed.

Was Darko Milicic entitled to a preliminary injunction against BMC?

19-5c **Reformation**

Reformation

A court may partially rewrite a contract to fix a mistake or cure an unenforceable provision.

The final remedy, and perhaps the least common, is **reformation**, a process in which a court will partially rewrite a contract. Courts seldom do this because the whole point of a contract is to enable the parties to control their own futures. But a court may reform a contract if it believes a written agreement includes a simple mistake. Suppose that Roger orally agrees to sell 35 acres to Hannah for $600,000. The parties then draw up a written agreement, accidentally describing the land as including 50 additional acres that neither party considered part of the deal. Roger refuses to sell. Hannah sues for specific performance but asks the court to *reform* the written contract to reflect the true agreement. Most but not all courts would reform the agreement and enforce it.

A court may also reform a contract to save it. If Natasha sells her advertising business to Joseph and agrees not to open a competing agency in the same city anytime in the next 10 years, a court may decide that it is unfair to force her to wait a decade. It could reform the agreement and permit Natasha to compete, say, 3 years after the sale. But some courts are reluctant to reform contracts and would throw out the entire noncompetition agreement rather than reform it. Parties should never settle for a contract that is sloppy or overbroad, assuming that a court will later reform errors. They may find themselves stuck with a bargain they dislike, or with no contract at all.

19-6 SPECIAL ISSUES

Finally, we consider some special issues of damages, beginning with a party's obligation to minimize its losses.

19-6a Mitigation of Damages

A party injured by a breach of contract may not recover for damages that he could have avoided with reasonable efforts. In other words, when one party perceives that the other has breached or will breach the contract, the injured party must try to prevent unnecessary loss. A party is expected to **mitigate** his damages; that is, to keep damages as low as he reasonably can.

Malcolm agrees to rent space in his mall to Zena, for a major department store. As part of the lease, Malcolm agrees to redesign the interior to meet her specifications. After Malcolm has spent $20,000 in architect and design fees, Zena informs Malcolm that she is renting other space and will not occupy his mall. Malcolm nonetheless continues the renovation work, spending an additional $50,000 on materials and labor. Malcolm will recover the lost rental payments and the $20,000 expended in reliance on the deal. He will *not* recover the extra $50,000. He should have stopped work when he learned of Zena's breach.

Mitigate
To keep damages as low as reasonable

19-6b Nominal Damages

Nominal damages are a token sum, such as one dollar, given to a plaintiff who demonstrates that the defendant breached the contract but cannot prove serious injury. A school board unfairly fires Gemma, a teacher. If she obtains a teaching job at a better school for identical pay the very next day, she probably can show no damages at all. Nonetheless, the school wrongfully terminated her, and a court may award nominal damages. Nominal damages provide plaintiff with a "moral victory."

Nominal damages
A token sum, such as one dollar, given to a plaintiff who demonstrates a breach but no serious injury

19-6c Liquidated Damages

It can be difficult or even impossible to prove how much damage the injured party has suffered. So lawyers and executives negotiating a deal may include in the contract a **liquidated damages clause**, a provision stating in advance how much a party must pay if it breaches. Assume that Laurie has hired Bruce to build a five-unit apartment building for $800,000. Bruce promises to complete construction by May 15. Laurie insists on a liquidated damages clause providing that if Bruce finishes late, Laurie's final price is reduced by $3,000 for each week of delay. Bruce finishes the apartment building June 30, and Laurie reduces her payment by $18,000. Is that fair? The answer depends on two factors: **A court will generally enforce a liquidated damages clause if** (1) **at the time of creating the contract, it was very difficult to estimate actual damages, and** (2) **the liquidated amount is reasonable.** In any other case, the liquidated damage will be considered a mere penalty and will prove unenforceable.

Liquidated damages
A clause stating in advance how much a party must pay if it breaches

We will apply the two factors to Laurie's case. When the parties made their agreement, would it have been difficult to estimate actual damages caused by delay? Yes. Laurie could not prove that all five units would have been occupied or how much rent the tenants would have agreed to pay. Was the $3,000 per week reasonable? Probably. To finance an $800,000 building, Laurie will have to pay at least $6,000 interest per month. She must also pay taxes on the land and may have other expenses. Laurie does not have to prove that every penny of the liquidated damages clause is justified, but only that the figure is reasonable. A court will probably enforce her liquidated damages clause.

On the other hand, suppose Laurie's clause demanded $3,000 per day. There is no basis for such a figure, and a court will declare it a penalty clause and refuse to enforce it. Laurie will be back to square one, forced to prove in court any damages she claims to have suffered from Bruce's delay.

EXAM Strategy

Question: In March, James was accepted into the September ninth-grade class at the Brookstone Academy, a highly competitive private school. To reserve his spot, James's father, Rex, sent in a deposit of $2,000 and agreed in writing to pay the balance due, $19,000. If James withdrew in writing from the school by August 1, Rex owed nothing more to Brookstone. However, once that date passed, Rex was obliged to pay the full $19,000, whether or not James attended. On August 5, Rex hand-delivered to Brookstone a letter stating that James would not attend. Brookstone demanded the full tuition and, when Rex refused to pay, sued for $19,000. Analyze the case.

Strategy: When one party seeks contract damages that are specified in the agreement, it is relying on a liquidated damages clause. A court will generally enforce a liquidated damages clause provided the plaintiff can prove two things. What are those two things? Can this plaintiff meet that standard?

Result: Brookstone must prove that at the time of creating the contract it was difficult to estimate actual damages and that the liquidated amount is reasonable. Rex will probably argue that the liquidated amount is unreasonable, contending that a competitive school can quickly fill a vacancy with another eager applicant. Brookstone will counter that budgeting, which begins in January, is difficult and imprecise. Tuition money goes toward staff salaries, maintenance, utilities, and many other expenses. If the school cannot not rely in January on a certain income, the calculation becomes impossible. Rex had four months to make up his mind, and by August 1, the school was firmly committed to its class size and budget. In a similar case, the court awarded the full tuition to the school, concluding that the sum was a reasonable estimate of the damages.

Chapter Conclusion

The powers of a court are broad and flexible and may suffice to give an injured party what it deserves. But problems of proof and the uncertainty of remedies demonstrate that the best solution is a carefully drafted contract and socially responsible behavior.

EXAM REVIEW

1. **BREACH**   Someone breaches a contract when he fails to perform a duty without a valid excuse.

2. **REMEDY**   A remedy is the method a court uses to compensate an injured party.

3. **INTEREST** An interest is a legal right in something, such as a contract. The first step that a court takes in choosing a remedy is to decide what interest it is protecting.

4. **EXPECTATION** The expectation interest puts the injured party in the position she would have been in had both sides fully performed. It has three components:

(a) Direct damages, which flow directly from the contract.
(b) Consequential damages, which result from the unique circumstances of the particular injured party. The injured party may recover consequential damages only if the breaching party should have foreseen them.
(c) Incidental damages, which are the minor costs an injured party incurs responding to a breach.

EXAM Strategy

Question: Mr. and Ms. Beard contracted for Builder to construct a house on property he owned and sell it to the Beards for $785,000. The house was to be completed by a certain date, and Builder knew that the Beards were selling their own home in reliance on the completion date. Builder was late with construction, forcing the Beards to spend $32,000 in rent. Ultimately, Builder never finished the house, and the Beards moved elsewhere. They sued. At trial, expert testimony indicated the market value of the house as promised would have been $885,000. How much money are the Beards entitled to, and why?

Strategy: Normally, in cases of property, an injured plaintiff may use specific performance to obtain the land or house. However, there *is* no house, so there will be no specific performance. The Beards will seek their expectation interest. Under the contract, what did they reasonably expect? They anticipated a finished house, on a particular date, worth $885,000. They did not expect to pay rent while waiting. Calculate their losses. (See the "Result" at the end of this section.)

5. **RELIANCE** The reliance interest puts the injured party in the position he would have been in had the parties never entered into a contract. It focuses on the time and money that the injured party spent performing his part of the agreement. If there was no valid contract, a court might still award reliance damages under a theory of promissory estoppel.

EXAM Strategy

Question: Bingo is emerging as a rock star. His last five concerts have all sold out. Lucia signs a deal with Bingo to perform two concerts in one evening in Big City for a fee of $50,000 for both shows. Lucia then rents the Auditorium for that evening, guaranteeing to pay $50,000. Bingo promptly breaks the deal before any tickets are sold. Lucia sues, pointing out that the Auditorium seats 3,000 and she anticipated selling all tickets for an average of $40 each, for a total gross of $120,000. How much will Lucia recover, if anything?

6. **RESTITUTION** The restitution interest returns to the injured party a benefit that she has conferred on the other party which would be unjust to leave with that person. Restitution can be awarded in the case of a contract created, for example, by fraud, or in a case of quasi-contract, where the parties never created a binding agreement.

7. **SPECIFIC PERFORMANCE** Specific performance, ordered only in cases of land or a unique asset, requires both parties to perform the contract.

8. **INJUNCTION** An injunction is a court order that requires someone to do something or refrain from doing something.

9. **REFORMATION** Reformation is the process by which a court will—occasionally—rewrite a contract to ensure that it accurately reflects the parties' agreement and/or to maintain the contract's viability.

10. **MITIGATION** The duty to mitigate means that a party injured by a breach of contract may not recover for damages that he could have avoided with reasonable efforts.

EXAM Strategy

Question: Ambrose hires Bierce for $25,000 to supervise the production of Ambrose's crop, but then breaks the contract by firing Bierce at the beginning of the season. A nearby grower offers Bierce $23,000 for the same growing season, but Bierce refuses to take such a pay cut. He stays home and sues Ambrose. How much money, if any, will Bierce recover from Ambrose, and why?

Strategy: Ambrose has certainly breached the contract. The injured party normally receives the difference between his expectation interest and what he actually received. Bierce expected $25,000 and received nothing. However, Bierce made no effort to minimize his losses. How much would Bierce have lost had he mitigated? (See the "Result" at the end of this section.)

11. **NOMINAL DAMAGES** Nominal damages are a token sum, such as one dollar, given to an injured plaintiff who cannot prove damages.

12. **LIQUIDATED DAMAGES** A liquidated damages clause will be enforced if and only if, at the time of creating the contract, it was very difficult to estimate actual damages and the liquidated amount is reasonable.

4. Result: The Beards' direct damages represent the difference between the market value of the house and the contract price. They expected a house worth $100,000 more than their contract price, and they are entitled to that sum. They also suffered consequential damages. Builder knew they needed the house as of the contract date, and he could foresee that his breach would force them to pay rent. He is liable for a total of $132,000.

5. Result: Lucia can easily demonstrate that Bingo's breach cost her $50,000—the cost of the hall. However, it is uncertain how many tickets she would have sold. Unless Lucia has a strong track record selling tickets to concerts featuring Bingo, a court is likely to conclude that her anticipated profits were speculative. She will probably receive nothing for that claim.

10. Result: Even if he had mitigated, Bierce would have lost $2,000. He is entitled to that sum. However, he cannot recover the remaining $23,000. After Ambrose breached, Bierce had identical work available to him, but he failed to take it. His failure to mitigate is fatal.

MULTIPLE-CHOICE QUESTIONS

1. ***CPA QUESTION*** Master Mfg., Inc. contracted with Accur Computer Repair Corp. to maintain Master's computer system. Master's manufacturing process depends on its computer system operating properly at all times. A liquidated damages clause in the contract provided that Accur would pay $1,000 to Master for each day that Accur was late responding to a service request. On January 12, Accur was notified that Master's computer system had failed. Accur did not respond to Master's service request until January 15. If Master sues Accur under the liquidated damage provision of the contract, Master will:

   (a) Win, unless the liquidated damages provision is determined to be a penalty

   (b) Win, because under all circumstances liquidated damage provisions are enforceable

   (c) Lose, because Accur's breach was not material

   (d) Lose, because liquidated damage provisions violate public policy

2. ***CPA QUESTION*** Kaye contracted to sell Hodges a building for $310,000. The contract required Hodges to pay the entire amount at closing. Kaye refused to close the sale of the building. Hodges sued Kaye. To what relief is Hodges entitled?

   (a) Punitive damages and direct damages

   (b) Specific performance and direct damages

   (c) Consequential damages or punitive damages

   (d) Direct damages or specific performance

3. A manufacturer delivers a new tractor to Farmer Ted on the first day of the harvest season. But, the tractor will not start. It takes two weeks for the right parts to be delivered and installed. The repair bill comes to $1,000. During the two weeks, some acres of Farmer Ted's crops die. He argues in court that his lost profit on those acres is $60,000. If a jury awards $1,000 for tractor repairs, it will be in the form

of _____ damages. If it awards $60,000 for the lost crops, it will be in the form of _____ damages.

(a) direct; direct

(b) direct; consequential

(c) consequential; direct

(d) consequential; consequential

(e) direct; incidental

4. Julie signs a contract to buy Nick's 2012 Mustang GT for $20,000. Later, Nick changes his mind and refuses to sell his car. Julie soon buys a similar 2012 Mustang GT for $21,500. She then sues Nick and wins $1,500. The $1,500 represents her _____ .

(a) expectation interest

(b) reliance interest

(c) restitution interest

(d) none of the above

5. Under the Uniform Commercial Code, a seller _____ generally entitled to recover consequential damages, and a buyer _____ generally entitled to recover consequential damages.

(a) is; is

(b) is; is not

(c) is not; is

(d) is not; is not

CASE QUESTIONS

1. Lewis signed a contract for the rights to all timber located on Nine-Mile Mine. He agreed to pay $70 per thousand board feet ($70/mbf). As he began work, Nine-Mile became convinced that Lewis lacked sufficient equipment to do the job well and forbade him to enter the land. Lewis sued. Nine-Mile moved for summary judgment. The mine offered proof that the market value of the timber was exactly $70/mbf, and Lewis had no evidence to contradict Nine-Mile. The evidence about market value proved decisive. Why? Please rule on the summary judgment motion.

2. Twin Creeks Entertainment signed a deal with U.S. JVC Corp. in which JVC would buy 60,000 feature-film videocassettes from Twin Creeks over a three-year period. JVC intended to distribute the cassettes nationwide. Relying on its deal with JVC, Twin Creeks signed an agreement with Paramount Pictures, agreeing to purchase a minimum of $600,000 worth of Paramount cassettes over a two-year period. JVC breached its deal with Twin Creeks and refused to accept the cassettes it had agreed upon. Twin Creeks sued and claimed, among other damages, the money it owed to Paramount. JVC moved to dismiss the claim based on the Paramount contract, on the ground that Twin Creeks, the seller of goods, was not entitled to such damages. What kind of damages is Twin Creeks seeking? Please rule on the motion to dismiss.

3. Racicky was in the process of buying 320 acres of ranchland. While that sale was being negotiated, Racicky signed a contract to sell the land to Simon. Simon paid $144,000, the full price of the land. But Racicky went bankrupt before he could complete the *purchase* of the land, let alone its sale. Which of these remedies should Simon seek: expectation, restitution, specific performance, or reformation?

4. Parkinson was injured in an auto accident by a driver who had no insurance. Parkinson filed a claim with her insurer, Liberty Mutual, for $2,000 under her "uninsured motorist" coverage. Liberty Mutual told her that if she sought that money, her premiums would go "sky high," so Parkinson dropped the claim. Later, after she had spoken with an attorney, Parkinson sued. What additional claim was her attorney likely to make?

5. *YOU BE THE JUDGE* **WRITING PROBLEM** John and Susan Verba sold a Vermont lakeshore lot to Shane and Deborah Rancourt for $115,000. The Rancourts intended to build a house on the property, but after preparing the land for construction, they learned that a wetland protection law prevented building near the lake. They sued, seeking rescission of the contract. The trial court concluded that the parties had reached their agreement under a "mutual, but innocent, misunderstanding." The trial judge gave the Verbas a choice: they could rescind the contract and refund the purchase price, or they could give the Rancourts $55,000, the difference between the sales price and the actual market value of the land. The Rancourts appealed. Were the Rancourts entitled to rescission of the contract? **Argument for the Rancourts:** When the parties have made a mutual mistake about an important factual issue, either party is entitled to rescind the contract. The land is of no use to us and we want our money back. **Argument for the Verbas:** Both sides were acting in good faith and both sides made an honest mistake. We are willing to acknowledge that the land is worth somewhat less than we all thought, and we are willing to refund $55,000. The buyers shouldn't complain—they are getting the property at about half the original price, and the error was as much their fault as ours.

DISCUSSION QUESTIONS

1. **ETHICS**   The National Football League owns the copyright to the broadcasts of its games. It licenses local television stations to telecast certain games and maintains a "blackout rule," which prohibits stations from broadcasting home games that are not sold out 72 hours before the game starts. Certain home games of the Cleveland Browns team were not sold out, and the NFL blocked local broadcast. But several bars in the Cleveland area were able to pick up the game's signal by using special antennas. The NFL wanted the bars to stop showing the games. What did it do? Was it unethical of the bars to broadcast the games that they were able to pick up? Apart from the NFL's legal rights, do you think it had the moral right to stop the bars from broadcasting the games?

2. Consequential damages can be many times higher than direct damages. Consider the "Farmer Ted" scenario raised in multiple-choice question 3, which is based on a real case.[10] Is it fair for consequential damages to be 60 times higher than direct damages?

---

[10]Prutch v. Ford, 574 P.2d 102 (Colo. 1977).

The Supreme Court is skeptical that *punitive* damages should be more than 9 times compensatory damages in a tort case. Should a similar "soft limit" apply to consequential damages in contract cases?

3. PepsiCo entered into a contract to sell its corporate jet to Klein for $4.6 million. Before the deal closed, the plane was sent to pick up PepsiCo's chairman of the board, who was stranded at Dulles airport. The chairman then decided that the company should not part with the plane. Klein sued PepsiCo for specific performance, arguing that he could not find a similar jet on the market for that price. Should a court force PepsiCo to sell its plane?

4. Walgreens operated a pharmacy in the Sara Creek mall. As part of this long-term lease, Sara Creek agreed not to lease mall space to another pharmacy. During an economic recession, Sara Creek's largest tenant left and the landlord informed Walgreens that it intended to rent that space out to a "deep discount" store that would contain a pharmacy. It was the only way to remain profitable, according to Sara Creek. Walgreens sued for an injunction against Sara Creek until its contract expired in 10 years. Should a court hold Sara Creek to its contract, even if this decision means bankrupting it?

5. Is it reasonable to require the mitigation of damages? If a person is wronged because the other side breached a contract, should she have any obligations at all? For example, suppose that a tenant breaches a lease by leaving early. Should the landlord have an obligation to try to find another tenant before the end of the lease?

CHAPTER 22

© Creative Travel Projects/Shutterstock.com

OWNERSHIP, RISK, AND WARRANTIES

This is the story of the Seated Woman with a Bent Left Leg. Only she knows where she went and what she saw between 1938 and 1963. The problem? She is a piece of work—artwork, that is.

Franz Friedrich Grunbaum was a famous Austrian Jewish songwriter and cabaret performer. In March of 1938, when the Nazis stormed into Austria, they caught Grunbaum and his wife at the Czech border and immediately imprisoned him at Dachau concentration camp. The law required Jews to submit a statement listing all of their property, so Mrs. Grunbaum filed the document, which included 81 drawings by modernist Egon Schiele.

Grunbaum died in Dachau in January of 1941, after performing a New Year's show for his fellow prisoners. At that time, Mrs. Grunbaum, who was still free, filed a death certificate claiming he had no property and making no mention of the art. Mrs. Grunbaum was arrested by the Nazis on October 5, 1942, and died shortly thereafter in a Minsk concentration camp. Nothing else is known about the whereabouts of the drawings at that time.

Fast-forward 65 years: A drawing entitled "Seated Woman with Bent Left Leg" went up for auction at the famed Sotheby's auction house. Its alleged owner, David Bakalar, claimed to have purchased it in good faith for $4,300 from a reputable art dealer in 1963. But the winning bid of $675,000 was suddenly withdrawn when Milos Vavra and Leon Fischer, Grunbaum's heirs, sent a letter claiming that Bakalar was not the Seated Woman's rightful owner—because the Nazis had stolen it from their family. Would Bakalar have to take a backseat to the heirs' ownership claims?[1]

> The problem? She is a piece of work—artwork, that is.

---

[1]Based on Bakalar v. Vavra, 500 Fed. Appx. 6 (2nd Cir. 2012).

22-1 LEGAL INTEREST

Who owns the drawing? Grunbaum's heirs wanted it back. But 44 years earlier, Bakalar had paid good money for it, without knowledge of its tumultuous past. Both parties to this lawsuit are unhappy, but fortunately for us, they have illustrated the theme for our chapter: When two parties claim a conflicting legal interest in particular goods, *who wins?* Who obtains the law's protection? These are disputes over *conflicting interests in goods.*

An interest is a legal right in something. More than one party can have an interest in particular goods. Suppose you lease a new car from a dealer, agreeing to pay $400 per month for three years. Several parties will have legal interests in the car. The dealer still *owns* the car—interest number one. At the end of three years, the dealer gets it back. For three years, you have the *use* of the car—interest number two. You may use the car for all normal purposes, and you are obligated to make monthly payments. Your payments go to a finance agency, which has made an arrangement with the dealer to obtain the right to your $400 monthly payment. The finance agency has a *security interest* in the car—interest number three. If you fail to pay on time, the finance company has the right to repossess your car. If you take the car to a garage for maintenance, the garage has *temporary possession* of the car—interest number four. The garage has the right to keep the car locked up overnight, to work on it, and to test drive it. Sometimes legal interests clash, and it is those conflicts we look at here.

Often the parties will claim ownership, each arguing that his interest is stronger than the other's. But in this chapter, we also consider cases where each party argues that the *other* one owns the goods. Suppose a seller manufactures products for a buyer, but while the goods are being shipped, they are destroyed in a fire. The seller may argue that it no longer owned the goods, and the fire is the buyer's misfortune. But the buyer will claim it had not yet acquired the items.

In other cases, a *third party* will be involved. You pay $30,000 cash to buy a new car and expect to pick it up in three days. But the day before you arrive, the dealer's bank seizes all of the cars on the lot, claiming the dealer has defaulted on loans. Now the fight over legal interest is between you and the bank, with the dealer a relatively passive observer.

22-2 IDENTIFICATION, TITLE, AND INSURABLE INTEREST

Historically, courts settled disputes about legal interest by looking at one thing: title. But the drafters of the UCC concluded that "title" was too abstract an answer for the assorted practical questions that arose. It sometimes could be hard to prove exactly who did have title, and it made no sense to settle a wide variety of business problems with one legal idea. Today, title is only one of several issues that a court will use to resolve conflicting interests in goods. *Identification* and *insurable interest* have become more important, and title has diminished in significance. We can begin to understand all three doctrines if we examine how title passes from seller to buyer.

22-1a **Existence and Identification**

Title in goods can pass from one person to another only if the goods exist and have been identified to the contract.

Existence

Goods must exist before title can pass.[2] Although most goods do exist when people buy and sell them, some have not yet come into being, such as crops to be grown later or goods that have not yet been manufactured. A farmer may contract to sell corn even before it is planted, but title to the corn cannot pass until it actually exists.

Identification

Goods must be identified to the contract before title can pass.[3] This means that the parties must have designated the specific goods being sold. Often, identification is obvious. If Dealer agrees to sell to Buyer a 60-foot yacht with identification number AKX472, the parties have identified the goods. But suppose Paintco agrees to sell Brushworks 1,000 gallons of white base paint at a specified price. Paintco has 25,000 gallons in its warehouse. Title cannot pass until Paintco identifies the specific gallons that will go to Brushworks.

The parties may agree in their contract how and when they will identify the goods.[4] They are free to identify them to the contract in any way they want. Paintco and Brushworks might agree, for example, that within one week of signing the sales agreement, Paintco will mark appropriate gallons. If the gallons are stored 50 to a crate, then Paintco will have a worker stick a "Brushworks" label on 20 crates. Once the label is on, the goods are identified to the contract.

If the parties do not specify any particular method, identification will occur according to these rules:

- Identification occurs when the parties enter into a contract if the agreement describes specific goods that already exist. If the Dealer agrees to sell a yacht and the parties include the ID number in their contract, the goods are identified (even though the parties never use the term *identify*).

- For unborn animals, identification generally takes place when they are conceived; for crops, identification normally happens when they are planted.

- For other goods, identification occurs when the seller marks, ships, or in some other way indicates the *exact* goods that are going to the buyer.[5]

Identification for crops generally happens when they are planted. Thus, they are identified before they have grown and produced their yield.

---

[2]UCC § 2-105 (2).
[3]UCC § 2-401 (1).
[4]UCC § 501 (1).
[5]UCC § 2-501.

EXAM Strategy

Question: Arielle, an artist, has 25 hand-painted room screens in her studio. She contracts to sell five of them to Retailer for $5,000 each. The contract allows Arielle to choose which five she will sell. Arielle moves five screens from her studio to a warehouse, but a week later, a fire destroys the building and its contents. Two insurance companies dispute whether title to the screens has passed to Retailer. The warehouse insurer claims the goods were identified and title passed; Retailer's insurer says the goods were not identified and title never passed. The contract says nothing about identification. Have the goods been identified?

Strategy: Title cannot pass until the goods have been identified to the contract. Identification can occur in three ways: The parties describe specific goods that already exist, animals are conceived or crops planted, or the seller marks, ships, or otherwise indicates which are going to the buyer. Did any of those things happen?

Result: The parties never described the goods. The goods are neither animals nor crops. However, when Arielle moved five of the screens to the warehouse, she "indicated which goods were going to the buyer." The goods were identified.

22-2b Passing of Title

Once goods exist and are identified to the contract, ownership can pass from one person to another. **Title may pass in any manner on which the parties agree (UCC §2-401).** Once again, the Code allows the parties to control their affairs with commonsense decisions. The parties can agree, for example, that title passes when the goods leave the manufacturer's factory or when they reach the shipper who will transport them or at any other time and place. If the parties do not agree on passing title, §2-401 decides. There are three possibilities:

- *When the goods are being moved*, title passes to the buyer when the seller completes whatever transportation it is obligated to do. Suppose the Seller is in Milwaukee and the Buyer is in Honolulu. The contract requires the Seller to deliver the goods to a ship in San Francisco. Title passes when the Seller completes its last *contractually required* step. In this example, that happens when the goods reach the ship in San Francisco.

- *When the goods are* not *being moved and a contract calls for delivery of ownership documents*, title passes when the seller delivers these documents to the buyer. Suppose Seller, located in Louisville, has manufactured 5,000 baseball bats, which are stored in a warehouse in San Diego. Under the terms of their contract, Buyer will take possession of the bats at the warehouse. When Seller gives Buyer ownership documents, title passes.

- *When the goods are* not *being moved and the contract does* not *call for delivery of ownership documents*, title passes when the parties form the contract. For example, if the Buyer owns the warehouse where the bats are stored, Buyer needs no documents to take possession; title passes when the parties reach agreement.

22-2c Insurable Interest

Closely related to identification and title is the idea of insurable interest. Anyone buying or selling expensive goods should make certain that the goods are insured. There are some limits, though, on who may insure goods, and when. As we saw in Chapter 13, a party may insure something such as property or a human life only when she has a legitimate interest in it. If the person buying the policy lacks a real interest in the thing insured, the law regards the policy as a gambling agreement and considers it void.

When does someone have an insurable interest in goods? The UCC gives one answer for buyers and one for sellers. **A buyer obtains an insurable interest when the goods are identified to the contract (UCC §2-501).** Suppose that in January, Grain Broker contracts with Farmer to buy his entire wheat crop. Neither party mentions "identification." In January, the crop is not identified and Broker has no insurable interest. In May, after weeks of breaking the soil, Farmer plants his wheat crop. Once he has planted it, the goods are identified. The Broker now has an insurable interest and purchases insurance. In July, a drought destroys the crop, and the Broker never gets one grain of wheat. The Broker need not worry: His insurance policy will cover his losses.

The seller's insurable interest is different. **The seller retains an insurable interest in goods as long as she has either title to the goods or a security interest in them (UCC §2-501).** "Security interest" refers to cases in which the buyer still owes money for the goods and the seller can repossess the goods if payment is not made. Suppose Flyola Manufacturing sells a small aircraft to WingIt, a dealer, for $300,000. WingIt pays $30,000 cash and agrees to pay interest on the balance until it sells the plane. Flyola has an insurable interest even while the aircraft is in WingIt's showroom and may purchase insurance anytime until WingIt pays off the last dime.

And so, a seller and buyer can have an insurable interest in the same goods simultaneously. Suppose the heavy-metal band Flulike Symptoms hires Inkem Corp., in Minneapolis, to make 25,000 T-shirts with the band's logo, for sale at rock concerts. The parties agree that the T-shirts are identified as soon as the logo is printed, and that title will pass when Inkem delivers the T-shirts to the office of the Symptoms' manager in Kansas City. Inkem obviously has an insurable interest while the company is making the T-shirts and continues to have an interest until it delivers the T-shirts in Kansas City. But the Flulike Symptoms' insurable interest arises the moment their logo is stamped on each shirt, so the Symptoms could insure the goods while they are still stored in Inkem's factory. Why would the Symptoms spend hard-earned cash to insure goods they do not have? They may be uncertain that Inkem has obtained proper insurance.

In the following case, a car accident leads several insurance companies to dispute who owned the damaged auto. Each company wants to claim that the car belonged to—someone *else*.

CODE PROVISIONS DISCUSSED IN THIS CASE

Issue	Relevant Code Section
1. Which party had title to the car?	UCC §2-401: Title to goods may pass in any manner on which the parties agree.
2. Did the seller have an insurable interest in the car?	UCC §2-501: The seller retains an insurable interest in the goods as long as it holds title to or a security interest in them.

VALLEY FORGE INSURANCE CO. v. GREAT AMERICAN INSURANCE CO.

1995 Ohio App. LEXIS 3939, 1995 WL 540128
Ohio Court of Appeals, 1995

Facts: On a Friday afternoon, Karl and Linda Kennedy went to John Nolan Ford to buy a new Mustang. The parties signed all necessary documents, including a New Vehicle Buyer's Order, an Agreement to Provide Insurance, and credit applications. The Kennedys made a down payment, but they could not arrange financing before the dealership closed. John Nolan Ford determined that the Kennedys were creditworthy and allowed them to take the car home for the weekend. That evening, Karl Kennedy permitted his brother-in-law, Cella, to take the car for a drive, along with a passenger named Campbell. Cella wrecked the car, injuring his passenger. Campbell sued, and the question was which insurance company was liable: John Nolan Ford's insurer (Milwaukee Mutual), Cella's insurer (Valley Forge), or Kennedy's insurer (Great American). The trial court ruled that title had never passed to Kennedy and found Milwaukee Mutual liable. The insurance company appealed.

Issue: *Had title passed to Kennedy at the time of the accident?*

Excerpts from the *Per Curiam* Decision: Milwaukee argues that the risk of loss and insurable interest had passed because the car had been delivered. Further, Milwaukee states that the Kennedys explicitly agreed to provide insurance. Great American counters that the parties had "otherwise explicitly agreed" in the New Vehicle Buyer's Order that any interest in the car would not pass until "either the full purchase price is paid in cash or a satisfactory deferred payment agreement is executed by the parties[.]" No financing had been arranged at the time of the accident.

Two terms of the New Vehicle Buyer's Order apply to the situation at bar. Under the "Agreement" provision, the contract states that "it is expressly agreed that the purchaser acquires no right, title or interest in or to the property which he agrees to purchase hereunder until such property is delivered to him and either the full purchase price is paid in cash or a satisfactory deferred payment agreement is executed by the parties hereto[.]"

Milwaukee also argues that the Kennedys explicitly agreed to provide insurance by signing the "Agreement to Provide Insurance." While the agreement does state that the Kennedys agreed to provide insurance, it is not clear when the Kennedys were to obtain the insurance. In fact, because the agreement refers to an "instalment [sic] contract," it is possible that the Kennedys were to provide insurance once a financing agreement was reached. In light of the fact that the agreement is ambiguous, we construe the contract strictly against the drafter and hold that any agreement to provide insurance was to take effect after financing was obtained.

We hold that because the parties had otherwise agreed that interest in the car, including insurable interest, would not pass until the financing was complete, John Nolan Ford still had the risk of loss and the insurable interest when the accident occurred. [Affirmed.]

22-3 IMPERFECT TITLE

22-3a Bona Fide Purchaser

Some people are sleazy, and sales law must accommodate that reality. Bad Guy Abe steals Marvin's BMW in the middle of the night and promptly sells it to Elaine for $35,000 cash. Two weeks later, the police locate the car. Abe skipped town, leaving a dispute between two innocent parties. Either the original owner (Marvin) or the buyer (Elaine) must bear the loss. Who loses?

> ### THE QUESTION: WHO MUST SUFFER THE LOSS?
>
> | Owner→ | Bad Guy→ | Buyer |
> |---|---|---|
> | (Has valid title) | (Obtains goods from Owner and sells) | (Buys goods from Bad Guy) |

First, we need to know what kind of title Bad Guy obtains: Is it void or voidable? The key is this: Did Bad Guy *take* the item against the will of the owner, or did he fraudulently *trick* the owner into voluntarily handing the item to him?

When Abe stole it, he obtained void title, which is no title at all. When Bad Guy sells the goods to Buyer, she also gets *no title at all*. Elaine must return the car to Marvin and suffer the $35,000 loss for Abe's theft. This policy makes sense because Marvin has done nothing wrong. If the law permitted Elaine to get valid title, it would encourage theft.

In the chapter opener, Grunbaum's heirs argued that Bakalar had void title to the drawing because he had purchased artwork taken by the Nazis and a thief cannot pass good title. Unfortunately for their heirs, they were not able to prove that the drawing was indeed stolen: Bakalar introduced evidence that Mrs. Grunbaum's sister, Mathilde Lukacs, sold it to a Swiss dealer in 1956, a fact inconsistent with the heirs' Nazi loot theory. In the absence of evidence that the drawing was originally stolen, Grunbaum's heirs did not succeed in their claim.[6]

The outcome is different in the case of voidable title. If Bad Guy attempts to purchase the goods from Owner using fraud or deception, he obtains voidable title, meaning limited rights in the goods, inferior to those of the owner. The owner should be able to recover the goods from Bad Guy (if he can be found), but not from anyone else who ends up with them. Suppose the Swiss dealer had convinced Lukacs to part with the drawing through deceit. As a result, the devious dealer obtains only voidable title. If Lukacs learns of the fraud before the dealer sells the drawing to someone else, she will get her drawing back.

Now assume that before Lukacs caught on, the sneaky dealer sold it to Bakalar, who did not know of the Swiss swindle. Who keeps the drawing? Bakalar wins the artwork if he is a bona fide purchaser. **A person with voidable title has power to transfer valid title for value to a good faith purchaser, generally called a *bona fide purchaser* or *BFP*.**[7]

Voidable title
Limited rights in goods, inferior to those of the owner

The collector can prove that he is a bona fide purchaser by showing two things:

- That he gave value for the goods, *and*
- That he acted in good faith.

It is generally easy for purchasers to show that they gave value. The real issue becomes whether the buyer acted in good faith. If Bakalar paid a reasonable purchase price and had no reason to suspect wrongdoing, he acted in good faith. Bakalar keeps the Seated Woman.

On the other hand, suppose Bakalar knew the drawing was worth much more than the dealer's $4,300 price. The Swiss dealer was in a frantic hurry to unload the drawing and would only meet in a dark alley in Zurich. The dealer would not produce any information about the provenance, or the origin, of the art. The dealer's conduct, together with the obvious discount, would make a reasonable person suspicious. In that case, the collector would not be acting in good faith and therefore is not a bona fide purchaser. The Grunbaum heirs would reclaim the drawing, and Bakalar would lose his $4,300.

---

[6]Bakalar v. Vavra, 500 Fed. Appx. 6 (2nd Cir. 2012).
[7]UCC §2-403(1).

22-3b Entrustment

Your old Steinway grand piano needs a complete rebuilding. You hire Fred Showpan, Inc., a company that repairs and sells instruments. Showpan hauls your piano away and promises to return it in perfect shape. Two months later, you are horrified to spot Showpan's showroom boarded up and pasted with bankruptcy notices. Worse still, you learn that Fred sold your beloved instrument to a customer, Frankie List. When you track down List, he claims he paid $18,000 for the piano and likes it just fine. Is he entitled to keep it?

Quite likely he is. Section 2-403(1), the BFP provision we just discussed, would not apply because Showpan did not *purchase* the piano from you. But §2-403(2) does apply. This is the "entrustment" section, and it covers cases in which the owner of goods voluntarily *leaves* them with a merchant, who then sells the goods without permission. According to **UCC §2-403(2), any entrusting to a merchant who deals in goods of that kind gives him power to transfer all rights of the entruster to a buyer in the ordinary course of business (BIOC).** There are several important ideas in this section:

Entrusting means delivering goods to a merchant or permitting the merchant to retain them.[8] In the piano example, you clearly entrusted goods to a merchant. If you buy a used car from Fast Eddie's and then leave it there for a week while you obtain insurance, you have entrusted it to Eddie.

Deals in Goods of That Kind

The purpose of the section is to protect innocent buyers who enter a store, see the goods they expect to find, and purchase something, having no idea that the storekeeper is illegally selling the property of others. Shoppers should not have to demand proof of title to everything in the store. Further, if someone has to bear the risk, let it be the person who has entrusted her goods; she is in the best position to investigate the merchant's integrity. But this protection does not extend to a buyer who arrives at a vacuum cleaner store and buys an $80,000 mobile home parked in the lot.

In the Ordinary Course of Business

Buyer in the ordinary course of business (BIOC)
One who acts in good faith, without knowing that the sale violates the owner's rights

A **buyer in the ordinary course of business (BIOC)** is one who acts in good faith, without knowing that the sale violates the owner's rights. If Frank List buys your piano assuming that Showpan owns it, he has acted in good faith. If Frank was your neighbor, recognized your instrument, and bought it anyway, he is not buying in the ordinary course of business and must hand over the piano.

Of course, a merchant who violates the owner's rights is liable to that owner. If Showpan were still in business when you discovered your loss, you could sue and recover the value of the piano. The problems arise when the merchant is bankrupt or otherwise unable to reimburse the owner.

EXAM Strategy

Question: Pamela went to University Used Auto and asked if the company had a Lincoln Navigator. University had no such SUV, but a sales representative told Pamela that he would find her one. The representative contacted Royal auto dealership, which sold new and used cars. Royal agreed to supply University with a car, on the understanding that an interested buyer would pay *Royal*, which in turn would give a finder's fee to University. The companies had worked this way in the past. Royal

---

[8]For a discussion of who is and who is not a merchant, see Chapter 21.

delivered a Navigator as requested. But when the used car company sold the vehicle to Pamela, the company instructed her to pay University directly, which she did. Royal sued Pamela, seeking the car, and the court had to determine whether there had been an entrustment. Royal argued that it never entrusted the Navigator to University because the parties agreed to require payment to Royal.

Strategy: Entrustment means delivering goods to a merchant who routinely deals in such articles.

Result: Royal delivered a used car to a used car dealer. That is entrustment. It is true that both dealers understood that Pamela was to pay Royal—but she did not know that. Entrustment protects good faith buyers, and Pamela wins.

22-4 RISK OF LOSS

Many of the issues we have looked at thus far involve someone doing something wrong, often a scoundrel selling goods that he never owned. Now we turn to cases where there may be no wrongdoer.

Accidents hurt businesses. When goods are damaged, the law may again need to decide whether it is the seller or buyer who must suffer the loss. In the cases we have seen thus far, the parties were arguing, "It's mine!"—"Like heck it is, it's *mine!*" In risk of loss cases, the parties are generally shouting, "It was yours!"—"No way, dude, it was *yours!*"

Athena, a seafood wholesaler, is gearing up for the Super Bowl, which will bring 150,000 hungry visitors to her city for a week of eating and gabbing. Athena orders 25,000 lobsters from Poseidon's Fishfoods, 500 miles distant, and simultaneously contracts with a dozen local restaurants to resell them. Poseidon loads the lobsters, still kicking, into refrigerated railcars owned by Demeter Trucking. But halfway to the city, the train collides with a prison van. None of the convicts escape, but the lobsters do, hurtling into swamps from which they are never recaptured. Athena loses all of her profits and sues. As luck would have it, Demeter Trucking had foolishly let its insurance lapse. Poseidon claims the goods were out of its hands. Who loses?

The common law answered this problem by looking at which party had title to the goods at the time of loss. But the Uniform Commercial Code again rejects the old concept, striving once more for a practical solution. The UCC permits the parties to agree on who bears the risk of loss. **UCC §2-509(4) states that the parties may allocate the risk of loss any way they wish.**

Often the parties will do just that, avoiding arguments and litigation in the event of an accident. As part of her agreement with Poseidon, Athena should have included a one-sentence clause, such as "Seller bears all risk of loss until the lobsters are delivered to Athena's warehouse." As long as the parties make their risk allocation clear, the Code will enforce their terms.

22-4a Shipping Terms

The parties can quickly and easily allocate the risk of loss by using common shipping terms that the Code defines. FOB means free on board; FAS indicates free alongside a ship; and CIF stands for cost, insurance, and freight. By combining these designations with other terms, the parties can specify risk in a few words:

- *FOB place of shipment.* The seller is obligated to put the goods into the possession of the carrier at the place named. The seller bears the expense and risk until they are in the carrier's possession. From that moment onward, the buyer bears the risk.

- *FOB place of destination.* The seller must deliver the goods at the place named and bears the expense *and risk* of shipping.

- *CIF.* The price includes in a lump sum: the cost of the goods and the insurance and freight to the named destination.

- *C&F.* The price includes in a lump sum: the cost of the goods and freight, but *not* insurance.

Thus, if Athena had put a clause in her contract saying, "FOB Athena's warehouse," Poseidon would have had the risk of any loss up to the time the lobsters were unloaded in Athena's possession. Poseidon would then have known that it must insure the lobsters during transit.

22-4b **When the Parties Fail to Allocate the Risk**

If the parties fail to specify when the risk passes from seller to buyer, the Code provides the answer. When neither party breached the contract, §2-509 determines the risk; when a party has breached the contract, §2-510 governs. The full analysis of risk is somewhat intricate, so we first supply you with a short version: **When neither party has breached the contract, the risk of loss generally passes from seller to buyer when the seller has transported the goods as far as he is obligated to. When a party has breached, the risk of loss generally lies with that party.**

And now, for the courageous student, the full version of how the UCC allocates the risk of loss when the parties failed to specify it.

When Neither Party Breaches

In the example of Athena and Poseidon, both parties did what they were supposed to do, so there was no breach of contract. To settle these cases, we need to know whether the contract obligated the seller to ship the goods or whether the goods were handled in some other way. There are three possibilities: (1) the contract required the seller to ship the goods, or (2) the contract involved a bailment, or (3) other cases.

If the Seller Must Ship the Goods.   Most contracts require the seller to arrange shipment of the goods. In a *shipment contract*, the seller must deliver the goods *to a carrier*, which will then transport the goods to the buyer. The carrier might be a trucking company, railroad, airline, or ship, and is generally located near the seller's place of business. **In a shipment contract, the risk passes to the buyer when the seller delivers the goods to the carrier.** Suppose Old Wood, in North Carolina, agrees to sell $100,000 worth of furniture to Pioneer Company, in Anchorage. The contract requires Old Wood to deliver the goods to Great Northern Railroad lines in Chicago. From North Carolina to Chicago, Old Wood bears the risk of loss. If the furniture is damaged, stolen, or destroyed, Old Wood is out of luck. But once the furniture is on board the train in Chicago, the risk of loss passes to Pioneer. If the train derails in Montana and every desk and chair is smashed to kindling, Pioneer must nevertheless pay the full $100,000 to Old Wood.

In a *destination contract*, the seller is responsible for delivering the goods *to the buyer*, and risk passes to the buyer when the goods reach the destination. If the contract required Old Wood to deliver the furniture to Pioneer's warehouse in Anchorage, then Old Wood bears the loss for the entire trip. If the train travels 3,000 miles and then plunges off a bridge in Alaska, 45 feet from its destination, Old Wood picks up the tab.

Bailor

The one who owns goods legally held by another

Bailee

The one with temporary possession of another's goods

If There Is a Bailment.   Freezem Corp. produces 500 room air conditioners and stores them in Every-Ware's Warehouse. This is a **bailment, meaning that one person or company is legally holding goods for the benefit of another.** Freezem is the **bailor**, the one who owns the goods, and Every-Ware is the **bailee**, the one with temporary possession. Suppose Freezem agrees to sell 300 of its air conditioners to KeepKool

Appliances. KeepKool does not need the machines in its store for six months, so it plans to keep them at Every-Ware's until then. But two weeks after Freezem and KeepKool make their deal, Every-Ware burns to the ground. Who bears the loss of the 300 air conditioners? **If the contract requires a bailee to hold the goods for the buyer, the risk passes when the buyer obtains documents entitling her to possession, or when the bailee acknowledges her right to the goods.** If fire broke out in Every-Ware's before KeepKool received any documents enabling it to take the air conditioners away, then the loss would fall on Freezem.

Other Cases.   The great majority of contracts involve either shipment by the seller or a bailment. In the remaining cases, if the seller is a *merchant*, risk passes to the buyer on receipt. This means that a merchant is only off the hook if the buyer actually accepts the goods. If the seller is *not a merchant*, risk passes when the seller tenders the goods, meaning that she makes them available to the buyer. The Code is giving more protection to buyers when they deal with a merchant.

When One Party Breaches

We now look at how the Code allocates risk when one of the parties *does* breach. Again there are three possibilities: (1) seller breaches and buyer rejects; (2) seller breaches, buyer accepts, but then revokes; or (3) buyer breaches.

Seller Breaches and Buyer Rejects.   PlayStore, a sporting goods store, orders 75 canoes from Floataway. PlayStore specifies that the canoes must be 12 feet long, lightweight metal, dark green. Floataway delivers 75 canoes to Truckit, a trucking company. When Truckit's trucks arrive, PlayStore finds that the canoes are the right material and color, but 18 feet long. PlayStore rejects the craft, and Truckit heads back to Floataway. But one of the trucks is hijacked and the 25 canoes it carries are never recovered. Floataway demands its money for the 25 lost canoes. Who loses?

Floataway had delivered **nonconforming goods**; that is, merchandise which differs from that specified in the contract. A buyer has a right to reject such goods. **When the buyer rejects nonconforming goods, the risk of loss remains with the seller until he cures the defect or the buyer decides to accept the goods.** In our example, Floataway must suffer the loss for the stolen canoes. If PlayStore had decided to accept the canoes, even though they were the wrong size, then the risk would have passed to the sports store.

Nonconforming goods
Merchandise that differs from what is specified in the contract

Seller Breaches, Buyer Accepts, but Then Revokes.   PlayStore orders 200 tennis rackets from High Strung. When the rackets arrive, they seem fine, so the store accepts them. But then a salesperson notices that the grips are loose. Every racket has the same problem. PlayStore returns the rackets to High Strung, but they are destroyed when a blimp crashes into the delivery truck. **When a buyer accepts goods but then rightfully revokes acceptance, the risk remains with the seller to the extent that the buyer's insurance will not cover the loss.** If PlayStore's insurance covers the damaged rackets, there is no problem. If PlayStore's insurance does not cover the loss of goods in transit, High Strung must pay.

Buyer Breaches.   One last time. PlayStore orders 60 tents from ExploreMore. About the time the tents leave the factory, PlayStore decides to drop its line of camping goods and specialize in team sports. PlayStore notifies ExploreMore that it wants to explore less and will not pay. The tents are destroyed in a collision involving a prison van and a train carrying lobsters. This time, PlayStore is liable. **When a buyer breaches the contract before taking possession, it assumes the risk of loss to the extent that the seller's insurance is deficient.**

Exhibit 22.1 should clarify.

Start Here

Did the Parties Allocate the Risk in Their Contract?

If the parties have allocated the risk in their contract, that agreement will control and everything on this chart is gloriously irrelevant.

If the parties have *not* allocated the risk of loss, then §2-509 and §2-510 will determine who suffers the loss.

In using the two Code sections to determine the risk, the first question is whether either party has breached the contract.

No Breach (§2-509)
If neither party breaches, there are three possibilities:

1 Contract requires Seller to ship goods by carrier.

2 Contract requires a bailee to hold goods for Buyer.

3 Other cases.

a *Shipment Contract* requires Seller to deliver the goods to a carrier.

Risk passes to Buyer when Seller delivers goods to carrier.

a If Seller *is* a merchant

Risk passes to Buyer on receipt of goods.

b *Destination Contract* requires Seller to deliver goods to a specified destination.

Risk passes to Buyer when carrier tenders goods at the destination.

Risk passes to Buyer when she obtains documents entitling her to possession, or when Bailee acknowledges she is entitled to possession.

b If Seller *is not* a merchant

Risk passes to Buyer on tender of delivery.

Breach (§2-510)
If a party breaches, there are three possibilities:

1 Seller breaches. The goods are nonconforming and the Buyer rightfully rejects them.

2 Seller breaches. The buyer accepts but then revokes his acceptance.

3 Buyer breaches. Buyer repudiates conforming goods or in some other way breaches the contract before he takes possession of the goods.

Risk remains with the Seller until he cures the defects or the Buyer decides to accept the goods.

Risk remains with the Seller to the extent that the Buyer's own insurance is deficient.

Risk passes to the Buyer to the extent that the Seller's insurance is deficient, for a commercially reasonable time.

EXHIBIT 22.1

CODE PROVISIONS DISCUSSED IN THIS CASE

Issue	Relevant Code Section
1. Did the parties create a bailment?	In a bailment, one person legally holds goods for the benefit of another.
2. Which party bore the risk of the horse's death?	UCC §2-509(2): If the contract requires a bailee to hold the goods for the buyer, the risk passes when the buyer obtains documents entitling her to possession, or when the bailee acknowledges her right to the goods.

In the following case, neither party breached, so §2-509 governs.

HARMON V. DUNN

1997 Tenn. App. LEXIS 217, 1997 WL 136462
Tennessee Court of Appeals, 1997

Facts: Bess Harmon owned a two-year-old Tennessee Walking Horse named Phantom Recall. Harmon, who lived in Tennessee, boarded her horse with Steve Dunn at his stables in Florence, Alabama. Dunn cared for Phantom Recall and showed him at equestrian events. Harmon instructed Dunn to sell the horse for $25,000, and Dunn arranged for his friend Scarbrough to buy the colt. On June 30, Dunn delivered Scarbrough's $25,000 check to Harmon, who handed over the horse's certificate of registration and a "transfer of ownership" document. That night at a horse show, Dunn told Scarbrough that he had delivered the check and had the ownership papers in his car. Dunn did not actually give the documents to his friend. Scarbrough knew that Phantom Recall was at Dunn's stable, where Scarbrough had boarded other horses. Sadly, the colt developed colitis and died suddenly, on July 4. Scarbrough stopped payment on his check, and Harmon sued for her money. The trial court found for Harmon, and Scarbrough appealed.

Issue: *Which party bore the risk of Phantom Recall's death?*

Excerpts from Judge Farmer's Decision: [UCC §2-509 states:] Risk of loss in the absence of breach …

(2) Where the goods are held by a bailee to be delivered without being moved, the risk of loss passes to the buyer:

    (a) on his receipt of a negotiable document of title covering the goods, or

    (b) on acknowledgment by the bailee of the buyer's right to possession of the goods, or

    (c) after his receipt of a non-negotiable document of title or other written direction to deliver…

Phantom Recall died of colitis—but that was just the beginning of the drama.

We conclude that the facts before us clearly establish a bailor-bailee relationship between Harmon and Dunn. It is not disputed that the latter was the agent of the former. Here, it was agreed that Dunn would train and care for Phantom Recall at the Dunn Stables in Florence, Alabama. He was also responsible for transporting the horse to various shows. The record establishes that prior to the horse's death, he had been entered and shown by Dunn himself in three separate events.

Having established Dunn a bailee for purposes of [§2-509(2)] and in the absence of any prior arrangement with Dunn or Harmon that the horse be delivered elsewhere upon purchase from the latter, we find that the risk of loss passed to Scarbrough if and when the applicable provisions under subsection (2) occurred. Subsection (2)(a) and (b) provide that the risk of loss passes to the buyer "on his receipt of a negotiable document of title covering the goods; or on acknowledgment by the bailee of the buyer's right to possession of the goods."

We find that Scarbrough received the ability to control possession of the horse no later than July 1 irrespective of the fact that he did not actually receive physical possession of the ownership documents at that time. The documents which were necessary for transfer of ownership and taking possession of the horse were already in the hands of the bailee. We find an actual physical back and forth exchange between the two unnecessary under these facts where the bailee and the seller's agent are one and the same. Certainly Scarbrough had the ability to control possession of the horse no later than July 1 when he was made aware that Dunn had the transfer papers.

[Affirmed.]

22-5 WARRANTIES

The *Harmon* case illustrates what happens when an accident destroys the goods sold and neither party is at fault. But what if Harmon had guaranteed Scarbrough a healthy horse and delivered a sick one? The UCC also addresses this issue in its warranty provisions. A **warranty** is a promise that goods will meet certain standards. Normally a manufacturer or a seller gives a warranty and a buyer relies on it. A warranty might be explicit and written: "The manufacturer warrants that the light bulbs in this package will illuminate for 2,000 hours." Or a warranty could be oral: "Don't worry, this machine can harvest any size of wheat crop ever planted in the state."

Warranty
A contractual assurance that goods will meet certain standards

Sometimes a manufacturer offers a warranty as a means of attracting buyers: "We provide the finest bumper-to-bumper warranty in the automobile industry." Other times, *the law itself* imposes a warranty on goods, requiring the manufacturer to meet certain standards whether it wants to or not. We will begin with the first option—when the seller voluntarily provides a warranty.

22-5a Express Warranties

Express warranty
One that the seller creates with his words or actions

An **express warranty** is one that the seller creates with his words or actions.[9] Whenever a seller *clearly indicates* to a buyer that the goods being sold will meet certain standards, she has created an express warranty. For example, if the sales clerk for a paint store tells a professional house painter that "this exterior paint will not fade for three years, even in direct sunlight," that is an express warranty and the store is bound by it. Or, if the clerk gives the painter a brochure that makes the same promise, the store is again bound by its express warranty. On the other hand, if the salesperson merely says, "I know you're going to be happy with this product," there is no warranty because the promise is too vague.

The UCC establishes that the seller may create an express warranty in three ways: (1) with an affirmation of fact or a promise; (2) with a description of the goods; or (3) with a sample or model. In addition, the buyer must demonstrate that what the seller said or did was part of the *basis of the bargain*.

---

[9] UCC §2-313.

Affirmation of Fact or Promise

Any affirmation of fact—or any promise—can create an express warranty.[10] An affirmation of fact is simply a statement about the nature or quality of the goods, such as "this scaffolding is made from the highest grade of steel available at any price" or "this car will accelerate from 0 to 60 in 5.3 seconds." A promise can include phrases such as, "we guarantee you that this air conditioning system will cool your building to 72 degrees, regardless of the outdoor temperature."

A common problem in cases of express warranty is to separate true affirmations of fact from mere sales puffery or seller's opinion, which creates no express warranty. "You meet the nicest people when you ride a Honda motorcycle," is mere puffery. If you purchase a Honda and meet only deadbeats, the manufacturer owes you nothing.

A statement is more likely to be an affirmation of fact if:

- **It is specific and can be proven true or false.** Suppose the brochures of a home builder promise to meet "the strictest building codes." Since there is a code on file, the builder's work can be compared to it, and his promise is binding.

- **It is written.** An oral promise *can* create an express warranty. But promises in brochures are more likely to be taken seriously. Statements in a *written contract* are the likeliest of all to create a binding warranty.

- **Defects are not obvious.** If a used car salesman tells you that a car is rust-free when the driver's door is pockmarked with rust, you should not take the statement seriously —since a court will not, either.

- **Seller has greater expertise.** If the seller knows more than the buyer, his statements will be more influential with buyer and court alike. If your architect assures you that the new porch will be structurally sound, the law recognizes that you will naturally rely on her expertise.

Description of Goods

Any description of the goods can create an express warranty.[11] The statement can be oral or written. A description might be a label on a bag of seed, referring to the seed as a particular variety of tomato; it could be a tag on airplane parts, assuring the buyer that the goods have met safety tests. Wherever the words appear, if they describe the goods as having particular characteristics or qualities, the seller has probably created an express warranty.

Sample or Model

Any sample or model can create an express warranty.[12] A sample can be a very effective way of demonstrating the quality of goods to a customer. However, a seller who uses a sample is generally warranting that the merchandise sold will be just as good.

Basis of Bargain

The seller's conduct must have been part of the basis of the bargain. To prove an express warranty, a buyer must demonstrate that the two parties *included the statements or acts in their bargain*. Some courts have interpreted this to mean that the buyer must have *relied* on the seller's statements. There is logic to this position. For example, suppose a sales brochure makes certain assurances about the quality of goods, but the buyer never sees the brochure until she files suit. Should the seller be held to an express warranty? Some courts would rule that the seller is not liable for breach of warranty.

---

[10]UCC §2-313(1)(a).

[11]UCC §2-313(1)(b).

[12]UCC §2-313(1)(c).

Other courts, however, have ruled that a seller's statement can be part of the basis of the bargain even when the buyer has not clearly relied on it. These courts are declaring that a seller who chooses to make statements about his goods will be held to them *unless the seller can convince a court that he should not be liable*. This is a policy decision, taken by many courts, to give the buyer the benefit of the doubt since the seller is in the best position to control what he says.

In the following case, was Sony just playing with its customers?

You be the Judge

In Re Sony PS3 "Other OS" Litigation

2014 U.S. App. LEXIS 187, 2014 WL 31217
United States Court of Appeals for the Ninth Circuit, 2014

Facts: In 2006, Sony Computer Entertainment America LLC introduced the PlayStation 3 (PS3) gaming system, as "the most advanced computer system that serves as a platform to enjoy next generation computer entertainment." Sony promoted PS3's innovative capabilities: access to online gaming through the PlayStation Network (PSN) and an "Other OS" feature, which enabled users to install other operating systems and use the console as a personal computer. In some promotional materials, Sony stated that it expected the PS3 to have a "ten year life cycle" and that it would "be a console that's going to be with you again for 10 years." However, the product license agreement and terms of service informed consumers that updates could result in some features losing functionality.

In 2010, Sony released a PS3 software update that posed a difficult dilemma for PS3 owners. Installing the update would improve online gaming, but disable the Other OS feature; declining it would maintain the Other OS, but disable access to the PSN.

A group of disgruntled gamers sued Sony, claiming breach of express warranty. They argued that Sony expressly promised that the PS3 and all of its features would work for ten years, but later unilaterally took away a fundamental product feature after only four years. The district court dismissed the claim, reasoning that the company's statements did not amount to express warranties. The plaintiffs appealed.

You Be the Judge:
Argument for Sony: Your honors, let's examine what Sony promised: The company predicted that the PS3 console would have a ten-year lifespan. That statement is not the same as a promise that all of the PS3's features would be available for that entire time period. Sony's statements only promise a ten-year lifespan for the PS3 itself. Moreover, Sony's license agreement and terms of service clearly informed consumers that updates "may cause some loss of functionality." It is clear that Sony's express warranty did not extend to all of the product's features.

Argument for PS3 Owners: Sony explicitly touted the PS3 as being with the consumer for "another ten years." It also promoted its fundamental features: the PSN and the Other OS. Any reasonable consumer would construe a promise of a ten-year product lifespan to extend to all of its features. And this was the basis of the bargain between Sony and its PS3 consumers. Imagine if the manufacturer of a hybrid car suddenly disabled the vehicle's electric feature, making it function solely on gasoline—years after it was sold. That manufacturer's switcheroo would change the fundamental nature of the product in the consumer's hands. This is what Sony did. And that is a breach of an express warranty.

22-5b Implied Warranties

Sean decides to plow driveways during the winter. Emily sells him a snowplow and installs it on his truck, but she makes no promises about its performance. When winter arrives, Sean has plenty of business, but he finds that the plow cannot be raised or lowered whenever the temperature falls below 40 degrees. He demands a refund from Emily, but she declines, saying, "I never said that thing would work in the winter. Tough luck." Is she off the hook? No. It is true she made no express warranties. But many sales are covered by implied warranties.

Implied warranties are those created by the UCC itself, not by any act or statement of the seller. The Code's drafters concluded that goods should generally meet certain standards of quality, regardless of what the seller did or did not say. So the UCC creates both an implied warranty of merchantability and an implied warranty of fitness.

Implied Warranty of Merchantability

This is the most important warranty in the UCC. Buyers, whether individual consumers or billion-dollar corporations, are more likely to rely on this than any other section. Sellers must understand it thoroughly when they market goods. **Unless excluded or modified, a warranty that the goods are merchantable is implied in a contract for their sale if the seller is a merchant with respect to goods of that kind. Merchantable** means that the goods are fit for the ordinary purposes for which they are used.[13] This rule contains several important principles:

- *Unless excluded or modified* means that the seller does have a chance to escape this warranty. We later discuss what steps a seller may take if she wants to sell goods that are *not* merchantable.

- *Merchantability* requires that goods be fit for their normal purposes. To be merchantable, a ladder must be able to rest securely against a building and support someone who is climbing it. The ladder need not be serviceable as a boat ramp.

- *Implied* means that the law itself imposes this liability on the seller even if it is not written down.

- *A merchant with respect to goods of that kind* means that the seller is someone who routinely deals in these goods or holds himself out as having special knowledge about such goods. When selling vehicles, a car dealer is acting as a merchant, but an accountant who sells his used car by listing it online is not.

Merchantable
The goods are fit for the ordinary purpose for which they are used.

Dacor Corp. manufactured and sold scuba diving equipment. It ordered air hoses from Sierra Precision, specifying the exact size and couplings so that the hose would fit tightly and safely into Dacor's oxygen units. Within about one year, customers returned a dozen Dacor units, complaining that the hose connections had cracked or sheared and were unusable. Dacor recalled 16,000 units and refit them with safe hoses, at a cost of more than $136,000. Dacor sued Sierra, claiming a breach of the implied warranty of merchantability. The Illinois court ruled that Sierra was a merchant with respect to scuba hoses because it routinely manufactured and sold them. Further, the court ruled that since use of the faulty hose assemblies under water would be life-threatening, they were clearly not fit for the purpose for which they were sold—which was, after all, scuba diving! The court ordered Sierra to pay the cost of Dacor's recall.[14]

The scuba equipment was not merchantable because a properly made scuba hose should never crack under normal use. But what if the product being sold is food, and the food contains something that is harmful—yet quite normal?

GOODMAN V. WENCO FOODS, INC.

333 N.C. 1
North Carolina Supreme Court, 1992

Facts: Fred Goodman and a friend stopped for lunch at a Wendy's restaurant in Hillsborough, North Carolina. Goodman had eaten about half of his double hamburger when he bit down and felt immediate pain in his lower jaw. He took from his mouth a one-half-inch piece of cow bone, along with several pieces of his teeth. Goodman's pain was intense, and his dental repairs took months.

---

[13]UCC §2-314(1).
[14]Dacor Corp. v. Sierra Precision, 19 F.3d 21 (7th Cir. 1994).

The restaurant purchased all of its meat from Greensboro Meat Supply Company (GMSC). Wendy's required its meat to be chopped and "free from bone or cartilage in excess of 1/8 inch in any dimension." GMSC beef was inspected continuously by state regulators and was certified by the United States Department of Agriculture (USDA). The USDA considered any bone fragment less than three-quarters of an inch long to be "insignificant."

Goodman sued, claiming a breach of the implied warranty of merchantability. The trial court dismissed the claim, ruling that the bone was natural to the food and that the hamburger was therefore fit for its ordinary purpose. The appeals court reversed this ruling, holding that a hamburger could be unfit even if the bone occurred naturally. Wendy's appealed to the state's highest court.

Issue: *Was the hamburger unfit for its ordinary purpose?*

Excerpts from Justice Exum's Decision: We hold that when a substance in food causes injury to a consumer, it is not a bar to recovery against the seller that the substance was "natural" to the food, provided that the substance's presence should not reasonably have been anticipated by the consumer.

A one-half-inch, inflexible bone shaving is indubitably "inherent" in or "natural" to a cut of beef, but whether it is so "natural" to hamburger as to put a consumer on his guard—whether it "is to be reasonably expected by the consumer"—is, in most cases, a question for the jury. We are not requiring that the respondent's hamburgers be perfect, only that they be fit for their intended purpose. It is difficult to conceive of how a consumer might guard against the type of injury present here, short of removing the hamburger from its bun, breaking it apart and inspecting its small components.

Wendy's argues that the evidence supported its contention that its hamburger complied with [legal] standards. Wendy's reasons that [regulators permit] some bone fragments in meat and that its hamburgers are therefore merchantable as a matter of law. The court of appeals rejected this argument, noting that compliance "with all state and federal regulations is only some evidence which the jury may consider in determining whether the product was merchantable." We agree.

We thus conclude, as did the court of appeals majority, that a jury could reasonably determine the meat to be of such a nature and the bone in the meat of such a size that a consumer should not reasonably have anticipated the bone's presence. The court of appeals therefore properly reversed the directed verdict for Wendy's on plaintiff's implied warranty of merchantability claim.

Implied Warranty of Fitness for a Particular Purpose

The other warranty that the UCC imposes on sellers is the implied warranty of fitness for a particular purpose. This cumbersome name is often shortened and referred to as simply the *warranty of fitness*. **Where the seller at the time of contracting *knows* about a particular purpose for which the buyer wants the goods, and knows that the buyer is relying on the seller's skill or judgment, there is (unless excluded or modified) an implied warranty that the goods shall be fit for the purpose.**[15] Here are the key points:

- **Particular purpose.** The seller must know about some *special* use that the buyer plans for the goods. For example, if a lumber salesman knows that a builder is purchasing lumber to construct houses in a swamp, the UCC implies a warranty that the lumber will withstand water.

- **Seller's skill.** The buyer must be depending upon the seller's skill or judgment in selecting the product, and the seller must know it. Suppose the builder says to the lumber salesman, "I need four-by-eights that I will be using to build a house in the swamp. What do you have that will do the job?" The builder's reliance is obvious, and the warranty is established. By contrast, suppose that an experienced Alaskan sled driver offers to buy your three huskies, telling you she plans to use them to pull sleds. She has the experience and you do not, and if the dogs refuse to pull more than a one-pound can of dog food, you have probably not breached the implied warranty of fitness.

- **Exclusion or modification.** Once again, the seller is allowed to modify or exclude any warranty of fitness.

---
[15]UCC §2-315.

Two Last Warranties: Title and Infringement

Strapped for cash, Maggie steals her boyfriend's rusty Chevy and sells it to Paul for $2,500. As we saw earlier in this chapter, Maggie gets no valid title by her theft, and therefore Paul receives no title either. When the boyfriend finds his car parked at a nightclub, he notifies the police and gets his wheels back. Poor Paul is out of pocket $2,500 and has no car to show for it. That clearly is unjust, and the UCC provides Paul with a remedy: **The seller of goods warrants that her title is valid and that the goods are free of any security interest that the buyer knows nothing about, unless the seller has clearly excluded or modified this warranty.**[16] Once again, the Code is imposing a warranty on any seller except those who explicitly exclude or modify it. When Maggie sells the car to Paul, she warrants her valid title to the car and simultaneously breaches that warranty since she obviously has no title. If he can find her, Paul will win a lawsuit against Maggie for $2,500.

The same Code section imposes what it calls an infringement warranty. This warranty means that, **unless otherwise agreed, a seller who is a merchant warrants that the goods are free of any rightful claim of copyright, patent, or trademark infringement.**[17]

Wesley sells to Komputer Corp. a device that automatically blasts purple smoke out of a computer screen anytime a student's paper is really dreadful. Unless Komputer Corp. agrees otherwise, Wesley is automatically giving the buyer a warranty that no one else invented the device or has any copyright, patent, or trademark in it.

22-5c Warranty Disclaimers

The Code permits a seller to *disclaim* some express or implied warranties. A disclaimer is a statement that a particular warranty *does not* apply.

Disclaimer
A statement that a particular warranty does not apply

Oral Express Warranties

Under the Code, a seller may disclaim an oral express warranty. Suppose Traffic Co. wants to buy a helicopter from HeliCorp for use in reporting commuter traffic. HeliCorp's salesman tells Traffic Co., "Don't worry, you can fly this bird day and night for six months with nothing more than a fuel stop." HeliCorp's contract may disclaim the oral warranty. The contract could say, "HeliCorp's entire warranty is printed below. Any statements made by any agent or salesperson are disclaimed and form no part of this contract." That disclaimer is valid. If the helicopter requires routine servicing between flights, HeliCorp has not breached an oral warranty.

Would you fly in a helicopter protected by an oral express warranty?

Written Express Warranties

This is the one type of warranty that is almost impossible to disclaim. **If a seller includes an express warranty in the *sales contract*, any disclaimer is definitely invalid.** Suppose HeliCorp sells an industrial helicopter for use in hauling building equipment. The sales contract describes the aircraft as "operable to 14,000 feet." Later, the warranty section of the contract specifically disclaims,

[16]UCC §2-312(1).
[17]UCC §2-313(3).

"any other warranties or statements that appear in this document or in any other document." That disclaimer is invalid and does not cancel the assurance that the helicopter can operate to 14,000 feet. The Code will not permit a seller to take contradictory positions in a document. The goal is simply to be fair, and the UCC assumes that it is confusing and unjust for a seller to say one thing to help close a deal and the opposite to limit its losses.[18]

What if the express written statement is in a different document, such as a sales brochure? The disclaimer is void if it would *unfairly surprise* the buyer. Assume, again, that HeliCorp promises a helicopter that requires no routine maintenance for six months, but this time, the promise appears in a sales brochure that Traffic Co. reads and relies on. If HeliCorp attempts to disclaim the written warranty, it will probably fail. Most people take written information seriously, and courts usually find that consumers would be unfairly surprised if a company tried to go back on promises made in a sales brochure.

Implied Warranties

A seller may disclaim the implied warranty of merchantability provided he *actually mentions the word* merchantability *and makes the disclaimer conspicuous.* Courts demand to see the specific word *merchantability* in the disclaimer to be sure the buyer realized she was giving up this fundamental protection. If the word is there, and the disclaimer is conspicuous enough that the buyer should have seen it, she has forfeited the warranty. A seller may disclaim the implied warranty of fitness with any language that is clear and conspicuous.

To make life easier, the Code permits a seller to disclaim *all* implied warranties by conspicuously stating that the goods are sold "as is" or "with all faults." Notice the tension between this provision and the one just discussed. A seller who wants to disclaim *only* the warranty of merchantability must explicitly mention that term; but a seller wishing to exclude *all* implied warranties may do so with a short expression, such as "sold as is."

Many states, though, prohibit a seller from disclaiming implied warranties in the sale of consumer goods. In these states, if a home furnishings store sells a bunk bed to a consumer, and the top bunk tips out the window on the first night, the seller is liable. Even if the sales contract clearly stated "no warranties of merchantability," the court would reject the clause and find that the seller breached the implied warranty of merchantability.

EXAM Strategy

Question: Marcos's backyard pool, which measured 35 feet by 18 feet, needed a new filter. A sales brochure stated, "This filter will keep any normal backyard pool, up to 50 feet by 25, clean and healthy all summer for a minimum of 5 years." Marcos signed a sales contract, which included this disclaimer: "The filter will work to normal industry standards. This is the only warranty. No other statements, written or oral, apply. Pools vary widely, and the Seller cannot guarantee any specific level of performance or cleanliness. Buyer agrees to this disclaimer." The filter failed to keep Marcos's pool clean, and he sued for breach of warranty. Who should win?

Strategy: Sellers are often able to disclaim oral warranties, but usually not written ones. Here, the initial promise and the disclaimer were in different documents. Does that change the outcome? Finally, Marcos was a consumer. Courts treat consumers differently from corporate buyers.

---

[18]UCC § 2-316(1).

Result: It is difficult or impossible for sellers to disclaim written warranties, even if the promise and disclaimer are in different documents. A disclaimer that would unfairly surprise the buyer is void. Marcos relied on the sales brochure—as the company intended—and the seller will probably lose. Furthermore, most states give extra protection to consumers, knowing that they are less sophisticated buyers. A court is likely to find in favor of Marcos based on the seller's express warranty, as well as the implied warranties of merchantability and fitness.

22-5d Remedy Limitations

The seller may also limit the buyer's *remedy,* which means that, even if there is a breach of warranty, the buyer still may have only a very limited chance to recover against the seller. Simon Aerials, Inc., manufactured boomlifts, the huge cranes used to construct multistoried buildings. Simon agreed to design and build eight unusually large machines for Logan Equipment Corp. Simon delivered the boomlifts late, and they functioned poorly. Logan requested dozens of repairs and modifications, which Simon attempted to accomplish over many months, but the equipment never worked well. Logan gave up and sued for $7.5 million, representing the profits it expected to make from renting the machines and the damage to its reputation. Logan clearly had suffered major losses, and it recovered—nothing. How could that be?

Simon had negotiated a **limitation of remedy clause,** by which the parties may limit or exclude the normal remedies permitted under the UCC.[19] These important rights are entirely distinct from disclaimers. A disclaimer limits the seller's warranties and thus affects whether the seller has breached her contract in the first place. A remedy limitation, by contrast, states that if a party *does* breach its warranty, the injured party will not get all of the damages the Code normally allows.

In its contract, Simon had agreed to repair or replace any defective boomlifts, but that was all. The agreement said that if a boomlift was defective, and Logan lost business, profits, and reputation, Simon was not liable. The court upheld the remedy limitation. Since Simon had repeatedly attempted to repair and redesign the defective machines, it had done everything it promised to do. Logan got nothing.[20]

Limitation of remedy clause

Contract clause allowing parties to limit or exclude applicable UCC remedies

Consequential Damages

Simon's contract clause is typical: Many sellers exclude liability for consequential damages, which can be so vast and unpredictable. Recall that a party injured by breach of contract normally gets direct, or *compensatory* damages.[21] In the sale of goods, that means the difference between the value of the goods promised and those actually delivered. A seller can anticipate and probably tolerate such damages since the seller understands exactly how much it costs to repair or replace the goods it has sold.

Consequential damages, however, are different. They are losses stemming from the buyer's particular circumstances. The buyer might have entered into dozens of contracts in reliance on the goods it expects from the seller. The seller will have no way of knowing how great the consequential damages could be. Logan Equipment claimed that it would have earned profits in the millions, and it was just such a claim that Simon had determined to avoid.

Consequential damages

Contract damages resulting as an indirect consequence of the breach

---

[19]UCC §2-719. A few states prohibit remedy limitations, but most permit them.

[20]Logan Equipment Corp. v. Simon Aerials, Inc., 736 F. Supp. 1188 (D. Mass. 1990).

[21]Compensatory, consequential, and incidental damages are discussed in Chapter 19, on remedies.

Notice that there is one major restriction on limitation of remedy clauses: **An exclusion of consequential damages is void if it is unconscionable.** The word *unconscionable* means that a remedy restriction is shockingly one-sided and fundamentally unfair. If the buyer is a consumer, a court will be likelier to consider such an exclusion unfair since the typical consumer will not understand the terms and may never even notice them.

If the buyer is a consumer who suffers a *personal injury*, a court is nearly certain to reject an exclusion for consequential damages. It is unfair for a corporation to market defective goods and escape liability because an unsuspecting consumer failed to understand contract language. Suppose Byron buys a hot-air popcorn popper that comes with a label that attempts to limit remedies. Byron is seriously burned when the popper ignites. Virtually all courts will ignore the label and permit Byron to recover his full damages, which in his case, might include such consequential items as lost wages or the cost of the nonrefundable airline ticket for the trip he cannot take as a result of the breach.

However, when the buyer is a corporation, courts assume it had adequate legal advice and an opportunity to reject unacceptable terms. When two companies agree to a remedy limitation, they are allocating the risk of loss as one part of their bargain. A court will seldom substitute its judgment for that of the contracting companies. In the *Logan Equipment* case, both parties were corporations, and sophisticated executives negotiated the boomlift sale. The court found nothing unconscionable in the bargain and enforced the limitation that the parties had agreed to.[22]

22-5e Privity

When two parties contract, they are *in privity*. If Lance buys a chainsaw from the local hardware store, he is in privity with the store. But Lance has no privity with Kwiksaw, the manufacturer of the chainsaw. Under traditional contract law, a plaintiff injured by a breach of contract could sue only a defendant with whom he had privity. So, many years ago, if Lance's chainsaw had been seriously defective, he could have sued only the store. Kwiksaw would have had no liability because it was not in privity with Lance. This rule hurt consumers because the local retailer often had fewer assets to compensate for serious injuries. Today, privity is gradually disappearing as a defense. Various states are approaching the issue in different ways, so there is no single rule. We can, however, highlight the trends.

Personal Injury

Where a product causes a personal injury, most states permit a warranty lawsuit even without privity. If the chain on Lance's power saw flies off and slashes his arm, he has suffered a personal injury. Of course, he may sue the store, with which he has privity. But he will want to sue the manufacturer, which has more money. In the majority of states, he will be able to sue the manufacturer for breach of warranty even though he had no privity with it. (Note that Lance is sure to make other claims against the manufacturer, including negligence and strict liability, both discussed in Chapter 9.)

Economic Loss

If the buyer suffers only economic loss, privity may still be required to bring a suit for breach of warranty. **If the buyer is a business, the majority of states require privity.** Fab-Rik makes fabric for furniture and drapes, which it sells to various wholesalers. Siddown makes sofas. Siddown buys Fab-Rik fabric from a wholesaler and, after installing it on

---

[22]Logan Equipment, 736 F. Supp. at 1195.

200 sofas, finds the material defective. Siddown may sue the wholesaler but, in most states, will be unable to sue Fab-Rik for breach of any warranties. There was no privity.

By contrast, when the buyer is a *consumer*, more states will permit a suit against the manufacturer, even without privity. Lance, the consumer, buys his power saw to landscape his property. This time, the saw malfunctions without injuring him, but Lance must buy a replacement for considerably more money. Many states—but not all—will permit him to recover his losses from Kwiksaw, the manufacturer, on the theory that Kwiksaw intends its product to reach consumers and is in the best position to control losses.

In the following case, a jailhouse tragedy prompts a product liability suit.

REED v. CITY OF CHICAGO

263 F.Supp.2d 1123
United States District Court for the Northern District of Illinois, 2003

Facts: J. C. Reed was arrested and brought to Chicago's Fifth District Police Station. Police were allegedly aware that he was suicidal, having seen him slash his wrists earlier. They removed his clothing and dressed him in a paper isolation gown. Sadly, Reed used the gown to hang himself.

Reed's mother, on his behalf, sued the police (for failing to monitor a suicidal inmate) and also Cypress Medical Products, the manufacturer of the isolation gown. The claim was that the gown should have been made of material that would tear if someone attempted to hang himself with it. Cypress moved to dismiss the suit, claiming that Reed had no privity with the company.

Issue: *Could Reed maintain a lawsuit against Cypress despite lack of privity?*

Excerpts from Judge Moran's Decision: The single issue we must decide is whether plaintiff, as a non-purchaser, can recover from the manufacturer and designer of the gown for breach of warranty. Historically, Illinois law has required privity. Lack of privity occurs when a user of the product, beside the purchaser, is injured. Section 2-318 of the Uniform Commercial Code (UCC), as adopted by the Illinois legislature, contains mandatory exceptions to the general requirement of privity:

> A seller's warranty whether express or implied extends to any natural person who is in the family or household of his buyer or who is a guest in his home if it is reasonable to expect that such person may use, consume or be affected by the goods and who is injured in person by breach of the warranty.

The Illinois Supreme Court has determined that privity is no longer an absolute requirement for breach of warranty actions. While section 2-318 lists specific exceptions to the privity requirement, Illinois courts have noted that this list is not necessarily exhaustive.

The vast majority of cases examining the limits of section 2-318 in Illinois have dealt with the employment context, expanding the class of potential breach of warranty plaintiffs to employees of the ultimate purchaser. In [a case called *Whitaker*,] plaintiff was injured while using a bandsaw that had been purchased by his employer. The court determined that the employee was essentially a third party beneficiary to the sale in that the employee's safety while using the bandsaw was "either explicitly or implicitly part of the basis of the bargain when the employer purchased the goods."

In cases examining the limits of section 2-318 in other contexts, courts have been reluctant to find additional exceptions to the privity requirement. In [a case called *Hemphill*,] the court refused to allow a breach of warranty claim by a university football player against the manufacturer of his helmet.

While no Illinois courts have expanded the plaintiff class for breach of warranty actions beyond employees, we believe that the law requires us to do so here. The beneficiary of any warranty made by the manufacturer and designer of the gown is necessarily a potentially suicidal detainee like Reed. If protection is not provided to plaintiffs like Reed, any warranty as to the safety of the gown would have little, if any, effect. In designing and manufacturing the gown, defendants contemplated that the users of the gown would be detainees. More-over, the safety of these detainees was necessarily a part of the bargain, whether explicitly or implicitly, between the seller and buyer. For these reasons, a detainee of the City like Reed must be able to enforce the protections of any warranties made by the manufacturer and designer of the gown.

For the foregoing reasons, defendants' motion to dismiss is denied.

22-5f Buyer's Misuse

Misuse by the buyer will generally preclude a warranty claim. Common sense tells us that the seller only warrants its goods if they are properly used. Lord & Taylor warranted that its false eyelashes would function well and cause no harm. But when Ms. Caldwell applied them, they severely irritated one eye. She sued, but the store prevailed. Why? Caldwell applied the eyelashes improperly, getting the glue into one eye. On her other eye, she used the product correctly and suffered no harm. Her misuse proved painful to her eye—and fatal to her lawsuit.[23]

22-5g Statute of Limitations and Notice of Breach

It is right that a seller be responsible for the goods it places in the market. On the other hand, a seller should not face potential liability *forever*. A company cannot be a perpetual insurer for goods that it sold decades earlier. So, the UCC imposes two important time limits on a buyer's claim of breach.

The Code sets a four-year statute of limitations. This means that the buyer must bring any lawsuit for breach of a warranty no later than four years after the goods were delivered. The Code puts an additional burden on a buyer asserting a breach of warranty. **The UCC requires that a buyer notify the seller of defects within a reasonable time.**[24] The purpose here is to enable the seller to cure, by repairing or replacing, any problems with the goods. Ideally, a seller that receives notice of a potential breach will fix the problem and there will *be* no lawsuit.

The circumstances will determine what is a "reasonable" amount of time. An inexperienced consumer could reasonably take many months to figure out that a new laptop computer had a serious operating defect. Further, a delay of six or eight months would not harm a large computer manufacturer. On the other hand, a corporate buyer of perishable food products must act very quickly if it wishes to claim the goods are defective.

Chapter Conclusion

Bad things happen. Deals fall through. Goods disappear. Products injure. Unfortunately, people often fail to consider these possibilities when making a contract. In that case, the UCC steps in with default rules that address critical issues in commercial transactions, such as when an insurable interest exists, the risk of loss shifts, and warranties are made. But these default rules will not always be in a party's best interest. Fortunately, the UCC gives buyers and sellers the freedom to change its default settings. Businesspeople who understand the UCC can tailor the rules to their own advantage. Armed with this chapter's information, they will know how and when to alter the UCC's rules to suit their business purposes and protect themselves if and when bad things *do* happen.

EXAM REVIEW

1. **INTEREST AND TITLE**   An *interest* is a legal right in something. *Title* means the normal rights of ownership.

---

[23]Caldwell v. Lord & Taylor, Inc., 142 Ga. App. 137 (Ga. Ct. App. 1977).
[24]UCC § 2-067.

2. **IDENTIFICATION**   Goods must *exist* and be *identified* to the contract before title can pass. The parties may agree in their contract how and when they will identify goods; if they do not specify, the Code stipulates when it happens. The parties may also state when title passes, and once again, if they do not, the Code provides rules.

Question: On September 10, Bell Corp. entered into a contract to purchase 50 lamps from Glow Manufacturing. Bell prepaid 40 percent of the purchase price. Glow became insolvent on September 19 before segregating, in its inventory, the lamps to be delivered to Bell. Bell will not be able to recover the lamps because:

a. Bell is regarded as a merchant.

b. The lamps were not identified to the contract.

c. Glow became insolvent fewer than 10 days after receipt of Bell's prepayment.

d. Bell did not pay the full price at the time of purchase.

Strategy: In analyzing issues about ownership, remember that title can never change hands until the goods have been identified to the contract. Identification can occur in three ways: the parties describe specific goods that already exist, animals are conceived or crops planted, or the seller marks, ships, or otherwise indicates which are going to the buyer. (See the "Result" at the end of this section.)

3. **INSURABLE INTEREST**   A buyer obtains an *insurable interest* when the goods are identified to the contract. A seller retains an insurable interest in goods as long as she has either title or a security interest in them.

4. **VOID AND VOIDABLE TITLE**   *Void title* is no title at all. *Voidable title* means limited rights in the goods, inferior to those of the owner. A person with voidable title has power to transfer good title to a *bona fide purchaser (BFP);* that is, someone who purchases in good faith, for value.

5. **ENTRUSTING**   Any *entrusting* of goods to a merchant who deals in goods of that kind gives him the power to transfer all rights of the entruster to a buyer in the ordinary course of business.

6. **BIOC**   A buyer in the ordinary course of business generally takes goods free and clear of any security interest.

Question: Fay Witcher owned a Ford Bronco. Steve Risher operated a used car lot. Witcher delivered his automobile to Risher, asking him to resell it if he could. Witcher specified that he wanted all cash for his car, not cash plus a trade-in. Risher sold the car to Richard Parker for $12,800, but he took a trade-in as part payment. Risher promised to deliver the Bronco's certificate of title to Parker

EXAM Strategy

EXAM Strategy

within a few days but never did. He was also obligated to deliver proceeds of the sale to Witcher, and, of course, he failed to do that. Parker claimed that the car was rightfully his. Witcher argued that Parker owned nothing because he never got the title and because Witcher never got his money. Who loses?

Strategy: Any *entrusting* of goods to a merchant who deals in goods of that kind gives him the power to transfer all rights of the entruster to a buyer in the ordinary course of business. A buyer in the ordinary course of business generally takes goods free and clear of any security interest. Did Witcher entrust the auto? Was Parker a BIOC? Why or why not? (See the "Result" at the end of this section.)

7. **RISK OF LOSS**   In their contract, the parties may allocate the *risk of loss* any way they wish. If they fail to do so, the Code provides several steps to determine who pays for any damage. When neither party has breached, the risk of loss generally passes from seller to buyer when the seller has transported the goods as far as he is obligated to. When a party has breached, the risk of loss generally lies with the party that has breached.

EXAM Strategy

Question: Bradkeyne International, Ltd., an English company, bought a large quantity of batteries from Duracell, Inc. The contract specified delivery "FOB cargo ship, Jacksonville, Florida." Duracell supervised the loading of the batteries onto a ship in Jacksonville in early July, and they arrived in England in August. When loaded onto the ship, the batteries were conforming goods that could be used for normal purposes. But on board the ship, excessive heat damaged them. By the time they reached England, they were worth only a fraction of the original price. Bradkeyne sued Duracell. Who loses?

Strategy: The advantage of standard shipping terms is that they make business predictable and exam questions easy. If you know what "FOB cargo ship, Jacksonville, Florida" means, you know the answer. (See the "Result" at the end of this section.)

8. **EXPRESS WARRANTY**   Seller can create an express warranty with any affirmation description of the goods, or sample or model, provided the promise part of the basis of the bargain.

9. **IMPLIED WARRANTY OF MERCHANTABILITY**   With certain exceptions, the Code implies a warranty that the goods will be fit for their ordinary purpose.

10. **IMPLIED WARRANTY OF FITNESS FOR A PARTICULAR PURPOSE**   With some exceptions, the Code implies a warranty that the goods are fit for the buyer's special purpose, provided that the seller knows of that purpose when the contract is made and knows of the buyer's reliance.

---

2. Result: The contract was silent about which goods were involved, neither animals nor plants were involved, and Glow never segregated the lamps. The lamps were never identified to the contract, and the correct answer is (b).

6. Result: Risher was a merchant dealing in automobiles, meaning that Witcher did entrust the car to him. Parker was a BIOC: He acted in good faith, without knowing that the sale violated the agreement between Witcher and Risher. Parker wins, and he keeps the car.

7. Result: "FOB cargo ship, Jacksonville, Florida" means that the seller bears all risks until the goods are placed in the carrier's possession. From that moment onward, the buyer bears the risk. The batteries were fine when delivered, so Duracell was off the hook once they were on board. Bradkeyne bears the loss.

MULTIPLE-CHOICE QUESTIONS

1. *CPA QUESTION* On Monday, Wolfe paid Aston Co., a furniture retailer, $500 for a table. On Thursday, Aston notified Wolfe that the table was ready to be picked up. On Saturday, while Aston was still in possession of the table, it was destroyed in a fire. Who bears the loss of the table?

   (a) Wolfe, because Wolfe had title to the table at the time of loss

   (b) Aston, unless Wolfe is a merchant

   (c) Wolfe, unless Aston breached the contract

   (d) Aston, because Wolfe had not yet taken possession of the table

2. Sheri signs a contract with Farmer Charlie on February 1. Under the deal, she will pay $25,000 for Charlie's entire pumpkin crop on October 1. Charlie plants pumpkin seeds on March 1, and they begin to sprout on April 1. When are the pumpkins identified?

   (a) February 1

   (b) March 1

   (c) April 1

   (d) October 1

3. Sam obtains a Patek Philippe watch from Greg by fraud. It has a retail price of $10,000. He sells it to Melissa for $9,000. She believes he owns the watch. Melissa _____ a bona fide purchaser. Sam disappears. If Greg discovers that she has the watch and demands that it be returned, Melissa _____ have to give the watch to Greg.

   (a) is; will

   (b) is; will not

   (c) is not; will

   (d) is not; will not

4. *CPA QUESTION* Vick bought a used boat from Ocean Marina that disclaimed "any and all warranties." Ocean was unaware the boat had been stolen from Kidd. Vick surrendered it to Kidd when confronted with proof of the theft. Vick sued Ocean. Who prevails?

   (a) Vick, because the implied warranty of title has been breached

   (b) Vick, because a merchant cannot disclaim implied warranties

   (c) Ocean, because of the disclaimer of warranties

   (d) Ocean, because Vick surrendered the boat to Kidd

5. *CPA QUESTION* Which of the following conditions must be met for an implied warranty of fitness for a particular purpose to arise?

   I. The warranty must be in writing.

   II. The seller must know that the buyer was relying on the seller in selecting the goods.

   (a) I only

   (b) II only

   (c) Both I and II

   (d) Neither I nor II

6. *CPA QUESTION* Under the UCC sales article, an action for breach of the implied warranty of merchantability by a party who sustains personal injuries may be successful against the seller of the product only when:

   (a) The seller is a merchant of the product involved.

   (b) An action based on negligence can also be successfully maintained.

   (c) The injured party is in privity of contract with the seller.

   (d) An action based on strict liability in tort can also be successfully maintained.

CASE QUESTIONS

1. Franklin Miller operated Miller Seed Co. in Pea Ridge, Arkansas. He bought, processed, and sold fescue seed, which is used for growing pasture and fodder grass. Farmers brought seed to Miller, who would normally clean, bag, and store it. In some cases, the farmers authorized Miller to sell the seed, in some cases not. Miller mixed together the seed that was for sale with the seed in storage so that a customer could not see any difference between them. Miller defaulted on a $380,000 loan from the First State Bank of Purdy. First State attempted to seize all of the seed in the store. Tony Havelka, a farmer, protested that his 490,000 pounds of seed was merely in storage and not subject to First State's claim. Who is entitled to the seed?

2. John C. Clark, using an alias, rented a Lexus from Alamo Rent-A-Car in San Diego, California. Clark never returned the car to Alamo and obtained a California "quick title" using forged signatures. He then advertised in the *Las Vegas Review Journal* newspaper and sold the car to Terry and Yvonne Mendenhall for $34,000 in cash. The Mendenhalls made improvements to the car, had it insured, smog- and safety-tested, registered, licensed, and titled in the state of Utah. When Alamo reported the car stolen,

the Nevada Department of Motor Vehicles seized the auto and returned it to Alamo. The Mendenhalls sued Alamo. The trial court concluded that the Mendenhalls had purchased the car for value and without notice that it was stolen, and so they were bona fide purchasers entitled to the Lexus. Alamo appealed. Please rule.

3. Universal Consolidated Cos. contracted with China Metallurgical Import and Export Corp. (CMIEC) to provide CMIEC with new and used equipment for a cold rolling steel mill. Universal then contracted with Pittsburgh Industrial Furnace Co. (Pifcom) to engineer and build much of the equipment. The contract required Pifcom to deliver the finished equipment to a trucking company, which would then transport it to Universal. Pifcom delivered the goods to the trucking company as scheduled. But before all of the goods reached Universal, CMIEC notified Universal it was canceling the deal. Universal, in turn, notified Pifcom to stop work, but all goods had been delivered to the shipper and ultimately reached Universal. Pifcom claimed that it retained title to the goods, but Universal claimed that title had passed to it. Who is right?

4. *YOU BE THE JUDGE* **WRITING PROBLEM** Construction Helicopters paid Heli-Dyne Systems $315,000 for three helicopters that were in Argentina. Two were ready to fly, and one was disassembled for routine maintenance. The contract said nothing about risk of loss (the parties could have saved a lot of money by reading this chapter). Heli-Dyne arranged for an Argentine company to oversee their loading on board the freight ship *Lynx*. The two helicopters and 25 crates containing the disassembled craft were properly loaded, but when the ship arrived in Miami, only 7 of the crates appeared. Heli-Dyne refused to supply more parts, and Construction sued. Who bears the loss? **Argument for Construction:** Construction had no control over the goods until they reached Miami. Although we do not know exactly what happened to the crates, we know the one party that had *nothing* to do with the loss: Construction. The company should not pay for damage it never caused. **Argument for Heli-Dyne:** Because the contract failed to specify risk of loss, it is a shipment contract. In such an agreement, risk of loss passes to the buyer when the seller delivers the goods to a carrier. Heli-Dyne delivered the goods and has no further responsibility.

5. Leighton Industries needed steel pipe to build furnaces for a customer. Leighton sent Callier Steel an order for a certain quantity of "A 106 Grade B" steel. Callier confirmed the order and created a contract by sending an invoice to Leighton, stating that it would send "A 106 Grade B" steel, as ordered. Callier delivered the steel, and Leighton built the furnaces, but they leaked badly and required rebuilding. Tests demonstrated that the steel was not in fact "A 106 Grade B," but an inferior steel. Leighton sued. Who wins?

6. Boboli Co. wanted to promote its "California-style" pizza, which it sold in supermarkets. The company contracted with Highland Group, Inc., to produce 2 million recipe brochures, which would be inserted in the carton when the freshly baked pizza was still very hot. Highland contracted with Comark Merchandising to print the brochures. But when Comark asked for details concerning the pizza, the carton, and so forth, Highland refused to supply the information. Comark printed the first lot of 72,000 brochures, which Highland delivered to Boboli. Unfortunately, the hot bread caused the ink to run, and customers opening the carton often found red or blue splotches on their pizzas. Highland refused to accept additional brochures, and Comark sued for breach of contract. Highland defended by claiming that Comark had breached its warranty of merchantability. Please comment.

DISCUSSION QUESTIONS

1. **ETHICS** Myrna and James Brown ordered a $35,000 motor home from R.V. Kingdom, Inc. The manufacturer delivered the vehicle to R.V. Kingdom, with title in the dealer's name. The Browns agreed to accept the motor home, but they soon regretted spending the money and asked R.V. Kingdom to resell it. The motor home stayed on R.V. Kingdom's lot for quite a few months, but when the Browns decided to come get it, they learned that R.V. Kingdom had illegally used the vehicle as collateral for a loan and that a bank had repossessed it. The Browns filed a claim with their insurance company, State Farm. The insurer agreed that the vehicle had been stolen and agreed that the Browns' policy covered newly acquired vehicles. But the company refused to pay, claiming that the Browns had not taken title or possession to the goods and therefore had no insurable interest. The Browns sued. Please rule on their case.

   Let's also look at the ethics of the case by creating a contrasting hypothetical. Suppose that among the insurance company's thousands of customers was Arvee, a recreational vehicle dealership similar to the one in the real case. Imagine that Arvee had taken in an automobile for resale from a customer named Parker and kept the vehicle on its lot. If Parker's auto were stolen, what argument would the insurance company be making? How would the company define insurable interest in *that* case?

2. Imagine that your laptop gets a virus, and you take it to a local computer repair shop. The shop sells your computer to Heidi. Under the entrustment rules in the UCC, Heidi is a buyer in the ordinary course of business. And so, even if you find Heidi and demand that she return your laptop, *she gets to keep it*. Is this fair? Does the law give too much protection to purchasers in this situation, and not enough to victims?

3. Greg manufactures and sells T-shirts. As a seller, would he be better off if his contracts indicated "FOB (place of shipment)" or "FOB (place of destination)"? Explain your answer.

4. A seller can disclaim all implied warranties by stating that goods are sold "as is" (or by using other, more specific language). Is this fair? The UCC's implied warranties seem reasonable—that goods are fit for their normal purposes, for example. Should it be so easy for sellers to escape their obligations?

5. After learning more about implied warranties and disclaimers, would you ever buy an item sold "as is?" Imagine a car salesman who offers you a car for $8,000, but who also says that he can knock the price down to $6,500 if you will buy the car "as is." If you live in a state that does not give consumers special protections, which deal would be more appealing?

Agency and Employment Law

CHAPTER 28

AGENCY LAW

Lauren Brenner had a great idea for a new kind of fitness studio in New York. Called Pure Power Boot Camp, Brenner's gym was modeled on a U.S. Marine training facility, with an indoor obstacle course, camouflage colors, and a rubber floor designed to look like dirt. Brenner's special insight was that people would be more likely to stick to an exercise regime if they worked out together in a small group. So she limited classes to 16 people (called "recruits") who went through the training program (a "tour of duty") together. Brenner also hired retired Marines as "drill instructors."

© Tomas Tichy/Shutterstock.com

Ruben Belliard, a retired Marine, was Pure Power's head drill instructor. On his recommendation, Brenner also hired Alexander Fell. But, as Brenner began plans to franchise her concept, the two men went to war against her. They decided to start their own copycat gym, which was to be called Warrior Fitness Boot Camp. Meanwhile, Fell began dating Jennifer Lee, a Pure Power client, which was wrong for two reasons: (1) Pure Power's policies prohibited instructors from dating clients, and (2) she was a business school grad, who helped the two men develop their competing business plan. (Clearly, she had been dozing through her business law class.)

> **As Brenner began plans to franchise her concept, the two men went to war against her.**

While still employed by Brenner, Belliard and Fell rented a gym space near Pure Power. Belliard stole copies of Pure Power's confidential customer list, business plan, and operations manuals. The two men sent marketing emails about Warrior to Pure Power's clients and even invited them to a cocktail party to announce Warrior Fitness's launch. On another front, Lee spread false rumors about Brenner—that she had fired an employee because he was gay.

Then one day at Pure Power, Fell openly defied Brenner's instructions, screaming at her that he dared her to fire him. She had little choice but to do so. Belliard then convinced her to fire another drill inspector. Two weeks later, Belliard quit without giving notice, intentionally leaving Brenner with only one drill instructor. Two months later, Fell and Belliard opened Warrior Fitness.

Thus far, this book has primarily dealt with issues of *individual* responsibility: What happens if *you* knock someone down or *you* sign an agreement? But most businesses need more than one worker. Certainly Lauren Brenner could not operate her business by herself.

That is where agency law comes in. It is concerned with your responsibility for the actions of others and their obligations to you. What happens if your agent assaults someone or signs a contract in your name? Or tries to leave with all of your clients?

Hiring other people presents a significant trade-off: If you do everything yourself, you have control over the result. But the size and scope of your business (and your life) will be severely limited. Once you bring in other people, both your risks and your rewards can increase immensely.

The Pure Power case highlights a common agency issue: If your employees decide to leave for greener pastures, what obligation do they owe you in that period before they actually walk out the door? The court's opinion is later in the chapter.

28-1 CREATING AN AGENCY RELATIONSHIP

Let's begin with two important definitions:

- **Principal:** A person who has someone else acting for him.

- **Agent:** A person who acts for someone else.

Principals have substantial liability for the actions of their agents.[1] Therefore, disputes about whether an agency relationship exists are not mere legal quibbles but important issues with potentially profound financial consequences.

In an agency relationship, someone (the agent) agrees to perform a task for, and under the control of, someone else (the principal). **To create an agency relationship, there must be:**

- a **principal** and

- an **agent,**

- who mutually **consent** that the agent will act on behalf of the principal and

- be subject to the principal's **control**

- thereby creating a **fiduciary relationship**.

Principal
In an agency relationship, the person for whom an agent is acting

Agent
In an agency relationship, the person who is acting on behalf of a principal

28-1a **Consent**

To establish consent, the principal must ask the agent to do something, and the agent must agree. In the most straightforward example, you ask a neighbor to walk your dog, and she agrees. Matters were more complicated, however, when Steven James met some friends one evening at a restaurant. During the two hours he was there, he drank four to six beers. (It is probably a bad sign that he cannot remember how many.) From then on, one misfortune piled upon another. After leaving the restaurant at about 7:00 p.m., James sped down a highway and crashed into a car that had stalled on the road, thereby killing the driver. James told the police at the scene that he had not seen the parked car (another bad sign). Evidently, James's lawyer was not as perceptive as the police in recognizing drunkenness. In a misguided attempt to help his client, James's lawyer took him to the local hospital for a blood test. Unfortunately, the test confirmed that James had indeed been drunk at the time of the accident.

---

[1]The word *principal* is always used when referring to a person. It is not to be confused with the word *principle*, which refers to a fundamental idea.

The attorney knew that if this evidence was admitted at trial, his client would soon be receiving free room and board from the Massachusetts Department of Corrections. So at trial, the lawyer argued that the blood test was protected by the client–attorney privilege because the hospital had been his agent and therefore a member of the defense team. The court disagreed, however, holding that the hospital employees were not agents for the lawyer because they had not consented to act in that role.

The court upheld James's conviction of murder in the first degree by reason of extreme atrocity or cruelty.[2]

28-1b Control

Principals are liable for an agent's acts because they exercise control over that person. If principals direct their agents to commit an act, it seems fair to hold the principal liable when that act causes harm. How would you apply that rule to the following situation?

William Stanford was an employee of the Agency for International Development. While on his way home to Pakistan to spend the holidays with his family, his plane was hijacked and taken to Iran, where he was killed. Stanford had originally purchased a ticket on Northwest Airlines but had traded it for a seat on Kuwait Airways (KA). The airlines had an agreement permitting passengers to exchange tickets from one to the other. Stanford's widow sued Northwest on the theory that KA was Northwest's agent. The court found, however, that no agency relationship existed because Northwest had no control over KA.[3] Northwest did not tell KA how to fly planes or handle terrorists; therefore, it should not be liable when KA made fatal errors. Not only must an agent and principal consent to an agency relationship, but the principal also must have control over the agent.

28-1c Fiduciary Relationship

A **fiduciary relationship** is one of trust: A trustee acts for the benefit of the beneficiary, always putting the interests of the beneficiary before his own. The beneficiary places special confidence in the fiduciary who, in turn, is obligated to act in good faith and candor, doing what is best for the beneficiary. **Agents have a fiduciary duty to their principals.**

All three elements—consent, control, and a fiduciary duty—are necessary to create an agency relationship. In some relationships, for example, there might be a *fiduciary duty* but no *control*. A trustee of a trust must act for the benefit of the beneficiaries, but the beneficiaries have no right to control the trustee. Therefore, a trustee is not an agent of the beneficiaries. *Consent* is present in every contractual relationship, but that does not necessarily mean that the two parties are agent and principal. If Horace sells his car to Lily, they both expect to benefit under the contract, but neither has a *fiduciary duty* to the other and neither *controls* the other, so there is no agency relationship.

28-1d Elements Not Required for an Agency Relationship

Consent, control, and a fiduciary relationship are necessary to establish an agency relationship. **The following elements are *not* required for an agency relationship:**

- **Written Agreement.** In most cases, an agency agreement does not have to be in writing. An oral understanding is valid, except in one circumstance—the **equal dignities rule**. According to this rule, if an agent is empowered to enter into a contract that must be in writing, then the appointment of the agent must also be written. For

Equal dignities rule

If an agent is empowered to enter into a contract that must be in writing, then the appointment of the agent must also be written.

---

[2]Commonwealth v. James, 427 Mass. 312 (S.J.C. MA 1998).
[3]Stanford v. Kuwait Airways Corp., 648 F. Supp. 1158 (S.D.N.Y. 1986).

example, under the Statute of Frauds, a contract for the sale of land is unenforceable unless in writing, so the agency agreement to sell land must also be in writing.

- **Formal Agreement.** The principal and agent need not agree formally that they have an agency relationship. They do not even have to utter the word *agent*. So long as they act like an agent and a principal, the law will treat them as such.

- **Compensation.** An agency relationship need not meet all the standards of contract law. For example, a contract is not valid without consideration, but an agency agreement is valid *even if the agent is not paid*.

28-2 DUTIES OF AGENTS TO PRINCIPALS

Agents owe a fiduciary duty to their principals. There are four elements to this duty.

28-2a Duty of Loyalty

An agent has a fiduciary duty to act loyally for the principal's benefit in all matters connected with the agency relationship.[4] The agent has an obligation to put the principal first, to strive to accomplish the principal's goals.

The following case reveals the outcome of the opening scenario.

PURE POWER BOOT CAMP, INC. v. WARRIOR FITNESS BOOT CAMP, LLC

813 F. Supp. 2d 489
United States District Court for the Southern District of New York, 2011

Facts: Based on the facts in the opening scenario, Brenner filed suit against Belliard and Fell, alleging that they had violated their duty of loyalty to her company.

Issue: *Did Belliard and Fell violate their duty of loyalty to Pure Power?*

Excerpts from Judge Katz's Decision: An agent is obligated under New York law to be loyal to his employer and is prohibited from acting in any manner inconsistent with his agency or trust and is at all times bound to exercise the utmost good faith and loyalty in the performance of his duties. This duty is not dependent upon an express contractual relationship, but exists even where the employment relationship is at-will.

When an employee uses an employer's proprietary or confidential information when establishing a competing business, the employee breaches his or her fiduciary duty to the employer. Although an employee may, of course, make preparations to compete with his employer while still working for the employer, he or she may not do so at the employer's expense, and may not use the employer's resources, time, facilities, or confidential information; specifically, whether or not the employee has signed an agreement not-to-compete, the employee, while still employed by the employer, may not solicit clients of his employer, may not copy his employer's business records for his own use, may not charge expenses to his employer, which were incurred while acting on behalf of his own interest, and may not actively divert the employer's business for his own personal benefit or the benefit of others. In addition, even in the absence of trade secret protection, employees are not permitted to copy their employer's client list, and such acts have been deemed to be an egregious breach of trust and confidence.

This ongoing and deliberate conduct, transpiring over the course of several months, constitutes a clear breach of the duty of loyalty owed by employees, Belliard and Fell, to their employer, Pure Power. [Belliard and Fell must pay Brenner $245,000.]

---

[4]Restatement (Third) of Agency §8.01.

The various components of the duty of loyalty follow.

Outside Benefits

An agent may not receive profits unless the principal knows and approves. Suppose that Hope is an employee of the agency Big Egos and Talents, Inc. (BEAT). She has been representing Robert Downey Jr. in his latest movie negotiations.[5] Downey often drives her to meetings in his new Aston Martin. He is so thrilled that she has arranged for him to star in the new movie *Little Men* that he buys her an Aston Martin. Can Hope keep this generous gift? Only with BEAT's permission. She must tell BEAT about the gift; the company may then take the vehicle itself or allow her to keep it.

Confidential Information

The ability to keep secrets is important in any relationship, but especially a fiduciary relationship. **Agents can neither disclose nor use for their own benefit any confidential information they acquire during their agency.** As the following case shows, this duty continues even after the agency relationship ends.

ABKCO MUSIC, INC. v. HARRISONGS MUSIC, LTD.

722 F.2d 988
United States Court of Appeals for the Second Circuit, 1983

Facts: Bright Tunes Music Corp. (Bright Tunes) owned the copyright to the song "He's So Fine," a chart-topping hit for the Chiffons. The company sued Beatle George Harrison alleging that his composition "My Sweet Lord" copied "He's So Fine." At the time the suit was filed, Allen B. Klein handled the business affairs of the Beatles.

Klein (representing Harrison) met with the president of Bright Tunes to discuss possible settlement of the copyright lawsuit. Klein suggested that Harrison might be interested in purchasing the copyright to "He's So Fine." Shortly thereafter, Klein's management contract with the Beatles expired. Without telling Harrison, Klein began negotiating with Bright Tunes to purchase the copyright to "He's So Fine" for himself. To advance these negotiations, Klein gave Bright Tunes information about royalty income for "My Sweet Lord"—information that he had gained as Harrison's agent.

The trial judge in the copyright case ultimately found that Harrison had infringed the copyright on "He's So Fine" and assessed damages of $1.6 million. After the trial, Klein purchased the "He's So Fine" copyright from Bright Tunes and with it, the right to recover from Harrison for his breach of copyright.

George Harrison, a few months after writing "My Sweet Lord."

Issue: *Did Klein violate his fiduciary duty to Harrison by using confidential information after the agency relationship terminated?*

Excerpts from Judge Pierce's Decision: There is no doubt that the relationship between Harrison and [Klein]

---

[5]Do not be confused by the fact that Hope works as an agent for movie stars. As an employee of BEAT, her duty is to the company. She is an agent of BEAT, and BEAT works for the celebrities.

prior to the termination of the management agreement was that of principal and agent, and that the relationship was fiduciary in nature. [A]n agent has a duty not to use confidential knowledge acquired in his employment in competition with his principal. This duty exists as well after the employment is terminated as during its continuance.

On the other hand, use of information based on general business knowledge or gleaned from general business experience is not covered by the rule, and the former agent is permitted to compete with his former principal in reliance on such general publicly available information. The evidence presented herein is not at all convincing that the information imparted to Bright Tunes by Klein was publicly available.

While the initial attempt to purchase [the copyright to "He's So Fine"] was several years removed from the eventual purchase on [Klein]'s own account, we are not of the view that such a fact rendered [Klein] unfettered in the later negotiations. Taking all of these circumstances together, we agree that [Klein's] conduct did not meet the standard required of him as a former fiduciary.

Ethics Both this case and *Pure Power* provide examples of agents who competed against their principal. You may well be in this situation at some point in your own life. As we saw in the Ethics chapter, rationalization is a common, and dangerous, trap. Imagine how Klein, Belliard, and Fell might have rationalized their wrong-doing. What steps can you take to ensure that you do not fall prey to this same ethics trap?

Competition with the Principal

Agents are not allowed to compete with their principal in any matter within the scope of the agency business. If Allen Klein had purchased the "He's So Fine" copyright while he was George Harrison's agent, he would have committed an additional sin against the agency relationship. Owning song rights was clearly part of the agency business, so Klein could not make such purchases without Harrison's consent. Once the agency relationship ends, however, so does the rule against competition. Klein was entitled to buy the "He's So Fine" copyright after the agency relationship ended (so long as he did not use confidential information).

Conflict of Interest between Two Principals

Unless otherwise agreed, an agent may not act for two principals whose interests conflict. Suppose Travis represents both director Steven Spielberg and actor Jennifer Lawrence. Spielberg is casting the title role in his new movie, *Nancy Drew: Girl Detective*, a role that Lawrence covets. Travis cannot represent these two clients when they are negotiating with each other unless they both know about the conflict and agree to ignore it. The following example illustrates the dangers of acting for two principals at once.

EXAM Strategy

Question: The Sisters of Charity was an order of nuns in New Jersey. Faced with growing healthcare and retirement costs, they decided to sell off a piece of property. The nuns soon found, however, that the world is not always a charitable place. They agreed to sell the land to Linpro for nearly $10 million. But before the deal closed, Linpro signed a contract to resell the property to Sammis for $34 million. So, you say, the sisters made a bad deal. There is no law against that. But it turned out that the nuns' law firm also represented Linpro. Their lawyer at the firm, Peter Berkley, never told the sisters about the deal between Linpro and Sammis. Was that the charitable—or legal—thing to do?

Strategy: Always begin by asking if there is an agency relationship. Was there consent, control, and a fiduciary relationship? *Consent:* Berkley had agreed to work for the nuns. *Control:* they told him what he was to do—sell the land. The purpose of a *fiduciary relationship* is for one person to benefit another. The point of the nuns' relationship with Berkley was for him to help them. Once you know there is an agency relationship, then ask if the agent has violated his duty of loyalty.

Result: You know that an agent is not permitted to act for two principals whose interests conflict. Here, Berkley was working for the nuns, who wanted the highest possible price for their land, and Linpro, who wanted the lowest price. Berkley has violated his duty of loyalty.

Secretly Dealing with the Principal

If a principal hires an agent to arrange a transaction, the agent may not become a party to the transaction without the principal's permission. Suppose Spielberg hires Trang to read new scripts for him. Unbeknownst to Spielberg, Trang has written her own script, which she thinks would be ideal for him. She may not sell it to him without revealing that she wrote it herself. Spielberg may be perfectly happy to buy Trang's script, but he has the right, as her principal, to know that she is the person selling it.

Appropriate Behavior

An agent may not engage in inappropriate behavior that reflects badly on the principal. This rule applies even to *off-duty* conduct. While off-duty (but still in uniform), a coed trio of flight attendants went wild at a hotel bar in London. They kissed and caressed each other, showed off their underwear, and poured alcohol down their trousers. The airline fired two of the employees and gave a warning letter to the third.

28-2b Other Duties of an Agent

Before Taylor left for a five-week trip to Antarctica, he hired Angie to rent out his vacation house. Angie neither listed his house on the Multiple Listing Service used by all the area brokers, nor posted it online, but when the Fords contacted her looking for rental housing, she did show them Taylor's place. They offered to rent it for $750 per month.

Angie emailed Taylor in Antarctica to tell him. He responded that he would not accept less than $850 a month, which Angie thought the Fords would be willing to pay. He told Angie to email him back if there was any problem. The Fords decided that they would go no higher than $800 a month. Although Taylor had told Angie that he had no cell phone service in Antarctica, she texted him the Fords' counteroffer. Taylor never received it, so he never responded. When the Fords pressed Angie for an answer, she said she could not get in touch with Taylor. Not until Taylor returned home did he learn that the Fords had rented another house. Did Angie violate any of the duties that agents owe to their principals?

Duty to Obey Instructions

An agent must obey her principal's instructions unless the principal directs her to behave illegally or unethically. Taylor instructed Angie to email him if the Fords rejected the offer. When Angie failed to do so, she violated her duty to obey instructions. If, however, Taylor had asked her to say that the house's basement was dry when in fact it looked like a swamp every spring, Angie would be under no obligation to follow those illegal instructions.

Duty of Care

An agent has a duty to act with reasonable care. In other words, an agent must act as a reasonable person would, under the circumstances. A reasonable person would not have texted Taylor while he was in Antarctica.

Under some circumstances, an agent is held to a higher—or lower—standard than usual. **An agent with special skills is held to a higher standard because she is expected to use those skills.** A trained real estate agent should know enough to post all listings online.

But suppose Taylor had asked his neighbor, Jed, to help him sell the house. Jed is not a trained real estate agent, and he is not being paid, which makes him a **gratuitous agent**. A gratuitous agent is held to a lower standard because he is doing his principal a favor and, as the old saying goes, you get what you pay for—up to a point. **Gratuitous agents are liable if they commit *gross* negligence, but not *ordinary* negligence.** If Jed, as a gratuitous agent, texted Taylor an important message because he forgot that Taylor could not receive these messages in Antarctica, he would not be liable for that ordinary negligence. But if Taylor had, just that day, sent Jed an email complaining that he could not get any text messages, Jed would be liable for gross negligence and a violation of his duty.

Gratuitous agent
Someone not paid for performing duties

Duty to Provide Information

An agent has a duty to provide the principal with all information in her possession that she has reason to believe the principal wants to know. She also has a duty to provide accurate information. Angie knew that the Fords had counteroffered for $800 a month. She had a duty to pass this information on to Taylor.

28-2c Principal's Remedies when the Agent Breaches a Duty

A principal has three potential remedies when an agent breaches her duty:

- **Damages**. The principal can recover from the agent any damages the breach has caused. Thus, if Taylor can rent his house for only $600 a month instead of the $800 the Fords offered, Angie would be liable for $2,400—$200 a month for one year.

- **Profits**. If an agent breaches the duty of loyalty, he must turn over to the principal any profits he has earned as a result of his wrongdoing. Thus, after Klein violated his duty of loyalty to Harrison, he forfeited profits he would have earned from the copyright of "He's So Fine." Some states also allow punitive damages against disloyal employees.

- **Rescission**. If the agent has violated her duty of loyalty, the principal may rescind the transaction. When Trang sold a script to her principal, Spielberg, without telling him that she was the author, she violated her duty of loyalty. Spielberg could rescind the contract to buy the script.[6]

---

[6]A principal can rescind his contract with an agent who has violated her duty but, as we shall see later in the chapter, the principal might not be able to rescind a contract that the agent has made with a third party.

28-3 DUTIES OF PRINCIPALS TO AGENTS

In a typical agency relationship, the agent agrees to perform tasks for the principal, and the principal agrees to pay the agent. The range of tasks undertaken by an agent is limited only by the imagination of the principal. Because the agent's job can be so varied, the law needs to define an agent's duties carefully. The role of the principal, on the other hand, is typically less complicated—often little more than paying the agent as required by the agreement. Thus, the law enumerates fewer duties for the principal. Primarily, the principal must reimburse the agent for reasonable expenses and cooperate with the agent in performing agency tasks. The respective duties of agents and principals can be summarized as follows:

Duties of Agents to Principals	Duty of Principals to Agents
Duty of loyalty	Duty to compensate as provided by the agreement
Duty to obey instructions	Duty to reimburse reasonable expenses
Duty of care	Duty to cooperate with the agent
Duty to provide information	

28-3a Duty to Indemnify

As a general rule, the principal must indemnify (i.e., reimburse) the agent for any expenses she has reasonably incurred. These reimbursable expenses fall into three categories:

- **A principal must indemnify an agent for any expenses or damages reasonably incurred in carrying out his agency responsibilities.** Peace Baptist Church of Birmingham, Alabama, asked its pastor to buy land for a new church. He paid part of the purchase price out of his own pocket, but the church refused to reimburse him. Although the pastor lost in church, he won in court.[7]

- **A principal must indemnify an agent for tort claims brought by a third party if the principal authorized the agent's behavior and the agent did not realize he was committing a tort.** Marisa owns all the apartment buildings on Elm Street, except one. She hires Rajiv to manage the units and tells him that, under the terms of the leases, she has the right to ask guests to leave if a party becomes too rowdy. But she forgets to tell Rajiv that she does not own one of the buildings, which happens to house a college sorority. One night, when the sorority is having a raucous party, Rajiv hustles over and starts ejecting the noisy guests. The sorority is furious and sues Rajiv for trespass. If the sorority wins its suit against Rajiv, Marisa would have to pay the judgment, plus Rajiv's attorney's fees, because she had told him to quell noisy parties and he did not realize he was trespassing.

- **The principal must indemnify the agent for any liability to third parties that she incurs as a result of entering into a contract on the principal's behalf, including attorney's fees and reasonable settlements.** An agent signed a contract to buy cucumbers for Vlasic Food Products Co. to use in making pickles. When the first shipment of

---

[7]*Lauderdale v. Peace Baptist Church of Birmingham*, 246 Ala. 178 (S. Ct. AL 1944).

cucumbers arrived, Vlasic inspectors found them unsuitable and directed the agent to refuse the shipment. The agent found himself in a pickle when the cucumber farmer sued. The agent notified Vlasic, but the company refused to defend him. He settled the claim himself and, in turn, sued Vlasic. The court ordered Vlasic to reimburse the agent because he had notified them of the suit and had acted reasonably and in good faith.[8]

28-3b Duty to Cooperate

Principals have a duty to cooperate with their agent:

- **The principal must furnish the agent with the opportunity to work.** If Lewis agrees to serve as Ida's real estate agent in selling her house, Ida must allow Lewis access to the house. It is unlikely that Lewis will be able to sell the house without taking anyone inside.

- **The principal cannot unreasonably interfere with the agent's ability to accomplish his task.** Ida allows Lewis to show the house, but she refuses to clean it and then makes disparaging comments to prospective purchasers. "I really get tired of living in such a dark, dreary house," she says. "And the neighborhood children are vicious thugs." This behavior would constitute unreasonable interference with an agent.

- **The principal must perform her part of the contract.** Once the agent has successfully completed the task, the principal must pay him, even if the principal has changed her mind and no longer wants the agent to perform. Ida is a 78-year-old widow who has lived alone for many years in a house that she loves. Her asking price is outrageously high because she does not really want to sell. She put her house on the market so that she could show it to all the nice young families who move to town. When Lewis actually finds a couple willing to pay Ida's price, she rejects the offer. But the contract had provided that Lewis would find a willing buyer at the asking price. Because he has done so, Ida must pay his real estate commission even if she refuses to sell her house.

28-4 TERMINATING AN AGENCY RELATIONSHIP

Either the agent or the principal can terminate the agency relationship at any time. In addition, the relationship terminates automatically if the principal or agent no longer can perform their required duties or a change in circumstances renders the agency relationship pointless.

28-4a Termination by Agent or Principal

The two parties—principal and agent—have these choices in terminating their relationship:

- **Term Agreement.** If the principal and agent agree in advance how long their relationship will last, they have a term agreement. For example:

  ○ **Time.** Alexandra hires Boris to help her add to her collection of guitars previously owned by rock stars. If they agree that the relationship will last two years, they have a term agreement.

---

[8]*Long v. Vlasic Food Products Co.*, 439 F.2d 229 (4th Cir. 1971).

○ **Achieving a Purpose.** The principal and agent can agree that the agency relationship will terminate when the principal's goals have been achieved. Alexandra and Boris might agree that their relationship will end when Alexandra has purchased 10 guitars.

○ **Mutual Agreement.** No matter what the principal and agent agree at the start, they can always change their minds later on, so long as the change is mutual. If Boris and Alexandra originally agree to a two-year term, but Boris decides he wants to go back to business school and Alexandra runs out of money after only one year, they can decide together to terminate the agency.

- **Agency at Will.** If they make no agreement in advance about the term of the agreement, either principal or agent can terminate at any time.

- **Wrongful Termination.** An agency relationship is a personal relationship. Hiring an agent is not like buying a book. You might not care which copy of the book you buy, but you do care which agent you hire. If an agency relationship is not working out, the courts will not force the agent and principal to stay together. **Either party always has the *power* to terminate. They may not, however, have the *right*.** If one party's departure from the agency relationship violates the agreement and causes harm to the other party, the wrongful party must pay damages. Nonetheless, he will be permitted to leave. If Boris has agreed to work for Alexandra for two years but he wants to leave after one, he can leave, provided he pays Alexandra the cost of hiring and training a replacement.

If the agent is a gratuitous agent (i.e., is not being paid), he has both the power and the right to quit any time he wants, regardless of the agency agreement. If Boris is doing this job for Alexandra as a favor, he will not owe her damages when he stops work.

28-4b Principal or Agent Can No Longer Perform Required Duties

If the principal or the agent is unable to perform the duties required under the agency agreement, the agreement terminates.

- **If either the agent or the principal fails to obtain (or keep) a license necessary to perform duties under the agency agreement, the agreement ends.** Caleb hires Allegra to represent him in a lawsuit. If she is disbarred, their agency agreement terminates because the agent is no longer allowed in court. Alternatively, if Emil hires Bess to work in his gun shop, their agency relationship terminates when he loses his license to sell firearms.

- **The bankruptcy of the agent or the principal terminates an agency relationship only if it affects their ability to perform.** Bankruptcy rarely interferes with an agent's responsibilities. After all, there is generally no reason why an agent cannot continue to act for the principal whether the agent is rich or poor. If Lewis, the real estate agent, becomes bankrupt, he can continue to represent Ida or anyone else who wants to sell a house. The bankruptcy of a principal is different, however, because after filing for bankruptcy, the principal loses control of his assets. A bankrupt principal may be unable to pay the agent or honor contracts that the agent enters into on his behalf. Therefore, the bankruptcy of a principal is more likely to terminate an agency relationship.

- **An agency relationship terminates upon the death or incapacity of either the principal or the agent.** Agency is a personal relationship, and when the principal dies, the agent cannot act on behalf of a nonexistent person.[9] Of course, a nonexistent person cannot act either, so the relationship also terminates when the agent dies. Incapacity has the same legal effect because either the principal or the agent is at least temporarily unable to act.

- **If the agent violates her duty of loyalty, the agency agreement automatically terminates.** Agents are appointed to represent the principal's interest; if they fail to do so, there is no point to the relationship. Thus, in the Pure Power case, Belliard's and Fell's agency relationship with Brenner automatically ended once they engaged in disloyal activities. She had the right to fire them on the spot, whether or not they had employment contracts.

28-4c Change in Circumstances

After the agency agreement is negotiated, circumstances may change. **If these changes are significant enough to undermine the purpose of the agreement, the relationship ends automatically.** Andrew hires Melissa to sell his country farm for $100,000. Shortly thereafter, the largest natural gas reserve in North America is discovered nearby. The farm is now worth 10 times Andrew's asking price. Melissa's authority terminates automatically.

Other changes in circumstance that affect an agency agreement are:

- **Change of law.** If the agent's responsibilities become illegal, the agency agreement terminates. Oscar has hired Marta to ship him succulent avocados from California's Imperial Valley. Before she sends the shipment, Mediterranean fruit flies are discovered, and all fruits and vegetables in California are quarantined. The agency agreement terminates because it is now illegal to ship the California avocados.

- **Loss or destruction of subject matter.** Andrew hired Damian to sell his Palm Beach condominium, but before Damian could even measure the living room, Andrew's creditors attached the condo. Damian is no longer authorized to sell the real estate because Andrew has "lost" the subject matter of his agency agreement with Damian.

28-4d Effect of Termination

Once an agency relationship ends, the agent no longer has the authority to act for the principal. If she continues to act, she is liable to the principal for any damages he incurs as a result. The Mediterranean fruit fly quarantine ended Marta's agency. If she sends Oscar the avocados anyway and he is fined for possession of a fruit fly, Marta must pay the fine.

The agent loses her authority to act, but some of the duties of both the principal and agent continue even after the relationship ends:

- **Principal's duty to indemnify agent.** Oscar must reimburse Marta for expenses she incurred before the agency ended. If Marta accumulated mileage on her car during her search for the perfect avocado, Oscar must pay her for gasoline and depreciation. But he owes her nothing for her expenses after the agency relationship ends.

- **Confidential information.** An agent is not entitled to use confidential information even after the agency relationship terminates. Remember the "He's So Fine" case earlier in the chapter? George Harrison's former agent was wrong to use confidential information to negotiate on his own behalf the purchase of the "He's So Fine" copyright.

[9]Restatement (Third) of Agency §§3.05, 3.06, 3.07, 3.08.

28-5 LIABILITY TO THIRD PARTIES

Thus far, this chapter has dealt with the relationship between principals and agents. Although an agent can dramatically increase his principal's ability to accomplish her goals, an agency relationship also dramatically increases the risk of legal liability to third parties. A principal may be liable in tort for any harm the agent causes and also liable in contract for agreements that the agent signs. Indeed, once a principal hires an agent, she may be liable to third parties for his acts, even if he *disobeys* instructions. Agents may also find themselves liable to third parties.

28-5a Principal's Liability for Contracts

Many agents are hired for the primary purpose of entering into contracts on behalf of their principals. Salespeople may do little other than sign on the dotted line. Most of the time, the principal is pleased to be liable on these contracts. But even if the principal is unhappy (because, say, the agent has disobeyed orders), the principal generally cannot rescind contracts entered into by the agent. After all, if someone is going to suffer, it should be the principal who hired the disobedient agent, not the innocent third party.

The principal is liable for the acts and statements of his agent if (1) the agent had authority, or (2) the principal ratified the acts of the agent. In other words, the principal is as responsible as if he had performed those acts himself. Thus, when a lawyer lied on an application for malpractice insurance, the insurance company was allowed to void the policy for the entire law firm. It was as if the firm had lied. In addition, the principal is deemed to know any information that the agent knows or should know.

Authority

A principal is bound by the acts of an agent if the agent had authority. There are three types of authority: express, implied, and apparent. Express and implied authority are categories of actual authority because the agent is truly authorized to act for the principal. In apparent authority, the principal is liable for the agent's actions even though the agent was *not* authorized.

Peter Casolino/Alamy

Did Nell have the authority to hire this auctioneer?

Express Authority. The principal grants express authority by words or conduct that, reasonably interpreted, cause the agent to believe the principal desires her to act on the principal's account.[10] In other words, the principal asks the agent to do something and the agent does it. Craig calls his stockbroker, Alice, and asks her to buy 100 shares of Banshee Corp. for his account. She has *express authority* to carry out this transaction.

Implied Authority. Unless otherwise agreed, authority to conduct a transaction includes authority to do acts that are reasonably necessary to accomplish it.[11] The principal does not have to micromanage the agent. David has recently inherited a house from his

---

[10]Restatement (Third) of Agency §2.01.
[11]Restatement (Third) of Agency §2.02.

grandmother. He hires Nell to auction off the house and its contents. She hires an auction-eer, advertises the event, rents a tent, and generally does everything necessary to conduct a successful auction. After withholding her expenses, she sends the tidy balance to David. Totally outraged, he calls her on the phone, "How dare you hire an auctioneer and rent a tent? I never gave you permission! I absolutely *refuse* to pay these expenses!"

David is wrong. A principal almost never gives an agent absolutely complete instruc-tions. Unless some authority is implied, David would have had to say, "Open the car door, get in, put the key in the ignition, drive to the store, buy stickers, mark an auction number on each sticker, ..." and so forth. To solve this problem, the law assumes that the agent has authority to do anything that is reasonably necessary to accomplish her task.

Apparent Authority.   **A principal can be liable for the acts of an agent who is not, in fact, acting with authority if the *principal's* conduct causes a third party reasonably to believe that the agent is authorized.**[12] In the case of *express* and *implied* authority, the principal has authorized the agent to act. Apparent authority is different: The principal has *not* authorized the agent, but has done something to make an innocent third party *believe* the agent is authorized. As a result, the principal is every bit as liable to the third party as if the agent had had authority.

Zbigniew Lambo and Scott Kennedy were brokers at Paulson Investment Co., a stock brokerage firm in Oregon. The two men violated securities laws by selling unregistered stock, which ultimately proved to be worthless. Kennedy and Lambo were liable, but they were unable to repay the money. Either Paulson or its customers would end up bearing the loss. What is the fair result? The law takes the view that the principal is liable, not the third party, if the principal, by word or deed, allowed the third party to believe that the agent was acting on the principal's behalf. In that case, the principal could have prevented the third party from losing money.

Although the two brokers did not have *express* or *implied* authority to sell the stock (Paulson had not authorized them to break the law), the company was nonetheless liable on the grounds that the brokers had *apparent* authority. Paulson had sent letters to its customers notifying them when it hired Kennedy. The two brokers made sales presentations at Paulson's offices. The company had never told customers that the two men were not authorized to sell this worthless stock.[13] Thus the agents *appeared* to have authority, even though they did not. Of course, Paulson had the right to recover from Kennedy and Lambo, in the unlikely event that they had assets.

Remember that the issue in apparent authority is always what the *principal* has done to make the *third party* believe that the *agent* has authority. Suppose that Kennedy and Lambo never worked for Paulson but, on their own, printed up Paulson stationery. The company would not be liable for the stock the two men sold because it had never done or said anything that would reasonably make a third party believe that the men were its agents.

Ratification

If a person accepts the benefit of an unauthorized transaction or fails to repudiate it, then he is as bound by the act as if he had originally authorized it. He has *ratified* the act.[14] Many of the cases in agency law involve instances in which one person acts *without* authority for another. But sometimes after the fact, the principal decides that he approves of what the agent has done even though it was not authorized at the time. The law would be perverse if it did not permit the principal, under those circumstances, to agree to the deal the agent has made. The law is not perverse, but it is careful. **Even if an agent**

---

[12]Restatement (Third) of Agency §2.03.

[13]Badger v. Paulson Investment Co., 311 Ore. 14 (S. Ct. OR 1991).

[14]Restatement (Third) of Agency §4.01.

acts without authority, the principal can decide later to be bound by her actions as long as these requirements are met:

- The "agent" indicates to the third party that she is acting for a principal.

- The "principal" knows all the material facts of the transaction.

- The "principal" accepts the benefit of the whole transaction, not just part.

- The third party does not withdraw from the contract before ratification.

A night clerk at the St. Regis Hotel in Detroit, Michigan, was brutally murdered in the course of a robbery. A few days later, the *Detroit News* reported that the St. Regis management had offered a $1,000 reward for any information leading to the arrest and conviction of the killer. Two days after the article appeared, Robert Jackson turned in the man who was subsequently convicted of the crime. But then it was Jackson's turn to be robbed—the hotel refused to pay the reward on the grounds that the manager who had made the offer had no authority. Jackson still had one weapon left: He convinced the court that the hotel had ratified the offer. One of the hotel's owners admitted he read the *Detroit News*. The court concluded that if someone reads a newspaper, he is sure to read any articles about a business he owns; therefore, the owner must have been aware of the offer. He accepted the benefit of the offer by failing to revoke it publicly by, say, announcing to the press that the reward was invalid. This failure to revoke constituted a ratification, and the hotel was liable.[15]

Subagents

Many of the examples in this chapter involve a single agent acting for a principal. Real life is often more complex. Daniel, the owner of a restaurant, hires Michaela to manage it. She in turn hires chefs, waiters, and dishwashers. Michaela is called an **intermediary agent**—someone who hires **subagents** for the principal. Daniel has never even met the restaurant help, yet they are his subagents.

As a general rule, an agent has no authority to delegate her tasks to another unless the principal authorizes her to do so. **But when an agent is authorized to hire a subagent, the principal is as liable for the acts of the subagent as he is for the acts of a regular agent.** After Daniel authorizes Michaela to hire a restaurant staff, she hires Lydia to serve as produce buyer. When Lydia buys food for the restaurant, Daniel must pay the bill.

Intermediary agent

Someone who hires subagents for the principal

Subagents

Someone appointed by an agent to perform the agent's duties

28-5b **Agent's Liability for Contracts**

The agent's liability on a contract depends upon how much the third party knows about the principal. Disclosure is the agent's best protection against liability.

Fully Disclosed Principal

An agent is not liable for any contracts she makes on behalf of a *fully* disclosed principal. A principal is fully disclosed if the third party knows of his *existence* and his *identity*. Augusta acts as agent for Parker when he buys Tracey's prize-winning show horse. Augusta and Tracey both grew up in posh Grosse Pointe, Michigan, where they attended the same elite schools. Tracey does not know Parker, but she figures any friend of Augusta's must be OK. She figures wrong—Parker is a charming deadbeat. He injures Tracey's horse, fails to pay the full contract price, and promptly disappears. Tracey angrily demands that Augusta make good on Parker's debt. Unfortunately for Tracey, Parker was a fully disclosed principal— Tracey knew of his *existence* and his *identity*. Although Tracey partly relied on Augusta's good

---

[15]Jackson v. Goodman, 69 Mich. App. 225 (Mich. Ct. App. 1976).

character when contracting with Parker, Augusta is not liable because Tracey knew who the principal was and could have (should have) investigated him. Augusta did not promise anything herself, and Tracey's only recourse is against the principal, Parker (wherever he may be).

To avoid liability when signing a contract on behalf of a principal, an agent must clearly state that she is an agent and also must identify the principal. Augusta should sign a contract on behalf of her principal, Parker, as follows: "Augusta, as agent for Parker" or "Parker, by Augusta, Agent."

Unidentified Principal

In the case of an *unidentified* principal, the third party can recover from either the agent or the principal. (An unidentified principal is also sometimes called a "partially disclosed principal.") A principal is unidentified if the third party knew of his *existence* but not his *identity*. Suppose that, when approaching Tracey about the horse, Augusta simply says, "I have a friend who is interested in buying your champion." Any friend of Augusta's is a friend of Tracey's—or so Tracey thinks. Parker is an unidentified principal because Tracey knows only that he exists, not who he is. She cannot investigate his creditworthiness because she does not know his name. Tracey relies solely on what she is able to learn from the agent, Augusta. Parker and Augusta are **jointly and severally liable** to Tracey. Thus, Tracey can recover from either or both of them. However, she cannot recover more than the total she is owed: If her damages are $100,000, she can recover that amount from either Parker or Augusta, or partial amounts from both, but in no event more than $100,000.

Undisclosed Principal

In the case of an *undisclosed* principal, the third party can recover from either the agent or the principal. A principal is undisclosed if the third party did not know of his existence. Suppose that Augusta simply asks to buy the horse herself, without mentioning that she is purchasing it for Parker. In this case, Parker is an undisclosed principal because Tracey does not know that Augusta is acting for someone else. Both Parker and Augusta are jointly and severally liable. As Exhibit 28.1 illustrates, the principal is always liable, but the agent is not unless the principal's identity is a mystery.

Jointly and severally liable
All members of a group are liable. They can be sued as a group, or any one of them can be sued individually for the full amount owed. But the plaintiff cannot recover more than the total she is owed.

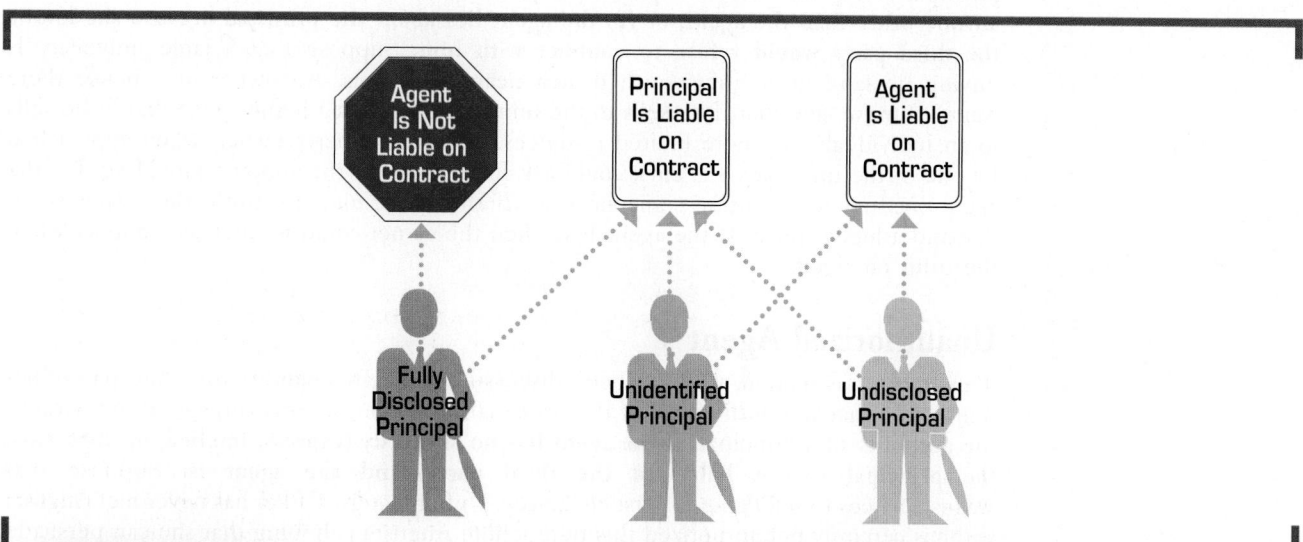

EXHIBIT 28.1

In some ways, the concept of an undisclosed principal violates principles of contract law. If Tracey does not even know that Parker exists, how can they have an agreement or a meeting of the minds? Is such an arrangement fair to Tracey? The following incident illustrates why this type of contract is permitted.

William Zeckendorf was a man with a plan. For years, he had been eyeing a six-block tract of land along New York's East River. It was a wasteland of slums and slaughterhouses, but he could see its potential. The meat packers had refused to sell to him, however, because they knew they would never be permitted to build slaughterhouses in Manhattan again. Finally, he got the phone call he had been waiting for. The companies were willing to sell—at more than three times the market price of surrounding land. Undeterred, Zeckendorf immediately put down a $1 million deposit. But to make his investment worthwhile, he needed to buy the neighboring property—once the slaughterhouses were gone, the other land would be much more valuable.

Zeckendorf was well known as a wealthy developer; he had begun his career managing the Astor family's real estate holdings. If sellers knew that he was involved in the deal, prices would skyrocket, and the project would become too costly. So he hired agents to purchase the land for him. To conceal his involvement further, he went to South America for a month. When he returned, his agents had completed 75 different purchases, and he owned 18 acres of Manhattan land.

Shortly afterward, the United Nations (UN) began seeking a site for its headquarters. President Truman favored Boston, Philadelphia, or a location in the Midwest. The UN committee suggested Greenwich or Stamford, Connecticut. But John D. Rockefeller settled the question once and for all. He purchased Zeckendorf's land and donated it to the UN (netting Zeckendorf a 25 percent profit). Without the cooperation of agency law, the UN headquarters would not be in New York today.

> **Without the cooperation of agency law, the UN headquarters would not be in New York today.**

Because of concerns about fair play, there are some exceptions to the rule on undisclosed principals. **A third party is not bound to the contract with an undisclosed principal if (1) the contract specifically provides that the third party is not bound to anyone other than the agent, or (2) the agent lies about the principal because she knows the third party would refuse to contract with him.** Suppose that a large university is buying up land in an impoverished area near its campus. An owner of a house there wants to make sure that if he sells to the university, he gets a higher price than if he sells to an individual with more limited resources. A cagey property owner, when approached by one of the university's agents, could ask for a clause in the contract providing that the agent was not representing someone else. If the agent told the truth, the owner could demand a higher price. If the agent lied, then the owner could rescind the contract when the truth emerged.

Unauthorized Agent

Thus far in this section, we have been discussing an agent's liability to a third party for a transaction that was authorized by the principal. Sometimes, however, agents act without the authority of a principal. **If the agent has no authority (express, implied, or apparent), the principal is not liable to the third party, and the agent is.** Suppose that Augusta agrees to sell Parker's horse to Tracey. Unfortunately, Parker has never met Augusta and has certainly not authorized this transaction. Augusta is hoping that she can persuade him to sell, but Parker refuses. Augusta, but not Parker, is liable to Tracey for breach of contract.

28-5c **Principal's Liability for Torts**

The general rule of tort liability is this: **An employer is liable for a *physical* tort committed by an employee acting within the scope of employment and a *nonphysical* tort of an employee acting with authority.**[16] This principle of liability is called *respondeat superior*, which is a Latin phrase meaning "let the master answer." Under the theory of *respondeat superior*, the employer (that is, the principal) is liable for misbehavior by the employee (that is, the agent) whether or not the employer was at fault. Indeed, the employer may be liable even if he *forbade* or tried to *prevent* the employee from misbehaving. Thus, a company could be liable for the damage an on-duty worker causes if speeding while driving, even if she is violating company policy at the time.

This rule sounds harsh. But the theory is that, because the principal controls the agent, he should be able to *prevent* misbehavior. If he cannot prevent it, at least he can *insure* against the risks. Furthermore, the principal may have deeper pockets than the agent or the injured third party and thus be better able to *afford* the cost of the agent's misbehavior.

To apply the principle of *respondeat superior*, it is important to understand these terms: employee, scope of employment, nonphysical tort, and acting with authority.

Employee

There are two kinds of agents: (1) employee and (2) independent contractor. **Generally, a principal *is* liable for the physical torts of an employee but is *not* liable for the physical torts of an independent contractor.** Because of this rule, the distinction between an employee and an independent contractor is important.

Employee or Independent Contractor?   The more control the principal has over an agent, the more likely that the agent will be considered an employee. Therefore, **when determining if agents are employees or independent contractors, courts consider whether:**

- The principal supervises details of the work.
- The principal supplies the tools and place of work.
- The agents work full time for the principal.
- The agents receive a salary or hourly wages, not a fixed price for the job.
- The work is part of the regular business of the principal.
- The principal and agents believe they have an employer-employee relationship.
- The principal is in business.[17]

Suppose that Mutt and Jeff work 40 hours a week at Swansong Media preparing food for the company's onsite dining room. They earn a weekly salary. Swansong provides food, utensils, and a kitchen. This year, however, Swansong decides to go all out for its holiday party, so it hires FiFi LaBelle to cater the event. She buys the food, prepares it in her own kitchen, and delivers it to the company in time for the party. She is an independent contractor, while Mutt and Jeff are employees.

Respondeat superior

An employer is liable for a physical tort committed by an employee acting within the scope of employment and a nonphysical tort of an employee acting with authority.

---

[16]Restatement (Third) of Agency §7.07.
[17]Ibid.

Ethics   For employers, the advantages of independent contractors extend beyond agency law. Contractors cost substantially less in payroll taxes and benefits, and require less paperwork. Also, companies with fewer than 50 employees are not required to provide health insurance under the Patient Protection and Affordable Care Act.

   To increase tax revenue, the federal government is aggressively auditing employers to ensure that workers are being properly classified as employees. Microsoft paid almost $100 million to settle such a case. But even apart from the legal issues, employees who are inaccurately classified as independent contractors suffer from a large tear in their financial safety net, with unemployment, Social Security, and healthcare benefits at risk. What ethical obligation do employers have? What would Mill, Kant and Milton Friedman say?

Negligent Hiring.   Although, as we have seen, principals are generally not liable for the physical torts of an independent contractor, there is one exception to this rule: **A principal is liable for the physical torts of an independent contractor *if* the principal has been negligent in hiring or supervising her.** Remember that, under *respondeat superior*, the principal is liable *without fault* for the torts of employees. The case of independent contractors is different: The principal is liable only if he was *at fault* by being careless in his hiring or supervising.

   Exhibit 28.2 illustrates the difference in liability between an employee and an independent contractor.

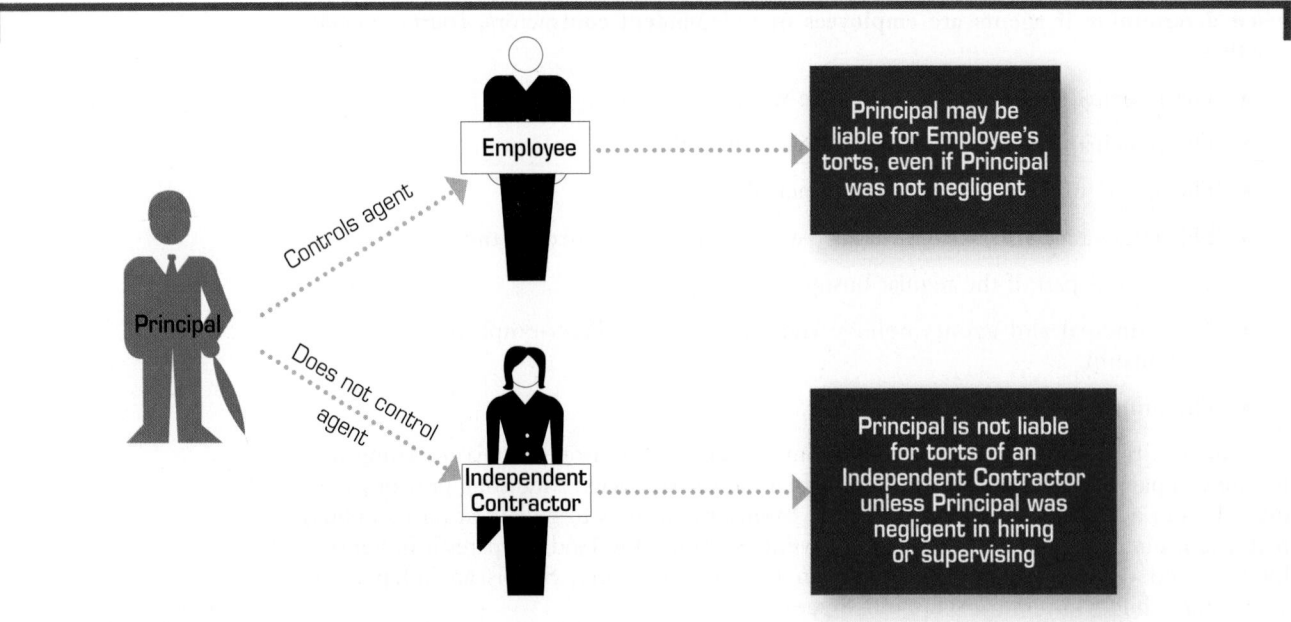

EXHIBIT 28.2

Scope of Employment

You remember that: An employer is liable for a physical tort committed by an employee acting within the scope of employment. **An employee is acting within the scope of employment if the act:**

- is one that employees are generally responsible for,
- takes place during hours that the employee is generally employed,
- is part of the principal's business,
- is similar to the one the principal authorized,
- is one for which the principal supplied the tools, and
- is not seriously criminal.

If an employee leaves a pool of water on the floor of a store and a customer slips and falls, the employer is liable. But if the same employee leaves water on his own kitchen floor and a friend falls, the employer is not liable because the employee is not acting within the scope of employment.

Scope of employment cases raise two major issues: authorization and abandonment.

Authorization.   In authorization cases, the agent is clearly working for the principal but commits an act that the principal has not authorized. Although Jane has often told the driver of her delivery van not to speed, Hank ignores her instructions and plows into Bernadette. At the time of the accident, he is working for Jane, delivering flowers for her shop, but his act is not authorized. **An act is within the scope of employment, even if expressly forbidden, if it is of the same general nature as that authorized or if it is incidental to the conduct authorized.** Hank was authorized to drive the van, but not to speed. However, his speeding was of the same general nature as the authorized act, so Jane is liable to Bernadette.

EXAM Strategy

Question: While on a business trip, Trevor went sightseeing on his day off. Although company policy forbade talking on a cell phone while driving, Trevor did answer his phone while in his car. Distracted, he crashed into Olivia's house, causing substantial damage. Was his employer liable for the damage?

Strategy: Whenever a case involves a company's liability for the acts of an employee, begin by asking if *respondeat superior* applies. Was he acting within the scope of employment? Does it matter that it was his day off and he was violating company policy?

Result: In a similar case, the court ruled that the employer was liable because it is foreseeable that travelling employees will go sightseeing and, therefore, companies should include this potential liability as a cost of doing business.[18] The fact that the employer's policy prohibits talking on a cell phone does not protect the company from liability if an employee violates that policy. The employer should not have hired such a disobedient worker.

---

[18]Potter v. Shaw, 60 Mass. App. Ct. 1112 (Mass. App. Ct. 2004).

Abandonment.   This Exam Strategy also illustrates the second major issue in a scope of employment case: abandonment. **The principal is liable for the actions of the employee that occur while the employee is at work, but not for actions that occur after the employee has abandoned the principal's business.** Although the rule sounds straightforward, the difficulty lies in determining whether the employee has in fact abandoned the principal's business. The employer is liable if the employee is simply on a *detour* from company business, but the employer is not liable if the employee is off on a *frolic of his own*. Suppose that Hank, the delivery van driver, speeds during his afternoon commute home. An employee is generally not acting within the scope of his employment when he commutes to and from work, so his principal, Jane, is not liable. On the other hand, if Hank stops at the Burger Box drive-in window en route to making a delivery, Jane is liable when he crashes into Anna on the way out of the parking lot because this time, he is simply making a detour.

Was the employee in the following case acting within the scope of his employment while driving to work? You be the judge.

You be the Judge

Facts: Staff Sergeant William E. Dreyer was a recruiter for the United States Marine Corps, which provided Dreyer with a car to drive while on government business. He was not permitted to use this car

ZANKEL V. UNITED STATES OF AMERICA
2008 U.S. Dist. LEXIS 23655, 2008 WL 828032 United States District Court for the Western District of Pennsylvania, 2008

acting within the scope of his employment at the time of the accident.

You Be the Judge: *Was Dreyer within the scope of employment when he killed Zankel? Is the government liable?*

while commuting to and from home unless he had specific authorization from his boss, Major Michael Sherman, but Sherman was lenient in giving authorization and even permitted his soldiers simply to leave a message on his voicemail. He had denied only about a dozen of such requests over a three-year period.

Each month, Dreyer was expected to meet specific quotas for the number of contracts signed and recruits shipped to basic training. However, despite working 16 to 18 hours every day of the week, Dreyer had not met his recruiting quotas for months. Sherman had formally reprimanded him and increased his target for the following month.

On the day before the accident, Dreyer left home at 6:30 a.m., driving his own car. At the office, he switched to a government car and worked until 10:45 p.m. He then discovered that his personal car would not start. He did not want to call Sherman that late, so he drove his government car home without permission. He believed that, had he called, Sherman would have said it was OK.

Dreyer arrived home at midnight. He was under orders to attend an early morning training session the next day. So he awoke early and left home at 6:35 a.m. At 6:40 a.m., his car struck and killed 12-year-old Justin Zankel. The child's parents sued the U.S. government, claiming that it was liable for Dreyer's actions because he had been

Argument for the Zankels: At the time of the accident, Dreyer was driving a government vehicle. Although he had not requested permission to drive the car, if he had done so, permission certainly would have been granted.

Moreover, even if Dreyer was not authorized to drive the Marine Corps car, the government is still liable because his activity was of the same general nature as that authorized and it was incidental to the conduct authorized. Driving the car was part of Dreyer's work. Indeed, he could not perform his job without it. In addition, Dreyer was on the road early so that he could attend a required training session. He was exhausted from trying to reach impossible goals. The Marine Corps must bear responsibility for this tragic accident.

Argument for the United States: The government had a clear policy stating that recruiters were not authorized to drive a government car without first requesting permission. Dreyer had not done so. Therefore, he was not authorized to drive the government car at the time of the accident.

Moreover, it is well established that an employee commuting to and from work is not within the scope of employment. If Dreyer had been driving from one recruiting effort to another, that would be a different story. But in this case, he had not yet started work for the Marine Corps, and therefore the government is not liable.

Intentional Torts

A principal is *not* liable for the *intentional* physical torts of an employee unless (1) the employee intended to serve some purpose of the employer, or (2) the employer was negligent in hiring or supervising this employee. Thieves have stolen a number of computers and purses from the desks of Compania employees. When Aubrey sees a stranger walking down the hallway carrying a computer, she tackles him from behind, breaking his nose. It turns out that he was an authorized computer repair person. Compania is liable for Aubrey's actions because she was motivated, at least in part, by a desire to help her employer. But if Aubrey attacks someone in the parking lot because he dented her car, Compania is *not* liable. Aubrey was acting out of personal revenge or frustration, not a desire to help her employer.

In the following case, a priest committed terrible crimes. Was the Church liable for his acts?

DOE v. LIBERATORE

478 F. Supp. 2d 742
United States District Court for the Middle District of Pennsylvania, 2007

Facts: A number of priests wrote to James Timlin, the Bishop of Scranton, warning him that Father Albert Liberatore was engaging in a sexual relationship with one of his adult male students at a seminary. Bishop Timlin transferred Liberatore from the seminary to the Sacred Heart church.

Fourteen year-old John Doe was a member of Liberatore's parish. Liberatore befriended Doe, taking him on outings and giving him expensive gifts. Doe routinely slept in Liberatore's bed. A number of priests told Bishop Timlin that they feared Liberatore was sexually abusing Doe. One witness reported that she had seen Doe put his hand down Liberatore's pants. Eventually, Doe himself told a priest that he was being sexually abused. The priest instructed Doe to forgive Liberatore and not to tell other people because it would ruin Doe's life and the lives of others.

Only after Liberatore pleaded guilty to multiple counts of sexual abuse did the Church dismiss him from the priesthood. Doe filed suit against the Church and Bishop Timlin, alleging that they were liable for the torts committed by Liberatore. The defendants filed a motion to dismiss.

Issues: *Was Liberatore acting within the scope of his employment? Was the Church liable for his criminal acts?*

Excerpts from Judge Caputo's Decision: Under Pennsylvania law, an employer is held liable for the negligent acts of his employee which cause injuries to a third party, provided that such acts were committed during the course of and within the scope of the employment.

The conduct of an employee is considered within the scope of employment if: (1) it is of a kind and nature that the employee is employed to perform; (2) it occurs substantially within the authorized time and space limits; (3) it is actuated, at least in part, by a purpose to serve the employer; and (4) if force is intentionally used by the employee against another, the use of force is not unexpected by the employer.[19]

Here, it is clear that Liberatore's sexual molestation of Plaintiff was not within the scope or nature of his employment as a priest. Indeed, the activity of which Plaintiff now complains is wholly inconsistent with the role of one who is received into the Holy Orders as an ordained priest of the Roman Catholic Church. Moreover, the acts of sexual abuse perpetrated by Liberatore were both outrageous and certainly not actuated by any purpose of serving the Diocese, Sacred Heart, or Bishop Timlin. Therefore, the Court will grant summary judgment in favor of the Diocese, Sacred Heart, and Bishop Timlin as to [this issue].

Plaintiff next claims that the Diocese, Sacred Heart, and Bishop Timlin are liable for negligence in their hiring, supervision, and retention of Liberatore as a Diocesan

---

[19]Note that Pennsylvania requires this fourth element but the Restatement (Third) of Agency does not.

priest. [A]n employer owes a duty to exercise reasonable care in selecting, supervising and controlling employees. In the instant case, the Diocese, Sacred Heart, and Bishop Timlin may be liable if they knew or should have known that Liberatore had a propensity for committing sexual abuse and his employment as Pastor at Sacred Heart might create a situation where his propensity would harm a third person, such as Plaintiff. [A] reasonable jury could conclude that the Diocese, Sacred Heart, and Bishop Timlin were negligent or reckless in supervising and retaining Liberatore. However, the Court concludes that a reasonable jury could not find that the Diocese, Sacred Heart, and Bishop Timlin were negligent or reckless in hiring Liberatore because there is no evidence suggesting that Liberatore was or would become a child sex predator when he was hired.

Nonphysical Torts

Nonphysical tort

One that harms only reputation, feelings, or wallet

So far, we have seen the rules on *physical* torts. A **nonphysical tort** is one that harms only reputation, feelings, or wallet. **Nonphysical torts (whether intentional or unintentional) are treated like a contract claim: The principal is liable only if the employee acted with express, implied, or apparent authority.**[20] Suppose that Dwayne buys a house insurance policy from Andy, who is an agent of the Balls of Fire Insurance Company. Andy throws away Dwayne's policy and pockets his premiums. When Dwayne's house burns down, Balls of Fire is liable because Andy was acting with apparent authority.

EXAM Strategy

Question: Daisy was the founder of an Internet start-up company. Jay was her driver. One day, after he had dropped her at a board meeting, he went to the car wash. There, he told an attractive woman that he worked for a money management firm. She gave him money to invest. On the way out of the car wash, he was so excited that he hit another customer's expensive car. Who is liable for Jay's misdeeds?

Strategy: In determining a principal's liability, begin by figuring out whether the agent has committed a physical or nonphysical tort. Remember that the principal is liable for physical torts within the scope of employment, but for nonphysical torts, she is liable only if the employee acted with authority.

Result: In this case, Daisy is liable for the damage to the car because that was a physical tort within the scope of employment. But she is not liable for the investment money because Jay did not have authority (express, implied, or apparent) to take those funds.

28-5d Agent's Liability for Torts

The focus of the prior section was on the *principal's* liability for the agent's torts. But it is important to remember that **agents are always liable for their own torts.** Agents who commit torts are personally responsible, whether or not their principal is also liable. Even if the tort was committed to benefit the principal, the agent is still liable. So the sailor who got into a fistfight while rousing a shipmate from bed is liable even though he thought he was acting for the benefit of his principal.

---

[20]Restatement (Third) of Agency §7.08.

This rule makes obvious sense. If the agent was not liable, he would have little incentive to be careful. Imagine Hank driving his delivery van for Jane. If he was not personally liable for his own torts, he might think, "If I drive fast enough, I can make it through that light even though it just turned red. And if I don't, what the heck, it'll be Jane's problem, not mine." Agents, as a rule, may have fewer assets than their principal, but it is important that their personal assets be at risk in the event of their negligent behavior.

If the agent and principal are *both* liable, which does the injured third party sue? The principal and the agent are *jointly and severally liable*, which means, as we have seen, that the injured third party can sue either one or both, as she chooses. If she recovers from the principal, he can sue the agent.

Chapter Conclusion

When students enroll in a business law course, they fully expect to learn about torts and contracts, corporations, and antitrust. They probably do not think much about agency law; many of them have not even heard the term before. Yet it is an area of the law that affects us all because each of us has been and will continue to be both an agent and a principal many times in our lives.

EXAM REVIEW

1. **CREATING AN AGENCY RELATIONSHIP** A principal and an agent mutually consent that the agent will act on behalf of the principal and be subject to the principal's control, thereby creating a fiduciary relationship.

2. **ELEMENTS NOT REQUIRED** An agency relationship can exist without either a written agreement, a formal agreement, or compensation.

3. **AN AGENT'S DUTIES TO THE PRINCIPAL** An agent owes these duties to the principal: duty of loyalty, duty to obey instructions, duty of care, and duty to provide information.

4. **THE PRINCIPAL'S REMEDIES IN THE EVENT OF A BREACH** The principal has three potential remedies when the agent breaches her duty: recovery of damages the breach has caused, recovery of any profits earned by the agent from the breach, and rescission of any transaction with the agent.

EXAM Strategy

Question: Jonah tells his friend Derek that he would like to go parasailing. Derek suggests that they try an outfit called Wind Beneath Your Wings because he has heard good things about it. Derek offers to arrange everything. He makes a reservation, puts the $600 fee on his credit card, and picks Jonah up to drive him to the Wings location. What a friend! But the day does not turn out as Jonah had hoped. While he is soaring up in the air over the Pacific Ocean, his sail springs a leak, he goes plummeting into the sea and breaks both legs. During his recuperation in the hospital, he learns that Wings is unlicensed. He also sees an ad for Wings offering parasailing for only $350. And Derek is listed in the ad as one of the company's owners. Was Derek Jonah's agent? Has he violated his fiduciary responsibility?

Strategy: There are three issues to consider in answering this question: (1) Was there an agency relationship? This requires consent, control, and a fiduciary relationship. (2) Is anything missing—does it matter if the agent is unpaid or the contract is not in writing? (3) Has the agent fulfilled his duties? (See the "Result" at the end of this section.)

5. **THE PRINCIPAL'S DUTIES TO THE AGENT** The principal has three duties to the agent: to compensate as provided by the agreement, to reimburse legitimate expenses, and to cooperate with the agent.

6. **POWER AND RIGHT TO TERMINATE** Both the agent and the principal have the power to terminate an agency relationship, but they may not have the right. If the termination violates the agency agreement and causes harm to the other party, the wrongful party must pay damages.

7. **AUTOMATIC TERMINATION** An agency relationship automatically terminates if the principal or agent no longer can perform the required duties or if a change in circumstances renders the agency relationship pointless.

8. **A PRINCIPAL'S LIABILITY FOR CONTRACTS** A principal is liable for the contracts of the agent if the agent has express, implied, or apparent authority.

9. **EXPRESS AUTHORITY** The principal grants express authority by words or conduct that, reasonably interpreted, cause the agent to believe that the principal desires her to act on the principal's account.

10. **IMPLIED AUTHORITY** Implied authority includes authority to do acts that are incidental to a transaction, usually accompany it, or are reasonably necessary to accomplish it.

11. **APPARENT AUTHORITY** Apparent authority means that a principal is liable for the acts of an agent who is not, in fact, acting with authority if the principal's conduct causes a third party reasonably to believe that the agent is authorized.

EXAM Strategy

Question: Dr. James Leonard wrote Dr. Edward Jacobson to offer him the position of chief of audiology at Jefferson Medical College in Philadelphia. In the letter, Leonard stated that this appointment would have to be approved by the promotion and appointment committee. Jacobson believed that the appointment committee acted only as a rubber stamp, affirming whatever recommendation Leonard made. Jacobson accepted Leonard's offer and proceeded to sell his house and quit his job in Colorado. You can guess what happened next. Two weeks later, Leonard sent Jacobson another letter, rescinding his offer because of opposition from the appointment committee. Did Leonard have apparent authority?

Strategy: In cases of apparent authority, begin by asking what the principal did to make the third party believe that the agent was authorized. What did the Medical College do? (See the "Result" at the end of this section.)

12. **AN AGENT'S LIABILITY FOR A CONTRACT** An agent is not liable for any contract she makes on behalf of a fully disclosed principal. The principal is liable. In the case of an unidentified or undisclosed principal, both the agent and the principal are liable on the contract.

13. **A PRINCIPAL'S LIABILITY FOR TORTS** An employer is liable for a physical tort committed by an employee acting within the scope of employment and a nonphysical tort of an employee acting with authority.

Question: While drunk, the driver of a subway car plows into the back of the car ahead of him, killing a passenger. It was against the rules for the driver to be drunk. Is the subway authority liable for the negligence of its employee?

Strategy: With a tort case, always determine first if the agents are employees or independent contractors. This worker was an employee. Then ask if the employee was acting within the scope of employment. Yes, he was driving a subway car, which is what he was hired to do. Does it matter than he had violated subway rules? No, his violation of the rules does not eliminate his principal's liability because his actions are of the same general nature as those that are authorized. (See the "Result" at the end of this section.)

14. **INDEPENDENT CONTRACTOR** The principal is liable for the physical torts of an independent contractor only if the principal has been negligent in hiring or supervising him.

15. **INTENTIONAL TORTS** A principal is not liable for the intentional physical torts of an employee unless (1) the employee intended to serve some purpose of the employer; or (2) the employer was negligent in hiring or supervising this employee.

16. **NONPHYSICAL TORTS** A principal is liable for nonphysical torts of an employee (whether intentional or unintentional) only if the employee was acting with express, implied or apparent authority.

17. **AGENT'S LIABILITY FOR TORTS** Agents are always liable for their own torts.

4. Result: There is an agency relationship: Derek had agreed to help Jonah; it was Jonah who set the goal for the relationship (parasailing); the purpose of this relationship was for one person to benefit another. It does not matter if Derek was not paid or the agreement not written. Derek has violated his duty to exercise due care. He should not have taken Jonah to an unlicensed company. He has also violated his duty to provide information: He should have told Jonah the true cost for the lessons and also revealed that he was a principal of the company. And he violated his duty of loyalty when he worked for two principals whose interests were in conflict.

11. Result: No. Leonard had told Jacobson that he did not have authority. If Jacobson chose to believe otherwise, that was his problem.

13. Result: The subway authority is liable.

MULTIPLE-CHOICE QUESTIONS

1. At Business University, semester enrollment begins at midnight on April 1. Jasper asked his roommate, Alonso, to register him for an important required course as a favor. Alonso agreed to do so but then overslept. As a result, Jasper could not enroll in the required course he needed to graduate and had to stay in school for an additional semester. Is Alonso liable to Jasper?

(a) No, because an agency agreement is invalid unless the agent receives payment.

(b) No, because Alonso was not grossly negligent.

(c) No, because the cost of the extra semester is unreasonably high.

(d) Yes, because Alonso disobeyed his instructions.

2. Finn learns that, despite his stellar record, he is being paid less than other salespeople at Barry Co., so he decides to start his own company. During his last month on the Barry payroll, he tells all of his clients about his new business. He also tells them that Barry is a great company, but his fees will be lower. After he opens the doors of his new business, most of his former clients move with him. Is Finn liable to Barry?

(a) No, because he has not been disloyal to Barry—he praised the company.

(b) No, because Barry was underpaying him.

(c) No, because his clients have the right to hire whichever company they choose.

(d) Yes, Finn has violated his duty of loyalty to Barry.

3. Kurt asked his car mechanic, Quinn, for help in buying a used car. Quinn recommends a Ford Focus that she has been taking care of its whole life. Quinn was working for the seller. Which of the following statements is true?

(a) Quinn must pay Kurt the amount of money she received from the Ford's prior owner.

(b) After buying the car, Kurt finds out that it needs $1,000 in repairs. He can recover that amount from Quinn, but only if Quinn knew about the needed repairs before Kurt bought the car.

(c) Kurt cannot recover anything because Quinn had no obligation to reveal her relationship with the car's seller.

(d) Kurt cannot recover anything because he had not paid Quinn for her help.

4. Figgins is the dean of a college. He appointed Sue as acting dean while he was out of the country and posted an announcement on the college website announcing that she was authorized to act in his place. He also told Sue privately that she did not have the right to make admissions decisions. While Figgins was gone, Sue overruled the admissions committee to admit the child of a wealthy alumnus. Does the child have the right to attend this college?

   (a) No, because Sue was not authorized to admit him.

   (b) No, because Figgins did not ratify Sue's decision.

   (c) Yes, because Figgins was a fully disclosed principal.

   (d) Yes, because Sue had apparent authority.

5. **CPA QUESTION** A principal will not be liable to a third party for a tort committed by an agent:

   (a) unless the principal instructed the agent to commit the tort.

   (b) unless the tort was committed within the scope of the agency relationship.

   (c) if the agency agreement limits the principal's liability for the agent's tort.

   (d) if the tort is also regarded as a criminal act.

6. **CPA QUESTION** Cox engaged Datz as her agent. It was mutually agreed that Datz would not disclose that he was acting as Cox's agent. Instead, he was to deal with prospective customers as if he were a principal acting on his own behalf. This he did and made several contracts for Cox. Assuming Cox, Datz, or the customer seeks to avoid liability on one of the contracts involved, which of the following statements is correct?

   (a) Cox must ratify the Datz contracts to be held liable.

   (b) Datz has no liability once he discloses that Cox was the real principal.

   (c) The third party can avoid liability because he believed he was dealing with Datz as a principal.

   (d) The third party may choose to hold either Datz or Cox liable.

CASE QUESTIONS

1. An elementary school custodian hit a child who wrote graffiti on the wall. Is the school district liable for this intentional tort by its employee?

2. What if the custodian hit one of the schoolchildren for calling him a name? Is the school district liable?

3. A soldier was drinking at a training seminar. Although he was told to leave his car at the seminar, he disobeyed orders and drove to a military club. On the way to the club, he was involved in an accident. Is the military liable for the damage he caused?

4. One afternoon while visiting friends, tennis star Vitas Gerulaitis fell asleep in their pool house. A mechanic had improperly installed the swimming pool heater, which leaked carbon monoxide fumes into the house where he slept, killing him. His mother filed suit against the owners of the estate. On what theory would they be liable?

5. *YOU BE THE JUDGE* **WRITING PROBLEM** Sarah went to an auction at Christie's to bid on a tapestry for her employer, Fine Arts Gallery. The good news is that she purchased a Dufy tapestry for $77,000. The bad news is that it was not the one her employer had told her to buy. In the excitement of the auction, she forgot her instructions. Fine Art refused to pay, and Christie's filed suit. Is Fine Arts liable for the unauthorized act of its agent? **Argument for Christie's:** Christie's cannot possibly ascertain in each case the exact nature of a bidder's authority. Whether or not Sarah had actual authority, she certainly had apparent authority, and Fine Arts is liable. **Argument for Fine Arts:** Sarah was not authorized to purchase the Dufy tapestry, and therefore Christie's must recover from her, not Fine Arts.

DISCUSSION QUESTIONS

1. **ETHICS** Mercedes has just begun work at Photobook.com. What a great place to work! Although the salary is not high, the company has fabulous perks. The dining room provides great food from 7 a.m. to midnight, five days a week. There is also a free laundry and dry-cleaning service. Mercedes's social life has never been better. She invites her friends over for Photobook meals and has their laundry done for free. And because her job requires her to be online all the time, she has plenty of opportunity to stay in touch with her friends by g-chatting, tweeting, and checking Facebook updates. She is, however, shocked that one of her colleagues takes paper home from the office for his children to use at home. Are these employees behaving ethically?

2. Kevin was the manager of a radio station, WABC. A competing station lured him away. In his last month on the job at WABC, he notified two key on-air personalities that if they were to leave the station, he would not hold them to their noncompete agreements. What can WABC do?

3. Jesse worked as a buyer for the Vegetable Co. Rachel offered to sell Jesse 10 tons of tomatoes for the account of Vegetable. Jesse accepted the offer. Later, Jesse discovered that Rachel was an agent for Sylvester Co. Who is liable on this contract?

4. The Pharmaceutical Association holds an annual convention. At the convention, Brittany, who was president of the association, told Luke that Research Corp. had a promising new cancer vaccine. Luke was so excited that he chartered a plane to fly to Research's headquarters. On the way, the plane crashed and Luke was killed. Is the Pharmaceutical Association liable for Luke's death?

5. Betsy has a two-year contract as a producer at Jackson Movie Studios. She produces a remake of the movie *Footloose*. Unfortunately, it bombs, and Jackson is so furious that he fires her on the weekend the movie opens. Does he have the power to do this?

CHAPTER 29

EMPLOYMENT AND LABOR LAW

> ... you would see them plunging their feet and ankles into the steaming hot carcass of the steer.

"On the killing beds you were apt to be covered with blood, and it would freeze solid; if you leaned against a pillar, you would freeze to that, and if you put your hand upon the blade of your knife, you would run a chance of leaving your skin on it. The men would tie up their feet in newspapers and old sacks, and these would be soaked in blood and frozen, and then soaked again, and so on, until by nighttime a man would be walking on great lumps the size of the feet of an elephant. Now and then, when the bosses were not looking, you would see them plunging their feet and ankles into the steaming hot carcass of the steer.... The cruelest thing of all was that nearly all of them—all of those who used knives—were unable to wear gloves, and their arms would be white with frost and their hands would grow numb, and then of course there would be accidents."[1]

---

[1] From Upton Sinclair, *The Jungle* (New York: Bantam Books, 1981), p. 80, a 1906 novel about the meat-packing industry.

29-1 INTRODUCTION

For most of history, the concept of career planning was unknown. By and large, people were born into their jobs. Whatever their parents had been—landowner, soldier, farmer, servant, merchant, or beggar—they became, too. People not only knew their place, they also understood the rights and obligations inherent in each position. The landowner had the right to receive labor from his tenants, but he also cared for them if they fell ill. Certainly, there were abuses, but at a time when people held religious convictions about their position in life and workers had few expectations that their lives would be better than their parents', the role of law was limited.

The primary English law of employment simply established that, in the absence of a contract, an employee was hired for a year at a time. This rule was designed to prevent injustice in a farming society. If an employee worked through harvest time, the landowner could not fire him in the unproductive winter. Conversely, a worker could not stay the winter and then leave for greener pastures in the spring.

In the eighteenth and nineteenth centuries, the Industrial Revolution profoundly altered the employment relationship. Many workers left the farms and villages for large factories in the city. Bosses no longer knew their workers personally, so they felt little responsibility toward them. The old laws that had suited an agrarian economy with stable relationships did not fit the new employment conditions. Instead of duties and responsibilities, courts emphasized the freedom to contract. Since employees could quit their factory jobs whenever they wanted, it seemed only fair for employers to have the same freedom to fire a worker. That was indeed the rule adopted by the courts: Unless workers had an explicit employment contract, they were employees at will. **An *employee at will* could be fired for a good reason, a bad reason, or no reason at all.** For nearly a century, this was the basic common law rule of employment. A court explained the rule this way:

> Precisely as may the employee cease labor at his whim or pleasure, and, whatever be his reason, good, bad, or indifferent, leave no one a legal right to complain; so, upon the other hand, may the employer discharge, and, whatever be his reason, good, bad, or indifferent, no one has suffered a legal wrong.[2]

However evenhanded this common law rule of employment may have sounded in theory, in practice, it could lead to harsh results. As the opening scenario illustrates, the lives of factory workers were grim. It was not as if they could simply pack up and leave; conditions were no better elsewhere. Courts and legislatures gradually began to recognize that individual workers were generally unable to negotiate fair contracts with powerful employers. Since the beginning of the twentieth century, employment law has changed dramatically. Now, the employment relationship is more strictly regulated by statutes and by the common law.

Note well, though: **In the absence of a specific legal exception, the rule in the United States is *still* that an employee at will can be fired for any reason. But today there are several important exceptions to this rule.** Many of the statutes discussed in this chapter were passed by Congress and therefore apply *nationally*. The common law, however, comes from state courts and only applies *locally*. We will look at a sampling of cases that illustrates national trends, even though the law is not the same in every state.

This chapter covers five topics in employment law: (1) employment security, (2) workplace freedom, (3) workplace safety, (4) financial protection, and (5) collective bargaining. Chapter 30 covers employment discrimination.

---

[2]Union Labor Hospital Association v. Vance Redwood Lumber Company, 158 Cal. 551, 554 (Cal. 1910).

29-2 EMPLOYMENT SECURITY

29-2a Family and Medical Leave Act

The Family and Medical Leave Act (FMLA) guarantees both men and women up to 12 weeks of *unpaid* leave each year for childbirth, adoption, or a serious health condition of their own or in their immediate family. This statute defines an immediate family member as a spouse, child, or parent—but not a sibling, grandchild, or in-law. An employee who takes a leave must be allowed to return to the same or an equivalent job with the same pay and benefits. The FMLA applies only to companies with at least 50 workers and to employees who have been with the company full time for at least a year, which means that only about 60 percent of workers are covered by this statute.

Here are some examples of what counts as a "serious health condition" under this statute:

- Any health issue that requires hospitalization.

- A condition that requires more than one visit to a healthcare provider. The visits may be spread out over as long as a year.

- A condition that requires only one visit to a healthcare provider but that also requires a course of treatment such as physical therapy or prescription medication.

Thus, the FMLA would apply in the case of a heart attack, ongoing kidney dialysis, and an ear infection that required antibiotics. It would generally not cover food poisoning that did not require hospitalization, the common cold, or a sprained ankle.

In many FMLA lawsuits, a worker claims that he or she was fired in retaliation for taking leave, while the employer argues that the termination was for some other reason. The following case illustrates this dynamic.

PETERSON V. EXIDE TECHNOLOGIES

477 Fed. Appx. 474
United States Court of Appeals for the Tenth Circuit, 2012

Facts: Exide Technologies issued repeated warnings to Robert Peterson for driving forklifts too fast and violating other safety rules. After he was injured in a forklift crash, Exide granted him FMLA leave for 10 days while he recovered.

Peterson's manager fired him during the leave period for "flagrant violations of safety rules." Peterson sued, claiming that he was terminated in retaliation for exercising his right to take FMLA leave. The lower court granted summary judgment to Exide, and Peterson appealed.

Issue: *Was Peterson fired in retaliation for claiming FMLA leave?*

Excerpts from Judge Baldock's Decision: The FMLA makes it unlawful for any employer to interfere with, restrain, or deny the exercise of the rights provided by the FMLA, or to discriminate against any individual for opposing any practice prohibited by the FMLA.

[I]f Plaintiff makes out a prima facie retaliation case, the burden shifts to Defendant to demonstrate a legitimate, nonretaliatory reason for its termination decision. If Defendant meets this burden, the burden shifts back to Plaintiff to show that there is a genuine dispute of material fact as to whether Defendant's explanations are pretextual.

Defendant asserts it dismissed Plaintiff for the legitimate reason that he violated company safety policies. According to Defendant's Plant Manager:

Based on my own review of the photographs and the damage they depicted, Plaintiff was driving too fast at the time of the crash and was not operating his forklift in a safe manner. Such conduct on Plaintiff's part was a flagrant violation of company health and safety policy and posed a threat to the safety of Plaintiff and other Exide employees.

The Plant Manager also based his decision to fire Plaintiff on the "history of careless and unsafe conduct" reflected in Plaintiff s personnel file. Defendant has adequately demonstrated a nonretaliatory reason for Plaintiff's termination: his repeated safety violations. Thus, the burden shifts back to Plaintiff to show pretext.

Plaintiff argues Defendant's asserted justification is pretextual because the forklift accident was a "minor incident." Whether the accident was "minor" is questionable. But even if it was, we see nothing that prevents Defendant from firing employees for minor safety violations. Particularly where, as here, the employee has a record of unsafe work performance, even a minor infraction could be the last straw.

Plaintiff has produced no evidence to undermine Defendant's nonretaliatory explanation for the termination. Aside from the fact Plaintiff was on FMLA leave when he was fired, no evidence suggests a causal connection between Plaintiff's firing and his exercise of FMLA rights. Therefore, the district court properly granted summary judgment.

AFFIRMED.

Ethics

Although the FMLA offers important protections, the time off it provides is unpaid. Some cities require employers to provide paid family leave, but currently, only 11 percent of private sector employees are eligible for this type of time off. The federal government provides none for its own employees, not even for childbirth. The United States is the only advanced country that does not require employers to provide paid maternity leave. Should Congress modify the FMLA to require some period of paid leave for new mothers? If so, for how long? A few weeks while they recuperate from childbirth? Or a few months to care for the newborn? What about paternity leave, which many countries require? And how about workers who take FMLA leave to deal with a serious illness? Should they be paid?

29-2b Common-Law Protections

The employment-at-will doctrine was created by the courts. Because that rule sometimes led to grossly unfair results, the courts created a major exception: **wrongful discharge**.

Wrongful Discharge: Violating Public Policy

Wrongful discharge
An employer may not fire a worker for a reason that violates basic social rights, duties, or responsibilities.

Olga Monge was a schoolteacher in her native Costa Rica. After moving to New Hampshire, she attended college in the evenings to earn U.S. teaching credentials. At night, she worked at the Beebe Rubber Co. During the day, she cared for her husband and three children. When she applied for a better job at her plant, the foreman offered to promote her if she would be "nice" and go out on a date with him. When she refused, he assigned her to a lower-wage job, took away her overtime, made her clean the washrooms, and generally ridiculed her. Finally, she collapsed at work, and he fired her.[3]

Imagine that you are one of the judges who decided this case. Olga Monge was an employee at will and therefore could be fired for any reason. But how can you let the foreman get away with this despicable behavior? The New Hampshire Supreme Court decided that even an employee at will has some rights:

> We hold that a termination by the employer of a contract of employment at will which is motivated by bad faith or malice or based on retaliation is not in the best interest of the economic system or the public good and constitutes a breach of the employment contract.[4]

---

[3]Monge v. Beebe, 114 N.H. 130 (NH 1974).
[4]Ibid at 133.

The *Monge* case illustrates the concept of **wrongful discharge, which prohibits an employer from firing a worker for certain particularly *bad reasons*.** A bad reason is one that violates public policy. Unfortunately, this public policy rule is easier to name than it is to define because its definition and application vary from state to state. **In essence, the public policy rule prohibits an employer from firing a worker for a reason that violates fundamental social rights, duties, or responsibilities.**

Almost every employee who has ever been fired feels that a horrible injustice has been done. The difficulty, from the courts' perspective, is to distinguish those cases of dismissal that are offensive enough to harm the community at large from those that injure only the employee. The courts have primarily applied the public policy rule when an employee refuses to violate the law, performs a legal duty, exercises a legal right, or supports fundamental societal values.

Refusing to Violate the Law.   Larry Downs went to Duke Hospital for surgery on his cleft palate. When he came out of the operating room, the doctor instructed a nurse, Marie Sides, to give Downs enough anesthetic to immobilize him. Sides refused because she thought the anesthetic was wrong for this patient. The doctor angrily administered the anesthetic himself. Shortly thereafter, Downs stopped breathing. Before the doctors could resuscitate him, he suffered permanent brain damage. When Downs's family sued the hospital, Sides was called to testify. A number of Duke doctors told her that she would be "in trouble" if she testified. She did testify, and after three months of harassment, she was fired. When she sued Duke University, the court held:

> It would be obnoxious to the interests of the state and contrary to public policy and sound morality to allow an employer to discharge any employee, whether the employment be for a designated or unspecified duration, on the ground that the employee declined to commit perjury, an act specifically enjoined by statute. To hold otherwise would be without reason and contrary to the spirit of the law.[5]

As a general rule, employees may not be discharged for refusing to break the law. Courts have protected employees who refused to participate in an illegal price-fixing scheme, falsify pollution control records required by state law, pollute navigable waters in violation of federal law, or assist a supervisor in stealing from customers.[6]

Performing a Legal Duty.   **Courts have consistently held that an employee may not be fired for serving on a jury.** Employers sometimes have difficulty replacing employees who are called up for jury duty and, therefore, prefer that their workers find some excuse for not serving. But jury duty is an important civic obligation that employers are not permitted to undermine.

Exercising a Legal Right.   **As a general rule, an employer may not discharge a worker for exercising a legal right if that right supports public policy.** Dorothy Frampton injured her arm while working at the Central Indiana Gas Co. Her employer (and its insurance company) paid her medical expenses and her salary during the four months she was unable to work. When she discovered that she also qualified for benefits under the state's workers' compensation plan, she filed a claim and received payment. One month later, the company fired her without giving a reason. When she sued, the court held that the gas company had violated public policy. If workers fear that making a claim for workers' comp will get them fired, then no one will file and the whole point of the statute will be undermined.[7]

---

[5]Sides v. Duke University, 74 N.C. App. 331 (N.C. Ct. App. 1985).
[6]Tameny v. Atlantic Richfield Co., 27 Cal. 3d 167 (Cal. 1980); Trombetta v. Detroit, T. & I. R., 81 Mich. App. 489 (Mich. Ct. App. 1978); Sabine Pilot Service, Inc. v. Hauck, 28 Tex. Sup. J. 339 (Tex. 1985); Vermillion v. AAA Pro Moving & Storage, 146 Ariz. 215 (Ariz. Ct. App. 1985).
[7]Frampton v. Central Indiana Gas Co., 260 Ind. 249 (Ind. 1973).

Supporting Societal Values.   **Courts are sometimes willing to protect employees who do the right thing, even if they violate the boss's orders.** Kevin Gardner had just parked his armored truck in front of a bank in Spokane, Washington, when he saw a man with a knife chase the manager out of the bank. While running past the truck, the manager looked directly at Gardner and yelled, "Help me, help me." Gardner got out of his truck and locked the door. By then, the suspect had grabbed another woman, put his knife to her throat, and dragged her into the bank. Gardner followed them in, tackled the suspect, and disarmed him. The rescued woman hailed Gardner as a hero, but his employer fired him for violating a "fundamental" company rule that prohibited drivers from leaving their armored trucks unattended. However, the court held for Gardner on the grounds that, although he had no affirmative legal duty to intervene in such a situation, society values and encourages voluntary rescuers when a life is in danger.[8] This issue is, however, one on which the courts are divided. Not all judges would have made the same decision.

In the following case, an employee was fired for exercising her legal right to use medical marijuana. Did her employer violate public policy?

---

[8]Gardner v. Loomis Armored, Inc., 128 Wn.2d 931 (Wash. 1996).

You be the Judge

Facts: The voters of Washington state passed the Medical Use of Marijuana Act (MUMA), which stated that:

> Humanitarian compassion necessitates that the decision to authorize the medical use of marijuana by patients with terminal or debilitating illnesses is a personal, individual decision, based upon their physician's professional medical judgment and discretion.
>
> Qualifying patients and medical practitioners shall not be found guilty of a crime under state law for their possession and limited use of marijuana. This act is intended to provide clarification to law enforcement and to all participants in the judicial system.
>
> Any person meeting the requirements appropriate to his or her status under this chapter shall not be penalized in any manner, or denied any right or privilege, for such actions.
>
> Nothing in this chapter requires any accommodation of any on-site medical use of marijuana in any place of employment.

Jane Roe suffered from debilitating migraine headaches that caused chronic pain, nausea, blurred vision, and

ROE V. TELETECH CUSTOMER CARE MGMT. (COLO.) LLC

171 Wn.2d 736
Washington Supreme Court, 2011

sensitivity to light. On a medical questionnaire, she described her average pain as an 8 on a scale of 1 to 10 where 10 represented "pain as bad as you can imagine." Because other medications were not effective, she obtained a prescription for medical marijuana. It alleviated her symptoms without side effects and allowed Roe to work and care for her children. She ingested marijuana only in her home.

TeleTech Customer Care Mgmt. offered Roe a position as a customer service representative but required that she first pass a drug test. She told the company about her medical marijuana use. On the day she started work, TeleTech received notice that Roe had failed the drug test. A week later, it fired her.

Roe sued TeleTech for wrongful discharge, alleging that her termination had violated public policy. (She filed suit under a pseudonym because medical marijuana use is illegal under federal law.) The trial court granted TeleTech's motion for summary judgment. The appeals court confirmed. The Washington Supreme Court agreed to hear the case.

You Be the Judge: *Did TeleTech violate public policy when it fired Roe? Was this discharge wrongful?*

Arguments for Roe: Roe is exactly the sort of person this statute is intended to protect. Medical marijuana changed her life—now she can hold a job and care for her family.

But, of course, she cannot hold a job if employers terminate her for using this legal medication. TeleTech is undermining the whole point of the statute and jeopardizing its clear policies. A ruling in favor of TeleTech would inhibit other people from using medication that citizens voted to make available.

Furthermore, the statute specifically states that, "No person … shall be penalized in any manner, or denied any right or privilege, for such actions." Being fired is a substantial penalty.

No one is asking TeleTech to tolerate drug-impaired workers. Marijuana should be treated like any other medication—it cannot be used if it hurts job performance. But there is no evidence that it did so.

Arguments for TeleTech: Just because medical marijuana is legal in Washington does not mean that it is an important social right. Indeed, employers can fire workers for many *legal* behaviors, such as smoking, or being disagreeable.

The purpose of MUMA is to protect doctors and patients from criminal liability, not to create an unlimited right to use medical marijuana. The statute does not explicitly prevent employers from banning its use. And how can marijuana use be an important public policy when it is still illegal under federal law?

Contract Law

Traditionally, many employers (and employees) thought that only a formal, signed document qualified as an employment contract. Increasingly, however, courts have been willing to enforce an employer's more casual promises, whether written or verbal. Sometimes courts have also been willing to *imply* contract terms in the absence of an *express* agreement.

Truth in Hiring. **Verbal promises made during the hiring process are generally enforceable, even if not approved by the company's top executives.** When the Tanana Valley Medical-Surgical Group, Inc., hired James Eales as a physician's assistant, it promised him that, as long as he did his job, he could stay there until retirement age. Six years later, the company fired him without cause. The Alaska Supreme Court held that the clinic's promise was enforceable.[9]

Employee Handbooks. The employee handbook at Blue Cross & Blue Shield stated that employees could be fired only for just cause and then only after warnings, notice, a hearing, and other procedures. Charles Toussaint was fired summarily five years after he joined the company. Although this decision was ultimately reviewed by the personnel department, company president, and chairman of the board of trustees, Toussaint was not given the benefit of all of the procedures in the handbook. The court held that **an employee handbook creates a contract.**[10]

Some employers have responded to cases like this by including provisions in their handbooks stating that it is not a contract and can be modified at any time. Generally, these provisions have been enforced.[11] However, employers cannot have it both ways. If a handbook states that it is not a contract, then employers cannot enforce provisions favorable to them, such as required arbitration clauses.[12]

---

[9]Eales v. Tanana Valley Medical-Surgical Group, Inc., 663 P.2d 958 (Alaska 1983).

[10]Toussaint v. Blue Cross & Blue Shield, 408 Mich. 579 (Mich. 1980).

[11]See, for example, Federal Express Corp. v. Dutschmann, 36 Tex. Sup. J. 530 (Tex. 1993).

[12]See, for example, Sparks v. Vista Del Mar Child & Family Services, 207 Cal. App. 4th 1511 (Cal. App. 2d Dist. 2012).

Covenant of Good Faith and Fair Dealing.   As we saw in Chapter 20 on practical contracts, about half the states imply a covenant of good faith and fair dealing in contracts. This covenant requires both parties to behave reasonably, making an honest effort to meet both the spirit and letter of the contract.

In the employment context, these cases mostly arise in situations in which an employer fires a worker to avoid paying promised income or benefits. When Forrest Fleming went to work for Parametric Technology Corp., the company promised him valuable stock options if he met his sales goals. He would not be able to *exercise* the options (that is, purchase the stock), however, until several years after they were granted, and then only if he was still employed by the company. During his four years with Parametric, Fleming received options for about 18,000 shares at a price as low as 25 cents each. The shares ultimately traded in the market for as much as $50. Although Fleming exercised some options, the company fired him three months before he became eligible to purchase an additional 1,000 shares. The jury awarded him $1.6 million in damages. Although Parametric had not violated the explicit terms of the option agreement, the jury believed it had violated the covenant of good faith and fair dealing by firing Fleming to prevent him from exercising his remaining options.[13]

Tort Law

Workers have successfully sued their employers under the following tort theories.

Defamation.   **Employers may be liable for defamation when they give false references about an employee.** In his job as a bartender at the Capitol Grille restaurant, Christopher Kane often flirted with customers. After he was fired from his job, his ex-boss claimed that Kane had been "fired from every job he ever had for sexual misconduct." In fact, Kane had never been fired before. He recovered $300,000 in damages for this defamation.

More than half of the states, however, recognize a qualified privilege for employers who give references about former employees. A qualified privilege means that employers are liable only for false statements that they know to be false or that are primarily motivated by ill will. After Becky Chambers left her job at American Trans Air, Inc., she discovered that her former boss was telling anyone who called for a reference that Chambers "does not work good with other people," is a "troublemaker," and "would not be a good person to rehire." Chambers was unable, however, to present compelling evidence that her boss had been primarily motivated by ill will. Neither Trans Air nor the boss was held liable for these statements because they were protected by a qualified privilege.[14]

To reduce the likelihood of defamation suits, many companies refuse to provide references for former employees. They instruct their managers to reveal only a person's salary and dates of employment and not to offer an opinion on job performance.

What about risky workers? Do employers have any obligation to warn about them? **Generally, courts have held that employers do *not* have a legal obligation to disclose information about former employees. But, in the case of violence, courts are divided.** While Jeffrey St. Clair worked as a maintenance man at the St. Joseph Nursing Home, he was disciplined 24 times for actions ranging from extreme violence to drug and alcohol use. When he applied for a job with another firm, St. Joseph refused to give any information other than St. Clair's dates of employment. After he savagely murdered a security guard at his new job, the guard's family sued, but a Michigan court dismissed the case.[15]

A California court, however, reached the opposite decision in a school case. Officials from two junior high schools gave Robert Gadams glowing letters of recommendation without mentioning that he had been fired for inappropriate sexual conduct with students. While an assistant principal at a new school, he molested a 13-year-old. The court held that

Qualified privilege

Employers who give references are liable only for false statements that they know to be false or that are primarily motivated by ill will.

---

[13]Fleming v. Parametric Tech. Corp., 1999 U.S. App. LEXIS 14864 (9th Cir. 1999).
[14]Chambers v. American Trans Air, Inc., 577 N.E.2d 612 (Ind. Ct. App. 1991).
[15]Moore v. St. Joseph Nursing Home, Inc., 184 Mich. App. 766 (Mich. Ct. App. 1990).

the writer of a letter of recommendation owes to third parties (in this case, the student) "a duty not to misrepresent the facts in describing the qualifications and character of a former employee, if making these misrepresentations would present a substantial, foreseeable risk of physical injury to the third persons."[16]

To assist employers in giving references, Lehigh economist Robert Thornton has written *The Lexicon of Intentional Ambiguous Recommendations* (LIAR). For a candidate with interpersonal problems, he suggests saying, "I am pleased to say that this person is a former colleague of mine." For a candidate with drug or alcohol problems, there are several possibilities: "She was always high in my opinion," "We remember the hours she spent working with us as happy hours," or "I would say that her real talent is getting wasted at her current job."[17]

Intentional Infliction of Emotional Distress. **Employers who condone cruel treatment of their workers may face liability under the tort of intentional infliction of emotional distress.** Morris Shields, a supervisor at GTE, was continuously in a rage. He would yell and scream profanity at the top of his voice while pounding his fists. He would charge at employees, stopping uncomfortably close to their faces while screaming and yelling. He regularly threatened to fire the clerks he supervised. At least once a day, he would call one of the clerks into his office and have her stand in front of him, sometimes for as long as 30 minutes, while he stared at her, read papers, or talked on the phone. Once, when Shields discovered a spot on the carpet, he made a clerk get on her hands and knees to clean it while he stood over her yelling. The Supreme Court of Texas upheld a jury award of $100,000 for the workers.[18]

29-2c **Whistleblowing**

No one likes to be accused of wrongdoing even if (or, perhaps, especially if) the accusations are true. This is exactly what **whistleblowers** do: They are employees who disclose illegal behavior on the part of their employer. Not surprisingly, some companies, when faced with such an accusation, prefer to shoot the messenger. Rather than fixing the reported problem, they retaliate against the informer.

Whistleblower
Someone who discloses wrongdoing

For eight years, medical device maker C.R. Bard paid kickbacks to doctors and hospitals to get them to buy its radioactive seeds for treating prostate cancer. To cover the cost of the kickbacks, the company inflated its bills to Medicare. Bard paid the government $48 million to settle this case. Of this amount, $10 million went to Julie Darity, a former Bard employee who was fired after she blew the whistle on the company's wrongdoing.

The law on whistleblowers varies across the country. As a general rule, however, whistleblowers are protected in the following situations:

- **The False Claims Act.** Darity recovered under the federal False Claims Act, a statute that permits lawsuits against anyone who defrauds the government. The recovery is shared between the government and the whistleblower. This act prohibits employers from firing workers who file suit under the statute.

- **The Dodd-Frank Wall Street Reform and Consumer Protection Act.** Anyone who provides information to the government about violations of securities or commodities laws is entitled to a payout of from 10 to 30 percent of whatever

---

[16]Randi W. v. Muroc Joint Unified School District, 14 Cal. 4th 1066 (1997), modified, 14 Cal. 4th 1282c, 97 Cal. Daily Op. Service 1439.

[17]Robert J. Thornton, *Lexicon of Intentionally Ambiguous Recommendations*, Barnes and Noble Books, 2005.

[18]Gte Southwest v. Bruce, 42 Tex. Sup. J. 907 (Tex. 1999).

award the government receives, provided that the award tops $1 million. If a company retaliates against tipsters, they are entitled to reinstatement, double back pay, and attorney's fees.

This whistleblowing provision is intended to encourage tips to the government, but companies fear it may also discourage employees from reporting wrongdoing to corporate compliance offices—why report a problem to your own company for free when you could get paid a lot of money to report it to the government?

- **Sarbanes-Oxley Act of 2002.** This act protects employees of publicly traded companies who provide evidence of fraud to investigators (whether in or outside the company). A successful plaintiff is entitled to reinstatement, back pay, and attorney's fees.

- **Constitutional protection for government employees.** Employees of federal, state, and local governments have a right to free speech under the United States Constitution. Therefore, the government cannot retaliate against public employees who blow the whistle if the employee is speaking out on a matter of *public concern*. A New York City social worker complained on TV that the city child welfare agency was not adequately protecting children from horrible abuse. When the city suspended her, she sued. The court ruled that the government has the right to prohibit some employee speech, but if the employee speaks on matters of public concern, the government bears the burden of justifying any retaliation. In this case, the court held for the social worker.[19]

- **Statutory protection for federal employees.** The Civil Service Reform Act and the Whistleblower Protection Act prevent retaliation against federal employees who report wrongdoing. They also permit the award of back pay and attorney's fees to the whistleblower. This statute was used to prevent the National Park Service from disciplining two managers who wrote a report expressing concern over development in Yellowstone National Park.

- **State laws.** The good news is that all 50 states have laws that protect whistleblowers from retaliation by their employers. The bad news is that the scope of this protection varies greatly from state to state. Most courts, however, prohibit the discharge of employees who report illegal activity. A Connecticut court held a company liable when it fired a quality control director who reported to his boss that some products had failed quality tests.[20]

EXAM Strategy

Question: When Shiloh interviewed for a sales job at a medical supply company, the interviewer promised that she would only have to sell medical devices, not medications. Once she began work (as an employee at will), Shiloh discovered that the sales force was organized around regions, not products, so she had to sell both devices and drugs. When she complained to her boss over lunch in the employee lunchroom, he said in a loud voice, "You're a big girl now—it's time you learned that you don't always get what you want." That afternoon, she was fired. Does she have a valid claim against the company?

[19]Harman v. City of New York, 140 F.3d 111 (2d Cir. 1998).
[20]Smith v. Calgon Carbon Corp., 917 F.2d 1338 (3rd Cir. 1990).

Strategy: Shiloh is an employee at will. Does she have any protection under the law? Shiloh has had two key interactions with the company—being hired and being fired. The employer's promises made during the hiring process are enforceable. Here, the company is liable because the interviewer clearly made a promise that the company did not keep. What about the way in which Shiloh was fired? Is it intentional infliction of emotional distress? Was this treatment cruel? Probably not cruel enough to constitute intentional infliction of emotional distress.

Result: The company is liable to Shiloh for making false promises to her during the hiring process, but not for the manner in which she was fired.

29-3 WORKPLACE FREEDOM

The line between home and workplace often blurs. Employees respond to customer emails 24/7, while their behavior at home (say, drug use) can have an impact on their employer. This section deals with worker freedom: The right to personal lifestyle choices and to the public expression of opinions about the workplace.

29-3a Off-Duty Activities

In the absence of a specific law to the contrary, employers *do* have the right to fire workers for off-duty conduct. Employees have been fired or disciplined for such extra-curricular activities as taking part in dangerous sports (such as skydiving), dating coworkers, smoking, or even having high cholesterol.

> **Employers *do* have the right to fire workers for off-duty conduct.**

Lifestyle Laws

A few states, such as California, have passed lifestyle laws that protect the right of employees to engage in *any* lawful activity or use any lawful product when off duty. Thus, if California residents skydive while smoking a cigarette, they may lose their lives, but not their jobs. Some laws also protect *particular* off-duty conduct.

Smoking

Smokers tend to take more sick days and have higher healthcare expenses than other employees. The federal government estimates that it costs an extra $3,400 a year to employ a worker who smokes. As a result, several thousand employers, including Union Pacific and Alaska Airlines, simply refuse to hire those who light up. **In roughly 60 percent of the states, however, employers cannot prohibit workers from smoking.**

Some workers have also claimed that nicotine addiction is a disability under the Americans with Disabilities Act (ADA; see Chapter 30 for more information about this statute), but so far, courts have been skeptical that Congress intended ADA coverage for the roughly 60 million Americans who smoke.[21] Several amendments to the ADA passed in 2008 could provide more protection for smokers, but the courts have not yet decided such a case.

---

[21]See Brashear v. Simms, 138 F.Supp.2d 693 (D.Md. 2001).

Alcohol and Drug Use

Private Employers.   Under *federal* law, *private* **employers are permitted to test job applicants and workers for alcohol and *illegal* drugs.** They may sanction workers who fail the test, even if the drug or alcohol use was off duty. *State* laws on drug testing vary widely.

Although employers were traditionally most concerned about illegal drugs, they now also worry about *legal* use of prescription drugs such as Xanax and oxycodone because these medications may cause impairment. In one study, workers drug-tested after accidents in the workplace were four times more likely to have opiates in their system than job applicants.

However, **the Equal Employment Opportunity Commission (EEOC), the federal agency charged with enforcing federal employment laws, prohibits testing for prescription drugs unless a worker seems impaired.** The EEOC filed suit against a company that randomly tested for legal use of prescription drugs, and a jury awarded substantial damages to the employees.[22]

Government Employers.   Governments are sometimes allowed to conduct drug and alcohol tests of their employees. Public safety workers, such as police and firefighters, can be randomly tested for illegal drugs, and they may also be required to report legal drug use that could compromise their ability to perform their jobs. If their drug use (legal or not) is a threat to public safety, they may be suspended or fired from their jobs. Other government employees, whose work does not involve public safety, can be tested only if they show signs of impairment.

29-3b Free Speech in the Workplace

The National Labor Relations Act (NLRA) is well known as pioneer legislation that protects employees' right to unionize. However, many people do not realize that **the NRLA protects *all employees* (1) who engage in collective activity (2) in connection with work conditions and (3) who are not supervisors.** Thus, the National Labor Relations Board (NLRB), which enforces this statute, has long held that even non-unionized workers cannot be fired for complaining about their jobs. When a hair salon fired two (non-unionized) hairdressers for violating the salon's "negativity policy" by complaining about work conditions, the NLRB ruled that this action was a violation of the statute.[23]

Recently, however, the NLRB has applied this principle online, ruling that company social media policies violate the NLRA if they unreasonably constrain employee speech about work conditions. In short, **workers (who are not supervisors) have the right to discuss work conditions, whether that discussion takes place in the lunchroom or in a chat room and whether or not the employee is engaged in union activities.** The following case illustrates the NLRB's views on this issue.

HISPANICS UNITED OF BUFFALO, INC. AND CARLOS ORTIZ BEFORE THE NLRB

359 NLRB No. 37
National Labor Relations Board, 2012

Facts: Lydia Cruz-Moore and Marianna Cole-Rivera worked at Hispanics United of Buffalo (the Agency), an organization that assisted victims of domestic violence. At work and at home, by phone and by text, Cruz-Moore routinely complained to Cole-Riviera that other employees provided poor service to their clients. At home one Saturday night, Cruz-Moore texted Cole-Riviera that she intended to tell the executive director, Lourdes Iglesias,

---

[22]Bates v. Dura Auto Sys Inc, 2011 U.S. Dist. LEXIS 97469 (M.D. Tenn 2011)
[23]Salon/Spa at Boro, 2010 NLRB LEXIS 533 (N.L.R.B. Dec. 30, 2010).

that these other employees had been performing poorly. Cole-Rivera then posted the following message on her Facebook page:

> Lydia Cruz, a coworker feels that we don't help our clients enough at [the Agency]. I about had it! My fellow coworkers how do u feel?

Four off-duty employees posted comments saying that they were upset with Cruz-Moore. She responded with a comment demanding that Cole-Rivera "stop with ur lies about me."

Cruz-Moore then complained to Iglesias that she felt defamed by the Facebook postings. After looking at them, Iglesias fired Cole-Rivera and the four coworkers on the grounds that their remarks violated the Agency's zero tolerance policy on bullying and harassment.

Issue: *Were these Facebook postings protected speech under the NLRA?*

Excerpts from the Decision of the NLRB:[24] [Two issues are] in dispute here: whether the employees' Facebook comments constituted concerted activity and, if so, whether that activity was protected by the Act.

The Board defined concerted activity as that which is engaged in with or on the authority of other employees, and not solely by and on behalf of the employee himself. Applying these principles, there should be no question that the activity engaged in by the five employees was concerted. As set forth in her initial Facebook post, Cole-Rivera alerted fellow employees of another employee's complaint that they "don't help our clients enough," stated that she "about had it" with the complaints, and

solicited her coworkers' views about this criticism. By responding to this solicitation with comments of protest, Cole-Rivera's four coworkers made common cause with her, and, together, their actions were concerted because they were undertaken with other employees.

As to the [other] element of the violation, whether the employees' concerted activity was protected, we find that the Facebook comments here fall well within the Act's protection. The Board has long held that [the NLRA] protects employee discussions about their job performance, and the Facebook comments plainly centered on that subject. As discussed, the employees were directly responding to allegations they were providing substandard service to the Agency's clients. Given the negative impact such criticisms could have on their employment, the five employees were clearly engaged in protected activity in mutual aid of each other's defense to those criticisms.

According to the Agency, it was privileged to discharge the five employees because their comments constituted unprotected harassment and bullying of Cruz-Moore, in violation of its "zero tolerance" policy. [We] reject this argument. First, the Facebook comments cannot reasonably be construed as a form of harassment or bullying within the meaning of the Agency's policy. Second, legitimate managerial concerns to prevent harassment do not justify policies that discourage the free exercise of [NLRA] rights by subjecting employees to discipline on the basis of the subjective reactions of others to their protected activity. Here, the Agency applied its harassment policy to the discharged employees based solely on Cruz-Moore's subjective claim that she felt offended by the Facebook comments.

Note, however, that to be protected, the employee speech must be "concerted." The *Arizona Daily Star* fired a reporter for tweeting a series of comments, including:

> You stay homicidal, Tucson. See Star Net for the bloody deets.
> What?!?!? No overnight homicide? WTF? You're slacking Tucson.

The NLRB ruled that this tweets were not protected activity because the reporter had been acting alone, not in concert with other workers.[25]

29-3c **Polygraph Tests**

A polygraph exam is a type of lie detector test. **Under the Employee Polygraph Protection Act of 1988, employers may not require, or even *suggest*, that an employee or job candidate submit to a polygraph test *except in the following cases*:**

- an employee who is part of an "ongoing investigation" into crimes that have already occurred,

---

[24]For ease of reading, we have replaced "Respondent" with "Agency."
[25]NLRB Case No. 28-CA-23267.

- an applicant applying for a government job, or
- an applicant for a job in public transport, security services, banking, or at pharmaceutical firms that deal with controlled substances.

If an employer requires a polygraph test, it must give advance written notice of when the test will be given and advise workers that they are entitled to legal counsel. A private employer may not fire or discriminate against an employee who fails a polygraph exam unless it also finds supporting evidence that the worker has done something wrong.

29-3d **Guns**

Employers have the right to prohibit guns in the workplace but, in almost half the states, Bring Your Gun to Work Laws prevent companies from banning firearms in the parking lot. Advocates for gun rights argue that workers have the right to protect themselves during their commutes and that, ultimately, such laws improve employee safety. However, a study found that a workplace that permits guns is five times as likely to suffer a homicide as one in which they are banned.[26]

Some executives worry about the dangers of disciplining workers in states with Bring Your Gun to Work laws. An employment lawyer reported that he had attended termination meetings in which executives had sought protection from bulletproof vests or armed guards. In one case, a company held a termination meeting in an airport conference room so that participants would have to pass through security first.[27]

EXAM Strategy

Question: To ensure that its employees did not use illegal drugs in or outside the workplace, Marvel Grocery Store required all employees to take a polygraph exam. Moreover, managers began to check employees' Facebook pages for reference to drug use. Jagger was fired for refusing to take the polygraph test. Pete was dismissed after revealing on his Facebook page that he was using marijuana (illegally). Has the company acted in accordance with the law?

Strategy: First: As employees at will, are Jagger and Pete protected by a statute? The Employee Polygraph Protection Act permits employers to require a polygraph test as part of ongoing investigations into crimes that have occurred.

Second: What about Pete's marijuana use? No statutes protect a worker for *illegal* off-duty conduct. Can the company punish Pete for what he wrote on his Facebook page? Not if it relates to work conditions and involves concerted activity.

Result: Here, Marvel has no reason to believe that a crime occurred, so it cannot require a polygraph test. Pete's Facebook postings have nothing to do with work conditions and illegal activity is not protected. So the company is liable to Jagger for requiring him to take the polygraph exam, but not to Pete for firing him over illegal drug use.

---

[26]Dana Loomis, Stephen W. Marshall, and Myduc L. Ta, "Employer Policies Toward Guns and the Risk of Homicides in the Workplace," *Am J Public Health*. 2005 May; 95(5): 830–832.
[27]Sara Murray, "Guns in the Parking Lot: A Delicate Workplace Issue," *The Wall Street Journal*, Oct. 15, 2013.

29-4 WORKPLACE SAFETY

29-4a OSHA

In 1970, Congress passed the Occupational Safety and Health Act (OSHA) to ensure safe working conditions. **Under OSHA:**

- Employers must comply with specific health and safety standards. For example, healthcare personnel who work with blood are not permitted to eat or drink in areas where the blood is kept. Protective clothing—gloves, gowns, and laboratory coats—must be impermeable to blood.

- Employers are under a general obligation to keep their workplace "free from recognized hazards that are causing or are likely to cause death or serious physical harm" to employees.

- Employers must keep records of all workplace injuries and accidents.

- The Occupational Safety and Health Administration (which is also known as OSHA) may inspect workplaces to ensure that they are safe. OSHA may assess fines for violations and order employers to correct unsafe conditions.

29-4b Workplace Bullying

Rich was on the company's leadership council, where one of his responsibilities was to help new employees. But he seemed to misinterpret his responsibilities—instead of helping, he singled out Jonathan, to whom he sent texts and voicemails that were racist, mocking, and threatening. Rich also publicly called Jonathan "the Big Weirdo" and told others that he was the easiest one to scare. After a series of incidents in which other employees joined with Rich to publicly embarrass him, Jonathan quit.

Studies estimate that as many as 60 percent of employees are bullied at some point in their careers. A bullying atmosphere is bad for two reasons. One, it impairs worker productivity. In the example above, Rich Incognito and Jonathan Martin were offensive linemen on the Miami Dolphins football team. Players had a practice of hazing rookies, but Incognito took the harassment to a new level with Martin. If a 300-pound lineman could be so troubled by bullying, imagine how more vulnerable employees might feel.

Two, bullying may also subject employers to liability. Half of the states have introduced anti-bullying legislation, although none has passed it. And the Supreme Court of Indiana ruled that "workplace bullying" is an entirely appropriate term to be used in front of a jury and could be considered a form of intentional infliction of emotional distress.[28]

29-5 FINANCIAL PROTECTION

Congress and the states have enacted laws designed to provide employees with a measure of financial security. All of the laws in this section were created by statute, not by the courts.

---

[28]Raess v. Doescher, 883 N.E.2d 790 (Ind. 2008).

29-5a Fair Labor Standards Act: Minimum Wage, Overtime, and Child Labor

Passed in 1938, the Fair Labor Standards Act (FLSA) regulates wages and limits child labor nationally. It provides that hourly workers must be paid a minimum wage of $7.25 per hour, plus time and a half for any hours over 40 in one week. These wage provisions do not apply to salaried workers, such as managerial, administrative, or professional staff. More than half the states and even some cities set a higher minimum wage, so it is important to check state guidelines as well.

One significant issue that employers face under the FLSA is: "What counts as work, and how do you keep track of it?" What if a worker answers email during lunch or takes a phone call on the train ride home? Although these activities count as work, how can the employer keep track of them? Carla Bird, an assistant at Oprah Winfrey's production company, submitted timesheets showing 800 hours of overtime in 17 weeks. She said she had worked 12 or 13 hours a day, seven days a week, for four months. The company paid her $32,000 in overtime.[29] If employees work all the time, or even if they are just on call, they are entitled to be paid for those hours.

Another issue facing employers: Are unpaid internships covered by the FLSA? Eric Glatt and Alexander Footman were unpaid interns at Fox Searchlight Pictures Inc., where they worked on the movie *Black Swan*. A court ruled that they were actually employees who were entitled to wages under the FLSA. **To be unpaid, an internship must:**

- provide training similar to that given in school,

- be for the benefit of the intern,

- not displace regular employees, and

- not provide any immediate advantage to the employer.[30]

The FLSA also prohibits "oppressive child labor," which means that children under 14 may work only in agriculture, entertainment, a family business, babysitting, or newspaper delivery. Fourteen- and fifteen-year-olds are permitted to work *limited* hours after school in nonhazardous jobs, such as retail. Sixteen- and seventeen-year-olds may work *unlimited* hours in nonhazardous jobs.

29-5b Workers' Compensation

Workers' compensation statutes ensure that employees receive payment for injuries incurred at work. Before workers' comp, injured employees could recover damages only if they sued their employer. It was the brave worker who was willing to risk a suit against his boss. Lawsuits not only poisoned the atmosphere at work, but employers frequently won anyway by claiming that (1) the injured worker was contributorily negligent, (2) a fellow employee had caused the accident, or (3) the injured worker had assumed the risk of injury. As a result, seriously injured workers (or their families) often had no recourse against the employer.

Workers' comp statutes provide a fixed, certain recovery to the injured employee, no matter who was at fault for the accident. In return, employees are not permitted to sue their employers for negligence. The amounts allowed (for medical expenses and lost wages) under workers' comp statutes are often less than a worker might recover in court, but the injured employee trades the certainty of some recovery for the higher risk of rolling the dice at trial. Payments are approved by an administrative board that conducts an informal hearing into each claim.

---

[29]Lisa Belkin, "O.T. Isn't as Simple as Telling Time," *The New York Times*, September 20, 2007.
[30]Glatt v. Fox Searchlight Pictures Inc., 293 F.R.D. 516 (S.D.N.Y. 2013).

29-5c Health Insurance

Under the Patient Protection and Affordable Care Act, employers with 50 or more full-time employees must pay a penalty if they do not provide basic health insurance. In addition, company insurance policies must cover employees' children up to the age of 26.

Losing your job does not mean that you must also give up your health insurance—at least not immediately. Under the Consolidated Omnibus Budget Reconciliation Act (COBRA), **former employees must be allowed to continue their health coverage for 18 months after leaving their job.** But they must pay the cost themselves, plus as much as an additional 2 percent to cover administrative expenses. COBRA applies to any company with 20 or more workers.

29-5d Social Security

The federal social security system began in 1935, during the depths of the Great Depression, to provide a basic safety net for the elderly, ill, and unemployed. **The Social Security system pays benefits to workers who are retired, disabled, or temporarily unemployed, and to the spouses and children of disabled or deceased workers.** The social security program is financed through a tax on wages that is paid by employers, employees, and the self-employed.

Although the social security system has done much to reduce poverty among the elderly, many worry that it cannot survive in its current form. The system was designed to be "pay as you go"; that is, when workers pay taxes, the proceeds do not go into a savings account for their retirement, but instead are used to pay benefits to current retirees. In 1940, there were 40 workers for each retiree; currently, there are 3.3. As a result, the system now pays out more in benefits each year than it receives in tax revenues. To ensure long-term viability, some aspects of social security will have to change.

The Federal Unemployment Tax Act (FUTA) is the part of the social security system that provides support to the unemployed. FUTA establishes some national standards, but states are free to set their own benefit levels and payment schedules. **A worker who quits voluntarily or is fired for just cause is ineligible for unemployment benefits.** While receiving payments, she must make a good-faith effort to look for other employment.

Before social security, breadlines were often the only safety net available to the unemployed.

29-5e Pension Benefits

In 1974, Congress passed the Employee Retirement Income Security Act (ERISA) to protect workers covered by private pension plans. Under ERISA, employers are not required to establish pension plans, but if they do, they must follow these federal rules. The law was aimed, in particular, at protecting benefits of retired workers if their companies subsequently go bankrupt. The statute also prohibits risky investments by pension plans. In addition, the statute sets rules on the vesting of benefits. (An employer cannot cancel *vested* benefits; *nonvested* benefits are forfeited when the employee leaves.) Before ERISA, retirement benefits at some companies did not vest until the employee retired—if he quit or was fired before retirement, even after years of service, he lost his pension. Under current law, employee benefits normally must vest within five years of employment.

29-6 LABOR UNIONS

The opening scenario of this chapter provides a graphic example of how painful (literally) working conditions could be in the past. In a desire for better pay and improved working conditions, workers in the nineteenth and early twentieth centuries sought strength through collective bargaining. They began to join together in unions.

But American courts treated any coordinated effort by workers as a criminal conspiracy. They convicted workers merely for the *act* of joining together, even if no strike took place. A company could usually obtain an immediate injunction merely by alleging that a strike *might* cause harm. Courts were so quick to issue injunctions that most companies became immune to union efforts.

But with the economic collapse of 1929 and the vast suffering of the Great Depression, public sympathy shifted to the workers. Congress responded with two landmark statutes.

29-6a **Key Pro-Union Statutes**

In 1932, Congress passed **the Norris-LaGuardia Act, which prohibited federal court injunctions in nonviolent labor disputes.** No longer could management stop a strike merely by saying the word *strike*. By taking away the injunction remedy, Congress was declaring that workers should be permitted to organize unions and to use their collective power to achieve legitimate economic ends. The statute led to explosive growth in union membership.

In 1935, Congress passed the Wagner Act, generally known as the National Labor Relations Act (NLRA). This is the most important of all labor laws. **The NLRA ensures the right of workers to form unions and encourages management and unions to bargain collectively and productively.** With the enactment of the NLRA, Congress put an end to any notion that unions were inherently illegal.

Section 7 of the NLRA is the cornerstone of union power. **It guarantees employees the right to organize and join unions, bargain collectively through representatives of their own choosing, and engage in other concerted activities.** Note, however, that for the purposes of this statute, **"supervisors" are not employees and do not have the right to form a union.** A **supervisor** is anyone with the authority to make independent decisions on hiring, firing, disciplining, or promoting other workers.[31] For example, the Supreme Court ruled that university faculty were supervisors and, therefore, were not covered by the NLRA.[32]

Section 8 prohibits employers from engaging in the following unfair labor practices (ULPs):

- Interfering with union organizing efforts
- Dominating or interfering with any union
- Discriminating against a union member
- Refusing to bargain collectively with a union

Later, Section 8 was amended to prohibit unions from engaging in these ULPs:

- Interfering with employees who are exercising their labor rights
- Causing an employer to discriminate against workers as a means to strengthen the union
- Charging excessive dues

When a union tried to organize Starbucks workers, the company prohibited employees from discussing the union or their working conditions and posting union material on employee bulletin boards. It also punished pro-union employees with unfavorable work assignments. All of these actions were ULPs.[33]

The NLRA also established the National Labor Relations Board (NLRB) to administer and interpret the statute and to adjudicate labor cases. For example, when a union charges that an employer has committed a ULP—say, by refusing to bargain—the claim goes first to the NLRB.

Supervisor

Anyone with the authority to make independent decisions on hiring, firing, disciplining, or promoting other workers

---

[31] 29 U.S.C. § 152(11).
[32] NLRB v. Yeshiva Univ., 444 U.S. 672 (U.S. 1980).
[33] NLRB v. Starbucks Corp., 679 F.3d 70 (2d Cir. 2012).

29-6b Labor Unions Today

Organized labor is in flux in the United States. In the 1950s, about 25 percent of workers belonged to a union. Today, only about 11 percent do. That is the lowest level since 1916. Even more remarkable, membership in private sector unions has declined from 35 percent in the 1950s to 6.6 percent now.

There are four major reasons for this decline. One: More states have passed right-to-work laws that permit employees in unionized workplaces to opt out of joining the union or paying dues. Two: Some large employers (such as Boeing) have relocated to states with little union presence. Three: Employment is increasing in industries, such as services, that have not traditionally been unionized. Four: Public employees (such as teachers and police officers) are much more likely to be unionized, but they are generally not covered by the NLRA. Instead, state labor laws apply, which tend to provide less protection than federal statutes.

This decline in strength reduces union bargaining power. Thus, the auto unions agreed to a two-tiered structure that pays new workers little more than half the wages of long-term employees. All of these factors have contributed to stagnation in pay for the bottom half of wage earners, even as their productivity has increased dramatically.

29-7 ORGANIZING A UNION

29-7a Exclusivity

Under §9 of the NLRA, a validly recognized union is the *exclusive* representative of the employees. This means that the union represents all of the designated employees, regardless of whether a particular worker *wants* to be included. The company may not bargain directly with any employee in the group, nor with any other organization representing the designated employees.

However, a union may not exercise power however it likes: Along with a union's exclusive bargaining power goes a duty of fair representation, which requires that a union treat all members fairly, impartially, and in good faith. A union may not favor some members over others, nor may a union discriminate against a member based on characteristics such as race or gender.

29-7b Organizing: Stages

A union organizing effort generally involves the following pattern:

Campaign

Union organizers talk—or attempt to talk—with employees and persuade them to form a union. The organizers may be employees of the company, who simply chat with fellow workers about unsatisfactory conditions; or a union may send nonemployees of the company to hand out union leaflets to workers as they arrive and depart from work.

Authorization Cards

Union organizers ask workers to sign authorization cards, which state that the particular worker requests the specified union to act as her sole bargaining representative.

If a union obtains authorization cards from a sizable percentage of workers, it seeks recognition as the exclusive representative for the bargaining unit. The union may ask the employer to recognize it as the bargaining representative, but most of the time, employers refuse to recognize the union voluntarily.

Petition

Assuming that the employer does not voluntarily recognize a union, the union generally petitions the NLRB for an election. It must submit to the NLRB regional office authorization cards signed by at least 30 percent of the workers. The regional office verifies whether there are enough valid cards to warrant an election and looks closely at the proposed bargaining unit to make sure that it is appropriate. If the regional office determines that the union has identified an appropriate bargaining unit and has enough valid cards, it orders an election.

Election

The NLRB closely supervises the election to ensure fairness. All members of the proposed bargaining unit vote on whether they want the union to represent them. If more than 50 percent of the workers vote for the union, the NLRB designates that union as the exclusive representative of all members of the bargaining unit. When unions hold representation elections, they win about 60 percent of the time.

29-7c Organizing: Actions

What Workers May Do

The NLRA guarantees employees the right (1) to talk among themselves about working conditions and forming a union, (2) to hand out literature, and ultimately, (3) to join a union.[34] Workers have the right to urge other employees to sign authorization cards and to push their cause vigorously. When employees hand out leaflets, the employer generally may not limit the content, as long as it is somewhat related to union activity.

There are, of course, limits to what union organizers may do. An employer may restrict organizing discussions if they interfere with business. A worker on a moving assembly line has no right to walk away from his task to talk with other employees about organizing a union; these discussions must be left until lunch or some other break time.[35] Likewise, management may prohibit union discussions in the presence of customers.

What Employers May Do

The employer may vigorously present anti-union views to its employees but may not use either threats or rewards to defeat a union drive.[36] A company may not fire a worker who favors a union; nor may it suddenly grant a significant pay raise in the midst of a union campaign.

EXAM Strategy

Question: The Teamsters Union is attempting to organize the drivers at We Haul trucking company. Workers who favor a union have been using the lunchroom to hand out petitions and urge other drivers to sign authorization cards. The company posts a notice in the lunchroom: "Many employees do not want unions discussed in the lunchroom. Out of respect for them, we are prohibiting further union efforts in this lunchroom." Is this sign legal?

Strategy: The NLRA guarantees employees the right to talk among themselves about forming a union and to hand out literature. Management has the right to present anti-union views.

---

[34]NLRA §7.
[35]NLRB v. Babcock & Wilcox Co, 351 U.S. 105 (S. Ct. 1956).
[36]NLRB v. Gissel Packing Co, 395 U.S. 575 (S. Ct. 1969).

Result: We Haul has violated the NLRA. The company has the right to urge employees not to join the union. However, it is not entitled to block the union from its organizing campaign. Even assuming the company is correct that some employees do not want unions discussed, it has no right to prohibit such advocacy.

29-8 COLLECTIVE BARGAINING

Once a union is formed, a company must then bargain with it toward the goal of creating a new contract, which is called a **collective bargaining agreement (CBA)**.

The NLRA *permits* the parties to bargain almost any subject they wish, but it only *requires* them to bargain certain issues. **Under the statute, mandatory subjects include wages, hours, and other terms and conditions of employment.** In addition, courts have interpreted the statute to include: benefits, order of layoffs and recalls, production quotas, work rules (such as safety practices), retirement benefits, and onsite food service and prices. An employer may not *unilaterally* make changes in conditions of employment without first bargaining with the union.

The union and the employer are *not* obligated to reach an agreement, but they are required to bargain in good faith. In other words, the two sides must meet with open minds and make a reasonable effort to reach a contract. In the following Landmark Case, a company violated this rule.

Collective bargaining agreement (CBA)

A contract between a union and management

Landmark Case

NLRB v. TRUITT MANUFACTURING CO.
351 U.S. 149
United States Supreme Court, 1956

Facts: A union representing workers at Truitt Manufacturing Company requested a raise of 10 cents per hour for all members. The company countered with an offer of 2.5 cents, arguing that a larger increase would bankrupt the company. The union demanded to examine Truitt's books, and when the company refused, the union complained to the NLRB.

The NLRB determined that the company had committed a ULP by failing to bargain in good faith and ordered it to allow union representatives to examine its finances. A court of appeals found no ULP and refused to enforce the Board's order. The Supreme Court granted *certiorari*.

Issue: *Did the company refuse to bargain in good faith?*

Excerpts from Justice Black's Decision: While Congress did not compel agreement between employers and bargaining representatives, it did require collective bargaining in the hope that agreements would result. [T]he Act admonishes both employers and employees to exert every reasonable effort to make and maintain agreements.

In their effort to reach an agreement here, both the union and the company treated the company's ability to pay increased wages as highly relevant. Claims for increased wages have sometimes been abandoned because of an employer's unsatisfactory business condition; employees have even voted to accept wage decreases because of such conditions.

Good-faith bargaining necessarily requires that claims made by either bargainer should be honest claims. This is true about an asserted inability to pay an increase in wages. If such an argument is important enough to present in the give and take of bargaining, it is important enough to require some sort of proof of its accuracy.

The Board concluded that under the facts and circumstances of this case, the respondent was guilty of an unfair labor practice in failing to bargain in good faith. We see no reason to disturb the findings of the Board.

Reversed.

29-9 CONCERTED ACTION

Concerted action
Tactics taken by union members to gain bargaining advantage

Concerted action refers to any tactics that union members take in unison to gain some bargaining advantage. It is this power that gives a union strength. **The NLRA guarantees the right of employees to engage in concerted action for mutual aid or protection.**[37] The most common forms of concerted action are strikes and picketing.

29-9a Strikes

The NLRA guarantees employees the right to strike, but with some limitations.[38] A union has a guaranteed right to call a strike if the parties are unable to reach a CBA. A union may also call a strike to protest a ULP, or to preserve work that the employer is considering sending elsewhere. Note that the right to strike can be waived. Management will generally insist that the CBA include a **no-strike clause**, which prohibits the union from striking while the CBA is in force. A strike is illegal in several other situations as well; here, we mention the most important.

No-strike clause
A clause in a CBA that prohibits the union from striking while the CBA is in force

Cooling-Off Period

Before striking to terminate or modify a CBA, a union must give management 60 days' notice. This cooling-off period is designed to give both sides a chance to reassess negotiations and to decide whether some additional compromise would be wiser than enduring a strike. Suppose a union contract expires July 1. The two sides attempt to bargain a new contract, but progress is slow. The union may strike as an economic weapon, but it must notify management of its intention to do so *and then must wait 60 days.*

Statutory Prohibition

Many states have outlawed strikes by public employees. The purpose of these statutes is to ensure that unions do not use public health or welfare as a weapon to secure an unfair bargaining advantage. However, even employees subject to such a rule may find other tactics to press their cause.

Sit-down strike
Members stop working but remain at their job posts, blocking replacement workers

Sit-down Strikes

In a **sitown strike**, members stop working but remain at their job posts, physically blocking replacement workers from taking their places. This type of strike is illegal.

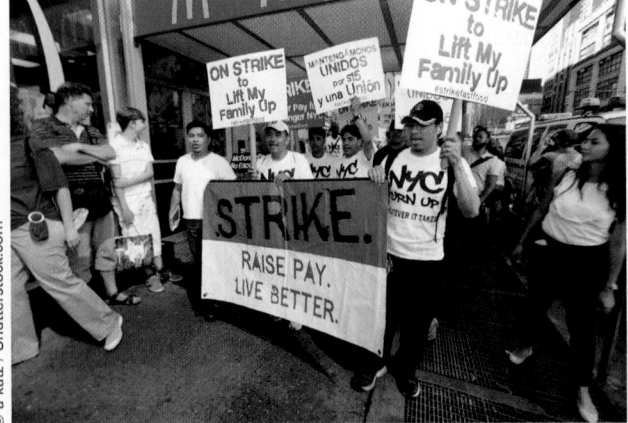

Fast food workers are using strikes as a means to raise their standard of living.

Partial Strikes

A partial strike occurs when employees stop working temporarily, then resume, then stop again, and so forth. This tactic is particularly disruptive because management cannot bring in replacement workers. **A union may either walk off the job or stay on it, but it may not alternate.**

29-9b Replacement Workers

When employees go on strike, management has the right to use replacement workers to keep the business operating. What about after the strike ends? May the employer offer the replacement workers *permanent* jobs, or must the company give union members their jobs back? It depends on the type of strike.

---

[37]NLRA §7.
[38]NLRA §13.

An **economic strike** is one intended to gain wages or benefits. **During an economic strike, an employer may hire** *permanent* **replacement workers.** When the strike is over, the company has no obligation to lay off the replacement workers to make room for the strikers. However, if and when the company does hire more workers, it may not discriminate against the strikers.

After an unfair labor practices (ULP) strike, union members are entitled to their jobs back, even if that means the employer must lay off replacement workers. In the *Truitt* case, the Supreme Court ruled that the company had committed a ULP. If the union had gone out on strike, the company would have had to hire back all the union members once the strike was over, regardless of how many replacement workers it had hired.

Economic strike
One intended to gain wages or benefits

29-9c Picketing

The goal of picketing is to discourage employees, replacement workers, and customers from doing business with the company. **Picketing the employer's workplace in support of a strike is generally lawful.** However, the picketers are not permitted to use physical force to *prevent* someone from crossing the line. The company may terminate violent picketers and permanently replace them, regardless of the nature of the strike.

Secondary boycotts are generally illegal. A **secondary boycott** is a picket line established not at the employer's premises but at a different workplace. If Union is on strike against Truck Co., it is free to picket Truck Co.'s office and terminal. But Union cannot set up a picket line at a supermarket where Truck Co. delivers in an effort to pressure Truck Co. by persuading shoppers and other workers to boycott the store.

Secondary boycott
A picket line established not at the employer's premises but at a different workplace

29-9d Lockouts

The workers have bargained with management for weeks, and discussions have turned belligerent. It is 6:00 a.m., the start of another day at the factory. But as 150 employees arrive for work, they are surprised to find the company's gate locked and armed guards standing on the other side. This is a **lockout**: Management has prohibited workers from entering the premises and earning their paychecks. **Most lockouts are legal.**

Lockout
Management prohibits workers from entering the premises

Chapter Conclusion

Since the first time one person hired another, there has been tension in the workplace. The law attempts to balance the right of a boss to run a business with the right of a worker to fair treatment. Different countries balance these rights differently. The United States, for instance, guarantees its workers fewer rights than virtually any other industrialized nation. American bosses have great freedom to manage their employees. Alternatively, in Canada, France, Germany, Great Britain, and Japan, employers must show just cause before terminating workers. Which system is best? On the one hand, being mistreated at work can be a terrible, life-altering experience, but on the other, companies that cannot lay off unproductive employees are less likely to add to their workforce, which may be one reason that Europe tends to have a higher unemployment rate than the United States.

EXAM REVIEW

1. **TRADITIONAL COMMON LAW RULE** The traditional common law rule of employment provided that an employee at will could be fired for a good reason, a bad reason, or no reason at all. But modern law has created exceptions to this rule that prohibit firing an employee-at-will for a bad reason.

2. **FMLA**   The Family and Medical Leave Act guarantees workers up to 12 weeks of unpaid leave each year for childbirth, adoption, or a serious health condition of their own or in their immediate family.

3. **WRONGFUL DISCHARGE AND PUBLIC POLICY**   Generally, an employee may not be fired for refusing to violate the law, performing a legal duty, exercising a legal right, or supporting fundamental societal values.

EXAM Strategy

Question: When Theodore Staats went to his company's "Council of Honor Convention," he was accompanied by a woman who was not his wife, although he told everyone she was. The company fired him. Staats alleged that his termination violated public policy because it infringed upon his freedom of association. He also alleged that he had been fired because he was too successful—his commissions were so high, he out-earned even the highest-paid officer of the company. Has Staats's employer violated public policy?

Strategy: Is Staats protected by a statute? No. Is he being asked to break the law? No. Is he trying to perform a legal duty? No. Is he being denied a legal right? Is he supporting fundamental societal values? (See the "Result" at the end of this section.)

4. **PROMISES MADE DURING THE HIRING PROCESS**   Promises made during the hiring process are generally enforceable, even if not approved by the company's top executives. An employee handbook also creates a contract.

EXAM Strategy

Question: When Phil McConkey interviewed for a job as an insurance agent with Alexander & Alexander, the company did not tell him that it was engaged in secret negotiations to merge with Aon. When the merger went through soon thereafter, Aon fired McConkey. Was Alexander liable for not telling McConkey about the possible merger?

Strategy: Was McConkey protected by a statute? No. Did the company make any promises to him during the hiring process? (See the "Result" at the end of this section.)

5. **COVENANT OF GOOD FAITH AND FAIR DEALING**   About half the states imply a covenant of good faith and fair dealing in contracts. This covenant requires both parties to behave reasonably, making an honest effort to meet both the spirit and letter of the contract.

6. **DEFAMATION**   Employers may be liable for defamation when they give false references about an employee.

7. **INTENTIONAL INFLICTION OF EMOTIONAL DISTRESS** Employers who condone cruel treatment of their workers may face liability under the tort of intentional infliction of emotional distress.

8. **WHISTLEBLOWERS** Whistleblowers receive some protection under both federal and state laws.

9. **OFF-DUTY ACTIVITIES** In the absence of a specific law to the contrary, employers have the right to fire workers for off-duty conduct.

10. **ALCOHOL AND DRUG USE** Under federal law, private employers are permitted to test job applicants and workers for alcohol and illegal drugs. The Equal Employment Opportunity Commission prohibits testing for prescription drugs unless a worker seems impaired.

11. **FREE SPEECH** Under the NLRA, workers (who are not supervisors) have the right to discuss work conditions, whether that discussion takes place in the lunchroom or in a chat room and whether or not the employee is engaged in union activities.

12. **GUNS** Employers have the right to ban guns from the workplace but, in almost half the states, laws prevent companies from banning firearms in the parking lot.

13. **OSHA** The goal of the Occupational Safety and Health Act is to ensure safe conditions in the workplace.

14. **WORKERS' COMPENSATION** Workers' compensation statutes ensure that employees receive payment for injuries incurred at work.

15. **HEALTH INSURANCE** Under the Patient Protection and Affordable Care Act, employers with 50 or more full-time employees must pay a penalty if they do not provide basic health insurance. In addition, former employees must be allowed to continue their health insurance for 18 months after being terminated from their job, but they must pay for it themselves.

16. **SOCIAL SECURITY** The Social Security system pays benefits to workers who are retired, disabled, or temporarily unemployed and to the spouses and children of disabled or deceased workers.

17. **UNEMPLOYMENT COMPENSATION** Workers are eligible for unemployment compensation unless they have quit their job voluntarily or were fired for just cause.

18. **ERISA** The Employee Retirement Income Security Act regulates private pension plans.

19. **RIGHT TO ORGANIZE** Section 7 of the NLRA guarantees employees the right to organize and join unions, bargain collectively, and engage in other concerted activities. Section 8 of the NLRA makes it a ULP for an employer to interfere with union organizing, discriminate against a union member, or refuse to bargain collectively. During a union organizing campaign, an employer may vigorously

present anti-union views to its employees, but it may not use threats or rewards to defeat the union effort.

20. **EXCLUSIVITY**   Under §9 of the NLRA, a validly recognized union is the exclusive representative of the employees.

EXAM Strategy

Question: Power, Inc., which operated a coal mine, suffered financial losses and had to lay off employees. The United Mine Workers of America (UMWA) began an organizing drive. Power's general manager warned miners that if the company was unionized, it would be shut down. An office manager told one of the miners that the company would get rid of union supporters. Shortly before the election was to take place, Power laid off 13 employees, all of whom had signed union cards. A low-seniority employee who had not signed a union card was not laid off. The union claimed that Power had committed ULPs. Comment.

Strategy: The NLRA guarantees employees the right to organize. An employer may vigorously advocate against a union organizing campaign. However, it is a ULP to interfere with union organizing or discriminate against a union member. (See the "Result" at the end of this section.)

21. **BARGAINING**   The employer and the union *must* bargain over wages, hours, and other terms and conditions of employment. They *may* bargain over other subjects, but neither side may insist on doing so. The union and the employer must bargain in good faith, but they are not obligated to reach an agreement.

22. **STRIKES**   The NLRA guarantees employees the right to strike, with some limitations. After an *economic* strike, an employer is not obligated to lay off replacement workers to give strikers their jobs back, but it may not discriminate against strikers when filling job openings. After a ULP strike, the striking workers must get their jobs back.

23. **PICKETING**   Picketing the employer's workplace in support of a strike is generally lawful. Secondary boycotts are generally illegal.

24. **LOCKOUTS**   Most lockouts are legal.

---

3. Result: The court held that freedom of association is an important social right and should be protected. However, being fired for bringing a lover to an employer's convention is not a threat to public policy. Nor is discharge for being too successful.

4. Result: The court held that when Alexander hired him, it was making an implied promise that he would not be fired immediately. The company was liable for not having revealed the merger negotiations.

20. Result: Each of the acts described was a ULP. Threatening layoffs or company closure are classic examples of ULPs. Laying off those who had signed union cards, but not those who refused, was clear discrimination.

MULTIPLE-CHOICE QUESTIONS

1. When Brook went to work at an advertising agency, his employment contract stated that he was "at will and could be terminated at any time." After 28 months with the company, he was fired without explanation. Which of the following statements is true?

   (a) The company must give him an explanation for his termination.

   (b) Because he had a contract, he was not an employee at will.

   (c) He could only be fired for a good reason.

   (d) He could be fired for any reason.

   (e) He could be fired for any reason except a bad reason.

2. **CPA QUESTION** An unemployed CPA generally would receive unemployment compensation benefits if the CPA _____.

   (a) was fired as a result of the employer's business reversals

   (b) refused to accept a job as an accountant while receiving extended benefits

   (c) was fired for embezzling from a client

   (d) left work voluntarily without good cause

3. During a job interview with Venetia, Jack reveals that he and his wife are expecting twins. Venetia asks him if he is planning to take a leave once the babies are born. When Jack admits that he would like to take a month off work, he can see her face fall. She ultimately decides not to hire him because of the twins. Which of the following statements are true?

   (a) Venetia has violated the FMLA.

   (b) Venetia has violated COBRA.

   (c) Both (a) and (b)

   (d) None of the above

4. Which of the following statements is true?

   (a) In about half the states, employees have the right to bring guns into their workplace.

   (b) In about half the states, employees have the right to bring guns into their workplace parking lot.

   (c) Both (a) and (b) are true.

   (d) None of the above is true.

5. Alpha Company's workers go on strike. The company hires replacement workers so that it can continue to operate its business. When the strike ends, Alpha must rehire the original workers if the strike was over _____.

   (a) wages

   (b) a ULP

   (c) both (a) and (b)

   (d) None of the above

CASE QUESTIONS

1. When Walton Weiner interviewed for a job with McGraw-Hill, Inc., he was assured that the company would not terminate an employee without "just cause." Weiner also signed a contract specifying that his employment would be subject to the provisions of McGraw-Hill's handbook. The handbook said, "[The] company will resort to dismissal for just and sufficient cause only, and only after all practical steps toward rehabilitation or salvage of the employee have been taken and failed. However, if the welfare of the company indicates that dismissal is necessary, then that decision is arrived at and is carried out forthrightly." After eight years, Weiner was fired suddenly for "lack of application." Does Weiner have a valid claim against McGraw-Hill?

2. Hugo's sister posted a message on his Facebook page asking him how his evening as a bartender had gone. He responded with complaints that he had not had a raise in five years and that his tips "sucked." He also called his customers "rednecks" and stated that he hoped they choked on glass as they drove home drunk. Can Hugo's boss fire him for these comments?

3. *YOU BE THE JUDGE* **WRITING PROBLEM** Apex gave Marcie an employment handbook stating that (1) she was an at-will employee, (2) the handbook did not create any contractual rights, and (3) employees who were fired had the right to a termination hearing. The company fired Marcie, claiming that she had falsified delivery records. She said that Apex was retaliating against her because she had complained of sexual harassment. Apex refused her request for a termination hearing. Did the employee handbook create a contract guaranteeing Marcie a hearing? **Argument for Apex:** The handbook could not have been clearer—it did not create a contract. Marcie is an employee at will and is not entitled to a hearing. **Argument for Marcie:** Apex intended that employees would rely on the handbook. The company used promises of a hearing to attract and retain good employees. Marcie was entitled to a hearing.

4. Triec, Inc., is a small electrical contracting company in Springfield, Ohio, owned by its executives, Yeazell, Jones, and Heaton. Employees contacted the International Brotherhood of Electrical Workers, which began an organizing drive, and 6 of the 11 employees in the bargaining unit signed authorization cards. The company declined to recognize the union, which petitioned the NLRB to schedule an election. The company then granted several new benefits for all workers, including higher wages, paid vacations, and other measures. When the election was held, only 2 of the 11 bargaining unit members voted for the union. Did the company violate the NLRA?

5. Sally is sent home from school with the chicken pox. Her father takes her to a pediatrician who says that she will be fine in about a week and in the meantime just needs bed rest and plenty of fluids. Is Sally's father entitled to leave under the FMLA to care for Sally?

DISCUSSION QUESTIONS

1. Debra Agis worked as a waitress in a Ground Round restaurant. The manager informed the waitresses that "there was some stealing going on." Until he found out who was doing it, he intended to fire all the waitresses in alphabetical order, starting with the letter "A." Dionne then fired Agis. Does she have a valid claim against her employer?

2. **ETHICS** Should employers be allowed to fire smokers? Nicotine is highly addictive and many smokers begin as teenagers, when they may not fully understand the consequences of their decisions. As Mark Twain, who began smoking at 12, famously said, "Giving up smoking is the easiest thing in the world. I know because I've done it thousands of times."

3. Noelle was the principal of a charter school and an employee at will. The head administrator imposed a rule requiring cafeteria workers to stamp the hands of children who did not have sufficient funds in their lunch accounts. Some of these children were entitled to free lunches, others needed to ask their parents to replenish their accounts. Noelle directed the cafeteria workers to stop this humiliating practice. The administrator fired her. Does Noelle have a valid claim for wrongful termination?

4. **ETHICS** As the manager of BigBox Store, you are afraid that, if your workers unionize, you will not be able to compete against stores with a non-union workforce. You would very much like to fire Geraldo, the employee who is leading the unionization effort. Of course, you know this action would be a violation of the NLRA. But you also know that, if you were found to have violated the law (after years of litigation), you would simply be required to reinstate Geraldo, pay him some back wages, and post a notice promising never to do it again.[39] (After all that time, Geraldo probably would not even want his BigBox job back.) In the meantime, all the other employees would be so scared, they would not support the union. This strategy is the most cost effective, but is it the right thing to do? What would Mill and Kant say?

5. Despite its detailed dress code for employees, Starbucks stores permitted workers to wear multiple pins and buttons, some of which, but not all, were related to its employee-reward and product-promotion programs. When a union tried to organize employees, management prohibited workers from wearing more than one pro-union pin at a time. (One employee had tried to wear eight union buttons.) Is this rule a ULP?

6. Catherine Wagenseller was a nurse at Scottsdale Memorial Hospital and an employee at will. While on a camping trip with other nurses, Wagenseller refused to join in a parody of the song "Moon River," which concluded with members of the group "mooning" the audience. Her supervisor seemed upset by her refusal. Prior to the trip, Wagenseller had received consistently favorable performance evaluations. Six months after the outing, Wagenseller was fired. She contends it was because she had not mooned. Should the hospital be able to fire Wagenseller for this reason?

---

[39]House Report 110-023 Employee Free Choice Act of 2007.

7. *YOU BE THE JUDGE* **WRITING PROBLEM** Nationwide Insurance Co. circulated a memorandum asking all employees to lobby in favor of a bill that had been introduced in the Pennsylvania House of Representatives. By limiting the damages that an injured motorist could recover from a person who caused an accident, this bill promised to save Nationwide significant money. Not only did John Novosel refuse to lobby, but he privately criticized the bill for harming consumers. Nationwide was definitely not on his side—it fired him. Novosel filed suit, alleging that his discharge had violated public policy by infringing his right to free speech. Did Nationwide violate public policy by firing Novosel? **Argument for Novosel:** The United States Constitution and the Pennsylvania Constitution both guarantee the right to free speech. Nationwide has violated an important public policy by firing Novosel for expressing his opinions. **Argument for Nationwide:** For all the high-flown talk about the Constitution, what we have here is an employee who refused to carry out company policy. If the employee wins in this case, where will it all end? What if an employee for a tobacco company refuses to market cigarettes because he does not approve of smoking? How can businesses operate without loyalty from their employees?

8. **ETHICS** Edward Snowden was a contractor at the National Security Agency (NSA) who publicly released a huge number of highly classified documents. From these files, the world learned for the first time that the NSA had been collecting vast amounts of information about the email, mail, and telephone usage of millions of people, many of them American citizens. In releasing this data, Snowden had embarrassed U.S. officials and possibly damaged spy operations. However, the NSA's own auditor found that the NSA had exceeded its authority. Two federal judges ruled that the NSA had violated the Constitution. Because Snowden broke the law, he was not protected by whistleblower statutes. He sought asylum overseas because, if he returned to the United States, he faced life in prison. Does he deserve life in prison? Should he be offered amnesty? A reduced sentence? How important is it to encourage whistleblowing?

CHAPTER 30

© Tomas Tichy/Shutterstock.com

EMPLOYMENT DISCRIMINATION

Imagine that you are on the hiring committee of a top San Francisco law firm. You come across a resume from a candidate who grew up on an isolated ranch in Arizona. Raised in a house without electricity or running water, he had worked alongside the ranch hands his entire childhood. At the age of 16, he left home for Stanford University, and from there had gone on to Stanford Law School, where he finished third in his class. You think to yourself, "This sounds like a real American success story. A great combination of grit and intelligence." But without hesitation, you toss the resume into the wastebasket.

> You think, "This sounds like a real American success story." But you toss the resume into the wastebasket.

This is a true story. Indeed, there was a candidate with these credentials who was unable to find a job in any San Francisco law firm. The only jobs on offer were as a secretary, because this candidate was a woman—Sandra Day O'Connor, who went on to become one of the most influential lawyers of her era and the first woman justice on the Supreme Court of the United States.

Before 1964, you might never see a female or African American doctor, engineer, police officer, or corporate executive. If a woman or minority did get a job, it was legal to treat them differently from white men. Women, for example, could be paid less for the same job and could be fired if they got married or pregnant.

30-1 INTRODUCTION

The United States has travelled a long and bumpy road toward equality of opportunity in the workplace. This story begins after the Civil War, when a torn and bleeding country sought to protect the rights of freed slaves and undo the terrible harm of a century of slavery. The country began by ratifying three Constitutional amendments: The Thirteenth prohibits slavery, the Fourteenth guarantees due process of law and equal protection under the law, and the Fifteenth prohibits restrictions on the right to vote because of race or color. In addition, Congress passed the Civil Rights Act of 1866, which provided that all people born in the United States (except Native Americans) were citizens of the United States and had the same rights as white citizens.[1]

However, in response to these laws, many states passed (and the Supreme Court upheld) statutes that made these protections worthless. The most notorious case was *Plessy v. Ferguson*, in which the Supreme Court upheld the constitutionality of a Louisiana law that prohibited blacks from riding in railroad cars reserved for whites. Blacks were provided with "separate but equal" cars.[2]

Not until 1954, almost a century after the Civil War, did the Supreme Court reverse its *Plessy* decision. In the landmark case *Brown v. Board of Education*, the high court ruled that "separate but equal" policies were unconstitutional.[3] In particular, it prohibited segregated public schools. However, many school districts were slow to comply with the case, and even ten years later, segregated public schools still existed in many parts of the country. Nonetheless, *Brown* inspired a generation of civil rights leaders such as Martin Luther King and Rosa Parks, who led protests, boycotts, and voter registration drives.

These actions influenced Congress to pass the Civil Rights Act of 1964. Title VII of this Act prohibits certain types of employment discrimination, which is the focus of this chapter. However, the statute was even more far-reaching because it prohibited a broad range of discrimination, including in education, voting, and public accommodations (such as hotels, restaurants, and movie theaters).

We begin now with a review of constitutional provisions that prohibit discrimination in the workplace and follow with a discussion of the major federal anti-discrimination statutes: the Civil Rights Act of 1866, the Equal Pay Act of 1963, Title VII of the Civil Rights Act of 1964, the Pregnancy Discrimination Act, the Age Discrimination in Employment Act, the Rehabilitation Act of 1973, the Americans with Disabilities Act, and the Genetic Information Nondiscrimination Act.

---

[1] 42 USC 21 §1981.
[2] 163 U.S. 537 (S. Ct. 1896).
[3] 347 U.S. 483 (S. Ct. 1954).

30-2 THE UNITED STATES CONSTITUTION

The Fifth Amendment to the Constitution prohibits the *federal government* from depriving individuals of "life, liberty, or property" without due process of law. The Fourteenth Amendment prohibits *state governments* from violating an individual's right to due process and equal protection. The courts have interpreted these provisions to prohibit employment discrimination by federal, state, and local governments.

30-3 CIVIL RIGHTS ACT OF 1866

As we have seen, the Civil Rights Act of 1866 was meant to provide freed slaves with the same rights as white citizens. It has been interpreted to prohibit *racial* discrimination in both private and public employment (except it does not apply to the federal government). As we will see later in the Enforcement section of this chapter, it offers plaintiffs some significant advantages over Title VII.

30-4 EQUAL PAY ACT OF 1963

Under the Equal Pay Act, a worker may not be paid at a lesser rate than employees of the opposite sex for equal work. "Equal work" means tasks that require equal skill, effort, and responsibility under similar working conditions. Citicorp rewarded Heidi Wilson's good work with a promotion to manager, but neglected to include a raise or even a bonus. She protested that the man she replaced had earned 75 percent more, but Citicorp argued that salaries were based not just on position but also on seniority and experience. Also, the economy was suffering through a recession. So Wilson requested a market analysis, but Citicorp refused. She also discovered that Citicorp had rewarded other employees with bonuses that were higher than Wilson's salary. An arbitrator awarded Wilson $340,000 in back pay.[4]

30-5 TITLE VII OF THE CIVIL RIGHTS ACT OF 1964

Under Title VII of the Civil Rights Act of 1964, it is illegal for employers with 15 or more employees to discriminate on the basis of race, color, religion, sex, or national origin. Discrimination under Title VII applies to every aspect of the employment process, from job ads to postemployment references, and includes hiring, firing, promoting, placement, wages, benefits, and working conditions of anyone who is in one or more of the so-called **protected categories** under the statute.

Protected categories
Race, color, religion, sex, or national origin

30-5a **Prohibited Activities**

There are four types of illegal activity under this statute: disparate treatment, disparate impact, hostile environment, and retaliation. All of these activities are illegal if used against anyone in a protected category.

---

[4]Elizabeth Behrman, "Tampa woman wins lawsuit against Citicorp for pay discrimination," *The Tampa Bay Times*, April 16, 2012.

Disparate Treatment

To prove a disparate treatment case, the plaintiff must show that she was *treated* less favorably than others because of her sex, race, color, religion, or national origin. Note that the burden of proof is on the plaintiff: She must prove that the employer *intentionally* discriminated, but this motive can be inferred from differences in treatment. The required steps in a disparate treatment case are:

1. The plaintiff presents evidence that:

- she belongs to a protected category under Title VII,

- she suffered adverse employment action, and

- this action occurred under conditions giving rise to an inference of discrimination.

Prima facie

From the Latin, meaning "from its first appearance," something that appears to be true upon a first look

If the plaintiff can show these facts, she has made a ***prima facie*** case. The plaintiff is not required to *prove* discrimination; she need only create a *presumption* that discrimination occurred.

Sandra Guzman was a reporter at the *New York Post*.[5] She was also black, Hispanic, Puerto Rican, and female. The company fired her, while keeping on a white editor. Although an editor's position was open, the company did not offer her that job. This evidence alone is not *proof* of discrimination because the *Post* may have had a perfectly good, nondiscriminatory explanation. However, its behavior *could have been* motivated by discrimination.

2. The defendant must present evidence that its decision was based on legitimate, nondiscriminatory reasons. The *Post* said that it had fired Guzman because the section she edited, Tempo, was unprofitable. The white editor had been kept on because she had an employment contract; Guzman did not. The company had not offered Guzman the open position because the pay was substantially less. The *Post* moved for summary judgement.

3. To win, the plaintiff must now prove that the employer intentionally discriminated. She may do so by showing either that (1) the reasons offered were simply a *pretext*, or (2) that a discriminatory intent is more likely than not. Guzman offered evidence that Tempo was not closed until after she was fired and that it had been more successful than the rest of the *Post*. She testified that she would have taken the open job, even at a lower salary. She also alleged that many *Post* employees had made racist and sexist remarks. Furthermore, the *Post* had run a cartoon, which was widely viewed as a racist insult to President Barack Obama, because it seemingly compared him to a monkey.[6] If Guzman can prove these facts to be true, she will win because she has offered evidence of both pretext and intent. Thus, the court denied the *Post's* request for summary judgment.

EXAM Strategy

Question: The appearance policy at Starwood Hotels prohibited employees from wearing hairstyles that showed excessive scalp. When Carmelita Vazquez repeatedly came to work with her hair in cornrows, Starwood fired her for violating its policy. Vazquez was African-American and Hispanic. White women were allowed to wear their hair in braids. Vazquez filed a disparate treatment claim under Title VII.

Strategy: The steps of a disparate treatment case are: One: Vazquez has presented a *prima facie* case—she is in a protected category and was treated differently from similar people who are not protected under Title VII, giving rise to an inference of discrimination.

---

[5]Guzman v. News Corp., 2013 U.S. Dist. LEXIS 155026, 2013 WL 580705 (S.D.N.Y. 2013).
[6]To see this cartoon, google "Obama chimp cartoon NY Post."

Two: Starwood presented evidence that its decision was based on legitimate reasons —
Vazquez had violated its appearance policy.

Three: To win, Vazquez must show that Starwood's decision was a pretext or had
a discriminatory intent.

Result: The court found for Vazquez, believing that Starwood did have a discriminatory
intent.[7]

Disparate Impact

We have already studied the *Griggs v. Duke Power* case in Chapter 4, but it is a landmark case
in employment law, so worth reviewing again.[8] Duke Power required all applicants to its
most desirable departments to have a high school education or satisfactory scores on two
tests that measured intelligence and mechanical ability. Neither test gauged the ability to
perform a particular job. The pass rate for whites was much higher than for blacks, and
whites were also more likely than blacks to have a high school diploma. Although Duke
Power was not, on its face, discriminating against blacks, the upshot of these employment
rules was that more whites got the good jobs.

The Supreme Court ruled that Duke Power was violating Title VII because its rules
had a disparate impact on a protected category. The court stated:

> Nothing in [Title VII] precludes the use of testing or measuring procedures; obviously they are
> useful. What Congress has commanded is that any tests used must measure the person for the job
> and not the person in the abstract.

**Disparate impact applies if the employer has a rule that, *on its face,* is not discriminatory,
but *in practice* excludes too many people in a protected category.** Unlike disparate treatment,
in a disparate impact case, the plaintiff does not have to prove *intentional* discrimination.

The required steps in a disparate impact case are:

1. **The plaintiff must present a *prima facie* case.** The plaintiff is not required to prove
    discrimination; he need only show a disparate impact—that the employment practice in
    question excludes a disproportionate number of people in a protected group (women
    and minorities, for instance). In the *Griggs* case, a far higher percentage of whites than
    blacks passed the tests required for one of the good jobs. The Equal Employment
    Opportunity Commission (EEOC) defines a disparate impact as one in which the pass
    rate for a protected category is less than 80 percent of that for others. (As we will see, the
    EEOC is the federal agency charged with enforcing most discrimination statutes.)

2. **The defendant must offer some evidence that the employment practice was a job-
    related business necessity.** Duke Power would have to show that the tests predicted
    job performance.

3. **To win, the plaintiff must now prove either that the employer's reason is a pretext or
    that other, less discriminatory, rules would achieve the same results.** The plaintiffs in
    Griggs showed that the tests were not a job-related business necessity—workers who had
    been hired before the tests were introduced performed the jobs well. Duke Power could
    no longer use them as a hiring screen. If the power company wanted to use tests, it
    would have to find some that measured an employee's ability to perform particular jobs.

Griggs was decided almost a half century ago. Yet, as the following case illustrates, hiring
tests remain a frequent subject of litigation.

---

[7]Vazquez v. Caesar's Paradise Stream Resort, 2013 U.S. Dist. LEXIS 170178, 2013 WL 6244568
(M.D. Pa. Dec. 3, 2013).
[8]401 U.S. 424 (S. Ct. 1971).

GULINO v. BD. OF EDUC. OF THE CITY SCH. DIST. OF N.Y.

907 F. Supp. 2d 492
United States District Court for the Southern District of New York, 2012

Facts: A New York State task force on teacher qualifications decided that all teachers needed a basic understanding of liberal arts and sciences. National Evaluation Systems (NES), a professional test development company, was hired to develop the Liberal Arts and Sciences Test (LAST) to measure this knowledge.

NES began by establishing two committees of teachers and professors (Committees) to ensure that the LAST was both relevant to the job of a New York public school teacher and free from bias. The Committees reviewed a draft framework, a list of exam subtopics, and sample questions. NES then sent its draft framework and subtopics for review to twelve hundred New York public school teachers and education professors. It also piloted some sample questions on students at various state education colleges.

To determine what a passing score should be, the Committees estimated what percentage of test-takers would answer each question correctly. They recommended a passing score of between 38 and 48. The New York State Education Commissioner ultimately established 43 as the required score.

Teachers could not be licensed to teach in New York City unless they passed the LAST. Whites succeeded at a higher rate than African-Americans and Latinos. A group of minority teachers filed suit against the Board of Education for the City of New York (Board) alleging that the LAST violated Title VII.

Issue: *Did the LAST violate Title VII?*

Excerpts from Judge Wood's Decision: Under Title VII, an exam is job related if it has been properly validated. The essence of validation is in the requirement that the content of the test be related to the content of the job.

There are several flaws in the way that NES developed [the LAST] that prevent the Court from finding that the company conducted a suitable job analysis. First, NES never created a list of the tasks teachers perform, nor determined whether the subtopics identify knowledge needed to perform those tasks.

Second, NES representatives testified that the company collected materials from schools and colleges throughout the state, interviewed deans and administrators of liberal arts programs at colleges and universities in New York, and consulted with education experts. The representatives, however, could not describe how the information collected was used or how it supported the choice of subtopics. It also appears that NES actually drafted the subtopics prior to collecting materials and conducting interviews.

The third requirement is that the content of the exam must be directly related to the content of the job. The fact that the LAST is related generally to the liberal arts and sciences does not prove that the exam is job related; indeed, the liberal arts and sciences is an extremely broad field that encompasses far more than the basic knowledge all teachers need in order to be competent. Rather, to be job related, the LAST must test for the minimum level of knowledge about the liberal arts and sciences that is necessary to ensure that all teachers are competent to teach. There is no evidence in the record establishing the minimum level of knowledge about the liberal arts and sciences needed by all teachers. Consequently, the Court finds that the Board has failed to establish that the LAST is directly related to teachers' jobs.

[A court must also] determine whether the exam is scored in a way that usefully selects those applicants who can better perform the job. There is no evidence that the committees were given any guidance as to the definition of minimally-competent. At the same time, there was no evidence that higher scores on the LAST correlated with better teacher or student performance in the classroom.

In conclusion, the Court finds that the LAST is not job related, and the Board violated Title VII by requiring Plaintiffs to pass the exam in order to receive a teaching license.

Hostile Work Environment

Employers violate Title VII if they permit a work environment that is so hostile toward people in a protected category that it affects their ability to work. This rule applies whether the hostility is based on race, color, religion, sex, or national origin. (As we will see, this rule also applies to those treated badly because of pregnancy, age, or disability.) This concept of hostile environment first arose in the context of sexual harassment.

Sexual Harassment. When Professor Anita Hill accused Supreme Court nominee Clarence Thomas of sexually harassing her, people across the country were glued to their televisions, watching the Senate hearings on her charges. Thomas was ultimately confirmed to the Supreme Court, but "sexual harassment" became a household phrase. The number of cases—and the size of the damage awards—skyrocketed.

> # Everyone has heard of sexual harassment, but few people know exactly what it is.

Sexual harassment involves unwelcome sexual advances, requests for sexual favors, and other verbal or physical conduct of a sexual nature which are so severe and pervasive that they interfere with an employee's ability to work. **There are two categories of sexual harassment:** (1) quid pro quo and (2) hostile work environment.

- *Quid Pro Quo.* From a Latin phrase that means "one thing in return for another," *quid pro quo* harassment occurs if any aspect of a job is made contingent upon sexual activity. In the Guzman case, the plaintiff alleged that a male editor had offered a permanent reporter job to a young female copy assistant in exchange for the type of sexual activity that President Bill Clinton made famous.

- **Hostile Work Environment.** An employee has a valid claim of sexual harassment if sexual talk and activity are so pervasive that they interfere with her (or his) ability to work. Courts have found that offensive jokes, intrusive comments about clothes or body parts, and public displays of pornographic pictures can create a hostile environment. Guzman claimed that a male editor had shown her a photo of a naked man while telling stories about another editor's "voracious sexual appetite."

In the following landmark case, the Supreme Court defined the standard for a hostile work environment.

Landmark Case

TERESA HARRIS V. FORKLIFT SYSTEMS, INC.

510 U.S. 17
United States Supreme Court, 1993

Facts: Teresa Harris was a manager at Forklift Systems; Charles Hardy was its president. Hardy frequently made inappropriate sexual comments to Harris and other women at the company. For example, he said to Harris, in the presence of others, "You're a woman, what do you know?" and "We need a man as the rental manager." He called her "a dumb-ass woman" and suggested that the two of them "go to the Holiday Inn to negotiate your raise." He also asked Harris and other female employees to get coins from his front pants pocket. He insisted that Harris and other women pick up objects he had thrown on the ground. While Harris was arranging a deal with one of Forklift's customers, he asked her, in front of other employees, "What did you do, promise the guy some sex Saturday night?"

Harris sued Forklift, claiming that Hardy had created an abusive work environment. The trial court ruled against Harris on the grounds that Hardy's comments might offend a reasonable woman, but they were not severe enough to have a serious impact on Harris's psychological well-being. The appeals court confirmed, and the Supreme Court granted *certiorari*.

Issue: *To be a violation of Title VII, must sexual harassment seriously affect the employee's psychological well-being?*

Excerpts from Justice O'Connor's Decision: Title VII of the Civil Rights Act of 1964 makes it "an unlawful employment practice for an employer to discriminate against any individual with respect to his compensation, terms, conditions, or privileges of employment, because of such individual's race, color, religion, sex, or national origin." [T]his language is not limited to economic or tangible discrimination. The phrase "terms, conditions, or privileges of employment" evinces a congressional intent to strike at the entire spectrum of disparate treatment of men and women in employment, which includes requiring people to work in a discriminatorily hostile or abusive environment. When the workplace is permeated with discriminatory intimidation, ridicule, and insult that is sufficiently severe or pervasive to alter the conditions of the victim's employment and create an abusive working environment, Title VII is violated.

This standard takes a middle path between making actionable any conduct that is merely offensive and requiring the conduct to cause a tangible psychological injury. [M]ere utterance of an epithet which engenders offensive feelings in an employee does not sufficiently affect the conditions of employment to implicate Title VII. Conduct that is not severe or pervasive enough to create an objectively hostile or abusive work environment—an environment that a reasonable person would find hostile or abusive—is beyond Title VII's purview. Likewise, if the victim does not subjectively perceive the environment to be abusive, the conduct has not actually altered the conditions of the victim's employment, and there is no Title VII violation.

But Title VII comes into play before the harassing conduct leads to a nervous breakdown. A discriminatorily abusive work environment, even one that does not seriously affect employees' psychological well-being, can and often will detract from employees' job performance, discourage employees from remaining on the job, or keep them from advancing in their careers. Moreover, even without regard to these tangible effects, the very fact that the discriminatory conduct was so severe or pervasive that it created a work environment abusive to employees because of their race, gender, religion, or national origin offends Title VII's broad rule of workplace equality.

Same-Sex Harassment.   Suppose that one man makes unwelcome sexual overtures to another man in the workplace. The Supreme Court ruled that same-sex harassment is also a violation of Title VII.[9]

Corning Consumer Products Co. provides a set of practical guidelines for eliminating sexual harassment. It asks employees to apply four tests in determining whether their behavior violates Title VII:

- Would you say or do this in front of your spouse or parents?

- What about in front of a colleague of the opposite sex?

- Would you like your behavior reported in your local newspaper?

- Does it need to be said or done at all?

Hostile Environment Based on Race.   Reginald Jones, who was African American, drove a truck for UPS Ground Freight. He began finding bananas and banana peels on his truck in the terminal. Some employees wore Confederate shirts and hats. After he reported these incidents to a supervisor, two other drivers came up to him one night in the parking lot holding a crowbar. They asked him if he had reported them to the supervisor. He again reported this event and again found banana peels on his truck. When Jones sued UPS Ground Freight, alleging a racially hostile work environment, the trial court granted UPS's motion for summary judgment. But the appellate court overturned this decision, ruling that the case should go to a jury because these events could, indeed, have created a hostile work environment.[10]

---

[9]Oncale v. Sundowner Offshore Services, Inc., 523 U.S. 75 (S. Ct. 1998).
[10]Jones v. UPS Ground Freight, 683 F.3d 1283 (11th Cir. 2012).

Hostile Environment Based on Color.   Title VII prohibits discrimination based on both race and color. Although many people assume that they are essentially the same, that is not necessarily the case. For example, Dwight Burch alleged that his coworkers at an Applebee's restaurant created a hostile work environment when they called him hateful names because of his dark skin color. These colleagues were also African American but had lighter skin. While denying any wrongdoing, Applebee's settled the case by paying Burch $40,000 and agreeing to conduct antidiscrimination training.

Hostile Environment Based on National Origin.   Title VII also prohibits a hostile environment based on national origin. While working at Steel Technologies, Inc., Tony Cerros was promoted several times. So what was the problem? Coworkers and supervisors called him names like "brown boy," "spic," and "wetback," They also told him that "if it ain't white, it ain't right," and wrote "Go Back to Mexico" on the bathroom wall. Although the company removed the bathroom graffiti, it did not investigate Cerros's complaints until he filed suit. At that point, it determined that Cerros had not faced discrimination. The trial court agreed because Cerros had, after all, been promoted. However, the appeals court overturned the decision, finding for Cerros on the grounds that he had suffered a hostile work environment, which is in itself a violation of Title VII, even if there is no evidence of adverse employment actions.[11]

Employer Liability for Harassment.   Employees who engage in illegal harassment are liable for their own misdeeds. But is their company also liable? The Supreme Court has held that:

- The company is liable if it knew or should have known about the conduct and failed to stop it.

- Even if the company was unaware of the misbehavior, it is nonetheless liable if the victimized employee suffered a "tangible employment action" such as firing, demotion, or reassignment.

- If the company was unaware of the behavior and the victimized employee did not suffer a tangible employment action, the company is still liable unless it can prove that (1) it used reasonable care to prevent and correct harassing behavior, and (2) the employee unreasonably failed to take advantage of the complaint procedure or other preventive opportunities provided by the company.[12]

Retaliation

Title VII also prohibits employers from retaliating against workers who oppose discrimination, bring a claim under the statute, or take part in an investigation or hearing. Retaliation means that the employer has done something that would deter a reasonable worker from complaining about discrimination. Research indicates that retaliation occurs in as many as 60 percent of discrimination cases.

However, the standard of proof is higher for retaliation claims than for the underlying discrimination issue. In basic discrimination cases, a plaintiff can win by showing that discrimination was a motivating factor, although other factors were also involved. But **in a retaliation case, the plaintiff must demonstrate that, but for the defendant's desire to retaliate, he would never have taken the harmful action.** (This standard is called **but-for causation**.)

But-for causation

The retaliatory action would not have occurred if it were not for the defendant's discriminatory intent.

---

[11]Cerros v. Steel Techs, Inc., 288 F.3d 1040 (7th Cir. 2002).

[12]Burlington Industries, Inc. v. Ellerth, 524 U.S. 742 (S. Ct. 1998); Faragher v. Boca Raton, 524 U.S. 775 (S. Ct. 1998). Although these cases involve sexual harassment, the EEOC has ruled that the same principles apply to other forms of illegal harassment. See the EEOC's "Questions & Answers for Small Employers on Employer Liability for Harassment by Supervisors."

A defendant can defeat a retaliation claim by showing that there were other, non-discriminatory reasons for his action.

Dr. Naiel Nassar taught at the University of Texas Southwestern Medical Center (University). He alleged that Dr. Beth Levine, who was one of his supervisors, was biased against him because he was Muslim and of Middle Eastern heritage. Among other claims, she allegedly said, "Middle Easterners are lazy." When Nassar left his job at the University, he sent a letter to Levine's boss, Dr. Gregory Fitz, and others, blaming her harassment for his departure. Fitz worried that these letters harmed Levine's reputation, so he persuaded a hospital to withdraw its job offer to Nassar. Fitz defended his actions by claiming that the University and the hospital had an exclusivity agreement, under which the hospital could only hire University faculty as staff physicians. The Supreme Court ruled that, to prevail in his lawsuit, Nassar would have to show that Fitz would not have interfered *but for* his discriminatory intent.[13] This standard is a high one to meet.

Title VII prohibits disparate treatment, disparate impact, hostile environment, and retaliation when used against any of the categories protected by Title VII—race, color, religion, sex, and national origin. Now we look at particular rules that apply to only some of these categories.

30-5b Religion

Employers cannot discriminate against a worker because of his religious beliefs. In addition, employers must make reasonable accommodation for a worker's religious practices unless the request would cause undue hardship for the business. A common issue involves employees who cannot work on their Sabbath. This refusal might be an "undue hardship" if there are no other employees who could perform that work on those days. What would you do in the following cases if you were the boss?

1. A Christian says he cannot work at Walmart on Sundays—his Sabbath. It also happens to be one of the store's busiest days.

2. A Jewish police officer wants to wear a beard and yarmulke as part of his religious observance. Facial hair and headgear are banned by the force.

3. Muslim workers at a meat-packing plant want to pray at sundown, but specific break times were specified in the labor contract and sundown changes from day to day. The workers begin to take bathroom breaks at sundown, stopping work on the production line.

4. A Jehovah's Witness needs to miss one of his scheduled shifts at UPS so that he can attend the Memorial, one of that religion's most important events.

Disputes such as these are on the rise and are not easy to handle fairly. In the end, Walmart fired the Christian, but when he sued on the grounds of religious discrimination, the company settled the case. A judge ruled that the police officer could keep his beard because the force allowed other employees with medical conditions to wear facial hair, but the head covering had to go. The boss at the meat-packing plant fired the Muslim employees who left their posts to pray. UPS paid $70,000 to settle the Jehovah's Witness suit.

Cynthia Johnson/The LIFE Images Collection/Getty Images

Price Waterhouse decided that Ann Hopkins was not feminine enough to to be a partner. But the Supreme Court disagreed.

---

[13]Univ. of Tex. Southwestern Med. Ctr. v. Nassar, 133 S. Ct. 2517 (S. Ct. 2013).

30-5c Sex

What does discrimination on the basis of sex mean? In a landmark case that defined this provision of Title VII, the Supreme Court ruled that **"gender must be irrelevant to employment decisions."**[14] In this case, the accounting firm Price Waterhouse had refused to promote Ann Hopkins to partner. Of the 88 people who came up for partner that year, she was the only woman. She was not only a high performer, she was also the most successful in bringing in business. The problem? She was "sometimes overly aggressive, unduly harsh, difficult to work with, and impatient with staff." Partners commented that she was macho, overcompensated for being a woman, and needed to take a course at charm school. They were opposed to her use of profanity because it was a "lady using foul language." A partner explicitly told her that she should "walk more femininely, talk more femininely, dress more femininely, wear makeup, have her hair styled, and wear jewelry."

In ruling in her favor, the Supreme Court held that **Title VII forbids sexual stereotyping.** The opinion said, "An employer who objects to aggressiveness in women but whose positions require this trait places women in an intolerable and impermissible catch-22: out of a job if they behave aggressively and out of a job if they do not. Title VII lifts women out of this bind."

30-5d Attractiveness

Attractive men and women have advantages in life: Voters, jurors, teachers, college admissions staffs, and bosses treat them better. Studies have shown that investors are willing to pay more for the stock of companies with attractive CEOs.[15]

Marissa Mayer, CEO of Yahoo, is ranked among the top 5 percent of executives for attractiveness. Does that increase the value of Yahoo stock?

Peter Kramer/NBC/NBC NewsWire/Getty Images

Is it legal for employers to discriminate on the basis of attractiveness, to hire the best looking? **Unattractiveness is not a protected category under Title VII**, so any discrimination claim would have to fit into one of the existing categories. (However, several jurisdictions—Washington, D.C., and San Francisco, for example—do have regulations prohibiting attractiveness discrimination.)

In 1966, Eastern Airlines placed the following ad for flight attendants in *The New York Times*:

> A high school graduate, single (widows and divorcees with no children considered), 20 years of age (girls 19 ½ may apply for future consideration). 5'2" but no more than 5'9," weight 105 to 135 in proportion to height and have at least 20/40 vision without glasses.

Airlines hoped that young, attractive, thin, single, female flight attendants would be a lure for the mostly male passengers. Ultimately, flight attendants (with the help of the EEOC) were able to make the case that most of these requirements were sex discrimination, largely because they did not also apply to men. Imagine an airline refusing to hire married pilots. Although airlines still set weight limits, now they are related to safety—helping passengers

---

[14]Price Waterhouse v. Hopkins, 490 U.S. 228 (S. Ct. 1989).
[15]Halford, Joseph Taylor and Hsu, Scott H. C., Beauty is Wealth: CEO Appearance and Shareholder Value (November 20, 2013). Available at SSRN: http://ssrn.com/abstract=2357756.

evacuate planes—not attractiveness. In a more recent case, Abercrombie & Fitch paid $50 million to settle a case alleging that it only hired young, white, physically fit salespeople because that was part of the Abercrombie "look."

What about the opposite problem—when an employee is *too* attractive? Melissa Nelson worked as a dental assistant for James Knight. When his wife found out that he was attracted to Nelson, she insisted that he fire her, which he did. The Iowa Supreme Court ruled that her termination did not constitute sex discrimination, partly because she was replaced by another (presumably unattractive) woman.[16]

In the following case, a casino fired a female bartender for refusing to wear makeup. Did the casino violate Title VII? You be the judge.

You be the Judge

JESPERSEN V. HARRAH'S

444 F.3d 1104
United States Court of Appeals
for the Ninth Circuit, 2006

Facts: Darlene Jespersen was a bartender at the sports bar in Harrah's Casino in Reno, Nevada. She was an outstanding employee, frequently praised by both her supervisors and customers.

After Jespersen had been at Harrah's for almost 20 years, the casino implemented a program that required bartenders to be "well groomed, appealing to the eye." More explicitly, for men:

- Hair must not extend below top of shirt collar. Ponytails are prohibited.

- Hands and fingernails must be clean and nails neatly trimmed at all times.

- No colored polish is permitted.

- Eye and facial makeup is not permitted.

- Shoes will be solid black leather or leather type with rubber (non-skid) soles.

The rules for women were:

- Hair must be teased, curled, or styled. Hair must be worn down at all times, no exceptions.

- Nail polish can be clear, white, pink, or red color only. No exotic nail art or length.

- Shoes will be solid black leather or leather type with rubber (non-skid) soles.

- Makeup (foundation/concealer and/or face powder, as well as blush and mascara) must be worn and applied neatly in complimentary colors, and lip color must be worn at all times.

An expert was brought in to show the employees (both male and female) how to dress. The workers were then photographed and told that they must look like the photographs every day at work.

Jespersen tried wearing makeup for a short period of time but then refused to do so. She did not like the feel of it and also believed that this new appearance interfered with her ability to deal with unruly, intoxicated guests because it "took away [her] credibility as an individual and as a person."

After Harrah's fired Jespersen, she sued under Title VII. The district court granted Harrah's motion for summary judgment. Jespersen appealed.

You Be The Judge: *Did Harrah's requirement that women wear makeup violate Title VII?*

Argument for Jespersen: Jespersen refused to wear makeup to work because the cost—in time, money, and personal dignity—was too high.

Employers are free to adopt different appearance standards for each sex, but these standards may not impose a greater burden on one sex than the other. Men were not required to wear makeup, but women were. That difference meant a savings for men of hundreds of dollars and hours of time.[17] Harrah's did not have the right to fire Jespersen for violating a rule that applies only to women, with no equivalent for men.

Argument for Harrah's: Employers are permitted to impose different appearance rules on women than on men as long as the overall burden on employees is the same. For example, it is not discriminatory to require men to wear their hair short. On balance, Harrah's rules did not impose a heavier burden on women than on men.

---

[16]Nelson v. James H. Knight DDS, P.C., 834 N.W.2d 64 (Iowa 2013).
[17]See for example, Michael Kinsley, "Making Up Is Hard to Do," *The Washington Post*, March 26, 2008.

30-5e Family Responsibility Discrimination

Suppose that you are in charge of hiring at your company. You receive applications from four people: a mother, a father, a childless woman, and a childless man. All have equivalent qualifications. Which one would you hire? In studies, participants repeatedly rank mothers as less qualified than other employees and fathers as most desirable, even when their credentials are exactly the same.

Family responsibility discrimination is a violation of Title VII if it involves men and women being treated differently—say, mothers being offered less appealing assignments than fathers or fathers being denied benefits that are available to mothers. After Dawn Gallina, an associate at a big law firm, revealed to her boss that she had a young child, he began to treat her differently from her male colleagues and spoke to her "about the commitment differential between men and women." A court ruled that her belief of illegal discrimination was reasonable.[18]

The EEOC has issued guidelines indicating that stereotypes are not a legitimate basis for personnel decisions and may violate Title VII. In addition, some state and local laws prohibit either parenthood discrimination or family responsibility discrimination.

30-5f Sexual Orientation

Neither Title VII nor any other *federal* statute protects against discrimination based on sexual orientation. However, by executive order, the federal government does prohibit discrimination based on sexual orientation among its own employees and also among companies that work for it. **In addition, almost half the states and hundreds of cities have statutes that prohibit discrimination based on sexual orientation.**

The Supreme Court has ruled that it is unconstitutional to withhold federal benefits from same-sex married couples.[19] But this inconsistency in federal law means that, in many places, a gay person could be fired for claiming these benefits.

30-5g Gender Identity and Expression

David Schroer was in the Army for 25 years, including a stint tracking terrorists. The Library of Congress offered him a job as a specialist in terrorism. (Who knew that libraries needed terrorism specialists?) However, when he revealed that he was in the process of becoming *Diane* Schroer, the Library of Congress withdrew the offer. As you can guess, he sued under Title VII.

Traditionally, courts took the view that sex under Title VII applied only to how people were born, not what they chose to become. Employers could and did fire workers for changing sex. About half of transgender people reported in a survey that they had experienced an adverse employment action because of gender nonconformity.[20] However, a federal court found the Library of Congress in violation of Title VII for withdrawing Schroer's offer.[21] And some other courts have reached a similar result, In addition, **the EEOC ruled that discriminating against someone for being transgender is a violation of Title VII** and about one-third of the states and hundreds of cities prohibit gender identity and expression discrimination. Also, the federal government prohibits discrimination on gender identity among its employees and in companies that work for it.

---

[18]Gallina v. Mintz, Levin, 123 Fed. Appx. 558 (4th Cir. 2005).
[19]United States v. Windsor, 133 S. Ct. 2675 (S. Ct. 2013).
[20]Jaime M. Grant, Lisa A. Mottet, Justin Tanis, Jack Harrison, Jody L. Herman, and Mara Keisling, Nat'l Ctr. for Transgender Equal. and Nat'l Gay and Lesbian Task Force, Injustice at Every Turn: A Report of the National Transgender Discrimination Survey 2 (2011) reported in Jason Lee, "Symposium: Lost in Transition: the Challenges of Remedying Transgender Employment Discrimination Under Title VII," 35 Harv. J. L. & Gender 423.
[21]Schroer v. Billington, 577 F. Supp. 2d 293 (U.S. Dt. Ct. 2008).

30-5h **Background and Credit Checks**

When a new contractor took over a BMW plant, it required existing employees to undergo criminal background checks. As a result of these checks, it fired 88 workers, some of whom had been at the plant for more than 10 years. Although only 55 percent of the plant's employees were black, 80 percent of the terminated workers were. The EEOC accused BMW of violating Title VII because its policy had a disparate impact on black employees.

EEOC regulations prohibit companies from using criminal history information in a way that has an adverse impact on employees in a protected category if the background information is irrelevant in determining whether the employee is appropriate for the job. In the BMW case, the EEOC argued that old data should not be used to terminate long-term workers with an unblemished employment record.

At least 10 states and more than 50 localities limit the ability of public employers to ask about an applicant's criminal record. Some jurisdictions extend this limitation to companies that work for the government, and a few also limit private employers.

Employers may not consider arrest records, because that is not evidence of wrongdoing. **The EEOC also discourages the use of credit checks because minorities tend to have worse credit ratings than whites.** In addition, one-quarter of the states and many cities have passed "ban the box" legislation that limits employer use of background checks.

30-5i **Immigration**

Under Title VII, it is illegal for employers to discriminate against non-citizens because "national origin" is a protected category. Therefore, employers should not ask about a job applicant's country of origin, but they are permitted to inquire if the person is authorized to work in the United States. If the applicant says, "Yes," the interviewer cannot ask for evidence until the person is hired. At that point, the employer must complete an I-9 form—Employment Eligibility Verification—within three days. This form lists the acceptable documents that can be used for verification. Employees have the right to present whichever documents they want from the list of acceptable items. The employer may not ask for some other document. The I-9 forms must be kept for three years after the worker is hired or one year after termination.

30-5j **Defenses to Charges of Discrimination**

Under Title VII, the defendant has four possible defenses.

Merit

A defendant is not liable if he shows that the person he favored was the most qualified. Test results, education, or productivity can all be used to demonstrate merit, provided they relate to the job in question. Harry can show that he hired Bruce for a coaching job instead of Louisa because Bruce has a master's degree in physical education and seven years of coaching experience. On the other hand, the fact that Bruce scored higher on the National Latin Exam in the eighth grade is not a good reason to hire him over Louisa.

Seniority

Many companies use seniority as an important factor in determining everything from compensation to layoffs. While such systems offer many advantages—they encourage a commitment to the company, an incentive to learn job-specific skills, and a willingness to train other workers without fear of losing one's job—they also tend to perpetrate prior discriminatory practices. If historic trends result in black employees having less seniority, they will also be paid less and laid off more. However, a seniority system violates Title VII only if it was designed with the *intention* to discriminate. **A legitimate seniority system is legal even if it perpetuates past discrimination.**

Bona Fide Occupational Qualification (BFOQ)

An employer is permitted to establish discriminatory job requirements if they are *essential* to the position in question. The business must show that it cannot fulfill its primary function unless it discriminates. Such a requirement is called a **bona fide occupational qualification (BFOQ)**. (Note that only religion, sex, or national origin can be a BFOQ—never race or color.)

Catholic schools may, if they choose, refuse to hire non-Catholic teachers; clothing companies may refuse to hire men to model women's attire. Generally, however, courts are not sympathetic to claims of BFOQ. They have almost always rejected BFOQ claims that are based on customer preference. For example, an employer violated the law when it refused to appoint a woman to a position as vice president of international operations because of its fear that men in other countries might not want to work with her.[22]

However, the courts recognize three situations in which employers may consider customer preference:

- **Safety.** The Supreme Court ruled that a maximum security men's prison could refuse to hire women correctional officers. If a woman wanted to risk her life, that was her choice, but the court feared that an attack on her would threaten the safety of both male guards and inmates.[23]

- **Privacy.** An employer may refuse to hire women to work in a men's bathroom, and vice versa.

- **Authenticity.** An employer may refuse to hire a man for a woman's role in a movie. In addition, a court ruled that Disney could fire an Asian man from the Norwegian exhibit at its Epcot international theme park, not because he was Asian, but because he was not culturally authentic. He did not have first hand knowledge of Norwegian culture and did not speak Norwegian.[24]

Bona fide occupational qualification (BFOQ)
An employer is permitted to establish discriminatory job requirements if they are essential to the position in question.

Affirmative Action

The goal of affirmative action programs is to remedy the effects of past discrimination. How people feel about affirmative action tends to be a function of how they define the term. Most people are opposed to quotas, but at the same time, they support outreach and recruitment efforts aimed at women and disadvantaged minorities.

Affirmative action is not required by Title VII, nor is it prohibited. Affirmative action programs have three different sources.

Litigation. Courts have the power under Title VII to order affirmative action to remedy the effects of past discrimination.

Voluntary Action. Employers can *voluntarily* introduce an affirmative action plan to remedy the effects of past practices or to achieve (but not to maintain) equitable representation of minorities and women, provided that the plan is not too unfair to majority members.[25] For example, in the university and community college system in Nevada, only 1 percent of the faculty were black (and roughly 25 percent were female). In response, the university instituted a policy that permitted any department that hired a minority candidate to also hire an additional candidate of any race. Although Yvette Farmer was one of three finalists for a job in the sociology department, it hired a black African male without even granting her an interview. The Court ruled that the university's affirmative action plan was legal.[26]

Government Contracts. The government may use affirmative action programs when awarding contracts only if (1) it can show that the programs are needed to overcome specific past discrimination; (2) they have time limits; and (3) nondiscriminatory alternatives are not available.

---

[22]Fernandez v. Wynn Oil Co., 653 F.2d 1273 (9th Cir. 1981).
[23]Dothard v. Rawlinson, 433 U.S. 321 (S.Ct. 1977).
[24]Gupta v. Walt Disney World Co, 256 Fed. Appx. 279 (11th Cir. 2007).
[25]In United Steelworkers of America v. Weber, 443 U.S. 193 (S. Ct. 1979).
[26]University and Community College System of Nevada v. Farmer, 113 Nev. 90 (S. Ct. Nev. 1997).

30-6 PREGNANCY DISCRIMINATION ACT

Under the Pregnancy Discrimination Act, an employer may not fire, refuse to hire, or fail to promote a woman because she is pregnant. An employer also violates this statute if the work environment is so hostile toward a pregnant woman that it affects her ability to do her job. And an employer must treat pregnancy and childbirth as any other temporary disability. If, for example, employees are allowed time off from work for other medical disabilities, women must also be allowed a maternity leave.

Jennifer Hitchcock worked at Angel Corps, a home care agency. When her supervisor learned that Hitchcock was pregnant, she asked whether Hitchcock was going to quit after she gave birth. The supervisor told her it was important to make a decision as soon as possible to ensure continuity of care for their clients. After this conversation, the supervisor significantly increased Hitchcock's workload and began scrutinizing her performance. This same supervisor had also counseled another worker to have an abortion because she already had two children. Within two weeks, Angel Corps fired Hitchcock on the grounds that she had made an improper assessment of a patient. When Hitchcock sued under the Pregnancy Discrimination Act, the court denied her employer's request for summary judgment because the evidence was sufficient to show that the reasons given for Hitchcock's termination were just a pretext.[27] This case offers an excellent example of what an employer should *not* do when an employee is pregnant.

The Pregnancy Discrimination Act also protects a woman's right to terminate a pregnancy. An employer cannot fire a woman for having an abortion.[28]

30-7 AGE DISCRIMINATION IN EMPLOYMENT ACT

Under the Age Discrimination in Employment Act (ADEA), an employer with 20 or more workers may not fire, refuse to hire, fail to promote, or otherwise reduce a person's employment opportunities because he is 40 or older. Nor may an employer require workers to retire at a certain age. (This retirement rule does not apply in some jobs, such as police officer, airline pilot, and top-level corporate executive.) The goal of the statute is to counteract stereotypes about the abilities of older workers. A plaintiff in an age discrimination case can show discrimination in three ways: disparate treatment, disparate impact, and hostile work environment.

30-7a Disparate Treatment

In a disparate treatment claim, the plaintiff must show that the employer intentionally discriminated against him because of his age, or enacted a policy that intentionally treated employees differently because of their age. Proof of intent involves obvious statements and behavior or more subtle circumstantial evidence.

Under the ADEA, a disparate treatment case requires three steps:

1. The plaintiff must show that:

- He is 40 or older;
- He suffered an adverse employment action;
- He was qualified for the job for which he was fired or not hired; and
- He was replaced by a younger person.

---

[27]Hitchcock v. Angel Corps, Inc., 718 F.3d 733 (7th Cir. 2013).
[28]Doe v. C.A.R.S Protection Plus, Inc., 527 F.3d 358 (3rd Cir. 2008).

2. The employer must present evidence that its decision was based on legitimate, nondiscriminatory reasons.

3. The plaintiff must show that the employer's reasons are a pretext and, in fact, the employer intentionally discriminated.

Note that the standard of proof is tougher in an age discrimination case than in Title VII litigation. **Under the ADEA, the plaintiff must show that but for his age, the employer would not have taken the action it did.** In other words, to win a case, the plaintiff must show that age was not just one factor, it was the deciding factor. When Jack Gross was 54 years old, his employer transferred most of his responsibilities to a younger woman and demoted him. Age may well have been one factor in his employer's decision, but there were other reasons as well. The Supreme Court ruled for the employer, on the grounds that Gross had not shown that age was the "but-for" cause of the disputed decision.[29] This case made the road much steeper for ADEA plaintiffs.

In passing the ADEA, Congress was particularly concerned about employers who relied on unfavorable stereotypes rather than job performance. The following case provides further support for the adage: "Loose lips sink ships."

REID v. GOOGLE, INC.

50 Cal. 4th 512
Supreme Court of California, 2010

Facts: Google's vice-president of engineering, Wayne Rosing (aged 55), hired Brian Reid (52) as director of operations and director of engineering. Reid had a Ph.D. in computer science and had been a professor of electrical engineering at Stanford University. At the time, the top executives at Google were CEO Eric Schmidt (47), Vice-President of Engineering Operations Urs Hölzle (38), and founders Sergey Brin (28), and Larry Page (29).

During his two years at Google, Reid's only written performance review stated that he had consistently met expectations. The comments indicated that Reid was very intelligent and creative and was a terrific problem solver, with an excellent aptitude and attitude. He also dealt confidently with fast-changing situations. However, the review also commented that "Adapting to Google culture is the primary task. Right or wrong, Google is simply different: younger contributors, inexperienced first-line managers, and the super-fast pace are just a few examples of the environment."

According to Reid, even as he received a positive review, Hölzle and other employees made derogatory age-related remarks such as his ideas were "obsolete," "ancient," and "too old to matter," that he was "slow," "fuzzy," "sluggish," and "lethargic," an "old man," an "old guy," and an "old fuddy-duddy," and that he did not "display a sense of urgency" and "lacked energy."

Nineteen months after Reid joined Google, he was fired. Google says it was because of his poor performance. Reid alleges he was told it was based on a lack of "cultural fit."

Reid sued Google for age discrimination. The trial court granted Google's motion for summary judgment on the grounds that Reid did not have enough evidence of discrimination. The Court of Appeal overruled the trial court. The California Supreme Court agreed to hear the case.

Issues: *Did Reid have enough evidence of age discrimination to warrant a trial?*

Excerpts from Justice Chin's Decision: Google contends that the Court of Appeal should have applied the stray remarks doctrine, i.e., should have categorized the alleged statements by Hölzle and Rosing as irrelevant stray remarks and disregarded them in reviewing the merits of the summary judgment motion. [S]trict application of the stray remarks doctrine, as urged by Google, would result in a court's categorical exclusion of evidence even if the evidence was relevant. An age-based remark not made directly in the context of an employment decision or uttered by a non-decision-maker may be relevant, circumstantial evidence of discrimination. [T]he United States Supreme Court indicates that even if age-related

---

[29]Gross v. FBL Fin. Servs., 557 U.S. 167 (S.Ct. 2009)

comments can be considered stray remarks because they were not made in the direct context of the decisional process, a court should not categorically discount the evidence if relevant; it should be left to the factfinder to assess its probative value.

[T]he stray remarks cases merely demonstrate the common-sense proposition that a slur, in and of itself, does not prove actionable discrimination. A stray remark alone may not create a triable issue of age discrimination. But when combined with other evidence, an otherwise stray remark may create an ensemble [that] is sufficient to defeat summary judgment.

For the reasons stated above, we affirm the judgment of the Court of Appeal.

30-7b Disparate Impact

Disparate impact claims arise when an employer's actions do not explicitly discriminate, but nonetheless have an adverse impact on people aged 40 or over. Here, too, the standards are different under the ADEA than under Title VII. **Under the ADEA a disparate impact case requires only two steps:**

1. The plaintiffs must present a *prima facie* case that the employment practice in question excludes a disproportionate number of people 40 and older.

2. The employer wins if it can show that the discriminatory decision was based on a *reasonable factor other than age.*

One reasonable factor other than age is cost. Sometimes companies fire older workers because they are paid more, receive higher pension benefits, or generally cost more (e.g., higher healthcare expenses). Courts have supported these decisions, holding that an employer is entitled to prefer *lower-paid* workers even if that preference results in the company also choosing *younger* workers. As the court put it in one case, "An action based on price differentials represents the very quintessence of a legitimate business decision."[30] Thus, Circuit City Stores fired 8 percent of its employees because they could be replaced with people who would work for less. The fired workers were more experienced—and older. This action was legal under the ADEA.

30-7c Hostile Work Environment

Diane Kassner (age 79) and Marsha Reiffe (61) worked for 2nd Avenue Delicatessen. They filed suit under the ADEA, alleging that their boss and coworkers made comments to them about their age, such as "Drop dead," "Retire early," "Take off all of that makeup," and "Take off your wig." In addition, their boss pressured the two women to retire and pointed to the front of the restaurant and said, "There's the door." But the two women were never fired.

The court ruled that the ADEA prohibits a hostile work environment based on age. A workplace is considered hostile if a reasonable person would find that intimidation, ridicule, and insult based on age are pervasive.[31] In short, this case, combined with the *Google* case, indicate that it is wise to avoid any comments about an employee's age.

30-7d Bona Fide Occupational Qualification

As is the case under Title VII, age is rarely a BFOQ. **To set a maximum age, the employer must show that:**

- The age limit is reasonably necessary to the essence of the business; and either
- Virtually everyone that age is unqualified for the job, or
- Age is the only way an employer can determine who is qualified.

---

[30]Marks v. Loral Corp., 57 Cal. App. 4th 30 (Cal. Ct. App. 1997).
[31]Kassner v. 2nd Ave. Delicatessen, Inc., 496 F.3d 229 (2nd Cir. 2007).

Although some courts have held that age can be a BFOQ in cases where public safety is at issue, such as for pilots and bus drivers, the EEOC is not always in agreement. In short, the BFOQ defense is very limited in ADEA cases.

EXAM Strategy

Question: Solapere ran a job ad on Monster.com, which said that the company would only consider hiring people who either had a job or had been unemployed for less than six months. The average length of unemployment in the United States at that time was nine months, which meant that such a policy eliminated millions of job applicants. Did this ad violate federal law?

Strategy: Solapere was not intentionally discriminating against anyone, thus no disparate treatment claim. What about a disparate impact claim? Did this policy exclude too many people in a protected category? The unemployed are not a protected category under Title VII, but this policy might have had an impact on groups that are protected.

Result: Older people and some minority groups have higher unemployment rates than other workers. Therefore, this practice could violate both Title VII and the ADEA unless Solapere could show that it was a job-related business necessity. Could it be a job-related business necessity?

30-8 DISCRIMINATION ON THE BASIS OF DISABILITY

30-8a The Rehabilitation Act of 1973

The Rehabilitation Act of 1973 prohibits discrimination on the basis of disability by the executive branch of the federal government, federal contractors, and entities that receive federal funds. It also requires these organizations to develop affirmative action plans for the hiring, placement, and promotion of the disabled. The same legal standards apply to both this statute and the Americans with Disabilities Act, discussed next. Cases interpreting one statute also apply to the other.

30-8b Americans with Disabilities Act

The Americans with Disabilities Act (ADA) prohibits employers with 15 or more workers from discriminating on the basis of disability.

Disability

A disabled person is someone with a physical or mental impairment that substantially limits a major life activity or the operation of a major bodily function or someone who is regarded as having such an impairment. Major life activities include the following tasks: caring for oneself, performing manual tasks, seeing, hearing, eating, sleeping, walking, standing, lifting, bending, speaking, breathing, learning, reading, concentrating, thinking, communicating, and working. Major bodily functions include functions of the immune system, normal cell growth, and digestive, bowel, bladder, neurological, brain, respiratory, circulatory, endocrine, and reproductive functions. The ADA applies to *recovered* drug addicts but not to the *current* use of drugs, sexual disorders, pyromania, exhibitionism, or compulsive gambling. Although the ADA protects alcoholics who can meet the definition of disabled, employers can nonetheless fire alcoholics if their drinking adversely affects job performance.

Suppose an employee has a disabling illness, but one that can be successfully treated. The employee is still considered to be disabled, even if the illness is well controlled. Thus, someone with diabetes is disabled, even if the illness is managed so well that it does not interfere with major life activities. There is one important exception—someone whose vision is normal when wearing glasses or contact lenses is not disabled for purposes of the ADA.

Accommodating the Disabled Worker

Once it is established that a worker is disabled, employers may not discriminate on the basis of disability as long as the worker can, with *reasonable accommodation*, perform the *essential functions* of the job. An accommodation is unreasonable if it would create *undue hardship* for the employer. Let's look at those terms more closely.

Reasonable Accommodation.   To meet this standard, employers are expected to:

- make facilities accessible,

- permit part-time schedules,

- acquire or modify equipment, and

- assign a disabled person to an open position that he can perform. (Note that the employer is not required to create a new job or find a perfect position, just a reasonable one.)

This discussion of the ADA reflects changes Congress made to the statute in the ADA Amendment Act of 2008 (ADAAA). This statute expanded the definition of "disability" as the term had previously been interpreted by the Supreme Court. The following case illustrates the impact of the ADAAA.

WILLOUGHBY v. CONN. CONTAINER CORP.

2013 U.S. Dist. LEXIS 168457, 2013 WL 6198210
United States District Court for the District of Connecticut, 2013

Facts: Anthony Willoughby worked for Connecticut Container Corp. (CCC), which made boxes. When Willoughby was diagnosed with diabetes, he submitted a doctor's form to CCC's Human Resources department. Despite treatment, Willoughby experienced side effects that included swelling, dizziness, blurred vision, and frequent bathroom use. Heat caused the symptoms to worsen.

One night, Willoughby reported to work feeling unwell. For two weeks, he had been assigned to the transfer car, which required particularly strenuous activity in the heat. That night, his ankles swelled and his vision deteriorated. When he told his supervisor, Darlene Bailey, she said "do the work or go home." Willoughby also informed the shift supervisor, who ignored him.

Later that night, after Willoughby did not respond to pages, Bailey found him in a chair. Willoughby says he had passed out; Bailey states that he was sleeping. He presented HR with a note from a physician verifying that he had passed out due to low blood sugar. Willoughby was fired for sleeping on the job.

Willoughby filed suit, alleging that CCC had violated the ADA because it had failed to provide reasonable accommodation for his disability. CCC filed a motion for summary judgment.

Issues: *Was Willoughby disabled? If so, did CCC provide reasonable accommodation?*

Excerpts from Judge Haight's Decision:[32]   The Court finds, given the expanded interpretation of the definitions of disability and major life activity directed by the ADAAA, that Willoughby could indeed easily be found by a jury to be an individual who has a physical impairment that substantially limits one or more major life activities of such individual and, accordingly, has a disability under the ADA. As EEOC regulations themselves note, diabetes substantially limits endocrine function, and therefore it should easily be concluded that diabetes will, at a minimum, substantially limit what amounts to a major life activity.

CCC avers that Willoughby's claim under the ADA that CCC failed to provide [him] with an accommodation is baseless in view of the fact that Willoughby himself testified he never asked for an accommodation. [W]hile generally, it is the responsibility of the individual with a disability to inform the employer that an accommodation is needed, it is, in fact, an employer's duty reasonably to accommodate an employee's disability if the disability is obvious—which is to say, if the employer knew or reasonably should have known that the employee was disabled. [T]he ADA contemplates that employers will engage in 'an interactive process' with their employees and in that way work together to assess whether an employee's disability can be reasonably accommodated.

Given that CCC did in fact have notice of Willoughby's disability, and given that CCC did not, prior to Willoughby's termination, engage with Willoughby in any sort of interactive process by which the parties worked together to assess whether Willoughby's disability could be reasonably accommodated, the Court finds that a jury could permissibly find that Willoughby is able to meet this claim that CCC failed to provide reasonable accommodation under the ADA.

Essential Functions of the Job. A juvenile corrections officer was hit by a baseball that fractured her wrist. Nine months after returning to her job, she was assigned to the night shift, where the only other officer was a newcomer. Concerned that her wrist was not strong enough for her to restrain some of the inmates on her own, she asked to be paired with an experienced officer. Her employer fired her on the grounds that she could not perform the essential functions of the job. But the court ruled that, since she had been working successfully as an officer during the day, clearly she could perform the essential functions.[33]

Undue Hardship. What constitutes undue hardship is the subject of much litigation. Many courts hold that employers may use cost–benefit analysis—they are not required to make an expensive accommodation that provides little benefit. Nor are they required to provide identical working conditions for all employees. For example, a woman who was wheelchair-bound asked that her employer lower the sink in the kitchenettes that were being built in her building. Otherwise, she would have to use the bathroom sink which, she felt, segregated and stigmatized her. The cost to lower the kitchen sinks ranged from as much as $2,000 (to do all the sinks in the building) to as little as $150 (for just the sink on her floor). The court ruled that the employer had no obligation to provide identical conditions and that it had already made a reasonable accommodation by lowering the sink in the bathroom. Although the employer could, in theory, afford this request, it did not have an obligation to spend so much money for so little benefit.[34]

Medical Exams

Employers interact with workers at three key stages: applying, entering (after hiring but before the job starts), and working. The ADA sets different standards for medical exams at these three stages:

- **Applicants.** An employer generally may not require a medical exam or ask about disabilities, except that the interviewer may ask:
  - whether an applicant can perform the work (provided that the same question is asked of all applicants),
  - for the applicant to demonstrate how he would perform the job, and
  - (in the event that a disability is obvious) what accommodation the applicant would need.

[32]For ease of reading, we have substituted the parties' names for Plaintiff and Defendant.
[33]Leuzinger v. County of Lake, 2007 U.S. Dist. LEXIS 35955 (N.D. CA 2007).
[34]Vande Aande v. Wisconsin Department of Administration, 44 F.3d 538 (7th Cir. 1995).

- **Entering employees**. The company may require a medical test and make it a condition of employment, but the test must be:
  - required of all employees, whether or not they are disabled, and
  - treated as a confidential medical record (except in the case of managers who need to know).

- **Existing employees**. An employer may require medical exams or discuss any suspected disability, but only to determine if a worker is still able to perform the existing functions of her job.

Relationship with a Disabled Person

An employer may not discriminate against someone because of his *relationship* with a disabled person.

Obesity

According to the EEOC, just being overweight is not a disability unless it has some underlying physiological cause, such as a thyroid disorder. **However, being morbidly obese (defined as having double the normal body weight) is a disability, no matter what the cause.**

Lisa Harrison weighed 527 pounds when Family House fired her. (Some family.) The normal weight for someone her height—five feet, two inches tall—was between 102 and 130 pounds. The EEOC filed suit, claiming that Family House had fired her for a perceived disability and had failed to make reasonable accommodation. Family House filed a motion for summary judgment alleging that it had fired Harrison because her obesity impaired her job performance. In denying this motion, the court ruled that her severe obesity was a disability under the ADA.[35]

Mental Disabilities

Under EEOC rules, physical and mental disabilities are to be treated the same. Physical ailments such as diabetes and deafness may sometimes be easier to diagnose, but psychological disabilities are also covered by the ADA. Among other accommodations, the EEOC rules indicate that employers should be willing to put up barriers to isolate people who have difficulty concentrating, offer flexible hours to allow for therapy, or provide detailed day-to-day feedback to those who need greater structure in performing their jobs.

Disparate Treatment and Disparate Impact

Both disparate treatment and disparate impact claims are valid under the ADA. The steps in a disparate *treatment* case are:

1. The plaintiff must offer *prima facie* evidence that the employer discriminated because of his disability.
2. The employer must then offer a legitimate, nondiscriminatory reason for its action.
3. To win, the plaintiff must now prove that the employer intentionally discriminated. She may do so either by showing that (1) the reasons offered were simply a *pretext* or (2) that a discriminatory intent is more likely than not.

To win a disparate *impact* case, the plaintiff must show that a policy that *looks* neutral falls more harshly on a protected group and cannot be justified by business necessity.

The following Exam Strategy illustrates how disparate treatment and disparate impact are applied in an ADA case and also demonstrates the importance of choosing the correct theory.

---

[35]EEOC v. Res. for Human Dev., Inc., 827 F. Supp. 2nd 688 (E.D. La. 2011).

EXAM Strategy

Question: Hughes Missile Systems fired Joel Hernandez because he tested positive for cocaine, which, not surprisingly, was a violation of workplace rules. He, however, had no hard feelings, and two years later, he reapplied for a job at Hughes. At the time, he provided evidence that he was clean. However, the company rejected his application because it had a policy against hiring anyone who had been fired for cause. Did the company violate the ADA?

Strategy: Under the ADA, it is legal to discriminate against a drug user, but not against a recovered drug addict. To win a disparate *treatment* case, Hernandez had to show that Hughes's excuse for not rehiring him was just a pretext and its decision was really motivated by an intent to discriminate based on his disability. To win a disparate *impact* claim, Hernandez had to show that the no-rehire policy affected disabled people more than others and that it was not justified by business necessity. Could he prove either of these claims?

Result: The Supreme Court ruled that Hernandez could not prove his disparate treatment claim because its no-rehire rule was legitimate and not just a pretext for discrimination. And because Hernandez had not raised the issue of disparate impact in the lower courts, the Supreme Court refused to consider it. So he lost his case.[36]

Hostile Work Environment

An employee is entitled to recovery under the ADA if she is subjected to a hostile work environment because of her disability. Sandra Flowers's boss fired her eight months after finding out that she was HIV-positive. During that eight months, Flowers's entire work environment changed. Before, Flowers and her boss had been friends who went out together for lunch, drinks, and the movies. Afterward, the socializing stopped, the boss began monitoring Flowers's phone calls, and then subjected her to four "random" drug tests in one week. A jury found that Flowers's termination was not based on her disability, but that her boss had nonetheless created a hostile work environment by unreasonably interfering with Flowers's ability to work.[37]

While lauding the ADA's objectives, many managers have been apprehensive about its impact on the workplace. Most acknowledge, however, that society is better off if every member has the opportunity to work. And as advocates for the disabled point out, we are all, at best, only temporarily able-bodied. Even with the ADA, only 35 percent of the disabled population who are of working age are employed, whereas 78 percent of able-bodied people have jobs.

30-9 GENETIC INFORMATION NONDISCRIMINATION ACT

Suppose you want to promote someone to CFO, but you know that her mother and sister both died young of breast cancer. Is it legal to consider that information in making a decision? Not since Congress passed the Genetic Information Nondiscrimination Act

---

[36]Raytheon Co. v. Hernandez, 540 U.S. 44 (S.Ct. 2003).
[37]Flowers v. S. Reg'l Physician Servs, 247 F.3d 229 (5th Cir. 2001).

(GINA). **Under GINA, employers with 15 or more workers may not require genetic testing, or use information about genetic makeup or family medical history as a factor in hiring, firing, or promoting employees.** Nor may health insurers use such information to decide coverage or premiums. Thus, even an employer Wellness Program cannot *require* participants to answer questions about their family medical history.

Note, however, that insurance companies may seek the results of genetic testing before issuing disability, life, or long-term care policies. At this writing, only three states prohibit the use of such information for these types of policies.[38]

30-10 HIRING PRACTICES

The hiring process is an easy place for employers to go wrong. Here are pitfalls to avoid.

30-10a Interviews

Most interviewers (and students who have read this chapter) would know better than Delta Airlines interviewers who allegedly asked applicants about their sexual orientation birth control methods, and abortion history. The following list provides guidelines for interviewers.

Don't Even Consider Asking	Go Ahead and Ask
Can you perform this function with or without reasonable accommodation?	Would you need reasonable accommodation in this job?
How many days were you sick last year?	How many days were you absent from work last year?
What medications are you currently taking?	Are you currently using drugs illegally?
Where were you born? Are you a United States citizen?	Are you authorized to work in the United States?
How old are you?	What work experience have you had?
How tall are you? How much do you weigh?	Could you carry a 100-pound weight, as required by this job?
When did you graduate from college?	Where did you go to college?
How did you learn this language?	What languages do you speak and write fluently?
Have you ever been arrested?	Have you ever been convicted of a crime that would affect the performance of this job?
Do you plan to have children? How old are your children? What method of birth control do you use?	Can you work weekends? Travel extensively? Would you be willing to relocate?
What is your corrected vision?	Do you have 20/20 corrected vision?
Are you a man or a woman? Are you single or married? What does your spouse do? What will happen if your spouse is transferred? What clubs, societies, or lodges do you belong to?	Talk about the weather instead!

---

[38]The states are California, Oregon, and Vermont.

The most common gaffe on the part of interviewers? Asking women about their child-care arrangements. That question assumes the woman is responsible for child care.

30-10b Social Media

Almost all employers now rely on social media as a part of their hiring process.[39] They may look at LinkedIn to find potential candidates or check Facebook for evidence of unprofessional behavior. These searches sometimes reveal information that is illegal for employers to act on, such as age, religion, pregnancy, or illness. Yet, sometimes employers do. In one experiment, researchers replied to job postings with identical (fake) resumes that were linked to a Facebook page identifying the applicant's religion as either Christian or Muslim. Christians were more likely to obtain an interview.

Such misuse of social media has consequences. A university decided not to hire an applicant after it learned from his website that, because of his religion, he doubted the theory of evolution. The university argued that these religious views would have impeded the performance of his job, which required him to raise funds in the science community and work with university scientists.[40] A federal judge denied the university's request for summary judgment, so the university settled the case for $125,000.

To help prevent this type of liability, some employers keep the role of "cyber-vetting" separate from that of hiring. A handful of states now prohibit employers from asking for social media passwords and many others have such legislation pending.

30-11 ENFORCEMENT

30-11a Constitutional Claims

People bringing a claim under the Constitution must file suit on their own.

30-11b The Civil Rights Act of 1866

For plaintiffs alleging racial discrimination, the Civil Rights Act of 1866 offers substantial advantages over Title VII:

- A four-year statute of limitations (versus less than a year under Title VII)

- Unlimited compensatory and punitive damages (which, in one case, amounted to $7 million)[41]

- Applicability to all employers, not just those with 15 or more employees

However, this statute is not enforced by the EEOC, which means that the plaintiff is on his own when it comes to negotiating with or filing suit against an employer.

30-11c The Rehabilitation Act of 1973

This statute is enforced by the EEOC (for claims against the executive branch of the federal government), the Department of Labor (for claims against federal contractors), and the Department of Justice (for claims against entities that receive federal funds).

---

[39]One study reported that 94% of employers "now use or expect to use social media."

[40]Gaskell v. Univ. of Ky., 2010 U.S. Dist. LEXIS 124572 (E.D. Ky. 2010).

[41]Edwards v. MBTA. (June 8, 2001) After the verdict, the case settled.

30-11d **Other Statutory Claims**

The EEOC is the federal agency responsible for enforcing Title VII, the Equal Pay Act, the Pregnancy Discrimination Act, the ADEA, the ADA, and GINA.

Before a plaintiff can bring suit under one of these statutes, she must first file a complaint with the EEOC. Generally, the plaintiff must file within 180 days of the wrong-doing.[42] But if the plaintiff is alleging that she was paid less than she should have been, each paycheck she receives starts the statute of limitations all over again. After it receives a filing, the EEOC conducts an investigation and also attempts to mediate the dispute. If it determines that discrimination has occurred, it will typically file suit on behalf of the plaintiff. This arrangement is favorable for the plaintiff because the government pays the legal bill. If the EEOC decides *not* to bring the case, or does not make a decision within six months, it issues a right to sue letter, and the plaintiff may proceed on her own in court within 90 days. Under the ADEA, a plaintiff may bring suit 60 days after filing a charge with the EEOC. Many states also have their own version of the EEOC.

Remedies available to the successful plaintiff include hiring, reinstatement, retroactive seniority, back pay, front pay (to compensate for future lost wages), and reasonable attorney's fees. Under Title VII and the ADA, plaintiffs are also entitled to compensatory and punitive damages up to $300,000, but only in certain disparate treatment cases, not disparate impact suits. Compensatory damages include future monetary losses, mental anguish, loss of enjoyment of life, and damage to reputation. Punitive damages are available if the defendant acted with malice or reckless indifference to the plaintiff's rights. Under the ADEA, plaintiffs can recover compensatory damages but are eligible for punitive damages only in the case of "willful" violations; that is, knowing or reckless disregard of the law. In the case of willful violations, the damage award is typically doubled.

Two trends, however, have reduced employees' chances of taking home substantial damages. Concerned about a rise in discrimination lawsuits, employers now often require new hires to agree in advance to arbitrate, not litigate, any future employment claims. The Supreme Court has upheld the enforceability of mandatory arbitration provisions.[43] Employees sometimes receive worse results in the arbitrator's office than in the courtroom, because arbitrators tend to favor repeat customers (such as management) over one-time users (such as employees). In addition, discovery is more limited in arbitration than in court, which means that the plaintiff may not be able to make the strongest case. Also, arbitration awards are usually not disclosed publicly, so employers have less incentive to avoid misbehavior.

But even if a case does go to trial, plaintiffs in job discrimination cases have a much worse track record than other types of plaintiffs—they win less often at trial, and they lose more often on appeal. As a result, the number of discrimination cases in the federal courts has declined.[44]

Chapter Conclusion

This chapter began with an example from the country's past, when discrimination was legal and many people were foreclosed from the American dream of opportunity and advancement. Anti-discrimination laws have had an enormous impact on the American workplace—half of all workers are now women. In 1960, about 5 percent of doctors and lawyers were women or minorities; now about one-third are. It is a sign of how much the world has

---

[42]This is the case unless he resides in a state with an appropriate state agency, in which case he has 300 days.

[43]Gilmer v. Interstate/Johnson Lane Corp, 500 U.S. 20 (S.Ct. 1991).

[44]Kevin M. Clermont and Stewart J. Schwab, "Employment Discrimination Plaintiffs in Federal Court: From Bad to Worse?" *3 Harv. l. & Pol'y Rev.* 103 (2009).

changed that, after finishing this chapter, the authors realized that female or minority judges wrote the opinions in four of the five cases (including Justice Sandra Day O'Connor). Economists estimate that about a quarter of the enormous increase in this country's GDP over the last 50 years came from admitting women and blacks more fully into the workforce.[45] And research indicates that companies with more women in high positions perform better.[46]

But discrimination has not disappeared. As we saw earlier in the chapter, at least one experiment showed that Muslims are less likely to be hired than Christians. In another study, almost one-third of recruiters reported that they would "react negatively" to "overly religious" posts on social media.[47] After being laid off, older workers take longer to find work and that new job is likely to pay less. Women and minorities remain underrepresented at the top of the employment ladder, as CEOs, partners in law and consulting firms, department heads in hospitals, or chaired professors in universities. On average, women working full time earn only 80 percent as much as male coworkers, even after accounting for occupation, industry, race, marital status, and job tenure. Although there are undoubtedly many reasons for this inequality, such as women taking time out of work to care for children, gender discrimination also seems to play a role. For example, male CFOs in public companies earn 16 percent ($215,000) more than female CFOs, even after controlling for age, time in the job, company size, and market capitalization.[48] And the CEO of Microsoft recently advised women that they should not ask for a raise, but instead should have faith in the system.

As adults, we spend more time working than in any other single activity. A job that we love can permeate our lives with satisfaction and even joy. Work that bores or bedevils us may shorten our lives. We have devoted two chapters to employment law precisely because work *is* so important in our lives. Now you know both your rights as a worker and your obligations as an employer. We hope that when you have other people's lives in your hands, you will treat them as you would wish to be treated.

EXAM REVIEW

1. **CONSTITUTION**   The U.S. Constitution prohibits employment discrimination by federal, state, and local governments.

2. **THE CIVIL RIGHTS ACT OF 1866**   The Civil Rights Act of 1866 prohibits racial discrimination in both private and public employment (except it does not apply to the federal government).

3. **EQUAL PAY ACT OF 1963**   Under the Equal Pay Act, a worker may not be paid at a lesser rate than employees of the opposite sex for equal work.

4. **TITLE VII**   Under Title VII of the Civil Rights Act of 1964, it is illegal for employers with 15 or more workers to discriminate on the basis of race, color, religion, sex, or national origin.

5. **TYPES OF DISCRIMINATION**   There are four types of prohibited activities under Title VII: disparate treatment, disparate impact, hostile environment, and retaliation.

---

[45]Data from David Wessel, "The Positive Economics of Leaning In," *The Wall Street Journal,*" April 3, 2013.
[46]"Closing the Gap," *The Economist,* Nov 26, 2011.
[47]Jobvite's 6th Annual Social Recruiting Survey.
[48]http://www3.cfo.com/article/2012/4/compensation_gmi-gender-gap-gofoernance-metrics

6. **DISPARATE TREATMENT**   To prove a disparate treatment case, the plaintiff must show that she was *treated* less favorably than others because of her sex, race, color, religion, or national origin.

7. **DISPARATE IMPACT**   Disparate impact applies if the employer has a rule that, *on its face*, is not discriminatory, but *in practice* excludes too many people in a protected group and the rule is not a job-related business necessity.

8. **HOSTILE WORK ENVIRONMENT**   Employers violate Title VII if they permit a work environment that is so hostile toward people in a protected category that it affects their ability to work.

9. **SEXUAL HARRASSMENT**   Sexual harassment involves unwelcome sexual advances, requests for sexual favors, or other verbal or physical conduct of a sexual nature that are so severe and pervasive that they interfere with an employee's ability to work.

10. **RETALIATION**   Title VII also prohibits employers from retaliating against workers who oppose discrimination, bring a claim under the statute, or take part in an investigation or hearing.

11. **RELIGION**   Employers cannot discriminate against a worker because of his religious beliefs. In addition, employers must make reasonable accommodation for a worker's religious practices unless the request would cause undue hardship for the business.

12. **SEX**   Title VII forbids sex stereotyping.

13. **ATTRACTIVENESS**   Unattractiveness is not itself a protected category under Title VII, so any discrimination claim would have to fit into one of the existing categories.

14. **FAMILY RESPONSIBILITY DISCRIMINATION**   Men and women may not be treated differently because of their family responsibilities.

15. **SEXUAL ORIENTATION**   Neither Title VII nor any other federal statute protects against discrimination based on sexual orientation but almost half the states and hundreds of cities do have statutes that prohibit such discrimination. Also, the federal government prohibits discrimination based on sexual orientation among its own employees and also among companies that work for it.

16. **GENDER IDENTITY AND EXPRESSION**   Traditionally, courts ruled that employees were not protected from discrimination based on gender identity. But some federal courts, the EEOC, about one-third of the states and hundreds of cities prohibit gender identity and expression discrimination. Also, the federal government prohibits discrimination on the basis of gender identity among its employees and in companies that work for it.

17. **BACKGROUND AND CREDIT CHECKS**   EEOC regulations prohibit companies from using criminal history information in a way that has an adverse impact on employees in a protected category if the background information is irrelevant in determining whether the employee is appropriate for the job. The EEOC also discourages the use of credit checks.

18. **IMMIGRATION**   Under Title VII, it is illegal to discriminate against non-citizens because "national origin" is a protected category.

19. **DEFENSES**   Under Title VII, the defendant has four possible defenses: merit, seniority, bona fide occupational qualification, and affirmative action.

20. **BONA FIDE OCCUPATIONAL QUALIFICATION**   Under the BFOQ standard, an employer is permitted to establish discriminatory job requirements if they are essential to the position in question.

EXAM Strategy

Question: When Southwest Airlines first started, it refused to hire male flight attendants because its strategy was to court its (mostly male) customers by promoting an image of "feminine spirit, fun, and sex appeal." Its ads featured women in provocative uniforms serving "love bites" (almonds) and "love potions" (cocktails). Its ticketing system featured a "quickie machine" to provide "instant gratification." Is this refusal to hire men a violation of Title VII?

Strategy: Southwest argued that its "Love" campaign was an essential marketing tool. Was being a woman a BFOQ? Remember that the courts have almost always rejected BFOQ claims that are based on customer preference. (See the "Result" at the end of this section.)

21. **PREGNANCY DISCRIMINATION ACT**   Under the Pregnancy Discrimination Act, an employer may not fire, refuse to hire, or fail to promote a woman because she is pregnant or because she has had an abortion. An employer must also treat pregnancy as it would any other temporary disability.

22. **AGE DISCRIMINATION IN EMPLOYMENT ACT**   Under the ADEA, an employer with 20 or more workers may not fire, refuse to hire, fail to promote, or otherwise reduce a person's employment opportunities because he is 40 or older.

EXAM Strategy

Question: Kathy was over 40 when SFI refused to hire her as an insurance agent, it said because she had no sales experience. But the job ad had not specified that sales experience was required. It turned out that when SFI hired agents from outside the company, it was much more likely to hire people under 40. But when promoting from within, it was much more likely to promote people over 40. Did SFI violate the ADEA when it refused to hire Kathy?

Strategy: An ADEA case involves a three-step analysis. One: Kathy must show that she is older than 40, suffered an adverse employment action, was qualified for the job, and a younger person actually got the job. Two: SFI has to show that its decision was based on a legitimate reason. No sales experience is a good reason. Three: Kathy must prove that her age was the deciding factor. (See the "Result" at the end of this section.)

23. **REHABILITATION ACT**   The Rehabilitation Act of 1973 prohibits discrimination on the basis of disability by the federal government, federal contractors, and all entities that receive federal funds.

24. **AMERICANS WITH DISABILITIES ACT** The ADA prohibits employers with 15 or more workers from discriminating on the basis of disability.

25. **DISABILITY** A disabled person is someone with a physical or mental impairment that substantially limits a major life activity or the operation of a major bodily function or someone who is regarded as having such an impairment.

26. **TREATMENT OF DISABLED WORKERS** Once it is established that a worker is disabled, employers may not discriminate on the basis of disability so long as she can, with reasonable accommodation, perform the essential functions of the job. An accommodation is not reasonable if it would create undue hardship for the employer.

EXAM Strategy

Question: When Thomas Lussier filled out a Postal Service employment application, he did not admit that he had twice pleaded guilty to charges of disorderly conduct. Lussier suffered from posttraumatic stress disorder (PTSD) acquired during military service. Because of this disorder, he sometimes had panic attacks that required him to leave meetings. He was also a recovered alcoholic and drug user. During his stint with the Postal Service, he had some personality conflicts with other employees. Once, another employee hit him. He also had one episode of "erratic emotional behavior and verbal outburst." In the meantime, a postal employee in Ridgewood, New Jersey, killed four colleagues. The postmaster general encouraged all supervisors to identify workers who had dangerous propensities. Lussier's boss discovered that he had lied on his employment application about the disorderly conduct charges and fired him. Is the Postal Service in violation of the law?

Strategy: Was Lussier disabled under the ADA? He had a mental impairment (PTSD) that substantially limited a major life activity. Could Lussier, with reasonable accommodation, perform his job? Yes. Was his firing illegal? (See the "Result" at the end of this section.)

27. **GENETIC INFORMATION NONDISCRIMINATION ACT** Under GINA, employers with 15 or more workers may not require genetic testing, or use information about genetic makeup or family medical history as a factor in hiring, firing, or promoting employees.

---

20. Result: Safety, privacy, and authenticity are three situations in which customer preference can be a BFOQ. None of these issues was a factor in this case. The court ruled against Southwest on the grounds that it was "not a business where vicarious sex entertainment is the primary service provided."[49]

22. Result: In the absence of specific comments about age, it is very difficult to show that age is the deciding factor. Kathy is likely to lose her case.

26. Result: The court held that the Postal Service was in violation of the law because Lussier had been dismissed solely as a result of his disability. Clearly, he could perform his job with reasonable accommodation.

---

[49]*Wilson v. Southwest Airlines,* 517 F. Supp 292 (N.D. Tex 1981).

Multiple-Choice Questions

1. Gregg Young, the CEO of BJY Inc., insisted on calling Mamdouh El-Hakem "Manny" or "Hank" even when El-Hakem asked him not to. El-Hakem was of Arab heritage. Young argued that a "Western" name would increase El-Hakem's chances for success and would be more acceptable to BJY's clientele. Does this behavior violate the law?

   (a) Yes, Young violated Title VII by discriminating against El-Hakem on the basis of his national origin.

   (b) Yes, Young was creating a hostile work environment.

   (c) Both (a) and (b)

   (d) No, Manny is just a nickname. No harm was intended and, indeed, no harm resulted.

   (e) No, because customers did prefer a Western name.

2. The CEO of BankTwo realized that not one single officer of the bank was female or minority. He announced that henceforth, the bank would only hire people in these two groups until they comprised at least 30 percent of the officers. Is this plan legal?

   (a) Yes, voluntary affirmative action plans are always legal.

   (b) Yes, because fewer than 20 percent of the officers are female or minority.

   (c) No, to be legal, the goal of an affirmative action plan cannot be greater than 20 percent female or minority.

   (d) No, the plan is too unfair to white men, who have no chance of being hired for a long time.

3. When Allain University was looking for a diversity officer, it decided it would only hire a person of color. Is this decision legal?

   (a) Yes, color is a BFOQ for this position.

   (b) No, color is never a BFOQ, but race could be.

   (c) No, neither race nor color can be a BFOQ.

   (d) No, race and color can be a BFOQ, but are not in this situation. A person does not have to be a member of a minority group to promote diversity.

4. Ralph has worked as a model builder at Snowdrop Architects for 30 years. The firm replaces him with Charlotte, who is 24 and willing to work for much less than Ralph. The firm never offered to let him stay for less pay. When he left, one of the partners told him, "Frankly, it's not a bad thing to have a cute young person working with the clients." Which of the following statements is true?

   (a) Snowdrop is liable because it had an obligation to offer Ralph the lower salary before firing him.

   (b) Snowdrop is liable because it is illegal to replace an older worker with a younger one just to save money.

   (c) Snowdrop is liable because age was a factor in Ralph's firing.

   (d) Snowdrop is liable under Title VII because it replaced an old man with a young woman.

   (e) Snowdrop is not liable because age was not the deciding factor in Ralph's firing.

5. During chemotherapy for bone cancer, Pete, a delivery man, is exhausted, nauseated, and weak. He has asked permission to come in later, work a shorter day, and limit his lifting to 10 pounds. Delivery people typically carry packages of up to 70 pounds. Does Pete's employer, Vulcan, have the right to fire him?

   (a) No, Vulcan must create a new position so that the employee can do something else.

   (b) No, Vulcan must transfer the employee to another position, but only if one is vacant and he is able to perform it.

   (c) Yes, Vulcan can fire Pete because none of his major life activities has been affected.

   (d) Yes, Vulcan can fire Pete because he cannot perform the essential functions of his job.

   (e) Yes, Vulcan can fire Pete because he is not disabled—once the chemotherapy treatments end, he will feel fine again.

CASE QUESTIONS

1. An employer placed a job advertisement for security guards, specifying that applicants had to be United States citizens. It also required applicants to present a Social Security card. Was this ad legal?

2. In the 2008 recession, Roger lost his job as a comptroller. Desperate for work after a year of unemployment, he began to apply for any accounting job at any company. But no one would hire him because he was "overqualified and overexperienced." He repeatedly explained that he was eager to fill the job that was available. Have these companies that refused to hire Roger violated the ADEA?

3. FedEx refused to promote José Rodriguez to a supervisor's position because of his foreign accent and "how he speaks." Is FedEx in violation of the law?

4. Pam Huber worked at Walmart as a grocery order filler, earning $13 an hour. While on the job, she suffered a permanent injury to her right arm and hand. Both she and Walmart agreed that she was disabled under the ADA. As a reasonable accommodation, she asked for a job as a router, which was then vacant. Although she was qualified for that job, she was not the most qualified. Walmart filled the job with the most qualified person. It offered Huber a position as a janitor at $6.20 per hour. Did Walmart violate the ADA?

5. Ronald Lockhart, who was deaf, worked for FedEx as a package handler. Although fluent in American Sign Language, he could not read lips. After 9/11, the company held meetings to talk about security issues. Lockhart complained to the EEOC that he could not understand these discussions. FedEx fired him. Has FedEx violated the law?

6. In 1961, NASA began admitting women into its astronaut training program. They performed well in the training but none of them ever served as astronauts because NASA changed its rules to require jet fighter experience for astronauts. Since women were not eligible to fly jet fighters, they could not qualify for space duty. Would these women have had a claim under Title VII?

7. After the terrorist attacks of 9/11, the United States tightened its visa requirements. In the process, baseball teams discovered that 300 foreign-born professional players had lied about their age. (A talented 16-year-old is much more valuable than a 23-year-old with the same skills.) In some cases, the players had used birth certificates that belonged to other (younger) people. To prevent this fraud, baseball teams began asking for DNA tests on prospects and their families to make sure they were not lying about their identity. Is this testing legal?

DISCUSSION QUESTIONS

1. You are the hiring manager for a bus company. One of the applicants for a job as a bus driver seems perfectly qualified and he is a minority. You would like to hire him, but a background check reveals that he was convicted of second degree murder 40 years before, when he was 15. Should you hire him?

2. Generally, the BFOQ defense does not apply to customer preference. But recently, some clients have been pressuring their law firms to staff their cases with female and minority lawyers. If a firm does so, would the BFOQ defense be valid? Should it be?

3. **ETHICS**   Mary Ann Singleton was the librarian at a maximum-security prison located in Tazewell County, Virginia. About four times a week, Gene Shinault, assistant warden for operations, persistently complimented Singleton and stared at her breasts when he spoke to her. On one occasion, he measured the length of her skirt to judge its compliance with the prison's dress code and told her that it looked "real good". He constantly told her how attractive he found her; made references to his physical fitness, considering his advanced age; asked Singleton if he made her nervous (she answered "yes"); and repeatedly remarked to Singleton that if he had a wife as attractive as Singleton, he would not permit her to work in a prison facility around so many inmates. Shinault told Singleton's supervisor in her presence, "Look at her. I bet you have to spank her every day." The supervisor then laughed and said, "No. I probably should, but I don't." Shinault replied, "Well, I know I would." Shinault also had a security camera installed in her office in a way that permitted him to observe her as she worked. Singleton reported this behavior to her supervisor, who simply responded, "Boys will be boys." Did Shinault sexually harass Singleton? Whether or not Shinault violated the law, what *ethical* obligation did Singleton's supervisor have to protect her from this type of behavior?

4. The Lillie Rubin boutique in Phoenix would hire only women to work in sales because fittings and alterations took place in the dressing room or immediately outside. The customers were buying expensive clothes and demanded a male-free dressing area. Has the Lillie Rubin store violated Title VII? What would its defense be?

5. Lisa T. Jackson, who was white, worked at Uncle Bubba's Seafood and Oyster House. She filed suit under Title VII, alleging that the restaurant discriminated against black employees. They had to enter through the restaurant's rear entrance and could not use the customer bathrooms. Neither of these prohibitions applied to white staff. Jackson's boss also repeatedly told racist jokes. Jackson stated that this behavior

caused her great difficulty in managing the staff and also immense emotional distress because she had biracial nieces. In addition, one of her bosses asked her how she "looked so white," given that her father was of Sicilian descent. Can Jackson recover under Title VII?

6. Peter Oiler was a truck driver who delivered groceries to Winn-Dixie stores. He revealed to his boss that in his free time he liked to dress as a woman, even though he was happily married to a woman. Oiler had been diagnosed with transvestic fetishism with gender dysphoria and a gender identity disorder. Winn-Dixie fired him for fear that, if customers found out, they would go elsewhere to buy their groceries. Does Oiler have a claim against Winn-Dixie?